CONTENTS

D0002919

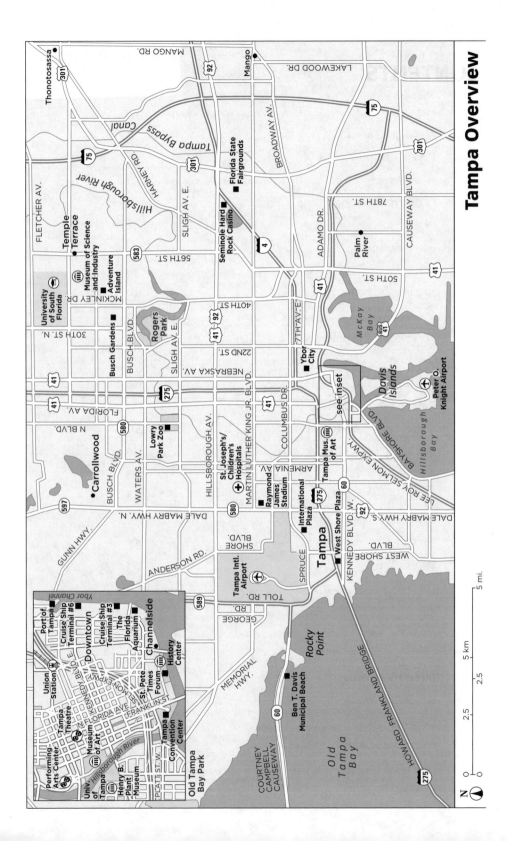

Tampa Overview

Inset (Downtown / Ybor Channel):

Ybor Channel

Port of Tampa
Cruise Ship Terminal #6
Cruise Ship Terminal #3
The Florida Aquarium
Channelside
Downtown
Union Station
Tampa Theatre
St. Pete Times Forum
History Center
Performing Arts Center
Museum of Art
Univ. of Tampa
Hillsborough River
Henry B. Plant Museum
Tampa Convention Center
Old Tampa Bay Park
PLATT ST. W.
FRANKLIN ST.
N FLORIDA AVE.
N KENNEDY BLVD. E.
SELMON EXPY.

Main map labels:

Thonotosassa
MANGO RD.
MANGO RD.
Mango
LAKEWOOD DR.
FLETCHER AV.
Temple Terrace
Tampa Bypass Canal
HARNEY RD.
Hillsborough River
Florida State Fairgrounds
SLIGH AV. E.
BROADWAY AV.
University of South Florida
Museum of Science and Industry
Adventure Island
MCKINLEY DR.
Seminole Hard Rock Casino
78TH ST.
CAUSEWAY BLVD.
ADAMO DR.
Palm River
50TH ST.
Busch Gardens
BUSCH BLVD.
30TH ST. N.
Rogers Park
SLIGH AV. E.
40TH ST.
7TH AV. E.
22ND ST.
NEBRASKA AV.
Ybor City
McKay Bay
Davis Islands
Peter O. Knight Airport
Carrollwood
N BLVD.
FLORIDA AV.
Lowry Park Zoo
HILLSBOROUGH AV.
MARTIN LUTHER KING JR. BLVD.
COLUMBUS DR.
see-inset
Tampa Mus. of Art
Hillsborough Bay
BAYSHORE BLVD.
LEE ROY SELMON EXPWY.
GUNN HWY.
DALE MABRY HWY. N.
597
580
WATERS AV.
BUSCH BLVD.
583
SLIGH AV.
St. Joseph's/Children's Hospitals
Raymond James Stadium
ARMENIA AV.
International Plaza
West Shore Plaza
Tampa
DALE MABRY HWY. S.
SHORE BLVD.
SPRUCE
KENNEDY BLVD. W.
WEST SHORE BLVD.
ANDERSON RD.
Tampa Intl. Airport
TOLL RD.
GEORGE RD.
589
MEMORIAL HWY.
Rocky Point
Ben T. Davis Municipal Beach
COURTNEY CAMPBELL CAUSEWAY
Old Tampa Bay
HOWARD FRANKLAND BRIDGE

Route shields: 301, 75, 92, 301, 583, 41, 580, 275, 41, 92, 41, 4, 41, 60, 275, 92, 580, BUS 41, 41

Scale:
0   2.5   5 km
0   2.5   5 mi.

N

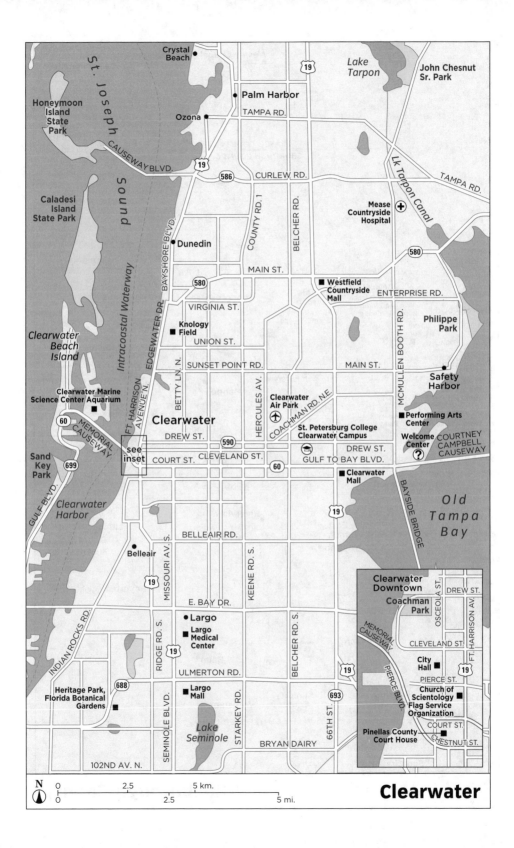

Clearwater

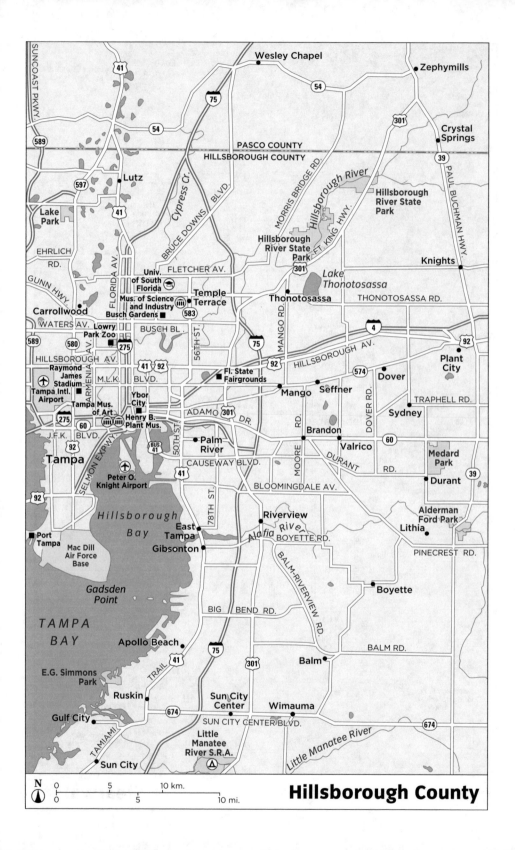

Hillsborough County

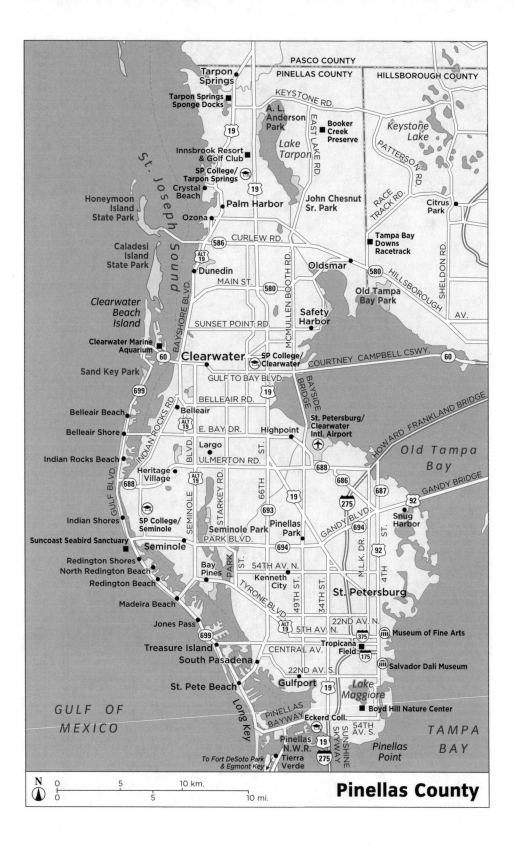

Pinellas County

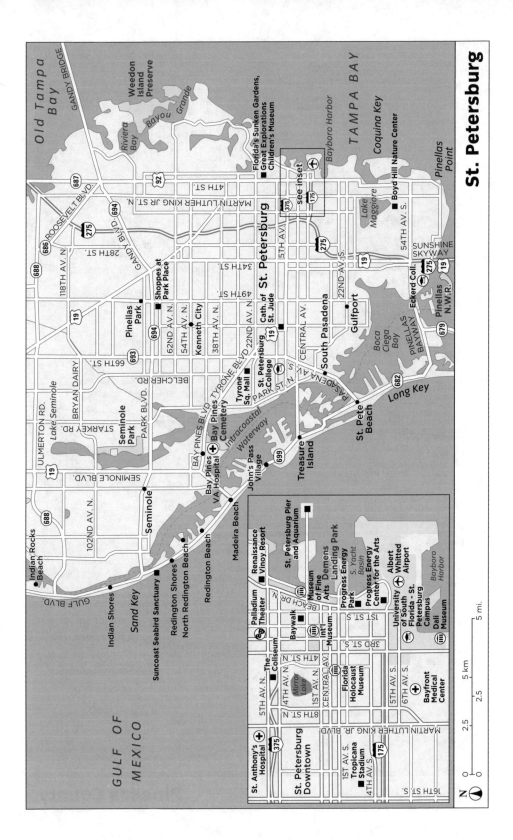

St. Petersburg

PREFACE

Welcome, welcome, welcome!

We're so glad you've picked up this *Insiders' Guide® to the Greater Tampa Bay Area*. We've been waiting to show you around the two counties surrounding Tampa Bay, Florida's largest open-water estuary—a place where salt water from the Gulf of Mexico mixes with fresh water flowing in from rivers and springs.

That's kind of what you'll find here—a mixture of south and north, as well as of east and west, of rural and urban, of uptown glitz and down home comfort.

It has been such fun to explore our home with you in mind, revisiting and learning more about familiar favorites, as well as discovering new places we can't wait to tell you about. And we're not the only ones welcoming you to the Tampa Bay area. Each person interviewed for this book—and there have been a lot of them!—has been eager to share what they know of Hillsborough and Pinellas Counties.

Hillsborough County, on Tampa Bay's east side, and Pinellas County, on Tampa Bay's west side, meet on the north side of the bay. Manatee County claims a portion of the southeastern side of Tampa Bay, but we'll only go there in our Day Trips chapter.

First, you'll read about this land as it was when the first Europeans came here in the 1500s. We'll show you how the Tampa Bay area grew—for good or ill—from a backwoods army outpost into a major metropolitan cultural and sports center.

Then we'll take you around to some of our favorite places to eat (behind a gas station?!), to play, to learn, and to celebrate every part of life. You'll meet cigar makers and artists, deep-sea sponge harvesters and philanthropists . . . and some scalawags and miscreants, as well.

Finally, if you fall in love with this land of sunshine, we'll give you the information you need to make it your home. In the last few chapters there's information about the schools, the major industries, the churches, and who to call to learn about xeriscaping your garden.

But we'll say right up front that this book is not the guide of all guides to Hillsborough and Pinellas County. We doubt there is one.

In fact, trying to cram information about the Tampa Bay area into one book turned out to be a fairly daunting task. Midway through the writing of this *Insiders Guide®*, we were floored momentarily by the audacity of trying to condense into one book all we thought you ought to know about the Tampa Bay area, its two counties, and its three major cities—each of which could have been the basis for its own book.

Even if we did manage to scrunch every last tidbit of info into the book, what fun would that be? Half the experience of going someplace new is the thrill of discovery when you find your own hidden treasures.

So—what we've done is to give you enough information to make you comfortable with being here. We'll show you how the main highways interconnect so you can get around. We'll tell you about where to see live theater, but we won't give away the plot. Fair enough?

Well, all right then. Let's get started!

ACKNOWLEDGMENTS

In one sense, every person who has ever lived within what we know today as Hillsborough and Pinellas Counties has contributed to this book. Their lives—whether recorded by historians or government vital statistics departments or not—made this area what it is.

Had the Tampa Bay area not grown to be a major metropolitan area with cosmopolitan connections, however, it would not have become a subject for a book of this type.

In that sense, we recognize the people of every generation who did more than just subsist—those who moved this area, for good or ill, onto the world-wide economic and entertainment playing field. We also recognize the people who have kept us from becoming collective victims of our own successes—those who have worked to balance that growth with a preservation of our natural and spiritual resources.

Every person who has ever put pen to paper—or fingers to keyboard—and left a written record of his or her experiences in the Tampa Bay area has also contributed to this book. From the unnamed Gentleman of Elvas, who recorded his and others' encounters with the native people in the 1500s, to a young Jewish bride who came to Tampa in the early 1900s and kept a diary, to the court stenographers who recorded depositions and proceedings during the Kefauver hearings in the 1950s, to the journalists and photojournalists of yesterday and today—each writer left his or her observations as a legacy to later generations.

The University of South Florida's Florida Studies Program works to make sense of this legacy. Led by co-directors Raymond Arsenault and Gary Mormino, scholars research land deeds, court documents, maps, and meeting minutes to fill in the gaps between diaries, reports, and newspaper clippings. As co-editors of the University Press of Florida's The Florida History and Culture series, Arsenault and Mormino also have written or helped produce a number of books that were invaluable resources in completing this project.

My thanks to Globe Pequot Press and to Insiders' Guide® editor Amy Lyons for recognizing the Tampa Bay area as a major destination point and relocation area and for producing this book.

My thanks to my friends and teachers along the way, for pushing me to do more and to be more; to Pam, my sister in spirit and in spirit of adventure, for sharing this ride; to my son, Brian, for helping me sound, in the outdoor chapter, like I know how to fish; to my husband, Lee, whose presence permeates this book, for many years of exploring trails and waterways, art studios and hot dog stands, and life; and to, as Shakespeare's *Hamlet* put it, the "divinity that shapes our ends, rough hew them how we will."

HOW TO USE THIS BOOK

Novel or cookbook. It's up to you.

Read this book from cover to cover, turning pages in breathless anticipation to learn how the Tampa Bay area grew from being ignored as an infant to being a major player in business, sports, and the arts.

No time? Then check the table of contents for the chapter on where cruise ships dock. Or use the index to find the page telling where to play disc golf. Find the recipe, mix it up, and dish it out.

This *Insiders' Guide® to the Greater Tampa Bay Area, Including Tampa, St. Petersburg, and Clearwater* was written with both kinds of readers in mind.

We wrote it for visitors—people coming to build sand castles on our beaches, to attend a conference at the Tampa Bay Convention Center, or to make this their base as they visit other parts of the central Florida region. We also wrote it for people moving to the Tampa Bay area—people needing to know who inspects child care facilities, where to get license plates for their cars, and how to cope with living in a state prone to tropical storms and hurricanes. We hope residents will read this book, too. We hope you'll nod as you read about a place you've been. And we hope you'll discover a few things you didn't know before, just as we did while we were writing the book.

START HERE

Use this book as a starting point—20 starting points, actually.

Want a quick rundown on the major cities, our overall climate, and notable industries, plus teasers for places to go and things to do? The Area Overview will acquaint you quickly with the Tampa Bay area. Learn about our airports, seaports, roads, and other transportation systems in Getting Here, Getting Around. Read about our roots and how we grew to where we are today in the History chapter. You'll find bits of history woven throughout the book, too.

The Accommodations chapter will tell you about hotels, spas, resorts, bed-and-breakfasts, RV and other commercial campgrounds, hostels—and how to rent a yacht.

Hungry? Restaurants and Other Eats tells you about many of our world-class dinner restaurants—as well as where to get a great breakfast. We'll tell you what kinds of things happen around here after the sun goes down in Nightlife.

Going Shopping? Come along to our major malls and to some one-of-a-kind stores that are attractions as much as stores. Speaking of Attractions and Kidstuff, that's where you'll find information on everything from Busch Gardens to a free train ride in a local park. Next we give you a January through December listing of Annual Events and Festivals—like the Gasparilla Pirate Fest in January and where to see fireworks on July 4.

Our Arts centers and programs and our Parks and Recreation centers are like two sides of the same coin, each enriching our lives with created and natural beauty. We're pros when it comes to Spectator Sports—football, baseball, hockey, automobile racing, and other major competitions are held here.

We'll take you north to where mermaids live, to the Enchanted Empire of the East, and south to the circus in Day Trips and Weekend Getaways.

Maybe you're ready to move here. Great! Our Relocation chapter will tell you how to find neighborhood-specific information, where dog parks are, a bit about the economy and politics, hurricane helps, and how to make your garden grow.

In separate chapters, we'll tell you about Education and Child Care—including our library systems and county extension offices—and Health Care, Wellness, and Senior Living. Our Worship chapter describes the rich diversity of faiths to be found here. You'll learn about our magazines, newspapers, and radio and television stations in our Media chapter. MacDill Air Force Base and our U.S. Coast Guard stations play major roles in the Tampa Bay area—look for information about our Military toward the end of the book.

GO THERE

Please remember, however, that these are only starting points.

Consider this: The Tampa Bay area—Hillsborough and Pinellas Counties, for the purposes of this book—has twice as many people as the state of Rhode Island. The Tampa Bay geographic area is slightly larger than Rhode Island's. Twenty starting points is about all we have room for here.

While we wish we could list every place to find great Greek food or every golf course to challenge, we can't. So we've given you other places to look for more detailed listings. Use the Web sites, blogs, publications, and other sources we've referenced to learn more. Keep your eyes open, too. We tried to take you to as many places

as possible, hoping you would spot an intriguing book store next to a restaurant we mentioned. Or vice versa.

SIGNPOSTS ALONG THE WAY

A couple of housekeeping notes, and then we'll be on our way.

We'll tell you in each chapter how we've arranged the information. Still, here's a quick and easy way to figure out if something is on the Tampa side of the bay (Hillsborough County) or on the St. Petersburg/Clearwater side of the bay (Pinellas County): 813 area code phone numbers are in Hillsborough County (plus Oldsmar in northeast Pinellas County); 727 area code phone numbers are in Pinellas County.

Look for Insiders' Tips, indicated by **i**, and for Close-up articles giving background information or spotlighting a place.

i **Look east and slightly north from the Tampa Bay area when the space shuttle launches from Cape Canaveral. You'll see the golden glow of the rocket for a couple of minutes as it ascends. The view is best at night, but it's usually visible during the day, too.**

AREA OVERVIEW

S ay "bay area'"and many people think only of cable cars and a famous bridge on the west coast of the continental United States. Ah, but there's another bay area on another west coast with another equally elegant bridge draped across its shoulders. And this bay area—the Tampa Bay area on Florida's west coast—basks in a whole lot more sunshine every day of the year.

Largely ignored for almost five centuries by Spanish conquistadors, French and English explorers, and post–Civil War land speculators, Tampa and its neighbors, St. Petersburg and Clearwater, grew at a more leisurely, more thoughtful pace. But grow they did! Today, the three cities form a business, entertainment, and sports triumvirate rivaling those of older communities around the country while retaining the flavor of their yesteryear charm.

Want proof? Home Shopping Network, Jabil Circuit, Inc., and Rooms to Go are among the national and international businesses headquartered in the Tampa Bay area. The internationally acclaimed Bern's Steak House leads a list of fine dining experiences awaiting you. We've got two international airports and two international seaports, three major-league sports teams—more, if you count the ones who make this area their spring training home—and three top-rated performing arts venues.

But that's not all. There's Ybor City, aka "Cigar City," where you can watch artisans handroll cigars the way they have since 1886 when two brothers moved their business from Cuba to Tampa. Or you can stroll the docks of Tarpon Springs, a Greek community just north of Clearwater that still harvests natural sea sponges from the ocean floor the way they do in the Aegean Sea.

Around late February and early March, when the sweet smell of thousands of acres of ripening strawberries fills the air around here, we kind of forget that Plant City is named after late-1800s railroad magnate Henry B. Plant. After all, this area produces three-quarters of the nation's winter strawberries, so you'd think the city would be named after these ruby-red globules of goodness. That's okay. We make up for it with an 11-day homage to the bountiful berry at the Florida Strawberry Festival.

Busch Gardens provides roller coaster thrills and chills and a world-class zoo, water slides of every configuration fill neighboring Adventure Island, and the beaches of Pinellas County are rated some of the best in the nation.

So whether your tastes run to Broadway musicals or Grand Prix–style racing, soaking up some oceanfront rays or bashing a golf ball toward some far off tiny little cup, you'll find all that and more when you visit our bay area.

And, after you've kayaked through a mangrove tunnel or windsurfed off the Gulf of Mexico, if you find you just can't bear the thought of returning home to icy sleet and mounds of snow, well then, consider that our cost of living is generally lower than that of the rest of the country's. Check out the relocation sections toward the back of the book and we'll get you started toward living permanently in the Sunshine State.

Right now, let's take the nickel tour so you can get your bearings. Then you can explore the greater Tampa Bay area to your heart's content. We've divided the region into three sections:

greater Tampa, which includes the City of Tampa and parts of Hillsborough County; greater St. Petersburg, which includes the City of St. Petersburg and parts of southern Pinellas County; and greater Clearwater, which includes the City of Clearwater and parts of northern Pinellas County.

GEOGRAPHY

Located halfway up Florida's west coast, the Tampa Bay area consists of two counties containing three major cities and a host of smaller towns and unincorporated areas. Pinellas County occupies the 280-square-mile peninsula on the Gulf of Mexico side—the western side—of Tampa Bay. Hillsborough County, with its almost perfectly square boundaries, claims most of the eastern shoreline of the bay.

Although Pinellas County is the largest peninsula in the Tampa Bay area, dividing the bay from the Gulf of Mexico, many smaller peninsulas split the bay into lesser bays and inlets. Numerous islands rim the coastal areas, ranging in size from those large enough to hold towns and cities to tiny plots home only to birds.

Altitude sickness isn't a concern as the highest point in these two counties is only about 120 feet above sea level.

Flat doesn't mean boring, however. Winding rivers flow through oak hammocks and past downtown office complexes. Deer and coyotes still inhabit palmetto thickets in parts of Pinellas County, even though technically Pinellas County has no rural land. Cypress swamps, salt marshes, and mangrove stands invite modern-day explorers to venture out of the concrete and asphalt world into the rhythms of the natural world.

Nor does flat and natural mean unpopulated and without the amenities of civilization. Almost 2.4 million people make the Tampa/St. Petersburg/Clearwater metro area (which includes smaller cities and unincorporated areas within a slightly larger geographic area) their home. That makes it more populated than any other metro area in the state, according to the 2000 census.

i The federal government includes Manatee County to the south and Pasco County to the north in designating this Tampa-St. Petersburg-Clearwater a Metropolitan Statistical Area (MSA).

Anchor Cities
Tampa
Tampa grew from a small military outpost, Fort Brooke, established in 1823 at the start of the Seminole Indian Wars. From this seed, the city became a seaport of sorts, trading mainly with Cuba, which came in handy after the Civil War—bringing in desperately needed gold to rebuild Florida—and during the Spanish-American War—shipping Teddy Roosevelt's Rough Riders and other troops to Cuba in the 1898 war that cost Spain Cuba, Guam, the Philippine Islands, and Puerto Rico.

i Florida is a Clean Indoor Air State, which means smoking is not allowed inside any public building with very few exceptions (tobacco shops, for one). Nor is smoking allowed inside any public or private enclosed workplace.

With the discovery of phosphate—used in fertilizers, animal feed, toothpaste, light bulbs, and more—and the arrival of the railroad in the 1880s—Tampa grew by fits and starts to its present population of approximately 343,000 people. Neighborhoods within the city limits include the formerly unincorporated areas of Sulpher Springs, Palma Ceia, and New Tampa plus the formerly incorporated towns of North Tampa, Ybor City, Fort Brooke, West Tampa, and Port Tampa City.

As the county seat for Hillsborough County, a county with only two other incorporated cities, Plant City and Temple Terrace, and one that is 84 percent rural, Tampa dominates the area. So much so, in fact, that there have been a few unsuccessful attempts to consolidate the City of Tampa and Hillsborough County governments.

Since Tampa is an international sea and air port of call, some foreign consulates have their offices here, including Greece, Panama, and Costa Rica. The Seminole Indian Tribe of Florida has a reservation inside the Tampa city limits on the premises of the Hard Rock Café and Casino.

The University of South Florida in Tampa houses cutting edge medical and other types of research facilities. Across the street from USF is MOSI, the Museum of Science and Industry, which brings in exhibits from around the world to help us understand the natural and techno-logical worlds. Sit in a wind tunnel at MOSI, for example, and see what hurricane force winds feel like. And, if shopping is your thing, then start by checking out Tampa's International Plaza or Westshore Mall.

But enough of bare-bones facts. Come play with pirates! No real pirates are known to have plagued Tampa Bay, but that didn't stop us from inventing one. Every January, Tampa goes a little crazy commemorating a pirate invasion that never really occurred. So grab a costume, join a krewe, and help Jose Gaspar invade the city all over again during Gasparilla, a month long series of parades, art festivals, and other festivities attracting pirate-loving participants from all over.

Gasparilla sets the tone for the rest of the year and for the area—we're serious about our fun and we work hard to make sure life is about more than the daily grind. Did we mention Tampa is home to one of the most child-friendly zoos in the country? Or that we have the largest performing arts complex south of Washington, D.C., the Straz Center, formerly the Tampa Bay Performing Arts Center? We'll save those for later chapters. Meantime, let's move on across the bay.

i A well-known evangelist cut his preaching teeth on the streets of Tampa in the late 1930s when he attended Florida Bible Institute in the Temple Terrace area. He had lots to preach about as Tampa simmered with mob activity and political corruption. FBI later became Trinity College, now in Pasco County. The preacher was William Franklin "Billy" Graham.

St. Petersburg

Named after St. Petersburg, Russia, the birthplace of one of the city's founders, the City of St. Peters-burg takes up most of southern Pinellas County. The city's current population of 248,098 makes it the fourth largest city in Florida, and its vibrant downtown belies its former reputation as "God's Waiting Room" where retirees whiled away their days sitting on city-provided green benches or playing shuffleboard.

Not that the reputation ever really was accu-rate. The nation's first scheduled commercial air-plane flight took off from St. Petersburg in 1914, the same year baseball's Grapefruit League—aka spring training—began in, you guessed it, St. Petersburg.

i In 1910, Lew B. Brown, owner of *The Evening Independent*, dubbed St. Petersburg "The Sunshine City" and said the paper would be free any day the sun didn't make an appearance in the paper's coverage area. That "Sunshine Offer" stood until the paper closed in 1986. In seventy-six years, the paper was free 296 times— about four times a year.

Incorporated in 1892, the city today is home to an impressive collection of Salvador Dalí works and Major League Baseball's Tampa Bay Rays. The City of St. Petersburg Municipal Marina, with 610 boat slips, is the largest public marina in either Pinellas or Hillsborough County.

In recent years, the city has expanded north-east until it bumps up against the southeastern part of Clearwater. In fact, the two cities share naming rights to the St. Petersburg-Clearwater International Airport, although the airport is on unincorporated Pinellas County land.

Not only is St. Petersburg surrounded by water on three sides, it also contains Lake Mag-giore, a lake large enough that, in less environ-mentally aware days, it was the site of hydrofoil boat races where a number of speed records were set. Today Lake Maggiore is part of the Boyd Hill Nature Preserve that boasts 3 miles

⊙ Close-up

Tampa Bay

Humans aren't the only inhabitants of the Tampa Bay area. Tampa Bay itself teems with fish, shellfish, reptiles and other critters that live among the sea grasses and mangroves. Sea birds nest in these watery areas, too, but sometimes encroach a bit into human territory. It's not uncommon to see an egret, miles inland, walking across your yard poking around for bugs, or to have an osprey pair nesting atop a highway road sign near one of the bridges spanning the bay. With 398 square miles of water at high tide, Tampa Bay is Florida's largest open-water estuary, where salt water from the Gulf of Mexico mixes with fresh water draining from nearby land.

Throughout this book, we'll spotlight human activity as it relates to Tampa Bay—check out the sport fishing, boating, cruises, and other activities in their various sections. For now, however, let's look more closely at the bay that gives the area its name and its predominant ecology.

GEOGRAPHY

Dangling off the west coast of Florida, about halfway up, is a 280 square-mile peninsula, Pinellas County. The City of St. Petersburg takes up much of the southern end of the peninsula, and the City of Clearwater anchors its northern end.

Off the western shore of Pinellas County, a series of barrier islands follows the contours of the peninsula, starting with Anclote Key and Honeymoon Island in the north and continuing south to Pass-a-Grille Beach and Tierra Verde. When the Pinellas peninsula ends, the barrier islands continue, stretching south toward the next part of the Florida mainland, the Bradenton-Sarasota area in Manatee County.

Mullet Key, the last island in the Pinellas County part of the chain and shaped like a V, points not quite 2 miles southwest toward a lone island, Egmont Key, claimed by Hillsborough County. South of Egmont Key across about 3 miles of water, Anna Maria Island, part of Manatee County, begins another stretch of barrier islands following Florida's coastline southward towards the Cape Coral/Fort Myers area.

Salt water from the Gulf of Mexico flows east and north through the miles-wide gaps between Mullet Key, Egmont Key, and Anna Maria Island, filling the 80-square mile or so space between the Pinellas Peninsula and the Florida mainland—Tampa Bay. Another peninsula extending south from Tampa International Airport to MacDill Air Force Base splits Tampa Bay into two lesser bays—Hillsborough Bay on the east and Old Tampa Bay on the west. Smaller islands dot the shoreline all around Tampa Bay, causing the water to swirl into lesser bays and bayous with such colorful names as Cockroach Bay on the Hillsborough County side and Coffeepot Bayou in St. Petersburg.

The bay is about 40 miles long and about 20 miles wide at its widest point. Except for a spot near Egmont Key where water rushing in and out has gouged a 90 foot deep hole, Tampa Bay is not quite 45 feet deep, and that's only because periodic dredging keeps the shipping channels open to that depth. The average depth of the bay is between 11 and 12 feet.

Four main freshwater rivers—the Hillsborough, the Alafia, the Manatee, and the Little Manatee—and more than 100 smaller tributaries from a watershed area of about 2,200 square miles empty into Tampa Bay.

ECOSYSTEM

The mixture of fresh and salt water nourishes a web of plant life that provides an incubator for sea creatures from microscopic phytoplankton to gigantic manatees.

As the freshwater rivers and streams get closer to the saltwater bay, the water becomes brackish and the land becomes marshy. Despite their somewhat desolate appearance, these salt marshes are, like rainforests, some of the most biologically productive places on earth. Salt marshes also protect the land against the erosion of the tides, act as a buffer during storms, and filter pollutants from the water before it reaches the bay.

During low tide, mud flats appear around the fringes of the bay. Wading birds gather and eat their fill of small crabs, clams, and other delicacies exposed by the receding water.

Stands of black, red, and white mangrove trees line the bay itself, their interlocked roots and branches trapping nutrient-rich sediment that feeds tiny worms and other invertebrates. These in turn are food for mollusks and crabs and newly hatched snook, mullet, and other fish.

Extending further into the bay past the mangroves, shallow flats form underwater meadows where sea grasses sway to the tides' rhythms, feeding and sheltering sea urchins, shrimp, and manatees.

Oyster bars or reefs dot the bay, especially near river mouths and other freshwater sources. Fishermen love spotting oyster bars, as they attract redfish, snook, and other game fish. Not so attractive, however, are the razor sharp oyster shells that can damage boat hulls and slice open unprotected feet.

More than 200 species of fish live in Tampa Bay and more than 25 species of birds nest along its shores.

Three National Wildlife Refuges have been designated in Tampa Bay: Pinellas National Wildlife Refuge, Egmont Key National Wildlife Refuge, and Passage Key National Wildlife Refuge.

RECLAIMING THE BAY

As the Tampa Bay area grew and as flat-bottomed skiffs powered by poles and oars gave way to gas- and diesel-powered inboard and outboard motor boats, the life hidden beneath the surface of the bay suffered.

Too much nitrogen running into the bay—the result of everything from an increase in industrial wastewater and an increase in the use of lawn fertilizer to a decrease in the amount of freshwater entering the bay—caused algae to grow at a more rapid rate than it should. The overabundance of algae reduced the level of oxygen in the water, which killed fish, reduced the clarity of the water, and killed underwater acres of sea grass.

Boat propellers razed sea grass meadows and killed or injured manatees. Bacteria from partially untreated wastewater closed beaches and swimming areas.

In 1990, Tampa Bay was designated by Congress as one of 28 estuaries in the National Estuary Program. Various local municipal, county, state, and federal governments and agencies formed the Tampa Bay National Estuary Program (www.tbep.org) to restore and preserve Tampa Bay's ecosystems.

Today, Tampa Bay has been partially restored, and residents and local governments have a greater understanding of the bay's importance to the region's economy and to the overall quality of life in the area defined by this body of water.

of walking trails and five different ecosystems nestled between suburban neighborhoods and a golf course.

Speaking of environmentally friendly, St. Petersburg built the first water reclamation system in the United States. Instead of using increasingly scarce drinking water for things like watering lawns, the city sends 37 million gallons of treated wastewater a day through almost 300 miles of a separate piping system to more than 10,000 customers. The system is still one of the largest in the world. What difference does it make? While the rest of the area is restricted to watering lawns one day a week, reclaimed-water users can soak their lawns three days a week.

i **Don't expect restaurant table servers to bring water automatically. Despite being surrounded by water, the central Florida area has experienced several years of drought. Water reserves are low, and we have contests to think up new ways to save water.**

Some people consider downtown St. Petersburg's nightlife, centered near the BayWalk complex of shops, restaurants, and entertainment venues, to be among the Tampa Bay area's best. With the American Stage Theatre producing at least one open-air performance each season and with musicians from around the country jamming at Jannus Landing and other spots, they just might be right.

The University of South Florida's St. Petersburg campus, the Poynter Institute for Media Studies, and a host of other resources make St. Petersburg an academic force to be reckoned with. Or is that "with which to be reckoned"? Guess we'd better check with one of the professors. Meantime, let's move along to Clearwater.

i **Did we mention the amount of sunshine for which St. Petersburg is noted? At one point, the city held a Guinness record for the most consecutive days with sunshine—786—logged between 1967 and 1968.**

Clearwater

Before Pinellas County came to be, the peninsula was part of Hillsborough County, and Clearwater was mostly farmland. When Punta Pinal ("Point of Pines") became separate from Hillsborough County in the early 1900s, Clearwater, sitting atop a bluff above a natural harbor, was the largest town and became the county seat.

Today, the City of Clearwater (population 107,742) stretches the width of northern Pinellas County from the Gulf of Mexico to Tampa Bay—hence the name of the major east-west road: Gulf-to-Bay Boulevard. A city-owned marina provides boat slips for 209 boats, and a number of charter fishing and day-cruise boats launch from the city's harbor.

Saxophones simper and trumpets wail each October as Coachman Park, a two-acre grassy basin with a performing pavilion near Clearwater's bluffs, hosts the Annual Clearwater Jazz Holiday. For 30 years Clearwater has drawn crowds from around the world for four days of non-stop music and art. Dave Brubeck, the Count Basie Orchestra, and Spyro Gyra are just a few of the many top-name musicians sharing their talents in Clearwater.

i **Rolling Stones fans probably already know that in May 1965, Keith Richards and Mick Jagger wrote the bulk of "(I Can't Get No) Satisfaction" at the Jack Tar New Fort Harrison Hotel in Clearwater.**

In 1975, the city gained notoriety when the Church of Scientology, founded by now deceased L. Ron Hubbard, bought the aging Fort Harrison Hotel and converted it into the Flag Service Organization, their worldwide spiritual headquarters.

Clearwater also is known for Ruth Eckerd Hall, which has been listed in *Variety* magazine's top 10 entertainment venues by ticket sales. Broadway musicals and rock bands, stand-up comics and the Miami Ballet all play at Ruth Eckerd Hall to sell-out crowds. Want to do some performing yourself? The Marcia P. Hoffman Institute for the

Vital Statistics

Mayors: Pam Iorio (Tampa), Bill Foster, (St. Petersburg), and Frank V. Hibbard (Clearwater)

Florida's governor: Charlie Crist

United States senators from Florida: Bill Nelson and George S. LeMieux

Average maximum temperatures (degrees Fahrenheit): 70 (January), 81 (April), 90 (July), 84 (October)

Average minimum temperatures (degrees Fahrenheit): 52 (January), 62 (April), 75 (July), 68 (October)

Average precipitation (in inches): 2.27 (January), 1.80 (April), 6.49 (July), 2.29 (October)

Average annual snowfall (in inches): Zero!

Total combined population of the two counties (2007 U.S. Census estimate): 2,092,164

Counties: Hillsborough (Tampa) and Pinellas (St. Petersburg and Clearwater)

Total combined land area of the two counties: 1,331 square miles

Median age: 35.1 years (Hillsborough County); 43.0 years (Pinellas County)

Average household income (2007): $50,485 (Hillsborough County); $44,325 (Pinellas County)

Median price for house (2007): $222,800 (Hillsborough County); $204,700 (Pinellas County)

Major airports: Tampa International Airport (TPA), St. Petersburg/Clearwater International Airport (PIE)

Major seaports: Port of Tampa (Florida's largest in area and cargo tonnage); Port of St. Petersburg

Major interstates: I–275 and I–4

Total consumer spending (2002): $40.1 billion (Hillsborough County); $31.3 billion (Pinellas County)

Hotel and motel rooms in the area: More than 30,000

Florida base sales tax rate (as of July, 2008): 6 percent, but many counties collect an additional 0.25 percent to 1.5 percent on sales and most charge an additional transient lodging tax. In both Hillsborough and Pinellas County rates are 7 percent sales tax and 12 percent lodging tax.

Major colleges and universities: University of South Florida, University of Tampa, St. Petersburg College, Eckerd College, Stetson Law School

Major league sports teams: Tampa Bay Buccaneers (NFL), Tampa Bay Lightning (NHL), Tampa Bay Rays (MLB)

Famous people from the Tampa Bay area: Angela Bassett, Ray Charles, Hulk Hogan, Lauren Hutton, Jack Kerouac, Evel Knievel, Butterfly McQueen, Jim Morrison, Lisa Marie Presley, among others

Companies headquartered or started in the Tampa Bay area: Home Shopping Network, Hooters, Jabil Circuits, Inc., OSI Restaurant Partners (Outback & Bonefish Grill), Raymond James Financial Services, Rooms to Go, WellCare Health Plans, Inc., Wikipedia

Military bases: MacDill Air Force Base (U.S. Central Command Headquarters, Tampa), U.S. Coast Guard Stations (St. Petersburg, Clearwater, and Tampa)

Motor vehicle laws: Move over: See flashing lights in the emergency lane up ahead? You are required to vacate the lane closest to the emergency vehicle (three or more lanes) or to slow down to 20 mph or less (two lanes). It's called the Move Over Law. **Car seats:** Children age three and under must ride in an approved car seat or carrier; children ages four and five must be properly restrained (approved car seat/carrier and/or seat belt). **Seatbelts:** Drivers and all front seat passengers must wear seat belts. **Motorcycles:** Motorcyclists over the age of 21 with proper proof of insurance can get a hel-met exemption; otherwise helmets and approved eyewear are required. Motorcyclists must have head-lamps on day and night. Go to the Florida Department of Highway Safety and Motor Vehicles' Web site at www.flhsmv.gov/fhp/cps for more laws and exact language.

Performing Arts brings top instructors in dance, acting, singing, and other performance arts to Ruth Eckerd Hall and offers classes for everyone from pre-school children to senior adults.

Other Towns

Pinellas County's beach cities are worlds of their own and deserve more mention than there is room for here, as do other communities in Pinel-las County.

So look for activities and places of interest in these communities to be listed along with those in St. Petersburg:

- Gulfport
- Kenneth City
- Lealman
- Madeira Beach
- North Redington Beach
- Pinellas Park
- Redington Beach
- Redington Shores
- Seminole
- South Pasadena
- St. Pete Beach
- Treasure Island

And look for activities and places of interest in these communities to be listed along with those in Clearwater:

- Belleair
- Belleair Beach
- Belleair Bluffs
- Belleair Shore
- Dunedin
- Indian Rocks Beach
- Indian Shores
- Largo
- Oldsmar
- Palm Harbor
- Safety Harbor
- Tarpon Springs

CLIMATE AND WEATHER

Maybe we've belabored the point about sun-shine. But it's true. The percentage of sunshine hours ranges from 61 percent in December to 75 percent in April and May. We don't buy chains or snow tires. Most of us don't have an ice scraper.

That doesn't mean it's always warm. There are a few nights each winter when we cover our shrubs and plants with sheets and light blankets. Not because there's been a collective breakdown of clothes dryers, but because of overnight frost and freeze warnings. Citrus and strawberry grow-ers camp outside those nights, tending to their plants and hoping to save their crops.

So while you won't need a snowsuit or insu-lated boots, pack a jacket and a sweater or two when you visit in the winter. Even in the summer-time you may want a light jacket handy for indoor areas where the air conditioning can sometimes make you wonder if you traveled too far south and landed in Antarctica.

Sunny days, balmy breezes, and mild winters can easily lull visitors and residents into forgetting about Mother Nature's less benevolent side.

Hurricanes and tropical storms spawn tor-nadoes and waterspouts and, combined with normal tidal fluctuations in sea levels, can flood coastal areas. Lightning strikes in the Tampa Bay

Visitor Centers and Other Helpful Links

Our two area visitors' centers have loads of information to share and staffs that can help you fine-tune your vacation. Call or e-mail and ask them to send you a free visitors guide to the area—you'll find shorter but more comprehensive listings of places to stay, places to eat, and things to do than we can provide in this book. Plus, you'll find discount coupons inside that will help you stretch your dollars. You can also go to their Web sites and explore online—look for coupons there, too.

Tampa/Hillsborough County
Tampa Bay and Company
401 E. Jackson St., Ste. 2100
Tampa
(813) 223-1111, (800) 44-TAMPA (448-2672)
www.visittampabay.com

St. Petersburg/Clearwater/Pinellas County
St. Petersburg/Clearwater Area Convention and Visitors Bureau
13805 58th St. N., Ste. 2-200
Clearwater
(727) 464-7200, (877) 352-3224
www.floridasbeach.com

area more often than in some other places in the country. Scorching summer days feel even hotter when the humidity rises, sapping energy from even the hardiest among us. Pollen and other particles in the air, especially in the early spring, can cause problems for people with allergies.

So plan ahead. Pack the sunscreen and use it. Drink lots of water. Pay attention to the pollen count, usually listed in the local weather reports. When severe weather threatens, tune to a local emergency broadcast channel and follow their directions.

The rest of the time? Enjoy that Florida sunshine!

GETTING HERE, GETTING AROUND

The Tampa Bay area may win the prize for the most ways to get to a major city in the United States. With two international airports and host of smaller municipal and executive airports, two international seaports and myriad smaller marinas, plus the usual highways, byways, and rail service, getting here should not be a problem.

Nor is getting around once you're here too terribly difficult, as most of the metropolitan areas are laid out in an orderly grid pattern. If you find yourself in the areas that aren't and that wind and meander like a confused snail's trail, just take a deep breath and remember: You're in Florida, Land of Flowers, where the pace is a tad more relaxed. Find someone to ask or pull over and pull out the maps. You'll get there.

BY AIR

Tampa International Airport (TIA)

Tampa International Airport (TIA) (www.tampa airport.com) qualifies as both a major travel hub and a not-to-be-missed attraction. So read through the information for travelers and then linger a bit over the why-you-ought-to-bring-your-date-or-the-kids-here bit that follows. You'll be glad you did.

TIA consistently gets high reviews from travelers for its easy-to-navigate design and for its friendly service and thoughtful amenities. The airport is arranged like a bicycle wheel with the terminal as the center hub and six airside buildings (five of which were operational at press time) on the rim. Two shuttle trams run back and forth from each airside building to the terminal. Traveling at a speed that reaches 12 mph, the trams

> **i** Local newscasters call Tampa International Airport "TIA," but remember to enter TPA when buying tickets online or you'll end up in Tirana, Albania. Not that we have anything against Albania, but we doubt you'll find a Busch Gardens theme park or a major league baseball team there. Around these parts, "TPA" means Tampa Port Authority, another major transportation hub.

make the trip every 37 seconds and can carry up to 17 passengers, so you never have to wait very long to catch a ride.

Information about the Marriot Hotel located at the airport is in the Accommodations chapter.

> **i** Super sleuths may notice Airsides B and D are not listed at TIA, where the airside buildings are lettered A through F. Airside B is there, kind of. Ask your checked-in bags. They may have stopped at what used to be Airside B and is now TIA's remote baggage sorting facility. Airside D was demolished in 2008. Planes park there overnight.

In the Terminal

Once you leave your plane, follow the crowd from your gate toward the center of the airside building to the security check-in area. You'll see a walkway to the side that will take you to the shuttle trams. There is limited seating at the front and back of each tram. Heed the canned advice—hold onto one of the poles and brace yourself as the trams accelerate and decelerate quickly.

Passengers exit the shuttle tram on the opposite side from which they entered and find themselves on the third level of the terminal building near either a red or a blue set of elevators. Look up at one of the overhead signs to confirm whether your flight was from a red or a blue airline. Take that color elevator or escalator down two flights to the baggage claim area, which also will be designated as either a red or a blue area. Ticket counters are on the second level.

i **T.G.I. Friday's, located inside the terminal at TIA, created the first World Bartending Championships in the 1980s. In 2006, the franchise located at TIA was named the chain's world-wide top performing franchise.**

If you decide to check out the many shops or to get a bite to eat before collecting your bags, remember whether you are red or blue—airlinewise, not politically. Take the wrong-colored elevator or escalator down, and you may end up purple, as you'll end up on the wrong side of the building and will have to go back upstairs, cross the lobby, and go down the correct set of elevators or escalators.

Ground Transportation from TIA

A Commercial Ground Transportation Quadrant is located at each of the four corners of TIA's baggage claim area. Here you will find:

- **Taxicabs:** Yellow Cab (813-253-0121) and United Cab (813-253-2424) serve airport travelers, and each charges the same rates: $15 minimum, $25 to downtown Tampa or the cruise port, or $2 plus $2.25 per mile.
- **Airport limos:** SuperShuttle (800-282-6817 or 727-572-1111), a shared-passenger van service, covers Hillsborough, Pinellas, Pasco, and Hernando Counties. Rates begin at $12 and include up to three pieces of luggage.
- **Rental car courtesy vehicle service:** Car rental companies located off of airport property (see list) provide free transportation to their facilities.
- **Charter buses:** If you are part of a tour, you will meet your driver or guide here, unless you are told otherwise.

Other ground transportation options include:

Color-Coding for Ease at TIA

TIA color-codes airlines for separate loading and unloading areas, separate baggage areas, and separate elevators and escalators to minimize overcrowding and keep foot, car, and plane traffic flowing smoothly. Here's a list of current red and blue airlines.

Follow RED signs for:
Air Canada
Air Tran
British Airways
Cayman Airways
Charters
Continental
Frontier
Midwest
Southwest
Spirit
Ted
United
West Jet

Follow BLUE signs for:
American
Delta
Freedom Airlines
Jet Blue
Northwest/KLM
US Airways

- **Local buses:** Hillsborough Area Regional Transit (HART) buses stop outside the east end of the red baggage claim area near baggage carousel #20. Route maps and schedules are available at the bus stop, or you can call (813) 254-4278 or go online to www.gohart .org, where you can even purchase fare cards in advance.

- **Rental cars:** Exit the baggage claim area and cross the walkway—which also consists of four lanes for cars arriving to pick up passengers—where a number of companies have their counters (see list).

Parking and Curbside Options

Generally speaking, motor vehicle traffic flows smoothly at the airport. All traffic enters from the south, circles the airport counter-clockwise, and exits to the south. All parking options are open 24/7. The maximum stay in any lot is 45 days. TIA provides wheelchair-accessible parking on all levels of all parking garages and near the bus stops in the Economy Lot.

i TIA broadcasts continuous updates on parking and other traffic information on 1610 AM radio. If you have a particular concern about parking, call (813) 870-8790.

ECONOMY PARKING

Just before entering the airport loop, a spur to the right takes drivers to the Cell Phone Waiting Lot, the U.S. Post Office (open until midnight on April 15), and the Economy Parking Garage and Lot, which holds 10,545 vehicles. Rates are $9 per day or $1 per 20 minutes. Clearance heights are 8 feet in the garage and 13 feet in the lot. Shuttles come by every three to seven minutes 24/7.

LONG-TERM GARAGE

This is the first large building drivers see to their left as they enter the airport loop. The Long Term Garage holds 7,635 vehicles. Rates are $15 per day or $1 per 20 minutes. The first hour is free. Clearance height is 7 feet, 10 inches, although there is a high vehicle area with a clearance of 10 feet. Go to Level 5 to take the monorail to the terminal or go to Level 2 to walk to the terminal.

SHORT-TERM GARAGE

This parking is actually on Levels 4 through 9 of the terminal building itself and will be the sec-

Rental Car Companies Serving Tampa International Airport

Located at the Airport

Avis
(800) 831-2847
(813) 396-3500
www.avis.com

Budget
(800) 527-0700
(813) 877-6051
www.budget.com

Dollar Rent A Car, Inc.
(800) 800-4000
(813) 396-3640
www.dollar.com

Enterprise Rent-A-Car
(800) 736-8222
(813) 396-4000
www.enterprise.com

Hertz Car Rental
(800) 654-3131
(813) 874-3232
www.hertz.com

Thrifty Car Rental
(800) 847-4389
(813) 348-0607
www.thrifty.com

Located Off-site

Alamo
(813) 396-4140
www.alamo.com

E-Z Rent-A-Car
(800) 277-5171
(813) 287-9787
www.e-zrentacar.com

National Car Rental
(813) 396-4140
www.nationalcar.com

Payless Car Rental
(813) 289-6554
www.paylesscarrental.com

Specialty Auto Rentals
(866) 825-7005
(813) 639-9611
www.bnm.com/special.htm

U-Save Auto Rental of Florida
(888) 440-8744
(813) 282-8619 or (813) 287-1872
www.usave.com

ond building seen to the left. This garage holds 3,612 vehicles. Rates are $20 per day or $1 per 20 minutes with the first hour free. Clearance height is 6 feet, 8 inches. As in the passenger areas, parking is divided into red and blue areas and color-coded elevators take passengers down to the terminal areas.

VALET PARKING

Need an extra hand or you're in a rush? Drop off your car at the blue departure curbside between 5:30 a.m. and 5:30 p.m. for valet service. For any-time valet service, go to Level 5 of the Short Term Garage and look for the Yeager elevators on the red side of the garage. Rates are $25 per day or $1 per half hour with a $5 minimum.

CURBSIDE DEPARTURES AND ARRIVALS

Not only is motor vehicle traffic directed to sepa-rate areas for red and blue airlines, traffic is also diverted to the upper ticketing level to drop off passengers for outgoing flights (Departures) and to the lower baggage level to pick up incoming passengers (Arrivals).

As with most major airports, security con-cerns do not allow drivers to park in these areas or to leave their vehicles. If someone is picking you up at the airport, have them wait in the Cell Phone Waiting Lot until after you have claimed your bags.

Leaving the Airport

All traffic exits to the south of the airport. Allow plenty of time to get to your destination. If you suddenly realize you're in the wrong lane to make an exit, go to the next exit, get off safely, and backtrack. We want you to arrive alive!

- To get to St. Petersburg, southern Pinellas County, and the southern Pinellas County beaches, look for I–275 west (Howard Frank-land Bridge).
- To get to Clearwater, northern Pinellas County, and the northern Pinellas County beaches, look for Hwy. 60 west or SR 60 west (Courtney Campbell Causeway).

- To get to downtown Tampa, look for Spruce Street.
- To get to east Tampa, east Hillsborough County, Lakeland, or Orlando, look for I–275 north and then I–4 east.
- To go north towards Brooksville, take the Vet-eran's Expressway to I–75 north.

i TIA's Web site (www.tampaairport .com/maps) contains clearly drawn interactive maps of each level. Click on the icons at the top of each map to locate rest-rooms, baggage carousels for each airline, and other necessities.

St. Petersburg-Clearwater Interna-tional Airport (PIE)

St. Petersburg-Clearwater International Air-port (PIE) (www.fly2pie.com) isn't a just pie-in-the-sky maybe-someday airport. It's been around almost as long as Tampa's mega-port, and it has seen upwards of 1.4 million passengers a year come and go through its gates. But this PIE defi-nitely has a flavor all its own.

It's tropical beach-chair relaxed, and it's easy to scoot into and out of.

And talk about being close to the beaches: You could step off a plane at PIE and be on a bayside white-sand beach within 30 minutes.

But what really sells people on the St. Petersburg-Clearwater International Airport are the low-cost, non-stop flights from many smaller markets in the U.S. and Canada.

PIE has built up such a loyal customer base, in fact, that when one airline announced they would be discontinuing service to PIE because of climbing fuel prices and other factors, they were flooded with almost 7,000 letters and e-mails from PIE fans asking them to reconsider. They did.

So here's the rundown on the St. Petersburg-Clearwater International Airport—our favorite PIE.

ℹ Why PIE? Built in the 1950s after the U.S. government turned over its World War II combat-training facility to Pinellas County, the airport was originally called Pinellas International Airport. PIA was already taken, however, by the airport at Peoria, Illinois. PIE it was and has been even when the name was changed again in 1957 to its present St. Petersburg-Clearwater International Airport.

Commercial Planes Servicing PIE

- Allegiant Air—Services smaller airports from Illinois to North Carolina and New York.
- Beau Rivage—Charter service to Gulfport-Biloxi, Mississippi.
- Seacoast Airlines—Charter service to Key West and Marathon, Florida.
- Sunwing Airlines—Seasonal service to Toronto, Canada.
- Transat Holidays—Seasonal service to Halifax, Nova Scotia.
- USA 3000 Airlines—Service to Chicago-O'Hare, Illinois.; Cleveland, Ohio; and St. Louis, Missouri.

In the Terminal

You'd have to work really hard to get lost here. Ticketing is at one end, baggage is at the other, and there are plenty of signs to point you in the right direction. Upstairs is a food-service concession and a lounge area. Scattered throughout the terminal are vending machines and newsstand-type vendors. Stroll through the terminal and see copper fish swimming through mangrove roots while a wading bird hunts nearby. Check out the other artwork throughout the tropically themed facility.

Even if you don't have baggage to claim, take a few minutes to be awed by the full-scale replica of an early 1900s airboat hanging from the ceiling. Remember what you just arrived in, and then imagine the pilot and passenger who flew in a craft like the one above you in 1914 from St. Petersburg to Tampa—the word's first heavier-than-air commercial airline flight. (Read more about the pilot, Tony Jannus, and this history-making flight in the History chapter.)

Ground Transportation

Exit the terminal through the baggage area to get to the short-term parking ($13 per day or $2 per hour) and long-term parking ($10 per day or $2 per hour) parking areas. Both lots are open-air and are open only during scheduled flight times. The remote lot ($8 per day) is open only during peak season when the long-term lot is full.

Taxis generally wait across the curbside drop-off/pick-up area, or you can call (727) 799-2222 for a Yellow cab or Yellow shuttle van or (727) 535-0000 for a United cab.

Car rental companies serving PIE are:
- Alamo/National, (727) 530-5491 (one counter services both companies)
- Avis, (727) 530-1407
- Budget, (727) 535-5263
- Dollar, (727) 531-3557 (off-site shuttle service)
- Enterprise, (727) 524-1239
- Hertz, (727) 531-3774

Leaving the Airport

All traffic exits onto SR 686 (Roosevelt Boulevard).

Turn left (east) at the stoplight to go to I–275 to Tampa or St. Petersburg or to get to SR 688 (Ulmerton Road), which takes you west to the Largo/Seminole area and the mid-county beaches.

Turn right onto SR 686, which becomes East Bay Drive and takes you west to Largo and the mid-county beaches. Or take the first turn to the right off of SR 686 to go over the Bayside Bridge, which becomes McMullen-Booth Road. At the northern end of the Bayside Bridge, exit for SR 60 west (Gulf-to-Bay Boulevard), which takes you to Clearwater and the north county beaches, or for SR 60 east which takes you over the Courtney Campbell Bridge to Tampa.

OTHER AIRPORTS

As many as 30 other smaller heliports and air-parks dot the Tampa Bay area. The ones listed below are the larger, publicly managed airports in Hillsborough and Pinellas Counties.

Tampa/Hillsborough County

In addition to Tampa International Airport, the Hillsborough County Aviation Authority oversees three other public airports, used primarily by corporate and private jets and airplanes. Each facility has rental cars, fuel, and maintenance services plus other amenities available.

Peter O. Knight Airport

Tampa's main airport from 1935 to 1945, Peter O. Knight Airport sits on the southern tip of the Davis Islands group and right across Seddon Channel from the Port of Tampa. Peter O. Knight Airport operates seven days a week, 12 hours a day, and the seaplane basin is still operational. Call (813) 251-1752 or go to www.airnav.com/airport/ktpf for more information.

Plant City Airport

Located in eastern Hillsborough County near I–4. Call (813) 752-4710 or go to www.pcairport.net for more information.

Tampa Executive Airport (formerly Vandenberg Airport)

Located in central Hillsborough County, this airport sits just north of I–4, making it convenient to travelers heading west into Tampa or east to Orlando. Call (813) 262-1515 or go to www.tampa airport.com for more information.

St. Petersburg/Southern Pinellas County

Albert Whitted Airport

Open 24/7, Albert Whitted Airport, owned and operated by the City of St. Petersburg, services commercial and private aviation as well as such organizations as the Civil Air Patrol, Bayflight Medavac and other medical flight services, area news organizations, and some military operations (U.S. Coast Guard and U.S. Army Reserve Helicopters). Call (727) 893-7654 or go to www.stpete .org/airport/index.asp for more information.

Each October the St. Petersburg AirFest brings airshows, displays, and concerts to Albert Whitted Airport. Each April Grand Prix racecars zoom across one of Albert Whitted's runways as part of the official racecourse (see the Spectator Sports chapter).

A nearby city park offers an observation area for people who just love to watch avionic activity (see the Parks and Recreation chapter).

Clearwater/Northern Pinellas County

Clearwater Airpark

Owned by the City of Clearwater and leased to Clearwater Aircraft, Inc., the Clearwater Airpark is open every day from 7 a.m. to 9 p.m. The airpark sits in a residential area in the middle of Clearwater, putting it close to area beaches and not far from U.S. 19, the main north-south road through Pinellas County. For more information, call (727) 443-3433 or go to www.clearwaterairpark.com.

> **i** Want to see the Tampa Bay area by hot air balloon? Go to www.blast valve.com/balloon_rides/usa/florida_balloon _rides for a list of links to companies providing a lofty view of beaches and bays.

BY LAND

Train Service

Trains brought people to Tampa and carried out valuable phosphate ore in the late 1800s. Tampa Union Station, built in 1912 when it served three passenger rail lines, reflects the preeminence of trains in the late 19th century and early 20th century. This magnificent Italian Renaissance style building is on the National Register of Historic Places and was restored in 2001.

Today, Amtrak (www.amtrak.com) offers two levels of daily train service from Tampa. Silver Service trains include the Silver Meteor and the Silver Star, both of which have sleeping accommodations, coach seating, and a dining car. Palmetto Service trains offer Business Class service, which includes complimentary non-alcoholic beverages, newspapers, and other services.

Both trains travel south to Miami and north as far as New York City.

Tampa Union Station station is located at 601 N. Nebraska Ave. (SR45), Tampa. The station is open 8:15 a.m. to 6:15 p.m., seven days a week. The Quick-Trak automated ticketing machine is available 8:15 a.m. to 6:30 p.m., seven days a week.

(Q) Close-up

Tampa International Airport

It's a shame most of the almost 20 million air travelers passing through Tampa International Airport each year zip through the terminal, focused on finding either a departing gate or a baggage carousel. And it's a shame most local people think of TIA as just a place to fly out of or into.

TIA is way more than that. It's a public art gallery. Educational field trip. Historical site. Shopping and dining destination. It's even a place to have a child's birthday party complete with scavenger hunt—for free!

So let's learn about this cornerstone of the Tampa Bay area.

HISTORY

By 1928, it was clear that airplanes were more than a passing fad and that air travel held real business potential. Fourteen years earlier the first commercially scheduled heavier-than-air flight had landed in Tampa, or more accurately in Tampa Bay near the mouth of the Hillsborough River.

But trains and ships still provided much of the Tampa Bay area's transportation, along with that newer invention, the automobile. So when Drew Field Municipal Airport opened on February 23, 1928, area residents might have wondered why anyone would want to put an airport 6 miles out in the boonies. Plus, rumor had it that another airport—what would become Peter O. Knight Airport—was in the works closer to downtown. That was another seven years away, however.

The 160 acres of mostly pine woodlands that made up Drew Field Municipal Airport had been obtained from land developer and citrus grower John H. Drew by the City of Tampa.

During World War II, Drew Field was leased to the U.S. government for use as a signal-air-warning training school and for combat air training. The government gave Drew Field back to the City of Tampa in 1945. By that point, people knew air travel was more than just a phase, so the Florida Legislature created the Hillsborough County Aviation Authority and a local tax was levied to fund the authority.

Because the U.S. Army Air Force had greatly enlarged Drew Field during World War II, commercial airline operations were moved from Peter O. Knight Airport to Drew Field in 1946. By 1952, Drew Field was serving four airlines and about one million passengers a year, and the name was changed to Tampa International Airport. By 1960, TIA was serving 11 airlines, had been designated an intercontinental airport, and could accommodate jet aircraft.

The current terminal building, with four separate airside buildings, opened in 1971. Although the design, which included an at-the-time futuristic unmanned shuttle system ferrying people between landside and airside buildings and the longest escalators in the state, was innovative, it has proved efficient. TIA has won a number of world-recognized awards for service and passenger satisfaction.

Over the years, various improvements and additions have been made to the facilities. Today, the airport occupies the original 160 acres plus another 3,140 acres—3,300 acres total—and is valued at nearly $2 billion.

TIA recognizes aviation history throughout its property. Travelers to the airport drive on Bessie Coleman Boulevard, named after the first African-American pilot (1892–1926) and the first American to obtain an international pilot's license. Elevators are named after Chuck Yeager, Ivan Sikorsky, and others.

PUBLIC ART PROGRAM

No matter where your eyes fall at TIA, they'll see art on the floors and walls and hanging from the ceiling. Look for mosaic medallions underfoot while you're waiting for the shuttle from Airside C to the terminal, for instance. See the manatee floating on its back amid blue and green carpet swirls of water and seagrass as you descend the escalators to claim your baggage. Both are part of TIA's Public Art Program, established in 1998 to give employees of and travelers to TIA an aesthetic pause.

But art at Hillsborough County airports is nothing new.

In the 1930s, local artist George Snow Hill painted a set of seven murals, depicting the history of flight. Hill's murals hung at Peter O. Knight airport until its demolition in 1965. In 1971, Mr. Hill himself restored the murals, and two of them were hung in TIA's terminal. The rest were put in storage until 1985 when Airside E was designed with all seven murals in mind.

Perhaps the most viewed artwork at the airport is the flock of life-sized metal pelicans hanging in suspended flight over the escalator wells between the Transfer and Baggage Claim Levels. Sculpted by Roy Butler, of Plantation, Florida, this flock has been part of a collection of metal bird scenes at the airport since the early 1970s. More of these birds swoop low over walkway areas and roost on a life-size mangrove right in the middle of all the bustle on the ticketing level (Level 2).

Glass art, paintings, tile work, photographs, sculptures, tapestries—they're all waiting to be discovered at TIA. Want to know more about the artwork? Stop at one of the information kiosks located at the top of the escalators or go to www.tampaairport.com/about/guest_services/public_art.

ACTIVITIES AT THE AIRPORT

Ever wonder what an airplane gas station looks like? Take the free airfield tour at TIA and visit the fuel farm to find out. Groups of up to 20 people tour the service roads in a minibus, talk to the fire fighters at the airport fire department, learn about the runways, and watch planes take off and land from really close-up ground level. Tours are offered seven days a week and last about an hour, and participants must be at least five years old.

Or take a free, one-hour guided walking tour of the terminal to learn about the airport design, public art program, and security measures. Tours are offered days and evenings, seven days a week, and participants must be at least five years old.

Want to explore the terminal on your own at 3 a.m.? Call ahead and you'll receive information that will allow you to conduct a self-guided tour any time of day or in the wee hours of the morning.

How about a scavenger hunt in the airport terminal? Or a birthday party—complete with airport games and a tour or scavenger hunt—for your child age 7 to 12? It's all free (you supply the cake and beverages) for the asking. If you come by during the Thanksgiving and Christmas holiday season, you just might catch a local band or chorus making merry with music.

Call (813) 870-8759 to arrange for any of the tours or activities.

SHOPPING AND DINING

Space prohibits our telling you about all the shops in the airport terminal and the dining options. Suffice it to say you could spend an afternoon browsing the sports and beach gear, clothing, books, and toys. Then have a humungous root beer float while watching planes land and take off. Or enjoy a table-service meal at one of several chain restaurants in the terminal. Really want to impress your significant other? Try dinner at The View at CK's (see Restaurants chapter), a revolving, roof-top restaurant capping the Airport Marriott Hotel (see Accommodations chapter). A complete listing of shops and restaurants can be found at www.tampaairport.com/about/shops.

So there you have it. And you thought an airport was just for catching a flight.

Bus Stations

Three Greyhound bus stations serve the Tampa Bay area. Each station offers package express and charter services. While the Web site (www.grey hound.com) list times of operations, each station cautions that these are subject to change.

The **Tampa Greyhound Station** is at 610 Polk St., Tampa, and the main phone number is (813) 229-2174. The station is open 24/7, but ticketing and package express hours vary.

The **St. Petersburg Greyhound Station** is at 180 9th St. N, St. Petersburg, and the main phone number is (727) 898-1496. The station is open from 8 a.m. until 7:30 p.m. Sunday through Thursday and until 10 p.m. on Friday and Saturday. Package express and ticketing hours are the same as station hours.

The **Clearwater Greyhound Station** is at 2815 Gulf-to-Bay Blvd., Clearwater, and the main phone number is (727) 796-7315. The station is open from 6 a.m. until 7 p.m. 365 days a year. Package express and ticketing hours are the same as station hours.

Charter Buses

The Federal Transit Administration, part of the U.S. Department of Transportation, oversees private charter operations. For information about charter bus services in the Tampa Bay area, search the FTA database at http://ftawebprod.fta.dot .gov/charterregistration.

Public Buses, Streetcars, and Trolleys

HART (HILLSBOROUGH AREA REGIONAL TRANSIT AUTHORITY)

www.hartline.org

HART operates more than just a bus system. Billing itself as being "in the business of connecting people," HART also provides paratransit service to people unable to use the regular bus system because of a disability, coordinates and underwrites vanpooling, and works with employers to offer public transportation passes to employees.

Trollies and streetcars, operated by HART on Tampa streets, add a touch of color and charm to downtown and historic sections of Tampa. If you visit the Ybor City area on just the right day, you just might catch the Birney—the only fully restored original streetcar in Florida. The Birney traveled Ybor City streets back in the early part of the 20th century. Then buses came along in 1946, and the street cars were sent to some place other than street car heaven. This particular car was found 45 years later, rusting away and being used as a storage shed. Some of the volunteers who restored the Birney remember riding it as youngsters.

For bus schedules and maps and to purchase fares online, go to HART's Web site, or call (813) 254-4278 for more information. A note of caution: We found 2006 rates on the streetcar page of the HART Web site in 2009. Look at the date at the bottom of the Web page to be sure the information is current—good advice anytime you look for information online!

PSTA (PINELLAS SUNCOAST TRANSIT AUTHORITY)

www.psta.net

PSTA's buses run the length of Pinellas County, or for a quarter you can ride the Looper, a trolley serving the downtown St. Petersburg area. Other trolleys connect the beach cities.

PSTA also provides on-demand service to disabled people through its DART program, and provides connector service to Tampa.

For information about routes and schedules or to purchase tickets online, go to www.psta.net. Or call (727) 540-1900 for more information.

Driving Around

Some people are born with maps and compasses in their heads. They only have to travel a road once and they know where it intersects with what and how it connects point Q with point Z.

Then there are the rest of us who do dry runs the day before we travel anywhere other than the grocery store. For those of us in this category, here's a breakdown of the major north-south and east-west roads in the Tampa Bay area.

i Call 5-1-1 or go to www.511tampabay .com for real-time traffic and road information in the Tampa Bay area.

North-South Main Highways

Stretching from Michigan to Miami, I-75 brings a steady flow of visitors to the Tampa Bay area from both north and south. Just inside the Pasco-Hillsborough County line and north of Tampa, I-275 splits off from I-75. I-75 veers to the east, skirts the downtown area, and runs through the New Tampa area (northeastern part of Tampa) and then south. While I-75 charts an inland course, I-275 bears slightly west before dropping straight south into downtown Tampa.

Just before reaching the downtown area proper, I-275 receives I-4 traffic coming from the east. Shortly past this junction, I-275 turns west. The last few Tampa-side exits take traffic slightly north to Tampa International Airport or to meet SR 60, which takes traffic to Clearwater over the Courtney Campbell Causeway (see Close-Up: Bridging the Bay).

I-275 continues west about 3 miles over the Howard Frankland Bridge. As the bridge ends, exits take traffic south to St. Petersburg via 4th Street N., west to SR 688 (Ulmerton Road) to Largo, Seminole, and the mid-County beaches (and also to SR 680/Roosevelt Boulevard and the St. Petersburg-Clearwater International Airport), and south to Pinellas Park/St. Petersburg via 9th Street N. (Dr. Martin Luther King Jr. Street N.).

I-275 continues south through Pinellas County until it joins U.S. 19 and crosses the Sunshine Skyway Bridge in south St. Petersburg. Once across the Sunshine Skyway Bridge, I-275 bears east and rejoins I-75 as the Interstate continues south to the Port Charlotte area and then to Fort Myers.

i Past visitors to the Tampa Bay area may remember the I-275/I-4 "Malfunction Junction" that backed traffic up for miles because of bottlenecks and accidents. Recent construction has traffic flowing smoothly in that area, although you still need to pay attention—a couple of I-4 eastbound exits are on the left.

Also running north-south through northwestern Hillsborough County is a toll road, the Veterans' Expressway, that begins just north of Tampa International Airport and just past where SR 60 takes traffic west to Clearwater. The Veterans' Expressway becomes the Suncoast Parkway, which shoots traffic north through two other counties. You can buy a pass at www.sunpass .com or at many area stores. Otherwise, stock up on quarters. Tolls range from 25 cents to $1.25, and the toll plazas tend to break up what is supposed to be a swift ride into chunks of stop-and-go traffic.

Before there were interstates bypassing city traffic, there were highways. U.S. 19, built in 1926, has carried long-haul trucks and winter snowbirds from Lake Eerie, Pennsylvania, to Pinellas County, Florida, for much of that time. In Pinellas County itself, U.S. 19 remains the main north-south route, running from the Pasco-Pinellas border in the north to the Sunshine Skyway Bridge in the south.

U.S. Hwy. 19—or just plain old 19, to us—in our area has had a bad reputation for the number of traffic deaths that have occurred along various stretches. In recent years, overpasses have been constructed at main intersections, a right-turn only lane has been added in stretches, and better signage and address markers have been added to alleviate some of the problems. "Pray for me—I drive U.S. 19," bumper stickers aren't as common as they once were. Still, 19 carries a lot of vehicles driven by drivers trying to get to work, by drivers unfamiliar with the area, and by big-rig truckers. It's worth using extra caution when traveling this busy road.

i To make matters more confusing, there's also Alternate U.S. 19, which splits from U.S. 19 just north of the Pasco-Pinellas County line. Alternate U.S. 19 runs down western Pinellas County and was the original route for U.S. Hwy. 19.

On the Tampa side of the bay, U.S. 41 connected Miami with Michigan long before I-75 was built, and the portion of U.S. 41 running between Tampa and Miami is still known as the Tamiami ("tammy-ammy") Trail. All the main north-south roads in Tampa, starting with Dale Mabry Hwy. in the west, Florida Ave., Nebraska Ave., and N. 56th/S. 50th streets, tie into U.S. 41 at one point or another.

East-West Main Highways

I–4 runs east-west through the middle of Hillsborough County across the middle of the state and connects the Tampa Bay area with Orlando and Daytona Beach.

Four roads running east-west connect Pinellas County to Hillsborough County. Tampa Road sounds like it should be in Hillsborough County, but it's actually in Pinellas County and takes people to Tampa from the Palm Harbor area. Once it crosses the Pinellas-Hillsborough County line, it jogs southeast and becomes West Hillsborough Avenue as it runs across the top of Tampa Bay itself. Then it turns straight east and becomes Hillsborough Avenue in Tampa. A couple of other Pinellas east-west roads run into Tampa Road before it hits Hillsborough County, most notably Curlew Road.

Gulf-to-Bay Boulevard (SR 60) in Clearwater carries traffic from Clearwater Beach on the Gulf of Mexico to the Courtney Campbell Causeway on the Tampa Bay side of the Pinellas peninsula. Once SR 60 crosses the water, it takes a little jog southeast on North Memorial Highway before running into I–275. SR 60 disappears and reappears further east in Hillsborough County, paralleling I–4.

From Indian Rocks Beach in the west, SR 688, aka Ulmerton Road (except for a short section just east of Indian Rocks Beach where it is Walsingham Road), has been the traditional north-south dividing line in Pinellas County for school and other zoning issues. As populations have shifted northward, the dividing line has shifted somewhat; but Ulmerton Road remains the major east-west route between Pinellas County and Tampa via I–275 and the Howard Frankland Bridge.

i For the most part, in Pinellas County streets and lanes run north-south while avenues and drives run east-west. Central Avenue in St. Petersburg is a main east-west dividing road. For example, 49th Street North is the portion of 49th Street running north of Central. Hence, there might be an address at 500 49th Street North and a different one at 500 49th Street South.

Park Boulevard in Pinellas County is the southernmost east-west route from Pinellas County to Tampa. Starting just south of the beach town of Indian Shores in the west, Park Boulevard, aka 78th Avenue North, moves east until it crosses 113th Street North where it takes a slight dog-tail to the southeast. It remains Park Boulevard, but now is also known as 74th Avenue North and SR 694. When Park Boulevard/74th Avenue North/SR 694 crosses U.S. 19, it bears northeast and becomes Gandy Boulevard/SR 694. Continuing east, Gandy Boulevard crosses the bay over the Gandy Bridge (U.S. 92) into Tampa.

From there, you can pick up the Lee Roy Selmon Expressway (formerly the Crosstown Expressway), which cuts across the southern part of Tampa. This toll road takes travelers through the old Hyde Park Historic District, near the Davis Islands and Peter O. Knight Airport, past the Channelside and Port of Tampa areas, and east of Tampa into Brandon.

i Drawbridges that open to let sailboats through, particularly in the Pinellas beach areas, can mean delays for car traffic.

Bicycles

Nationwide, pedacycle (one- or two-wheeled nonmotorized vehicles) fatalities accounted for almost 2 percent of all traffic fatalities, according to 2007 National Highway and Traffic Safety Administration (NHTSA) report. In Florida, pedacycle fatalities were almost 4 percent of the total.

That doesn't mean you should forget about bicycling here. It just means you need to use extra caution when cycling, especially when you are sharing the road with motorized vehicles.

That said, some, but not all, roads in both Hillsborough and Pinellas Counties have marked bike lanes. Better yet, Pinellas County has several trails—one extending the full length of the county—that are for pedestrians and cyclists only and can be used for commuting (see the Parks and Recreation chapter). Hillsborough's trails are mostly loops in park areas.

For more information about bicycling in the Tampa Bay area, try these Web sites:

- Look for the "Florida Bicycling Street Smart" brochure, available online or in PDF format, on the Florida Department of Transportation's pedestrian and bicycle safety page (www.dot .state.fl.us/safety/ped_bike/ped_bike.shtm). Also on this page are links to "Bicycle Laws" and to "Bicycle Touring Information" (maps, lists of trails, etc.).
- Look for "Bicycle Suitability Maps" on Hillsborough County's Metropolitan Planning Organization Web site (www.hillsboroughmpo.org).
- Tampa BayCycle's Web page (www.tampa baycycle.com) lists clubs and events and also information about the Emergency Ride Home Program offering free transportation home to cyclists who commute to work at least two days a week.

i **All bicyclists age 16 and under must, by law, wear a properly fitting helmet. Bicycles are considered vehicles and must obey all traffic laws. There is no state law prohibiting riding on sidewalks, but a few neighborhoods have outlawed it.**

BY SEA

Most people reading this book won't be travelling to the Tampa Bay area by boat.

But there may be a number of people coming here to go somewhere else via cruise ship, and some people may do some boating once they get here.

Segue into the Sunshine

See the Tampa Bay area via a Segway tour or rent one of these self-propelled gliders. Go to www.segway guidedtours.com for a list of Segway tours throughout the United States, including those in the Tampa Bay area, or try one of these vendors:

Tampa Bay Segs
101 2nd Ave. N., St. Petersburg
(727) 772-3639
www.tampabaysegs.com
Magic Carpet Glide
Channelside Bay Plaza, Tampa
(813) 380-1916
www.magiccarpetglide.com

So first we'll tell you about the Port of Tampa and give you information about the cruise industry here, then we'll talk a bit about other boat traffic. More detailed information about pleasure boating can be found in the Parks and Recreation chapter.

Port of Tampa

TAMPA PORT AUTHORITY
1101 Channelside Dr.
Tampa
(813) 905-7678, (800)741-2297
www.tampaport.com
If you've driven across Boston's Storrow Drive connector bridge or the Casco Bay drawbridge in Portland, Maine, you've driven across bridge components made here and shipped out of the Port of Tampa. Spread fertilizer on your lawn lately? We're one of the largest phosphate producers in the country and it gets shipped out of the Port of Tampa, too.

The Tampa Port Authority administers Florida's largest port, the Port of Tampa, which sits at the upper end of Hillsborough Bay, a smaller bay on the northeast side of Tampa Bay.

⊙ Close-up

Bridging the Bay

For early settlers, it was a long row across the bay for mail and to buy supplies. The alternative was to slog around the top of the bay through snake-infested marsh and patches of palmetto thickets. Building bridges, however, isn't cheap. Currently, five bridges span Tampa Bay from east to west. One bridge spans a section of the bay on the Pinellas side from north to south.

SUNSHINE SKYWAY BRIDGE

Completed in 1987, the southernmost bridge, the Bob Graham Sunshine Skyway Bridge, is also the largest cable-stayed bridge in the world and is considered by some sources to be among the top 10 bridges in the world. The original steel-cantilevered bridge, built in 1954 was destroyed during a storm in May 1980, when a freighter rammed into it, causing more than 1,000 feet of the center span to fall into the bay below. A number of vehicles also fell into the bay, and 35 people were killed.

The new bridge is not only stronger and higher, it also has a series of concrete islands, called dolphins, which were added around the six main piers of the bridge to absorb the impact of errant boats. The bridge, designed by the Figg and Muller Engineering Group, and the dolphin system, designed by Parsons Brinkerhoff, have won many awards.

The remaining sections of the old bridge still stretch out from land on either side of the bay and are now part of the state park system, being used as fishing piers (see Parks and Recreation chapter).

The Sunshine Skyway connects Pinellas County to Manatee County via I–275 and U.S. 19, passing over Hillsborough County waters in its 5.5 miles. During severe weather, the bridge may be closed. The Sunshine Skyway is a toll bridge, so be prepared with cash or a SunPass card.

GANDY BRIDGE

About halfway up the Pinellas peninsula, the land bulges into Tampa Bay as though reaching toward Hillsborough County's Interbay Peninsula. Here, the Gandy Bridge, about 2.5 miles long, connects north St. Petersburg to south Tampa on U.S. 92.

This is the oldest crossing point on the bay. In 1924, the first Gandy Bridge was built by Philadelphia contractor George Gandy. At the time, it was the world's longest automobile toll bridge.

Since that first bridge, three other Gandy Bridges have been built at this spot, the most recent span in 1996. Because the bridge is actually comprised of two separate spans completed decades apart, the design of each span is different, giving it a bit of a gimpy look.

For a while, a span built in 1956 was used as a pedestrian trail and fishing pier called the Friendship Trail. Deterioration of the bridge and prohibitive repair costs closed the trail in 2008.

HOWARD FRANKLAND BRIDGE

The 3-mile-long Howard Frankland Bridge, named for a Tampa businessman who proposed the route, connects mid-Pinellas County with Tampa on I–275 and is the most traveled of the bridges.

Originally opened in 1960 as a single-span, four lane (two lanes in each direction) crossing, the bridge was quickly dubbed the Howard "Frankenstein" because of the horrendous mid-bridge traffic accidents and resulting traffic tie-ups on both sides of the bay.

Separate four-lane spans, one completed in 1990 and a slightly higher one completed in 1992, now bridge the bay at this point. The approaches on both sides of the bay were also reconfigured.

Regardless of its past history, the Howard Frankland Bridge has always provided motorists traveling east with an impressive view of the Tampa skyline. Motorists traveling west on I-275 emerge from Tampa's waterfront concrete-and-glass Westshore district, finding themselves rather suddenly on the Howard Frankland Bridge. Stretching ahead and for miles on either side of the bridge is the vast body of water that is Tampa Bay. We still get a catch in our throat when we cross this bridge, even after several decades of living here.

COURTNEY CAMPBELL CAUSEWAY

With waves breaking just below eye level not many yards from the roadway, the Courtney Campbell Causeway gives travelers an unforgettable view of the upper end of Old Tampa Bay. Palm trees and scrub cedars, permanently bent from the prevailing winds, line its sides, and public beach and boat ramp access make it a popular recreational area.

Begun in 1927 by former steamboat captain Ben T. Davis, a descendent of Jefferson Davis, the causeway was finally completed in 1934 and opened as a toll bridge. At the time, it was the country's longest over-water fill across an open body of water. In 1944, the bridge, along with other property in the area, was appropriated by the federal government as part of the war effort. It was named the Courtney Campbell Causeway in 1948, honoring a U.S. Congressman from Clearwater Beach who led the effort to repair the causeway and to add the park system. In 2004, the State of Florida designated the Courtney Campbell Causeway an official Scenic Highway.

The 9.9 mile Courtney Campbell Causeway carries traffic along SR 60 between Clearwater and mid-Tampa. For information about the causeway, the hiking trail that runs along its sides, and other amenities, go to the Parks and Recreation chapter.

SR 580 BRIDGE

A short but graceful unnamed bridge connects Safety Harbor with Oldsmar at the very top of Old Tampa Bay.

BAYSIDE BRIDGE

This north-south bridge on the northwestern side of Tampa Bay connects McMullen-Booth Road in Clearwater with 49th Street North from SR 60 to Roosevelt Boulevard near the St. Petersburg-Clearwater International Airport. Completed in 1993, the twin-span bridge is about 3 miles long and has relieved traffic congestion on U.S. 19.

Encompassing 5,000 acres, the Port of Tampa is Florida's, and one of the nation's, largest ports. Cargo including petroleum, phosphates (mostly used in fertilizer), cement, citrus, and just about everything else you can think of gets shipped in and out of here every day.

Additionally, the Port of Tampa is one of the largest shipbuilding and repair centers in the southeastern United States, and it is a major cruise ship port.

Plan on spending some time in the Channelside area or along the Riverwalk just watching these leviathans dock or weigh anchor and get underway for other ports around the world.

Cruise Terminal 2 (651 Channelside Dr., Tampa)

CARNIVAL CRUISE LINES
(888) CARNIVAL (888-227-6482)
www.carnival.com

Cruise Terminal 3 (815 Channelside Dr., Tampa)

ROYAL CARIBBEAN INTERNATIONAL
(800) 398-9819
www.royalcaribbean.com

HOLLAND AMERICA LINE
(877) 932-4259
www.hollandamerica.com

Cruise Terminal 6 (1333 McKay St., Tampa)

PARKING GARAGE FOR TERMINALS 2 AND 3
810 Channelside Dr.
Tampa

Cruise parking for Terminals 2 and 3 is in the parking garage located across the street from the terminals, which are located near Channelside BayPlaza and the Florida Aquarium. Rates are $14 per day. Valet parking is available for an additional charge.

Cruise parking for Terminal 6 is adjacent to the terminal, which is just north of the Florida Aquarium and near the offices of the Tampa Port Authority. The rate at this terminal is also $14 per day.

ℹ The Port of Tampa is not to be confused with Port Tampa, listed on www.ghosttowns.com. Railroad magnate Henry B. Plant ended his rail line at this point just northwest of where MacDill Air Force Base is today. Plant's train ran out onto the dock so Plant's steamship passengers could step from one to the other (see History chapter).

Port St. Petersburg

PORT ST. PETERSBURG
250 85th Ave. S.E.
St. Petersburg
(727) 893-7053, (800) 782-8350
www.stpete.org/port/index.asp

Port St. Petersburg only encompasses three acres, but those three acres regularly host some of the world's largest yachts—the kind that carry a helicopter or two and an extra sailboat or powerboat, and have their own movie theaters and lobster tanks. Because Port St. Petersburg's regular residents are mostly support vessels such as dredges and barges working offshore or tugs plying back and forth to change crews on larger rigs, the port is much cleaner than one serving more industrial customers. Additionally, the port's proximity to both Albert Whitted and Tampa International airports makes it easy for both yacht owners and crews to make this a base from which to travel elsewhere.

Arriving by Boat

The amount of boat traffic on Tampa Bay rivals the amount of car traffic on the surrounding roads. With two major ports—the Port of Tampa and Port Manatee—and a third international port, the Port of St. Petersburg, on Tampa Bay, boats of many sizes—a few in excess of 800 feet long—are on the water at any given time. Boaters of all types need to be mindful of boating laws and etiquette, especially in the areas around major shipping channels.

Boaters in the Tampa Bay area tune their radios to Channel 16 for hailing and distress calls and for marine advisory information. Channel 9 is a secondary vessel-to-vessel hailing channel. Channels 1 through 4 provide weather information.

The Office of Coast Survey publishes a series of books called United States Coast Pilot. *Coast Pilot 5* covers the Gulf coast from Key West to Texas. The books, along with nautical charts and other navigational aids, can be purchased or the books can be downloaded for free. Go to www .nauticalcharts.noaa.gov/nsd/coastpilot.htm for more information.

Gulf Intracoastal Waterway

In 1919, Congress authorized the creation of a system of waterways along the Atlantic and Gulf coasts of the United States, using existing protected passages between barrier islands and the mainland and building man-made canals. The 3,000-mile Intracoastal Waterway allows low-draft barges and other watercraft to travel from New Jersey to Texas without having to venture for long distances into the open ocean.

The U.S. Army Corps of Engineers built and maintains most of the Intracoastal Waterway, including the shipping channels in the Tampa Bay area.

U.S. Coast Guard

Two United States Coast Guard units serve the Tampa Bay area from Pinellas County. The Tampa office is part of the St. Petersburg sector.

AIR STATION CLEARWATER
15100 Rescue Way
Clearwater
(727) 535-1437
http://uscg.mil/d7/airstaclearwater/baseinfo
.asp

SECTOR ST. PETERSBURG COMMAND CENTER
600 8th Ave. S.E., St. Petersburg
(727) 824-824-7506

Helpful Web Pages

- For online information about the marine weather forecast and tides, go to the National Weather Service/National Oceanic and Atmospheric Administration Web page at www.srh.noaa.gov/tbw/tampabaymarine weather.htm
- For a list of public marinas and boat ramps in Pinellas County, go to **www.pinellasmarina .com**
- For a list of links and phone numbers to other boating helps in Pinellas County, go to **www .stpete.org/marina/boating_and_marine_ links.asp**
- For a list of Hillsborough County marinas, go to **www.centralfloridafishingreport.com/ FishingInfo/212.html**
- For a list of other boating helps and organizations in Hillsborough County, go to **www .floridasmart.com/local/counties/ hillsborough/sports_boating.htm**
- For a list of Florida's seaports, go to **http:// dlis.dos.state.fl.us/fgils/seaports.html**

From Minnesota to Florida by Boat

Adventurous boaters can navigate the inland waterways from the Midwest to Florida via the Tennessee-Tombigbee Waterway, or Tenn-Tom (www.tenntom.org). Via this system of locks and dams completed in 1984 and linking the Tennessee River with the Tom Bigbee-Black Warrior River in Alabama, it is possible to travel from Minneapolis, Minnesota, to Mobile, Alabama, by pleasure boat. From Mobile, follow the Intracoastal Waterway system along the Gulf side of Florida to Pensacola and Panama City, and then down to Pinellas County and the Tampa Bay area. Most marinas are required to hold a few slips open for transient boaters, but you'll want to call ahead whenever possible to make reservations.

HISTORY

Look around the Tampa Bay area, with its high-rise buildings, bridges spanning the bay, and more than two million residents, and it's hard to imagine a time when only a handful of people lived here, a time when there were only a few small huts and no bridges or roads.

Only within the last 150 years or so has the Tampa Bay area gone from being ignored as unimportant to being a major metropolitan area and international destination.

For centuries, Spanish, French, and English explorers dismissed the Tampa Bay area as not worth settling. Even post–Civil War land speculators went elsewhere first because there was no railroad into the Tampa Bay area and not much in the way of roads. People who wanted to come here came primarily by boat.

In the mid-1800s, there was a military fort here and a small town with a harbor. Tampa became a shipping point for scrub cattle raised by Florida Cracker cowboys—so called because of the cracking sound of the whip they used to communicate with each other and to kill rattlesnakes and other dangerous critters—and sold to Cuban markets.

During the Civil War the cattle went north to feed the Confederate Army. After the war, cattle trade with Cuba resumed, and the gold that came back in return helped Florida recover from the war.

This established route to Cuba conveniently allowed the United States to send Teddy Roosevelt's Rough Riders and other troops to take San Juan Hill during the Spanish-American War.

By then, phosphate had been discovered nearby and the railroad had come in. The railroad brought tourists, and many of them decided they liked not having to fight blizzards in January. Clear Water Harbor and St. Petersburg began to grow on the Pinellas side of the bay.

Commercial aviation got its start in 1914 right here in the Tampa Bay area, and the 1940s war years brought Army airfields to both Hillsborough and Pinellas Counties.

But it was the invention of affordable air-conditioning that really changed the Tampa Bay area from a wintering ground for Northern snowbirds, as the locals call them, to a permanent home for 2.4 million people by the first decade of the 21st century.

Before we delve into the recorded history of the Tampa Bay area, let's look further back into what this spot on earth might have seen over thousands of years. For even before Europeans "discovered" the Tampa Bay area, and even before earlier peoples settled here, these rivers and seas, swamps and marshes, lands and skies were home to other creatures.

PREHISTORIC ERA TO THE COMING OF THE EUROPEANS

The Unpeopled Past

As far as we know, there were no social columnists for the *Dinosaur Daily Times* reporting a gazillion years ago on which mammoth invited which glyptodon (think armadillo as big as a small car) over for a dinner of swamp grass last Tuesday.

Clues to the Tampa Bay area's prehistoric past, however, are still being discovered today.

In 2007, for instance, a local high-school student out taking pictures at Boca Ciega Millennium Park in Pinellas County discovered what turned out to be a tooth and part of a jaw from a Columbian mammoth. That's an elephant-like animal that hasn't been around for at least 9,000 years.

Volunteers helped researchers from the University of South Florida and Tampa's Museum of Science and Industry (MOSI) dig up even more bones and other fossils—30 boxes full—through which scientists are still sorting.

Then there's the Fossil Park neighborhood of St. Petersburg, so named for a shell pit of—yup!—fossils found in the early 1960s.

In 1907, a mastodon skeleton was dug up near Lake Maggiore in St. Petersburg.

And in the Four Corners area of Hillsborough, Polk, Hardee, and Manatee counties is Bone Valley, where phosphate mining has exposed skeletal relics from a time we can only imagine. Even today, visitors to the Mulberry Phosphate Museum in Polk County (see Day Trips chapter) can sift through shovels full of dirt in search of fossilized shark teeth and other treasures.

i You'll find other bits of historical information scattered throughout the book. Look for a history of the area's news media in the Media chapter, for instance, or for tidbits about how the arts developed here in the Arts chapter. There's a write-up about the Grapefruit League in the Sports chapter and one about area historic hotels in the Accommodations chapter.

First Peoples

At some point, however, people moved in. Those people didn't leave a written history.

It's hard for us to imagine a civilization without books like the one you're holding. Or to imagine a civilization with no writing at all—no clay tablets marked with a stylus, no quill pens and parchment, no computers or cell phones. No grocery lists, no written agreements, no text messaging, no love notes, no birth or death certificates—and no written history except, perhaps, pictures scratched onto stone or shell.

What we think we know about how those people lived is based on the few surviving clues they left and on the writings of European people raised in a very different culture who did not speak the native language right away and who may not have understood everything they saw.

Some historians and archaeologists say the very first people who came here were the descendents of people who had migrated across a bridge of land in what is now Siberia to what is now Alaska about 30,000 to 35,000 years ago. Their descendents came to the Tampa Bay area about 10,000 to 12,000 years ago. In other words, these people might very well have encountered that Columbian mammoth whose bones were found by a high-school girl just a couple of years ago!

Other anthropologists believe the people who came here were part of a different group of people, the Taíno, who came from the Andes area of South America. These Taíno people migrated through the Amazon area and into the Caribbean Islands. From there, they came to what they called Bimini—what we call Florida—and spread northward.

Various names have been given to these cultures—names of our making—and refer to different time periods and to concentrations of people within different geographic regions.

Archaeologists and anthropologists say the people who lived in the Tampa Bay area and north to Alabama after 500 BC were part of the Deptford culture. Then the Deptford culture disappeared, and after about AD 1400, the people here were part of the Safety Harbor culture.

The earliest peoples here seem to have been hunter-gatherers. It wasn't until about 5000 BC that they began to live in villages, and not until about 1000 BC that they began farming in any sense.

Either way, there were several subgroups of people, one of which was the Timucua (Tee-MOO-qwah).

The Timucuan people, who lived here before Europeans arrived, lived from the Tampa Bay area northward into southern Alabama and Georgia. The Timucuan nation included tribes such as the Pensacola, the Apalachee, (who may have been a larger separate group), the Ocale, and other tribes. At least one writer refers to Timucuan towns of Tocobaga, Ucita, and Mocoso families or tribes living in the Tampa Bay area.

Geographically, the Tocobagan people lived in the southernmost region of what is generally considered to be Timucuan territory. Some linguists say the Tocobagan people and some of the other north-Florida tribes were not Timucuan because they spoke different languages and sometimes fought with each other.

Regardless of their origins, an estimated 100,000 to 350,000 native people lived in Florida at the time the Europeans arrived. About 7,000 of those were Tocobagans.

A few Taíno words survive into our language today. "*Barbacoa*," meaning "roasted over an open flame," is one such word. We call it barbecue.

Notes and drawings from early European explorers indicate the Tocobaga people farmed the land—growing corn, beans, and other vegetables—speared gilled fish, and harvested shellfish. They hunted alligator, sea cow or manatees, and deer. Men wore breechcloths of woven fiber and women wore skirts of Spanish moss. They built villages of round houses with palm-thatched roofs and created raised mounds of shells and earth.

Some of the mounds were burial and religious mounds. Others, called middens, were formed from the empty shells and other materials left over after meals—lots of meals. Some of these mounds can still be seen in the area today. At Pinellas County's Philippe Park in Safety Harbor, at the upper end of Tampa Bay, visitors can climb to the top of a shell mound and can try to imagine what life was like for those long-ago people.

Clashing Cultures

European explorers came to this country off and on through the centuries. But Christopher Columbus's 1492 voyage was the beginning of intentional colonization by Europeans in the Western Hemisphere. It was also the beginning of the end of the early peoples who lived here.

Before the Europeans came, the various Native American peoples had fought with each other, but they fought using similar weapons. Before the Europeans came, they had gotten sick and had died from disease. Over time, their immune systems had developed some resistance, and they had learned which herbs helped them fight which illnesses.

When the Europeans arrived, however, they brought with them deadlier weapons and new diseases that the native peoples couldn't fend off easily. The Europeans also brought different ways of thinking about property, wealth, social order, and religion. It's hard to say which element ultimately defeated the Native American peoples the Europeans found here. Most likely it was a combination of factors.

In 1513, Juan Ponce de Léon discovered this peninsula, thinking it was an island. He landed on the Atlantic side of the peninsula near the St. Johns River. Because it was Easter time and spring in Florida, de Léon named this land after *Pascua Florida*, the Feast of Flowers.

De Léon returned to Florida in 1521 and went up the west side of the peninsula to what is now Charlotte Harbor near Fort Myers, about 100 miles south of Tampa Bay. The Spaniards started to build a village there, but the native peoples, part of the Calusa tribe living in south Florida, drove the Spaniards away. De Léon was fatally wounded, and he died in Cuba.

One of the members of de Léon's expedition, Hernando de Escalante Fotaneda, was held captive by the Calusa. Many years later, Fotaneda wrote in his memoir that the Calusa called the place "*tanpa*." Linguists disagree on whether this means "the place to gather sticks," "sticks of fire" (which may refer to the prevalence of lightning in the area), or whether Fotaneda misheard the native word "*itimpi*," which just means "near it."

Regardless, when a later group of Spaniards ventured up Florida's west coast, they apparently missed the Charlotte Harbor bay. Instead, they landed in a larger bay further north, and called this larger bay by the wrong name, Tampa. And the name stuck.

In 1528, a group of Spanish soldiers led by Pánfilo de Narváez landed in the Tampa Bay area. Narváez and his men most likely pulled into a small sheltered area, what is now called Boca Ciega Bay on the Pinellas peninsula, and then scouted inland until they found a deserted village, perhaps in today's Weedon Island area or as far north as Safety Harbor. A marker commemorates the landing, although another marker in downtown Tampa also marks Narváez's landing.

Narváez did not endear himself to the Tocobagans, who had hidden to see what these strangers would do. At least one report says Narváez's men ransacked the village, looking for gold.

When the Tocobagans rushed in to protest, the report goes on, Narváez pulled his sword and slashed off Chief Hirrihigua's nose. The chief's mother tried to help her son, but Narváez turned his dogs on her, and the dogs killed the old woman. The Tocobagans got rid of Narváez by convincing him there was gold to be found further north.

Narváez and many of his men hacked their way north through the underbrush to the Apalachee area near present-day Tallahassee. The rest of Narváez's crew were supposed to sail the boats north and meet Narváez, but some returned to Cuba and others were lost at sea. Of the group that did not return to Cuba, only three people apparently survived, turning up in Mexico City eight years later.

In 1539, Hernando de Soto made the next known landing in Tampa Bay, which he named *La Bahia del Espiritu Santo* (The Bay of the Holy Spirit). De Soto took Calusa warriors with him in hopes of intimidating the Tocobagans. An uneasy peace was established that didn't last long. Like the gullible Narváez before him, de Soto was persuaded there was gold to be found elsewhere. De Soto managed to hike even further north—some accounts say he got as far as present-day Kansas—but he never returned to the Tampa Bay area.

In 1549, Father Luis Cancer de Barbastro, who had won over hostile Guatemalan Indians by going to them without a Spanish military escort, decided to try reach the Indians of *La Florida*. He asked to be taken where the Indians had had no previous dealings with the Spaniards, but—

whether by design or by accident—he landed in Tampa Bay where the Tocobagans, having had enough of the Spaniards, clubbed him to death as he waded ashore.

The last Spanish garrison in the Tampa Bay area apparently was established by Pedro Menéndez de Avilés in the late 1560s. Menéndez drove out a French colony that had established itself in the St. Johns River area on the east coast and then deposited Spanish settlers—both military and civilian—in key areas along both coasts of Florida.

Both the Charlotte Harbor and the Tampa Bay areas intrigued the Spanish because they thought that one or both of these bays might be the western outlet of the St. Johns River. So, Menéndez tried to establish a settlement at Charlotte Harbor and posted a garrison at Tampa Bay. But Indian hostilities in both places caused the Spanish to withdraw.

Menéndez's experience ended formal attempts by Europeans to colonize the Tampa Bay area for the next 200 years. Cuban fisherman fished Tampa Bay's waters and took their catch back to Cuba. Runaway slaves from the north gathered here and created a settlement called Angola. Eventually the Timucuans, the Tocobagans, and the Calusa died out or were displaced by other tribes, most notably the Seminole, who moved in from the northeast.

COLONIAL ERA TO PRE-CIVIL WAR

Pedro Menéndez de Avilés had made a concerted effort to colonize Florida in the late 1560s, but he had also been charged with protecting the trade routes against pirates and privateers. He didn't have the resources to do both. The garrison Menéndez posted in the Tampa Bay area in the late 1560s—and withdrew a short time later—was the last official European post in the area had for almost 200 years.

From the mid-1500s, then, until well after the American Revolution, the Tampa Bay area remained largely ignored by the three European superpowers of the day. Spain had decided the

Close-up

The Real Pocahontas Story?

Was John Smith really Juan Ortiz?

Some 80 years before the English Captain John Smith—with a reputation for tactless arrogance and incessant bragging—landed up north in Virginia at Jamestown, a cabin boy named Juan Ortiz had already seen the New World.

Ortiz was part of Pánfilo de Narváez's 1528 expedition. Ortiz worked on one of the vessels anchored in what would later be called Tampa Bay, where they waited for Narváez to return. When Narváez didn't come back, having decided to march inland, Ortiz was on one of the ships that sailed back to Cuba.

Eight years later, Narváez's wife funded another expedition to try to find out what had happened to her husband. Ortiz, now eighteen, went along to help the sailors find the spot. When they found what Ortiz thought was the right bay, Ortiz and a friend rowed to shore in a small boat.

As it happened, it was near the same spot where Narváez had mutilated the Tocobagan Chief Hirrihigua and killed the chief's mother eight years earlier. Chief Hirrihigua and his men captured the youths and dragged them off to their village, killing Ortiz's friend on the way and intending to kill Ortiz.

The chief's daughter, Ulele, hiding nearby, saw what was happening and felt sorry for Ortiz. She asked her mother to intervene. The chief relented, and Ortiz was made a slave instead of being killed.

One of Ortiz's tasks was to keep animals from eating the bodies of dead Tocobagans during the time between their death and their burial.

One night, Ortiz fell asleep and an animal stole the body of the chief's grandchild. Chief Hirrihigua decided to roast Ortiz alive as punishment. As Ortiz screamed in pain outside over the open flame, the Tocobagans celebrated inside in a hut. Ulele slipped out, cut Ortiz free, and tended his burns.

Then she led him to another village, home to the Macoso (sometimes spelled "Mocoso"), another tribe living near the Alafia River near what is now Riverview in Hillsborough County. Here, Ortiz found safety, and he lived among the Macoso for the next 10 years.

Ulele had been engaged to a Macoso chief, but saving Ortiz cost her the marriage.

When Hernando de Soto landed in Tampa Bay in 1539, he thought Ortiz was one of the native people, and took him captive. After telling de Soto his story, Ortiz became de Soto's translator. Ortiz and de Soto both died a couple of years later.

But another member of de Soto's party, known to us only as the Gentleman of Elvas, included Ortiz's story in his account of the expedition, which was published in 1557 and translated into English in 1605.

Some researchers believe that Captain John Smith read Ortiz's story and based his story about Pocahontas saving him from her father, Powhatan, on Ortiz's story of Ulele and Hirrihigua.

No one else in Jamestown left any record of Smith's story, and Smith apparently didn't start talking about it until after Pocahontas died in 1617. The incident is included in a revised version of Smith's adventures published in 1624. Because of this, and because of Smith's reputation for bragging, some historians believe Smith may have "borrowed" Ortiz's story and made it his own.

west coast of Florida wasn't worth colonizing—they had enough to do to try to hold onto St. Augustine in the northeast and their other more southerly possessions. The French had tried to establish a settlement in the St. Johns River area, but it had not survived. The English, too busy colonizing the area north of Florida, didn't have the resources to move into territory already claimed by the Spanish.

Plus, each of the three countries had pressing demands on the home front—often involving fighting with each other. It was hard to convince royal governments struggling to pay for armies and navies to defend their native countries that they also should invest in colonizing a seemingly impenetrable wilderness halfway around the world. Promised gold hadn't materialized and the expeditions that had been sent had died in the attempt.

So Florida as a whole, and the Tampa Bay area in particular, remained mostly untouched by Europeans.

The rest of the country? That was a different story. As often happens, events that occurred hundreds, even thousands, of miles away eventually determined Florida's fate and planted the seeds for what would become today's City of Tampa.

A Three-Way Tie for Last Place

After the Spanish military tried and failed to colonize Florida in the 1500s, the Spanish church tried to set up missions—without Spanish military protection, as that had proved counterproductive.

Between 1602 and 1674, Jesuit priests and, later, Franciscan friars established more than 40 missions throughout northern Florida. They did so under, to them, primitive and hostile conditions and with little in the way of regular support from the church that had sent them. As happens with missionaries of many types and times, the Spanish missionaries not only tried to change religious beliefs but also cultural thinking, introducing the idea that parcels of land could belong to an individual rather than to a whole tribe, for instance, or that systematically cultivating the land—under Spanish employers, of course—was more productive than subsistence farming.

Meanwhile, the English had settled the Carolinas and Georgia. The English and the Spanish were almost always fighting each other back in Europe, and they carried that enmity into the New World. Only they didn't just fight each other. They also tried to get different native tribes to fight for them.

Beginning about 1680, Indians in the South Carolina area who sided with the English began attacking Spanish missions in that area and further south. Between this pressure from the English and the Florida natives' lack of enthusiasm toward the teachings of the Church, most of the Spanish missions were gone within 20 years. By 1708, only the missions in St. Augustine remained.

The French, meanwhile, had settled in the Mississippi River area and eastward to Mobile Bay. For a while, relations between the French and Spanish were cordial. But in 1719, back in Europe, France joined Austria, Holland, and England in attacking Spain. That led to fighting between the French and the Spanish in Florida, with the English as occasional participants.

Land went back and forth during various conflicts between the three powers until 1763. That year, the First Treaty of Paris ended the Seven Years' War—as it was known in Europe—or the French and Indian War—as it was known on this side of the Atlantic. The French lost Canada to the English and lost Louisiana to the Spanish. In exchange for Havana, which England had captured, Spain gave Florida to the English.

The English found little opposition to their rule in Florida. The Spanish and some remaining native peoples, who had mostly died out due to disease and fighting, withdrew to Cuba and other Caribbean islands. The majority of Seminoles hadn't yet moved in from the west. At least one writer believes Florida, divided at that time into East Florida and West Florida, could have become the fourteenth and fifteenth of the American colonies.

English governor James Grant in East Florida won the loyalty of the remaining natives through gifts and diplomacy. Governor George Johnstone in West Florida didn't fare as well and was eventually replaced.

The Tampa Bay area still didn't attract much attention. In 1745, an English captain named Braddock mapped the Tampa Bay area. Spain, in turn, sent Don Francisco María Celi in 1757, to inventory the area's natural resources. María Celi recorded the name of the piney peninsula on the west side of the bay as *Punta Pinal de Jiménez* and called the river he found near Tampa *El Rio San Julián de Arriaga*. Never mind that the native people who lived by the river called it *Cotanchobee*—"Where the Big Water Meets the Land."

English surveyors, probably using Braddock's map, reached the Tampa Bay area during this time and gave English place-names to some of the previously Spanish ones. *El Rio San Julián de Arriaga* became the Hillsborough River, named after the Earl of Hillsborough, the Colonial Secretary at the time. Hillsborough probably never visited the Tampa Bay area, but a river, an island, a county, and the east fork of Tampa Bay all bear his name.

Some English settlers arrived in Florida to claim land grants. But Mississippi and other areas were more attractive and easier to settle, so Florida remained largely uninhabited, except for the Pensacola area in West Florida and the St. Johns River area in East Florida, where planters grew rice, indigo, citrus, and sugarcane, and tapped the trees for turpentine.

Up north, however, discontent in the colonies had become out and out war. While England was distracted by the upstart American revolutionaries, Spain retook West Florida in 1781. Thousands of English loyalist refugees from northern colonies made their way to East Florida, but under the terms of the Second Treaty of Paris, England abandoned East Florida to the Spanish in 1784.

However, some English people stayed in Florida and some citizens of the new United States began to drift southward. Runaway slaves fled from Georgia across the border to Spanish West Florida, and raiders came to steal them back. Timber rights and other border issues caused problems for the Spanish.

Spain couldn't govern the Louisiana area and the now-reunited Florida and at the same time deal with newly inspired revolutionaries in Spain's southern holdings.

Spain transferred control of Louisiana to the new Republic of France in 1800. The French republic, needing money and not having the means to oversee so much land, sold the Louisiana Territory to the United States in 1803. Florida was now bordered only by one young, aggressive nation that didn't have to try to maintain and defend land on two continents.

Again, war in Europe—this time the French Revolution and the Napoleonic Wars from 1789 to 1814—caused turmoil. Once Napoleon was defeated, the Americans feared the English would try to get back the American colonies, using Florida as one of their bases. After a series of incidents unrelated to Florida, the United States declared war on England. The War of 1812 ensued, ending two years later in a draw.

In the middle of this tug-of-war between the Spanish, the Americans, and the English, pirates and other bandits plagued the coasts. Slavers of many nationalities flourished, although the trade was officially illegal. Briefly, the flags of Venezuela and Mexico flew over parts of Florida. The Creek Indians, part of the Seminoles, began fighting their way into northern Florida, incited in part by the English.

The United States government sent General Andrew Jackson to the southern border areas (at that time southern Alabama and Georgia) to subdue the Indians, which he did during the Creek War (1813 to 1814) and the First Seminole War (1817 to 1818). Jackson exposed England's covert involvement in inciting the Seminole to attack, and demonstrated the lack of Spanish control in the area.

Finally, in 1821, Spain yielded control of Florida and Oregon to the United States in exchange for the Texas territory, which the United States had acquired as part of the Louisiana purchase.

Florida had been fought over by Spain, England, and France, the three superpowers of the day, but it was the United States that won.

ⓘ Just south of Tampa Bay, on the Manatee River in what is now the Sarasota
area, Angola, a free-black town of about
750 people, had formed, built by runaway
slaves from the north. When Florida became
part of the United States, Governor Andrew
Jackson ordered the destruction of Angola.
Some survivors escaped to the Bahamas.

The Florida Frontier

Spain withdrew her military from Florida in 1821,
but left something else. Animals.

From highly bred Arabian horses to swine
and Spanish cattle to packs of dogs, lost and
abandoned non-native animals multiplied
throughout Florida. American settlers, coming
south, caught horses and branded cows, building
herds in Florida that they would then drive back
north to Georgia and South Carolina to sell.

It wasn't an easy life. These American pio-
neers contended with thick underbrush and
palmettos that covered over trails within days of
being cleared, swampy areas writhing with water
moccasin snakes and alligators, and swarms of
mosquitoes and other insects. In those days
before televised weather warnings, they also
dealt with devastating hurricanes that seemed to
come from nowhere.

And there was another nation of people in
Florida, struggling to find a place to call home and
also building herds of cattle and other livestock.

Survivors from many native tribes, mostly
Creek people driven out of their land by Europeans moving in, had moved into Florida from
Georgia, Alabama, and Louisiana. Some sources
say the Spanish called these groups *cimaronnes*
or "free people." Other sources say the natives
called themselves the *yat'siminoli* or "wild men,
roamers." Either way, they began to be called
Seminole. They were joined by the remnants of
other Florida tribes and by runaway black slaves,
known as Black Seminole.

As early as 1760, some of these Creek/Semi-
nole people were raising cattle in the Brookesville
area just north of Tampa Bay. Before 1812, the
Creek/Seminole people may have numbered
about 25,000 people.

The United States waged various campaigns
against these native peoples from 1813 until
1858, killing many and forcibly removing others
to Arkansas. A few survivors—estimates range
from less than 100 to as many as 300—slipped
into the swamps and wild areas and lived in
hiding.

Fort Brooke

The Spanish explorers had marched on through
the Tampa Bay area, lured by the promise of gold
elsewhere. The English had looked the bay over,
renamed a few spots, and moved on.

After 1700, however, commercial fishermen
from Cuba made Tampa Bay one of their fishing
grounds. During the fall and winter, these fishermen would catch and dry vast numbers of red
snapper, snook, grouper, pompano, tarpon, and
other fish to take back to Havana. A few of them
camped out year round. By the early 1800s there
were a couple of Cuban families growing citrus
and corn, but there still was no permanent Euro-
American settlement in the Tampa Bay area.

That was about to change.

In 1823, two years after the United States
gained control of Florida, the government
decided that all the Seminole people needed
to live in one spot far away from where white
settlers were likely to venture. That spot, they
decided, was near Tampa Bay. Reluctantly, the
Seminole agreed to the terms of the Treaty of
Moultrie Creek, which prohibited them from living within 20 miles of the coast.

In January 1824, Brevet Colonel George Mercer Brooke brought four companies of soldiers
from Pensacola to the Tampa Bay area to establish a military post and to find a suitable spot
where the Florida Seminole could be relocated.

To Brooke's pleasant surprise, he found the
beginnings of a plantation owned by Richard S.
Hackley, who had been the American consul in
Madrid during the time the Spanish and Americans were negotiating over Florida. Hackley, seeing what he thought was a great opportunity,
had bought a huge tract of land in the Tampa Bay
area from the Spanish Duke of Alagon in 1819,

intending to farm it himself. But on his return to New York, Hackley found his law practice demanded his attention. A couple of years later, he sent his son, Robert, to Florida to begin building and planting.

Robert Hackley hired 16 men and brought a boatload of supplies into Tampa Bay in November, 1823. Before long, he had built a house and planted rows of citrus trees near the Hillsborough River. Robert Hackley then left to go to Pensacola for a few weeks.

As Hackley sailed north, Brooke sailed south. He commandeered Hackley's house and refused to relinquish it when young Hackley returned. Hackley's father sued, and his heirs fought the case all the way to the Supreme Court, where their claim was denied. Hackley and his heirs were never compensated for either the land or the improvements.

This house on the northeast bank of the Hillsborough River became the captain's headquarters for Fort Brooke, the first permanent non-native settlement in the Tampa Bay area. The government named the county in which it sat "Mosquito County."

i For a time, Colonel Zachary Taylor was stationed at Fort Brooke. Taylor became commander of the U.S. Army's southern forces in 1841 and was elected president of the United States in 1848.

Fort Brooke became known as a trading post with the Seminole. In 1828, a trader named William G. Saunders built the first general store on Florida's west coast. Other civilians came to set up businesses serving the soldiers and fishermen, and in 1831 the first post office on the west coast, Tampa Bay Post Office, was established with Saunders as postmaster.

Hillsborough County came into being in 1834, but the 1840 census showed fewer than 100 civilians living in all of Hillsborough County, which at that time included land that would later become 10 separate counties in Central Florida.

Odet Phillippe and St. Helena

While American soldiers established the first settlement on the east side of Tampa Bay, the western side became home to a refugee from Napoleon's France.

Odet Phillippe (some sources spell it "Philippe") claimed to have been of royal birth and a surgeon in Napoleon's army who was captured by Admiral Horatio Nelson. Imprisoned in the Bahamas, Count Phillippe was released two years later. Eventually he married in Charleston, made and lost money, and determined to start over in Florida. On the way he was captured by pirates, tended their sick, and was shown a map of the Espiritu Santo (Tampa) Bay as a reward.

In 1832, Phillippe sailed up the west coast of Florida into Tampa Bay and settled near a Tocobaga mound. He built a citrus plantation he called St. Helena after Napoleon's place of exile, sold produce to the soldiers at Fort Brooke, and even built ten-pin alleys and billiards parlors for the soldiers' amusement in the infant Tampa.

Phillippe's grave has never been found, but a marker commemorating this first non-native settler of Pinellas County is in Philippe [sic] Park in Safety Harbor.

The Second Seminole War (1835 to 1842)

Most of the Seminole were moved to an area east of Tampa Bay, although a few lived on very small reservations established in the Apalachicola area. Drought, lack of sufficient space, and inadequate food supplies soon made the Tampa area Seminoles' situation desperate. Each side charged the other with failing to live up to the terms of the Treaty of Moultrie Creek. By 1834, the United States government decided to move the Seminole to lands west of the Mississippi River—with or without their cooperation.

The Seminole were leery of this new move. Some of the Seminole prepared to make the move. Others advocated resisting by force.

In November 1835, an army private was killed as he left Fort Brooke headed to Fort King near Ocala. A month later, a Seminole chief was killed in an ambush as he left Fort Brooke, where he had just sold his cattle in preparation for the move west.

Fourteen Seminole chiefs and 500 of their people retreated to Fort Brooke for protection against the almost certain war to come. White settlers abandoned more remote settlements and gathered together. Several spots in central Florida came under Seminole attack over the next few weeks.

On December 28, two Fort Brooke companies under the command of Major Francis Langhorne Dade were ambushed north of Tampa near Bushnell, and 108 soldiers were killed. Three soldiers escaped, but one was killed the next day.

By June 1837, the number of Seminole at Fort Brooke, by now the U.S. Army's southern headquarters, had grown to about 700, and plans were made to move them west. Something, however, made the Seminole people afraid, and one night almost all of them slipped away into the woods. Some were captured and removed west. Others made their way to the Everglades. Still others lived hidden in the wilds of the Tampa Bay area.

The conflict would continue for the next five years, with some of the Seminole actively resisting and others still hoping to make a peaceful, if coerced, move to a land they hoped they could call their own.

By the early 1840s, however, Fort Brooke had been displaced by Fort Harvie, which later became Fort Myers, 100 miles south as Army headquarters in Florida.

The Armed Occupation Act of 1842, which promised 160 acres to any adult, white male willing to bear arms and build a home, brought settlers. Tampa began to grow as a livestock-trading center, and cattle shipped to Cuba brought in gold.

But the land grants were only offered for nine months because slave-owning southerners didn't want abolitionist non-slave owners to move into the south. The next time land grants were offered was in 1862.

In the meantime, Florida became a state in 1845. Tampa legally became a town in July 1848—until that time it had been an appendage of Fort Brooke.

Just two months later, a hurricane destroyed most of Tampa and Fort Brooke. But what seemed to doom the infant town actually sealed its future. The federal government decided to rebuild Fort Brooke, which meant builders and tradesmen came to Tampa. That, in turn, meant increased business for merchants.

Tampa incorporated in 1850. But the new city had no power to levy taxes and soon found itself in debt. It dissolved in October 1852. Less than a year later, however, the city reincorporated. In 1855, Tampa adopted its first city charter and elected its first mayor, Judge Joseph B. Lancaster.

There was no railroad and not much in the way of roads beyond game trails. Ships still brought most people into and out of the area until 1853 when a stagecoach established a run—an optimistic term, considering it took two days—to Gainesville.

Third Seminole War (1855 to 1858)

As more white settlers came further into Florida, they began to encroach on the land the government had assigned to the Seminole. In August 1850, a young settler was killed in northern Hillsborough County. Three Seminoles were caught, taken to Fort Brooke and lynched—although the official explanation given was that they had committed suicide.

All the remaining Seminole left Hillsborough County and joined those living in the Everglades area. From there, the 150 or so Seminole warriors, who were all that remained of a nation that once numbered in the tens of thousands, began attacking settlers.

The U.S. Army responded, but were somewhat ineffective against the stealthy Seminole. Finally, in 1858, the federal government offered to move the rest of the Seminole to Arkansas. Most Seminole, recognizing the ultimate futility of trying to hold onto land against increasingly poor odds, accepted the offer. The rest were left without a reservation, but with lots of wilderness in which to hide and live as best they could.

ℹ️ Until the Vietnam War, the Second Seminole War (1835 to 1842) was the longest and costliest war involving U.S. troops. The Seminole never surrendered, and today the Seminole exist as a sovereign nation within the United States. The United States government didn't reimburse Florida for expenses incurred in the Seminole Wars until 1903, when they paid Florida $700,000.

CIVIL WAR TO WORLD WAR I

By 1860, Tampa was a growing town of 885 people, and it was the Hillsborough County seat.

Hillsborough County had birthed Manatee County to the south in 1856. Losing that land and the people who lived on it hurt the tax base of Hillsborough County's fledgling government. A bout of yellow fever had come and gone, and a promised railroad had failed to materialize. Still Tampa grew.

Herding cattle became big business in central Florida. As many as 250 head of cattle a week were shipped from Tampa.

On the other side of the bay, in what was still western Hillsborough County, Clear Water Harbor had grown, too, after some ups and downs. Fort Harrison had been built in 1841 overlooking Clear Water Harbor to care for sick and wounded soldiers and as a refuge for settlers in the area. Just a few months later, however, it was clear that the Second Seminole War was largely over, so the fort was abandoned.

Clear Water Harbor became an official Post Office in 1859. Seven McMullen brothers had settled in the area and, while most of the area was given to small-scale farming, there was at least one large farm in the area growing cotton and raising cattle on a larger scale than most.

But neither Tampa nor Clear Water Harbor was more than a blip on the map.

Maybe it was just as well the Tampa Bay area was still a bit isolated. Another war was about to begin, one that would sweep hurricane-like over the South for five years. The full fury of that hurricane would fall in bigger places than Tampa.

Fort Harrison

In one of the ironies of history, Fort Harrison, which existed for only a few months in 1841, is commemorated in the name of one of the major north-south streets in Clearwater and in the name of a historic hotel, now the headquarters for the Church of Scientology.

Not much in Tampa commemorates Fort Brooke, which gave Tampa its start, existed for almost four decades, and was at one time the headquarters for the southern U.S. Army. One downtown parking garage bears the name Old Fort Brooke Municipal Parking Garage and two cannons sit on the University of Tampa grounds. The parking garage probably would have been given some other name, except that construction workers stumbled on the fort's cemetery when they were building the garage in 1980.

Within just the last few years, Cotanchobee Park, a city park along the Hillsborough River bearing the native people's name for the river, was renamed Cotanchobee Fort Brooke Park. A memorial to all the lives lost during the Seminole Wars was placed in the park.

"Let Us Alone"

Florida's first state flag, presented in 1845 at the inauguration of its first governor, consisted of five colorful horizontal stripes—blue, orange, red, white, and green. Stitched into the second stripe were the words "Let Us Alone."

Most Floridians at the time may have hoped the rest of the country would let them alone, given the political turmoil growing around the issues of slavery and the right of states to chart their own courses, but it was probably wishful thinking. The words didn't profess the proper spirit of being part of a union of states, and another flag soon took its place.

By 1860, however, the whole South was telling the Union to let the South alone.

Politically, Democrats controlled Florida in 1860. The Democrats of that day defended slavery as an economic necessity and they were ready to secede. The Constitutional Union Party in Florida felt secession was not the answer to solving the problems, while the Republican Party was so new that it didn't even have an organized presence in Florida. In any case, many Southerners felt they would be well rid of their ties to the Union.

Interestingly, some people saw secession as treason, and instead advocated out-and-out revolution.

Not surprisingly, the Democrats won the 1860 election. In early January 1861, Florida became the third state to secede from the Union, joining South Carolina and Mississippi. Because the Confederacy had not yet been formed, Florida existed for a few short weeks as a sovereign state.

Florida had more liabilities than assets to offer the Confederacy. The whole state had fewer than 150,00 people, and almost half of those were black slaves. The only commodities Florida could offer the Confederacy were cotton, cattle, and salt. Getting them out of the state was a problem, as the bit of railroad that existed didn't connect with the rail lines in any other states. Finally, Florida had a vast amount of coastline that needed defending, but the Confederacy was more concerned about defending other places they thought were more key to their cause.

The Confederacy formed in February 1861, and a month later Floridians were mustered into the Confederate Army. By the end of 1861, Florida had provided the Confederate Army with 5,000 troops—and had to provide those troops with food, uniforms, weapons, and other gear on short notice and without any in-state resources on which to draw. Almost everything Florida's troops needed had to be bought from other Confederate states.

Tampa Bay During the War of Northern Aggression

By July 1860, Tampa had nine general stores and Captain James McKay had just purchased a 450-ton, 161-foot long steamer, the *Salvor*, for weekly Tampa–Key West–Havana runs. McKay, mayor at the time, also was the agent for other, larger steamers connecting Tampa and New Orleans, and he owned a saltworks further north on the east side of Tampa Bay.

McKay also was working to get the federal government to turn over the Fort Brooke property—empty, now that the Seminole Wars were over—to the City of Tampa so it could grow.

McKay tried to buy the property in the fall of 1860, but the government wasn't ready to sell. Instead, the United States Department of the Interior agreed to rent the property to McKay. McKay posted a $1,000 bond and took possession on January 1, 1861. Ten days later, Florida seceded, and a few days after that the Confederate Army moved into the fort.

Not long after that, the Federal navy landed on Egmont Key, a large island at the mouth of Tampa Bay where just a few years before the Seminole people had been penned like animals, awaiting transport west. The Federal troops built a fort, and the cat-and-mouse game of blockade running began.

In October 1861, Captain McKay's *Salvor* was caught by the U.S. Navy and confiscated. The South lost weapons, clothing, coffee, and cigars, and McKay and his son were imprisoned. When they were released five months later, they resumed smuggling supplies.

But a year later, in 1863, Federal troops burned two more of McKay's ships in the Hillsborough River, where the ships had been taken so their hulls could be scraped.

On their way home from burning McKay's boats, however, the Federal troops were ambushed by Confederate troops at Ballast Point. A few men were killed on either side and a few captured on either side.

But the end of Fort Brooke was more one-sided. When three Federal gunboats landed in

Tampa one spring day in 1864, not a Confederate soldier was there to stop them. They were all rounding up cattle in the interior or were foraging further south.

The Federal troops pulled down Fort Brooke's stockades, destroyed the cannon and machine shops, and ransacked the town. A month later, the Federal troops decided Tampa wasn't important enough to bother with further, and they left—much as the Spaniards and the English before them had done.

Tampa had, indeed, been left alone.

i In 1865, the writer of the science fiction book *From the Earth to the Moon* used "Tampa Town" as the setting for the launch of a manned rocket. A century later, in 1969, *Apollo 11* launched from Cape Canaveral just a couple of hundred miles east of Tampa, landed on the moon, and Neil Armstrong took a giant leap for mankind. Who was that prescient 19th century writer? Jules Verne.

Tawdry Tampa, Pristine Pinellas

Of the 15,000 Florida men who enlisted in the Confederate forces, 10,000 died fighting or of disease. Other families who had lived in Florida before 1861, but had Northern sympathies, had left early on. Losing so many people seemd to take a toll on Florida's morals and morale.

For the next 20 years or so, Tampa's reputation was far from wholesome. Food was hard to come by, businesses were boarded up, and the town became known for prostitution, gambling, and drunkenness. Tampa reincorporated after the war in 1866, but disbanded in 1869, then reincorporated in 1872.

Malaria, yellow fever, and other diseases made regular appearances. By 1880, the population had dropped from its 1860 high of 885 to 720—and that included the few Reconstruction-minded northerners who had gambled on Tampa's future and moved in.

Federal troops occupied Fort Brooke from 1866 until 1869. The fort, no longer needed, was decommissioned in 1883, and its land sold for commercial development.

Pinellas, on the other hand, hadn't had much to lose to begin with. During the war, a couple of lone settlers at the tip of the peninsula, Abel Miranda, in particular, harassed the Federal troops on Egmont Key. In turn, troops destroyed Miranda's home in 1862 and slaughtered his livestock. Miranda moved his family to Tampa, then returned to plague the Yankees for the duration of the war. Miranda's was the only home in Pinellas destroyed during the war.

By 1876, there were only 25 families, including one black family, on the entire Pinellas peninsula south of Clear Water Harbor. The isolation of these early settlers cannot be exaggerated. There were no roads linking Pinellas with Tampa. There were no bridges spanning the bay. Travel was mostly by boat. If the wind was favorable, that could be a journey of a few hours. If not, families risked being stranded on an island or worse.

A couple of Northern visitors, however, had made their way to Pinellas and were taken with its natural beauty and mild climate. Things in the Tampa Bay area were about to change.

Cattle, Railroads, and Cigars

Cattle ranching had been a major industry in Florida before the war, and the cattle trade helped Florida recover economically after the war. In Tampa, the only way to get the cattle to market was by boat, and most cattle were shipped to Cuba.

Cuba, long a trading partner with Tampa, revolted against Spain in 1868. For 10 long years things were in such turmoil in Cuba that they couldn't raise enough cattle to supply their own needs, so Tampa area ranchers made money— some estimates say as much as $2 million—during the decade.

But the cattle trade wasn't enough to solve all of Florida's money woes. By the early 1880s, Florida owed $1 million, and interest was accumulating at the rate of almost $70,000 each year. Much public land tied to pre–Civil War railroad expansion was mortgaged. Florida put land up for sale, hoping to attract businesses that would bring settlers. Buyers paid next to nothing for land, but instead of bringing in settlers, buyers cut the virgin timber and then left.

Then Hamilton Disston stepped up to the plate. Disston, a Philadelphia tool-making magnate, bought four million acres of Florida land for 25 cents an acre and set about draining swamps and making marshy land inhabitable. The sale solved Florida's debt problem and freed up land to be used by railroads.

In 1882, Disston established the town of Tarpon Springs, Pinellas County's northernmost town, near a pinpoint settlement called Anclote. (Read more about Tarpon Springs in the Attractions chapter.)

Henry B. Plant came up to bat next. Plant, a Connecticut railroad developer, bought up bankrupt railroads in Georgia and South Carolina after the war and by 1881 had extended rail service into Jacksonville. Disston's purchase opened up the sale of land for railroads in central Florida, and Plant jumped at the opportunity. By January 1884, Plant's railroad ran from Jacksonville to Tampa, cutting what used to be an arduous four-day journey to a just-over-12-hour jaunt.

Tampa became a boom town, getting hotels, an opera house, and a roller-skating rink in short order. The fishing industry took hold, now that fish could be shipped north by rail at the rate of 50,000 pounds a day, and that brought in an ice machine. Congress designated Tampa as an official port.

Vicente Martínez Ybor, a Cuban cigar manufacturer, was the third player up in the Tampa area's grand-slam batting order. Cigar workers in Cuban-owned cigar-manufacturing plants in Key West and New York had begun to organize, as the labor movement gained momentum. Ybor and another owner, Serafin Sanchez, thought they could avoid labor problems by moving their plants to Tampa.

Ybor negotiated with Tampa's Board of Trade, bought 70 acres about 2 miles northeast of Tampa, and built a town. Unfortunately, Ybor made the mistake of bringing one Spanish worker from New York to work with the rest of his Cuban workforce. Given that Cuba was still trying to shake off Spanish rule, the Cubans refused to work with the Spaniard, so Sanchez's plant opened first in April 1886. Before long, however, Ybor's plant and others were open, and Ybor City became known as the Cigar Capital of the World.

The strikes Ybor had hoped to avoid came anyway, but an influx of Cuban, Spanish, Italian, and German immigrants made both Ybor City and Tampa grow. In 1887, Tampa incorporated as a city (as opposed to a town), and Ybor City became part of the City of Tampa. (Learn more about Ybor City in the Parks and Recreation chapter.)

Pinellas Prospers

Hamilton Disston had his pick of places to build. After all, at one point he owned four million acres of Florida—reputedly the largest single purchase of land ever by one person. But he chose the Pinellas peninsula to build Tarpon Springs and, in 1885, Disston City—where the city of Gulfport is today—in the southern part of Pinellas.

Both model cities attracted Civil War veterans and families from England, and before long there were a school and a newspaper on Pinellas Point.

One of those Civil War veterans was John Constantine Williams, son of Detroit's first mayor, who had bought 1,600 acres in the Pinellas Peninsula in 1875, as well as some land in Tampa. Williams wasn't impressed enough to live in either place, however, until a second visit a couple of years later. In 1879, Williams moved his family to the Pinellas area to try farming. That didn't work out very well, and Williams returned to Detroit in 1881.

Pinellas's climate, however, drew Williams back in 1886. By that time, Hamilton Disston, whose property bumped up against Williams' property, had built Disston City and was doing everything he could to bring a railroad to Pinellas—while Henry B. Plant, not wanting to see business diverted from Tampa, was doing everything he could to prevent it.

By that time also, Russian immigrant Pyotr Alexeyevitch Dementyev had made his way to northern Florida. Dementyev built a sawmill that provided railroad ties and other materials to the Orange Belt Railway. When the Orange Belt defaulted on money it owed Dementyev, now known as Peter Demens, he took over the railroad's charter.

Disston approached Demens with an offer of 60,000 acres of land and legislative support to run the narrow-gauge Orange Belt south to Disston City. Demens decided he wanted to run the line even further south to Mullet Key, the furthest barrier island off the point of the peninsula, and asked for more land to do so.

Disston's board of directors refused.

John Williams, newly returned to the area, was more receptive to Demens' dream. In return for 250 acres of waterfront property along the Pinellas peninsula's east side and support for eventually running the railroad to Mullet Key, Williams wanted Demens to run the line through what Williams envisioned as a new town and to build a wharf there large enough to accommodate boats with a 12-foot draw. Despite Demens' running into financial difficulties, he completed his end of the bargain by 1889, and—although there are differing stories of how it came to pass—ended up naming the new city after his Russian birthplace of St. Petersburg.

By 1890, St. Petersburg, with 273 people, was the largest community on the Pinellas peninsula. Local fishermen no longer had to take their catch to Tampa, so an ice house came in and mackerel and snapper were soon on their way north via train. St. Petersburg residents voted to incorporate in 1892, the same year John Williams died. A freeze during the winter of 1894 to 1895 moved citrus growers southward from north Florida, where most of the groves had been lost. Another freeze in 1897 pushed growers and tourists into the Pinellas area.

As for Disston, he soon ran into difficulty. He had bought all that land with a $200,000 down payment and signed a note for the rest. He had planned to develop and sell the land to make the rest of the payments due. But when the railroad bypassed Disston City, those sales didn't happen as quickly as Disston needed them to. Before

long, Disston's world, based on growth, growth, and more growth, started collapsing around him. He died in 1896—various reports are given as to the cause of death, but heartbreak figures in them all.

A Grand Slam Home Run

The turn of the century saw the Tampa Bay area on the verge of changing from a team behind by three in the bottom of the ninth inning to one ready to make history. Hamilton Disston had demonstrated that Florida's swamps and jungle-like interior, including the Pinellas peninsula, could be drained and developed. Henry B. Plant's railroads had connected Tampa Bay to the rest of Florida and the rest of the country. Vicente Martínez Ybor had brought industry and a slew of immigrants who pulled Tampa into the world arena—mainly through their connection with Cuba, a Cuba struggling to become independent of Spanish rule.

Cuban immigrants in Ybor City funded revolutionaries like José Martí. The signal to attack sent to General Maxímo Gomez in 1895 was smuggled to him inside a cigar made in Ybor City. The United States became involved, for various and somewhat spurious reasons, in the Cuban War of Independence in 1898. Henry Plant persuaded the military to use his gargantuan Tampa Bay Hotel as their base of operations during the Spanish-American War. Colonel Theodore Roosevelt and his troops, the Rough Riders, stayed in Tampa before shipping out to Cuba and the Battle of San Juan Hill. (See the Accommodations chapter for more information about the hotel.)

And so the Tampa Bay area grew. Phosphate, used in everything from fertilizer to toothpaste, had been discovered east of Tampa, and most of it was shipped out from the Port of Tampa. People flocked to St. Petersburg for their health and to invest in land. Greek immigrants developed the sponge industry in Tarpon Springs. The Chicago Cubs decided on Tampa as their spring training home.

The folks on the Pinellas peninsula got tired of paying taxes to Hillsborough County and seeing very little in the way of benefits, particularly when it came to roadways. In 1911, Pinellas staged its own revolution and seceded from Hillsborough County. Clearwater was named the county seat and quickly built a courthouse to keep St. Petersburg from challenging the decision.

And the winning run—the one that would, eventually, bring the entire Tampa Bay area into its current position as a major metropolitan area—was warming up just outside the batter's box.

Not that anyone was going to recognize the batter as a history maker. Few people today, outside this area, even know his name or the name of his partner, Percival Elliot Fansler, who funded the venture.

But the swing Tony Jannus took on New Year's Day of 1914, when he flew the first ever regularly scheduled, commercial, winged flight, connected with a ball lobbed into the air by the Wright brothers just a few years earlier and sent it—and the world—soaring into the future.

The flight from St. Petersburg to Tampa lasted 22 minutes. Compared to the almost 3 hours such a trip took by ship, the 12 hours it took by train, or the days it took by automobile or horse, 22 minutes seemed miraculous. Local merchants began touting cross-bay air delivery as a selling point. The flights scheduled were full and ran on time. In fact, the airline—the St. Petersburg–Tampa Airboat Line—ran five weeks beyond its contracted March 31 end date.

It took a while for other investors to step forward and establish the airline industry. But today the Tampa Bay area boasts two international (one of which is intercontinental) airports, a host of smaller fields, and a major Air Force base.

i You can see a full-sized replica of the airboat that Tony Jannus flew back in 1914 at the St. Petersburg–Clearwater International Airport (see Getting Here, Getting Around). The airboat—and, yes, we mean boat—hangs from the ceiling in the baggage claim area.

WORLD WAR I THROUGH THE 1960S

Boom Time and World War I

All the growth in the Tampa Bay area brought diverse groups of people together in a very short period of time. At the end of the Civil War, for instance, Tampa had fewer than 1,000 residents. Only 25 families—one African-American—lived south of Clearwater on the Pinellas peninsula.

Within 20 years, railroad crews and other workers, many of whom were African-Americans, poured into the area. The hotels and other tourist attractions needed service workers. Again, many of the people who found jobs here in the service industries were African-Americans, many of whom had been sharecroppers in Alabama and Georgia and saw this as an opportunity to do better. By 1910, more than a quarter of St. Petersburg's population was African-American.

Ybor's cigar industry also created a need for new merchants and other workers in Ybor City. Immigrants from many parts of Europe came, bringing their ways of doing things.

Old-timers who had wrestled a living from the land, and who still farmed and ranched just outside the city limits, resented newcomers with their easy money and lah-dee-dah ways—never mind that that easy money was bringing in electricity, sewer systems, and more. White northerners had definite ideas about the place of African-Americans, free or not, that encouraged the revival of white southern supremacy movements. Pinellas residents broke away from Hillsborough County after a several-year-long bitter fight.

But whatever hostilities roiled underneath the surface, the boosters of the Tampa Bay area covered with a film of life-is-perfect publicity.

Then World War I devastated much of Europe and cost the United States more than 176,000 troops. Tampa lost 23 men in one day when their ship, ironically the U.S.S. *Tampa*, was torpedoed in Bristol Channel in 1918 and sank, taking all aboard with her.

In the Tampa Bay area, the war halted tourism and the flow of dollars tourists brought.

Some merchants shut down. Land speculators—in 1914 there were 83 real estate agencies in St. Petersburg, a town of fewer than 8,000 people—who had bought up land before the war couldn't make their payments on various loans and lost property.

But as soon as the war was over, tourists again flocked to the area—partly to escape labor and racial tensions in the north, to avoid an influx of socialists and the resulting "Red Scare," and to flee the influenza epidemics of 1918 to 1920.

Even the 1921 hurricane, which destroyed several piers and bridges and caused massive flooding in Tampa, didn't stop people from coming to the Tampa Bay area. All those people needed places to stay, and that set off a building boom that filled the air with the sounds of saws and hammers. Huge hotels, including the Vinoy Park Hotel and the Don Ce-Sar, were built during the 1920s (see the Accommodations chapter).

By and large, the people who came here wanted to play and they had the money to pay for it. So play they did. The Coliseum, at the time one of the nation's premier dance halls, booked top-name acts like Rudy Vallee, big-band leader Harry James, and humorist Will Rogers. Police departments looked the other way when Prohibition laws were broken, and a city-owned solarium permitted nude sunbathing.

i **Four years before the Nineteenth Amendment was ratified, giving women across the United States the right to vote, Clearwater became one of the first communities in the nation to recognize women as equal citizens. In October 1916, Sue Barco became the first woman to vote in Clearwater when she cast her ballot during a special bond election.**

Bust Time

What goes up must come down, the old adage says.

Land prices inflated like a hot air balloon during the early part of the 20th century. But those prices deflated when people figured out that a lot of the prices were based on just that—the hot air promises of the "knickerbocker boys" who promised small investors quick and easy returns in a year or two on undeveloped land ("Why, in just a few months, ma'am, you'll have doubled the amount your husband left you!") or that burst when the grandiose schemes of the overextended large investors got too big.

Like Hamilton Disston before him, D. P. Davis—for whom Tampa's Davis Islands are named—saw Tampa's future and tried to make it all happen overnight. He bought land in the harbor area, as well as land in St. Augustine where he saw similar possibilities, and figured all he had to do was build paradise and people would come and buy or lease it from him.

But a cold and rainy winter of 1925 to 1926 drove people home where they had left their warm woolies. It didn't help that the Investment Bankers Association of America's convention, held in St. Petersburg that year, witnessed first hand this shuttering of the fabled sunshine.

Before long, those who had bet on the short-term future had no tenants, no buyers, and couldn't afford to continue building. Workers were laid off of construction projects, and lumberyards were stuck with boards and building materials no one was buying. Davis and others had to sell out. Again like Disston before him, Davis was soon dead under less than clear circumstances.

Historians point out that the rest of the area's economy progressed quite nicely, thank you. Libraries, colleges, and other foundational institutions opened during this era. And eventually the tourists and other investors returned, albeit a bit wiser.

Depression and World War II Years

Just as the area was getting back on track, everything went topsy-turvy when the stock market crashed in 1929 just as a worldwide depression was brewing. Like the rest of the country, the Tampa Bay area struggled to stay afloat during the 1930s.

Tin-Can Tourists of the World

Road trips in the 1920s usually meant chugging along for days on end, bouncing over ruts in your car and camping out at night. Roads in many places were barely cow trails. Motels hadn't yet come into existence and even gas stations were few and far between.

Still, the call of the open road proved irresistible for many people—especially frost-bitten northerners yearning for the warm sunny days they read about in their local papers, courtesy of enterprising marketing stunts that originated in Tampa and St. Petersburg.

The more adventuresome locked up their homes, stocked up their Model Ts with tents, cookware, and a supply of tinned food, and headed south for the season. Tin-can tourists, as they were called, stopped wherever they pleased—or at least where there was no landowner to object—and pitched their tents. Sometimes the tin-canners were tidy and considerate. Sometimes they weren't. They made themselves less than welcome in many south Florida cities.

When multitudes of tin-can campers descended on the Tampa Bay area, they overwhelmed local public areas. Both St. Petersburg and Tampa at first set aside specific camping areas for tin-canners—Tampa's camp even had running water and plumbing. These winter semi-residents enrolled their children in school, paying 50 cents or so per week for the privilege.

Other tent cities sprouted in other Florida towns, but Tampa's de Soto Park was the tin-can capital. Tin-Can Tourists of the World, an actual organization that grew from 30,000 members in 1922 to over 147,000 members by the mid-1920s, held conventions in Tampa.

Tin-canners seemed to have it made—lots of sunshine for little more than the cost of gas to get down here. The Depression kept many of them home, but by the mid-1930s they returned. In 1938, The Tampa Missionary Board even appointed a chaplain to the tin-canners who still came to Florida, a young seminary student from North Carolina by the name of William Franklin "Billy Frank" Graham.

The problem was, the locals grumbled, the tin-canners didn't spend a whole lot of money while they were here. And when the tin-canners started looking for seasonal employment to pass the time or to take a few bucks back when they returned home, the locals grumbled louder that the tin-canners were taking jobs.

Eventually, St. Petersburg withdrew its official welcome and closed the tent city. Commercial campgrounds opened elsewhere in the area—the forerunners of today's travel trailer and mobile home parks.

In an effort to help homeowners, the state legislature instituted the Homestead Exemption on property taxes (see Relocation chapter). To raise money, the legislature also approved pari-mutuel wagering at horse and dog tracks.

A couple of good things happened during the Depression: St. Petersburg was one of few cities to get federal help, mainly because the city had land in abundance to offer in exchange for funding. The Veterans' Administration's offices and hospital at Bay Pines, built during the early 1930s with federal funds, employed construction workers and then medical professionals and office workers.

Tampa got funds to build the Peter O. Knight Airport on Davis Islands and to build new seawalls along Bayshore Boulevard. Both counties put people to work on mosquito abatement and malaria control programs.

Tourists began returning in the mid-1930s, which helped some. But when Germany invaded Poland in 1939, Tampa's shipbuilding industry got multimillion-dollar contracts to build military ships. And Tampa became home to MacDill Field, now MacDill Air Force Base, built on the Interbay Peninsula at Catfish Point.

Soldiers poured into the Tampa Bay area. The Army leased many of the area's mega-hotels to house and train troops. Drew Field Municipal Airport became a military signal-air-warning and combat air training school (see Close-up: Tampa International Airport in the Getting Here, Getting Around chapter).

Because of Tampa's importance as a sea port, as an air base, and as an army training center, the possibility existed that German submarines would find their way into the bay and attack. In 1942, four Nazi spies actually landed on the Atlantic side of Florida near Jacksonville, so most people took blackouts and other wartime measures seriously.

A Pinellas Park company turned palm fibers into gun wadding at the Palma-tex company, and Clearwater's Donald Roebling, grandson of the builder of the Brooklyn Bridge, invented the amphibious landing craft, the Alligator.

One War Ends Over There, Another Begins Right Here

Once the threat of a world-wide fascist empire had been dealt with, and once life returned to some semblance of "normal," people began to fight a more insidious local threat: crime and corruption.

In every age and in every community around the world, there are always people who look for ways to control other people and to beat the

system. If they can't beat the system, then they'll create a system of their own with their own rules, their own means of making money, and their own procedures for dealing with rule breakers.

The Tampa Bay area has had its share of people like this. The Native Americans who were here before Europeans came fought among themselves. Europeans from Spain fought against Europeans from England and neither group treated the Native Americans well. The United States' record is no better.

The cigar industry moved here to avoid labor organizers. But labor organized anyway and there were strikes in the late 1880s and early 1900s among the cigar workers as well as among rank-and-file carpenters and other builders.

Workers envied their bosses' wealth. Business owners resented being envied for what they saw as their return on millions of dollars invested in land, buildings, equipment, and even housing and other amenities for workers.

Bootlegged liquor brought in to keep the wealthy tourists happy during Prohibition also brought in bootleggers. Illegal gambling games, especially *bolita* in the Ybor area, came under the control of gangsters quick to see an opportunity to exploit players' hopes and fears. The legalized parimutuel racetrack gambling soon spawned illegal off-track betting—which in turn caused the hoped-for state revenues to fall.

i For a guide to a historical tour of underworld crime spots, check out Scott Dietche's 2001 article, "A Drive-By Historical Tour of Tampa's Notorious Wise Guys," at Creative Loafing's Web site (www .creativeloafing.com). We doubt the visitors' centers have copies.

Politicians, too, played power games and bent the rules. The hard-fought 1935 Tampa mayoral election, for instance, ended with people on both sides shouting "Fraud!" City police monitored the voting areas and arrested 100 voters, while sheriff's deputies, who supported the other candidate, arrested the police officers. The National Guard restored order.

The Depression heightened all this activity as desperate people became more willing to look for answers outside of what they perceived as a broken system. Socialists, communists, and anarchists, who had not received much of a hearing earlier in the century, found new followers. In response, the Ku Klux Klan re-emerged, kidnapping and beating—even killing—suspected communists. Tampa city police officers were implicated in the activities.

Legendary gangster Al Capone built a home in St. Petersburg, ostensibly for his mother.

While the Depression went on, most people were too occupied with survival to do more than look the other way. During World War II, the enemy was "over there."

But from May 1950 to August 1951, Tennessee Senator Carey Estes Kefauver forced the nation, including the Tampa Bay area, to confront the problem of organized crime right here. Kefauver headed the Special Committee on Organized Crime in Interstate Commerce, which conducted nationally televised hearings in 14 cities, including Miami and Tampa.

The Kefauver hearings were not the first congressional committee hearings to be nationally televised. In 1948, some Senate Armed Services Committee meetings were broadcast. But more people had television sets in 1950 than in 1948.

Nor did the 1948 hearings hold the same kind of drama the Kefauver hearings held two years later—the same kind of drama that keeps crime shows near the top of the ratings today. The hearings captured more public attention than had ever occurred before.

Florida's governor, Fuller Warren, had already come under statewide scrutiny because his 1948 campaign had been financed mainly by three people, one of whom owned Chicago and Florida racetracks. The Kefauver hearings, which revealed widespread illegal gambling throughout Florida and tied at least one county sheriff to ownership of a gambling establishment, increased the scrutiny of Governor Warren fifty-fold.

In Tampa, Kefauver's committee got the unexpected help of Charlie Wall. Wall, the privileged son of a Confederate army surgeon and a society denizen, had controlled the *bolita* and other illegal gambling rackets as well as the drug and alcohol traffic in the Tampa Bay area, for most of the early part of the 20th century. Wall's "employees" came from many ethnic backgrounds.

Other crime bosses coveted Wall's Tampa territory, however. In the mid 1940s, a Sicilian immigrant with wider Mafia connections, Santo Trafficante Sr., deposed Wall. Policemen and politicians were bought and bribed to look the other way as Trafficante moved in.

Wall's testimony during the Kefauver hearings exposed Trafficante's work, and it likely cost Wall his life. Wall's 1955 murder was never solved.

Trafficante moved his base of operations to Miami. His son, Santo Trafficante Jr., became involved in pre-Castro Cuban underworld activities. The CIA later took advantage of Trafficante's connections and hired him to try to help overthrow Castro. Some people say Trafficante and other mobsters were involved in the assassinations of the Kennedys.

> **i** The 1963 assassination of President John F. Kennedy in Dallas cut the Tampa Bay area deeply. Kennedy gave what turned out to be his last public speech—20 minutes or so about the economy—on November 18 at Al Lopez Field in Tampa.

Civil Rights Act

Even while the Kefauver hearings caused people across the country to demand that law enforcement officials and politicians clean up their acts—even if they couldn't eradicate organized crime—racial tensions that had simmered for more than 200 years began to boil over.

The Tampa Bay area had not had the kind of widespread slavery other Southern states had—mainly because the area was undeveloped. Nevertheless, the African-Americans who came here looking for work after the Civil War or who were recruited by local building contractors in the early 1920s soon found themselves under a more subtle, but no less restrictive, form of oppression.

Poll taxes undermined the Fifteenth Amendment's extension of voting rights to African-Americans and poor whites. Deed restrictions prevented African-Americans from purchasing or even renting property in certain areas, effectively creating racial ghettos that were last on the list when it came to publicly funded improvements such as sewer systems and electricity. African-Americans—and to some extent Jews—were confined to particular social and economic strata, and woe betide anyone of any race who questioned the rationale of these measures.

St. Petersburg's 1931 city charter, for instance, prohibited whites from moving into or even establishing businesses in African-American neighborhoods and vice versa. Despite its name, the city's Inter-Racial Relations Committee spent its time trying to figure out how to enforce the charter and keep the races separated.

Violence was not unknown. While racial lynching happened in greater numbers in Alabama and Mississippi, Florida had the highest per capita rate of racial lynching between 1900 and 1930. Two particularly heinous racial murders occurred in Pinellas County in 1905 and 1914, one of which was officially sanctioned and possibly officially instigated.

As with the issue of organized crime, World War II postponed any definitive action. But there were hints that change was coming.

The *St. Petersburg Times* added a "Negro News Page" in 1939, which gave the various African-American neighborhoods a means by which to communicate with each other and which openly accorded African-American men and women respect by using the courtesy titles of "Mr." and "Mrs.", "Dr.", etc. in the paper.

The National Urban League came to the Tampa Bay area in the mid-1940s and wrote an in-depth report analyzing the deplorable living conditions in and the overall status of the African-American communities, particularly in St. Petersburg.

Violence still occurred. In 1951, African-Americans and Jewish synagogues were the targets of a series of bombings throughout Florida.

It wasn't until the Civil Rights Act of 1964 outlawed racial segregation in schools, in public places, and in employment that African-Americans and other minority groups had the force of law behind them in their quest to live their lives on the same terms as whites, to enjoy the same liberties, and to pursue their visions of happiness.

1960S TO THE PRESENT

It would be nice to think that the Kefauver hearings eliminated corruption and that the Civil Rights Act of 1964 wiped away racial inequalities in the Tampa Bay area. They didn't, and legislation alone never will.

But the Kefauver hearings, the Civil Rights Act, and other similar acts made the people of this area take stock of themselves as citizens and as neighbors. We began to remember that we are the government and that we can't wait for someone else to "do something." We began to learn that we can accomplish more together than separately.

This remembering and learning didn't happen all at once—and we often need reminding today. But the hard lessons of the 1950s and 1960s allowed the Tampa Bay area to turn a corner and to grow in some new ways.

Meanwhile, other social sands were shifting.

The Carrier Corporation Conquers the South

Many of those soldiers who had passed through the Tampa Bay area during World War II remembered the balmy weather and the pristine beaches when they returned home. They also remembered sweating in the steamy summers and suffocating in the humidity.

People had fans, of course, and other forms of cooling—evaporative swamp coolers, for one. But fans and swamp coolers did nothing to decrease the humidity. Plus, air conditioning wasn't affordable, except for places like movie theaters and stores, which began to use chilled air as an advertising draw during summer months.

People began to get used to being cool, man.

(Oops, sorry. Must have been a passing Jack Kerouac moment—he lived in St. Petersburg for a while. Died here, actually, in 1969.)

In 1951, the Carrier Corporation made it possible for us to crawl into the ice box, as it were, when they introduced a low-cost window air conditioning unit that not only cooled the air, but also lowered the humidity.

Before long, architecture changed. Concrete block homes with smaller windows that trapped the artificial arctic air replaced wooden-framed, more open homes that encouraged breezes to blow in from outside. Verandas and porches disappeared—who sat out there anymore in the heat and the bugs?

Before long, American culture, particularly Southern culture, changed. As a people, we moved indoors. Snowbirds—winter-only tourists—began to stay longer. Businesses moved in, and the population grew.

Agricultural land disappeared from Pinellas County, in particular. In 1943, only 10 percent of all of Pinellas County land was developed, and commercial citrus groves covered more than 13,540 acres. Not quite 50 years later, more than 73 percent of the Pinellas peninsula was developed, and there were no commercial citrus groves left. Housing units grew from 40,525 in all of Pinellas County in 1940 to almost half a million in 2000.

Tampa Bay Hits the Major Leagues

Perhaps no event so signified the Tampa Bay area's coming of age as did the 1974 awarding of a National Football League franchise. The Tampa Bay Buccaneers kicked off in 1976, and they've had their ups and downs since.

But the Tampa Bay area has since hosted four Super Bowls, the first in 1984, bringing the attention of the nation, even the world, to Florida's west coast.

The Tampa Bay Rowdies (1975) and the Tampa Bay Lightning (1990) brought professional soccer and hockey to the Tampa Bay area. Major league baseball took longer to convince, but in 1995 the Tampa Bay Devil Rays were approved

as an expansion team. The Devil Rays (now called the Rays) became the first major league sports team based in St. Petersburg. (See the Spectator Sports chapter for more information.)

The Tampa Bay area also grew as a national performing arts venue during these years. This time St. Petersburg took the lead, opening the Mahaffey Theater in 1965 as part of the Bayfront Center. Clearwater's Ruth Eckerd Hall broke ground in 1979, and the Tampa Bay Performing Arts Center (now the Straz Center) in Tampa opened in 1987. Each facility has seen renovation and upgrades over the years.

In 1980, St. Petersburg spearheaded a drive, ultimately involving the entire Tampa Bay area and the State of Florida, to acquire one of the world's largest collections of Salvador Dalí works. The Museum of Fine Arts in St. Petersburg recently doubled in size, and the Tampa Museum of Art's new facility will open in 2010. (See the Arts chapter for more information.)

The University of South Florida, the area's first public university, was founded in 1956 and opened in 1960. The USF College of Medicine opened in the 1970s, and the H. Lee Moffitt Cancer Center & Research Institute opened in the 1980s. (See the Education and the Health Care, Wellness, and Senior Living chapters for more information.)

Large-scale theme parks were just beginning elsewhere in the country when Tampa's Busch brewery initiated a beautification program and opened Busch Gardens in 1959. In 1965, Busch Gardens added the Serengeti Plain, the largest, free-roaming habitat outside of Africa. Visitors could see giraffes, elephants, ibexes, lions, and other animals in a more natural environment than in caged zoos. Today, the brewery is gone, but the animals remain. Roller-coaster rides and live entertainment have taken the brewery's place, drawing visitors from around the world. (See the Attractions and Kidstuff chapter for more information.)

Politically, the Tampa Bay area has produced two Florida governors within recent years. Bob Martinez (1987 to 1991) was mayor of Tampa. Charlie Crist (2007–present) represented parts of St.

Petersburg in the Florida Senate before becoming Florida's attorney general and then governor.

MacDill Air Force Base grew to become headquarters for United States Central Command and other commands. (See the Military chapter for more information.)

In the late 1970s the Church of Scientology bought the old Fort Harrison Hotel in Clearwater and began the process of establishing its worldwide spiritual headquarters. Today, the Church of Scientology owns many buildings in Clearwater and throughout the area. (See the Worship chapter for more information.)

In the 1970s, the City of St. Petersburg built the first water reclamation system in the United States. As far back as 1920, the City of St. Petersburg recognized its population would grow beyond the ability of the city's land's to supply drinking water. So it bought some land in northwest Hillsborough County in 1930 where they could sink deep wells and ran 26 miles of pipe to bring the water to the city. St. Petersburg's water reclamation system, built in the 1970s, provides more than 37 million gallons of non-drinkable water each day that are used mainly to water lawns, golf courses, and other green areas. Because of this system, the city has also reduced the amount of drinking water it uses. St. Petersburg's water reclamation system is still one of the largest in the world.

Major Heartaches

We've had our share of hard times the last 50 years or so. We've ridden the national economy up and down along with everyone else. We've sent our sons and daughters off to Korea, Vietnam, the Persian Gulf, and other places around the world.

We've avoided major losses of life due to natural disasters, but we've sent volunteers to help pick up the pieces after Hurricanes Andrew (Category 5, 1992), Charley (Category 4, 2004), and Katrina (Category 5, 2005), and we've had narrow misses with Frances and Jeanne, both in 2004. In the Tampa Bay area, we've felt the economic impact of property damage due, primarily, to coastal flooding.

And we've had our share of other kinds of heartaches.

1980 was particularly devastating. In January 1980, 23 U.S. Coast Guard crew members died when their cutter, *Blackthorn*, collided with the tanker *Capricorn* in the shipping channel near the Sunshine Skyway Bridge. Just five months later, the Sunshine Skyway Bridge itself collapsed when the freighter *Summit Venture* hit a support column during a storm. Thirty-five people died when their vehicles dropped into the waters below.

In 1983, three of Hillsborough County's five commissioners were convicted of accepting bribes.

In 1988, two Pinellas County high-school students shot and killed their principal and wounded two other faculty members.

Along with the rest of the nation, we were horrified by the September 11, 2001 attacks on the World Trade Center and the Pentagon. Many of us had relatives and friends who died that day. We sent people, money, and prayers to New York and Washington.

But our grief twisted deeper just a few months later when a local teenager died after he deliberately flew a small, private airplane into a downtown Tampa building on a Saturday morning.

In the News Today

Crime and Corruption: A mob-related racketeering and murder trial, involving a crime family allegedly trying to move into the Tampa Bay area, was moved to New York in 2009 for various technical reasons. And a local official responsible for Hillsborough County's election office is under scrutiny for possibly funneling public funds into his re-election campaign.

Cuba: President Obama has abolished decades-old travel restrictions for Americans wanting to visit family in Cuba and eased other restrictions. Now Cuban-Americans in the Tampa Bay area wait to see what happens in their homeland.

Environment: Water restrictions continue throughout the area, meaning most people can only water their lawns one day a week and then just for a few hours. Population growth, combined with years of drought, have officials worried. Most of the rest of us don't get it. As long as water still flows out when we turn on the tap to brush our teeth, we figure there's no problem. **Roads:** In 2007, the Florida Legislature established the Tampa Bay Regional Transportation Authority to develop a master plan for transportation within a seven-county area. Public meetings are currently being held to discuss the draft version of the master plan, released in April 2009. **Seminole Tribe of Florida:** When last we left the Seminoles, back in 1858, all but 300 or so of the tribe had been relocated out West. The remnant had slipped into the Florida wilderness, most into the Everglades. In 2007, in what has to be one of the most ironic come-full-circle stories of history, the Seminole Tribe of Florida purchased the Hard Rock International network of cafes, hotels, and casinos around the world—including one in downtown Tampa, not far from Fort Brooke. Governor Crist signed a compact that allowed for casino gambling with the Seminole. The issue continues to be debated (see Spectator Sports).

Some of the issues we're dealing with now sound terribly familiar. Maybe history does repeat itself. Maybe, even when we learn from history, we're still doomed to repeat it because of some other more innate fatal flaw. We'll leave that to the playwrights and the preachers.

> **i** Within Tampa's city limits are at least two pieces of foreign soil. One is the Hard Rock Casino, part of the Seminole Tribe of Florida's property. The other is a small park in downtown Ybor City honoring Jose Martí and owned by the Cuban government.

So here we are, almost 500 years after those first Spaniards landed in the Tampa Bay area.

The sparsely inhabited land surrounding Tampa Bay in the 1500s is now home to more than two million people. We live in climate-controlled, pest-controlled environments that limit our contact with the outdoor environment that was home to those early people.

But our children play on the middens made by Chief Hirrihuiga and his daughter, Ulele—the same land on which Odet Phillippe grew citrus trees and called it St. Helena. The Amtrak train still follows much the same route that Henry Plant laid out. Planes still take off from where Tony Jannus flew his airboat.

Life goes on.

> **i** Football fans may know this one: Tampa hosted Superbowl XVIII in 1984 and Superbowl XLIII in 2009. Tampa also hosted two others: Superbowl XXV in 1991 and Superbowl XXXV in 2001.

HISTORY TIMELINE

Before Europeans arrived in the New World, with their innate need to assign numbers to years and chronicle events on paper, a number of Native American tribes lived in the area. This timeline begins with the first known European landing in the Tampa Bay area.

1492—Christopher Columbus lands in Hispaniola.

1513—Juan Ponce de Léon sails from Puerto Rico and lands on Atlantic side of Florida peninsula. It is spring and Easter time, so he names it after *Pascua Florida*, the Feast of Flowers.

1528—Pánfilo de Narváez, leading an expedition commissioned by Charles V, emperor of Spain, sails into what is now Boca Ciega Bay, on the Pinellas peninsula. Narváez alienates the native peoples and marches inland and north to Apalachee territory (near present-day Tallahassee).

1539—Hernando de Soto lands in Tampa Bay, alienates the native peoples, and marches north to Apalachee territory (near present-day Pensacola).

1549—Father Luis Cancer de Barbastro lands in Tampa Bay and is clubbed to death by the alienated native peoples before ever reaching shore.

1565—Pedro de Menéndez de Avilés establishes St. Augustine, the first permanent

European settlement in the United States, and posts a garrison to the Tampa Bay area soon after. The garrison withdraws because of Indian hostilities.

1607—Jamestown, the first permanent English settlement in the New World, is founded.

1670—Charleston, in what would become South Carolina, is settled by the English. The English begin to encroach on Spanish territory to the south.

1763—Florida is ceded to Great Britain by Spain as part of the treaty ending the Seven Years War, known on this side of the Atlantic as the French and Indian War.

1783—Great Britain loses Florida as part of the Treaty of Paris, which ended the American Revolution, and control reverts to Spain.

1813–1819—United States battles Creek and Seminole people in the Creek and First Seminole Wars in Georgia and Alabama. This pushes the Creek/Seminole into Florida.

1821—The United States buys Florida from Spain and destroys Angola, a colony on the eastern shore of Tampa Bay built by escaped slaves who had fled south from the American colonies.

1824—Colonel George Mercer Brooke establishes Fort Brooke at the mouth of the Hillsborough River in what is called Mosquito County. A town grows around the fort.

1832—Odet Phillippe builds his plantation, St. Helena, in what is now Safety Harbor.

1834—Hillsborough County is established.

1835–1842—Second Seminole War begins when two Fort Brooke companies are ambushed on their way to the Ocala area. Fort Brooke becomes the headquarters for the Army of the South (1837 to 1840).

1845—Florida becomes a state.

1848—Tampa becomes a town. Two months later, a hurricane destroys much of Fort Brooke and Tampa, and blows a pass (John's Pass) through one of the barrier islands along the Pinellas peninsula.

1850—Tampa incorporates as a city, but has no power to levy taxes.

1852—Tampa dissolves the city.

1853—Tampa reincorporates as a town again, and stagecoach service arrives.

1855—Tampa elects its first mayor, Judge Joseph B. Lancaster.

1855–1858—Third Seminole War.

1856—Manatee County separates from Hillsborough County.

1859—Clear Water Harbor becomes an official post office.

1861—Florida secedes from the Union and joins the Confederacy. Federal naval forces take hold of Egmont Key to halt blockade runners. Polk County separates from Hillsborough County.

1863—Battle of Ballast Point between Federal and Confederate forces in Tampa Bay is pretty much a draw.

1864—Union forces take Fort Brooke without a battle, as the troops are out rounding up cattle.

1865—The Civil War ends.

1866–1869—Reconstruction troops occupy Fort Brooke.

1866—Tampa reincorporates.

1869—Tampa disbands.

1872—Tampa reincorporates.

1881—Hamilton Disston buys up four million acres of Florida interior lands at 25 cents an acre.

1882—Disston draws up plans for a town at Tarpon Springs.

1883—Fort Brooke is decommissioned and the land sold for commercial development. Phosphate is discovered in Bone Valley near Tampa.

1884—Henry B. Plant establishes railroad service between Tampa and Jacksonville.

1886—Vicente Martinez Ybor buys 70 acres northeast of Tampa and builds a cigar factory. The Statue of Liberty arrives in New York from France.

1887—Tampa incorporates as a city, and Ybor City becomes part of Tampa. Tarpon Springs becomes first Pinellas peninsula town to incorporate. Yellow fever kills 79 people between September and December.

1888—Peter Demens's Orange Belt Railroad comes to John Williams's town, soon to be known as St. Petersburg.

1891—Clearwater incorporates.

1892—St. Petersburg incorporates.

1898—Colonel Theodore Roosevelt and his Rough Riders stay in Tampa before shipping out to Cuba during the Spanish-American War.

1905—Beginning of commercial harvesting of natural sponge beds off of Tarpon Springs.

1911—Pinellas residents secede from Hillsborough County. Clearwater becomes the county seat.

1913—Baseball's Grapefruit League begins when Chicago Cubs make Tampa their spring training home.

1914—The world's first commercial winged airline flight carries passengers between St. Petersburg and Tampa.

1914–1918—World War I.

1921—A hurricane destroys bridges and piers and causes massive flooding in Tampa Bay area.

1920–1925—Florida land boom.

1925–1928—Florida land bust.

1929—Stock market crashes.

1930–1935—Great Depression years.

1939—Germany invades Poland. Tampa's shipbuilding industry takes off. *St. Petersburg Times* adds "Negro News Page," distributed in African-American neighborhoods only.

1940–1945—World War II.

1951—Kefauver hearings expose organized crime and corruption in Tampa. Carrier Corporation begins to sell low-cost window-unit air conditioners.

1956—The University of South Florida is founded. It opens in 1960.

1959—Busch Gardens opens as a garden area.

1964—Civil Rights Act passes.

1974—National Football League awards Tampa an expansion team franchise and Tampa Bay Buccaneers are formed.

1980—USCGC *Blackthorn* sinks; 23 crew killed. Sunshine Skyway Bridge struck by a freighter and collapses; 35 die.

Selected Reading List

While this is by no means a complete list of the sources we used, we found the following books invaluable in helping us see the Tampa Bay area of long ago. We also are grateful for the extensive bibliographies in each that led us on a treasure hunt of our own.

Arsenault, Raymond. *St. Petersburg and the Florida Dream: 1888–1950.* Gainesville, FL: University Press of Florida, 1996.

Grismer, Karl H. *Tampa: A History of the City of Tampa and the Tampa Bay Region of Florida.* St. Petersburg, FL: The St. Petersburg Printing Company, Inc., 1950.

Jahoda, Gloria. *River of the Golden Ibis.* New York: Holt, Rinehart, and Winston, 1973.

Mormino, Gary R., and George E. Pozzetta. *The Immigrant World of Ybor City: Italians and Their Latin Neighbors in Tampa, 1885–1985.* Gainesville, FL: University Press of Florida, 1998.

Tebeau, Charlton W., and William Marina. *A History of Florida.* 3rd ed. Miami: University of Miami Press, 1999.

Young, June Hurley. *Florida's Pinellas Peninsula.* St. Petersburg, FL: Byron Kennedy and Co., 1984.

1984—Tampa hosts Superbowl XVIII.

1987—Bob Martinez becomes Florida's first governor of Hispanic heritage and the third from the Tampa Bay area.

2004—Four hurricanes hit Florida in one season.

2007— Seminole Tribe of Florida purchases Hard Rock International.

2009—Florida Legislature establishes Tampa Bay Area Regional Transportation Authority.

ACCOMMODATIONS

Now that you're here, you need a place to stay. So what's your pleasure? Want to save money by going the economy route? Want to pamper yourself a bit with something more luxurious? Looking to get to know the area and figure a bed-and-breakfast host can give you the local lowdown?

Or maybe you want something more adventuresome. How about letting yourself be rocked to sleep each night on a yacht?

With more than 30,000 hotel rooms and a host of other options from which to choose, the Tampa Bay area opens its doors to more than 20 million visitors each year. Even when we've hosted major events like four Super Bowls since 1984, we've managed to make room for everyone who has wanted to come.

This area was built with tourists in mind. Those silver-topped minarets you see that are now part of the University of Tampa? Those used to be part of Henry B. Plant's palatial Tampa Bay Hotel. And Pinellas County has two historic *grande dame* hotels and two historic "jazz queen" hotels that you'll read about later in this chapter. Each of those places, designed to accommodate the rich and famous from around the world, still stands. Each still pampers its guests with facials and massages, individualized regimens of exercise and treatments, and culinary creations to die for.

We also have some newer resort hotels that provide the kind of over-the-top experience Henry Plant provided for his guests. We'll definitely take you to some of those!

For people who prefer portable palaces, Tampa is the home of Lazydays, the country's largest single-site RV dealership in North America, where you can browse, buy, and learn to drive one of their super-sized homes on wheels. Or bring your RV here from wherever you are, and stay in their full-amenities RallyPark.

Whether you want to be able to step from your room onto a world-class golf course or you want to rough it in a log cabin or stay in a hostel, we'll find a place for you to rest your weary head. We'll find a base from which you can enjoy all the Tampa Bay area has to offer.

First, we'll take you to several of the places where hotels tend to cluster. You know, the ABCD's—near the airports and attractions, along the beaches, and by the convention centers downtown. We'll also show you some of the unusual and the historic places along the way. Then, we'll take you to other types of accommodation, such as RV parks, bed and breakfasts, and golf and tennis resorts. Within each heading, we'll give you Web sites for more thorough listings, and then we'll spotlight a really cool place or two.

Just a reminder: Florida is a Clean Air state and many hotels and motels have designated their entire building as being smoke-free. Other hotels still have some designated smoking rooms, and may or may not charge an extra fee. Check with the management before making reservations and for information about designated outdoor smoking areas.

Price Code

Prices reflect the average rate for high season (generally, November through April) double-occupancy rooms. Prices may vary depending on location within the building—waterfront rooms often cost more than landside rooms, for instance. Extra services such as parking (if applicable), telephone calls, laundry, and taxes are not included in these prices. Check for packages that include tickets to attractions or amenities such as spa services. Unless specified otherwise, the usual credit cards are accepted.

$................ Less than $75
$$ .... $75 to $125
$$$ .... $126 to $175
$$$$.............. $ 176 and up

HOTELS AT AIRPORTS AND ATTRACTIONS, BEACHES, AND CONVENTION CENTERS

Hillsborough County

Airports and Attractions

TAMPA INTERNATIONAL AIRPORT

The area surrounding Tampa International Airport, International Mall, Raymond James Stadium, and the Westshore area boasts some of the area's biggest hotels. We've listed several here.

i The Florida Department of Environmental Protection's Florida Green Lodging program encourages the lodging industry to reduce water use, conserve energy, improve air quality, and reduce solid waste. Hotels and resorts that do so are awarded a One, Two or Three Palm rating. Only 449 hotels in the state are designated "green" at this point, but the number is growing.

**DOUBLETREE HOTEL TAMPA
WESTSHORE AIRPORT** $$$$
4500 W. Cypress St.
Tampa
(813) 879-4800
http://doubletree1.hilton.com

Who can say no to the warm chocolate chip cookies offered to guests at the Doubletree Hotel Westshore? With almost 500 rooms and suites and more than 16,000 square feet of meeting space, the Doubletree hosts conferences and events of many types. The hotel has a business center, a fitness center, and heated pool. Snacks are offered in the HHonors VIP Lounge. Plus, the Doubletree Hotel also offers complimentary shuttle service to the Tampa Port Authority's cruise berths (ask for the park and cruise package). The Cypress Café & Grille serves breakfast, lunch, and dinner, while the Player's Sports Bar and Lounge offers an after-hours time out. No pets.

EMBASSY SUITES WESTSHORE $$$$
555 N. Westshore Blvd.
Tampa
(813) 875-1555
http://embassysuites1.hilton.com
The Embassy Suites Westshore is near Tampa International Airport, and also near Westshore Plaza and the business district near International Plaza. Look for a full business center and meeting space on premises. The complimentary breakfast here features cooked-to-order eggs and hot meats along with other items. There's a complimentary manager's reception each evening, and the Bay Café serves lunch and dinner. No pets. Self-parking is $7 per night; valet parking is $12 per night.

i He was called the "Sultan of Swat" and he was a frequent guest in the grand hotels of the Tampa Bay area. A 1966 article in the (now defunct) *Tampa Times* started the story that he signed his first contract in the Grand Dining Room of Henry B. Plant's Tampa Bay Hotel. He was George Herman "Babe" Ruth. However, according to Baseball's National Hall of Fame, Ruth actually signed the 1914 contract with the Boston Red Sox in Boston before coming to Tampa. The story persists.

Hotels, Motels, and Inns

With over 30,000 hotel and motel rooms in the area, we can't tell you about every one. We don't really need to either. If you have a favorite chain with which you've grown comfortable or that you use to add points to your frequent flyer card, you'll find most of the major ones and a few of the lesser ones here.

For a listing of smaller hotels and motels in Pinellas County, go to Superior Small Lodging's Florida Web site at www.floridassl.com. This non-profit network of smaller, often individually owned places conducts an annual on-site assessment of each business to ensure it meets SSL's standards. If you choose one of these smaller places, ask your host about its history. George Washington didn't sleep in the Tampa Bay area, but plenty of other notable people did.

For a more complete listing of hotels and motels in Hillsborough County, go to Tampa Bay and Company—our online visitor center—at www.visittampabay.com/hotels. The same information for Pinellas County can be found through the St. Petersburg/Clearwater Area Convention and Visitors Bureau, online at www.floridas beach.com.

RENAISSANCE TAMPA HOTEL INTERNATIONAL PLAZA **$$$$**
4200 Jim Walter Blvd.
Tampa
(813) 877-9200
www.marriott.com/hotels/travel/tpaim-renaissance-tampa-hotel-international-plaza
Rich, jewel-toned colors and gorgeous Mediterra-nean décor greet guests to the Renaissance Tampa Hotel at International Plaza. We mention this hotel in the Shopping chapter because it is so close to International Plaza, and we've included its award-winning Pelagia Trattoria in the Restaurant chapter under both Breakfasts and Fancy Dining. Here, we'll say that the hotel hosts events and weddings in its 12,500 square feet of meeting space; there is a full-service business center, fitness center, and pool; and area golf courses are close by. Self-parking is free; valet parking is $16 per night. No pets.

SHERATON SUITES TAMPA AIRPORT **$$$-$$$$**
4400 W. Cypress St.
Tampa
(813) 873-8675
www.starwoodhotels.com
In the atrium area at the Sheraton Suites Tampa Airport, you'll find it hard to believe you're not outside. Lush plantings and lots of light let guests enjoy *al fresco* dining in a more climate-controlled setting. Look for the St. James Grill (breakfast, lunch, and dinner) and St. James Bar (sports bar–themed) in the atrium at the Shera-ton Suites. There's also a business center, fitness center, indoor heated pool, and free shuttle service to nearby attractions. Meeting space is available. Some pets are allowed—contact the hotel for restrictions. Parking is free.

THE WESTSHORE HOTEL **$$$-$$$$**
1200 N. Westshore Blvd.
Tampa
(813) 282-3636, (800) 449-4343
www.thewestshorehotel.com
The Westshore Hotel's 237 rooms include Inter-net access and a work area in addition to the creature comforts. With over 11,000-square-feet of event space, the Westshore can accommodate meetings of up to 400 people. Guests have use of a business center, a fitness center, and heated pool. Dining options include the Green Iguana Bar & Grill (breakfast, lunch, and dinner) and the Buddha Lounge (sushi) at the Westhore Hotel, which is within walking distance of Westshore Mall and International Mall. Parking is free.

Staying at the Airport

**Tampa Airport Marriott
Hotel** $$$$
5503 W. Spruce St.
Tampa
(813) 879-5151, (800) 564-3440
www.marriott.com

Walk from your airside shuttle, on the transfer level of Tampa International Airport's terminal, down a wide corridor lined with shops and filled with artwork, right to the lobby of the Tampa Airport Marriott Hotel. Even locals book a room here when they've got an early flight out and want to catch an extra hour or so of shut-eye. Triple-paned windows and lots of soundproofing mean you won't even remember you're at an airport. Unless, that is, you happen to look out one of the many windows and notice a jet taking off or landing.

Plus, with 15 meeting rooms—the largest of which accommodates up to 800 people—it's a popular place for weddings and for business symposiums. The hotel includes 292 rooms and four suites. Rooms include the usual amenities, and the hotel offers a fitness room, outdoor pool and whirlpool, and massage service by appointment.

Parking can be a bit pricy at $6 per hour or $22 per day, but most people coming by air won't be parking here. A coffee house and a cafe in the lobby offer breakfast and lunch; a lounge area offers lunch and dinner. For really elegant dining, go up to The View at CK's, a revolving rooftop restaurant located on the top floor (see Restaurant chapter). The Tampa Airport Marriott Hotel just earned its Two Palm rating from the Florida Green Lodging program, one of very few hotels in the state to do so.

Busch Gardens/University of South Florida

The University of South Florida's Web site lists more than 30 hotels and motels, including some extended-stay hotels, near its various campuses (www.usf.edu/about-usf/hotels-near-the-tampa-campus.asp). Many of them offer discounts to travelers staying for USF–related events. Here are five hotels near the main USF campus and in proximity to Busch Gardens.

BEST WESTERN ALL SUITES HOTEL $$$
3001 University Center Dr.
Tampa
(813) 971-8930
www.bestwestern.com

This Best Western All Suites Hotel offers two-room suites with separate bedroom and living area, meeting space, pool and hot tub, plus billiards tables on the sun deck. A complimentary breakfast is offered each morning, and the Parrot's Cove Bar and Grill serves dinner. No pets and parking is free.

EMBASSY SUITES HOTEL
(ON THE MAIN USF CAMPUS) $$-$$$
3705 Spectrum Blvd.
Tampa
(813) 977-7066
http://embassysuites1.hilton.com

Located on the main campus of the University of South Florida, this Embassy Suites Hotel features a fitness room, heated pool, video arcade, and complimentary shuttle service to Busch Gardens. A 9,800-square-foot ballroom hosts a number of events throughout the year. Dining options include a complimentary, cooked-to-order breakfast, a manager's reception, and Mangroves Grille, located inside the seven-story atrium and serving lunch and dinner. No pets. Some smoking rooms available.

HOLIDAY INN EXPRESS HOTEL & SUITES $$-$$$

2807 E. Busch Blvd.
Tampa
(813) 936-8200
www.tampaholidayinn.com

Walk to Busch Gardens or Adventure Island or take advantage of the complimentary shuttle. After a day at the parks—look for package deals on the hotel's Web site—come back and wind down in the hotel pool or use the fitness area. Enjoy a complimentary hot breakfast each morning or choose from many nearby restaurants. The hotel's meeting space accommodates up to 60 people. No pets.

WINGATE BY WYNDHAM INN $$-$$$

3751 E. Fowler Ave.
Tampa 33612
(813) 979-2828
www.wingatetampa.com

Fitness area, hot tub, swimming pool—what more could there be? At the Wingate, there's also the AquaMassage bed, a 20-minute soothing body massage guests can enjoy while fully clothed. There's also a business center and shuttle service to nearby attractions. Dining options include a complimentary 40-item breakfast buffet, and the hotel has meeting space for up to 50 people.

CASINO GAMBLING

SEMINOLE HARD ROCK HOTEL & CASINO, TAMPA $$$$

5223 N. Orient Rd.
Tampa
(813) 627-7625, (866) 502-PLAY (7529)
www.seminolehardrocktampa.com

In the east end of Tampa, the Seminole Hard Rock Hotel & Casino draws vacationers and day-trippers from around the area (see Sports chapter). The Tribe bought the Hard Rock business in 2007, five years after building the licensed Tampa facility. The high-rise hotel features rooms and suites "designed to make you feel like a rock star," including in-room sound systems, plush bedding, lots of natural lighting, and oversized bath areas.

An outdoor pool, a complete fitness center, a Body Rock Spa, and a gift shop offer respite from the non-stop gaming, which is the biggest draw. Half a dozen or more different card games go on 24/7. Rooms and rooms of slot machines emit an incessant music that's a bit like electronic wind chimes. Guitars, keyboards, costumes, and other music memorabilia from rock's golden era convey the Hard Rock theme throughout. Watch a rock video projected onto a waterfall mid-casino and check out the artistically arranged Van Halen drum set in the well over the escalator near the entrance from the South Garage. Smoking is allowed in the casino.

There are several dining options, including the Council Oak Steaks & Seafood, a restaurant where you can view the evening's uncut steaks hanging in the cooler as you enter the restaurant; Floyd's, an upscale nightclub/restaurant; the marketplace-style Fresh Harvest, which features everything from dim sum to pasta; or the Green Room, which never closes. You'll find live entertainment in some of the restaurant areas. But you won't find the all-out rock concerts hosted at some of the other Hard Rock Cafés around the world. That's because the Ford Amphitheatre, an outdoor concert venue, sits right across I–4 from the casino.

Beaches

PIRATE'S POINTE FISHING RESORT $$-$$$

1800 Kofresi Court
Ruskin
(813) 641-2052, (877) 641-2052
www.piratespointeresort.com

Located on the Hillsborough County side of Tampa Bay and south of Tampa itself, Pirate's Pointe Fishing Resort offers an old-Florida fishing camp atmosphere with modern accommodations including a dock with boat slips, bricked courtyard patios, airy rooms, an outdoor swimming pool and cooking area, and free Internet service in the clubhouse. Rent a canoe or kayak and explore the Little Manatee River. Fish the river, or ask about guided off-shore fishing trips. Swap fish tales at a Saturday night cookout at the clubhouse. Pirate's Pointe Fishing Resort is just minutes away from E. G. Simmons Park (see

Parks and Recreation chapter). Units range from an efficiency to a five-bedroom cottage. Pets on leashes are welcomed.

SAILPORT WATERFRONT SUITES $-$$
2506 N. Rocky Point Dr.
Tampa
(813) 281-9599, (800) 255-9599
www.sailport.com

Sailport Waterfront Suites sits on a point of land at the north end of Old Tampa Bay on the Tampa side of the Courtney Campbell Causeway and minutes from Tampa International Airport. Sailport offers beach volleyball, tetherball, and the likes of Whiskey Joe's, the Rusty Pelican, Bahama Breeze, and other restaurants nearby. Although there is a sandy beach area with an incredible view of Tampa Bay, there is no access to the bay itself—the Rocky Point part of the address means just that. Not to worry, however. Sailport has a nice-sized pool and deck area that also overlooks Tampa Bay. A snack room in the main lobby is open 24/7 and sells soda, beer, wine, snacks, and forgot-to-pack items. Plus, guests enjoy complimentary coffee, pastries, and the morning paper.

Convention Center/Downtown Hotels

EMBASSY SUITES TAMPA $$$$
13 South Florida Ave.
Tampa
(813) 769-8300
http://embassysuites1.hilton.com

With a connecting sky bridge to the Tampa Convention Center, Embassy Suites Tampa wins the award for being the hotel closest to the Convention Center and to the city's Gasparilla Days pirate invasion (see Annual Events and Festivals chapter). But that's not the Embassy Suites' only claim to fame. A rooftop pool deck provides an incomparable view of the city, the fitness and business centers keep everything in top-form, and walking through the atriums—furnished with fountains and pools and foliage—reminds the weariest soul there's beauty in the world. With 9,000 square feet of meeting space and all-suite guest rooms, the Embassy is a convenient place for meetings and events.

Dining options for breakfast include a complimentary breakfast buffet with cooked-to-order omelets or grab-and-go choices. Trolleys American Café is open for lunch, dinner, and late-night snacks. A Starbucks is in the lobby. The manager's reception each evening offers an opportunity to introduce yourself to someone you've seen across a conference room. The trolley terminal is right outside the front door, so it's an easy ride to Channelside Bay Plaza or Ybor City (see Nightlife and Attractions chapters). No pets. Valet parking only at $20 per night, plus tax.

HOWARD JOHNSON PLAZA $$-$$$
111 W. Fortune St.
Tampa
(813) 223-1351
www.hojo.com

This downtown Tampa Howard Johnson Plaza features sophisticated décor throughout and meeting space that can accommodate up to 350 people. Plus, it's right across the river from Tampa's Riverfront Park. A fitness center and outdoor pool provide both workout and cool-down time. Complimentary shuttle service takes guests to many area destinations including the University of Tampa, Channelside, the Convention Center, and Tampa General Hospital. Dining options include the Waterworks Restaurant (breakfast, lunch, and dinner) and a lounge area. Pets are allowed, and on-site parking is $8 per night.

HYATT REGENCY TAMPA $$$$
211 N. Tampa St.
Tampa
(813) 225-1234
www.tamparegency.hyatt.com

The Hyatt Regency Tampa may not be right on the water, but that doesn't stop it from bringing the water to you—with an atrium-area waterfall cascading down from five stories above. Located in the heart of downtown Tampa, the Hyatt Regency Tampa offers 521 guest rooms, including some that allow smoking.

Business travelers will find a business center for updating proposals and preparing reports based on the meeting just concluded. Interna-

Close-up

Victorian Era *Grande Dame* and Jazz Age Queen Hotels

Back in the days when people traveled south to "take the cures," Florida was a favorite destination. Four hotels define this era from 1890 to 1929—two *grande dames* and two jazz babies gracefully reigning over their surroundings and graciously welcoming the well-heeled and well-connected from around the world. We've left the Web address here, but look for addresses and phone numbers elsewhere in this chapter.

Tampa Bay Hotel
Now the University of Tampa and the Henry B. Plant Museum
www.ut.edu / www.plantmuseum.com

When Henry B. Plant brought the railroad to Tampa in the late 1880s, he planned to bring a very select group of investors to town. The kind of people Plant wanted to attract wouldn't stay in Mrs. So-and-So's boarding house. So Plant built a hotel embodying the Gilded Age. Those silver-topped minarets in Tampa's skyline are stainless steel and are part of the University of Tampa now. Originally they topped Plant's Tampa Bay Hotel, once known as "Plant's Palace," which hosted more than 1,000 visitors at a time in its 511 rooms and suites.

The quarter-mile-long building covered six acres and housed the first elevator installed in Florida. The hotel grounds covered 150 acres and included a casino, a racetrack, a bowling alley, a golf course, tropical gardens, and a zoo. Guests fished for tarpon during the day and dined on a 10-course meal at night.

The Moorish Revival building, designed by New York architect John A. Wood, cost $2.5 million to build and was filled with opulent furnishings in the overstuffed Victorian manner. Rooms rented for $5 to $15 per night at a time when $2 per night for a room in Tampa was considered high.

Then again, not just anyone stayed at the Tampa Bay Hotel. The Queen of England, Sarah Bernhardt, and Stephen Crane were guests. So were Colonel Theodore Roosevelt and his Rough Riders. During the Spanish-American War, officers planned the invasion in the luxurious suites while the troops camped out and drilled on the grounds.

The Tampa Bay Hotel was empty from 1930 to 1933, when Tampa Bay Junior College moved in, eventually becoming the University of Tampa (see Education chapter). The southeast wing of the building is now the Henry B. Plant Museum (see Attractions chapter).

Belleview Biltmore Resort
www.belleviewbiltmore.com

One hotel in the area wasn't enough for Henry B. Plant. In 1897, Plant opened the Belleview Hotel on the Gulf of Mexico side of the Pinellas peninsula. Over the next several years, the hotel grew to 820,000 square feet, sitting on 20 acres of land that included a world-class golf course designed by Donald Ross in 1925.

Constructed of Florida and Georgia heart-of-pine wood in a Queen Anne shingle-style design by architects Michael J. Miller and Francis J. Kinnard, the Belleview Biltmore is thought to be the largest occupied wood-frame structure under one contiguous roof in the world. Its gleaming white exterior and dark-green sloped roof made it the "White Queen of the Gulf."

When Plant died in 1899, ownership passed to his son, Morton. Eventually the Belleview became part of the Biltmore hotel family. During World War II, the military requisitioned the hotel, which was used to house soldiers stationed at nearby airfields. Celebrities of many kinds—from Thomas Edison to President Barack Obama, Joe DiMaggio to Bob Dylan, Joan Baez to Prime Minister Margaret Thatcher—have danced in the Belleview Biltmore's ballrooms and slept in her bedrooms.

After narrowly escaping demolition, the Belleview Biltmore Resort was purchased by Legg Mason Real Estate Investors, Inc., and is being renovated. It will be closed until 2012.

The Vinoy Park Hotel
Now the Renaissance Vinoy Resort and Golf Club
www.vinoyrensaissanceresort.com

As the Gilded Age of the Victorian era yielded to the equally lavish Jazz Age of the Roaring Twenties, Aymer Vinoy Laughner, a Pennsylvania oil tycoon who wintered in St. Petersburg, opened his 375-room, $3.5-million Vinoy Park Hotel. It was 1925, and St. Petersburg was bustling. With the Vinoy Park Hotel, St. Petersburg could attract the kind of clientele Henry Plant's hotels were drawing.

Designed by architect Henry L. Taylor, the Mediterranean Revival–style, salmon-colored main building rose seven stories above the St. Petersburg waterfront and was flanked by two five-story buildings and by two two-story buildings. The grounds covered 12 acres, and the interior was furnished as befitted a Jazz Age queen. Calvin Coolidge, Admiral Byrd, the Pillsburys, and Babe Ruth, among others, stayed here.

During World War II, the Vinoy was commandeered for use by the Army Air Corps. Military bakers and cooks trained in the kitchens. From 1945 to 1974, the Vinoy operated as a hotel, although Laughner sold it in late 1946 to Chicago hotelier Charles Alberding. Eventually, however, the hotel deteriorated and closed. It sat empty—except for vagrants and those who braved rumors of ghosts and ignored "No Trespassing" signs—for almost 20 years.

In 1992, a $93-million renovation, with a Ron Garl designed golf course, revived the Vinoy.

The Don Ce-Sar
(Now the Don CeSar, a Loews Hotel)
www.loewshotels.com/en/hotels/st-pete-beach-resort

Thwarted love, a tragic death, and a $1.25-million American Taj Mahal rising like a shimmering pink mirage from the white sands of St. Petersburg beach—sounds like a bodice-ripping romance novel. Grab the tissues, and get ready for the real-life story of Thomas Rowe.

Rowe studied in London, returned to the States, and built commercial buildings in New York. Eventually he married a Virginia woman. In the early 1920s, Rowe came to Florida alone. Mary Lucille Rowe followed, but the Rowes were estranged and lived apart.

Unsubstantiated legend says Rowe had fallen in love with an opera singer named Lucinda while abroad, but her parents thwarted the romance. Lucinda died, and the broken-hearted Thomas Rowe never recovered. When, at 47, Rowe saw the white sands of St. Pete Beach, he determined to build a memorial to the lost Lucinda.

Because Lucinda had sung the title role in *Maritana*, which tells of a beautiful gypsy, courted by Spain's King Charles II but won by the mercenary knight Don César de Bazan, Rowe named his monument the Don Ce-Sar. One of the restaurants is the Maritana. The ballroom is dubbed the King Charles.

The Army bought the Don in 1942, making it a military convalescent center and later a Veteran's Administration office until 1969. The government planned to demolish the Don, but local people protested. Holiday Inn franchise owner William Bowman Jr. bought it in 1972. It is currently a Loew's hotel.

And Thomas Rowe and Mary Lucille? Thomas died in 1940. Mary Lucille entertained a group at the Don Ce-Sar shortly afterward. Some say it was the first time she had stepped foot in the building. Rowe's will was contested. By the time Mary Lucille obtained title, the military had its eye on it. Mary died in 1944.

tional travelers will find a currency exchange service on site and a multilingual staff. When it's time to relax, the rooftop sundeck and heated pool offer a way to get above the hustle and bustle. Adjacent to the pool area, the Health Club offers an array of fitness equipment. Or, if you'd rather play a bit harder, a full-service YMCA is next door and there are jogging paths to explore. The Hyatt Regency has arrangements with many area golf courses, to help guests keep their swing in shape.

With 30,000 square feet of event space, the Hyatt Regency Tampa hosts many conferences and gala events. Dining options include the atrium-area Avanzare Restaurant (breakfast, lunch, and dinner; call 813-222-4975 for dinner reservations) and the Avanzare Lounge (light food, full bar), and a Coffee Bar. No pets. All-valet parking is $14 for daytime guests and $18 overnight.

SHERATON TAMPA RIVERWALK HOTEL $$$$
200 N. Ashley Dr.
Tampa
(813) 223-2222
www.sheratontampariverwalk.com
There's just something awesome about being on the river—watching the cruise ships leave and return, marveling at the mega-tankers transporting commodities we too often use without thinking about how they got to us. The Sheraton Tampa Riverwalk Hotel gives guests a close-up view of the traffic on the Hillsborough River. And it's not all big boats, either. Watch for sculling teams and dragon boat paddlers—maybe from the riverfront pool deck or from the Ashley Street Grille. If you have your own boat, tie it up at the Sheraton's 200-foot dock.

When it's time to get back to work, the Sheraton will help you do it in style. With 12,000 square feet of event space, it can handle groups as large as 500. There's a full-service business center, free Internet service, and a fitness center. The Ashley Street Grille serves breakfast, lunch, and dinner. The Ashley Street Bar has a nice wine list. Some rooms are pet-friendly. Valet parking is $16 per night.

TAHITIAN INN $$–$$$$
601 S. Dale Mabry Hwy
Tampa
(800) 876-1397
www.tahitianinn.com
Whether you're looking for a hotel room for a night or two, or need a three-bedroom villa for a couple of months—Tahitian Inn just might be your island refuge right on the edge of Tampa's corporate center. Family-owned since 1958, the Tahitian Inn today offers classically subtle island décor in the suites and rooms. Visit the Serenity Spa's fitness center, steam room, or pool—or indulge in one of their many services, including various types of massages, waxings, facials, and other treatments.

The on-site Tahitian Café opens at 6 a.m. and closes at 9 p.m. Monday through Saturday and is open 7 a.m. to 3 p.m. on Sunday. Plus there's a full-service bar available on the patio area in front of the ponds and a poolside bar called The Torch. The Tahitian Inn has 79 rooms and four villas, some of which are pet-friendly. Children are welcome, too.

TAMPA MARRIOTT WATERSIDE HOTEL AND MARINA $$$$
700 S. Florida Ave.
Tampa
(813) 221-4900, (888) 268-1616
www.marriott.com/hotels/travel/tpamc-tampa-marriott-waterside-hotel-and-marina
Sitting between the Tampa Convention Center and the St. Petersburg Times Forum—as well as just up from the Channelside BayPlaza, the Florida Aquarium, and the Tampa Bay History Center (see Sports, Shopping, and Attractions chapters) the Tampa Marriott Waterside Hotel overlooks the point where the Hillsborough River becomes the upper end of Hillsborough Bay. With around 700 guest rooms and suites, the classically decorated and furnished Tampa Marriott Waterside Hotel knows how to host business travelers, providing a full-service business center to help with last-minute printing and other have-to-get-it-done needs.

Even business people need a break, however. The Marriott's fitness center helps keep guests at their physical best, while the Spa Waterside's services help refresh and reenergize them. The Tampa Marriott Waterside Hotel hosts conventions of its own, too. With 50,000 square feet of meeting space, the hotel can handle meetings of up to 2,500 people, and the hotel has its own marina.

Dining options include the elegant Il Terrazzo (dinner), the more casual Café Waterside (breakfast, lunch, and dinner), Champion Sports Bar (lunch and dinner), the poolside Pool Bar & Grill (lunch), a Starbucks Coffee Bar, and the Lobby Bar. No pets. Parking is $20 per day; $12 for short-term parking.

Pinellas County
Airports and Attractions
St. Petersburg–Clearwater International Airport

St. Petersburg–Clearwater International Airport lists a number of hotels near the airport on its Web site at www.fly2pie.com/visitor_info/hotels_restaurants.asp. Other hotels not far from the airport are along U.S. Hwy 19. Most of the hotels listed offer free shuttle service from the airport and various business-center type services. Some include a continental breakfast bar. Here are a few places to start.

CANDLEWOOD SUITES
(EXTENDED STAY) $–$$
13231 49th St. N.
Clearwater
(727) 573-3344
www.candlewoodsuites.com
Many people who come to the Tampa Bay area want to stay more than just a few days or even more than a week or two. Some people want to stay here for several months. Candlewood Suites is one of several places specializing in giving people a home away from home. Suites include full-size refrigerators, overstuffed recliner chairs, and a video and CD library through which

to browse. The Candlewood Cupboard on-site convenience store offers snacks, beverages, and frozen entrees at any hour. Pets are welcome. Smoking is allowed in some rooms.

CLEARWATER GRAND HOTEL $$
20967 U.S. 19 N.
Clearwater
(727) 799-1181
www.clearwatergrand.com
Located near Brighthouse Field where the Philadelphia Phillies come for spring training (see Spectator Sports chapter), the Clearwater Grand Hotel offers 148 rooms and suites with business workstations and free Internet access. Other amenities included a fitness center and pool area, a laundry area, and a business center. The Clearwater Grand Hotel has 6,000 square feet of meeting room space, which can accommodate up to 200 people. Guests will find a continental breakfast in the lobby area; the Bayside Bar & Grille serves breakfast, lunch, and dinner. Pets are allowed, and parking is free.

DAYS INN ST. PETERSBURG /
CLEARWATER AIRPORT HOTEL $–$$
3910 Ulmerton Rd.
Clearwater
(727) 573-3334
www.daysinnclearwater.com
Travelers coming to the Tampa Bay area on a tighter budget will find a good selection of lower cost accommodations. In addition to comfortable rooms with attractive décor, the Days Inn St. Petersburg/Clearwater Airport Hotel offers meeting space for smaller get-togethers and corporate meetings. Ask about the Corporate Connection Club that includes free passes to area Lifestyle Family Fitness locations and other amenities.

HAMPTON INN & SUITES $$–$$$
4050 Ulmerton Rd.
Clearwater
(727) 572-7456
http://hamptoninn1.hilton.com

Conveniently located near the St. Petersburg/ Clearwater International Airport and I–275, this Hampton Inn & Suites offers a complimentary hot breakfast. No time for breakfast? Grab one of their On the Run Breakfast Bags™ and hit the road.

SLEEP INN $–$$
3939 Ulmerton Rd.
Clearwater
(727) 573-5049
www.sleepinn.com
Travelers will find rooms with walk-in showers, heated pool and hot tub, and a free deluxe continental breakfast in the lobby each morning. No pets.

Beaches

You'll find hotels, motels, and resorts all along the 25 miles or so of barrier islands hugging Pinellas County's western side. The towns along that stretch are in almost alphabetical order, which makes it easy to start in the north with Clearwater Beach and work south to St. Petersburg Beach. Here, we've listed both larger hotels and resorts as well as some smaller places.

CLEARWATER BEACH AND SAND KEY

BAREFOOT BAY RESORT MOTEL AND MARINA $$–$$$$
401 E. Shore Dr.
Clearwater Beach
(727) 447-3316, (866) 447-3316
www.barefootbayresort.com
Not quite a bed and breakfast—there's no breakfast, although there's no lack of places to eat on Clearwater Beach—but not quite your typical motel, either. For one thing the Barefoot Bay Resort Motel sits on Clearwater Bay and right across from the municipal marina. Watch sailboats glide on by, and stroll across the street when the fishing boats come in to see the day's catch. Or do some fishing of your own on nearby Pier 60 or from the dock at the motel. Fifteen rooms, plus one two-bedroom apartment, a two-level pool deck with a barbecue grill, an ice

machine, soda machine, and laundry facilities make this place sound a bit more like home than a road-side pit stop.

No pets, but children are welcome. The marina has only an occasional transient slip available—most of the slips are rented on a long-term basis. Barefoot Bay Resort Motel accepts most credit cards, but not American Express. There is a minimum two-night stay.

CLEARWATER BEACH MARRIOTT SUITES ON SAND KEY $$$$
1201 Gulf Blvd.
Clearwater Beach
(727) 596-1100
www.marriott.com/hotels
This Marriott offers suite-only accommodations, which are especially appealing to guests planning to stay for an extended visit or needing a bit more room. A fitness center keeps guests in tip-top shape, and Antonio's Salon & Day Spa provides head-to-toe pampering. Enjoy the lagoon pool with waterfall, along with poolside pizza and ice cream service. Dining options include the Java Café coffeehouse, Kokomos Grille & Bar (lunch and dinner), and Watercolour Steakhouse and Grille (breakfast, lunch, and dinner—see Restaurant chapter for more information). No pets. Parking is free for hotel guests. Valet parking is $12.

HILTON CLEARWATER BEACH RESORT $$$$
400 Mandalay Ave.
Clearwater Beach
(727) 461-3222, (866) 203-6397
www.clearwaterbeachresort.com
Had enough of the winter doldrums and you *must* get away to somewhere, anywhere with skies colored something other than gray? Someplace you can shed your snowsuit and galoshes for a swimsuit and sandals? Right this way!

The Hilton Clearwater Beach Resort features the three S's—surf, sand, and sun. Guests will find an abundance of all three at this One-Palm certified Florida Green Lodging resort right on the Gulf of Mexico. Sitting on 10 acres of prime beachfront property, the resort offers guests a view of either the Gulf of Mexico or of Clearwater Harbor from most of its 400-plus rooms. Play in the surf on waverunners or boogie boards, go snorkeling or fishing, or parasail and view the sea from above. Build a sandcastle—we've seen some massive ones along these beaches!—or spike a beach volleyball over the net. Or just stretch out on a beach chair in the privacy of your own cabana and let the sun shoo the drearies away. In the evening, walk next door to Pier 60 for the nightly put-the-sun-to-bed party (see Attractions and Kidstuff chapters).

The Hilton Clearwater Beach Resort also has 32,000 square feet of meeting space, including a ballroom that can seat 1,200 people. Dining options include the Tiki Bar's beachside food-and-beverage service, the Sand Bar & Grill offering poolside lunch and dinner, Reflections Restaurant serving breakfast, lunch, and dinner (6:30 a.m. to 10 p.m.), and room service. Children ages four and up can enjoy the Fun Factory Kids Club activities. Have a younger child? The resort can provide you with a list of private care options. The resort has a few pet-friendly rooms.

HOLIDAY INN HOTEL & SUITES $$-$$$$
521 S. Gulfview Blvd.
Clearwater Beach
(727) 447-6461, (877) 863-4780
www.holidayinn.com

This Holiday Inn is right on the Gulf of Mexico— the water comes up to the sea wall on the beach side of the property. Not to worry—a public beach is just a few steps away, and the hotel's pool overlooks the gulf. There's an arcade game room and a fitness center. Guests have 189 rooms—half of them suites—from which to choose. Dining options include Jimmy's Fish House, Jimmy's Stone Creek Coffee Shop, the Jimmy Iguana Bar, and the Rum Runners Tiki Bar. No pets. Parking is $10 per day.

QUALITY HOTEL ON THE BEACH $$-$$$$
655 S. Gulfview Blvd.
Clearwater Beach
(727) 442-7171
www.qualitybeachresort.com

Every room has a private patio or balcony at this Quality Hotel overlooking Clearwater Pass and Sand Key Park. Plus there's an on-site 24-hour IHOP Restaurant, the Tropix Island Tiki Bar, a swimming pool, and a business center. The beach chaises and towels are complimentary, as is the parking. No pets.

SANDPEARL RESORT $$$$
500 Mandalay Ave.
Clearwater Beach
(727) 441-2425, (877) 726-3111
www.sandpearl.com

Like the pearl for which it is named, the Sandpearl Resort offers guests a touch of quiet elegance in its 250-plus rooms and more than 50 suites. Rooms are filled with the usual resort amenities, but Sandpearl guests can also arrange for a private chef to prepare an in-room dinner for two. Enjoy the beach or swim in the lagoon-like pool, or treat your body to a Salt Scrub and Vichy Energizer in the resort spa. Walk on the beach at dawn, or sit around a beachside fire pit at dusk. Camp Ridley provides activities for children ages 5 to 10. Young at heart guests can enjoy scavenger hunts on the beach, meeting with a visiting artist, or savoring new vintages at an in-house wine tasting.

The first new resort built on Clearwater Beach since the early 1980s, Sandpearl Resort is also the first resort or hotel in Florida, and one of only 15 in the world, to be awarded LEED (Leadership in Energy and Environmental Design) Silver Certification by the U.S. Green Building Council. Dining options include Caretta on the Gulf (serving breakfast, lunch, and dinner including a sushi buffet on Monday and Tuesday), Tate Island Grill (serving lunch and lighter fare dinners), and The Marketplace (featuring Starbucks coffee, pastries, and other items). The Sandpearl Resort offers 25,000 square feet of indoor and outdoor meeting space and wedding packages that include on-the-beach nuptials. All-valet parking is $16 per day. No pets.

SHEPHARD'S BEACH RESORT $$$
619 S. Gulfview Blvd.
Clearwater Beach
(727) 442-5107, (800) 237-8477
www.shephards.com

You want to play in the sun, but you also want to howl at the moon a bit? Shephard's Beach Resort bills itself as "Clearwater Beach's Premier Entertainment Resort," meaning you don't need the sun to have some fun. By day, you can zip around on jet skis or dangle in the sky from a parachute as you're towed by a boat along the shoreline. By night, you can ride The Wave—a party-hearty night club (see Nightlife chapter)—or dance to live music by moonlight at the Backyard Tiki Bar or indoors at the Sunset Lounge. Look for Beach Party Sundays and loads of special events.

Dining options include the Shephard's Waterfront Restaurant with a Prime Rib and Seafood Buffet (breakfast and lunch buffets are also offered) and the Margarita Grill. Parking is free for hotel guests and is sometimes free for restaurant or nightclub guests—special events may mean a parking charge. No pets.

SHERATON SAND KEY RESORT $$$$
1160 Gulf Blvd.
Clearwater Beach
(727) 595-1611, (800) 456-7263

Located next door to Sand Key Park and Preserve (see Parks and Recreation chapter), Sand Key Resort lets you explore acres of unspoiled wild beach, then lets you spoil yourself a bit with a Swedish or hot stone massage. Play tennis during the day at one of three courts overlooking the beach, then play beach volleyball by moonlight. Borrow some sand or pool toys from the beach or pool hut and set your inner child free to play a while, then settle back and listen to a jazz pianist play the ivories and ebonies.

The Sheraton Sand Key Resort has almost 400 rooms and suites offering resort amenities including use of the Sand Key Beach Club gathering room, stocked with snacks and beverages throughout the day and evening and offering a business workstation along with a ninth-floor panoramic view of the Gulf. A fully equipped fit-

ness center is on the top floor. Shopping options include Sea Grapes Apparel, which also sells art work, jewelry, and accessories, and Blue Water Provisions, a convenience mart. Rusty's Bistro offers guests a full breakfast buffet in the morning (including breakfast pizzas, in addition to more traditional fare) and "sun-drenched cuisine" in the evenings. More casual meals can be had at the Island Grille (lunch and dinner) and the Poolside Café (lunch and afternoon only). Chalk up a cue or pull out the darts at the Mainstay Tavern or enjoy poolside service at the Turtle Bar.

With 24,000 square feet of meeting and event space, the Sheraton Sand Key's staff can help guests plan conferences, weddings, and other events—even a golf tournament, if you'd like. No pets. Ask about activities for children. Parking is free for guests.

SILVER SANDS MOTEL $$
415 Hamden Dr.
Clearwater Beach
(727) 442-9550
www.silversandsflorida.com

Nothing big and nothing fancy, but clean, comfortable, and friendly are words you'll find in reviews of the Silver Sands Motel. Located at the southern end of Clearwater Beach, just before you go over the bridge to Sand Key, the Silver Sands Motel sits on the Intracoastal Waterway side of Gulf Boulevard.

Silver Sands Motel has nine rooms, and you're on your own when it comes to food and drink. But there are a host of restaurants from which to choose, and some rooms have a small kitchen area. Sit out by the pool and enjoy the Florida sunshine, or walk over to the beach and feel the sand between your toes. No pets, but children are welcome. Silver Sands Motel accepts most major credit cards, but not American Express. There is a minimum two-night stay.

MID-COUNTY BEACHES

BAREFOOT BEACH HOTEL $$$$
13238 Gulf Blvd.
Madeira Beach
(727) 393-6133, (800) 853-1536
www.barefootbeachhotel.com

The Barefoot Beach Hotel sits right on the beach just north of John's Pass Village (see Shopping chapter) and offers one- and two-bedroom suite units with kitchen areas. Play in the heated pool overlooking the beach or frolic in the ocean waves. There is free Internet access, and some meeting space is available. Rent a scooter on site and explore the beach cities, or the hotel will arrange for limo service. No pets. Parking is free.

BEST WESTERN SEA CASTLE SUITES $$–$$$
10750 Gulf Blvd.
Treasure Island
(727) 367-2704
www.bestwestern.com
The beachfront Best Western Sea Castle Suites offers 42 two-room suites, a heated pool, and a volleyball area, plus miles of sandy beach and a whole Gulf of Mexico in which to play. You'll find ice and vending machines on site, with many restaurants nearby—look for information about nearby John's Pass Village in the Shopping chapter. No pets. Parking is free for guests.

BILMAR BEACH RESORT $$$–$$$$
10650 Gulf Blvd.
Treasure Island
(727) 360-5531, (877) 834-0441
www.bilmarbeachresort.com
The Bilmar Beach Resort offers two heated pools and whirlpool, a mile-long beachside fitness trail, a fitness center, and meeting space for up to 250 people, in addition to its roomy guest suites and studios that are just steps away from the ocean. On-site dining options include Sloppy Joe's On the Beach (www.sloppyjoesonthebeach.com, lunch and dinner every day; live music Friday, Saturday, and Sunday until 11 p.m.) and Bazzie's Beach Bar (7 a.m. to 10 p.m., also with evening entertainment). No pets. Parking is free.

D&W'S SUN N FUN $$$–$$$$
20116 Gulf Blvd.
Indian Shores
(727) 595-3611, (800) 595-6774
www.beachdirectory.com/sunfun

Located on the Narrows—a strip of Pinellas County's barrier island wide enough for only one row of houses and Gulf Boulevard—D&W's Sun N Fun gives guests a glimpse of time gone by. Built in 1925, at the peak of the Pinellas land boom, this six-unit guest home once was a beach getaway for a Tampa merchant. Later, it hosted major-league baseball players and internationally known circus trapeze artists.

Today, each unit carries a different flavor of Florida—the two-bedroom suite features heart-of-pine flooring and other units feature the work of local artists. But the real attractions are outside. Step out one door and you're on the beach. Look out the window in the other direction, and watch sailboats slip by along the Intracoastal Waterway. Close your eyes a bit and you can easily imagine the ferry that once brought folks—and the lumber that built the house—across from the mainland.

Read the rate information carefully, as a cleaning fee is charged separately. No pets, but children are welcomed.

DOUBLETREE BEACH RESORT $$–$$$$
17120 Gulf Blvd.
North Redington Beach
(727) 391-4000
www.doubletreebeachresort.com
The Doubletree Beach Resort offers 125 rooms with West Indies décor, a beachside heated pool and Tiki Bar, and lots of sugar-fine sand waiting to be sifted through your fingers as you play on the semi-private beach. Nearby is the Suncoast Seabird Sanctuary (see Attractions chapter). Dining options include Mangos Restaurant (www.mangosrestaurant.com), open 6 a.m. to 11 p.m. and serving indoors or outdoors on the Verandah; the Copper Cove lounge area, open from 5 p.m. to midnight; and the Tiki Bar open from 11 a.m. until the sea cows come home, weather permitting. No pets. Self-parking.

MARRIOTT RESIDENCE INN $$$$
11908 Gulf Blvd.
Treasure Island
(727) 367-2761
www.marriott.com/hotels/travel/tpati-residence-inn-st-petersburg-treasure-island

The Marriott Residence Inn is an all-suite hotel for a home-away-from home experience on the Gulf of Mexico. The kitchen is stocked with cooking tools and dishes, or guests can enjoy the complimentary breakfast buffet and manager's evening reception. A fitness center is open all the time. Pets are allowed. Parking is free.

THUNDERBIRD BEACH RESORT $$-$$$
10700 Gulf Blvd.
Treasure Island
(727) 367-1961, (800) 367-2473
www.thunderbirdflorida.com

For decades, the Thunderbird Beach Resort has greeted people coming over the Treasure Island Causeway from St. Petersburg's Central Avenue. Guests will find a hot tub and heated pool in addition to the waters of the Gulf—and beach and pool towels are provided. Dining options include Groupers Seafood Grill (8 a.m. to 8 p.m.) and Ikki Woo Woo's Tiki Hut poolside beach bar with live music. The Sunset Meeting room can accommodate up to 100 people. No pets. Parking is free.

ST. PETE BEACH, PASS-A-GRILLE, AND TIERRA VERDE

BEACHCOMBER BEACH RESORT HOTEL $$$$
6200 Gulf Blvd.
St. Pete Beach
(727) 367-1902, (800) 544-4222
www.beachcomberflorida.com

The Beachcomber offers casual tropical décor, a children's game room, fitness center, two heated pools, free Internet access, and a business center for those who must work instead of play. Accommodations include both rooms and suites. Meeting space and event coordination are offered by the Beachcomber's sister facility, the Grand Plaza Hotel (see listing under Spas and Resorts). Dining options include Players Sports Bar & Grille with 34 television screens (lunch to late-night), Jimmy B's Beach Bar (lunch to late night, live entertainment). No pets. Parking is free.

THE DON CESAR, A LOEWS HOTEL $$$$
3400 Gulf Blvd.
St. Pete Beach
(727) 360-1881, (800) 282-1116 (reservations)
www.loewshotels.com/en/hotels/st-pete-beach-resort

Other coastal communities have lighthouses. We have the Don CeSar—a hotel sitting right on St. Pete Beach that is so big, boats use it as a navigational marker. Known as either the "Pink Palace," the "Pink Lady," or just "the Don," the Don CeSar is an icon on St. Pete Beach. (See a close-up of the Don elsewhere in this chapter.)

Currently part of the Loews Hotel family, the Don may be one of the most child- and pet-friendly hotels in the area. While parents are shopping for beachwear or fine accessories on the Garden Level or are being pampered at Spa Oceana, kids can attend Camp Cesar or an Etiquette Class that includes a four-course tutorial dinner. Kidbanas by the pool and a lending library of toys and games, plus healthy children's menu options, make the Don a great place for families. Pets, too, receive the royal treatment with food dishes and pet beds available. There is an extra charge for pets.

With 277 rooms and suites—all furnished with luscious linens and all the goodies you would expect—two beachfront pools, two ballrooms, a 24-hour business center, and loads of other features, the Don is a popular spot for weddings, conventions, and other functions. Dining choices range from the Sea Porch Café to the Chef's Table at the Maritana Grille (see Restaurant chapter).

Parking is included in the resort fee and is also free for Spa Oceana guests. Otherwise, parking ranges from $10 to $18 depending on whether it is self-serve or valet and on whether it is a weekday or weekend. In addition to the usual credit cards, the Don also accepts Diners, Carte Blanche, and JCB.

GRAND PLAZA HOTEL BEACHFRONT RESORT & CONFERENCE CENTER $$$$
250 Gulf Blvd.
St. Pete Beach
(727) 360-1811, (800) 448-0901
www.grandplazaflorida.com

Built in the almost-round, the Grand Plaza Hotel offers beachfront resort-style facilities including private balconies overlooking either the Gulf of Mexico or Boca Ciega Bay, tropical décor, a kids' game room, fitness center, heated pool, and free Internet access throughout. The Grand Plaza Hotel has 8,000 square feet of meeting space for conferences and business meetings, but the staff is equally willing to help organize a beach bash complete with volleyball on a professionally lit court.

Dining options include the Spinners Rooftop Revolving Bistro (lunch and dinner, reservations not required), the indoor-outdoor Palm Room (breakfast), and BongoBongos Beach Bar and Grille (lunch to late-night, live entertainment, right on the beach). No pets. Parking is free. Look for information about their sister facility, the Beachcomber Hotel, elsewhere in this chapter.

HOLIDAY INN SUNSPREE MARINA COVE RESORT $$-$$$
6800 Sunshine Skyway Lane
St. Petersburg
(727) 867-1151, (877) 863-4780
www.sunspreeresorts.com

The Holiday Inn SunSpree Marina Cove Resort has all the typical waterfront resort features—swimming pools, health and fitness center, children's activities—plus one you won't find many other places: The International Sailing School is located at the Holiday Inn's marina. Make arrangements for a sunset cruise, sign up for lessons or private instruction, or just watch the sailboats go by. Big boats, too.

Located near the approach to the Sunshine Skyway Bridge, this Holiday Inn offers a different view of the area where the estuarial waters of Tampa Bay meet the Gulf of Mexico. Dining options include Periscopes Waterfront Restaurant (breakfast and dinner), Banyon Tree Marketessan (lunch), Nemo's Lounge, and the Nepa Hut Bar. No pets. Parking is free.

PAGE TERRACE MOTEL $$-$$$
10500 Gulf Blvd.
Treasure Island
(727) 367-1997, (800) 532-6569
www.pageterrace.com

The 36-unit Page Terrace Motel offers beachfront accommodations ranging from efficiency units with kitchenettes to two-room suites and studio apartments. The somewhat secluded, heated pool overlooks the private beach area, and guests can test their skill on the shuffleboard court. Laundry facilities are on site and Internet access is free. Page Terrace Motel lists complimentary daily sunsets among their amenities—why not!

Children are welcome (cribs are available), but pets are not. Parking is free.

PLAZA BEACH HOTEL—BEACHFRONT RESORT $$
4506 Gulf Blvd.
St. Pete Beach
(727) 367-2791
www.plazabeach.com

BAY PALMS RESORT
4237 Gulf Blvd.
St. Pete Beach
(727) 360-7642
www.baypalmsresort.com

BAYVIEW PLAZA WATERFRONT RESORT
4321 Gulf Blvd.
St. Pete Beach
(727) 367-2791
www.thebayviewplaza.com

This trio of decorative, similarly priced, small hotels offers a variety of experiences. Stay in the 39-unit Plaza Beach Hotel and you're right on the beach. Literally. Guests can watch the surf roll in as they swim in the pool. Across the street, the 15-room Bay Palms Resort boasts one of the largest privately owned fishing decks in the area. Next door to the Bay Palms Resort is the seven-room Bayview Plaza Waterfront Resort, a boutique-type resort with another small fishing pier. Best of all, guests staying at any of the facilities get to enjoy the amenities at all three. Free Wi-Fi, too.

Pets are accepted at the Bayview and Bay Palms, but not at the Plaza Beach. Children are welcome at all three locations.

SANDPIPER HOTEL AND SUITES $$$$
6000 Gulf Blvd.
St. Pete Beach
(727)360-5551, (800) 360-4016
www.tradewindsresort.com/sp_default.asp
Sandpiper Hotel and Suites is sister to the TradeWinds Island Grand Beach Resort, located just south of the Sandpiper. Guests can enjoy the coziness of a smaller facility—159 guest rooms and suites—plus all the activities and services available at the TradeWinds—activities and services such as the Bodyworks Salon, the paddleboats, the tennis courts, golf privileges at area courses, the beaches, the kids' club (KONK), and everything else located at the TradeWinds (see listing for Tradewinds).

The Sandpiper has its own two pools, dining facilities, laundry and business areas, and 8,400 square feet of meeting room space. Pet-friendly accommodations are available, including a Pet Play Zone, dog walking area, and Paw Court Bistro room service menu. Read the pet policy, as it requires a veterinarian's certificate of health well in advance of the stay in addition to other requirements. Parking is included in the required nightly resort fee.

SIRATA BEACH RESORT & CONFERENCE CENTER $$$-$$$$
5300 Gulf Blvd.
St. Pete Beach
(727) 363-5100, (800) 344-5999
www.sirata.com
Play all day on the beach, then let the sound of the ocean waves lull you to sleep at the Sirata Beach Resort & Conference Center, located on 23 acres of beachfront property. Guests will find three swimming pools, whirlpools, a fitness center, paddleboats, golf privileges at area course, a children's playground, and meeting space for up

to 500 people. That's not enough? Let the staff help you make a parasailing reservation, find a charter fishing boat, or rent a waverunner. Lots of shopping nearby, too.

On-site dining options include the Compass Grille (breakfast, lunch, and dinner), Rum Runner Bar & Grille (lunch and dinner, live music), Harry's Beach Bar (lunch and dinner, live music), and the Lobby Lounge. No pets. Parking is $8 per night for hotel guests; validation is provided to restaurant guests with a receipt.

TRADEWINDS ISLAND GRAND BEACH RESORT $$$-$$$$
5500 Gulf Blvd.
St. Pete Beach
(727) 367-6461, (800) 360-4016
www.tradewindsresort.com
My, my, my—the TradeWinds Island Grand Beach Resort brings the outdoors indoors with its 8,000-square-foot lush, Grand Palm Colonnade, a sweeping gesture that says they'll stop at almost nothing to create a tropical paradise for their guests. Outdoors, guests can take a paddleboat and pedal their way around shaded waterways filled with swans and Nile perch, play beach volleyball or miniature golf, relax in one of five swimming pools, or serve it up on the tennis courts.

The Bodyworks Salon offers more than 40 salon and spa services including a certified La Stone warm-stone massage, Chocolate Wasabi Facials, and a Satin Body Scrub. The Kids Only, No Kidding! (KONK) Club offers crafts, games, and other activities for children ages 4 through 11, and the Tradewinds Action Zone (T.A.Z.) Team keeps the fun flowing for everyone with activities like glow-in-the-dark volleyball, poolside bingo, and other games. All this plus 18 acres of white sand beaches and the Gulf waters to play in.

The TradeWinds Island Grand Resort has almost 600 rooms and suites, including seven penthouse suites, waiting for guests. Dining options include the Palm Court Island Grill (lunch, dinner, and the Sunday Mimosa Brunch), Bermudas (breakfast and dinner), Flying Bridge (lunch and dinner), Beef O'Brady's (lunch and dinner), Capt. RedBeard's Sharktooth Tavern (live entertainment, crab races, and other activities), plus the Deli, a Pizza Hut Express, an Old Meeting House Ice Cream store, and Perks Up! Coffee and Cocktails.

Many activities and services such as cabanas, paddleboats, parking, tennis, Internet service, and more are included in the required nightly Resort Amenity Fee. With 56,000 total square feet of meeting space, the TradeWinds Island Grand Resort hosts weddings, conferences, and other events year round. See also the listing for the Sandpiper Hotel, an adjoining property, elsewhere in this chapter.

Convention Center/Downtown Hotels
St. Petersburg
HILTON ST. PETERSBURG BAYFRONT $$$$
333 1st St. S.
St. Petersburg
(727) 894-5000
www1.hilton.com

Located in St. Petersburg's waterfront district, the Hilton St. Petersburg Bayfront sits in the hub of the city's business and entertainment activity. Walk to the nearby Mahaffey Theater or the St. Petersburg Museum of Fine Arts (see Arts chapter), shop at the Baywalk Entertainment Complex (see Shopping chapter), or watch the planes land at nearby Albert Whitted Airport (see Getting Here, Getting Around). Go for a jog along Tampa Bay, work out in the fitness center, soak in the hot tub, and swim in the pool. The Olimpia Spa offers a variety of body-soothing services, and an on-site beauty salon keeps travelers looking their best. Business guests have the use of two workstations and a business center, plus the hotel has videoconferencing capabilities.

The soothing, airy, neutral tones throughout the hotel's décor highlight the colorful view out the windows—vibrant blue sky, rich green tropical foliage, sundrenched buildings and boats—an ever-changing picture viewed from within a sophisticated frame. The touches of interior color, which might be considered minimal in other surroundings, stands out and refreshes—as with the shades of orange in the Tangerine, the Hilton St. Petersburg Bayfront's restaurant, which serves

breakfast, lunch, and dinner. Brandi's Lobby Bar (lunch and dinner), and a Starbucks complete the on-site dining options, while the Corner Pantry (open 24/7) stocks pre-made salads and sandwiches, beverages, ice creams, snacks, clothing, and sundry items.

Pets are allowed. Self-parking is $12 per day.

HOTEL INDIGO ST. PETERSBURG
DOWNTOWN $$$$
234 3rd Ave. N.
St. Petersburg
(727) 822-4814, (877) 846-3446
www.ichotelsgroup.com

The Hotel Indigo St. Petersburg began as a 1920s-era hotel, recently renovated to a contemporary boutique-style establishment. Hotel Indigo offers many of the same amenities as other area hotels—fitness center, whirlpool, heated pool, business center, in-room Internet access—but with a slightly different flavor. Maybe it's the photomurals covering occasional walls—Fibonacci sequence math-inspired décor blending nature and numbers—and the touches of bold color against a softer palette. Or maybe it's the spa-style showers and hardwood flooring evoking a this-is-different *oh!*

In any case, Hotel Indigo St. Petersburg guests are in the middle of all the downtown business and entertainment action. Meeting space at the hotel can accommodate up to 250 people, and the on-site Phi Café serves breakfast and dinner in the bar area. Pets are allowed, and parking is free.

THE RENAISSANCE VINOY RESORT
AND GOLF CLUB $$$$
501 5th Ave. N.E.
St. Petersburg
(727) 894-1000, (888) 303-4430
www.renaissancevinoyresort.com

The name says "resort," the description says "luxury hotel." We figure the Vinoy's private 74-slip marina, private golf course, salon and day spa, and 12-court tennis complex pull it into the resort category. Plus the Vinoy offers a number of dining options. Guests can choose from Alfresco's

A Second Life for Two Boutique Hotels

One hotel began life in the 19th century as a real estate office. The other, newer by about 25 years, has always been used as a hotel. Both deteriorated over time until someone saw beauty beneath the aging skin.

Don Vicente de Ybor Historic Inn $$$

1915 Republica de Cuba (corner of 14th St. and 9th Ave.)
Tampa
(813) 241-4545, (866) 206-4545
http://donvincenteinn.com

Ybor city founder Vicente Martínez Ybor built this building in 1895 as the Ybor Land and Improvement Company. Eventually it became a health care clinic known first as *El Bien Publico* ("The good of the public") and later as the Gonzalez Clinic. The clinic closed in 1980 and sat empty until 1998 when Jack Shiver, credited with redeveloping much of downtown Ybor City, envisioned the building as an inn.

From the richly paneled walls to the stamped-tin ceilings to the hardwood floors, the Don Vicente Inn oozes historic elegance. Chandeliers, sconces, and period furnishings bespeak a quiet dignity that slows the rush-rush of modern visitors' steps and beckons them to linger. Sixteen high-ceilinged guest rooms upstairs are furnished with king-sized four-poster or queen-sized sleigh beds. Other amenities include cable TV, voicemail, broadband access, and a complimentary deluxe continental breakfast.

There is no on-site dining, but the Don Vicente Inn offers catered meals for meetings and is a favorite with wedding parties. Look for the two-story building with the word "INN" in big black letters on the back of the building as you're driving Ybor's narrow, bricked streets. Free parking for guests is behind the inn.

The Pier Hotel $$$

253 2nd Ave. N.
St. Petersburg
(727) 822-7500, (800) 735-6607
www.thepierhotel.com

The Pier Hotel opened in 1921 as The Hotel Scott. It was sold in 1923 to the Cordova family, who renamed it the Hotel Cordova. Although it changed hands several times, the Hotel Cordova it remained until 1999. After undergoing extensive renovations and restoration, the hotel reopened during the 2000 to 2001 season, making it the oldest continuously operating hotel in St. Petersburg.

Today, the Pier Hotel offers a step back into an elegantly appointed yesteryear when some of the world's most famous people stayed in her rooms. Notice the washbasins outside each room—in an era before hand sanitizer and plastic gloves, hotel staff washed their hands here before serving guests. The boutique hotel's 33 guest rooms feature period furniture with luxury linens, plus modern amenities such as microwave ovens, refrigerators, wet bars, and Internet access.

Guests enjoy a complimentary breakfast buffet and the concierge reception each evening in the parlor or on the veranda. Some event space is available. Children are welcome, but pets are not. Parking next door is $4 per night.

tropical fare; Fred's, a dinner-only steak and sea-food restaurant in a polo-club setting; or the elegantly stylish Marchand's Bar and Grill.

The Vinoy is a Marriott hotel on St. Petersburg's northeast waterfront. There are art museums and galleries and more to explore within walking distance. You could spend hours, however, just exploring this Jazz Age–era hotel—was that Zelda who just slipped around a corner?—with its Mediterranean Revival architecture and furnishings to match. (Read more about the Vinoy's history elsewhere in this chapter.)

The Vinoy offers a number of packaged stays—golf, spa, and other packages—as well as other offers. And, if you can arrange your stay during the off-season, you can enjoy yesteryear luxury at (almost) yesteryear rates. On-site parking starts at $12 per day. No pets.

CLEARWATER

Clearwater's downtown, on the west side of Clearwater, is served by hotels on Clearwater Beach, just across the Memorial Causeway. Hotels on the east side of Clearwater are mostly in the St. Petersburg–Clearwater Airport area or along U.S. 19. Hotels in both areas were listed earlier in the chapter.

GOLF, TENNIS, AND OTHER RESORTS

BELLEVIEW BILTMORE RESORT   NA
25 Belleview Blvd.
Clearwater
(727) 373-3000
www.belleviewbiltmore.com

We'd love to tell you about what to expect when you visit this *grande dame* hotel on Clearwater Bay. At the moment, however, we'd be doing little more than teasing you. The Belleview Biltmore Resort just closed for renovations and isn't expected to reopen until 2012. You can read a bit about the Belleview Biltmore's history elsewhere in this chapter. Go online to see what was and what is to come.

INNISBROOK RESORT AND
GOLF CLUB $$$$
36750 U.S. 19 N.
Innisbrook
(727) 942-2000, (800) 456-2000
www.innisbrookgolfresort.com

Admit it—you've always wanted to see how you stack up against the pros. Innisbrook's Copperhead Course, home of the PGA's Transitions Championship held in March (see Spectator Sports chapter), lets you do just that. And that's only one of Innisbrook's four demanding courses designed by Lawrence Packard waiting for you, daring you to take them on.

Golf, however, isn't the only reason guests dally a while at Innisbrook. Twenty-eight separate lodges, nestled among the pines and oaks, house the 620 guest rooms and suites. Colors are muted, and buildings blend into the natural beauty, which guests can enjoy on foot or by bicycle (child- or adult-sized), with or without a guide. Go fishing on Lake Innisbrook—tackle and bait are available on site—or check out the charter fishing possibilities. Did we mention the 11-court Tennis Center that offers clinics and private instruction? Or the Indaba Spa at Innisbrook with Shiatsu massages and Reiki sessions among its many services? There's more, including a children's playground, a putt-putt golf course, and loads of water fun at the Loch Ness Monster Pool. Dining options range from a take-out deli and dine-in grill to Packard's Steakhouse with a full menu of offerings from land and sea.

Still, if it weren't for the Spanish moss dripping from the cypress and other trees, you might think you were back in the birthplace of golf. Rolling hills, woods, names like St. Andrews and Turnberry on the signs, and those four daunting courses make Innisbrook Resort and Golf Club seem a little more than just par for the course. Since 2007, Innisbrook has been part of the Salamander Hospitality group of resorts. It underwent a $25 million renovation in 2008.

SADDLEBROOK RESORT $$$$
5700 Saddlebrook Way
Wesley Chapel
(813) 973-1111, (800) 729-8383
www.saddlebrookresort.com

Saddlebrook Resort, just north of Tampa, is for those who want to get away from it all and have it all at the same time. With two championship golf courses designed by Arnold Palmer, one of the country's largest tennis complexes, a 7,000-square-foot European-style spa, a half-million-gallon Superpool, and all sorts of dining and entertainment options, why would you ever leave to go anywhere else?

Saddlebrook's 95,000 square feet of meeting space can accommodate groups as large as 2,000, making this a top choice for weddings, business conferences, and other groups. Special activities for children, bike rentals, walking and jogging trails, and more appeal to a wide range of guests' interests. Also on the resort property is Saddlebrook Preparatory School, which provides college preparatory curriculum with intense golf and tennis instruction to more than 100 students in grades 3 through 12.

Parking for day events is $5 per day and it is an all-valet parking facility.

SAFETY HARBOR RESORT
AND SPA $$$–$$$$
105 N. Bayshore Dr.
Safety Harbor
(727) 726-1161, 888-BEST SPA (237-8772)
www.safetyharborresort.com

Come. Immerse yourself in the waters of the *Espiritu Santo* mineral springs as the long ago Tocobagan and other original peoples did. Partake of the waters Hernando de Soto called the Fountain of Youth. Follow in the footsteps of people from around the world who have come to these natural springs, which produce almost two million gallons of water each month. Stay for a day or for as long as you like in one of the almost 200 rooms and suites, most of which look out onto the upper end of Old Tampa Bay.

Let the dawning light nudge you awake, then follow its lure to a Sunrise Yoga session. Head to the tennis courts for private or group instruction, or slip into one of several pools—filled with mineral spring water, of course. Enjoy the tranquil gardens or the salon and spa services—which include medical skin-care treatments under the care of a licensed physician—or wander down Safety Harbor's Main Street with its shops and galleries filled with unexpected treasures. Dining options at the resort include the Fountain Grille or the poolside Tiki Bar. Three classically designed and decorated ballrooms draw wedding parties and other events to the Safety Harbor Spa and Resort.

The mineral springs are recognized by the U.S. Department of the Interior as an historical landmark. The Safety Harbor Spa and Resort, first developed in 1945 as a resort by Dr. Salem Baranoff, recently completed extensive renovations. Its water fitness program, including kaylates, a combination of kayaking and Pilates, is nationally recognized. Children are welcome at the resort, although there are no activities especially for children. No pets. Valet parking is available, or there is a large, shady area of unpaved parking under the oaks.

BED-AND-BREAKFASTS

As with the other types of accommodations, we can't list them all. But we know a couple of Web sites that try. Check out the St. Petersburg Association of Bed and Breakfast Inns at www.spaabbi.com or the American Bed and Breakfast Association (Tampa) at www.abba.com/b/274.

ASHLEY'S VICTORIAN HAVEN
BED & BREAKFAST $$–$$$
313 N. Grosse Ave.
Tarpon Springs
(727) 505-9152
www.ashleysvictorianhaven.com

Antique lovers will feel right at home in this Victorian two-story home, built about 1894, restored by proprietors Barbara and Larry Lawrence, and furnished with antiques from the early 1800s to the early 1900s (except, of course, for the beds). Luscious linens and spacious rooms allow guests to settle in for their stay. Visit the historic sponge docks, or roam the antiques shop district downtown.

A full breakfast is served each morning at 9 a.m. and might include quiche or French toast (made with real French bread, eggs, and cream), fresh fruit, and other goodies. Parking behind the home is abundant and large enough for a rig with a boat trailer. Guests enjoy evenings relaxing around the wood-burning stove in the spacious courtyard out back. The locked courtyard has also sheltered guests' motorcycles overnight.

No pets and no children under age 13. However, the Lawrences have a cottage to rent elsewhere in town—also period decorated—that is pet- and child-friendly.

THE BLUE MOON INN $$–$$$$
2920 Alternate U.S. 19 N.
Dunedin
(727) 784-371, (800) 345-7504
www.carefreervresorts.com

The amenities of a hotel—heated swimming pool, playground, volleyball—and the privacy of a B&B make this Key West–style retreat a great place for a family vacation. Each of the nine rooms is on the ground floor, making it easily wheelchair accessible. The high-ceilinged rooms are large—some have a separate lounge area that can be shut off from the sleeping area—and all have private patios that look out over a shady, grassy lawn. Each room also has a mini-kitchen including dishes, sleeper sofa, and iron and ironing board.

A Continental breakfast spread is available from 6:30 to 10 a.m. in the common kitchen/dining room and includes an assortment of cereals, fruit, yogurt, breads, juices, and hot beverages—plus the morning newspaper. Celtic music softly playing in the background reminds guests they are in Dunedin.

The Blue Moon Inn shares the clubhouse, pool, and other facilities with the Dunedin RV Resort (see listing elsewhere in this chapter). Pets are not allowed in the inn. Even though the inn is on a busy road, the rooms are very quiet and the pool and playground are behind the inn and well away from the road. The inn is right off the Pinellas Trail and very near the causeway to Honeymoon Island State Park.

**DICKENS HOUSE BED &
BREAKFAST** $$$–$$$$
335 8th Ave. N.E.
St. Petersburg
(727) 822-8622, (800) 381-2022
www.dickenshouse.com

This 1912 Craftsman home nestled under the trees in St. Petersburg's Old Northeast section exudes warmth and welcome. Each of the five rooms reflects a different aspect of the history of the house, its original owners, and the area. From the elegant Dickens Suite with its four-poster cherry wood canopied bed to the Orange Blossom nest tucked under the roof upstairs, the house has been carefully restored and furnished by proprietor Ed Caldwell.

Breakfasts are some of the most intriguing we've found—from the Puff Pastry Fruit Roll-up to the Eggs Tempura (a poached egg dipped in tempura batter, fried crisp, and served with a light sour cream and wasabi sauce) to the Danish *Ableskivers* (small breakfast cakes) served on sliced apples. Other amenities include an evening wine time and a business center. If going to the beach is on your list of things to do, Ed will load you up with beach chairs and towels. Then he'll hand you a picnic cooler and direct you to Mazzaro's Italian Market (see Shopping chapter)—an experience in itself—where you can pick and choose from their full deli or order take-out. After you've made your purchases—this kind of detail is why you go to a B&B, right?—follow Ed's directions to Fort De Soto Park (see Parks and Recreation chapter). Enjoy the white sand beaches—rated number one according to Dr. Beach (www.drbeach.org)—then head to the Hurricane (see Restaurant chapter) for dinner. Finally, stop at the big, pink Don CeSar (see listing in this chapter) for an ice cream cone at Uncle Andy's Ice Cream Parlor (street level).

No pets, and no children under age nine. The Dickens House is within walking distance of waterfront parks and the downtown area.

EQUUS MEADOW INN & RIDING STABLE $$$$
6812 George Road
Tampa
(813) 806-5566
www.equusmeadowinn.com

Equus Meadow Inn sits at the end of a lane—look for the white gate—and at the beginning of a little bit of country heaven. To the right are the horse stables and trails. To the left is the Carriage House Cottage, a romantic suite with its king-sized bed, comfortable sitting room, and kitchenette (no stove). Straight ahead is the main house—complete with white picket fence—where Sandy Roussé will greet you. Up an outside flight of stairs is the Meadowlook Private Quarters with a queen-sized bed. The balcony overlooks Equus Meadow Pond where guests can paddle a canoe or just sit and watch the ducks, guinea hens, or other fowl wander along the banks.

Come into the dining room off of the veranda for breakfast—maybe a veggie soufflé or maybe sausage sautéed with from-the-garden rosemary and then drizzled with honey. But you probably came here to ride, so get your jeans on and saddle up. Riding instructor/trail guide Ken Boyung will help select your horse, then off you go! There's lots of room to ride here and, yes, you can trot and canter. Adjoining the property is the Town 'n' Country Greenway, a Hillsborough County park, that includes several miles of unpaved horse trail along with paved bike trail.

Rooms accommodate one or two people only. No pets. While the riding instruction and trail rides are open to the public (see Attractions chapter), the overnight accommodations are available to guests ages 16 and up.

LAUGHING LIZARD BED & BREAKFAST $$$–$$$$
2211 Gulf Blvd.
Indian Rocks Beach
(727) 595-7006
www.laughinglizardbandb.com

Bed, breakfast, and beach is more like it at the Key West–style Laughing Lizard. Only 400 feet separate guests from the Gulf of Mexico. Owner Bill Ockunzzi will see that you have beach chairs and towels to take with you—after a leisurely breakfast of Mexican quiche or waffles or something equally scrumptious, served in Lizard Hall. And that's after a peaceful night's sleep in one of four remarkably decorated rooms—maybe the black-and-white Shy Salamande or the equally striking Island Iguana suite on the lower level. The colors are bold, the accessories and furnishings clever. And the lizards are everywhere—brightly painted metal ones climbing the walls, satiny fabric ones peeking out from behind lamps—all chuckling over some lizard-y jest, no doubt. You can't help but chuckle right back.

Don't let the thought of lugging luggage up three stories keep you away. There's a real elevator that bypasses all those stairs. No pets and no children. The Laughing Lizard is within walking distance of several local restaurants, shops, and galleries.

HOSTELS

Make that hostel—singular. As far as we could determine, this is the only one in the Tampa Bay area. But you never know. Another one might open up. Check with www.Hostelworld.com, www.Hostelbookers.com, or Hostels.org to see the latest listings.

GRAM'S PLACE $
3109 N. Ola Ave.
Tampa
(813) 221-0596
www.grams-inn-tampa.com

As the Web page says, if you have to ask what a hostel is, you probably don't want to stay here. But if you're a bit Bohemian of spirit or have trekked through just about anywhere else in the world, you know you'll find clean sheets and towels and a place to shower for way fewer bucks than you'll pay at a motel. At Gram's Place, you'll find more.

Named in honor of country-rock musician Gram Parsons, Gram's Place consists of two fence-enclosed 1940s-era homes decorated with a kaleidoscopic mix of memorabilia. Dorm-style and private rooms are named after various music styles. The most unusual room is Train Room #9 (think Jimmie Rodgers), a co-ed dorm that looks like the inside of a sleeper car. While a few rooms have private baths, most are shared. There's even a room with an outdoor shower and toilet area, for those who prefer not to have a roof over their heads all the time. View the surrounding area from the Crow's Nest, soak in the Jacuzzi, or play one of the house instruments (such as a piano, keyboard, or guitar). Owner Bruce Holland, brother of founder Mark Holland, regrets that the recording studio is no longer operational—see the Web page for a list of artists and recordings made at Gram's Place—but jam sessions are a given. House concerts featuring professional musicians passing through are in the works. Meals are not served, but there are two self-serve kitchens and a small mini-mart selling frozen dinners and other items.

Kids, yes. Pets, outside in carriers only. Bruce has bikes, canoes, and kayaks to rent for exploring the outdoors. There's free Wi-Fi, or he'll rent you a mini-laptop while you're visiting. Bring your own lock and you can use one of the outdoor lockers for extra gear. Parson's Pub (outdoors) is BYOB. Please call after 7 a.m. and before 11 p.m.

COMMERCIAL CAMPGROUNDS AND RV PARKS

Here's what you won't find in this section: You won't find tent camping or even RV camping at publicly owned parks. We have lots of that, too, but you'll find those places listed in the Parks and Recreation Chapter.

Here, we've listed commercial campgrounds that offer more than just a place to pitch a tent or hook up a sewer. We've paid special attention to places that take the really big motor homes. Check www.gocampingamerica.com for a more comprehensive list of commercial campgrounds.

DUNEDIN RV RESORT $
2920 Alternate U.S. 19 N.
Dunedin
(727) 784-3719, (800) 345-7504
www.carefreervresorts.com

Dunedin RV Resort has lots of pull-through and back-in sites and accommodates even the biggest RVs. Guests can enjoy the heated pool, play bocce or horseshoes, then join a woodcarving session or do some line dancing in the recreation room. There's a general store and laundry room on site, along with Internet access and RV supplies.

Lots of people come and stay for the winter. Even in summer, however, the park is busy, as many rally groups make this their destination. Want to have guests stay overnight but don't have room in your rig? See the listing under Bed-and-Breakfasts for the Blue Moon Inn, which shares the property.

LAZYDAYS RV SUPERCENTER $
RallyPark
6130 Lazy Days Blvd.
Seffner
(888) 500-5299 ext. 4261
www.lazydays.com/rallypark.html

Tennis courts, heated pool and whirlpool, shuffleboard courts, complimentary breakfast and lunch—the list goes on. RallyPark is *the* place for RVers needing a break from the scenic highway. The park has 300 sites with full 50-amp hook-ups, an air-conditioned laundry facility, a business area with Internet ports as well as wireless connection available, and an on-site Cracker Barrel Restaurant, Flying J RV Travel Plaza, and a Camping World store.

Lazydays opened in Tampa in 1976, and grew in the next 20 years from a 1.75-acre site to a 126-acre nicely landscaped facility just east of Tampa. The Lazydays RV Supercenter services more than 20,000 RVs a year. While staying at RallyPark, guests can also improve their driving skills with the RV Driver Confidence Course. Other seminars and fun off-site excursions also are offered, and RallyPark hosts several RV rallies each year.

Children and pets are welcomed. RallyPark offers first timers a three-day/two-night stay-free special. During peak season (January through March), the maximum stay is two weeks.

ST. PETERSBURG/MADEIRA
BEACH RESORT KOA $–$$$$
5400 95th St. N.
St. Petersburg
(727) 392-2233, (800) 562-7714
www.stpetersburgkoa.com
www.koa.com/where/fl/09144/

You'd never know you're in the middle of one of the most populous parts of Florida when you turn into this full-service KOA in mid-Pinellas County. Hidden among the mangroves along Boca Ciega Bay, campers can pitch their tents or stay in one of the heated/air-conditioned Kamping Kabins. Got a big group? No problem—their Kamping Lodge sleeps six. Not only will you be just minutes away from the beaches, you can also step right onto the Pinellas Trail, a paved walking, biking, and skating trail that runs the length of Pinellas County (see Parks and Recreation chapter). Rent a banana bike, rent a canoe, or just fish off the dock—or, if you must, log on through free Wi-Fi and tend to business.

Pets on leashes are welcomed in most parts of the campground. No pets and no smoking are permitted in the lodges. Class A RVs will find a spot here, too. There is a small playground area for children. Because this KOA offers such a wide variety of accommodations, from tent camping to deluxe lodges, the prices vary accordingly.

NOT YOUR ORDINARY PLACES TO STAY

Having a family reunion? Maybe you want to rent a bungalow or even a house while you're here. Check with the Chambers of Commerce listed in the Relocation chapter for businesses that handle rentals in other areas of our region. Or try www.vacationrentals.com or www.floridasmart.com.

SAILING FLORIDA CHARTERS &
SAILING SCHOOL, INC. $$$$
1421 Bay St. S.E., Ste. #2
St. Petersburg
(727) 894-SAIL (7245), (866) 894-SAIL (7245)
www.sailingflorida.com

If you're going to come to the ocean, why not stay on the ocean. Whether you want to charter their motor- and sail-powered yachts on a bareboat, crew-it-yourself basis or with a professional captain, you'll want to see what Sailing Florida Charters has to offer. From the 2005 Martinique 33 *Yachta Yachta* to the Catalina 440 *Suite Jolene,* or something even larger, Sailing Florida Charters can put you on the water for a half a day or half a year.

RESTAURANTS AND OTHER EATS

Hungry? Good!

Grab your appetite and let's go for . . . Greek food! Or Spanish. Or barbecue. Or knishes. Or steak and shrimp. Or Thai. Or a Chicago dog. Or—we'd probably better stop listing the types of foods you can find in the Tampa Bay area or we'll never get to the eating part.

Let's just say that whether you want to get all gussied up and visit Tampa's world-renowned Bern's Steak House—where they grow their own organic vegetables, age their own beef, and keep a saltwater fish tank in the kitchen for really fresh catch-of-the-day—or whether you want to eat just-off-the-grill barbecue at a picnic table under the trees alongside the Pinellas Trail in Dunedin, we've got you covered. We know that breakfast meals can be an art unto themselves, so we'll make special note of places where the morning meal is an event.

But you don't have to take our word for it. St. Petersburg is home to *Florida Trend* magazine, which has issued the Golden Spoon Awards to top restaurants around the state since 1977. Over the years, several of those awards have gone to Tampa Bay area restaurants. Go to www.floridatrend.com/dining_spirits.asp where you can read the reviews and columns by *Florida Trend*'s restaurant editor, Chris Sherman, who previously reviewed restaurants for the *St. Petersburg Times*.

Or check out *Tampa Tribune* writer Jeff Houck's "Restaurant" page at TBO.com (http://tboextra .com/dining/). From there, you can follow Houck's food news blog, "The Stew" (on Twitter, if you like) or click on the Restaurant Report Card icon to get health inspection and other reports. www .Tampagold.com is another source for restaurant reviews. And Laura Reilly, food critic for the *St. Petersburg Times*, writes "The Mouth of Tampa Bay" at http://blogs.tampabay.com/dining/.

You'll find most of the usual chains here, but a few deserve up-front recognition because here is where it all began for Hooters, although they are now headquartered in Atlanta, for Outback Steakhouse (which also owns Carrabas, Bonefish Grill, and several other chains), and for Checkers (which was founded in Mobile, Alabama, moved to Clearwater, and now has headquarters in Tampa). You'll also notice another chain in this area that you might not find in other parts of the country. Crispers is a soup-salad-and-sandwich eatery owned by Lakeland-based (just east of Hillsborough County) Publix Super Markets, Inc.

Another local chain, whose flagship restaurant just happens to be the world's largest Spanish restaurant, is based in Ybor City. Look for a close-up on Columbia Restaurants later in the chapter.

For the most part, this section is devoted to the local one-of-a-kind restaurants that make the Tampa Bay area a food lover's delight. We'll take you to tea lounges and taco stands, delis and dens of decadently delectable delights. But we can't take you to them all. Our greatest regret is that we're leaving out many really good places to eat. Pick up a copy of the latest *Restaurant Guide* for each area, distributed free at most hotels, area attractions, welcome centers, and at other merchants. You'll find many more great dining adventures waiting for you—and coupons!

Don't forget all the food festivals listed in the Festivals and Events chapter. Taste of Pinellas, in particular, features dozens of different restaurants all in one spot—a good way to sample foods from many different eateries.

You'll find Greek food listed along with burgers and fries in many non-Greek sounding restaurants, so we've included a glossary to help you figure out what's on the menu.

Note: Po-TAY-to, po-TAH-to—omelet, omelette. Whichever spelling the restaurant uses on their menus is the spelling we've used in referring to that scrambled egg creation stuffed with veggies, meat, and cheese that is good any time of day—no matter how you spell it. Conversely, we've seen a number of spellings for *prix fixe* (sounds like "prefix"), meaning a multi-course meal at one set, or fixed, price. We're sticking with *prix fixe*.

Price Code

We've based our code on dinner for two, without appetizers, dessert, alcoholic beverages, tax, or tip, i.e., an entrée and a non-alcoholic beverage for each person. Your bill may vary depending on menu changes and what you order. Lunch prices are often lower, especially in the pricier restaurants. Some restaurants have early bird and other specials. Enjoy!

$................. Less than $20
$$ .... $20 to $50
$$$ .... $51 and up

ALL ABOUT BREAKFAST

FIRST WATCH   **$$**
Carrollwood
13186 N. Dale Mabry, Tampa
(813) 961-4947

Countryside Village Square
2569 Countryside Blvd., Clearwater
(727) 712-8769

Downtown Tampa
520 Tampa St., Tampa
(813) 307-9006

Palm Harbor-Alderman Plaza Shopping Center
35150 U.S. 19 N., Palm Harbor
(727) 789-3447

The Shoppes at New Tampa
1648 Bruce B. Downs Blvd., Wesley Chapel
(813) 929-3947

University Collection
2726 E. Fowler Ave., Tampa
(813) 975-1718
www.firstwatch.com
Headquarters for First Watch is right across the Sunshine Skyway Bridge in Bradenton (Manatee County), and has been since 1986, so this chain with restaurants in 11 states qualifies as mostly locally grown. They're known for their creative combining of ingredients that wakes up breakfast with wow! flavor. Go for their Bacado omelette stuffed full of bacon, avocado, and Monterey Jack cheese, topped with sour cream, and served with freshly made salsa on the side. Or try their First Watch creations called Crepeggs, thin, sweet crepes wrapped around all sorts of savory fillings. Lovely pancakes, French toast, and Belgian waffles can be topped with fruit, granola, and other delectable delights. Menu choices include egg-white only, low-carb, gluten-free, and veggie options.

Lunch options include burgers, salads, and wraps. Kids have their own menu. First Watch restaurants are open 7 a.m. until 2:30 p.m. each day except Thanksgiving and Christmas.

i What's a Cuban sandwich? Split open an 8- to 12-inch section from a loaf of crusty Cuban bread. Layer roast pork, ham, Swiss cheese, and dill pickles inside and top with mustard. In the Tampa Bay area, add sliced salami. Press the sandwich in a *plancha* until the bread is toasted crispy and the cheese is melty.

KING CHARLES BALLROOM $$$
Don CeSar Loews Hotel
3400 Gulf Blvd.
St. Pete Beach
(727) 360-1881
www.loewshotels.com/en/hotels/st-pete-
beach-resort/dining/overview.aspx

Sunday Brunch at the Don features almost 200 items—a sumptuous repast, indeed, especially as guests can feast on an unimpeded view of the Gulf of Mexico as they sip mimosas and dine on made-to-order crepes, cheeses, smoked salmon, scrambled eggs with their choice of add-ins, carved-to-order meats, seafood galore, and more. Brunch is served from 10:30 a.m. to 2 p.m. with seatings every 30 minutes. Reservations are required.

LENNY'S RESTAURANT $–$$
21220 U.S. 19 N.
Clearwater
(727) 799-0402

Yes, they serve lunch, too—good deli food like Mettayya's Knish-Wich (corned beef, pastrami, or turkey on a grilled potato knish) as well as a variety of burgers, including one that's vegetarian. But Lenny's for breakfast is not to be missed. Plan on several minutes just to work your way through the menu, which lists everything from oatmeal to Stuffed Crab Benedict to one of Lenny's Bagel City creations. Or you can go with the more usual eggs, pancakes, French toast, or waffles. But many of their full breakfasts start with an appetizer basket of Danish pastry to take the edge off while you wake up—and it's good pastry, not convenience-store stuff. There's a kids' menu (ages 10 and under) and a seniors menu (ages 55 and older—seven forms of picture I.D. required). Plus you'll never run out of things to talk about—just look up and read the ceiling to each other.

Lenny's is open 6 a.m. to 3 p.m. all year long except for a few days in September. Both breakfast and lunch items can be ordered anytime during the day. There is a $1 charge for shared plates. Lenny's marks vegetarian items on their menu.

ℹ️ Cartoonist Frank Willard, creator of the *Moon Mullins* comic strip, often ate at Rubin's Spanish Restaurant in Tampa in the 1930s. So did another cartoonist, who turned the restaurant's loaded-to-the-max Cuban sandwich into a recurring gag in his series, still running today. The cartoonist was Chick Young, creator of *Blondie* and of the Dagwood sandwich.

MARCHAND'S BAR & GRILL $$–$$$
Renaissance Vinoy Resort & Golf Club
501 5th Ave. N.E.
St. Petersburg
(727) 824-8072
www.marchandsbarandgrill.com

If you just want a bowl of cold cereal or warm oatmeal with bananas, fresh berries, and steamed milk, you can get it. But if you want to try something more filling like the Florida Lobster Hash with soft poached eggs, potatoes, sausage, peppers, sweet onion, and a tomato hollandaise, Marchand's Bar & Grill at the Renaissance Vinoy can handle that, too. Try a Tropical Fruit Waffle, served with coconut cream and passion fruit syrup, or go for the low-cholesterol Egg White Omelette with spinach, tomato, and feta cheese.

Breakfast is served from 6:30 to 11:30 a.m. Monday through Saturday. Sunday brunch—complete with carving stations, hot seafood pot and cold raw bar, fruit and cheese cornucopia, chocolate fondue fountain, and an ice-your-own-cookie station for children—is served every Sunday from 10 a.m. to 2 p.m.

PELAGIA TRATTORIA $$
4200 Jim Walter Blvd.
Tampa
(813) 313-3235
www.pelagiatrattoria.com

You'll pay a bit more for breakfast here, but with items like Torched Oatmeal Créme Brûlée with Dried Fruit, or Banana and Nutella French Toast with a Berries Coulis, on the menu, heftier prices are to be expected. You'll also find more standard eggs-and-bacon type fare, including omelets and breakfast smoothies. Pelagia Trattoria is located in the Renaissance Tampa Hotel—see more information about their lunches and dinners later in this chapter. Breakfast is served daily from 6:30 to 10:30 a.m.

SKYWAY JACK'S $
2600 34th St. S.
St. Petersburg
(727) 866-3217

This iconic eatery has been around since 1976, although it used to be closer to the water and to the fishermen who could come in sandy, sunburned, and sometimes shoeless to wolf down eggs cooked just about anyway you can think of, salt-cured and country-aged ham, and grits. The restaurant moved up the road, and the fishermen and the locals followed. The menu is mostly breakfasts, but they also serve salads and sandwiches—chili mac, steak hoagie, and so forth. Skyway Jack's is open from 5 a.m. to 3 p.m. every day. No credit cards, and watch your step going in.

ASIAN

CHINA YUAN $$
8502 N. Armenia Ave.
Tampa
(813) 936-7388
www.chinayuanrestaurant.com

Hot pot dishes (Braised Lamb and Bean Curd), Crispy Roast Duck, and Dungeness Crab with Ginger are just a few of the traditional Hong Kong, Peking, and Szechuan dishes you'll find at China Yuan—rated by at least one food critic as the best in the Tampa Bay area. The fish, crab, and eel are saltwater tank fresh at China Yuan, and there's a full dim sum menu (although no cart service). They cook as many as 20 ducks each day served several ways—and the adventuresome can order a dish of boneless duck feet.

China Yuan is open Monday through Thursday from 11 a.m. to 10 p.m., Friday and Saturday from 10:30 a.m. to 11 p.m., and Sunday from 10:30 a.m. to 10 p.m.

HA LONG BAY $$
5944 34th St. N.
St. Petersburg
(727) 522-9988
www.ha-long-bay.com

Polished black tables and exquisite color landscape photos on the shades-of-green walls give this dim sum/Chinese/Vietnamese restaurant a sophisticated look. The extensive menu is written in three languages and the selections are not your typical fried rice and eggrolls—although those are on the menu, too. But you'll also find Clams with Ginger Scallion Sauce, Seafood in Bird Nest, Stuffed Tofu Pot, Shark Fin with Crab Meat Soup, and Sizzling Sirloin Steak with Black Bean Sauce. Ha Long Bay specializes in authentic Hong Kong–style dim sum, as well as classic Chinese and Vietnamese cuisine.

Dim Sum is served from 11 a.m. to 3 p.m. Monday through Thursday, and from 10 a.m. to 3 p.m. Friday through Sunday. Dinner is served from 5 to 10 p.m. Monday through Thursday and from 5 to 11 p.m. Friday through Sunday. The restaurant is closed between 3 and 5 p.m.

KOBÉ JAPANESE STEAK HOUSE AND SUSHI BAR $$–$$$
28775 U.S. 19 N.
Clearwater
(727) 791-1888

14401 N. Dale Mabry Hwy
Tampa
(813) 908-8909
www.kobesteakhouse.com

Cooking as entertainment has become an art, one which Japanese Teppanyaki chefs perfected long ago. At Kobé Japanese Steakhouse and Sushi Bar, guests watch their chef slice, sear, and sauté with abandon a variety of meats, poultry, seafood, and vegetables right in front of them. Not just any beef is served—Kobé beef cattle have been fed a special diet of rice, beans, rice bran, and beer, and their muscles massaged to make the meat oh-so-tender. Vegetarian dishes are also available, and an extensive sushi menu offers guests a tempting array of choices pre-

Hot Diggety! Seven Heavenly Hot Dog Joints

Here are a few of our favorite dog houses. Price? Are you kidding? We're talking $ meals here, even if you splurge and get the basket—but they come with $$$ flavor!

Bono's Famous Chicago Style Hot Dogs
6721 66th St. N.
Largo
(727) 535-1111

Nothing fancy at Bono's—dogs, subs, and salads—but you'll stand in line at lunchtime. Look for a small yellow house with three small, white, stone tables out front. Bono's is open Monday through Friday from 10 a.m. to 3 p.m.

Bruce's Chicago Grill & Dog House
7733 Ulmerton Rd.
Largo
(727) 524-1146

Bruce's wins for best décor and biggest menu. Iconic yellow walls covered with Chicago stuff make Windy City wanderers feel at home. Get the Chicago dog, Da Beef, or burn-your-throat Wisconsin brats. Bruce's opens at 11 a.m. Monday through Saturday, closes at 7 p.m. every day except Saturday when they close at 4 p.m.

Chi-Town Dogs
4115 66th St. N.
St. Petersburg
(727) 343-9003
www.chi-towndogs.com

The Chicago-style hot dogs with the neon green relish, onions, mustard, dill pickle, tomato, sport peppers, and a dusting of celery salt are heavenly and the fresh-cut fries are so-o good! Do NOT ask for ketchup on your dog—on the fries, okay. Chi-Town Dogs opens at 11 a.m. every day Monday through Saturday. Tuesdays they close at 5:30 p.m. and Saturdays they close at 4 p.m.—other days they stay open until 7 p.m.

Coney Island Grill
250 Dr. Martin Luther King Jr. St. N.
St. Petersburg
(727) 822-4493

Maybe you grew up in a different part of the country where the dogs were served with onions, mustard, and no-bean, all-meat Michigan-style chili on a plain bun. Coney Island Grill has been a St. Petersburg fixture since 1926. They open at 10 a.m. Monday through Saturday. They're open until 7 p.m. Monday through Friday and close at 3:30 on Saturday.

Mel's Hot Dogs
4136 E. Busch Blvd.
Tampa
(813) 985-8000
www.melshotdogs.com

The dogs are Chicago-style, natural-casing dogs on poppyseed buns and served 12 different ways. Mel's is in the last remaining building from Henderson Air Field, a World War II army base. Mel's opens Monday through Saturday at 11 a.m. and closes every day at 8 p.m. except Saturday when they close at 9 p.m.

Placy's Italian Beef & Sausage Restaurant
1359 S. Fort Harrison Ave.
Clearwater
(727) 443-0444
www.placys.us

Look for the red and white umbrellas outside—and Chicago dogs fixed different ways inside. You'll also find a peppers-and-eggs dog and a veggie California Surfer (avocado, cheese, sprouts). Placy's opens Monday through Saturday at 11:30 a.m. and closes at 7:30 p.m. Monday through Friday. Saturday at 5:30 p.m.

sented in picturesque settings of sauces, greens, and shredded carrots. There's a full bar, wine list, children's menu, early bird specials, and more. For dessert? Try the green tea ice cream—or maybe the fried cheesecake.

Kobé Japanese Steakhouse and Sushi Bar is open from 5 to 10 p.m. Monday through Saturday and from 4:30 to 10 p.m. on Sunday. Reservations can be made online or by calling the restaurant. There are other Kobé Japanese Steakhouse restaurants in the Orlando area.

LEE GARDEN $-$$
4447 4th St. N.
St. Petersburg
(727) 522-8580

8309 W. Hillsborough Ave.
Tampa
(813) 887-5077

You can't miss the pink-and-purple St. Petersburg restaurant on 4th St. North. Inside you'll find the traditional Chinese reds and golds. But we love the distinctive exterior. Lee Garden features a Chinese buffet that includes everything from lo mein to Egg Foo Young—very complete and very good. The dinner buffet includes sushi and steak. Or you can order from the menu—dishes like Seafood Goba, a shrimp, scallops, lobster, and crab dish cooked with vegetables; or Eight Delicious Chicken, with both white meats (chicken and pork) plus shrimp and cashew nuts. Some dishes are spicy, but you can always ask them to tone down the heat.

Lee Garden is open every day. They serve lunch from 11:30 a.m. to 3:30 p.m. and dinner from 3:45 to 9:30 p.m.

THAI COCONUT $$
1280 S. Missouri Ave.
Clearwater
(727) 441-1650
thethaicoconut.com

Royal Thai cuisine artistically presented—that pretty much sums up Clearwater's Thai Coconut restaurant. As the menu explains, Thai cuisine draws from Indian and Chinese culinary cultures,

mingling the flavors sometimes in unexpected ways. You'll find curry dishes, for instance, as well as fried rice, but you'll also find a Thai Coconut Combo Fried Rice and a Pad Thai dish of rice noodles sautéed with shrimp, chicken, ground peanuts, bean sprouts, green onion, and egg that some say is the best in the nation. Thai Coconut offers a selection of meats cooked to order with your choice of vegetables and sauces, an extensive sushi menu, and a variety of beers and wines. They grow many of their own herbs.

Lunch is served Monday through Friday from 11:30 a.m. to 2:30 p.m. Dinner is served every day beginning at 4:30 p.m., until 9:30 p.m. Sunday through Thursday and until 10 p.m. Friday and Saturday.

CASUAL CLOTHES, CLASSY COOKING

CAFÉ ALFRESCO $$
344 Main St.
Dunedin
(727) 736-4299
www.cafelafrescoonline.com

Nothing fancy means you can wear shorts and flip-flops and not feel out of place. But the food is definitely a cut above at Café Alfresco. That's because they're owned by Bon Appétit just down the road (150 Marina Plaza, 727-733-2151, $$$). There is no indoor waiting area—when it's busy, people line up outdoors and even down alongside the Pinellas Trail.

Sandwiches, salads—try the Thai Sesame Salmon Salad—and pastabilities are lighter fare. Or go for the Pork Diane, Cajun Meatloaf, or Orange Chicken Stir-Fry. Whatever you order, it will be creatively presented and yummy. Saturday and Sunday they serve brunch from 10 a.m. to 2 p.m. Otherwise, they're open from 11 a.m. to 10 p.m.

DANNY K'S ALLEY CAFÉ $
118 E. Court St.
Tarpon Springs
(727) 938-9452

Danny K's sits in the interior courtyard of the

downtown Taylor Arcade, an early 20th-century office/small-business two-story building. That means people can—and do—walk through from Court Street on one side to Tarpon Avenue on the other. The building is no longer in its prime, but it's a reminder that there are other ways of using space than strip stores and high-rise buildings. People come here to chat about the latest doings at City Hall or to talk shop. They come for breakfast, for lunch, and, except for Sundays, for dinner—and for coffee in between.

Breakfast is served all day, and there's a good selection of omelettes and Eggs Benedicts, including a Smoked Salmon Benedict and a Greek Benedict with gyro meat, tomatoes, and feta cheese plus hollandaise sauce. Waffles are made with a malted mix, and French toast can be made with regular, sourdough, or raisin bread. You'll find a Greek salad with non-traditional garbanzo beans in addition to the usual ingredients. And there are other creative salads on the menu—a Philly Supreme Salad with shaved ribeye steak (or chicken) with sautéed onions, peppers, and Provolone cheese over a large house salad. Mushrooms, too, if you want to pay a bit extra for them. Burgers, Cuban sandwiches, and pita wraps round out the menu. There are a number of vegetarian choices.

Danny K's opens every day at 7 a.m. They close Monday through Saturday at 9 p.m. and on Sunday at 2 p.m.

SPRING GARDEN FAMILY RESTAURANT $–$$
1018 62nd Ave. N.
St. Petersburg
(727) 528-2722

Like the name says, this is a family restaurant—the kind that fills up on Sunday mornings with the after-church crowd. The kind where the server might call you "Honey" or ask you how your cat is doing. Nothing fancy. Just good food—including breakfast all day—lots of coffee, and the price is right, too. Breakfasts are the usual eggs, pancakes, French toast, and waffles, although they also do Eggs Benedict and Eggs Florentine. There's a nice selection of omelets,

too. Try the spinach, feta cheese, and tomato stuffed omelet or the a corned beef and Swiss omelet. Lunches are burgers, hot or cold sandwiches, salads, and the like—Greek salads and gyros, too. Dinners are comfort-food favorites like liver and onions, meatloaf, and roast pork, but you can also get ribs, steak, and seafood. There's a children's menu, too.

The Spring Garden Family Restaurant opens at 6 a.m. every day. The lunch and dinner menu kicks in at 11 a.m., and the restaurant is open until 9 p.m.

COFFEE, TEA, AND THEE

BREW GARDEN $–$$
904 N. McMullen Booth Rd.
Clearwater
(727) 797-6622
www.thebrewgarden.com

By day it's the Kona Koffee Café, featuring Kona press coffee, lattes, espressos, hot chocolate treats, smoothies, and even Japanese-style tea service. By night it's the Belgian Tap House, serving beers and wines from around the world—think Youngs Double Chocolate Draft from England, Canadian Ephemere draft beer made with Granny Smith apples, Irish Guiness, Mexican Corona, Belgian Kasteele, Dominican Republic Presidente, and more. More as in 32 varieties on tap, as many varieties in bottles, and a decent selection of wines.

The limited food menu includes sandwiches, salads, and pastries—just enough selection to satisfy most tastes, but not enough to pull the attention away from the brews. The Brew Garden is developing an evening and late-night following, especially as they offer live music on Friday and Saturday evenings featuring local musicians (jazz, acoustic, etc.)—not hard to do, considering they're across the street from Sam Ashe Music (see Shopping) and from Ruth Eckerd Hall (see Art).

The Brew Garden opens Monday through Friday at 6:30 a.m. Saturday and Sunday they open at 7 a.m. They close at 11 p.m. Sunday through Thursday, and close at midnight Friday and Saturday.

🔍 Close-up

Columbia Restaurant $$–$$$

You sit in the airy Andalucían courtyard–like Patio Dining Room, near one of the tropical palms. The table setting is elegant, the service gracious. Your server sets Arroz con Pollo Valenciana in front of you—a plate full of steaming yellow rice topped with sautéed bone-in chicken, onions, tomatoes, green peas, and red pimientos. Your first forkful of tender, flavorful chicken tells you: This signature dish of the Columbia Restaurant—one the founder, Casimiro Hernandez, brought with him from Cuba more than 100 years ago—was worth the wait.

In 1898, Casimiro Hernandez was impressed into the Spanish navy against his will. He jumped overboard and swam home to Cuba, where he worked until he saved enough to come to the United States. He came to Tampa.

Hernandez opened a saloon, the Columbia Café, in 1905. The Columbia Café offered the local cigar workers a Spanish garbanzo bean soup with chorizo (sausage), ham, and potato; relleno con picadillo sandwiches; a signature "1905 salad"; strong coffee and drink; and a place to talk politics. During Prohibition, the Columbia—named after the song, "Columbia, Gem of the Ocean," which referred to America—expanded its restaurant operations. Before long, the Columbia Restaurant, "The Gem of Spanish Restaurants," had developed a statewide reputation for its classic Spanish food.

In 1935, having survived the worst of the Great Depression, the Columbia, now owned by Casimiro Hernandez Jr., opened the first air-conditioned dining room in Tampa, the Don Quixote Room. The air in the Don Quixote Room may have been cool, but the music and the dancing in it sizzled. Flamenco, salsa, and jazz musicians and dancers performed in the richly decorated room. Two years later, the Patio Room, an Andalucían courtyard–inspired open-air seating area with a retractable glass skylight, opened. People from outside of Tampa began making their way to Ybor City to eat at the Columbia and to hear Latin music.

In the 1950s, Casimiro Jr.'s daughter Adela and her husband Cesar Gonzmart became the third generation to own and operate the Columbia. The Siboney Room, a 300-seat theater, was added in 1956, and in 1959 the Columbia opened its second restaurant on St. Armand's Key in Sarasota.

Today, the original Columbia Restaurant, Florida's oldest restaurant, consists of 15 dining rooms that take up an entire city block and can seat 1,700 people. Flamenco dancers entertain guests with two shows each Monday through Saturday night. Seven Columbia restaurants or cafés bring authentic Spanish and Cuban food to communities around Florida. Four of the seven are listed below. The other three are in Sarasota (opened in 1959), St. Augustine (opened in 1983), and Disney's Celebration (opened in 1997).

KALEISIA TEA LOUNGE $
1441 E. Fletcher Ave., Ste. #133
Tampa
(813) 977-8266
www.thetealounge.com

Steeped in serenity, the Kaleisia Tea Lounge is about more than just drinking tea. Students from USF come here to sink into a sofa and rest their weary brains over a cup of tea or a chai latte. Business people stop in to recharge with a fruit smoothie or Vietnamese coffee. Neighbors drop by to play chess or to listen to local artists play anything from soft rock to harp music. A knitting circle and a book club meet here. Owners Kim Pham and Lan Ha, cousins, might say that's the power of tea.

Tea is definitely the focus at Kaleisia. The Wall of Tea holds a hundred different types—white, black, green, oolong—that customers can see, smell, and feel. Kaleisia staff will teach you about

The Columbia Restaurant has been recognized more than once by *Southern Living* magazine, has earned the Distinguished Restaurants of North America award, and was named to the Golden Spoon Hall of Fame in 2006 after having been named one of Florida's top restaurants every year since 1967. The University of South Florida awarded the Columbia the Celebration of Free Enterprise Award in 2007.

In addition to providing lovely surroundings, hospitable service, and delectable food at very reasonable prices, the Hernandez-Gonzmart family has been recognized for its philanthropic contributions to the community.

Reservations are recommended on weekends, are accepted other days, and can be made online at www.columbiarestaurant.com/reservations.asp. The Columbia offers extensive gluten-free information and a special menu for children ages 10 and under. Most of the restaurants also have a store where you can purchase cookbooks featuring Hernandez and Gonzmart family recipes as well as other items. The Columbia's Web site says dress is casual. But their less-than-casually furnished establishments provide a good excuse to dress accordingly. Each establishment, except the downtown Tampa location, is open every day of the year, but hours vary, so call ahead.

Ybor City (est. 1905)
2117 East 7th Ave.
Tampa
(813) 248-4961

The original Columbia Restaurant offers live jazz entertainment on Saturday in the Columbia Café. Reservations are required for dinner seatings that include the flamenco show, and there is an additional $6 cover charge.

St. Petersburg (est. 1988)
800 2nd Ave. N.E.
St. Petersburg
(727) 822-8000

Located on the fourth floor of the the Pier (see Attractions chapter), the St. Petersburg Columbia Restaurant offers a panoramic view of St. Petersburg's waterfront.

Clearwater Beach (est. 1989)
1241 Gulf Blvd.
Clearwater 33767
(727) 596-8400

The Clearwater Beach Columbia offers waterfront deck as well as indoor dining.

Downtown Tampa (est. 2009)
The Columbia Café
801 Old Water St., #1905
Tampa
(813) 229-5511

Located inside the Tampa Bay History Center (see Attractions chapter) overlooking the river, the Columbia Café offers an abbreviated menu containing many of the Columbia's favorites. Banquet space is available. Closed Thanksgiving and Christmas.

how tea is grown and processed and how to make a perfect cup of tea. In fact, Kaleisia offers private tea workshops, tea tastings, and Japanese, Chinese, and Korean tea ceremonies performed for large groups or small parties.

Kaleisia also serves vegan food including Vegan Spring Rolls, Cranberry-Walnut Salad, Pumpkin Coconut Soup, and a non-vegan item or two including Fruity Curry Chicken Salad. Kaleisia is open Monday through Saturday from 10 a.m. to 10 p.m. and on Sunday from noon to 6 p.m. Kaleisia offers a free tea tasting the last Saturday of each month from 1 to 5 p.m.

MARCHAND'S BAR & GRILL $$
501 5th Ave. N.E.
St. Petersburg
(727) 824-8072

Afternoon tea is an event at Marchand's. We're not talking a cuppa and a biscuit or two. This is a dress-to-the-nines and curl your pinkie affair. Perhaps Madame would like the Queen Elizabeth, with its selection of traditional tea sandwiches, scones, pastries, fresh fruit, homemade cream, and choice of tea? The Napoleon Bonaparte— pâtés, cornichons, wild berry flambé, tea, and a drop of something stronger—for the Gentleman? Tea is served at Marchand's on Wednesdays and Saturdays between 2:30 and 3:30 p.m. Linger as you like. Reservations are required.

SACRED GROUNDS COFFEE HOUSE $
4819 E. Busch Blvd.
Tampa
(813) 983-0837
www.sacredgroundstampa.com
Located in a two-story plaza near the University of South Florida, Sacred Grounds Coffee House serves veggie wraps, quesadillas, nachos, pitas and hummus, smoothies, coffee, and tea—foods you and your body can both enjoy. But it's not just the food for the body that brings people to Sacred Grounds Coffee House. There's food for the soul here, too—neighbors coming together to play board games that leave you anything but bored, study groups meeting in the library, people looking for a little peace and quiet along with a cup of coffee.

Friday and Saturday nights there's live music—anything from acoustic folk music to rock, but nothing too heavy. During the week various groups meet here—a Reiki circle, knitters, vegans, pagans, drum circle, and others. Check the calendar for days and times. And look for more information in the Arts chapter about open-mike and jam sessions.

Sacred Grounds Coffee House opens each evening at 6 p.m. and closes at midnight Sunday through Thursday. Friday and Saturday they're open until 2 a.m.

GREAT GREEK

ATHENIAN GARDEN $$
www.atheniangarden.com

Largo/Mid-County
12670 Starkey Rd.
Largo
(727) 518-8888
Opens at 11 a.m. Monday through Saturday and at noon on Sunday. Closes at 9 or 10 p.m., depending on the crowd.

St. Petersburg/Downtown
21 3rd St. N.
St. Petersburg
(727) 822-2000
Open at 7:30 a.m. Monday through Friday and at 9 a.m. Saturday and Sunday. Monday and Tuesday, they close at 8 p.m., Wednesday and Thursday at 9 p.m.; Friday and Saturday they're open until the crowd thins, and Sunday they close at 8 p.m.

St. Petersburg/North
9047 Dr. Martin Luther King Jr. St. N.
St. Petersburg
(727) 570-4500
Open Monday through Friday from 7 to 11 a.m. and from 7 a.m. to 1 p.m. Saturday and Sunday. Breakfast served.

St. Petersburg/Tyrone area
6940 22nd Ave. N.
St. Petersburg
(727) 345-7040
Opens at 11 a.m. Monday through Saturday and at 11:30 a.m. on Sunday. Closes at 10 p.m.

You'll find the usual gyros and Greek salads on the menu at Athenian Garden. But there are a few surprises, too, like the *Saganaki* appetizer, a kefalograviera cheese flamed with brandy and lemon. Or the Tabouleh and Hummus Salad, the Grouper and Avocado Wrap, and the *Guivesti* (Lamb Shank with Orzo). There's a children's menu, a large vegetarian meal selection, and desserts, too. Two of the locations serve a full breakfast menu.

Outback Steakhouse and Lee Roy Selmon's

Almost a decade before the Tampa Bay Buccaneers won their first, and to date only, Super Bowl, they produced a National Football League Hall of Fame gridiron giant named Lee Roy Selmon. Selmon was the Bucs' first ever draft pick in 1976, and he quickly became a cornerstone on the Bucs' defense. A back injury ended his football days in 1985, but Selmon, born in Oklahoma and an All-American at the University of Oklahoma, had made Tampa his home. Selmon worked in the banking business and, with two of his brothers, developed a line of barbecue sauce they sold in local markets.

A few years after Selmon retired from football, another team formed. This team of three—Bob Basham, Tim Gannon, and Chris Sullivan—had worked for various restaurants around the state and had an idea for a restaurant of their own. None of them had ever been to Australia, but Crocodile Dundee was popular at the time, and beef on the barbie sounded familiar but a twist. Today, Outback Steakhouse has restaurants around the nation. OSI Restaurant Partners, LLC, headquartered in Tampa, also developed other chains, including Carrabba's Italian Grill, Bonefish Grill, Fleming's, and Roy's.

In the mid-1990s, team Selmon and team Outback met when Selmon called to pitch his barbecue sauce for use in the steakhouse chains. OSI didn't take the sauce, but they did take Selmon to be on their board of directors. As the relationship matured, the next step was to develop a restaurant around the sauce and, more importantly, around Selmon. Credited with developing the brand-new football program at USF in the early 1990s, Selmon eventually became USF's athletic director from 2001 to 2004. The Lee Roy Selmon Crosstown Expressway in Tampa bears his name, symbolizing how he has cut through the typical "work together" rhetoric and has connected disparate parts of the community with hard work, grace, and good barbecue sauce.

The first Lee Roy Selmon's opened in Tampa in 2000. Today there are two restaurants in Tampa, another in St. Petersburg, and three south of the Skyway Bridge. You'll find home-style foods like Hall of Fame Ribs, Mama's Meatloaf, Sweet Heat Fried Chicken Platter, and Melt In Ya' Mouth Pecan Pie on the menu.

Each Lee Roy Selmon's is independently managed, so hours vary a bit from place to place. They're open every day of the year except Thanksgiving and Christmas Day. Go to www.leeroyselmons.com for updates and more information. $–$$

St. Petersburg
2424 Tyrone Blvd.
(727) 347-5774
Opens every day at 11:30 a.m. Closes at 10 p.m. Sunday through Thursday, and at 11 p.m. Friday and Saturday.

Tampa/South
4302 W. Boy Scout Blvd.
(813) 871-EATS (3287)
Open Monday through Thursday from 11 a.m. to 10:30 p.m., Friday and Saturday from 11 a.m. to 11:30 p.m., and Sunday from 11:30 a.m. to 10 p.m.

LOUIS PAPPAS MARKET CAFÉ $–$$
www.louispappas.com

Clearwater/Northwood Plaza
2560 McMullen Booth Rd.
Clearwater
(727) 797-3700

Tampa/Bay to Bay Center
3409 W. Bay-to-Bay Blvd.
Tampa
(813) 839-0000

Tampa/Shoppes at Citrus Park
7877 Gunn Hwy.
Tampa
(813) 926-5202

Tampa/Oak Ramble Plaza
14913 Bruce B. Downs Blvd.
Tampa
(813) 910-9000

For a long time Pappas Riverside Restaurant in Tarpon Springs was *the* place for Greek food. Opened in 1925 as the Riverside Café, Pappas, owned by the Pappamichalopolous family (shortened to Pappas soon after they came here in 1904 from Sparta), introduced the region to Greek food—gyros, souvlaki, herb-roasted chicken, and more. So successful was Pappas that the family opened other restaurants in the South Pasadena area of St. Petersburg and another on the Hillsborough River in Tampa.

Pappas became a victim of its own success when other Greek restaurants sprang up and even non-Greek restaurants began adding Greek items to the menu. Today Pappas Riverside Restaurant in Tarpon Springs is a special-events meeting place called Riverside Venue. Grandson Louis Pappas, however, continues the Pappas restaurant tradition with a number of smaller market cafés—meaning you can eat it there or take it home—throughout the Tampa Bay area. A fifth store is in Lakeland.

Louis Pappas Market Café serves breakfast—breakfast sandwiches, eggs, omelets, and Greek yogurt with honey and nuts (yes!)—Monday through Saturday from 7:30 to 11 a.m. and Sunday from 9 a.m. to noon. Lunch and dinner—Greek dishes as well as flatbread pizzas, salads, wraps, sandwiches and entrées—are served from 11 a.m. to 9 p.m. Monday through Saturday and until 7 p.m. on Sunday.

MIRAGE RESTAURANT $$
2284 Gulf-to-Bay Blvd.
Clearwater
(727) 724-3604
www.miragerestaurant.com

This is Greek, but it's also Persian, so you'll find many of the same types of foods with slightly different names. Shish kabob of filet mignon, for instance is served with rice topped with saffron. Their gyro is served with tabouli salad and hummus, as well as tzatziki sauce. There's Greek salad and also a Shirazi salad of chopped cucumbers, tomatoes, parsley, and onion. Try the lamb shank served with basmati rice, fresh lima beans, chopped dill, and saffron. Desserts range from baklava to faloodeh.

A belly dancer performs on Friday and Saturday evenings. Mirage Restaurant offers a lunch buffet from 11 a.m. to 2:30 p.m. Monday through Friday and from 11 a.m. to 3 p.m. Saturday and Sunday. They are open for dinner until 9 p.m. Sunday through Thursday and until 11 p.m. Friday and Saturday.

PANOS KOUZINA $$
3101 SR 580
Safety Harbor
(727) 797-2667
www.panoskouzina.com

On the south side of SR 580, as you're headed from Clearwater to Tampa, sits a bit of Mediterranean heaven. Don't let the fact that its strip-center neighbors are a coin laundry, a wireless store, and a drug store fool you into thinking Pano Kouzina isn't worth a stop. It is.

Panos Kouzina's menu blends Greek and Italian favorites from gyros on pitas to hand-tossed pizzas with any number of toppings. You can have your spaghetti Italian-style with meatballs and marinara sauce or Greek-style with feta and Parmesan cheeses, garlic, and butter sauce. Desserts include peanut butter brownie cake as well as tiramisu and baklava. Salads, sandwiches (The Greek from Philly?), even burgers and fries round out the menu. The food is presented with flair and the décor is sleek.

Owner Nick Pano majored in music and is a professional trumpet player. But he also makes music in the kitchen—check out the Web site videos of Nick cooking. Panos Kouzina is open Monday through Thursday from 11 a.m. to 9 p.m., Friday and Saturday from 11 a.m. to 10 p.m., and Sunday from noon to 8 p.m.

ONE-OF-A-KINDS

BAHAMA BREEZE $$
3045 N. Rocky Point Dr. E.
Tampa
(813) 289-7922
www.bahamabreeze.com

The only Bahama Breeze restaurant in the Tampa Bay area sits on a lagoon in Rocky Point just off the Clearwater Causeway on the Tampa side. Part of the Darden groups of restaurant—which means you can use your Olive Garden and Red Lobster gift cards here—Bahama Breeze offers Caribbean flavored food, colorful island décor, and an outdoor bar that hosts many a party.

Back to the food. The Bahama Breeze Web site contains a full glossary of Caribbean cooking terms, but one of the most common you'll see on their menu is "jerk" meat. No, this doesn't mean the meat acted like a cad. "Jerk" refers to dry-rubbing meat with various spices, as when making jerky. The Jamaican Grilled Chicken Breast, for instance, is prepared with Jamaican jerk seasonings, glazed with mango, and served with mango-pineapple salsa, cinnamon mashed sweet potatoes, and vegetables. Just want a sandwich? Try their Cuban or the Wood-Grilled Angus Burger. The beverage list is full of those island-inspired imbibibles with names like Bahamarita, Caipirinha (national drink of Brazil), Mojito Cubano, and the Bahamartini.

Bahama Breeze opens every day at 11 a.m., closes at midnight Sunday through Thursday, and is open until 2 a.m. on Friday and Saturday. They are closed Christmas and Thanksgiving Day.

THE CHEESECAKE FACTORY $$–$$$
2223 N. West Shore Blvd., Ste. B201
Tampa
(813) 353-4200
www.thecheesecakefactory.com

The Cheesecake Factory's menu is a small book with chapters dedicated to pizzas, pastas, specialties, sandwiches, fish and seafood, steaks and chops, and more. For the uninitiated, dinners range from comfort food like the Famous Factory Meatloaf served with mashed potatoes to the less predictable Hibachi Steak served with wasabi mashed potatoes. Egg and omelettes—served all day, every day—include dishes such as the Morning Quesadilla and a California Omelette. Plus there's a generous listing of specialty drinks, wines, beers, and spiked coffees.

And the cheesecake? Never fear. You'll find more than two dozen varieties on the menu—Craig's Crazy Carrot Cake Cheesecake, Chocolate Raspberry Truffle Cheesecake, Dutch Apple Caramel Streusel Cheesecake, just to name a few—along with a full page of other delectable desserts.

Located on the Bay Street side of International Mall, the Cheesecake Factory offers both indoor and outdoor dining for lunch, dinner, late night supper, dessert and coffee, and Sunday brunch. Plus they'll ship their cheesecakes just about anywhere in the country. The Cheesecake Factory opens Monday through Saturday at 11 a.m. and 10 a.m. on Sunday. The restaurant closes at 11 p.m. Sunday through Thursday and at 12:30 a.m. Friday and Saturday.

ELI'S BBQ $
360 Skinner Blvd.
Dunedin
(727) 738-4856

Eli's is only open on Fridays and Saturdays, and then the locals line up at the little white building just off the Pinellas Trail for pulled pork, sausage, chicken, and ribs smoked in another little building out back. Get your meal—meat, white bread, beans, and slaw—to go, or settle in at one of the picnic tables under the trees and watch the cyclists and skaters pass by while you

Close-up

Greek Food

Because the Tampa Bay area has become home to a large Greek population, many local restaurants offer a smattering of Greek food in addition to their other menu listings. You may see Greek salad listed along with house and chef's salads, gyros listed along with subs, and moussaka listed with lasagna. Of course, we have a number of Greek restaurants that also serve the occasional burger and fries.

Spice combinations used in Greek foods can be different from what non-Greeks are used to. Many people tend to think of cinnamon, nutmeg, and allspice as spices for sweet foods. But Greek and other Middle Eastern cuisines use these spices—and others—in meat and savory dishes, as well.

This quick guide will tell you about several of the most common Greek dishes you'll find listed. But don't be afraid to ask—we haven't met a chef yet who didn't delight in talking about food.

As with omelet/omelette, spellings vary. We've tried to include all the spelling variations we've seen.

Opa!

Baklava or baclava (BAH-klah-va): Layers and layers of crispy filo pastry filled with a ground walnut and honey mixture and soaked in a honey-flavored syrup.

Dolmades (dol-MAH-dehs): Grapevine leaves stuffed with seasoned rice and/or meat, rolled tightly, and steamed or simmered. We have had these served both hot and cold.

Feta (FEH-tah): The ubiquitous white goat cheese that is, like olive oil, one of the defining ingredients of Greek food. Feta is a semi-soft cheese with a sharp, somewhat salty flavor and can be cubed or crumbled.

Filo, fila, or phyllo (FEE-lo): Tissue-paper thin pastry dough made of flour, water, and oil. Many types of dessert and appetizer pastries are made with layers of filo dough, which becomes crispy when baked or fried.

Galatoboureko (gah-LAH-to-boo-REH-ko): Layers of filo filled with custard and topped with a honey syrup.

Greek salad: Traditionally, Greek salad is mostly sliced or chopped tomatoes, cucumbers, red onion, feta cheese, and kalamata olives with a sprinkling of salt and pepper, oregano and basil, and a drizzling of olive oil. Anchovies, lettuce, bell pepper, and vinegar are also common additions. What you will most often be served here is a lettuce salad with tomatoes, cucumber, onion, feta cheese, kalamata olives, and peperoncini peppers sprinkled with oregano and basil and an oil-and-vinegar-and-spices dressing that sometimes is on the sweet side. You might also find beets on the salad (pickled or not) and a scoop of potato salad buried in the middle of the lettuce—originally added to salads and fed to World War I troops by Louis Pappas of Tarpon Springs when he was an Army cook. Very occasionally, anchovies might be included—you can often ask for anchovies on the side, if you like them. Greek salad is most often served here with Greek bread—crusty loaf bread—rather than with pita.

Gyros (YEE-ros): The word refers both to a way of cooking meat and to the sandwich made from the meat. Traditionally, thin slices of raw meat are cooked on a vertical spit that turns in front of a heat source. In the United States, health laws have meant making changes. What you generally will see in this area is ground, processed meat (lamb, veal, or a combination) packed around a vertical rotisserie, and roasting merrily away. As orders come in, the cook slices thin strips of the gyros from the cylinder as it's turning. If the meat is for an entrée, it goes on the plate with some raw onions, tomatoes, and tzatziki sauce (see below). If the meat is for a gyro sandwich, the slices are placed on a grilled pita, along with raw onions, tomatoes, and tzatziki. Some people prefer their onions grilled, and most cooks will accommodate such orders.

Kadaife, kadaif (kah-DAY-if): Shredded dough filled with chopped or ground nuts and cinnamon, topped with a honey syrup and baked until golden.

Kafes (kah-FEYS): Coffee—but watch out! Greek coffee is super strong and the very fine grounds are not strained out. The grounds settle to the bottom of the cup.

Kalamata (kah-lah-MAH-tah): A type of Greek olive.

Moussaka (MOO-sah-kah): A layered casserole of sautéed eggplant and ground lamb or other meat cooked with onion, garlic, tomatoes, and spices. The last layer is a white sauce (scalded milk mixed into a flour-butter *roux)*, which is poured over the top. The casserole is baked until the top is browned.

Orzo (OR-tso): A small oval-shaped pasta that looks, at first glance, like rice.

Ouzo (OO-zo): An anise-flavored, colorless alcoholic beverage.

Pastitsio (Pah-STEE-see-oh): A layered casserole of pasta and cheese (sometimes with egg) on the bottom, ground beef, veal, or lamb cooked with tomatoes and spices in the middle, another layer of pasta, and either a white sauce or a custard topping.

Peperoncini, pepperoncini (peh-per-o-CHEE-nee) peppers: Mild, pickled small green peppers that often appear as a garnish on Greek salads.

Pilaf, pilafi (PEE-lahf): Rice cooked with broth and maybe some onion and other spices.

Pita (PEE-tah): These are not the thin pocket breads sold in grocery stores. These pitas, made with yeast, are thick and are often oiled and then grilled. Pitas may be served on the side with an entrée, but more commonly are the basis for a gyro or souvlaki sandwich.

Souvlaki, Souvlakia (soov-LAH-kee): Skewered and grilled chunks of meat, traditionally pork. Chicken and other meats and vegetables served souvlaki-style are also common.

Spanakopita, spanakopeta (spah-no-ko-PEE-tah): Spinach pie made with layers of filo and a spinach and feta cheese filling. Sometimes these are bite-sized appetizers. Sometimes a large panful is cut into sections and served as quiche would be.

Tiropita, tyropita (tee-ro-PEE-ta): Cheese pie made with filo layers and a mixture of feta and other cheeses. As with the spanokopita, tiropita is served as an appetizer or as a light entrée.

Tsatziki, tzatziki (tsah-TSEE-kee): A creamy sauce made of yogurt, cucumbers, garlic, dill, and other spices. It is generally served with gyro sandwiches and as a side dish to other meat entrées. Non-Greeks sometimes refer to it as cucumber sauce.

Yogurt with honey: Thick plain yogurt scooped like soft ice cream, topped with honey, and served as dessert.

fill up on oh-so-tender barbecue. When they sell out, that's it.

No dress code, no reservations, no dine-in eating. Cash only, cold canned sodas (no cups, no ice). Feel free to talk ribs or turkey to Elijah Crawford or whoever is minding the grill in the screened-in smokehouse out back.

KELLY'S $-$$
319 Main St.
Dunedin
(727) 736-5284
www.kellyschicaboom.com

The mannequin greeting you at the door tells you this isn't Kansas, Toto. The menu reinforces the feeling with items like the Seafood Omelet, which sounds harmless enough until you see it consists of shrimp, scallops, vegetables, provolone cheese, and a "Hellfire and Damnation" sauce. Tamer dishes include a fabulous Fruit & Nut French Toast, smoked salmon and bagel, and lots of the usuals. Lunch oddities include a Grilled Brie Sandwich and a Monte Cristo. Dinners are mostly steak and seafood, but kicked up a notch or two with offerings like the Wasabi Grilled Rib Eye Steak.

Kelly's has been a fixture in downtown Dunedin for 20 years, dishing up breakfast, lunch, and dinner from 8 a.m. until 9:30 p.m. on weekdays and 10:30 p.m. on Friday and Saturday. It's not big, but there's a spacious patio area out back. Next door is the Chic-a-Boom-Room Martini Bar and Lounge and next to that is the Blur Nightclub and Show Bar—all under the same ownership (see Nightlife chapter).

QUAKER STEAK AND LUBE $-$$
10400 49th St. N. (at U.S. 19)
Clearwater
(727) 572-WING (9464)
www.quakersteak.com

This looks like an old-fashioned gas station, and, when Quaker Steak and Lube first opened, we weren't sure whether we should bring our car in for an oil change or come for dinner. Now it's one of our favorite places to bring visitors for wings, burgers, and more, as much for the atmosphere as for the food.

Racing fans, little kids, and anyone who appreciates themed décor will feast their eyes on vintage cars and motorbikes, rescued from the scrap yard and hung from every imaginable surface, while waiting for the order of piping hot onion rings served on an antenna with dipping sauces on the side. Try the wings, served with one of the largest arrays of sauces in the area, or go for the ribs. Both seem taste-accelerated when eaten under a classic car in the middle of a service bay or next to a collection of license plates from around the country. The food is good and the décor is fun. Quaker Steak and Lube has a full bar and there is often music on the patio.

Wednesday night is bike (as in motorcycle) night and Saturday night is truck night. Check the online calendar for other events and promotions.

THE SPAGHETTI WAREHOUSE $$-$$$
1911 13th St.
Tampa
(813) 248-1720
www.meatballs.com

Spaghetti lovers, rejoice! The only Spaghetti Warehouse you'll find in Florida is in Tampa. And, while most of the menu features straightforward Italian fare—spaghetti and meatballs, 15-Layer Lasagne, spaghetti and meat sauce, veal parmigiana, spaghetti and Italian sausage—you'll also find an eyebrow raiser or two. Spaghetti and Beer Chili? Hmmmmm. Crab Crusted Tilapia with Garlic Shrimp? Double hmmmmm.

The Spaghetti Warehouse opens every day at 11 a.m., is open until 10 p.m. Sunday through Thursday, and is open until 11 p.m. Friday and Saturday. They offer a children's menu, beer, and wine.

OOH LA LA FINE DINING EXPERIENCES

Jackets are seldom required, even at fine restaurants in the Tampa Bay area, partly because of our climate. However, most of these restaurants expect at least casual business attire—and food always seems to taste better when the couture complements the cuisine. Call ahead if you want to be double sure.

Pete & Shorty's—One to Watch?

Back in 1983, the first Hooters Restaurant opened in Clearwater, Florida. Today, they're pretty much everywhere—in 43 states and more than two dozen foreign countries. They're also headquartered in Atlanta, so we can't exactly say they're a local company anymore.

But in 1998 several of the original founders of Hooters, along with others, opened a neighborhood tavern called Pete & Shorty's. In Clearwater. Next to a Hooters.

Eleven years later, Pete & Shorty's is beginning to branch out. A second one opened a few months ago in Pinellas Park. (Correction: It's actually a fourth one. A Tampa one that opened in 2002 is no longer open and a Las Vegas one by the same name, part of the Hooters Casino Hotel, is just a bar and not part of this group.)

Is this the start of another chain? Might be worth watching.

Pete & Shorty's menu features comfort food—Soup du Decade, Pete's Reel Fish Good Fish Dinner piled high, Shorty Burgers, and more. Nothing fancy—and the pot roast isn't quite like mom used to make—but the barbecue has a kick, the sandwiches are hefty, and they have a full bar. Did we mention they do deep-fried Oreo cookies for dessert?

Pete & Shorty's opens every day at 11 a.m. They're open until midnight on Monday through Thursday, until 2 a.m. Friday and Saturday, and until 10 p.m. Sunday.

Pete & Shorty's $$
2820 Gulf-to-Bay Blvd.
Clearwater
(727) 799-0580

7402 49th St. N.
Pinellas Park
(727) 549-8000
www.peteandshortys.com

ALFANO'S   **$$$**
1702 Clearwater-Largo Rd.
Clearwater
(727) 582-2125
www.alfanorestaurant.com

Alfano's isn't big and it isn't loud. It isn't on the beach or on a major highway. But look at the newspaper clippings and photos in the hallway, and you'll see an international who's who of famous people who have eaten Alfano's classic Italian cuisine. From the extra light and tender *Calamari Friti* to the prepared-at-your-table Caesar Salad to the Smoked Chicken *Ravioli Carbonera*, the food is elegant without being pretentious. There's a full bar, an extensive dessert menu, and background live piano music.

Alfano's serves lunch Monday through Friday from 11:30 a.m. to 2:30 p.m. and serves dinner from 5 to 9 p.m. Monday and Tuesday and 5 to 10 p.m. Wednesday through Saturday. They are closed Sunday. Alfano's offers a *prix fixe* menu from 5 to 6 p.m.

BOB HEILMAN'S BEACHCOMBER $$–$$$
www.heilmansbeachcomber.com
BOBBY'S BISTRO AND WINE BAR $$–$$$
447 Mandalay Ave.
N. Clearwater Beach
(727) 442-4144 (Beachcomber), (727) 446-9463 (Bistro)
www.bobbysbistro.com

Bob Heilman's Beachcomber has been around since 1948 and is a Golden Spoon Hall of Famer. You'll find classic menu items like the Back-to-the-Farm Chicken Dinner, sautéed fresh chicken livers, jumbo Gulf shrimp—try these bronzed—lamb chops, prime rib, and steak. Not just any old steaks from the grocery store, either. The Beachcomber selects theirs from a particular region and has them privately dry aged for maximum flavor control. Appetizers are decidedly on the seafood side—it is the Beachcomber, after all—and there's a full bar.

Bobby's Bistro puts a next-generation spin on the décor, the dining, and the wine list (allow extra time just to read it!). This menu features gourmet pizzas, a sandwich board, and salads. Heartier appetites aren't forgotten, however. You'll also find char-grilled steak, lamb chops, salmon, and ribs, each with carefully crafted touches that make for a memorable meal.

Both Bob Heilman's Beachcomber and Bobby's Bistro and Wine Bar are open every day of the year. At the Beachcomber, lunch is served from 11:30 a.m. to 4 p.m., and dinner is served from 4 p.m. until whenever. Bobby's Bistro opens at 5 p.m. each day and also is open until they decide to close.

CAFÉ ALMA $$–$$$
260 1st Ave. S.
St. Petersburg
(727) 502-5002
www.cafealma.com

Café Alma can't quite decide if it's European with a Middle Eastern streak or vice versa. Which is fine by us because that means we get to enjoy the best of both worlds. Tapas, for instance, may strictly speaking be of Spanish origin, but you'll find Curried Chicken Thighs, smoked Norwegian salmon, and a Hummus Platter along with Pineapple Citrus Ceviche, Pulled Duck Quesadillas, and other appetizers on the menu. Menus change according to the seasons, but entrées might include Pan Roasted Pork Tenderloin or Wild Mushroom and Grilled Vegetable Risotto.

Café Alma features an extensive wine, beer, and ale list, but you'll also find a nice selection of after-dinner liqueurs and coffees. Café Alma serves lunch Monday through Friday from 11 a.m. to 3 p.m. and serves soups, salads, and desserts from 3 p.m. to 5 p.m. Dinner is served at Café Alma from 4:30 to 10 p.m. Monday through Thursday, from 4:30 p.m. to midnight on Friday, and from 5 p.m. to midnight on Saturday. A very reasonably priced *prix fixe* dinner menu is available from 4:30 to 6 p.m. Monday through Friday. Saturday morning, Café Alma offers a brunch menu—omelettes, Benedicts, pancakes, soups, salads, and a make-your-own Bloody Mary bar—from 10:30 a.m. to 3 p.m. Reservations are suggested—Café Alma sometimes is rented for corporate and other private parties.

CAFÉ PONTE $$$
13505 Icot Blvd., Ste. 214
Clearwater
(727) 538-5768
www.cafeponte.com

It's not quite a Cinder-fella story, but almost. Owner/chef Christopher Ponte (the e is silent) had graduated from college in Rhode Island and was working in a Clearwater Beach restaurant. After several months of providing exemplary, special-request meals to a particular customer, the customer asked Ponte about his goals. Long story short, the customer sent Ponte to Paris to study at the Cordon Bleu. Afterwards, Ponte worked for and studied with many of the top chefs on both sides of the Atlantic before returning to Clearwater to open his own restaurant.

Café Ponte, a Golden Spoon restaurant for 2008, serves exquisitely presented dishes that mingle tastes from a variety of cuisines from around the world. Ponte's Maple Leaf Duck Breast, for instance, sounds like a fairly straightforward entrée, complete with seared foie gras and a ginger sweet potato pancake—until, that is, you see that it is served with an orange Szechwan peppercorn sauce.

The menu isn't set in stone, but people who don't like surprises can read it on their Web site. You'll find a number of imaginative martinis plus a carefully selected wine and liquor list.

Lunch at Café Ponte is served Monday through Friday from 11:30 a.m. to 2 p.m. Dinner is served Monday through Thursday from 5:30 to 9 p.m. and Friday and Saturday from 5:30 to 10 p.m. Café Ponte offers a *prix fixe* menu that includes a choice of appetizer, entrée, and dessert from 5:30 to 6:30 p.m. Reservations are suggested for all meals.

MARCHAND'S BAR & GRILL $$–$$$
Renaissance Vinoy Resort & Golf Club
501 5th Ave. N.E.
St. Petersburg
(727) 824-8072
www.marchandsbarandgrill.com

The entire resort was named to the Golden Spoon Hall of Fame in 2003, so we'll also mention Fred's, a surf-and-turf steakhouse open for dinner only; Alfresco's, a more casual indoor-outdoor bistro; the Promenade Lounge and Coffee Bar, which serves breakfast in addition to lunch and dinner; and Marchand's Bar, the dress code for which is "No bathing suits."

Then there's Marchand's Bar & Grill, featuring the Floribean-accented dishes of Executive Chef Mark Heimann, who oversees all the Vinoy's restaurants and their banquet department. You'll find an eclectic combination of tastes and textures at Marchand's. The Vinoy's crab cake appetizer, for instance, is served with an avocado-tomatilla salsa and plantain puree. Entrées include a New York strip steak served with mushroom and bacon hash, sturgeon presented with a black lentil risotto, and pasta dishes such as *Bolognese Tagliatelle*. You'll find the wines and liquors you'd expect at a Golden Spoon Hall of Famer. You'll also find Heimann's cookbook for sale in the hotel shop.

Dinner isn't the only meal featured at Marchand's. Breakfasts receive the same careful attention—especially the Sunday Brunch (see Breakfast section)—and Afternoon Tea is an occasion (see Coffee, Tea, and Thee, above).

Marchand's serves lunch Monday through Saturday from 11:30 a.m. to 2:30 p.m. and dinner every day from 5 to 10 p.m. Reservations are strongly suggested.

THE MARITANA GRILLE $$$$
Don CeSar Hotel
3400 Gulf Blvd.
St. Pete Beach
(727) 360-1881, (800) 282-1116
www.loewshotels.com/en/hotels/st-pete-beach-resort/dining

Chef Eric Neri welcomes you to the area's only Chef's Table, accessible to the kitchen area of the Maritana Grille. Watch as Chef Neri prepares a New American cuisine five-course tasting meal accented with Floribean touches selected just for you. Will the chef choose the Marmalade Roasted Gulf Red Snapper or the Porcini Rubbed Bone-in Ribeye—or something not on the menu at all, but equally delectable and prepared for you alone?

Or perhaps you'll choose to enjoy the aquatic atmosphere of the Maritana's dining room. Remember hearing the Hans Christian Andersen version of *The Little Mermaid* and wishing you could dine in a mermaid palace? The Maritana Grille must have heard your heart. Come, dine among aquariums full of exotic fish darting amid sea grasses and coral.

The Maritana Grille opens at 6 p.m. Tuesday through Sunday. It closes at 10 p.m. Tuesday through Thursday, at 11 p.m. Friday and Saturday, and at 10 p.m. Sunday. Reservations are recommended and may be made online or by calling the number listed above. Jackets are not required, but jeans, shorts, and T-shirts are not allowed. The Chef's Table experience requires at least 48 hours advance notice and accommodates groups of from two to eight people.

MISE EN PLACE $$-$$$
442 W. Kennedy Blvd.
Tampa
(813) 254-5373
www.miseonline.com

The plate containing your Mis en Place meal arrives at your table, and now you're in a quandary. Do you pick up your fork and disturb the creative composition of color and texture? Or do you frame the plate, preserving the visual artistry, and walk away, knowing you've sacrificed your hunger for a higher cause?

Head Chef Marty Blitz would have you do both. Frame the plate in your mind's eye and acknowledge the culinary painting before you. Then savor the equally artistic arrangement of the tastes and textures of a luncheon chipotle grilled shrimp; black bean, jicama, and corn salad; and avocado with a lime-mojo vinaigrette, for instance. From the dinner menu select something more exotic such as the Sous Vide Venison Loin or Lemon Thyme Seared Tofu. Or, as the menu suggests, get blitzed—with their Get Blitzed Tasting Menu, that is. A lovely selection of cheeses, wines, and desserts rounds out the meal.

Mis en Place, a Golden Spoon Hall of Fame establishment, is open for lunch Tuesday through Friday from 11:30 a.m. to 2:30 p.m., and reopens for dinner at 5:30 p.m., closing at 10 p.m. On Saturday, the restaurant is open from 5:30 to 11 p.m. The bar opens at 5 p.m. Tuesday through Saturday.

ℹ **Mise en Place's address says W. Kennedy Blvd., but park on the Grand Central Avenue side of the building. Head east on Kennedy from anywhere west of Howard Avenue. Just past N/S Blvd., Kennedy will make a distinct jog to the left. Go straight, and you're on Grand Central Avenue. Mise en Place is in the triangular building between the two roads.**

PELAGIA TRATTORIA $$$
4200 Jim Walter Blvd.
Tampa
(813) 313-3235
www.pelagiatrattoria.com

The classic flavors of Italy and the Mediterranean permeate the menu at Pelagia Trattoria, the restaurant of Executive Chef Fabrizio Schenardi. Located in the Renaissance Tampa Hotel (see Lodging chapter), Pelagia Trattoria offers a mosaic of dishes taking diners from *Stuzzichini,* teasers such as Manchego Cheese with Honey Comb, to *La Fine,* desserts such as a Walnut Crème Brûlée with Nocello. The rest of the menu is equally classic and creative. A "Fabrizio favorite"—there are many on the menu—is the Double Lamb Chops Scottadito Style with Fig Port Sauce and Gnocchi Romana. Seasonal offerings add a touch of mystery to the experience. Pelagia Trattoria offers a full wine and cigar list.

A 2008 Golden Spoon restaurant, Pelagia Trattoria serves lunch, and we've also listed this place under "Breakfasts." Lunch is served every day from 11 a.m. to 3 p.m. and dinner is served nightly from 5:30 to 10 p.m. Seating is both indoors and *al fresco.* Reservations are suggested.

ℹ **Look on Pelagia Trattoria's Web site for a current recipe from Chef Fabrizio Schenardi. Sign up for a quarterly newsletter, and you'll receive more recipes and culinary news.**

RESTAURANT BT $$-$$$
1633 W. Snow Ave.
Tampa
(813) 258-1916
www.restaurantbt.com

Combining a love of Vietnamese and French cuisines inherited from her father, with her own background in the fashion industry, local restaurateur BT has gone from creating lavish dinner parties for friends to operating one of the Tampa Bay area's finest restaurants. Restaurant BT, a 2008 Golden Spoon Restaurant, offers diners two very different taste choices. Go European with the filet mignon served with wild mushrooms, a veal reduction red wine sauce, organic seasonal vegetables, and pommes frites. Or have that same very rare filet mignon diced and tossed in lime juice with chili, ginger, and fresh herbs, and served with crushed peanuts and roasted shallots as Bo Tai Chanh.

Restaurant BT's wine and bar list is quite global—beers from Vietnam, Japan, England, and Germany; wines from Australia, France, and Italy; sake from Japan and California; and martinis with an Asian twist.

Restaurant BT serves lunch from 11:30 a.m. to 2:30 p.m. Monday through Saturday. Dinner is served Monday through Saturday beginning at 5:30 p.m. Last seating is at 9:30 p.m. Monday through Thursday, and at 10:30 p.m. Friday and Saturday. Sunday brunch—the full lunch menu plus breakfast omelets and crêpes—is served from 11 a.m. to 3 p.m. Dinner reservations are suggested. Ask about BT's customized eight-course chef's tasting menu.

RUTH'S CHRIS STEAK HOUSE $$$
1700 N. Westshore Blvd.
Tampa
(813) 282-1118
www.ruthschris.com
Many people consider Ruth's Chris Steak House the authority on preparing perfect steaks and on creating an ambiance worthy of their namesake entrée. The Tampa Ruth's Chris Steak House has upheld that reputation admirably since the mid-1990s. Guests can expect elegant beginnings (the Crabtini lump crab appetizer, for instance, served in a martini glass), magnificent middles (did we mention the sumptuous steaks served sizzling with a touch of butter?), and satisfying endings (bread pudding is anything but blasé at Ruth's Chris Steak House). Meals are under the direction of Chef George Snyder.

Non-beef eaters might try the Ahi Tuna Stack, featuring seared rare tuna and lump crab with a red pepper pesto. Vegetarians are offered a selection of six types of potato dishes and other vegetable creations. Guests will find a nice, not overwhelming, selection of wines and cocktails from which to choose.

Ruth's Chris Steak House also offers private dining experiences for those planning special events. The Tampa Ruth's Chris Steak House opens every day at 5 p.m. and closes at 10 p.m. Monday through Thursday, at 11 p.m. Friday and Saturday, and at 9 p.m. on Sunday. In addition to the usual credit cards, Ruth's Chris Steak House also accepts Diners, Discover, and Carte Blanche. Valet parking is complimentary or self-parking is available behind the restaurant.

THE VIEW AT CK'S $$$
5503 W. Spruce St.
Tampa
(813) 878-6500
www.ckstampa.com
Sitting atop the Tampa Airport Marriott Hotel (see Accommodations chapter), The View at CK's slowly revolves a full 360 degrees, presenting diners with an unparalleled view of the Tampa Bay area. Open for dinner only, guests can watch the sun fade and the lights come on as they linger over their meal.

Prepared under the direction of Chef Debra Desaulniers, each item is presented with an eye toward both the palate and the palette. A full sushi menu includes nigiri, makimono, and itamae selections accompanied by Japanese beer or sake. The dinner menu features a signature all-jumbo lump crab cake appetizer with snow pea pods and drizzled with a key lime mustard sauce, and such creations as Macadamia Grouper (from Florida, see sidebar) served with shrimp, a mango relish piña colada sauce and grilled asparagus, and a Thai Basil Fried Lobster Tail with Asian vegetable slaw and buttermilk mashed potatoes. Their certified Black Angus steaks are specially seasoned, then topped with the View's signature butter and caramelized cipollini onions. There's a lovely dessert selection, as well. Sweet.

The View at CK's is open Tuesday through Thursday from 5 to 9 p.m., and Friday and Saturday from 5 to 10 p.m. They are closed Sunday and Monday. On special holidays (see their Events calendar) the View at CK's offers a buffet brunch from 11 a.m. to 5 p.m. and has a children's buffet brunch menu. The View at CK's also offers such services as roses on the table, pre-selected wine from their extensive list, and other amenities that can be arranged when making dinner reservations. Parking in the Marriott Hotel parking area (go past the long-term and short-term parking) will be validated by the restaurant.

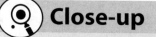

Close-up

Bern's Steak House $$$

Bern Laxer's vision, when he opened his steakhouse in 1956, was to provide Tampa with a dining experience at the level of a work of art. Laxer considered every detail, and Bern's continues his traditions. It isn't enough to buy good vegetables; Bern's grows them on its own organic farm. Bern's hand-sorts and roasts its own coffee. Chefs cut and trim each steak to order. The wine cellar is the largest private collection in the world. Bern's has two in-house cheese caves in which it stores and ages its own cheese.

One does not merely go to Bern's Steak House for dinner. One prepares oneself to participate in a performance—a *pas de deux* of the palate, as it were, between chef and client. One reviews one's calendar and makes an appointment for an evening of fine dining at Bern's. One may wish to consult in advance with one of Bern's three expert sommeliers for assistance in orchestrating, from among the 6,500-label wine collection, just the right accompaniments to the planned evening's several acts. One dons one's evening dress—or, at the least, one exchanges one's beach attire for business casual wear.

Once seated in one of Bern's intimate, lavishly decorated dining parlors, one is presented with the *programme du jour*, an 18-page novelette from which one selects the main characters in the evening's epicurean entertainment. One also reserves a private "wine cask" in the Harry Waugh Dessert Room for postprandial delights.

One orders an appetizer—Oyster Beignets, perhaps, or the Golden Steak Tartare with rye caraway toasts, or one of the 21 varieties of caviar from around the world. Then one settles back and lets the performance unfold—trusting in the talents of Bern's two culinary artisans—Chefs de Cuisine Andy Minne or Habteab Hamde, who come from opposite sides of the world but who are united in their passion to create epicurean adventures for their guests.

At some point in the evening, guests are offered a backstage tour of the kitchen and wine cellar. One accepts, and marvels at the behind-the-scenes meticulous attention to detail in the preparation of each dish Bern's serves.

WATERCOLOUR STEAKHOUSE & GRILLE $$$

Clearwater Beach Marriott Suites on Sand Key
1201 Gulf Blvd.
Clearwater Beach
(727) 953-1661
www.watercolourgrille.com

Special nights out might call for sizzling "Certified Angus Beef" steaks prepared to please the eye and the tongue and served at the Watercolour Steakhouse & Grille overlooking the Clearwater area Intracoastal Waterway. Your server will help you select just the right cut of meat—lamb, pork, and veal choices, too—unless, of course, your tastes run more to, say, a Gulf Grouper Oscar-style with lump crab and hollandaise.

You'll find an extensive wine list and the desserts are works of art in themselves. Let's see—will it be the Decadent Chocolate Ganache Cake or the Watercolour Bread Pudding presented with white chocolate, dried cherries, and a whiskey sauce?

Dinner is served daily from 5 to 10 p.m. Watercolour Steakhouse & Grille is also open for lunch Monday through Friday from 11 a.m. to 2 p.m. and on Saturday and Sunday from noon to 2 p.m. They're open for breakfast, as well, from 6:30 to 11 a.m. Monday through Friday and from 7 a.m. to noon Saturday and Sunday. You'll find live entertainment in the Lounge piano bar during the evenings Wednesday through Sunday.

THE WINE CELLAR RESTAURANT $$–$$$

17307 Gulf Blvd.
North Redington Beach
(727) 393-349
www.thewinecellar.com

After savoring each morsel of one's perfectly cooked Chateubriand with, perhaps, carmelized red onions or roasted garlic, one makes one's way upstairs to the Harry Waugh Dessert Room, named for the author of *Bacchus on the Wing*, who was a wine consultant to Queen Elizabeth II.

Wine, pastry, and cheese or a sweet something and coffee—then the evening ends, the curtain descends, and one carries away the sweet memory of a rare encounter, a magnificent meal.

A Golden Spoon Hall of Fame establishment, Bern's today is owned by David Laxer, Bern's son, who also owns SideBern's, a sleekly modern, award-winning restaurant featuring modern Mediterranean cuisine prepared by Executive Chef Chad Johnson and Chef de Cuisine Courtney Orwig.

Bern's Fine Wines and Spirits sells wines, cordials, coffees, and spirits. Bern's hosts a four-day Winefest each April that includes seminars, soirees, tastings, and dinners.

Bern's Steak House is open from 5 to 10 p.m. Sunday through Thursday and from 5 to 11 p.m. on Friday and Saturday. Bern's is closed on Christmas Day and Labor Day, and may be closed on other holidays. Bern's advises making reservations at least two weeks in advance during October through March. Online reservations must be confirmed.

SideBern's is open Monday through Thursday from 6 to 10 p.m. and Friday and Saturday from 6 to 11 p.m. with lounge menu items available until midnight. SideBern's occasionally holds private events when it is closed to the public.

Bern's Steak House
1208 S. Howard Ave.
Tampa
(813) 251-2421
www.bernssteakhouse.com

SideBern's
2208 W. Morrison Ave.
Tampa
(813) 258-2233
www.sideberns.com

A member of the *Chaîne des Rôtisseurs,* an international gastronomic guild, the Wine Cellar has been bringing European-style fine dining to the Tampa Bay area since 1975. From the beef Wellington to the rack of lamb carved tableside to the Jumbo Gulf Shrimp "In the Robe"—served in a puff pastry with a number of other surprises—the menu offers classic Continental cuisine. It goes without saying that the Wine Cellar's wine cellar is stocked with the finest wines from around the world.

The Wine Cellar also offers a children's menu of familiar favorites—corn dogs and french fries, no less!—to allow families to introduce their youngsters to fine dining experiences without forcing unfamiliar flavors. The Wine Cellar serves dinner Tuesday through Saturday from 4:30 p.m. to "late," and Sunday from 4 to 10 p.m. They offer a special dinner for early guests until 6 p.m. Tuesday through Sunday. On Monday, the Wine Cellar serves a Continental Buffet (only) from 5 to 9 p.m., consisting of an assortment of side dishes, salads, seafood dishes, Design-Your-Own-Pasta Extravaganza, two chef-carved meat selections, and desserts.

The Wine Cellar also offers catered meals and private banquets, including certified Kosher catering.

SEAFOOD

CRABBY BILL'S $$
401 Gulf Blvd.
Indian Rocks Beach
(727) 595-4825
www.crabbybills.com

The Web site picture of Bill and Delores Loder shows a smiling guy who looks anything but crabby. The Loders came here from New Jersey, took their love of fishing, clamming, and crabbing—and then cooking it all up into a seafood feast—and shared it with the public in a couple of different restaurants they started. But the one they opened in Indian Rocks Beach in 1983 as Crabby Bill's is the one that took off and became a bit of a seafood icon in the Tampa Bay area. The restaurant grew until today there are several Crabby Bill's in the area and as far away as Kissimmee near Orlando.

Today, the original Indian Rocks Beach restaurant—open 7 a.m. to 2 a.m. seven days a week—is still family owned and operated, with son Matt Loder now in charge. Some of the other restaurants are franchises, but the Loder family still oversees them all. They've also branched out a bit with an IRB Sushi next door to the original restaurant and the Loading Dock bar nearby as well.

Crabby Bill's serves five different types of crabs as well as the usual assortment of scallops, shrimp, oysters, lobster, and fish. Or go for their fried frog legs or St. Louis–style ribs. They also have a sandwich menu featuring grouper sandwiches, crab cake sandwiches, burgers, a children's menu and early-bird dinners served until 6 p.m.

Other Crabby locations include:
- Clearwater Beach: 37 Causeway Blvd., (727) 210-1313. Opens every day at 11 a.m.; closes Sunday through Thursday at 10 p.m., Friday and Saturday at 11 p.m.
- Clearwater Beach: 333 S. Gulfview Blvd., (727) 608-2065. Open every day from 11 a.m. to 2 a.m.
- St. Pete Beach: 5100 Gulf Blvd., (727) 360-8858. Opens every day at 11 a.m.; closes Sunday through Thursday at 10 p.m., Friday and Saturday at 11 p.m.
- Tampa: 7700 W. Courtney Campbell Causeway, (813) 281-0566. Open every day from 6:30 a.m. to 3 a.m.
- Tarpon Springs: 900 Pinellas Ave., (727) 934-7484. Opens every day at 11 a.m.; closes Sunday through Thursday at 10 p.m., Friday and Saturday at 11 p.m.

FOURTH STREET SHRIMP STORE $$
1006 4th St. N.
St. Petersburg
(727) 822-0325
www.theshrimpstore.com

Once upon a time in 1928, this building used to be a service station for Model T Fords. Then it got turned into a laundry/seafood market that became a restaurant. Before long, the laundry was gone to make room for the people wanting shrimp boiled, broiled, fried, sautéed, or added to pasta and other dishes. The market is still there, however—right up front, and it does a good bit of business.

The Fourth Street Shrimp Store's straightforward menu offers shrimp (you were expecting caribou?), a selection of other shellfish and seafood, burgers, salads, and sandwiches. A full bar is available, as are kids' menus and an early-bird menu (no orders after 6 p.m.). Feast your eyes on the hodgepodge of items hung from the ceiling or tacked to the wall—old signs, fishing floats, a canoe—while you wait for the smoked-fish spread appetizer served with saltines or a pound of you-peel-'em boiled shrimp. The Shrimp Store opens at 11 a.m. each day, and closes early (8:30 p.m. Sunday and Monday, 9 p.m. Tuesday through Saturday), so plan accordingly.

THE HURRICANE $–$$$
807 Gulf Way
St. Pete Beach
(727) 360-9558
www.thehurricane.com

Drive to the southern tip of the barrier islands that hug Pinellas County, and there you'll find the Hurricane with its unmatched, unobstructed, mesmerizing view of the Gulf that soothes the stress right out of you. Plus you get to eat, and eat good. Yes, there are a couple of steaks on the menu and you can even get a hot dog—if you must. But you came to Florida for seafood, didn't you? So start with the Pearls in a Blanket (scallops, water chestnuts, and pea pods wrapped in bacon and grilled or fried) or nicely spiced peel-and-eat shrimp. Then try the succulent stone crab dinner (October 15 through May 15 only) or the grouper cooked

What's Up with Florida Grouper?

A couple of years ago, the *St. Petersburg Times* discovered that some of the fish being sold in restaurants as Florida grouper wasn't really grouper and it wasn't really from Florida. In many cases, restaurants said they thought they were buying and paying for grouper. Suppliers said they thought they were selling grouper. It turned out that much of the fish was actually tilapia, catfish, hake, or Alaskan pollack caught in other places around the world.

Part of the problem developed because the number of grouper in Florida waters had decreased.

Grouper was "the" fish restaurants built their reputations on. As the population in this area grew, the demand for grouper grew. Fishermen found ways to catch more and more grouper. Before long, there weren't many grouper left. For several months in 2004 and 2005, fishing for grouper was banned to allow the fish populations to replenish.

Restaurants, however, didn't change their menus. Until, that is, the *Times* pointed out that much of what they were selling wasn't Florida grouper. Some restaurants dropped grouper altogether from their menus. Others changed their menus to read "grouper" rather than "Florida grouper." Still others became more conscious about what they were purchasing.

Florida's attorney general at the time, now Governor Charlie Crist, investigated. But it was difficult to prove intentional fraud on anyone's part. There are as many as 300 different species of grouper around the world, for one thing. But not all have been DNA tagged, so not all fish fillets can be identified as one kind of fish or another.

Another problem was that many kinds of fish swim together and get caught by the same fishnets. More than one kind of fish may be processed in one batch—and that batch may weigh as much as 50,000 pounds.

In 2008, the state dropped its case against the one supplier investigated when the supplier agreed to pay investigative costs and to donate $100,000 worth of food to a soup kitchen.

Florida's Department of Agriculture and Consumer Services' Web site says the following about grouper sold in restaurants:

"When purchasing grouper, look for a label on the menu or at the store. If the grouper bears the "Fresh from Florida" logo, it is required by law that the grouper be from Florida. (Grouper from another country can be labeled as "grouper" but not as "Florida grouper.")

Deal with merchants that you trust. There are many markets and restaurants in Florida that pride themselves on serving Florida seafood.

your favorite way. Want just a sandwich? Go for the grouper—deep-fried, char-grilled, blackened, jerked, or broiled in a butter sauce—or the crab melt on focaccia bread. The imaginative specialty drink menu features everything from a traditional margarita to frozen treats like the Sandy Banana to after-dinner coffees like the Nutty Irishman—but check the prices before you order.

The Hurricane opens at 10:30 a.m. The lower level dining area operates on beach time and closes between 9 and 10 p.m. or maybe as late as 11 p.m. on the weekends. The upper level dining area closes at midnight.

SOUL FOOD

JOSEPHINE'S AUTHENTIC SOUL FOOD RESTAURANT $
20729 Center Oak Dr.
Tampa
(813) 929-6767
www.josephinessoulfood.com
Sit down and set a spell. Think about what food was like when you were growing up. Owners Tony and Lisa Herlong remember, 'cause Mama Josephine Herlong fed her eight children and a host of others and taught them well. Now they have recreated many of Mama's recipes for us to enjoy. Choose your meat—chicken cooked four ways, smothered pork chops, catfish, meatloaf, pot roast, neck bones, ribs—and choose your sides—collard greens, black-eyed peas, candied yams, macaroni 'n' cheese—and sit back and savor. Breakfast is served, too, all day if you want. Choose from eggs and bacon, pancakes or waffles, or catfish-n-grits. Wash it down with Jo's Special Punch, or sweet tea, soda, plain tea, juice, or milk. Save room for dessert? Good. 'Cause there's sweet potato pie, fruit cobblers, cake, and other treats.

Josephine's Authentic Soul Food is open Tuesday through Friday from 10 a.m. to 8 p.m., Saturday from 8 a.m. to 8 p.m., and Sunday from noon to 6 p.m. They close on major holidays, but they also do catering. Check their Web site for specials and coupons.

The Price You Pay for Grouper

Be wary of grouper prices that are suspiciously low. Because the supply of Florida grouper is limited, the price is generally around $11 to $13 per pound for wholesale filet, and the retail value—the price paid by consumers—will be even higher. Prices that are considerably lower likely mean that the fish is not grouper, but instead is a substitute species of lesser value, such as basa, Asian swai, sutchi, or tra catfish.

Florida seafood industry experts say you should expect to pay the following approximate prices for Florida grouper in restaurants:
High-end, white tablecloth restaurant
Entree: $21 to $27
Sandwich: $13 to $16
Middle-price restaurant
Entree: $16 to $20
Sandwich: $10 to $12
Lower-price restaurant
Entree: $14 to $16
Sandwich: $8 to $10

The full article can be found on the Florida Department of Agriculture and Consumer Services' Web site at www.flseafood.com/consumers/grouper_substitution.htm.

SHIRLEY & LEE'S SOUL FOOD $
1789 34th St. S.
St. Petersburg
(727) 328-9467
Owner Shirley Tigg welcomes you into her place for all those *mmm-mmm* comfort food favorites. Fried chicken, turkey wings, smothered pork chops, chitlins on Saturdays, oxtails on Sundays. Served with sides like collard greens, candied

yams, mac 'n' cheese, black-eyed peas, okra and tomatoes, corn, cornbread, and yellow or white rice. Clean your plate and there's peach cobbler or banana pudding. Homemade lemonade and other beverages help quench your thirst. Breakfast includes the usual eggs and bacon or sausage and grits. But try the salmon patties or corned beef hash.

Shirley & Lee's Soul Food is open Tuesday through Sunday from 7 to 10 a.m. for breakfast and from 11:45 a.m. to 4 p.m. for lunch.

TACOS AND MORE

CARMELITA'S MEXICAN RESTAURANT $$
5211 Park St. N.
St. Petersburg
(727) 545-2956
www.carmelitas.net

This is the original Carmelita's, opened in 1983 by the Lopez family. Serving family-recipe dishes including chiles relleno, Del Ray burrito, and carne asada, Carmelita's developed a following that allowed it to expand in many ways. Today, there are five Carmelita's—four in Pinellas County and one in Pasco County. The menu has grown, too, to accommodate families with bilingual tastes. While part of the family enjoys enchiladas banderas, another part of the family can go for a burger and fries. Two of the stores serve breakfast on Sunday—dishes like chorizo potatoes or huevos rancheros and also like eggs, bacon, and pancakes. There's a children's menu and a full bar.

The original restaurant, listed above, is open from 11 a.m. to 9:30 p.m. Sunday through Thursday, from 11 a.m. to 10 p.m. Friday and Saturday. Breakfast on Sunday is served from 8 a.m. to 2:30 p.m. Space is limited at this location—call ahead for reservations if your party is six or larger. Other locations are:

- Clearwater: 5042 E. Bay Dr., (727) 524-8226. Opens at 11 a.m. every day. Closes at 9:30 p.m. Sunday through Thursday and at 10 p.m. Friday and Saturday.
- Largo: 7705 Ulmerton Rd., (727) 533-8555. Opens Monday through Saturday at 11 a.m. and at 9 a.m. on Sunday. Closes at 9 p.m. Sun-

day through Thursday and at 9:30 p.m. Friday and Saturday. Serves breakfast on Sunday from 9 a.m. to 1 p.m.
- Pinellas Park: 6218 66th St. N., (727) 545-8226. Opens at 11 a.m. Monday through Saturday and at 9 a.m. on Sunday. Closes at 9:30 p.m. Sunday through Thursday and at 10 p.m. Friday and Saturday. Serves breakfast on Sunday from 9 a.m. to noon.

DON PANCHO VILLA RESTAURANT & MARKET $-$$
2551 Drew St.
Clearwater
(727) 799-0253

4010 N. Armenia Ave.
Tampa
(813) 872-6387

Don Pancho Villa's started as a Mexican grocery store that cooked really good food and served it between the stalks of sugarcane and the stacks of tortillas. Eventually, they added booths—and then they outgrew that. Now the Clearwater restaurant and market are across the street from each other. This is the real deal where the *sopa de mariscos* (seafood soup) has whole mussels, crab claws, and shrimp, and your choices of meat for your tacos includes—in addition to the familiar *pollo* (chicken), *bistec* (steak), and *carnitas* (shredded pork)—*chorizo* (sausage), *barbacoa* (lamb), *cabeza* (beef head), *lengua* (beef tongue), and *cueritos* (fried pork skin), and they're served with chopped onions, cilantro, and lime. The Clearwater market is across the street at 21563 U.S. Hwy 19 N., (727) 799-0453, and they're open every day from 9 a.m. to 10 p.m.

MEMA'S ALASKAN TACOS $-$$
1724 E. 8th Ave.
Ybor City
(813) 242-TACO (8226)

Alaskan tacos in a town built on Cuban cigars? You'd better believe it. The food is wrapped in tortillas and, yes, the standard toppings are there. But the fillings are way more than your standard ground beef or chicken—although those are on the menu, too—and the secret, apparently, lies in cooking the meat and shell together. Try a gator, salmon, shrimp, or tofu Alaskan taco. Refried black beans are made from scratch. Vegetarians will find meatless tamales, chimichangas, and quesadillas. Wash it all down with beer, soda, energy drinks, or vitamin water.

Mema's opens at 11 a.m. each day and stays open until 1 a.m. Sunday through Wednesday and until 3 a.m. Thursday through Saturday for the after-party crowd. Counter service only. Limited seating inside and out.

RED MESA RESTAURANT
4912 4th St. N.
St. Petersburg 33703
(727) 527-8728

RED MESA CANTINA
128 3rd St. S.
St. Petersburg
(727) 510-0034
www.redmesarestaurant.com

The Red Mesa offers Mexican food as most of us have probably never had it—upscale, with an emphasis on seafood, and served with an occasional twist of the Far East. You can order tacos and quesadillas if you must—and they'll be *muy bueno*—but why not be a bit more adventuresome? Go for the Fried Oysters Chipotle or the Southwestern Tuna Sashimi, a daring fusion of East meets West tastes. Or try the *Corazon con Café*—espresso-encrusted filet mignon with chipotle chili mashed potatoes—if you happen to come on an evening when it's on the specials list. Desserts, too, are not your everyday fried ice cream and sopapillas. Think Guava Empanada or Plantains Foster.

The Red Mesa serves lunch Monday through Saturday from 11 a.m. to 4 p.m. Dinner is served from 4 to 9:30 p.m. Monday through Thursday and from 4 to 10:30 p.m. Friday and Saturday. On Sunday, breakfast is served from 9 a.m. to 2 p.m. and dinner is served from 2 to 9 p.m. A sunset *prix fixe* menu is available Monday through Friday from 4 to 5:45 p.m. Red Mesa Cantina serves many of the same dishes, has two bars, and is open for the late-night crowd.

NIGHTLIFE

When the sun goes down over the Gulf of Mexico, we're not quite ready to tuck ourselves in for the night and call it a day. Instead, you might find us shimmying and shaking to a Latin salsa or doin' some boot-scootin' two-steppin' at one of the area's dance clubs.

Others of us cheer on our favorite teams at a local sports bar or rack the balls and chalk up a cue for a friendly game of billiards. Still others prefer the uptown sophistication of places like the Blue Martini or the old-world atmosphere they find at Four Green Fields, an Irish pub with an authentic thatched roof.

And sometimes we head to one of many hangouts on the water just to escape four walls and air conditioning. Frenchy's Rockaway Grill on Clearwater Beach and the Hula Bay Club in Tampa are a couple of spots from which to toast the sunset, but there are others. Lots of others.

The nightspots in Tampa tend to be clustered in particular areas, so we'll give you a run-down on each cluster plus info on a spot or two in each area that seems unique. Pinellas nightspots are spread out a bit more.

Sometimes we just want to take in a movie, so we've listed the major movie complexes here, too. There's also a listing of Irish pubs, with a brief note about their St. Patrick's Day activities.

Don't forget to check the Arts chapter for live-performance theaters and the Parks and Recreation chapter to find out where to go night fishing. Some of the Annual Events and Festivals have late night activities, so look there, too.

Some places have cover charges—an entrance fee you pay just to get in and enjoy the music—some places don't, and some places it depends on who's playing. Call ahead or check the Web site to be sure before you go.

The legal drinking age is 21 in Florida, and many places won't allow anyone younger inside. There are a few places open to all ages until evening, at which time they are adults-only places. Pinellas County bars close at 2 a.m., while Hillsborough County bars close at 3 a.m.

Be careful where you park. If it's posted "Residents Only" or "No Parking," they mean it. Tow trucks make money every weekend because some people don't take the signs seriously.

Finally, this is a family guide, so we've tried to be circumspect. For a less inhibited view of Tampa Bay's nightlife, check out *Wingman: The Guy's Guide to Tampa Bay* (http://blogs.tampa bay.com/wingman), which is published by *tbt* Tampa Bay Today* (see Media chapter)—the tabs are "Gawk," "Gulp," "Brag," "Gamble," and "Recover." TBO.com's "Nightlife" tab is another source of information, which includes a calendar of events (www.tboextra.com/nightlife).

ℹ️ Drinking responsibly doesn't just mean having a designated driver or staying away from the wheel of a car. Drinking and boating or jet-skiing is just as dangerous. And any time your judgment is impaired you want to be sure you are with people you can trust not to take advantage of you.

HOT SPOTS

Tampa/Hillsborough County

BAYSTREET AT INTERNATIONAL PLAZA
2223 N. West Shore Blvd., #2000
Tampa
(813) 342-3790
www.shopinternationalplaza.com

Located near Tampa International Airport, the open-air Baystreet stays open long after the indoor mall, International Plaza, closes. Here you'll find the Blue Martini,The Grape, and several other upscale restaurants and nightspots.

CENTRO YBOR
1600 East 8th Ave.
Tampa
(813) 242-4660
www.centroybor.com
Ybor City's nightlife grew out of the social and dance clubs the cigar workers created for their after-work enjoyment. Today, Centro Ybor is home to the Improv Comedy Theater, Game-Works, Tampa Bay Brewing Company, Muvico Theaters, and other eat-drink-and-make-merry venues. Nor are the nightspots confined to Centro Ybor. Gaspar's Grotto, the Green Iguana, and other places are within walking distance. The GAYbor area includes several gay-friendly spots.

CHANNELSIDE BAY PLAZA/TAMPA RIVERWALK
615 Channelside Dr., Ste. 117
Tampa
(813) 223-425
www.channelsidebayplaza.com
Located on the water near the Port of Tampa, Channelside Bay Plaza has a Muvico IMAX theater, and several restaurants and nightspots including Splittsville, Stumps Supper Club, and Howl at the Moon. The Tampa Riverwalk, currently stretching from USF Park on the Riverwalk—near the Tampa Bay Convention Center—to Cotanchobee/Fort Brooke Park—just past the Marriott Waterside Hotel & Marina—will soon extend to Channelside Bay Plaza. Future plans call for the Riverwalk to run from The Heights, a residential area, to where the cruise ships dock at the Port of Tampa.

SOHO TAMPA
South Howard Avenue
Tampa
http://sohoonthestreet.blogspot.com
This area includes Old Hyde Park Village and is where you'll find Bern's Steak House, St. Bart's

Island House and Rhum Bar, and Ceviche Tapas Bar and Restaurant, as well as others. The blog link above is fairly new, and is posted by a local publication called *South Tampa Community News* (www.southtampatoday.com), owned by Tampa Marketing Company. Or check the South Howard Chamber of Commerce's (www.southtampa chamber.org) listing of restaurants and clubs for more places to visit.

> **i** Beat Generation writer Jack Kerouac's ghost is said to haunt the bars of St. Petersburg. Interestingly, Kerouac, author of *On the Road*, learned English as a second language. His first language, the language of his parents, was Quebec French.

St. Petersburg/South Pinellas
DOWNTOWN ST. PETERSBURG
www.discoverdowntown.com
Downtown St. Petersburg's offers a wide variety of nightlife within in one spot. Central Avenue between Beach Drive N.E. and about 15th Street or so is lined with cafés, bistros, and taverns. A couple of blocks north, you'll find BayWalk (www.newbaywalk.com), which has a 20-screen Muvico theater complex (see Movies, later in this section). Quiet little spots, like The Rare Olive and Café Alma (listed in the Restaurants and Other Eats chapter), feature a more intimate setting. Then again, there's Jannus Landing, which hosts some fairly upbeat, outdoor concerts, and the Push Ultra Lounge where you can dance, dine, and drink in a former train station. The Mahaffey and the American Stage Theaters (see The Arts chapter) are nearby.

JOHN'S PASS VILLAGE AND BOARDWALK
150 John's Pass Boardwalk
Madeira Beach
(727) 393-8230
www.johnspass.com
Shopping area by day, waterfront hangout by night. Located on the inland Madeira Beach side of John's Pass, this is where fishing boats and dolphin-watch and casino-cruise boats dock. And

Getting Home Safe and Sound

We all know the drill: Drink responsibly. Appoint a designated driver who chooses not to drink at all. Be a real friend: Take the keys from someone who's had too much to drink. Take a cab instead of a chance.

Partiers in the Tampa Bay area get some help with being responsible. To encourage the use of designated drivers, Anheuser-Busch promotes the **Who's Your Bud?** program. The Web site (www.whosyourbud.com) talks about the gift of being the designated non-drinker in the party and even has free thank-you cards friends can e-mail their DD buddies the next day. Some restaurants and bars provide free non-alcoholic beverages and discounts on food to designated drivers.

No designated driver in the group? Pepin Distributing Company, which serves Hillsborough County and other parts of the state, underwrites **free cab rides home** from United Cab and a free ride back to your car the next day. Look for the Alert Cab logo posted in Hillsborough County establishments, including Raymond James Stadium and the St. Pete Times Forum.

Taking a taxi home is great, unless you've parked in an area that tows cars after the bars close. To solve this problem, all Budweiser distributors in Florida have partnered with AAA Auto Club South provide **Tow to Go**, a free, confidential towing service to your home for several days near major holidays (including Cinco de Mayo and other such non-federal holidays) and every day from Thanksgiving through New Year's Day. Call 800-AAA-HELP (800-222-4357) or go to www.aaasouth.com/acs_new/tow_to_go.asp for a list of days the service is available.

Or you can **Zingo** your way home. Call Zingo Transportation, Inc., at 1-888-946-4611 (www.zingotampa.com) and they send out a fully insured driver to drive you home in your own car. The driver arrives on a De Blasi folding motorbike that gets folded, bagged, and placed in your trunk.

Drivers are available, for a fee, seven nights a week from 9 p.m. to 4 a.m. and are also available by appointment during the day (maybe you're planning on enjoying the bubbly at a champagne brunch or maybe you're having a wisdom tooth pulled and need a ride while you're still groggy). Zingo offers gift cards and memberships, and partners with some events and establishments in the area to provide free services to their patrons.

Think it's too much trouble or you don't want to pay the few bucks to take a cab or a Zingo? Think again. A December 2007 *Tampa Bay Today* article, "The $9,000 Drink," estimated that between lawyer's fees, bail, fines, fees, and increased insurance rates, the average DUI costs the driver $9,000.

And, as Zingo's VP Greg Bradley noted, every time there's a horrific alcohol-related accident, they start getting more calls.

Don't wait to be safe.

when the sun goes down, this is where the beach crowd finds live music and Texas hold-'em fun at places like the Daiquiri Deck and Oceanside Grille, enjoys a quiet glass of wine and a Cuban cigar at the Casa Havana Cigar and Café, or hangs out at the Hut's 70-foot-long waterfront bar to listen to live music or to keep tabs on the game of the week on one of the many TVs scattered around. There are lots of other places to explore here, too.

THE PIER
800 2nd Ave. N.E.
St. Petersburg
(727) 821-6164
www.stpete-pier.com
Captain Al's Waterfront Grill & Bar and an outdoor Tiki Bar are on the main level. The fourth floor houses one of the famous Columbia Restaurants (read about it in the Restaurants chapter), and the fifth floor has an observation area and an indoor Cha Cha Coconuts Tropical Bar and Grill. Enjoy live music and other entertainment and one of the best views—day and night—of St. Petersburg's waterfront.

Clearwater/North Pinellas
CLEARWATER BEACH CHAMBER OF COMMERCE
33 C South Gulfview Blvd.
Clearwater Beach
(727) 447-7600, (888) 799-3199
www.beachchamber.com
Drive over the Memorial Causeway from downtown Clearwater or come north on Gulf Boulevard from any of the other beach areas. When you can't go further, you're in Clearwater Beach. Sunset on Pier 60 (see Attractions chapter) means vendors and street entertainers from balloon artists to musicians. For a bit more elegance, there's Shepard's Wave Night Club. Sports fans can catch the action and enjoy live music at SouthBeach Grill. Or toast the sunset from Frenchy's Rockaway Grill on the Beach—and when they say "on the beach," they mean you can step off of their porch and onto the white sands of Clearwater Beach.

BEACH BARS
The beach bars listed here are just a few of the many places you'll find lining the beaches. Many places are open from the beach, so walk on up if you see a party going on without you. Also, check the resorts and hotels listed in the Accommodations chapter—many have beach bars that are open to the public.

FRENCHY'S ROCKAWAY GRILL
7 Rockaway St.
Clearwater Beach
(727) 446-4844
www.frenchysonline.com
Walk from the white-sand beach to the outdoor patio deck of Frenchy's—or vice versa. There's music and dancing. There's good food—a tropical chicken-and-walnut salad served in a tortilla shell, fajitas, fish tacos, steak—and plenty to drink. But mostly there's the Gulf of Mexico right there in front of you. So put up your feet ,and watch as the sun sinks behind the horizon. Lift your glass in a silent toast to another day done—then join the party.

Frenchy's Rockaway Grill opens every day at 11 a.m. They close at midnight Sunday through Thursday and at 1 a.m. on Friday and Saturday.

HULA BAY CLUB
5210 W. Tyson Ave.
Tampa
(813) 837-4852
www.hulabayclub.com
Dedicated to surfing legend Duke Kahanamoku, who also won Olympic medals in swimming, the Hula Bay Club and Duke's Retired Island Surfers' Bar brings a touch of the Hawaiian tropics to the Caribbean. Eat burgers, fish sandwiches, sushi, and more inside amidst classic island décor, or take your party outside where there's plenty of patio, deck, and poolside space from which to choose. Friday and Saturday nights feature live entertainment. The Hula Bay Club is on Tampa Bay near the Gandy Bridge, making it, too, a perfect place to salute the setting sun with an "Aloha!"

The Hula Bay Club opens each day Tuesday through Sunday at 11 a.m., closes at 10 p.m. Tuesday through Thursday, and closes at midnight on Friday and Saturday.

KA'TIKI SUNSET BEACH
8803 W. Gulf Blvd.
Treasure Island
(727) 360-2272
www.katikisunsetbeach.com
Live bands every night, pool table, multiple TVs so no one misses the big game, and the "no shirt" rule doesn't necessarily apply to the guys here—meaning walk in from the beach and you're dressed just fine. Open Monday through Saturday from 8 a.m. to 2 a.m. and Sunday from 11 a.m. to 2 a.m.

MAHUFFER
19201 Gulf Blvd.
Indian Shores
(727) 596-0226
www.mahuffer.com
"Politically incorrect" may be the most tactful way to describe Mahuffer, which advertises "Warm beer . . . lousy food . . . wurst place on the beach." Regardless, Mahuffer has been around since 1975 when local legend John "Mahuffer" Susor, aka "Sloppy John," began turning his bait shop into a place with, shall we say, character. The food is simple—hot dogs and chips kind of fare—and the beer choices are limited. But there's live music Friday, Saturday, and Sunday from 3 p.m. until the consensus is it's time to call it quits. Sometimes there are open jam sessions. Mahuffer is open every day from 11 a.m. to 2 a.m. Look for the colorfully painted junk car out front on the east side of Gulf Boulevard.

THE UNDERTOW
3850 Gulf Blvd.
St. Pete Beach
(727) 368-9000
www.undertowbeachbar.com
Located next door to the Don CeSar (see Accommodations chapter), the Undertow almost never closes. It's open from 8 a.m. to 2 a.m., so you can get breakfast the morning after or any of 150-plus beers the night before. Or something like that. There's also a full bar, beach volleyball, and music. Food is pizza, wings, burgers, and salads. Parking, however, is limited. No pets. Conditions, says the Web site, are "Righteous."

WHISKEY JOE'S BAR AND GRILL
7720 W. Courtney Campbell Causeway
Tampa
(813) 281-0770
www.whiskeyjoestampa.com
Located right next to Ben T. Davis Beach on the Tampa side of the Courtney Campbell Causeway, Whiskey Joe's offers indoor seating and a waterfront patio just off the beach. TVs are tuned to Rays, Bucs, and Lightning games, there are six live shows a week, and Sunday is Reggae Unleashed day featuring various bands. The menu includes soups and salads, sandwiches, burgers, seafood, and steaks. Whiskey Joe's opens every day at 11 a.m. and closes at 12:30 a.m. Sunday through Thursday and at 1:30 a.m. Friday and Saturday.

BREWERIES & BEER BARS

Check Beer Expedition's Web site at www.beer expedition.com/fl for a listing of Florida breweries, beer laws, beer stores, and more. Beer Me! is another Web site listing breweries around the world (www.beerme.com).

DUNEDIN BREWERY
937 Douglas Ave.
Dunedin
(727) 736-0606
www.dunedinbrewery.com
The Dunedin Brewery does just that—brews its own ales. Ales like Piper's Pale Ale, Apricot Peach Ale, and the darker Beach Tale Brown Ale. Nine of them are brewed year 'round, another five change with the seasons, and occasionally a guest beer fills out a slot. Salads, sandwiches, and wraps are on the menu. Live music, open mike nights, and other entertainment are on the playbill. Tuesday, the Dunedin Brewery is open from 4 p.m. to midnight, Wednesday from 4 p.m. to 1 a.m., Thursday from

noon to 1 a.m., Friday and Saturday from noon to 2 a.m., and Sunday from noon to 10 p.m.

DUNEDIN HOUSE OF BEER
927 A Broadway
Dunedin
(727) 216-6318
www.dunedinhob.com

The names alone are rich with flavor and colorful enough to conjure up enough plot, character, and scenic setting to write their own novels. SmuttyNose Old Brown Dog Ale. SeaDog Blueberry Wheat. Hook and Ladder Golden Ale. HobGoblin Ale. Hofbrau Dunkel. Just reading the list is heady stuff. But most people are going to come here to actually taste what's behind the labels—selections from around the world. So check out their "Events" calendar because they've got tastings listed and brewers coming to talk about their particular process—in between quaffs, of course. Sit inside, or there's a patio out back. Dunedin House of Beer opens Monday through Thursday at 4 p.m., Friday through Sunday at 2 p.m.

TAMPA BAY BREWING COMPANY
1600 E. 8th Ave.
Tampa
(813) 247-1422
www.tampabaybrewingcompany.com

Located in Centro Ybor, Tampa Bay Brewing Company not only brews its own beers and ales, it then cooks with them. Starting with Hummus Dip made with their True Blonde Ale, moving on to Iron Rat Stout Shepherd's Pie, and finishing up with Home Made Jack the Quaffer Bread Pudding, made with porter-soaked cherries. They even use the ale in their pizza dough. Tampa Bay Brewing Company is open from 11 a.m. to 11 p.m. Monday through Thursday, from 11 a.m. to midnight on Friday and Saturday, and from noon to 11 p.m. on Sunday. Indoor and outdoor seating.

WORLD OF BEER
9524 W. Linebaugh Ave.
Tampa
(813) 852-2337
www.worldofbeerusa.com

With more than 500 beers of every type from every part of the world filling coolers and on tap, World of Beer befits its name. Shh—a few wines are listed, too, as are cigars. Watch for cookouts held now and again. World of Beer has both indoor and outdoor seating. Sports fans have TVs to watch and occasionally live music fills the airwaves. World of Beer opens Monday through Friday at 3 p.m. and Saturday and Sunday at noon.

COUNTRY STOMPIN' GROUNDS
THE DALLAS BULL
3322 U.S. 301 N.
Tampa
(813) 987-2855
www.dallasbull.com

Who hasn't watched televised rodeo and wanted—just once—to see what it's like to try for eight seconds on a bucking bull? See for yourself at The Dallas Bull, Tampa's largest nightclub and one of the nation's oldest country music clubs, where the mechanical bull isn't the only attraction. Live concerts with name country artists—think Rascal Flatts, Joe Diffie, and others—line dancing classes, pool tables, a Western wear store, and more bring more than 20,000 visitors to The Dallas Bull each month. The Dallas Bull is open Wednesday through Saturday from 1 p.m. to 3 a.m. Minimum age is 18. Bar 9, located in the back of the Bull, is open Sunday through Tuesday, from 5 p.m. to midnight. Rumor has it Top 40 stuff plays on the second level. Look for the big barn on the east side of Tampa.

STUMPS SUPPER CLUB
615 Channelside Dr.
Tampa
(813) 226-2261
www.stumpssupperclub.com

"Southern cooking and deep-fried dancing" is how Stumps Supper Club puts it. Southern food, it is, with items like Fried Chicken and Waffles, Pulled Pork BBQ, and Gertie's Fruit Cobbler for dessert. Rock Star Friday means live-band karaoke night with singers backed by the Jimmy James Explosion—yes, you may end up on YouTube!—

and Saturday nights feature Jimmy James and the Velvet Explosion house band playing everything from James Brown to ABBA. OK—not strictly country, but the atmosphere counts.

Stumps Supper Club is open Wednesday and Thursday from 4 to 10 p.m., Friday from 4 p.m. to 3 a.m., Saturday from 3 p.m. to 3 a.m., and Sunday from 3 p.m. to 9 p.m. Stumps is closed Monday and Tuesday, plus Thanksgiving, Christmas Eve, and Christmas Day.

DANCE CLUBS

Most of these places suggest you "dress to impress." They want you spiffed up from head to toe, and they insist you put your dancing shoes on and leave other pairs in the closet. Seriously—some places are "no sneakers." Call ahead to be sure.

BLUE MARTINI
2223 N. W. Shore Blvd., #B203
Tampa
(813) 873-BLUE (2583)
www.bluemartinilounge.com
Just the fact that the Blue Martini is located at International Plaza's Bay Street tells you this is not just another bar. Mondays salute hospitality industry workers, Azul Tuesdays feature Latin dance lessons and music, and each of the other days has its own theme, live music, and special offers, too. Three-dozen or so specialty martinis are on the drink list along with wines and champagnes. A dinner menu includes flatbreads, steak, salads, a lobster taco, and desserts, but the focus is definitely on the title drink served in elegant surroundings. The Blue Martini is open Monday through Thursday from 4 p.m. to 3 a.m., Friday and Saturday from 1 p.m. to 3 a.m., and Sunday from noon to 3 a.m.

CLUB PRANA
1619 E. 7th Ave.
Tampa
(813) 241-4139
www.clubprana.com
Five levels of partying and dancing the night away, starting with the Lounge (dance floor in the center and bar area under the mezzanine), the Mezzanine (red velvet seating, small tables, overlooking the dance floor), the Sanctuary (VIP floor for elites—think plush purple floor to ceiling, a 1,000-gallon saltwater aquarium holding exotic fish and sharks—watch them feed!—and plasma screens so you can keep an eye on the dance floor action), the Nightclub (high energy music with a live stage dance show and a glass dance floor with views of the Sanctuary), and—finally—the Sky Bar (a rooftop live band area with two bartending stations where up to 300 people dance and party to hip-hop, reggae, and Latin music.

Club Prana allows patrons ages 18 and up to party, but you have to be 21 or older to drink. Club Prana is open Thursday through Saturday from 9 p.m. to 3 a.m. Make VIP reservations online.

FLOYD'S
Seminole Hard Rock Hotel & Casino
5223 N. Orient Rd.
Tampa
(813) 627-7625, (866) 502-PLAY (7529)
www.seminolehardrocktampa.com
Aside from its upscale glitz and reputation for rockin' music—it is, after all, part of the Hard Rock family—Floyd's other distinction is that the party goes on until 6 a.m. How does that work? The Seminole Tribe has sovereign nation status and can pretty much write its own laws. (See the Spectator Sports chapter for more information about the gambling industry in Florida.) Floyd's serves dinner Wednesday through Sunday from 5 to 10 p.m. and the nightclub is open Thursday through Saturday from 11 p.m. to 6 a.m.

HYDE PARK CAFÉ
1806 W. Platt St.
Tampa
(813) 254-2233
www.thehydeparkcafe.com
Glamour and glitz on Tuesday nights? The Hyde Park Café has become known for its Tuesday night see-and-be-seen parties, as well as for its lineup of DJs, five bars, and three distinct atmo-

spheres. Go for Velociti's disco-ball dance-floor glitter, Wally & Bernie's somewhat quieter tone, or the Café Courtyard's open-air glamour. The Hyde Park Café is open Tuesday, Thursday, Friday, and Saturday from 10 p.m. to 3 a.m. in addition to a full bar, they serve pizza, sandwiches, and small plates. Girls ages eighteen and up and guys ages twenty-one and up are welcome all nights. Thursdays only for guys ages eighteen to twenty.

JACKSON'S BISTRO
601 S. Harbour Island Blvd.
Tampa
(813) 277-0112
www.jacksonsbistro.com

A sophisticated waterfront setting, classy cuisine, professionally produced parties, and top-name talent like Jenny McCarthy, Carmen Electra, and Kim Kardashian, who performed during Super Bowl Week 2009, draw the Tampa Bay area's sophisticated, classy, professional, top-name partiers to Jackson's Bistro. Fantasy Friday's, in particular, are orchestrated events with music and other performers. Saturday Night has a South Beach flavor, and look for themed events throughout the year. Reservations strongly suggested (813-265-1234). Jackson's Bistro serves lunch Monday through Saturday from 11 a.m. to 2:30 p.m. and Sunday brunch from 10:30 a.m. to 2:30 p.m. Dinner is served Sunday through Thursday from 5 to 10 p.m., Friday and Saturday from 5 to 11 p.m. Sushi is served all day. The bar menu is served 2:30 p.m. until closing.

PUSH ULTRA LOUNGE
128 3rd St. S.
St. Petersburg
(727) 871-7874
www.pushlounge.com

Once the McNulty Station firehouse, today the Push Ultra Lounge shares the two-story brick building with the Red Mesa Cantina (see Restaurants and Other Eats chapter). With an indoor dance floor, an outdoor covered patio, and a rooftop deck, Push offers several upscale entertainment and bar choices. Thursday night, for instance, is Latino/International Night with salsa

lessons offered from 9 to 10 p.m. Push Ultra Lounge is open Thursday through Sunday from 8 p.m. until the wee hours.

SHEPHARD'S
619 S. Gulfview Blvd.
Clearwater Beach
(727) 442-5107
www.shephards.com

Shephard's offers three kinds of nightlife experiences. Put on the ritz with a full light-and-sound extravaganza at The Wave, dance to a mix of music from the '70s to today in the Sunset Lounge, or look for reggae and rock in the Tiki Bar. Thursday from 8 to 11 p.m. is Comedy Night at The Wave. Sunday the Tiki Bar boasts the biggest beach party around—not strictly at night, but where else should we list it? The Tiki Bar opens every day at 11 a.m., The Sunset Lounge opens every day at noon, and The Wave is open Friday through Sunday from 9 p.m. to 2 a.m.

THE VENUE
2675 Ulmerton Rd.
St. Petersburg
(727) 571-2222
www.thevenueclub.com

The address says St. Petersburg, but The Venue is up near the St. Petersburg–Clearwater International Airport. The Venue features two restaurants—Takara, a sushi and sake place, and Viaggio, serving an internationally influenced tapas menu—several bar areas, and the more exclusive Club V. Club V, on The Venue's upper level, has a a Champagne Lounge (two bottle minimum, one of which must be from their reserve), a Sky Bar, and other settings. Club V is open Friday and Saturday from 10 p.m. to 2 a.m., and for private receptions at other times. The Venue's restaurants open for lunch at 11 a.m. Monday through Friday, offer a *prie fixe* menu in the early evening, and serve until 11 p.m. on weekdays and until 1 a.m. on weekends. The Martini Bar and Deck Bar are open Monday through Saturday from 4 p.m. to 2 a.m. Usually, there are several choices of live music.

Not Your Mama's Concert Venues

People don't generally think of the concert venues listed here when they think Broadway or classical music. But they draw huge crowds for other kinds of concerts.

Ford Amphitheater
4802 U.S. 301 N.
Tampa
(813) 740-2446
www.livenation.com/venue/ford-amphitheatre-tickets

This open-air facility with covered stage and seating area, plus uncovered open lawn-seating area, hosts performers like Rascal Flatts, Def Leppard, and Crue Fest 2. Shows are rain or shine, and traffic can be an issue.

Jannus Landing
16 2nd St. N.
St. Petersburg
(727) 896-2276
www.jannuslandingconcerts.com

An outdoor courtyard featuring stand-up concerts for the younger crowd. Recent performers at Jannus Landing include Cky, ABSU, and Edwin McCain.

St. Pete Times Forum
401 Channelside Dr.
Tampa
(800) 745-3000
www.sptimesforum.com

Yes, this is where the Tampa Bay Lightning play. But when the Lightning aren't heating up the ice, performers ranging from Miley Cyrus to Judas Priest are heating up the stage.

Sun Dome
4202 E. Fowler Ave.
Tampa
(813) 974-3002
www.gousfbulls.com

Located on the main campus of the University of South Florida, the USF Sun Dome hosts concerts and events of all types—everything from Robin Williams to the Killers, Snoop Dogg to Men at the Cross, Pop Warner Cheer and Dance Competition to WFC Battle of the Bay.

DINNER CRUISES

CALYPSO QUEEN
Clearwater Marina
25 Causeway Blvd., Slip #18
Clearwater Beach
(727) 461-3113
http://calypsoqueen.com

For a more casual dinner cruise, this one aboard a triple-decked, tropical-decked-out ship—think colorful paddlewheel body with a tiki-hut on top—the *Calypso Queen* offers a sunset dinner and tropical party. The dinner buffet includes a variety of entrées, salads, and fruit, along with a cash bar. Party time afterwards features dancing, conga lines, and what-next kind of fun. Thursday evenings, they offer a Gospel Dinner Cruise with live music.

STARLITE CRUISES
Clearwater Marina
25 Causeway Blvd., Slip 58
Clearwater Beach

Corey Causeway
3400 Pasadena Ave. S.
St. Petersburg
(727) 462-2628, (800) 444-4814
www.starlitediningcruises.com

Dine aboard the *StarLite Majesty* dining yacht, sailing out of Clearwater and St. Petersburg, for a truly waterfront meal featuring a choice of entrees and full cash bar. A live band plays dance music after dinner—or lunch, for that matter. The *StarLite Majesty* sails Tuesday through Sunday at 7 p.m., but that's cast-off-the-lines times. You'll want to arrive at least thirty minutes prior so you can check in, be seated, place your order, and get settled. The dining area is elegant, so dress accordingly.

YACHT STARSHIP DINING CRUISES
603 Channelside Dr.
Tampa

Clearwater Marina
25 Causeway Blvd., Slip 55
Clearwater
(813) 223-7999
www.yachtstarship.com

Sailing out of both Tampa and Clearwater, the *Yacht StarShip* offers (seasonal) Sunday brunch cruises, as well as year-round lunch and dinner cruises. Cruise the harbor area of Hillsborough Bay or the Intracoastal Waterway of northern Pinellas County while being served a three-course meal with a choice of several entrées. Afterwards, there's dancing on the lounge deck or the stars up above on the promenade deck. Cash bar. There is a dress code, even for lunch. Check the Web site for details or ask when you call. This is a yacht, after all.

GAMES AND MORE GAMES

Just sitting around yakking—even in a club setting—a bit boring for you? Maybe you'd rather play video arcade games or maybe go for some bowling—in a more adult setting. During the day, kids with an adult are welcomed in these play spots. But at night, each has an age restriction.

GAMEWORKS TAMPA
1600 E. 8th Ave., Space A147
Tampa
(813) 241-9675
www.gameworks.com

Move over, kids! The grownups want to play, too. GameWorks is loaded with all kinds of simulator games in which you steer motorbikes or snowmobiles through an on-screen course and interactive ones in which you try to make your feet match the flashing lights on the floor as the music heats up—plus basketball and skee-ball and a whole lot more. A full-service bar in the center and the Hopscotch Lounge to one side allow for quieter conversation or a game of pool or darts. Jax Grill serves pizza, salads, burgers, and more. Look for specials on the Web site.

Located at 8th Ave. and 17th St. in Ybor City, GameWorks opens at 11 a.m. each day. Adults only (18 and above) after 10 p.m. There is a dress code (check the Web site), so spruce up before you come in.

SPLITSVILLE
615 Channelside Dr., Ste. 120
Tampa
(813) 514-BOWL (2695)
www.splitsvillelanes.com

You can't miss the gigantic ten-pin outside Splitsville at Channelside's Bay Plaza. Walk inside, and you'll wonder why bowling took so long to up its game a notch. Clusters of lanes with billiards tables and cushy booths in between give this bowling bar a classy look. Upscale cuisine (think sushi, edamame, shrimp quesadillas, steak, and more) four bars, music, and a dance floor make this a one-stop night out.

Splitsville opens at 4 p.m. during the week and 11 a.m. Friday through Sunday. Age 21 and above after 8 p.m.

UNITED SKATES OF AMERICA, INC.
5121 N. Armenia Ave.
Tampa
(813) 876-5826
www.usa-skating.com

Want to do some roller-skating without dodging little ones? Thursday from 9 p.m. to midnight is Roller Heat Adult Skate (ages 17 and older only) and Sunday from 9 p.m. to midnight is the Adult Soul Roll (ages 18 and older only). The snack bar is basic pizza, but there's a good-sized arcade game area, the décor is colorful, and they do some neat things with the lighting. Worth looking into when you want to do something a little more casual.

GAY-FRIENDLY BARS

AZALEA LOUNGE
1502 N. Florida Ave.
Tampa
(813) 228-0139
www.myspace.com/azalealounge
Karaoke three nights a week, DJ-led music other nights, pool tables, darts, and there's an outdoor patio area. The Azalea Lounge is open every day from 3 p.m. to 3 a.m.

CHIQ BAR
4900 66th St. N.
St. Petersburg
(727) 546-7274
www.clubzone.com/c/Saint_Petersburg/
Gay_Club/ChiQ_Bar.html
Lesbian bar featuring karaoke, drag king shows, beer pong, dancers, game room, live music and dancing—or head to the patio where there's a fire pit. ChiQ Bar is open Tuesday through Sunday from 4 p.m. to 2 a.m.

G.BAR
1401 E. 7th Ave.
Ybor City
www.gbartampabay.com
Colorful lights, lots of glitz, amateur strip nights, live music, themed events, male revue show, and they claim to host central Florida's largest lesbian party every Friday. G.Bar is open Tuesday through Sunday from 9 p.m. to 3 a.m. Wednesday is generally reserved for private events.

GEORGIE'S ALIBI
3100 3rd Ave. N.
St. Petersburg
(727) 321-2112
www.georgiesalibi.com/stpeteevents.aspx
Part sports bar—pool tables and thirty-one flatscreen sets tuned to Rays games, college games, and other sports events. Part dance club—drag contests, strip contests, dancers, music. Food options include salads and appetizers, hot and cold sandwiches, burgers, etc. Patio bar outside for smokers. Open every day 11 a.m. to 2 a.m.

IRISH PUBS

Come March 17, ye might be wantin' t' raise a wee glass t' the Emerald Isle. Or maybe more than just a wee glass. Either way, here's one place to start making your St. Patrick's Day plans or to enjoy the flavor of Ireland all year long. For more family-oriented St. Patrick's Day celebrations, see the Annual Events and Festivals chapter.

Tampa/Hillsborough County

DUBLINER IRISH PUB
2307 West Azeele St.
Tampa
(813) 258-2257

12836 Henderson Rd.
Tampa
(813) 300-2076
www.thedublineririshpub.com
The original Dubliner on West Azeele Street has often been voted among the top three Irish pubs in the area. Four full bars, including a tiki bar (in an Irish pub?), serve up the brews, and the décor adds all the Irish flavor a leprechaun could wish for. The newer Henderson Road Dubliner has a full liquor license.

FOUR GREEN FIELDS
205 W. Platt St.
Tampa
(813) 254-4444
www.fourgreenfields.com
Traditional Irish musicians perform each weekend at Four Green Fields, a cottage-like Irish pub boasting an authentic thatched roof and staff who really are Irish. Four Green Fields is also among the top three Irish pubs in the area. Did we mention it's probably also the most authentically Irish?

MACDINTON'S
405 Howard Ave. S.
Tampa
(813) 251-8999
www.macdintons.com
MacDinton's rivalry with the Dubliner and Four Green Fields has made for many a friendly debate.

MacDinton's serves hard liquor in addition to 18 brews on tap and tends to attract a younger crowd. Maybe that's because of the stage area and dance floor or the five full bars plus a tiki bar (What is it with tiki bars in Irish pubs?).

O'BRIEN'S IRISH PUBS AND RESTAURANT

701 W. Lumsden Rd.
Brandon
(813) 661-9688

1701 South Alexander St.
Plant City
(813) 764-8818

11744 N. Dale Mabry
Tampa
(813) 961-4092
www.obrienspub.com

In addition to serving up lunch, dinner, brews, and blarney each day, O'Brien's sponsors a number of fishing events in the area. Go to their Web site and click on the link "O'Brien's Fishing Club" to learn about tournaments and fun fishing festivities. But this is the Nightlife chapter, so we should mention they also have live entertainment, trivia contests, karaoke, and other events most nights.

WHITEY'S FOX & HOUNDS IRISH PUB

229 E. Brandon Blvd.
Brandon
(813) 685-8151
www.whiteysfoxandhounds.com

Look for Brandon Area Darts Association events held here throughout the year and a day-long party on St. Patrick's Day.

Pinellas County

COURIGAN'S IRISH PUB

1 Beach Dr.
St. Petersburg
(727) 551-9019

Get to Courigan's early—they close at 10 p.m.—to enjoy an uptown flavor of Ireland in downtown St. Petersburg. You'll find a full bar and live music in addition to Irish food and fun.

FLANAGAN'S IRISH PUB

465 Main St.
Dunedin
(727) 736-4994
www.flanagansirishpub.net

Every day is St. Patrick's Day at Flanagan's Irish Pub—according to Flanagan's, that is. And when March 17 rolls around for real, Flanagan's really lets loose (see Annual Events and Festivals). The rest of the year, you'll find traditional Irish entertainment and an "Auld Country Traditions" section on their menu, which includes Bangers and Mash, Irish stew, and other good grub. Flanagan's is closed on Mondays.

O'KEEFE'S FAMILY TAVERN AND GRILLE

1219 S. Fort Harrison Ave.
Clearwater
(727) 442-9034
www.okeefestavernonline.com

O'Keefe's claims to be home to Florida's biggest and best St. Patrick's Day celebration ($5 cover charge). The rest of the year, you'll find a St. Patty'O party every first Thursday of the month, live entertainment, and the ubiquitous tiki bar with tropical sunset specials on Fridays and Saturdays. The outside dining area is pet-friendly.

TOMMY DUFF'S IRISH AVIATION PUB

126 Island Way
Clearwater
(727) 449-1366
www.tommyduffs.com

Tommy Duff's claims the world's shortest St. Patrick's Day parade—a costumed pub crawl from Tommy Duff's to another nearby non-Irish bar and back. The rest of the year, Tommy Duff's is known for its aviation themed décor—model airplanes dangle from the ceiling and photos from every era of flying history plaster the walls.

MOVIE THEATERS

AMC Theaters

(888)AMC-4FUN (262-4386) (showtimes)
www.amctheatres.com

REGENCY (SQUARE MALL) 20
2496 W. Brandon Blvd.
Brandon
(813) 685-3396

TRI-CITY PLAZA 8
5140 East Bay Dr.
Clearwater
(727) 531-5796

VETERANS 24 & IMAX
9302 Anderson Rd.
Tampa
(813) 243-4881

WESTSHORE PLAZA 14
210 Westshore Plaza
Tampa
(813) 637-8225

WOODLANDS SQUARE 20
3128 Tampa Rd.
Oldsmar
(727) 771-6643

Drive-In Theaters

FUN-LAN DRIVE IN
2302 E. Hillsborough Ave.
Tampa
(813) 234-2311
www.fun-lan.com

RUSKIN FAMILY DRIVE-IN THEATRE
5011 U.S. 41 N.
Ruskin
(813) 645-1455
www.ruskinfamilydrivein.com

Independent Theaters

THE BEACH THEATRE
315 Corey Ave.
St. Pete Beach
(727) 360-6697
www.beachtheatre.com
The Beach Theatre offers both first-run and classic movies, as well as free kids' matinees on Saturday

mornings. (*Rocky Horror Picture Show* fans, see the Arts chapter.)

CHANNELSIDE CINEMAS 9 AND IMAX
615 Channelside Dr.
Tampa
(813) 221-0700
www.channelsideimax.com

CLEARWATER CINEMA CAFÉ
24095 U.S. 19 N.
Clearwater
(727) 799-3531 (showtimes)
(727) 797-9808 (information)
www.clearwatercinemacafe.com
This theater features a full dinner menu, full bar menu, and two screens.

TAMPA PITCHER SHOW
14416 N. Dale Mabry Hwy
Tampa
(813) 963-0578
www.tampapitchershow.net
In addition to movies, you'll find a full dinner menu and a lounge area with bar and live music on Fridays and Saturdays.

TAMPA THEATRE
711 N. Franklin St.
Tampa
(813) 274-8981
www.tampatheatre.org
Classic movies in an historic theater—go early to marvel at the architecture and ornamentation. See the Arts chapter for more information about the theater and its offerings.

Muvico Theaters
www.muvico.com

BAYWALK 20 AND IMAX
151 2nd Ave. N.
St. Petersburg
(727) 502-0965
A supervised children's playroom is available for children ages three and up.

CENTRO YBOR PREMIER (AGES 21 AND OVER, ALCOHOL SERVED)

CENTRO YBOR 20 (GENERAL SEATING)
1600 E. 8th Ave.
Tampa
(813) 242-0664

PALM HARBOR 10
37912 U.S. 19 N.
Palm Harbor
(727) 944-2282

STARLIGHT 20
18002 Highwood Preserve Parkway
Tampa
(813) 558-9745
A supervised children's playroom is available for children ages three and up.

Regal Theaters
www.regmovies.com

CITRUS PARK STADIUM 20
7999 Citrus Park Town Center Mall
Tampa
(813) 920-9471

LARGO MALL 8
10500 Ulmerton Rd. E.
Largo
(727) 581-7389

PARK PLACE STADIUM 16
7200 U.S. Hwy 19 N.
Pinellas Park
(727) 527-1930

UNIVERSITY 16
12332 University Mall Court
Tampa
(813) 975-0361

NOT YOUR ORDINARY SPOT

THE CASTLE (GOTH CLUB)
2004 N. 16th St.
Ybor City 33605
(813) 247-7547
www.castleybor.com
We're not talking Cinderella's castle here. This is more like a glammed up Wicked Witch of the West's lair. From the lavishly lit Main Hall to the Dungeon—our family-friendly constrictions won't let us go there—The Castle features dark-side music and parties. The Castle is open Thursday through Monday from 10:30 p.m. to 3 a.m.

CHIC-A-BOOM ROOM / THE BLUR
319-325 Main St.
Dunedin 34698
(727) 736-5284
www.kellyschicaboom.com
Artsy décor and not terribly fancy might describe Dunedin's best-known martini bar. Aside from their two dozen creatively named martinis with equally creative ingredients (think a Chica-Mocha-Lattetini with Stoli Vanil, White and Dark Starbucks Liquer, espresso, and caramel—Whatever happened to gin and vermouth?), the Chic-a-Boom Room also has more than eighty brands of bottled beer and an extensive wine list. Next door, The Blur features live music and other entertainment including Drag Queen Bingo, female impersonators, and karaoke. The Chic-a-Boom Room is open every day from 11 a.m. to 2 a.m. The Blur is open Tuesday through Saturday from 8 p.m. to 2 a.m.

CZAR
1402 E. 7th Ave.
Ybor City 33605
(813) 247-6838
www.myspace.com/czarvodkabar
The "vodka bar" part of the Web name ought to clue you as to what you'll find at Czar. Gotta love the name of one dance spot—Cyberia features electro, funk, and indie remixes. Plus Czar hosts live concerts and various parties (www.pulp theparty.com).

GASPAR'S GROTTO
1805 E. 7th St.
Ybor City 33605
(813) 248-5900

Couldn't get to Tampa for the Gasparilla Pirate Fest in January? Not to worry—you can get a taste of what you missed all year long at Gaspar's Grotto. Pirate-y décor and costumed serving wenches, video games and live music—what more could a brigand desire? Well, how about special Pets on the Patio parties the first Saturday of each month, a full lunch and dinner menu, and a kids menu. Gaspar's Grotto is open every day from 11:30 a.m. to 3 a.m.

ST. PETERSBURG NIGHTS
6800 Sunset Way
St. Pete Beach 33706
(727) 644-4839
www.stpetersburgnights.com

This Russian restaurant and bar features DJ'd music, live belly dancing, and magic shows. Some shows are dinner-theater style, including a Russian Accents variety show. Other times order from the menu and watch Russian videos (with subtitles), and enjoy Herring Napoleon, Ukranian Borscht, Chicken Kiev, Fried Pirogues, and other traditional Russian foods. Saturday nights, the Sunset Hookah Lounge on the beach offers water pipes. St. Petersburg Nights opens at 5 p.m. Tuesday through Sunday and closes Tuesday through Thursday at midnight, Friday and Saturday at 2 a.m., and Sunday at 10 p.m. Check the calendar closely and call for reservations before you go.

SPORTS BARS

COOTERS SPORTS BAR & GAME ROOM
Cooters Raw Bar and Restaurant
423 Poinsettia Ave.
Clearwater Beach
727-462-COOT (2668)
www.cooters.com/sportsbar.asp

Watch satellite-fed college and pro games—with fans from all over, but everyone plays nice—and NASCAR races on the multiple TVs or get up and play darts, video games, or virtual bowling. Every Wednesday there's a Guitar Hero tournament—we know you play when no one's watching, so go for it! There are prizes and everything.

Cooters Sports Bar & Game room offers a full lunch and a steak-and-seafood dinner menu—try their Old Bay Steamer Bucket full of mussels, oysters, shrimp, crab legs, and corn, or go for their Black Angus New York strip steak. And on Monday and Tuesday there's all you can eat snow crab. Age 18 and above after 9 p.m.

FERG'S SPORTS BAR AND GRILL
1320 Central Ave.
St. Petersburg
(727) 822-4562
www.fergsonline.com

Located near Tropicana Field, Ferg's has been around since the Rays were just a gleam in Tampa Bay area sports fans' eyes. But owner Mark Ferguson invested himself in area youth sports and built a following, never losing faith that Major League Baseball would eventually come to St. Petersburg. Today, Ferg's hosts sports fans of many types, but particularly baseball fans, who stop in before and after home games and come to watch away games on TV.

Ferg's opens every day at 11 a.m. Monday through Thursday, they're open until midnight, Friday and Saturday they're open until 2 a.m., Sunday they're open until 10 p.m.

HATTRICK'S
107 S. Franklin St.
Tampa 33602
(813) 225-4288

Hattrick's caters to Tampa Bay Lightning and other hockey fans, but it speaks other sports languages with equal fluency. Set in a three-story brick building filled with sports memorabilia, TV sets, and a video arcade area, Hattricks's menu ranges from hearty appetizers to hefty sandwiches. Hattricks is open 11:30 a.m. to 3 a.m., with happy hour from 4 to 8 p.m.

THE ARTS

The arts are pretty much unique to the human experience. Birds sing, but that's their way of talking to each other. Some elephants and chimpanzees have been taught to wield a paintbrush, but that's not their natural behavior. We humans appear to be the only creatures who intentionally create "non-essential" sounds and sights, who rearrange our environment to be more aesthetically pleasing, and who appreciate others peoples' efforts to do so.

We do a lot of creating and appreciating others' creations in the Tampa Bay area.

The State of Florida, both Hillsborough and Pinellas counties, and all three major Tampa Bay area cities incorporate art into public projects through public arts funding commitments. We've already noted the art that abounds at Tampa International Airport (see Getting There, Getting Around chapter).

But also check out the mural atop the fire station on Main Street in downtown Safety Harbor, just northeast of Clearwater. And you can't miss the "Security Lizard" atop the City of St. Petersburg's Fleet Maintenance Building—this 30-foot-long steel lizard zapping a hapless steel fly can be enjoyed from I–375!

We're home to the Florida Orchestra and the Tampa Bay Master Chorale. We have world-class art museums and artists who make their homes here. We have all sorts of smaller artsy districts tucked away in various neighborhoods in both counties. We have not one, but three world-class performing arts centers that attract touring Broadway shows and internationally recognized performers.

Our commitment to the arts begins in our local communities, many of which have fine arts centers offering classes in everything from sculpting to singing. Many of these art centers also have performance venues that host smaller-stage professional acts and community theater productions.

We teach our children to create and to appreciate others' creations. From the Pinellas Youth Symphony to the Tampa Bay Children's Chorus to the art and theater summer camps hosted by local artists, we give young creators a foundation on which to build. Look also in the Education chapter for information about our public school fine arts magnet programs: Pinellas County Center for the Arts in St. Petersburg, Leadership Conservatory for the Arts in Tarpon Springs, and Blake High School for the Arts in Tampa.

In this chapter we'll point out some of our better known art spots as well as some of the hidden gems. We'll also give you a calendar listing art events, and we'll introduce you to performance venues, arts organizations, and places to express your own creativity.

We've organized this chapter in alphabetical order by discipline: Art Museums, Galleries, and Fine Art Centers; Ceramics, Clay, and Glass; Dance; Film; Literary Arts; Music; and Theater. Please understand, however, that we could write a whole book just about the art scene here. Think of this chapter as hors d'oeuvres. You're on your own for dinner.

Bon appétit!

ART MUSEUMS, GALLERIES, AND FINE ART CENTERS

CARROLLWOOD CULTURAL CENTER
4537 Lowell Rd.

Tampa

Annex: 13345 Casey Rd.

Tampa

(813) 269-1310

www.carrollwoodcenter.org

It's hard to know where to list the Carrollwood Cultural Center. With art galleries and hands-on art classes, as well as a performing arts stage and resident professional theater company, the Carrollwood Cultural Center offers the community a well-stocked smorgasbord of arts opportunities. So, we'll list it in two places. In this listing, we'll mention only the gallery, which features local professional artists and student exhibitions, and the classes. Especially the classes. There are the usual drawing, jewelry making, and ceramics classes. But, what's this? A philosophy class? A French class? A candy-making class? Plus a community band, a community chorus, and an African dance class. From chess clubs to book clubs and many other activities in between, people of all ages should find a new skill, a new appreciation for art in the widest sense at the Carollwood Cultural Center. Administrative hours are 8 a.m. to 6 p.m. Monday through Friday. Classes are offered days, evenings, and weekends.

i *Creative Loafing,* an alternative weekly newspaper, usually includes comprehensive listings and in-depth reviews of art events. The paper is distributed in more than 1,500 locations around the Tampa Bay area, or go to www2.tampa.creativeloafing.com. Parents should know that the language in the paper can be a bit salty.

DUNEDIN FINE ART CENTER
1143 Michigan Blvd.

Dunedin

(727) 298-DFAC (3322)

www.dfac.org

Galleries, classes, and a hands-on children's art museum—the Dunedin Fine Art Center does it all, and does it all well. Past exhibits have ranged from the Miniature Art Society of Florida's Annual Competition (almost 1,000 works by artists from around the world) to the National Quilt Museum's biannual art-quilt competition to the works of contemporary ceramicists from around the country. Plus, the Dunedin Fine Art Center displays its quirky side with annual events that have included a Wearable ART fashion show with *haute couture* creations made entirely of balloons and a PODS (Portable on Demand Storage) installation art show.

The Gladys Douglas School for the Arts at the Dunedin Fine Art Center offers more than 100 classes throughout the year to people of all ages. Whether you want to play with clay or with computer manipulated photography, learn to draw or dabble in watercolor, carve stone or create jewelry, you'll find experienced artists who will teach you the basics and help you develop your own style. The David L. Mason Children's Art Museum, one of only three such facilities in Florida, provides guided, learn-by-doing activities to help preschool and elementary-school aged children explore various art concepts and media. Ask about their summer camps for children and teens. Gallery hours at the Dunedin Fine Art Center are Monday through Friday from 10 a.m. to 5 p.m., Saturday from 10 a.m. to 2 p.m., and Sunday from 1 to 4 p.m. Admission costs vary for the exhibits. Admission to the David L. Mason Children's Art Museum is $4 for non-members and $3 for seniors. Members and children ages two and under are free. There is a gift shop and a café on the premises.

HILLSBOROUGH COMMUNITY COLLEGE YBOR CITY CAMPUS ART GALLERY
Performing Arts Building Room 114

2204 N. 15th St.

Tampa

(813) 253-7674

www.hccfl.edu/yc/art-gallery.aspx

This small gallery on the Hillsborough Community College Ybor City campus features local artists' and students' work that ranges from the traditional to the *avant garde*. Who knows? You just might be viewing the next Dalí or Rembrandt. The gallery is open Monday, Wednesday, Thursday, and Friday from 10 a.m. to 4 p.m. On Tuesday, the gallery is open from noon to 7 p.m. The gallery is free and is open to the public.

LEEPA-RATTNER MUSEUM OF ART
600 Klosterman Rd.
Tarpon Springs
(727) 712-5762
www.spcollege.edu/central/museum
Located on the Tarpon Springs campus of St. Petersburg College, the Leepa-Rattner Museum of Art holds a collection of 20th century art by Abraham Rattner, Esther Gentle, Allen Leepa and other works by artists of the period including Pablo Picasso, Henry Moore, Max Ernst, and others. In addition to the museum itself, the complex, designed by E. C. Hoffman Jr., also includes the Ellis Foundation Art Education Center and the Michael M. Bennett Library.

Visitors to the Leepa-Rattner Museum of Art don't just contemplate artwork hanging on walls—although that is an important part of the overall collection. In the Challenge of Modern Art Interactive Gallery, visitors become part of the art as they step into a painting or manipulate colored panels to create a spontaneous work of art.

The Leepa-Rattner Museum of Art opens at 10 a.m. Tuesday through Saturday and closes at 5 p.m. except on Thursday when it is open until 9 p.m. The museum is open on Sunday from 1 to 5 p.m. Admission is $5 for adults and $4 for seniors. Admission is free to children, members, and students with ID, and is free to all on Sundays.

MOREAN ARTS CENTER
719 Central Ave.
St. Petersburg
(727) 822-7872
www.theartscenter.org
The Morean Arts Center's history goes back to 1917, with the founding of the St. Petersburg Art Club. Today, in addition to providing children and adults with classes in printmaking, paint-

ing, drawing, and digital art, as well as other art forms, the Morean Arts Center brings exhibits to St. Petersburg in media ranging from fiber art to photography by nationally and internationally acclaimed artists.

In 2004, the center provided live, narrated glassblowing demonstrations as part of the Museum of Fine Arts' Dale Chihuly exhibition. The center also hosted a related exhibit of other world-class glass artists. As a result of that collaboration, 2010 will see the opening of the Chihuly Collection at the Beth Ann Morean Arts Center (see listing elsewhere in this chapter). Ground was broken in 2008 for a new building, which will house the collection and provide space for a glassblowing hot shop with stadium seating so people can watch the process of creating glass art.

Gallery hours at the Morean Arts Center are 10 a.m. to 5 p.m. Monday through Saturday. Admission to exhibits is free. Call or go online for information about the Morean Arts Center's studio classes, KidVentures, and summer camps.

MUSEUM OF FINE ARTS
255 Beach Dr. N.E.
St. Petersburg
(727) 896-2667
www.fine-arts.org
An eclectic assortment of more than 4,600 works from the ancient worlds of Greece, Rome, South America, and Asia and more modern works of 17th- to 20th-century European and American artists, including Claude Monet and Georgia O'Keefe, makes this the most comprehensive art collection on Florida's west coast. Tucked in the back of the Mackey Gallery is a collection of Steuben and other glass art, housed in the Helen Harper Brown Gallery. In this black-box room, crystalline creations by Tiffany, Galle, and others, lit from below and behind, seem suspended in mid-air.

The Museum of Fine Arts has also hosted impressive traveling exhibits including works from around the world and by such noted artists as Andy Warhol and Dale Chihuly. Lectures and intimate music events are held in the auditorium and the courtyards. A café in the new addition makes it easy to enjoy part of the museum's collections in the morning and part in the afternoon. (You can also stop in just for lunch without paying the museum admission fee.)

Admission is $12 for adults, $10 for seniors ages 65 and up, $8 for students with I.D., $6 for children ages 7 to 18. Children ages 6 and under are free. The museum also has summer camps for children.

SALT CREEK ARTWORKS AND THE GALLERIES AT SALT CREEK

1600 4th St. S.

St. Petersburg

(727) 896-6594

www.saltcreekartworks.com

Salt Creek Artworks leases studio space to more than three dozen area artists and provides a classroom for the St. Petersburg campus of the University of South Florida's art department. Studio artists create in a variety of media, and visitors to the galleries may catch them at work or see finished pieces displayed. The Galleries at Salt Creek provides the area's largest gallery space outside of our museums. Artists from around the nation have displayed their works here. The Galleries at Salt Creek are open Tuesday through Saturday from 11 a.m. to 4 p.m. Check the Web site for current exhibits.

SALVADOR DALÍ MUSEUM

1000 3rd St. S.

St. Petersburg

(727) 823-3767, (800) 442-3254

www.salvadordalimuseum.org

The Salvador Dalí Museum is as much a tribute to a community pulling together to accomplish a task as it is to the genius of Salvador Dalí. In January 1980, the *Wall Street Journal* published an article, "Art World Dilly Dallies over Dalís," describing the offer of the most comprehensive collection of original Dalí artwork in the world to any museum willing to preserve the body of work intact. Established museums seemed lukewarm about the offer.

St. Petersburg attorney James W. Martin read the article and organized a group of community leaders who acted quickly and decisively. By mid-1980, the group had garnered government support, contacted the donors—A. Reynolds and Eleanor Morse, personal friends and patrons of Dalí and his wife—and established the necessary foundations to receive and manage the collections. The first part of the museum opened in 1982 and has been expanded several times since then. In December 2008, the community broke ground for a new Dalí museum a few blocks north of the existing building. The new museum will be twice the size of the current building and is expected to open in 2011.

Meanwhile, visitors to the Salvador Dalí Museum can see Dalí grow as an artist and in his understanding of the world around him as they move from gallery to gallery. The works— oils, watercolors, sketches, sculptures, and other works completed during the period from 1917 to 1970—are arranged, for the most part, in chronological order. The final gallery consists of massive paintings as high as 14 feet tall.

The museum is open seven days a week and is open in the evening on Thursdays. Admission is $17 for adults, $12 for students ages 10 to 17 (and older students with I.D.), $4 for children ages 5 to 9, and $14.50 for seniors ages 65 and older and for teachers, military personnel, and some public safety officers with I.D. Guided tours are available for an extra fee—and they are worth the cost.

i Look for the "Tips" page on the Dalí Museum's Web site (under the "Visit" tab), especially if you plan to take children. Some of Dalí's works are sexually explicit or grotesque, as he intended to shock people into seeing things differently. The "Tips" page helps parents and teachers focus children's attention on the optical illusions and suggests "I Spy" type games.

SYD ENTEL GALLERIES AND SUSAN BENJAMIN GLASS, ETC.

247 Main St.

Safety Harbor

(727) 725-1808

Syd Entel Galleries and Susan Benjamin Glass,

Etc., is one of those larger-on-the-inside places that has enriched the Tampa Bay area for almost 30 years. Featuring original artwork, limited edition prints, and a collection of fine art glass work, Syd Entel Galleries and Susan Benjamin Glass, Etc., have brought high-quality smaller shows to north Pinellas County. During the 2008 presidential election, for instance, we were treated to the *Dr. Seuss for President* exhibit, a collection of works by Theodore Geisel, who started his career as a political cartoonist.

Syd Entel Galleries and Susan Benjamin Glass, Etc., are open Monday through Friday from 9:30 a.m. to 5 p.m. and Saturday from 10 a.m. to 3 p.m., or by appointment.

TAMPA MUSEUM OF ART
120 Gasparilla Plaza
Tampa
(813) 274-8130
www.tampamuseum.org
Look for a brand-new facility in early 2010 as the Tampa Museum of Art spreads its wings in the Curtis Hixon Waterfront Park, roughly between the David A. Straz Jr. Center for the Performing Arts Center and the Tampa Convention Center along the Hillsborough River. The Tampa Museum of Art's permanent collections range from Greek and Roman antiquities to contemporary art works in many media, including an eclectic collection of sculpture. Past exhibits have included a collection of photographic portraits spanning the life of Mexican artist Frida Kahlo and "It's Not Easy Being Green," a collection of conceptual drawings, artwork, and design products that could move us toward a more sustainable society.

The Tampa Museum of Art offers classes for budding artists of all ages, including a summer art camp for children and programs for preschoolers. Popular adult events have included the Art Lovers' Tea, an afternoon gallery discussion, and Art After Dark, an evening of art, music, and mingling.

The Tampa Museum of Art will be open seven days a week, and there will be a café on the premises. At this writing, hours and admission details had not been finalized, so call or visit their Web site before you go.

USF CONTEMPORARY ART MUSEUM
4202 E. Fowler Ave. CAM 101
Tampa
(813) 974-4133
www.usfcam.usf.edu
It's easy to look back over the millennia and see the differences and similarities between, for instance, Ancient Roman art and French Impressionism. It is harder to follow the development from the Impressionists through the Cubists and on to today's work—which may be of a yet unnamed school or style. Part of the Institute for Research in Art, USF's Contemporary Art Museum displays works by artists of the 20th and 21st centuries—some internationally recognized and some student works—and lets us watch art evolve, almost from exhibition to exhibition.

You can visit the USF Contemporary Art Museum on your own, or you can request, with at least two weeks' advance notice, a guided tour. The museum is free and is open Monday through Friday from 10 a.m. to 5 p.m. and on Saturday from 1 to 4 p.m. The museum is closed on all state holidays.

i Ybor City artist Arnold Martinez, whose studio/gallery is catty-corner from the Ybor City museum, uses the coffee, wine, beer, and cigars preferred by his subjects to paint their portraits. (1909 N. 19th St., Tampa, 813-248-9572).

CERAMICS, CLAY, AND GLASS

THE CHIHULY COLLECTION AT THE BETH ANN MOREAN ARTS CENTER
719 Central Ave.
St. Petersburg
www.moreanartscenter.org
Opening 2010
Construction has begun on a building at the Morean Arts Center (see listing elsewhere in this chapter) to house the first permanent collection of Dale Chihuly glass installation works, a project that began after St. Petersburg's Museum of Fine Arts brought a Chihuly exhibit, *Masterworks in Glass*, to the area in 2004. The building also will

include a glassblowing hot shop with stadium seating and a children's center.

People stood in line to view the 2004 exhibit in St. Petersburg—an exhibit stunning for its use of space in addition to its interplay of color, light, and shape. Whole rooms became works of art, such as *Cranberry Red Persian Wall* with its massive glass shapes suggestive of a Georgia O'Keefe field full of red poppies. Another room was best seen lying on the floor looking up at the *Persian Pergola* ceiling. For a retrospective of the exhibit, go to the *St. Petersburg Times'* collection of articles, photographs, and videos at www.sptimes.com/2004/webspecials04/chihuly/index.shtml.

CREATIVE CLAY, INC.
Cultural Arts Center
1124 Central Ave.
St. Petersburg
(727) 825-0515
http://creativeclay.org
Creative Clay recognizes the intrinsic need to express oneself artistically and provides children and adults with various physical and developmental challenges with opportunities to explore all the arts including dance, theater, music, painting, sculpting, and writing. In 2003, Creative Clay representatives traveled to Japan to teach 25 communities the ARTLINK concept of pairing professional artists in various disciplines with students to produce a collaborative work. Visit the gallery, visit the studios—and come away with a new understanding of creativity.

ST. PETERSBURG CLAY COMPANY
420 22nd St. S.
St. Petersburg
(727) 896-CLAY (2529)
www.stpeteclay.com
St. Petersburg's 1920s-era Seaboard Train Station has become the Tampa Bay area's clay conclave. St. Petersburg Clay Company rents studio space to clay artists, hosts clay artists from around the world who present intensive workshops, and provides classes and kiln space for non-resident artists. Additionally, Highwater Clays, an Asheville, North Carolina clay producer, has located

their Florida distributorship at St. Petersburg Clay Company.

Inside, the St. Petersburg Clay Company offers members use of slab-rollers, extruders, clay mixers, and more than a dozen electric kilns. Outdoors, the Clay Company's kiln collection ranges from gas kilns to soda and salt kilns to wood-fired, raku, and pit kilns. The *piece de resistance*, however, is the 16th-century Japanese-style anagama kiln. Fired only once a year, this behemoth takes about a week of round-the-clock care and feeding and can hold several hundred pieces. St. Petersburg Clay Company is open Tuesday through Saturday from 10 a.m. to 5 p.m.

SUSAN BENJAMIN GLASS, ETC.
247 Main St.
Safety Harbor
(727) 725-1808
See Syd Entel Galleries and Susan Benjamin Glass, Etc. under Art Museums, Galleries, and Fine Art Centers.

DANCE

How we move to music varies with our culture—but has there ever been a culture that didn't at least step, stomp, jump, or clap in rhythm? From ballet to hip-hop, the Tampa Bay area has a wealth of dance experiences for you to explore.

COMOTION DANCE THEATER
St. Petersburg College
P.O. Box 13489
St. Petersburg 33733-3489
(727) 341-4686
www.spcollege.edu/central/comotion/program.htm
St. Petersburg College's resident dance company, CoMotion Dance Theater, has been exploring contemporary dance since 1985. Past performances have included works set to everything from Shel Silverstein poetry to folk music to more contemporary musical compositions. CoMotion Dance Theater performs two on-campus and several off-campus programs each year. The on-

campus performances are free, but donations are gratefully accepted.

THE DANCE PROJECT
204 N. 12th St.
Tampa
(813) 221-1042
www.thedanceproject.org

Before there was ballet as we know it, with tutued swans and sugar plum fairies pirouetting on a stage to unseen music—the orchestra having been consigned to the pit—dancers and musicians performed as an integrated unit. Musicians shared the stage with the dancers, who were seen as additional, if visual, instruments completing the composition. Instrumental music scores included space for the choreography. Luisa Meshekoff, owner and artistic director of the Dance Project, performs dance from the Baroque period, recreated using manuscripts from the Dance Collection of the Lincoln Center library in New York, where Meshekoff was part of the New York Baroque Dance Company. Meshekoff performs with Florida Pro Musica (see the music section later in this chapter) at various venues around the Tampa Bay area. Additionally, the Dance Project provides rehabilitative classes for injured dancers and for non-dancers who want to learn to use their bodies more efficiently and to avoid injury.

DUNDU DOLE URBAN AFRICAN BALLET
Life Force Cultural Arts Academy
P.O. Box 383
Clearwater 33757
(727) 481-8091

Dundu Dole Urban African Ballet dancers perform throughout the nation, but we get to see their high-energy African-influenced dance—often performed to the accompaniment of traditional African instruments—at places like St. Petersburg's First Night or as part of the Mahaffey Theater's Class Acts series. They may be most well known for their performances of LaVerne Reed's *Chocolate Nutcracker*, a full-length, upbeat retelling of the Christmas classic set in 1950s Harlem. Life Force Cultural Arts Academy offers inter-generational drumming, dancing, singing, and folklore classes (the Bantaba) in St. Petersburg and in Clearwater each week. Check the Web site for a schedule. Some classes charge a nominal per-class fee ($3 to $10).

MOVING CURRENT DANCE COLLECTIVE
5501 N. Branch Ave.
Tampa
(813) 237-0216
www.movingcurrent.com

Moving Current Dance Collective, a contemporary dance group, is the University of South Florida's company-in-residence. In addition to producing numerous performances throughout the year featuring local and national performers, choreographers, musicians, and visual and spoken-word artists, Moving Current also promotes dance as a lifelong expression through programs like Forever Moving (a troupe of dancers ages 50 to 85) and its work with Hillsborough County Public School students in grades kindergarten through 12. On the Spot, an improvisational series performed in non-traditional venues such as outdoor locations, brings dance to audiences instead of waiting for audiences to come to them.

FILM

THE BEACH THEATRE
315 Corey Ave.
St. Pete Beach
(727) 360-6697
www.beachtheatre.com

Rocky Horror Picture Show fans, this is your place each Saturday night at 11:30 p.m. or so, when a live cast, Interchangeable Parts, performs various versions of this cult favorite. R-rated and adult-oriented means no one under 17 is admitted without a parent. Audience participation is expected.

Other shows include first-run movies in the evening, classics, and free Saturday morning children's movies. The theater is a holdover from the pre-stadium theater days, so don't expect anything fancy. Just enjoy it for what it is—an anachronism.

THE TAMPA THEATRE

711 Franklin St.
Tampa
(813) 274-8981 (24-hour event info)
(813) 274-8286 (business and box office)
www.tampatheatre.org

Designed by famed theater architect John Eberson and built in 1926 by Paramount Studios, the Tampa Theatre was one of the country's most elaborate "movie palaces," which were as much an attraction as were the movies they played. For 10 cents, people who had to scrimp and save to survive could sink into plush seats surrounded by lavish décor. Stars twinkled overhead and clouds floated by while viewers waited for the latest film to start.

Anti-trust legislation passed in 1948 forced major studios to sell their theaters. Suburbia sprang up and downtowns deteriorated. Many movie palaces met their demise at the business end of a wrecking ball when the land they were on became more valuable than the theater. Tampa's residents rode to the rescue, however, in 1973. The city assumed the lease and the Arts Council of Hillsborough County took over management of the theater.

Today, the Tampa Theatre hosts first-run and classic films, concerts—including such performers and speakers as Ray Charles, Joan Baez, Harry Connick Jr., Sinbad, and Elie Wiesel—live theater, children's programs, and other events. Come early to hear the Mighty Wurlitzer Theatre Organ played by a Central Florida Theatre Organ Society volunteer—the way movie music used to sound.

GRAPHIC ARTS

USF GRAPHICSTUDIO

3702 Spectrum Blvd., Ste. 100
Tampa
(813) 974-3505
www.usfcam.usf.edu

Browse the Graphicstudio's Web page to see some of the limited-edition, fine-art graphics pieces that have been produced at the USF Graphicstudio, an art-world leader in developing new techniques.

Want to learn how a graphic-arts print production facility works? Call the USF Graphicstudio, at least two weeks in advance, to arrange for a tour. The studio's hours are Monday through Friday from 10 a.m. to 5 p.m. They are closed on all state holidays.

LITERARY ARTS

FLORIDA WRITERS ASSOCIATION

www.floridawriters.net

Three groups meet in the Tampa Bay area. The Brandon Writers Critique Group meets the second and fourth Thursday of each month from 7 to 9 p.m. at the Barnes & Noble store at Westfield Mall in Brandon (459 Brandon Town Center). The St. Petersburg Writers Group meets for critiques on the first and third Thursday of the month from 6:30 to 8:30 p.m. and for speakers and discussion on the second Thursday of the month from 5:30 to 8 p.m. The latter meetings are held at the St. Petersburg Main Library (corner of 9th Ave. N. and 38th St. N.). Check the group's blog (www.fwastpete.blogspot.com) for more information.

The Tampa Writers Group (www.fwatampa .blogspot.com) meets for critiques the second and fourth Monday at the Barnes & Noble bookstore at 11802 N. Dale Mabry. The Tampa group also meets at the same store for discussion and speakers on the third Saturday of the month from 10 a.m. to noon.

PINELLAS AUTHORS AND WRITERS ORGANIZATION

(727) 736-1026
www.pinawor.org

PINAWOR meets each Saturday from 9:30 a.m. to noon at the Largo Recreation Center (400 Highland Ave. N.E., Largo). Visitors can attend up to three meetings, but only members' work is reviewed. Members wanting feedback on a work in progress sign up before the meeting begins to read five minutes' worth of their work to the group. Parts-reading sessions for playwrights and screenwriters are scheduled about once a month. Occasionally, PINAWOR has a guest speaker, but mostly the meetings consist of candid comments about each other's writing. PINAWOR also offers occasional writing classes.

TAMPA WRITERS ALLIANCE

www.tampawriters.org

Go to the Tampa Writers Alliance Web site for current contact information—officers tend to change. General meetings are held the first Wednesday of each month, beginning at 7 p.m., at various locations—often a Barnes & Noble bookstore. Check the Web site for particular information as to location and guest speaker. The Tampa Writers Alliance also has a critique group meeting from 7 to 9 p.m. the second and fourth Wednesday of each month at the 11802 N. Dale Mabry Barnes & Noble bookstore. You can listen in, but only members' work is discussed. The poetry group meets at the same Barnes & Noble bookstore the fourth Thursday of each month beginning at 7 p.m.—sometimes there's music, too.

WRITERS IN PARADISE

Eckerd College—Special Programs
4200 54th Ave. S.
St. Petersburg
(727) 864-7994
http://writersinparadise.eckerd.edu

This intensive writing conference is for serious writers only—except for the Evening Reading Series, that is, which is free and open to the public. Come and listen to such highly regarded writers as Dennis LeHane (*Mystic River*), Peter Meinke (*The Shape of Poetry*), Ann Hood (*The Knitting Circle*), and others read from their works and discuss the writing process. No tickets or reservations are required—in fact, it's best if you let go all your reservations and bring an inquiring mind. Readings begin at 8 p.m. in the Miller Auditorium on the Eckerd College Campus. A wine-and-cheese reception from 7:30 to 8 p.m. precedes the readings each evening. Books are available for sale and authors for signing following the readings.

MUSIC

Jam Sessions and Open Mike

BAY AREA FIDDLERS ASSOCIATION

(727) 321-2379
www.bayareafiddlers.com

Rosin up your bow, and head on over to the Dunedin Community Center (1920 Pinehurst Road, 727-812-4530) for some foot-stomping old-time Irish fiddle music. The Bay Area Fiddlers Association meets the first and third Saturday of each month from 1 to 4 p.m., and they can always use another fiddle, mandolin, or guitar player. Listeners are welcome, too. There is no charge.

SACRED GROUNDS COFFEE HOUSE

4819 E. Busch Blvd.
Tampa
(813) 983-0837
www.sacredgroundstampa.com

Monday nights are open-mike nights beginning around 9 p.m. for poets, musicians, actors, and other artists. Each fourth Tuesday evening from 8 to 11 p.m. acoustic musicians—any instrument, but they don't want to mess with P.A. systems—gather at Sacred Grounds Coffee House for an any-kind-of-music-goes jam session. In fact, they've met at Sacred Grounds for so long they've been nicknamed the Tampa Jammers. There is no cover charge, but you ought to at least buy a cup of coffee, yes? Sacred Grounds Coffee House opens each evening at 6 p.m. and closes at midnight Sunday through Thursday. Friday and Saturday they're open until 2 a.m. (See Restaurants chapter.)

Marching Bands

AWESOME ORIGINAL SECOND TIME AROUNDERS MARCHING BAND, INC.

P.O. Box 15062
St. Petersburg 33733-5062
(727) 420-5717
www.secondtimearounders.com

Does the scent of valve oil or the remembered taste of dry, woody, just-out-of-the-pack reeds take you back to high school or college band days? Or maybe you never had the chance to be part of a marching band or drill team, but always wanted to give it a try. The Greater St. Petersburg Area Awesome Original Second Time Arounders Marching Band, Inc., is calling your name.

Back in 1983, 75 people responded to a newspaper ad inviting former band and auxiliary members to march in the St. Petersburg Festival of States parade. Today, the band fields around 500 members, including musicians, twirlers, drill, flag, and rifle teams. The Rounders have played in Oregon, Texas, Disney World, and Dublin, Ireland, and they have spawned at least one other marching band of second-timers. In 2008, the Second Time Arounders marched in the parade of all parades, the Macy's Thanksgiving Day parade in New York City.

Rehearsals begin in January and there are spots for people with no previous experience.

Orchestras

THE FLORIDA ORCHESTRA
244 2nd Ave. N., Ste. 421
St. Petersburg
(727) 892-3337, (800) 662-7286
www.floridaorchestra.org

The birth of the Florida Orchestra reveals a bit about the rivalry between Tampa and St. Petersburg—and also about the importance of the arts in the Tampa Bay area. The Tampa Symphony, later the Tampa Philharmonic Symphony, was birthed in 1947, largely through the efforts of a University of Tampa professor of music. A November 1949 *St. Petersburg Times* article focused on 11 members of the Tampa Symphony living across the bay in various Pinellas communities—many in St. Petersburg. Two years later, in February 1951, the 65-member strong St. Petersburg Symphony presented its inaugural concert, with Leon Poulopoulos as conductor—who also directed the Clearwater Symphony. Other groups also provided classical music of various kinds to the Tampa Bay area.

A 1963 *St. Petersburg Times* article lists the Tampa Philharmonic Orchestra, the "newly formed" St. Petersburg Philharmonic Orchestra, the St. Petersburg "Pops" Orchestra, the Clearwater Symphony Orchestra, and the Florida Philharmonic Orchestra—in addition to concert seasons sponsored by the St. Petersburg Music Association, the Carreno Music Club, and the St. Petersburg Civic Opera Association.

By 1966, however, supporters of the Tampa Philharmonic Symphony and the St. Petersburg Symphony recognized they could accomplish more by pooling their resources and funding one orchestra. In November 1966, each group sailed to the middle of Tampa Bay to sign the agreement creating the Florida Gulf Coast Symphony, whose inaugural 1968 to 1969 season was under the direction of Irwin Hoffman, previously director of the Chicago Symphony Orchestra.

Since then, the Florida Gulf Coast Symphony has become the Florida Orchestra, currently under the direction of Stefan Sanderling and performing more than 150 concerts each year in Tampa, St. Petersburg, and Clearwater. It has not been an easy 40-plus years, and at times the Florida Orchestra has struggled to adapt to changing financial priorities, changing tastes in music, and competition from other types of entertainment. Nor did the Florida Orchestra have a permanent home.

Despite these obstacles, the Florida Orchestra has become a respected organization in the music world. Each season, the Florida Orchestra performs a variety of music ranging from Masterworks series to Pops concerts and attracts such guest artists as violinist James Ehnes and guitarist Jason Vieaux. Recognizing that today's audiences must be both caught and taught, the Florida Orchestra offers coffee concerts complete with refreshments and explanatory remarks by the conductor, an orchestra petting zoo available to schools, and other outreach efforts.

In 2007, the Florida Orchestra and St. Petersburg College created a long-term partnership, part of which provides both office space and a rehearsal stage to provide the stability and physical base needed for the Orchestra to expand and to reach its full potential.

The Florida Orchestra performs at the Mahaffey Theater in St. Petersburg, at Ruth Eckerd Hall in Clearwater, and at the David Straz Jr. Center for the Performing Arts in Tampa, as well as at smaller venues throughout the Tampa Bay area. Watch for their free Pops concerts in parks and other locations for a taste-whetting sampling of marvelous music.

FLORIDA PRO MUSICA
P.O. Box 1754
Tampa 33601-1754
www.floridapromusica.com
(813) 258-4226

Florida Pro Musica, a Tampa Bay area chamber orchestra and chorus and the resident ensemble at Sacred Heart Church in Tampa, specializes in music from the Renaissance, Baroque, and Classical periods. Florida Pro Musica's reflective Advent concerts have become something of a tradition in the Tampa Bay area. In addition to presenting concerts at Sacred Heart Church, Florida Pro Musica also performs at other venues around Florida, sometimes with the Dance Project (see description earlier in this chapter).

MUSIKONG KAWAYAN BAMBOO ORCHESTRA
Bayanihan Arts Center
14301 Nine Eagles Dr.
Tampa
(813) 925-1232
www.pcfitampa.org

This 30-some-piece ensemble group playing traditional Philippine instruments sometimes is accompanied by the Philippine Choral Group, dancers from the Philippine Performing Arts Company, Inc., and soloists. Look for them at AsiaFest and other area festivals, or attend their one of their concerts at the Bayanihan Arts Center.

PINELLAS YOUTH SYMPHONY
P.O. Box 4106
Seminole 33775-4106
(727) 438-3149
www.pysmusic.org

Founded in 1958, the Pinellas Youth Symphony provides symphonic music instruction and performance experiences to young musicians ages five years through high school age. All rehearsals are held at Ruth Eckerd Hall in Clearwater, and the artistic and teaching staff includes members of area professional orchestras. Beginning instruction is available to children ages 5 to 14, and ensemble experience also is offered.

SUNCOAST SYMPHONY ORCHESTRA
P.O. Box 6126
Clearwater 33758-6126
(727) 787-8335
www.suncoastsymphony.org

The 65 members of the volunteer Suncoast Symphony Orchestra gather at a northeast Clearwater church each week to rehearse music ranging from Rossini to Mancini. They begin rehearsing in September and play three series of concerts at various venues around Pinellas County. Want to join them? Musicians range in age from late teens to—let's just say there's no such thing as "too old to play." The Suncoast Symphony Orchestra just celebrated its 25th year of making music.

TAMPA BAY SYMPHONY
P.O. Box 4653
Clearwater 33758
(727) 442-3696
http://tampabaysymphony.com/home.htm

Ninety-some volunteer musicians from around the Tampa Bay area rehearse at a church just northwest of St. Petersburg and play everything from Beethoven to Broadway. The Tampa Bay Symphony performs three concert series each year at each of the three major venues—Mahaffey Theater, Ruth Eckerd Hall, and the David Straz Jr. Center for the Performing Arts—plus a number of other concerts. For almost a quarter century, the Tampa Bay Symphony has also sponsored a Young Artist Competition, awarding cash prizes and providing performance opportunities for instrumentalists, vocalists, and pianists under age 21.

THE ARTS

Vocal

CLEARWATER CHORUS
1111 McMullen Booth Rd.
Clearwater
(727) 953-3121
www.clearwater-fl.com/gov/depts/parksrec/
arts_culture/chorus.asp
The Clearwater Chorus is sponsored by the City of Clearwater, but you don't have to live in Clearwater to be a part of the group. You do, however, have to drive to Clearwater for rehearsals, which are held Tuesday evenings at Ruth Eckerd Hall's Murray Studio Theater. About 100 singers strong, the Clearwater Chorus sings everything from light classics to Broadway show tunes, and presents two main concerts each year at Ruth Eckerd Hall. Auditions are held in August and January.

MASTER CHORALE OF TAMPA BAY
30382 USF Holly Dr.
Tampa
(813) 974-7726
www.masterchorale.com
The Master Chorale of Tampa Bay is a volunteer chorus, but that doesn't mean they aren't highly regarded. Designated as the principal chorus of the Florida Orchestra in 1989, the Master Chorale and the Florida Orchestra have produced some innovative and intensive works including Orff's *Carmina Burana* and Einhorn's *Voices of Light* with the 1928 silent film *The Passion of Joan of Arc*. In addition to performing classic works of the past, the Master Chorale also promotes the continuance of choral music by commissioning new works such as Eleanor Daley's *Listen to the Sunrise* and Paul Basler's *Missa Kenya*. In 1999, the Master Chorale was appointed as Artist-in-Residence at the University of South Florida.

Auditions for the Master Chorale are held in August. Performances are at the three major Tampa Bay area venues and also at churches and other sites around Florida.

ST. PETERSBURG OPERA COMPANY
P.O. Box 238
St. Petersburg 33731
(727) 823-2040
www.stpeteopera.org
Housed at the Palladium Theater, the St. Petersburg Opera Company presents three full-length operas each year, ranging from Stephen Sondheim's *Into the Woods* to Verdi's *La Traviata*. Most productions are held at the Palladium, but occasionally they take their show on the road to other area venues. Want to learn more about opera? The first Thursday of each month, beginning at 6 p.m., artistic director Mark Sforzini presents *Evenings with the Maestro* at the Music Gallery of Clearwater (5590 Ulmerton Road, Clearwater, 727-530-3304). These 90-minute programs feature live performances by singers. Check the Web site for ticket information.

TAMPA BAY HERALDS OF HARMONY
P.O. Box 274076
Tampa 33688-4076
(813) 228-7730
www.heraldsofharmony.org
Lovers of four-part barbershop-style harmony will be glad to hear we have several active groups in the Tampa Bay area. The Heralds of Harmony is among the largest men's groups in the area, drawing members from several communities and performing at venues throughout central Florida. They also compete internationally and have placed as high as ninth in the world. Several quartets have formed from the larger group, including the Harmonious Hunks, the Wise Guys, and others. The Heralds of Harmony rehearse Tuesday evenings from 7 to 10 p.m. at the Scottish Rite Masonic Lodge Theater (5500 Memorial Blvd., Tampa). Rehearsals are open; membership is by audition.

THEATER

AMERICAN STAGE THEATRE COMPANY
163 3rd St. N.
St. Petersburg
www.americanstage.org

Over the past 30 years, American Stage Theatre Company, St. Petersburg's resident theater ensemble, has grown to become a major player in the Tampa Bay area theater world. The first Tampa Bay area non-profit theater company to operate under a full contract with Actors' Equity Association, American State Theatre Company helped pioneer the Small Professional Theatre contract with Actors' Equity. Not enough seating? Then take the show outdoors! Since 1986, one full production a year has been performed outdoors in Demens Landing near the Pier.

American State Theatre Company recently has partnered with St. Petersburg College, which has meant a new theater building with more space for education and outreach programs in addition to their six Mainstage productions each year.

ECKERD THEATER COMPANY
Ruth Eckerd Hall
1111 McMullen Booth Rd.
Clearwater
(727) 712-2743
www.rutheckerdhall.com/etc/home.cfm
Eckerd Theater Company is a resident program at the Marcia P. Hoffman Performing Arts Institute at Ruth Eckerd Hall, but they're hardly ever home. That's because they tour much of the Eastern United States, bringing quality productions to younger audiences in schools and other organizations. Not only do Eckerd Theater Company actors perform, they also may lead post-performance workshops or discussions about the play. Study guides for teachers are available for many of the performances. To date, they have reached more than one million children.

We try to catch Eckerd Theater Company's productions before they hit the road. Although these performances are billed as being for younger audiences, we've seen grandparents laughing right along with their grandkids at the antics in *Aesop's Fables*—and we've seen teachers as absorbed as their students in the drama of *I Never Saw Another Butterfly*, a child's-eye view of the Holocaust.

GORILLA THEATER
4419 N. Hubert Ave.
Tampa
(813) 354-0550
www.gorilla-theatre.com
Gorilla Theater began as a place for husband-wife writing and production team Aubrey Hampton, also a ventriloquist and magician, and Susan Hussey to produce their own plays and to provide a venue for other local playwrights to produce their work. It has become a place where theatergoers can find seldom-produced works (or adaptations) by such writers as George Bernard Shaw and Henrik Ibsen. The Gorilla Theater also hosts the Tampa Bay Jazz Club's "Jazz at the Gorilla" and sponsors the Young Dramatists' Project, which offers full-scale, professional production of works written by teens.

Thursday performances are $20 or $15 for students with I.D. and for seniors ages 55 and up. Friday, Saturday, and Sunday performances are $25 and $20. If any of the 47 seats are still available 30 minutes before a show begins, student rush tickets are $10. Call the box office or order online. Other prices may apply for special performances. The Gorilla Theater is in a warehouse in an industrial area-—look for the bright yellow awning and big yellow signs. Free parking is available in front of the theater. Help the Gorilla Theater be a good neighbor by obeying the signs and not parking in front of other businesses.

JOBSITE THEATER, INC.
David Straz Jr. Center for the Performing Arts
Shimberg Playhouse
1010 N. W.C. MacInnes Place
Tampa
(813) 229-STAR (7827)
www.jobsitetheater.org
Jobsite Theater, Inc., is a professional exploratory theater company—exploratory in the sense that they are more interested in developing new on- and off-stage talent than in relying on familiar faces and in rehashing old territory. They deliberately seek out the new and the overlooked, producing, for instance, an entire season of unpublished work by various playwrights.

All the Community a Stage

We haven't even begun to tell you about our dedicated and very talented local community theater. Here's a quick list 50 you can explore on your own.

Tampa/Hillsborough

Carrollwood Players
(813) 265-4000
www.carrollwoodplayers.com

Masque Community Theatre of Temple Terrace
(813) 983-1710
www.masquetheatre.net

New Tampa Players
(813) 386-6687
www.newtampaplayers.org

St. Petersburg/South Pinellas

Gulfport Community Players
(727) 322-0316
www.gulfportcommunityplayers.org

Island Community Theatre
(727) 430-2328
www.islandcommunitytheatre.com

St. Petersburg Little Theatre
(727-866-2059)
www.splt.org

Clearwater/North Pinellas

City Players
(727) 531-8026
www.clearwater-fl.com/gov/depts/parksrec/
arts_culture/city_players.asp

Eight O'Clock Theatre
(727) 587-6793
www.eightoclocktheatre.com

Francis Wilson Playhouse
(727) 446-1360
www.franciswilsonplayhouse.org

Gilbert & Sullivan Players
(727) 536-6250

West Coast Players
(727) 734-7100
www.wcplayers.org

Because of their unique offerings and because of the quality of their productions, the Straz Center named Jobsite their resident theater company for its Shimberg Playhouse, beginning with the 2003 to 2004 season.

Jobsite is also an ensemble artists' company, meaning they rely exclusively on local talent, some of whom are members of Actors Equity Association or United Scenic Artists and others of whom are not, to produce their work. This arrangement and the commitment of ensemble members allows secondary works to be produced by ensemble members late at night or during other off-hours.

SALERNO THEATRE CO., INC.
13046 Race Track Rd., Ste. 253
Tampa
(877) 275-7050
www.salernotheatre.com

Salerno Theatre Co., Inc., is a professional, non-Equity, regional touring company that performs at various venues around the Tampa Bay area, and they are the resident company at the Carrollwood Cultural Center. Salerno Theatre produces only family-friendly Broadway musicals. That means you won't see them doing *Hair*, but you might see *Godspell* or *Oklahoma!*

Salerno's sister company, American Concert Company (www.americanconcertcompany.com, 813-846-0617), produces original Vegas-style

Art in Funky Places

You just never know when you're going to walk into a bank, for instance, and be taken aback by a work of art on display. Here are a few treasures we've found in the Tampa Bay area. But keep your eyes open for other unexpected art.

Bank Lobby
Don Quijote Segunda Parte by Izhar Patkin (1987–1989). The intrepid knight on his faithful steed, Rocinante, is caught looking in a mirror in this brilliantly colored, anodized aluminum sculpture that greets visitors to the SunTrust Financial Centre lobby (401 E. Jackson St., Tampa). Or go to YouTube.com and search for the video.

Cemetery
In addition to the more traditional marble and stone art works, look for the animals created in the chain-saw carved tree trunks and stumps at Sylvan Abbey Memorial Park (2860 Sunset Point Rd., Clearwater). Tree critters are by Keith Carroll.

Church Exterior
The whole east side of St. Alfred's Episcopal Church (1601 Curlew Rd., Palm Harbor) is a Christopher M. Still mural, *Ecce Homo* ("Behold the Man"), depicting scenes from the life of Jesus. If the office is open, ask to see the artwork inside the church.

Entire House
The Whimzey Twinz, Safety Harbor artists Todd Ramquist and Kiaralinda, didn't stop at one wall. Their whole house is one wild and crazy work of art—and it seems to be contagious. Check out the neighboring homes, as well, at the corner of 12th Ave. N. and 4th St. in Safety Harbor (www.kiaralinda.com).

Financial Center Parking Area
Turn off of SR 688 just over the Howard Frankland Bridge from Tampa and into Carillon Parkway toward the Raymond James Financial Center, and you'll be greeted by a full-sized bronze Native American on horseback. Pull into the small parking area in front of the building and explore the sculpture garden in front of the building. Want to see the extensive art collection inside? Call (727) 567-5896 to arrange for a tour (880 Carillon Pwy., St. Petersburg).

Water Tower
The City of Seminole's water tower rises 60 feet above the city and is painted like a giant bird cage filled with—what else?—birds. Titled *Florida Birds in Flight* by Tom Stovall, the water tower has been a bit controversial, but most residents flock protectively around it whenever anyone talks about opening the cage and letting the birds fly free. Trust us, you don't need an address for this one—intersection of Park Blvd. and 113th St. N. in Seminole is close enough.

cabaret and review shows such as the Bobby Darin Tribute Concert (www.bobbydarintribute .com) for corporate and other venues. American Concert Company's shows are both full-length (two hours) and abbreviated for assisted living facilities, senior centers, and other institutions.

SPANISH LYRIC THEATER
2819 Safe Harbor Dr. (mailing address only)
Tampa 33548
(813) 936-0217
www.spanishlyrictheatre.com

Spanish Lyric Theater celebrated its 50th anniversary in 2009—but the history of Spanish theater in Tampa goes back well over 100 years. In the late 1890s and early 1900s, early "Cigar Town" workers in the Ybor area built clubhouses with grand theaters capable of hosting professional theater productions. The Centuro Asturiano, the Centro Español, and the Círculo Cubano hosted traveling companies from Spain and Cuba as well as local theater groups. As the movie industry gained hold, some of the theaters became movie theaters. The Depression and other factors limited the number of live performances offered.

In 1959, some University of Tampa students and other community members discovered hidden treasure in the archives of the Centuro Asturiano. Old *zarzuela* (Spanish musical theater) scores and librettos begged to be revived. Thus began the Spanish Lyric Theater.

Today, the Spanish Lyric Theater offers an intriguing mixture of theatrical forms—reviews or *variedades*, Spanish *zarzuelas*, Broadway musicals, and operettas—in both Spanish and English. They have performed both *El Rey y Yo* and *The King and I*—alternating Spanish and English performances with the same cast. Their signature piece, however, may be an adaptation by Artistic Director René Gonzalez of the Cinderella story, *La Cenicienta de Ybor*, about a poor girl from 1950s Ybor City who wants to go to the Gasparilla Ball.

Cast artists are professional, non-Equity performers, and the Spanish Lyric Theater performs at venues including the Straz Center and the Florida State Fair. Check their Web site for a current production schedule.

STAGEWORKS THEATRE
1120 E. Kennedy Blvd.
(P.O. Box 3428)
Tampa (33601)
(813) 251-8984
www.stageworkstheatre.org

After 27 years of being a gypsy theater, producing a variety of works ranging from *Private Lives* to *Waiting for Godot* on a variety of stages around Tampa, Stageworks Theatre will be settling into its own space early in 2010. Stageworks Theatre relies primarily on local actors, both Equity and non-Equity performers, and encourages mixing veteran performers with less experienced actors as a means of continually renewing the theater tradition. Stageworks Theatre was, for many years, in residence at the University of Tampa's Falk Theatre, has performed at the Straz Center's Shimberg Theatre, and has co-produced works with the Gorilla Theatre. Their outreach programs include work with youth in the juvenile justice system.

THEATER VENUES AND PERFORMING ARTS SCHOOLS

Our three largest performing arts venues—the Mahaffey Theater in St. Petersburg, Ruth Eckerd Hall in Clearwater, and the Straz Center in Tampa—as well as other, smaller theaters host a variety of acts throughout the year. We'll break this section into geographic regions: Tampa/Hillsborough County, St. Petersburg/South Pinellas, and Clearwater/North Pinellas.

Tampa/Hillsborough County
CARROLLWOOD CULTURAL CENTER
4537 Lowell Rd.
Tampa
(813) 269-1310
www.carrollwoodcenter.org
Box office: The office is open Monday through Friday from 8 a.m. to 6 p.m.
Theaters: Main hall (212 seats, regular; 120 seats, cabaret)
Built: 2008

Education and Outreach: Various theater, dance, and other performance classes are offered at the Carrollwood Cultural Center.
Notable fact: Salerno Theatre Co., Inc., is the theater-in-residence at Carrollwood.
Parking: Free, onsite parking

DAVID A. STRAZ JR. CENTER FOR PERFORMING ARTS
1010 N. W.C. MacInnes Place
Tampa
(813) 222-1000
Box office: (813) 229-STAR (7827), (800) 955-1045. The ticket office is open Monday through Saturday from noon to 8 p.m. and Sunday from noon to 6 p.m.
Built: 1987
Theaters: Carol Morsani Hall (2,610 seats); Ferguson Hall (1,042 seats); the Jaeb Theater (268 seats); the TECO Energy Foundation Theater (250 seats); the Shimberg Playhouse (130 seats)
Education and Outreach: Patel Conservatory, which features 20 studios, a sound and lighting laboratory, a technical theater workshop, media arts/TV studio, and its own rehearsal hall and black-box theater.
Notable fact: The Straz Center (formerly the Tampa Bay Performing Arts Center) is the largest performing arts complex south of Washington, D.C.'s John F. Kennedy Center for the Performing Arts.
Parking: The Poe Garage ($6) is at Ashley Street and Cass Street. It connects via a covered walkway bridge to the Performing Arts Center. Other parking garages are nearby, and valet parking ($12) is available.

St. Petersburg/South Pinellas
THE PALLADIUM THEATER
253 5th Ave. N.
St. Petersburg
(727) 822-3590
www.mypalladium.org
Box office: (727) 822-3590. The box office is open one hour prior to performances. Otherwise, box office hours vary. Call for more information.
Built: 1925

> **i** The seats in the Palladium Theater date back a ways. One clue as to the vintage of the seats can be found right under them. Fastened to the bottom of each seat is a wire rack that, once upon a time, was used to hold a gentleman's hat.

Theaters: Hough Concert Hall (850 seats)
Education and Outreach: In 2007, the Palladium Theater came under the umbrella of St. Petersburg College for use as a community theater, to showcase student productions, and to allow emerging artists a venue.
Notable fact: The building originally was a First Church of Christ Science meeting hall and holds a full-sized Skinner Pipe Organ.
Parking: Free parking is available in the lots next door and across the street.

PINELLAS PARK PERFORMING ARTS CENTER
4951 78th Ave. N.
Pinellas Park
(727) 541-0721
www.pinellas-park.com/events/performing_arts_center.asp
Box office: Event line is (727) 541-0895.
Built: 1970s
Theaters: Main Hall (500 seats)
Education and Outreach: The Pinellas Park Civic Orchestra gives a free evening concert the first Sunday of each month.
Notable fact: The Pinellas Park Performing Arts Center was a church until the city bought it in 2007. The Classical Christian School for the Arts is located next door, but is not affiliated with the city.
Parking: Free, on-site parking.

PROGRESS ENERGY CENTER FOR THE ARTS
400 1st St. S.
St. Petersburg
(727) 892-5798
Box office: (727) 892-5767. The ticket office is open Thursday through Saturday from noon to 6 p.m. and two hours prior to any ticketed event.
Built: 2005 ($20-million major renovation and expansion)
Theaters: Mahaffey Theater (2,030 seats)

Education and outreach: The Class Acts program offers local school children live-theater performances both at the Mahaffey Theater and at their schools.

Notable fact: The Progress Energy Center for the Arts includes the Mahaffey Theater, offices for the Mahaffey Theater Foundation, the Center Plaza Waterfront Park, and the new Salvador Dalí Museum (under construction and opening in 2011).

Parking: On-site parking is available for $6.

Clearwater/North Pinellas

LARGO CULTURAL CENTER

105 Central Park Dr.
(P.O. Box 296)
Largo (33779-0296)
(727) 587-6751

Box office: (727) 587-6793. Box office hours are Tuesday through Friday from 10 a.m. to 6 p.m. and Saturday from 10 a.m. to 2 p.m.

Built: 1996

Theaters: Tonne Playhouse (333 seats, tiered; 250 seats, cabaret)

Education and outreach: Largo Cultural Center includes in its programs performances that are part of its Children's Educational and Family Theatre Series. They also offer a Summer Theatre Camp.

Notable fact: On the grounds of the Largo Cultural Center is the original Largo Feed Store, a historic building now used for rehearsal dinners and other parties. Eight O'Clock Theatre is the resident community theater company at Largo Cultural Center.

Parking: There is free parking in lots on either side of the theater.

RUTH ECKERD HALL

1111 McMullen Booth Rd.
Clearwater
(727) 791-7060
www.rutheckerdhall.com

Box office: (727) 791-7400, (800) 875-8682. The box office is open Monday through Saturday from 10 a.m. to 6 p.m. and one hour prior to performances.

Built: 1983. Officially, the center is the Richard B. Baumgardner Center for the Performing Arts, but very few people know it by that name.

Theaters: Ruth Eckerd Hall (2,180 seats), Murray Studio (200 seats, black-box)

Education and outreach: Marcia P. Hoffman Performing Arts Institute offers music, theater, dance, and technical classes and workshops to people of all ages. The institute also hosts the Family Theater Series performances, is the home of Eckerd Theater Company, and partners with Morton Plant Mease Hospital to provide the Arts in Medicine program.

Notable fact: *Billboard* magazine ranked Ruth Eckerd Hall number one in ticket sales and gross dollars for venues of its size for the period November 2007 through May 2008.

Parking: Parking lots and valet parking are available on-site. Parking fees start at $5.

TARPON SPRINGS PERFORMING ARTS CENTER

324 Pine St.
Tarpon Springs
(727) 937-0686
www.tarponarts.org

Box office: (727) 942-5605. Box office hours are 9 a.m. to 5 p.m. Monday through Friday and noon to 4 p.m. on Saturday, as well as before and during shows that are not sold out.

Built: 1925 (restored 1987)

Theaters: Main Stage (350 seats)

Education and outreach: The Cultural Arts Department has traveling local-history trunks available for teachers, especially fourth grade teachers. Some performances at the Performing Arts Center are available for school field trips.

Notable fact: The theater is located inside the City Hall building, which originally was a school building.

Parking: Parking is free in any of the lots surrounding City Hall.

FINE ARTS CALENDAR

So many of our festivals combine activities from cooking to jazz jamming that it's hard to classify them as one particular kind of event. Combination festivals—and music festivals other than classical music events—are listed in the Annual Events and Festivals chapter. Many of them attract artists of various genres and disciplines.

The events listed below, however, are more exclusively arts-oriented. Visual arts events listed are juried and usually include cash awards.

These are not the only events in our two-county area. Check museum and gallery Web sites for in-house and local showings. Look for commercial art and craft fairs throughout the year—many of the artists who exhibit their work at these fine arts festivals also sell their work at local fairs.

February

GASPARILLA INTERNATIONAL FILM FESTIVAL

(813) 514-9962

www.gasparillafilmfestival.com

The Gasparilla Film Festival, sponsored by the Tampa Film Institute, brings several art films to the Tampa Bay area each February. Films are shown at venues including the Tampa Theater, a Channelside theater, and the University of Tampa, as well as at the Beach Theater in St. Pete Beach and Studio 620 in St. Petersburg. The Tampa Film Institute sponsors other projects throughout the year as well, such as the Global Film Initiative.

March

GASPARILLA FESTIVAL OF THE ARTS

Franklin Street and Lykes Gaslight Square Park

Tampa

(813) 876-1747

www.gasparilla-arts.com

Originally part of the Gasparilla festivities, the Gasparilla Festival of the Arts now takes place after the pirates leave—we wouldn't want to have all that luscious artwork on display with marauding mavericks roaming around, now would we? (See description of Gasparilla in the Annual Events and Festivals chapter.) Three hundred artists from around the world fill the Franklin Street pedes-

trian mall in downtown Tampa with two- and three-dimensional products of their imaginations and compete for $75,000 in cash awards. Serious collectors are invited to an after-hours viewing of the works.

An Emerging Artists program, a Young Artist Showcase, musical artists performing a range of styles from jazz to opera, a children's hands-on-art activity area, and food vendors make this two-day festival a satisfying event. No wonder it's one of the nation's top art festivals.

Admission is free. No pets, and no wheeled transportation (such as bicycles, skateboards, or rollerblades). Parking is available in several parking garages or on the street.

TAMPA BAY JEWISH FILM FESTIVAL

Tampa Jewish Community Center

13009 Community Campus Dr.

Tampa

(813) 264-9000

www.festivalfocus.org

The Tampa Bay Jewish Film Festival features films about the Jewish or Israeli experience at various times and in various places around the world. For viewing dates, locations, and submission information, check the Web site or give them a call.

April

AMERICAN STAGE IN THE PARK

Demens Landing Park

Corner of 1st Ave. N. and Bayshore Blvd. S.E.

St. Petersburg

(727) 823-PLAY (7529)

www.americanstage.org

Each spring, American Stage, St. Petersburg's professional regional Equity theater, takes its show on the road—or at least to the waterfront park area at the entrance to the Pier—and invites the public to join them for an *al fresco* performance. Theatergoers arrive up to two hours before curtain—er, starting—time to stake out the best seats and enjoy the outdoors. Some people come bearing all the fixings for an elegant picnic dinner. Others opt to purchase a meal from one of the food vendors (usually only a few choices, but they're good). Some people go all out, decking out small portable tables with linens, candles, and flowers. Other diners are more casual. No matter. The show—in 2009 it was *Altar Boyz*—itself is always high-energy and professionally produced.

Performances begin at 8 p.m. Wednesday through Sunday evenings, and the plays run about six weeks. Ticket prices range from $11 to $27. Bring your own blanket or lawn chairs, or sit in the reserved chair seating. Children ages 12 and under are free on the lawn seating. Two nights have a "Pay What You Can" rate. Theatergoers may not bring pets or alcohol, although beer and wine are sold at the park.

MAINSAIL ARTS FESTIVAL
Vinoy Park
701 Bayshore Dr. N.E.
St. Petersburg
(727) 892-5885
www.mainsailartsfestival.org

Some 250 juried fine artists from around the country gather in St. Petersburg's waterfront Vinoy Park to share their work with us and to compete for more than $50,000 in cash awards. The two-day event features top artists in oil, watercolor, mixed media, clay, and other media, many of whom demonstrate their technique throughout the weekend. Young artists from Pinellas County schools display their work in the Young at Art Student Show. A Kids Create activity tent lets kids try their hands at mixing colors or making their own masterpiece to take home.

A culinary arts food court features a variety of local foods—fajita wraps! Mmmmmm! Sweet potato pie! Double-mmmmm!—as well as the standby hot dogs and lemonade. Strolling minstrels and live entertainment on the stage make this a performance arts as well as a visual arts festival. *Sunshine Artists* magazine says this is one of the "100 Best" fine arts events in the country.

Admission is free. No pets, no coolers. Park in any of the downtown parking areas and take the free shuttle to the park.

July
COOL ART SHOW
The Coliseum
535 4th Ave. N.
St. Petersburg
(727) 892-5202
www.pava-artists.org

Come in out of the summer heat into the air-conditioned Coliseum and browse the works of the Professional Association of Visual Artists (PAVA)—works so cool they sizzle. About 80 local artists participate in this juried, members-only showing of fine art and crafts created in a variety of media from wood to glass, jewelry to watercolors, photography to ceramics, and more. While you're there, cast an appreciative eye over this historic building, built in 1924, with its oak dance floor.

Admission and parking are free for this two-day show. The Coliseum's concessions serve food and beverages, including beer and wine.

October
ART HARVEST
Highlander Park
1920 Pinehurst Rd.
Dunedin
(727) 738-5523
www.jlcd.org

When the air goes from hot and humid to cool and crisp, we know the two-day Art Harvest in Dunedin can't be far off. The area's largest autumn juried fine art show, a fund-raiser for the Junior League of Clearwater-Dunedin's local projects, attracts more than 225 artists from around the country who pitch their tents under the oaks and around Wee Loch Ness and exhibit their works. Cash awards of $27,500 were presented last year to the top artists.

Admission is free. Parking is $5 per vehicle at the park or $3 per vehicle at Dunedin High School (1651 Pinehurst Rd.; a shuttle is provided). Food vendors and a children's activity area keep everyone fed and occupied. Plus the Dunedin Fine Arts Center is open to visitors (see description elsewhere in this chapter).

CLEARWATER JAZZ 'N ART WALK
Downtown Clearwater
Clearwater
(727) 461-5200
www.jazznartwalk.com
Held in conjunction with the Clearwater Jazz Holiday (see Annual Events and Festivals), this juried two-day fine art show offers a $5,000 total purse to the top three entries. Visitors strolling through the downtown area can chat with the artists about their works and purchase a great find to take home. Entertainment and a youth art display add to the walk. Buy food from pushcart vendors or stop in at any of the downtown restaurants. Hours are 10 a.m. to 5 p.m.

CLIP FILM FESTIVAL
Various venues
P.O. Box 18445
Tampa 33679-8445
(727) 828-0735, (813) 879-4220
www.cliptampabay.com
Formerly the Tampa International Gay and Lesbian Film Festival, the Clip Film Festival held each October brings people from around the state—and from other states, too—to view films with various sexual themes and perspectives. Awards are presented to the best films and best actors in several categories. The Friends of the Festival also sponsor a year-round film outreach series.

NECRONOMICON CONVENTION
Hilton Bayfront Hotel
333 First St. S.
St. Petersburg
(813) 982-9616
www.stonehill.org/necro.htm
Sci-fi, fantasy, and horror buffs from around the country have gathered in St. Petersburg each October for the past almost 30 years to meet favorite authors, play games, and have fun at Necronomicon, a three-day convention hosted by Tampa Bay's Stone Hill Science Fiction Association. Gaming—including more than 90 video networked games, role playing games, and live-action role playing games—goes on pretty much around the clock. If you can break away from the game

---

More Information on the Arts

The three organizations listed below maintain comprehensive listings of arts- and humanities-related organizations, schools, events, and festivals. Additionally, each organization administers grant funding of arts- and humanities-related projects.

Arts Council of Hillsborough County
1000 N. Ashley Dr., Ste. 105
Tampa
(813) 276-8250
http://tampaarts.com
Request or print out their 16-page Multicultural Visitors Guide, which lists everything from ethnic restaurants and associations to historic information about African-Americans, Asians, and Hispanics in the Tampa Bay area.

Florida Humanities Council
599 2nd St. S.
St. Petersburg
(727) 873-2000
www.flahum.org
The Florida Humanities Council, headquartered on the St. Petersburg campus of the University of South Florida, publishes *FORUM* magazine and produces radio programs.

Pinellas County Cultural Affairs
13805 58th St. N. Ste. 2450
Clearwater
(727) 453-7860
www.pinellasarts.org
Request or print out their 12-page Public Art brochure—then spend the day on a treasure hunt that will take you everywhere from the medical examiner's office to Boca Ciega Millenium Park.

room, however, you can attend one of the author panel discussions or visit the art show. Previous conventions have featured guest authors including Catharine Asaro, Lloyd Kaufman, and others. Experts in the fields of space travel, medicine, and other sciences come to discuss the reality behind the genre. In the evening, costume contests and a prom round out the fun. In short, the convention pretty much takes over all the meeting space available at the Hilton. Proceeds from the convention are donated to local charities.

The Necronomicon Web site says the convention is for members only, but don't let that stop you—you become a member of the convention when you buy your ticket. Admission starts at $30 for all three days (pre-paid), which includes everything but meals (on your own at nearby local eateries) and hotel room (optional). Daytime activities are family friendly, but after 10 p.m. discussion topics and activities are of a more adult nature. Parents are advised to preview the art exhibit, as they may wish to steer their children clear of some images. A phone number is listed above, but the preferred means of contact is via email at raggedyann@stonehill.org.

November

CRAFTART
Florida Craftsmen Gallery
501 Central Ave.
St. Petersburg
(727) 821-7391
www.floridacraftsmen.net

Florida fine craft artists from around the state gather outside the Florida Craftsmen Gallery for a two-day showing of their work and to compete for $15,000 in cash awards. This is where you'll find one-of-a-kind furniture pieces; architectural details like hand-painted, somewhat surreal tiles; and functional art. The exhibit is inside and just outside the gallery, so there are no additional activities going on—except for whatever's happening in downtown St. Petersburg that weekend, of course!

ATTRACTIONS AND KIDSTUFF

We thought about splitting this chapter into two parts, but so many attractions are kid-friendly. And so much so-called "kidstuff" appeals to the inner kid in all but the most curmudgeonly of us that we're keeping it all together.

Up front, however, you'll find Pint-Sized Fun for Little Ones. Here we feature attractions that are less overwhelming to the ages seven-and-under crowd—and to anyone looking for simpler pleasures than seeing just how many times one can be spun, looped, and twisted before flying apart at the joints.

We'll give you the get-you-started info on Adventure Island and Busch Gardens, our major theme parks, as well as on zoos, aquariums, and historical museums.

Look for a Close-up on an entire town. Tarpon Springs, home to the United States' largest concentration of people with Greek heritage, invites visitors to explore this north Pinellas town.

Many events listed in the Annual Events and Festivals chapter have carnival-type rides and other activities to keep kids busy. A couple of game places are listed in the Nightlife chapter. These places serve alcohol and are adults-only at night, but welcome parent-supervised children during the daytime.

Most attractions require shirts, pants or shorts, and shoes of some kind. Most outdoor attractions permit smoking only in designated areas, for the convenience of other guests. Smoking is not permitted in indoor attractions.

This chapter is organized by type of activity—Pint-Sized Fun for Little Ones, It Takes a Village, Amusement Parks, Aquariums and Zoos, History and Science Museums, Roller Rinks, and Skateboarding. Within each category, the attractions are listed alphabetically.

PINT-SIZED FUN FOR LITTLE ONES

For the times when you want to experience something less intense—regardless of your age!

DINOSAUR WORLD
5145 Harvey Tew Rd.
Plant City
(813) 717-9865
www.dinoworld.net

More than 150 life-sized dinosaurs roam the woods in Dinosaur World (exit 17 off I–4). Even with no scary sounds or animatronics, these gargantuan creatures impress visitors of all ages. Let the sandbox set dig in the boneyard. A playground, museum, and movie cave add to the fun.

Admission is $12.95 for adults, $10.75 for seniors (sixty and up), and $9.75 for children three

to twelve. Parking is free. Bring a cooler for an *al fresco* lunch, or have pizza delivered to the park. Vending machines sell chips and sodas. Friendly pets on leashes are welcome.

GREAT EXPLORATIONS CHILDREN'S MUSEUM
1925 4th St. N.
St. Petersburg
(727) 821-8992
www.greatex.org

Great Explorations Children's Museum invites preschoolers through elementary-age children to explore communities through exhibits like a child-sized market, a veterinary office, and a life-sized tree house. Look also for a laser operated harp, a climbing wall, and a robot lab plus more.

Great Explorations Children's Museum is open Monday through Saturday from 10:00 a.m.

to 4:30 p.m. and Sunday from noon to 4:30 p.m. Admission is $9 for ages eleven months and older, $8 for seniors ages sixty-five and older. No pets. Closed Christmas and New Year's Day.

GLAZER CHILDREN'S MUSEUM
110 Gasparilla Plaza
Tampa
(813) 277-3199
www.glazermuseum.org
Opening in 2010, the Glazer Children's Museum plans 175 interactive, accessible, bilingual exhibits featuring everything from a drop of water to a cruise ship. Check the Web site for opening date, hours, and fees.

LARGO CENTRAL RAILROAD
Largo Central Park
101 Central Park Dr.
Largo
(727) 585-9835
www.lcrailroad.com
All aboard! The first full weekend of each month, from 10 a.m. to 4 p.m., volunteers at Largo Central Railroad offer free rides to the public on a large scale-model railroad running on 1.2 miles of track through Largo Central Park. This is the kind of train you sit on, not in, as it chugs along, passing bronze sculptures as it travels through the park.

THE PIER AQUARIUM
800 Second Ave. N.E.
St. Petersburg
(727) 895-7437
www.pieraquarium.org
Twelve well-lit, not-too-deep aquariums keep marine creatures from around the world front and center. Adults may need to lift little ones up to see some of the exhibits, but it's worth doing so. Touch Tank Experience Time is from 1 to 4 p.m. each day. Visitors can hold sea stars, tulip snails, hermit crabs, and other critters. Fish feeding time is 3 p.m. each day. Story and craft times are on Wednesday.

The Pier Aquarium is open 10 a.m. to 8 p.m. Monday through Saturday ($5 for adults, $4 seniors and students) and noon to 4 p.m. Sunday

($2.50 for all). Children age six and under are free. The Pier Aquarium is closed Christmas Day.

SUNSETS AT PIER 60
10 Pier 60 Dr.
Clearwater
(727) 461-7732
www.sunsetsatpier60.com
Late each afternoon, buskers—street performers—appear on Pier 60, on Clearwater Beach. Steel drummers, living statues, balloon artists—you never know who will show up. Artists and other vendors sell their wares starting about two hours before sundown. The park has a snack bar, restrooms, and a large covered playground on the beach area. Sunsets at Pier 60 runs every day, weather permitting.

IT TAKES A VILLAGE

Some of our attractions are parts of towns or offer more than one kind of activity.

HERITAGE VILLAGE
11909 125th Street N.
Largo 33774
(727) 582-2123
www.pinellascounty.org/heritage

FLORIDA BOTANICAL GARDENS
12520 Ulmerton Road
Largo, FL 33774
(727) 582-2100
www.flbg.org
Heritage Village and the Florida Botanical Gardens, part of Pinellas County's Pinewood Cultural Center, are linked by walking paths. Thirty historic buildings from around the county have been moved to Heritage Village's twenty-one acres. Walk through the McMullen Log Cabin, the oldest existing structure in the county, or sit at a desk in part of the 1915 Union Academy, one of the county's first "Negro schools." Visit the tiny Safety Harbor Church, or see the Sulphur Springs Depot.

See Heritage Village through self-guided tours or join a docent-led group. Some buildings may be closed for school tours during the morning. See the Annual Events and Festivals chapter to learn about events held here featuring blacksmithing, cane syrup boiling, and other demonstrations. Admission is free, but donations are appreciated. Heritage Village is open 10 a.m. to 4 p.m. Tuesday through Saturday and 1 to 4 p.m. Sunday every day except Thanksgiving and Christmas. Parking inside the gate is limited, so park just outside the gate along the fence. Bring a picnic lunch. Vending machines sell sodas and snacks.

Cultivated gardens occupy thirty acres of the Florida Botanical Gardens. Another ninety acres are home to wetland and woodland plants and animals. The Pinellas County Extension offices are inside the Welcome Center. Experts can answer questions about soil pH or other gardening questions. Admission is free and there is plenty of parking, also free. The Florida Botanical Gardens is open 7 a.m. to 7 p.m. every day. The Welcome Center is open 8 a.m. to 5 p.m. Monday through Friday. Pets on leashes are permitted in the garden area, but not the natural wooded area. No bicycles, skateboards, or roller skates.

JOHN'S PASS VILLAGE
150 John's Pass Boardwalk
Madeira Beach
(727) 391-6025 x303
www.johnspassfestivals.com
This two-story fishing village at John's Pass, a water passage from the Intracoastal Waterway to the Gulf of Mexico, hosts parasailing, jet-ski, and fishing or casino charter cruise adventures. Pirate ships cater to visitors yearning for a little yo-ho-ho. A game arcade offers landside fun. Restaurants and ice cream shops keep tummies full. (See Shopping chapter)

A couple of attractions at the village cost nothing. Watch the boats sail in and out or watch fishermen unload their catch. Or cross under the bridge to the beach and marvel at the underside of the drawbridge mechanism!

THE PIER
800 2nd Ave. N.E.
St. Petersburg
(727) 821-6164
www.stpete-pier.com
Some people ridicule its design, but to us the five-story upside down pyramid at the end of The Pier says St. Petersburg turns things on end and shows us new possibilities, just as Peter Demens and John Williams did in 1889. That's when Demens built the first wharf on this spot and ran his Orange Belt Railroad to it because Williams envisioned what the area could be. The first Pier Pavilion was built in 1895, the current structure in 1973.

With an aquarium, shops, and restaurants, including one of the world famous Columbia Restaurants, The Pier is a microcosm of the Tampa Bay area. The top observation deck offers a great view of the city and the harbor. Rent fishing poles and catch a shark, or rent bikes and roam the downtown area. Charter boats do sunset cruises and out-to-sea weddings.

Park in one of the two lots at the approach to The Pier ($3 per day; $5 during special events) and ride the red trolley for free.

AMUSEMENT PARKS

ADVENTURE ISLAND
10001 N. McKinley Dr.
Tampa
(888) 800-5447
www.adventureisland.com
Slip-slidin' or floatin' along, Adventure Island offers both kinds of watery fun. Drift along the Rambling Bayou, or launch yourself down the Gulfscream's 225-foot long body slide at 42 mph—or try one of the kinder, gentler water slides, a 17,000-gallon wave pool, a sandy beach, or the Splash Attack fun maze. Fabian's Fun Port, for smaller children, lets youngsters play in bubbling springs or on a watery jungle gym. Spike Zone, an 11-court white-sand volleyball complex, hosts professional tournaments.

You'll get your exercise—many rides require climbing several flights of stairs. Some rides have wheelchair access. Adventure Island's Web site lists restrictions and accessibility information for each ride.

Adventure Island is open mid-March to mid-October. Hours and days vary. We strongly suggest you call or go online before you visit.

Admission is $39.95 for guests ages ten and up, $35.95 for children ages three to nine. Ages two and under are free. Parking is $10. Rented Cabanas ($125 per day) or Chiki Huts ($50 per day) include a small refrigerator, chairs, and towels. Small coolers are permitted. Check the Web site for clothing requirements.

Buy a bar-coded, waterproof wristband loaded with Caribbean Coin to pay for food and other items in the park. Unspent money will be refunded. Food options range from snacks to burgers, wraps, and pizza. Parents of teenaged eating machines might want to consider an all-day, all-you-can eat dining pass for $22.95 ($13.95 for children ages three through nine).

BUSCH GARDENS
10165 N. McKinley Dr.
Tampa
(888) 800-5447
www.buschgardens.com
Busch Gardens has come a long way since it began in 1959 as Anheuser Busch brewery's free gardens. The brewery closed in 1995, but Busch Entertainment Corp. eventually amassed the world's second-largest theme park collection. In October 2009, the Blackstone Group, which owns Merlin Entertainments and half of Universal Orlando, bought Busch Entertainment Corp.

Today, the African-themed Busch Gardens in Tampa lets visitors explore bat caves and bird gardens, ride body and brain boggling coaster rides, and watch 4-D comedy-adventure shows. Wear clothing that dries quickly—some rides can leave you damp or even soaking wet. Land of the Dragons is for the youngest visitors, and the Cheetah Chase's top speed of 22 mph makes it among the tamest of coaster rides. The Serengeti

Plain contains one of the largest collections of African animals outside of Africa itself.

Busch Gardens is open 10 a.m. to 6 p.m. every day. Hours are extended during special events. Admission is $74.95 for adults, $64.95 for children ages three to nine. Children two and under are free. Additional charges apply to some activities. Parking starts at $11. Strollers, wheelchairs, and pet kennels can be rented. Dining options are typical, but varied.

i Your party split up, and you're waiting for them. Slip on over to the Scorpion, Busch Garden's shortest coaster, which does anything but coast and packs a sting. Plus the line is generally shorter—perfect for when you're in between events or waiting for friends.

CELEBRATION STATION
24546 U.S. 19 N.
Clearwater
(727) 791-1799
www.celebrationstation.com
Celebrate fun with go-karts, batting cages, arcade games, a Playland with gentler rides, bumper boats, laser tag, and miniature golf. There's no admission fee, and activity prices vary. Most start at $2.50 each (arcade games use quarters or tokens). Ask about all-day play passes and packages that include meals. The on-site restaurant serves burgers, pizza, soft drinks, and the like, but Celebration Station will cater barbecue and other dinners for groups. Hours are noon to 9 p.m. Monday through Thursday, noon to 11 p.m. Friday, 10 a.m. to 11 p.m. Saturday, and 11 a.m. to 9 p.m. Sunday.

GRAND PRIX TAMPA
14320 N. Nebraska Ave.
Tampa
(813) 977-6272
www.grandprixtampa.com
Go Karts aren't the only thing going at Grand Prix Tampa. Bat, bungee, golf, or play games in the Castle Arcade. Or splat your friends with paintballs ($12.95 plus cost of paintballs). No admis-

sion fee means you pay only when you play. The Pit Stop Cafe serves food, soft drinks, and beer. Grand Prix Tampa is open 3 to 10 p.m. Monday through Thursday, noon to midnight Friday, 10 am. to midnight Saturday, and 10 a.m. to 10 p.m. Sunday.

AQUARIUMS AND ZOOS

CLEARWATER MARINE AQUARIUM
249 Windward Passage
Clearwater 33767-2244
(727) 441-1790
www.cmaquarium.org
The Clearwater Marine Aquarium is a marine rehabilitation center open to the public. Visitors see people working to help injured turtles, dolphins, stingrays, and other animals, some of which are permanent residents. The Clearwater Marine Aquarium offers educational shows and presentations throughout the day. See the Parks and Recreation chapter to learn about kayak tours.

The Clearwater Marine Aquarium is open 9 a.m. to 5 p.m. Monday through Thursday, 9 a.m. to 7 p.m. Friday and Saturday, and 10 a.m. to 5 p.m. Sunday. They are closed New Year's Day, Easter Sunday, Thanksgiving, Christmas Eve, and Christmas Day. Admission is $11 for adults, $9 for seniors (ages sixty and above), $7.50 for children ages three through twelve.

THE FLORIDA AQUARIUM, INC.
701 Channelside Dr.
Tampa 33602
(813) 273-4000
www.flaquarium.org
The multi-level Florida Aquarium explores the watery environments found in Florida. See how water bubbles up from the Florida aquifer into springs that form ponds and lakes where bluegill and bass live. Explore streams, rivers, and salt marshes where alligators swim r-e-a-l-l-y close to the thick acrylic wall separating them from visitors. Stand in front of a 42-foot-wide, 14-foot-high acrylic wall and see into a coral reef. Or bring a swimsuit and swim in the 500,000-gallon

Coral Reef ($85, ages six and up). Kids can play in an outdoor water park with a two-story pirate ship complete with water cannons. See Tampa Bay from a 49-foot powered catamaran on an Eco-Tour.

The Florida Aquarium is open 9:30 a.m. to 5:00 p.m. every day except Thanksgiving and Christmas. Admission is $19.95 for adults, $16.95 for seniors ages sixty and above, $14.95 for children ages three to eleven. Children two and under are free. Eco-Tours are extra. A café and restaurant are on-site.

SUNCOAST SEABIRD SANCTUARY
18328 Gulf Blvd.
Indian Shores 33785
(727) 391-6211 or (727) 391-2473
www.seabirdsanctuary.com
Each year, the Suncoast Seabird Sanctuary rescues and treats about 10,000 injured birds—that's twenty to thirty birds each day. Some birds are treated and released back into the wild. Some birds become permanent residents of the sanctuary.

Visitors to the Sanctuary, open 9 a.m. to sunset every day, can walk through the exhibit areas and see different species of birds. Free, guided tours are at 2 p.m. on Wednesday and Sunday afternoons. Private group tours also can be scheduled. Free.

TAMPA'S LOWRY PARK ZOO
1101 W. Sligh Ave.
Tampa 33604-5958
(813) 935-8552
www.lowryparkzoo.com
Named the number-one zoo for kids by *Parent's Magazine* (2009), Tampa's Lowry Park Zoo lets visitors explore eight different habitats with more than 2,000 animals from around the world. Ride a camel, touch a rhinoceros, or feed a giraffe! The zoo also has two water play areas and a climb-on playground. Rides include a flume, roller coaster, sky-tram, and others. Shows and talks throughout the day teach visitors about the animals. Or take a pontoon-boat River Odyssey Eco-Cruise on the Hillsborough River.

Tampa's Lowry Park Zoo is open 9:30 a.m. to 5:00 p.m. every day except Thanksgiving and Christmas. Admission is $19.95 for adults, $17.95 for seniors ages sixty and up, and $14.95 for children ages three through eleven. Children ages two and under are free. An unlimited ride wristband costs $20. The Eco-Cruise costs $14 for adults, $13 for seniors, and $10 for children. Parking is free. Nine different dining options range from snacks to full meals, or bring a picnic cooler and eat in the park area outside the zoo.

HISTORY AND SCIENCE MUSEUMS

FLORIDA HOLOCAUST MUSEUM
55 5th St. S.
St. Petersburg
(727) 820-0100
www.flhm2.org
Over the past 30 years, the Florida Holocaust Museum has grown from an idea to being one of the largest Holocaust museums in the United States. The centerpiece exhibit is an original boxcar from Gdania, Poland, used during World War II to transport Jews and other victims of the Nazi regime to the concentration camps. Visitors view scenes from pre-war Jewish life, learn about the history of anti-Semitism, see a scale model of Birkenau, and learn about "righteous Gentiles," who risked their lives to save others. The museum has also spotlighted other victims of discrimination including Carl Wilkins, the only American who stayed in Rwanda in 1994 rather than be evacuated.

The Florida Holocaust Museum is open 10 a.m. to 5 p.m. every day except Rosh Hashana, Yom Kippur, Thanksgiving, Christmas, and New Year's Day. The last admission is at 3:30 p.m. Admission is $14 for adults, $12 for seniors ages sixty and above, $10 for college students, and $8 for students under age eighteen. Members of the military and children ages six and under are free. Children under age sixteen must be accompanied by an adult. Parking in the museum's lot is free; otherwise look for metered parking along the streets.

Black enamel metal hands reach through barbed wire and fencing at the rear corner of the parking area behind the Florida Holocaust Museum. The small sculpture, "Let My People Go," by Dr. Ken Olshansky, reminds passersby—those who notice it, that is—of the price of looking the other way.

HENRY B. PLANT MUSEUM
401 W. Kennedy Blvd.
Tampa
(813) 254-1891
www.plantmuseum.com
Built in 1891 by railroad magnate Henry B. Plant at a cost of $2.5 million, the Tampa Bay Hotel covered six acres of land in an area inhabited primarily by mosquitoes and alligators. Plant furnished the hotel with treasures from around the world—at a cost of another half million dollars. The rich and famous came to hunt, fish, and dine in elegance. When Plant died in 1904, the City of Tampa bought the hotel. In the 1930s, it became home to the University of Tampa. The southeast wing, however, became the Henry B. Plant Museum. (Read more in the Accommodations chapter).

The museum is open 10 a.m. to 4 p.m. Tuesday through Saturday and noon to 4 p.m. Sunday. The museum is closed Thanksgiving, Christmas Eve, and Christmas Day. Donations of $5 for adults and $2 for children under age twelve are requested. Guided tours begin at 1 p.m. Tuesday through Friday. There are only eleven parking places in front of the museum, but there is free parking a few blocks away.

From December 1 through December 23, visitors enjoy a Victorian Christmas Stroll through decorated rooms. Carolers perform in the evenings and spiced cider and cookies are served on the veranda. Admission is $10 for adults, $5 for children twelve and younger.

MUSEUM OF SCIENCE AND INDUSTRY (MOSI)
4801 E. Fowler Ave.
Tampa 33617
(813) 987-6100
www.mosi.org

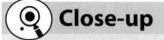

Close-up

Tarpon Springs

Tarpon Springs Chamber of Commerce
11 E. Orange St.
Tarpon Springs
(727) 937-6109
www.tarponspringschamber.com

Most people think of the sponge docks first when they think of Tarpon Springs. But there's also shopping in downtown Tarpon Springs (see Shopping chapter), an Epiphany celebration you won't find many other places in the world outside of Greece (see Annual Events and Festivals), and both a cultural arts center and a performance arts center you'll want to visit (see Arts chapter).

HISTORY

Tarpon Springs sits in the northernmost part of Pinellas County where the Anclote River empties into the Gulf of Mexico. Wealthy northerners built winter homes here in the 1870s. Seeing an abundance of tarpon coming into the river to spawn, they named the area Tarpon Springs.

Hamilton Disston, the Philadelphia tool manufacturer who saved Florida's post–Civil War government from bankruptcy when he purchased four million acres of land—16,000 square miles—for $1 million in 1881 (see History chapter), knew some of those northerners.

Disston built first in Tarpon Springs. He founded the Lake Butler Villa Co., hired an attorney, a surveyor, and a manager (Anson P. Safford, the former governor of Arizona), and started building hotels. Visitors who came to fish and stay in the hotels often liked the area so much that they bought houses. By 1887, Tarpon Springs had grown to the point that it became the first incorporated town on the Pinellas Peninsula.

One of the newcomers to the area was John Cheyney, a banker. Cheyney brought sponge rakers from the Bahamas and Cuba—where the sponge industry was suffering because of two kinds of bad climates: the weather and the Cuban revolution—to Tarpon Springs. Cheyney made connections with the northern markets that used sponges in their industries.

In 1905, John Cocoris came from New York to work for Cheyney. Cocoris, a sponge bleacher, knew that the Greek sponge divers could harvest more sponges from the deeper waters than the sponge rakers could from the shallows. Cocoris's brothers came over from Greece. Together they mapped the sponge beds and then brought a crew of divers from the Dodecanese Islands of Greece. Before long, they had set up their own business.

The Cocoris brothers' success brought immigrants from Greece and those who had settled else-

MOSI (pronounced mosey), is the largest science center in the southeastern United States. With more than 450 interactive permanent exhibits and as host to top-notch traveling exhibits, MOSI makes science understandable, relevant—and fun! Sit in a wind tunnel and feel what Category One hurricane force winds are like, or become an astronaut in the Challenger Learning Center. The IMAX Dome Theater, the Science Works Theater, and the Planetarium teach us about our world. The Kids in Charge! area provides activities for toddlers and for older children.

MOSI opens at 9 a.m. every day of the year and closes at 5 p.m. Monday through Friday and at 6 p.m. Saturday and Sunday. Admission begins at $20.95 for adults, $18.95 for seniors ages sixty and above, and $16.95 for children ages two to twelve. An on-site café serves snacks and meals.

where in the United States into Tarpon Springs. Before long, Tarpon Springs had become home to the greatest concentration of Greek people in the United States.

For 30 years, sponging was Florida's leading industry. But in 1947, a red tide algae bloom killed most of the sponge fields in the area. Spongers became shrimpers and fishermen. The sponge docks became a tourist attraction, and most of the sponges sold there are imported from other areas.

More recently, however, the sponge beds have recovered. In the 1980s, the sponge industry revived. In 2007, a record harvest of sponges by a single boat was reported.

The influence of Greek culture in the area has spread beyond Tarpon Springs and beyond the tourist industry. Two Pinellas County charter schools—public schools that use different curricula but are still required to meet state testing standards—include instruction in Greek language and culture (see Education chapter).

Tarpon Springs Trolley: Park in one of the free city-owned lots and take the Tarpon Springs Trolley on a Treasure Trail tour to get a feel for the area. Make stops along the way or go the distance in one shot. The trolley runs September through April (11 a.m. to 5 p.m., Tuesday through Sunday and until 7 p.m. on Friday and Saturday) and cycles every 25 to 30 minutes. Cost is $1 per ride or $3 all day and you must have exact change. Call (727) 942-5605 for reservations.

Walking Tour: Stop in at the Chamber of Commerce office for information on sights to see within walking distance of downtown, including the beautiful St. Nicholas Greek Orthodox Cathedral, the Historic Railroad Depot Museum, and other spots.

Downtown: Many antiques stores and other shops are in the downtown area, along with the old City Hall, which is now the Tarpon Springs Cultural Arts Center. Look also for the Classic Corvettes and Collectables Gallery (see Shopping chapter).

Sponge Docks: From the downtown area, drive on up North Pinellas Avenue to Dodecanese Boulevard and take a left. You might find a free parking spot or two, but you'll probably pay a few dollars to park in one of the lots at the east end of the docks. The docks lie in the mouth of the Anclote River where it empties into the Gulf of Mexico. You can walk the docks and watch the boats or take a dolphin-watching or sponge-diving cruise to learn about the sponge business that for 30 years was Florida's largest industry. There's a museum or two—just don't expect animatronics or special effects. In the evening, there's usually a game of backgammon going on outside a shop. Or just sit near the statue dedicated to the sponge divers, close your eyes, and listen to the sounds of Greek music and Greek conversation flowing around you. Smell the peppers and onions grilling and the *gyro* meat cooking. *Opa,* indeed.

TAMPA HISTORY CENTER
801 Old Water St.
Tampa
(813) 228-0097
www.tampabayhistorycenter.org
Located on the banks of the *Cotanchobee* ("Where the Big Water Meets the Land"), today's Hillsborough River, the Tampa Bay area's newest history center, opened in January 2009. Here's where history meets high-tech. Upstairs is an interactive Google Earth–type view of the Tampa Bay area. Or sit in a sculling boat and row through a course on the Hillsborough River—on the overhead monitor, anyway!

The Tampa Bay History Center is open 10 a.m. to 5 p.m. every day except Thanksgiving and Christmas. Admission is $12 for adults; $10 for seniors sixty-five and older, students, and youth ages thirteen to seventeen; and $7 for children ages four to twelve. Children three and under are free. Parking is $5 at the lot next door. Inside you'll find a gift store and a Columbia Cafe (see Restaurant chapter).

YBOR CITY MUSEUM STATE PARK
1818 East 9th Ave.
Tampa
(813) 247-1434
www.floridastateparks.org/yborcity
www.ybormuseum.org
Yes, it's a Florida State Park, but the Ybor City Museum State Park is smack dab in the middle of Ybor City so we're including it here in the Attractions chapter. Step into the former Ferlita Bakery building where, up until the 1920s, thousands of loaves of bread each week were baked in the huge brick ovens at the back of the building. Wander through the exhibits, reminders of what life was like more than a century ago for Cuban, Spanish, Italian, and Eastern European immigrants to Tampa. Tour the *casitas* next door—small homes in which a cigar worker and his family might have lived.

The museum is open 9 a.m. to 5 p.m. every day except Thanksgiving, Christmas, and New Year's Day. *La Casita* is open from 10 a.m. to 3 p.m. Guided tours are available Monday through Saturday. Admission is $3 for everyone ages six and older. Children ages five and under are free. Some metered parking is available on surrounding streets, or there are two parking garages within a few blocks of the museum—one on 9th Ave. near 13th St. and one at 15th St. and 5th Ave. (Read about the November Cigar Heritage Festival in the Annual Events and Festivals chapter.)

ROLLER RINKS

For a comprehensive listing of Florida roller rinks, speed clubs, derby and hockey teams, and other activities, go to Quad Club Dot Com at www.quadskating.com/rinks/us/fl.htm. Check the calendars of the rinks listed below for adults-only, all night, cheap, and open skate times. Prices listed below do not include skate rental.

ASTRO SKATING CENTER OF TARPON SPRINGS
875 Cypress St.
Tarpon Springs
(727) 938-5778
http://astroskatingcenter.com
A recent week's events included an All Day Skate from 9 a.m. to 5 p.m. ($9.99) that included free pony rides, inflatable activities, and free pizza and soda. Friday listed an Adult Organ Music Skate from 10:00 a.m. to 12:30 p.m. ($6) and the Big Show from 7:30 to 10:30 p.m.

ASTRO SKATING CENTER OF PINELLAS PARK
10001 66th St.
Pinellas Park
(727) 546-0018
http://astroskatingcenter.com
Look for an Adult Organ Music Skate from 10:00 a.m. to 12:30 p.m. ($6), a Wednesday Adult Night Party (ages 17 and older only, $6), the Big Show on Friday from 7:30 to 10:30 p.m. (suggested for ages 9 to 15, $8), and a Sunday Cheap Skate from 4 to 6 p.m. ($1).

SKATELAND OF BRANDON
750 Robertson St.
Brandon
(813) 681-3635
www.skatelandofbrandon.com
Wish you could skate all night? You can—check Skateland of Brandon's calendar to see when their next All Night Skate (7 p.m. to 7 a.m.) will be held. They even sell milk and donuts at 3 a.m. to intrepid skaters who need an energy boost. Note that their "Who We Are" page includes a dress code and other rules.

UNITED SKATES OF AMERICA, INC.
5121 N. Armenia Ave.
Tampa
(813) 876-5826
www.usa-skating.com
In addition to open and special skate times, United Skates of America hosts summer youth roller hockey leagues and roller derbies. Check

their online calendar for other days and times, as well as for coupons and specials.

USA'S SKATEPLEX
5313 E. Busch Blvd.
Temple Terrace
(813) 989-2100
www.usa-skating.com
USA's Skateplex has Adult Fitness Skates on Monday and Wednesday from 11:00 a.m. to 1:00 p.m. ($5). The Sunday 6:30 to 9:00 p.m. session is a Family Soul Skate with family-friendly R&B Soul music ($3 per person or $10 per family).

SKATEBOARDING

See the Parks and Recreation chapter for information about outdoor skateboard courses.

SKATEPARK OF TAMPA
4215 E. Columbus Dr.
Tampa
(813) 621-6793
www.skateparkoftampa.com
Take on the 8,000-square-foot indoor course at Skatepark of Tampa, home of worldwide professional and amateur skateboarding championship battles and the only indoor course in the Tampa Bay area. Or go for the 40-foot vert outside. Then there's the second indoor area with an indoor bowl and mini-ramp and a 4,500-square-foot beginners' course. Skatepark of Tampa also has a pro shop and a lounge for parents.

Check the Web site for hours and prices. If you're coming for the first time, bring a parent to sign the waiver or print one out from the Web site (must be notarized).

SHOPPING

Before there was a Tampa, there was a U.S. Army outpost, Fort Brooke. And just outside the gates of Fort Brooke, William Saunders built a place to shop—a small general store, the first on Florida's lower west coast.

Shopping in the Tampa Bay area has come a long way since Saunders's store, which sold basic necessities to Army families and settlers. From the high-end stores in International Plaza near Tampa International Airport to the bargains at the Big Top Flea Market in Tampa, you'll find a wide selection of shopping experiences.

Plus, we have some really great specialty shops like the Bill Jackson Shop for Adventure in Pinellas Park, where you can test drive a pair of skis, or Haslam's in St. Petersburg, Florida's largest new-and-used bookstore. And the architecture and décor of the Sam Ashe Music Store in Clearwater is a treat in itself.

Beach area shops, in places like John's Pass Village in Madeira Beach and the Tarpon Springs Sponge Docks, sell tropical everything and bikinis and sarongs year round.

So whether it's a middle of July sun-scorching day outside and you just want to cool off by watching the ice skaters at the Westfield Countryside Shopping Center in Clearwater, or it's a balmy December day and you want to ship Plant City oranges to your poor freezing friends up north, come along.

Let's go shopping!

We've arranged this chapter by type of shopping activity: Malls and Shopping Areas, Antiques Stores, Bookstores, Children's Stores, Classic Cars, Citrus, Flea Markets, Furniture, Music, Specialty Foods, and Sports and Outdoors. Within each category, the stores are arranged alphabetically.

> **i** The Better Business Bureau of West Florida can be reached at (727) 535-5522 or online at www.westflorida.bbb.org.

MALLS AND SHOPPING AREAS

BAYWALK
151 2nd Ave. N.
St. Petersburg
www.newbaywalk.com
Shops in the downtown St. Petersburg BayWalk include Shapiro's Art Gallery with one-of-a-kind furniture, clocks, home accessories, and jewelry; various women's clothing stores; shoe stores; and more. Or go for a beauty makeover at Lola Jane's Beauty Lounge or enjoy lunch at one of the great restaurants. There is no one main phone number for BayWalk, but the Web site lists each shop and

its phone number. BayWalk also has a Muvico theater (check the Nightlife chapter for more information).

CLEARWATER MALL
2747 Gulf-to-Bay Blvd.
Clearwater
There's no main phone number and no Web site, but this open-air mall on the corner of U.S. 19 N. and Gulf-to-Bay Boulevard in Clearwater hosts a Target Superstore, a Costco, Lowe's Building Supply, and other smaller shops. Restaurants include Smokey Bones, Moe's Southwest Grill, Panera Bread, and others. Careful—if you try to look up this mall online, you're apt to find yourself perusing a page for a similarly named mall in New Zealand!

INTERNATIONAL PLAZA AND BAY STREET
2223 N. West Shore Blvd., #2000
Tampa
(813) 342-3790
www.shopinternationalplaza.com
Ever dream of living in a shopping mall? International Plaza and Baystreet just might be the place where that dream comes true. Located adjacent to Tampa International Airport, you can stay at the luxurious Renaissance Tampa Hotel at International Plaza, a Mediterranean-style villa (see Accommodations chapter). Step from the hotel onto Bay Street, an open-air shopping village, or into the Plaza, an elegant two-story mall, and let the shopping begin!

With over 200 stores, including anchor stores Nordstroms, Nieman Marcus, Dillard's, and Robb & Stucky Interiors, and 16 restaurants including a Cheesecake Factory, a Café Japon, and the Capital Grille, you could spend your whole vacation exploring this world-within-a-world. There's even a spot just for kids—check out the Looney Tunes Ball Park play area sponsored by the Tampa Bay Rays. And when the sun goes down and the stores close up, the nightlife is just beginning at the Blue Martini and other upscale gathering spots.

i Attention Mac users: There is a full-service Apple Store at International Plaza on the second floor near Dillard's. Go to www.apple.com/retail/plaza for hours and to make service reservations.

JOHN'S PASS VILLAGE
150 John's Pass Boardwalk
Madeira Beach
(727) 391-6025 x303
www.johnspassfestivals.com
With over 100 merchants in this two-story, turn-of-the-century fishing village, John's Pass Village has lots of shopping you won't find anywhere else. Look for name-brand beachwear at the Hurricane Pass Outfitters and Margaritaville footwear at the Wild Time Boutique. Load up on souvenirs at Carribean Jubilee or kites and windsocks at Windworks. The Overhead Surf Shop (see description later in this chapter) sells surf, skim, and skate gear. You'll find artwork by local artists, beads, spices, and teas—and lots more.

LARGO MALL
10500 Ulmerton Rd.
Largo
(727) 518-2074
www.largomall.com
From Advance Auto Parts and PetSmart to Wigs by Abby, this open-air mall in mid-Pinellas County covers most shopping needs from groceries to gadgets. Other anchor stores include Bealls, Marshalls, Target, and Staples, and there's a host of smaller stores and businesses. The Regal Largo Mall 8 Cinemas (see Nightlife chapter for contact information) draw the movie crowd, and there are lots of places to eat. The Web site lists promotions and sales, and you can print coupons.

THE SHOPPES AT PARK PLACE
400 U.S. 19 N.
Pinellas Park
www.theshoppesatparkplace.com
The mall at the corner of U.S. 19 and Gandy/Park Boulevard has had a number of lives, and you'll hear it called by several names. For a long time it was Pinellas Square Mall, an indoor mall with an ice-skating rink in the center. For a short time, it was Parkside Mall—same setup, new owners. The indoor mall is gone and a large open-air shopping area has taken its place. There is no main phone number, but the Web page directory includes links to most of the shops (Office Depot, Michaels, and PetCo are among the larger stores) and businesses. Park Place Stadium 16 is part of the Regal movie chain (see Nightlife chapter for contact information).

THE SPONGE EXCHANGE
735 Dodecanese Blvd.
Tarpon Springs
(727) 934-8758
www.thespongeexchange.com
Thirty-one shops and restaurants fill this shopping village in Tarpon Springs. The Sponge Exchange used to be where the sponge boats sold their wares to buyers—like a livestock exchange only

selling the natural sea sponges that are used in a variety of industries. You can still see a bit of what the original sponge exchange looked like—wooden bins and shelves filled with sponges of many shapes and sizes and textures—at the family-owned Tarpon Sponge Company that anchors the Exchange. You'll find clothing, antiques, children's items, cigars, home décor, and gift items here, plus ice cream and other treats as well as two Greek restaurants.

TYRONE SQUARE MALL
6901 Tyrone Sq.
St. Petersburg
(727) 347-3889
www.simon.com

Located near the Bay Pines area of St. Petersburg, Tyrone Square Mall, a Simon-owned mall, includes 170 specialty shops anchored by Dillard's, JCPenney, Macy's, and Sears. When the kids—parents, too!—need a break from all that shopping, look for the Kidgets Korner Soft Play area in front of the JCPenney store. In fact, look on the Web site for the Kidgets link—the specials and freebies might be worth the $5 membership. Bonefish Grill, Lee Roy Selmon's, and Ruby Tuesday are the main restaurants at the mall.

UNIVERSITY MALL
2200 East Fowler Ave.
Tampa
(813) 971-3465
www.universitymalltampa.com

Located near the University of South Florida and Busch Gardens, University Mall offers a good mix of stores from Dillard's, Macy's, Sears, and Burlington Coat Factory to shoe repair and alterations services. A Regal Cinema draws crowds to the movies. University Mall just completed the first phase of a $10-million renovation.

WESTFIELD BRANDON SHOPPING CENTER
459 Brandon Town Center
Brandon
(813) 661-5100
http://westfield/com/brandon

Anchored by Dillard's, JCPenney, Macy's, Sears,

Dick's Sporting Goods, and Books-a-Million, the Brandon Shopping Center also hosts community events like the Brandon Blast and Rock, Rib & Ride Festival. (See Annual Events and Festivals for more information on this July 4 bash).

WESTFIELD CITRUS PARK
8021 Citrus Park Town Center
Tampa
(813) 926-4644
www.westfield.com/citruspark

Located in the northwest corner of Tampa, the Westfield Citrus Park shopping mall has over 150 stores including Dick's Sporting Goods, JCPenney, Macy's, Pottery Barn, and many others. Two Playtowns give kids—and parents—a break from shop-'til-you-drop-induced fatigue, and a Family Lounge with private nursing stations, child-sized restroom facilities, a microwave, and baby-changing stations makes shopping with tiny tots a breeze. Dining choices are a bit limited here, but there are mall standards such as Chick-Fil-A and Blimpie, so no one will starve. Moviegoers come here to see one of the not-quite-20 movies playing at the Regal Citrus Park 20.

WESTFIELD COUNTRYSIDE SHOPPING CENTER
27001 U.S. 19 N.
Clearwater
(727) 796-1079
www.westfield.com/countryside

Anchored by Dillard's, JCPenney, Macy's, and Sears, the Westfield Countryside Shopping Center has 160 merchants, a large food court on the upper level, and an NHL-sized ice skating rink in the center. The center just began extensive renovations, so you'll probably see "Excuse our dust" signs for a while.

i Looking for something to do on Sundays? The Williams-Sonoma store at the Westfield Citrus Park shopping mall offers free cooking classes. Learn how to cook for kids or how to make your family go bananas over breakfast. Call Williams Sonoma at (813) 920-6939 for times and details.

WESTSHORE PLAZA
250 Westshore Plaza
Tampa
(813) 286-0790
www.westshoreplaza.com

You knew one day it would come to that—you would actually need to have a license to shop. OK, so you don't exactly *need* to have such a license, but WestShore Plaza partners with local non-profit organizations to help them raise needed funds and to help you save money. Here's how it works: You buy a License to Shop from a participating NPO, then go shopping at Westshore Plaza. On any given shopping trip, you might save up to 20 percent at several participating stores or get some buy-one-get-one-free deals at others.

Shops at Westshore Plaza include Saks Fifth Avenue, Macy's, Rosetta Stone, and White House Black Market, and dining options include Mitchell's Fish Market, P. F. Chang's China Bistro, Maggiano's Little Italy, and the Palm Restaurant.

i Maybe it's just us—we don't see it mentioned in any of the reviews—but the parking lot design at most of the open-air malls drives us nuts. Watch carefully where you're going, and take pity on people trying to make turns.

ANTIQUES STORES

Antiques stores seems to cluster rather than scatter. So rather than give you a blow-by-blow account of each and every antiques store in the area, we'll tell you where some of those clusters are.

Belleair Bluffs

Along Indian Rocks Road near West Bay Avenue in Pinellas County, just south of Clearwater, you'll find half a dozen or more antiques and art shops including places like Lejans Antiques and Fine Art (727-586-7515) and Jewel Antique Mall (727-585-5568).

Businesses Banding Together

These merchants haven't formed their own chamber of commerce, but they're not in a mall with a marketing presence. There may be others, but here are a few Tampa Bay area merchants' associations. Look on their Web sites to find even more places to shop.

Carrollwood Area Business Association (Tampa)
(813) 264-0006
www.usecaba.com

Corey Area Business Association (St. Pete Beach)
(727) 366-2003
www.coreyave.com

Downtown St. Petersburg
www.discoverdowntown.com

Plant City

Along Collins Street—both North Collins and South Collins—in Hillsborough County just east of Tampa, there is a cluster of antiques stores including Collin Street Junction (813-659-2585) and Antiques & Treasures (813-752-4626).

St. Petersburg

Along Central Avenue are a number of antiques shops—not clustered, so much as strung like beads on a necklace with spaces in between. On the east end, close to downtown, is the Gas Plant Arcade Antique Mall near 12th St. (727-895-0368). A few blocks west, you'll find Asian Willow Antiques, specializing in Qing Dynasty antique Chinese furniture (727-321-1100).

Tampa

One of the largest clusters of antique shops in Tampa is on the Interbay Peninsula in what is called the Palma Ceia area. You'll find shops along Henderson Boulevard, South MacDill Avenue, and West El Prado Boulevard—places like Gas Light Antiques (813-870-0934) and Palma Ceia Antiques (813-254-7149).

BOOKSTORES

Some people say books are becoming obsolete in favor of the Internet. We find carrying our laptop to the beach cumbersome; the amount of text we can read at one time on our cell phone is miniscule.

You'd never know print is going the way of the dinosaur from the number of bookstores in our area. We've got our share of Barnes & Nobles, Books-a-Million, Borders, and Waldenbooks. We also have a number of independent book dealers, including Florida's largest and oldest new-and-used bookstore—Haslam's in St. Petersburg—and a rare book store, the Old Tampa Book Company.

BLUE MOON BOOKS AND COLLECTIBLES
1413 Cleveland St.
Clearwater
(727) 443-7444
www.bluemoonbooksandcollectibles.com
You have to be fairly thin to work your way between the stacks and shelves of books and odd collectibles stuffed into this store. But if you've ordered rare or hard-to-find books over the Internet, they may have come from owner Lowell Kelly's collection. Note that the "Ambiance" page of the Web site is a bit optimistic. But confirmed book addicts won't mind. They may even enjoy becoming bookworms and crawling through the selections.

BOOK SWAP OF CARROLLWOOD
13144 N. Dale Mabry Hwy
Tampa
(813) 963-6979
www.bookswapfl.com
Owner Cynthia Floyd bills this as "Tampa's most unique bookstore" because of its large selection of new and used fiction, non-fiction, classics, children's, and audio books. As the name implies, you can bring books you've read to the Book Swap and exchange them for store credit. Occasionally they have book signings at the store; a paranormal romance book club meets there Monday evenings.

HASLAM'S BOOK STORE
2025 Central Ave.
St. Petersburg
(727) 822-8616
www.haslams.com
Opened in 1933 by John and Mary Haslam, this 30,000 square foot building holds over 300,000 bestsellers, technical and trade books, religious books, and children's books, making it Florida's largest new-and-used independent book store. Now owned by a third generation of the Haslam family, Ray and Suzanne Hinst, the store serves third- and fourth-generation customers, as well. Check their Web site for author visits, book signings, and other events. Haslam's is closed on Sundays. Note to classic video gamers: If you play *Doom*, go to any of Haslam's Web site's inside pages (pages past the 'Home' page), scroll to the very bottom of the page, and click on "*Doom* Level." You can chase monsters and hunt for treasure throughout a virtual Haslam's.

INKWOOD BOOKS
216 S. Armenia Ave.
Tampa
(813) 253-2638
www.inkwoodbooks.com
Housed in an inviting 1920s bungalow painted in Key West colors, Inkwood Books holds new books, books, and more books chosen for a wide range of readers by owners Carla Jimenez and Leslie Reiner. Inkwood Books often handles the book sales and signings for nationally recognized authors such as Cokie Roberts and Kathie Lee Gifford when they present programs at the Tampa Convention Center and the Straz Center. Look for staff favorites, called Unchained Choices, throughout the store.

OLD TAMPA BOOK COMPANY
507 N. Tampa St.
Tampa
(813) 209-2151

The Old Tampa Book Company is Tampa's downtown general bookstore, but it's also the place to try for hard-to-find limited editions and rare books. Owners David and Ellen Brown will guide you through the more than 40,000 titles to help you find books about ships and sailing, literary criticism, regional history, and a host of other subjects. While you will find children's fiction and popular fiction here, the emphasis is on nonfiction. Not all the books are in English, either. The Browns carry about 1,500 titles in more than a dozen languages. The Old Tampa Book Company is closed on Sundays. Check out their sidewalk sale of $1 books.

CLASSIC CARS

CLASSIC CORVETTES & COLLECTIBLES, INC.
304 S. Pinellas Ave.
Tarpon Springs
(727) 945-1500
www.classiccorvettes.com

Muscle car lovers and those who appreciate museum-quality cars will want to visit Classic Corvettes & Collectibles, Inc., climate-controlled showroom in downtown Tarpon Springs. Or if you have a classic car that has seen better days, Classic Car Center just down the street will help you bring your baby back to prime condition. Classic Corvettes & Collectibles is a member of the Specialty Vehicle Dealers Association. The showroom is open to the public Monday through Friday from 9 a.m. to 6 p.m. and Saturday from 10 a.m. to 5 p.m. No drooling on the cars, please.

CHILDREN'S STORES

Yes, we have Toys 'R' Us stores in the Tampa Bay area, and almost every department store and bookstore has a children's section. But the stores listed below offer a little more guidance to parents and teachers looking for learning tools as well as play toys.

LAKESHORE LEARNING STORE
4501 W. Kennedy Blvd.
Tampa
(813) 207-0468
www.lakeshorelearning.com

More than just a toy store, Lakeshore Learning Store offers kids ages three and up free crafts sessions each Saturday and holds workshops for teachers and child-care workers that meet some continuing education requirements. Parents, too, can find ideas to keep their kids learning, even when they're not in school.

LEARNING EXPRESS
Brandon-Valrico
3454 Lithia Pinecrest Rd.
Valrico
(813) 643-1762
www.brandonvalrico.learningexpress-toys
.com

South Tampa
800 South Village Circle
Tampa
(813) 250-6200
www.southtampa.learningexpress-toys.com

St. Petersburg
6796 Tyrone Sq.
St. Petersburg
(727) 344-2711
www.saintpetersburg.learningexpress-toys
.com

Tampa-Westchase
12950 Race Track Rd.
Tampa
(813) 818-8697
www.westchase.learningexpress-toys.com

The four Learning Express stores in the Tampa Bay area offer toys and learning tools for children. Each of these stores have special events at the stores, but only the Tampa-Westchase Web site has a calendar listing events including story and craft times.

🔍 Close-up

Home Shopping Network—Making Shopping as Easy as ABC

Take one advertiser who can't pay for airtime, add one radio station willing to barter the bill away, then stir in 112 olive-green electric can openers. Mix well with a liberal dose of schlock-jock pitter-patter and a twist of why-not humor, then serve it up on an AM radio station in Clearwater, Florida.

What you get is a mega-industry that has changed the way we shop and the way we use television.

Back in 1977, Clearwater radio station WWQT-AM 1470 had an advertiser who couldn't pay his bill, but who had can openers. News talk show host Bob Circosta shrugged his shoulders and gave selling can openers a shot after his regular newscast.

All 112 can openers, priced at $9.95, sold in about an hour.

Selling items and gadgets became the format for a regular five-minute program called the Suncoast Bargaineers that ran each afternoon at 2 p.m.

In 1982, station owners Lowell "Bud" Paxson and Roy Speer moved the show to a local public access TV channel, figuring they could sell even more items if people could actually see them. For three hours each day Circosta pitched products, chatting with call-in buyers, and even delivering items occasionally.

The Home Shopping Channel became the 24-hour Home Shopping Club in 1985, then morphed into the Home Shopping Network. Today the business has been restructured as HSN.com and markets several of its own brands of home interior and clothing items.

Celebrities including Wolfgang Puck, Senator Orrin Hatch, Vanna White, and Dennis Rodman have pitched products over the years.

Countless viewers have become enthralled in watching HSN—not just by watching Omar Sharif carry on a love affair with cologne, but also by watching the number of buyers climb up while the little clock on the screen ticks down the number of seconds left before another product and another personality take their places.

HSN did more than create a shopping empire. It also changed both the computer software and cable television industries.

Today, we think nothing of going online to order anything from gold-plated toothpicks to gold-leafed artwork to gold-premium bonds. We hardly remember when there were more than three major television networks to watch. But in the mid-1980s, the software HSN needed hadn't been written yet. Cable television wasn't the pervasive contender for network viewers that it is now.

HSN, as the first shop-at-home network, spurred the development of software that could handle massive amounts of information and deal with transactions and credit checks in seconds. HSN's computer was reputedly second in size in Florida only to NASA's computer at the time.

CITRUS

Whether you want to ship a bushel of sunshine up north or just want to pick up a few grapefruit for breakfast, the citrus sellers listed below can help. Most of these places are also fruit and veg-gie markets, and sell jams, salsas, candies, and gifts. Most also sell soft-serve orange-and-vanilla twist ice cream cones and juice samples (first little cup is usually free; pay a dime for each one after that). Some have hard ice cream and other goodies, too. Call or check each market's Web

HSN also became a selling point for cable companies and spawned rivals like QVC Network, Inc. People started talking about whether it was the beginning of the end for the mail-order industry and its print catalogues.

Paxson left HSN in 1987, after a personal crisis, and went on to create the PaxNet television network and the Worship Network. Speer sold out in 1992—having seen HSN grow from a couple of million dollars annual revenue to over a billion dollars annual revenue. In 1993, however, a couple of class-action lawsuits against Speer were settled before going to trial, but not before attracting the attention of the IRS, who eventually determined that various losses Speer had claimed were legitimate.

In any case, when Barry Diller acquired HSN in 1995, HSN was losing money. Diller—who pioneered the miniseries format (think *Roots*) and Movie of the Week at ABC, took Paramount Pictures to top-of-the-heap status with hits like *Raiders of the Lost Ark,* and then created the Fox network—saw possibilities for electronic retailing that were way outside the television box.

HSN bought controlling interest in Ticketmaster.com, Hotels.com, Match.com, and other direct-sell businesses including Expedia and USA Network. HSN's Cornerstone Brands include Ballard Design, Garnet Hill, and The Territory Ahead.

Today's CEO, former Nike apparel guru Mindy F. Grossman, has upped the quality of the merchandise and has put HSN.com on Facebook and YouTube. Today's celebrities like Serena Williams and Paula Abdul still line up to promote products. Many of those celebs are coached by the original pitchman Bob Circosta, who teaches his techniques in seminars and private coaching sessions.

Viewers now can shop by remote or by mouse. "If you're one of the lucky first 900 callers" still brings in the buyers—more than 50 million of them a year. The clock still ticks down, and the items-purchased numbers still rise.

In 2006, HSN.com added a new feature. Shoppers in a few spots around the country can get in their cars, drive to retail locations, and shop in person. Go figure.

Here in the Tampa Bay area, you can get some real bargains at HSN's two retail outlet stores. Hours at both stores are Monday through Saturday from 10 a.m. to 9 p.m. and Sunday from noon to 6 p.m. (www.hsn.com).

HSN Retail Outlet of Bardmoor

10801 Starkey Rd.

Largo

(727) 872-4200

HSN Retail Outlet of Brandon

225 W. Brandon Blvd.

Brandon

(813) 654-4192

site for days and hours, which sometimes vary by season. Remember that it is illegal to ship fruit out of state that has not been inspected. Protect plants and the agricultural economy by dealing only with reputable growers and citrus shippers.

CITRUS COUNTRY GROVES

18200 U.S. 19 N.

Clearwater

(727) 536-9100, (800) 940-2601

5800 Seminole Blvd.
Seminole
(727) 392-1277, (800) 940-2601
www.holidaycitrus.com

GOLDEN VALLEY GROVES
601 N. Valrico Rd.
Valrico
(813) 689-1724, (800) 714-6322
www.goldenvalleygroves.com

PARKSDALE FARM MARKET
3702 W. Baker St.
Plant City
(813) 754-2704, (888) 311-1701
www.parkesdale.com

SUN GROVES
3393 SR 580
Safety Harbor
(727) 726-8484, (800) 672-6438
www.sungroves.com

FLEA MARKETS

Today's flea market vendors may be tomorrow's tycoons. Because they are generally open only on weekends, cost less to rent than regular store space, and often provide cooperative marketing programs, flea markets offer new businesses a way to test the waters with innovative products and services. Buyers trade the risk of dealing with less established businesses for reaping the reward of finding bargains before they become the next big ticket item. So support good old-fashioned American enterprise—you never know what you'll find at the flea market.

BIG TOP FLEA MARKET
Tampa
(813) 986-4004
www.bigtopfleamarket.com
Open Saturday and Sunday from 9 a.m. to 4:30 p.m., the Big Top Flea Market has more than 500 vendors including Dollar Store and a Mary Kay distributor. A food court and restrooms are in the middle core building—shops radiate from the center hub like spokes on a wheel.

49ER FLEA MARKET
10525 49th St. N.
Clearwater
(727) 573-3367
49er Flea Market is open Saturday and Sunday from 7 a.m. to 1 p.m. While the mailing address says "Clearwater," the location is just north of Pinellas Park and east of U.S. 19.

FUN-LAN DRIVE-IN THEATER AND SWAP SHOP
2302 E. Hillsborough Ave.
Tampa
(813) 237-0886
www.fun-lan.com/flea.html
By day, Fun-Lan is a flea market and swap shop; by night it's a drive-in theater. The flea market part is open Thursday through Sunday beginning at 6 a.m.

INTERNATIONAL FLEA MARKET
11309 N. Nebraska Ave.
Tampa
(813) 975-8888
International Farmer's Flea Market is open Wednesday and Thursday 10 a.m. to 6:30 p.m., Friday 10 a.m. to 8:30 p.m., Saturday from 9 a.m. to 8:30 p.m., and Sunday from 9 a.m. to 6:30 p.m.

MAGIC MALL
8330 N. Florida Ave.
Tampa
(813) 935-8871
Magic Mall is open Sunday, Wednesday, and Thursday from 10 a.m. to 6:45 p.m. and on Friday and Saturday from 10 a.m. to 8:45 p.m. They are closed Monday and Tuesday.

MUSTANG FLEA MARKET
7901 Park Blvd.
Pinellas Park
(727) 544-3066
Open Wednesday, Saturday, and Sunday from 6 a.m. to 2 p.m., the Mustang Flea Market is located next to the Wagon Wheel Flea Market.

"Doc" Webb's Most Unusual Drug Store

St. Petersburg may have been the birthplace of the loss-leader sales gimmick, thanks to a gung-ho businessman who saw opportunity where everyone else saw ruin. Who in their right mind, for instance, would expand a business that targeted the working class during the Great Depression?

James Earl Webb, that's who.

What? You've never heard of "Doc" Webb and his famous Webb's City, "The World's Most Unusual Drug Store" that covered 10 city blocks and inspired a musical more than 50 years later?

Step this way, ladies and gentlemen, and listen closely to the tale of the man who concocted cures for what ailed people—in the days before government regulation was common practice—and hawked them with the skill of a circus barker.

Plus he threw in the circus as a bonus.

Webb came to St. Petersburg in 1925 from Knoxville, Tennessee, having already earned the nickname "Doc" from his grateful customers who swore by his remedies for everything from constipation to venereal disease. With a partner, Webb opened a drug store in a less than prosperous area of St. Petersburg and soon built a bustling business.

Then the bottom dropped out of the land boom, and business fell off. Webb's answer was to cut prices. And cut and cut and cut until his partner couldn't take any more and sold his interest in the business to Webb.

When the Depression hit, Webb's response was to expand. He made Webb's Cut Rate Drug Store a one-stop shopping center where people could get their dry cleaning done, buy fresh-roasted coffee, and still pick up toothpaste and headache powder.

Webb's store grew and grew until it became Webb's City, housing 77 stores including a florist, an automobile service station, and a beauty salon. People could even take dance lessons up on the roof. When people didn't have money to pay with, Webb accepted the scrip that the local governments issued.

More than good deals, Webb also offered entertainment. It was gimmicky entertainment, sometimes, like dancing chickens and mermaid shows, but it worked.

Once, Webb sold 2,000 one-dollar bills for 95 cents each. The second day he sold another 2,500 one-dollar bills for 89 cents each. The third day he offered to buy back the bills for $1.35 each, but most of the bills—serial numbers having been recorded, of course—were already in Webb's cash register along with other dollars people had spent at his store.

After World War II, more sophisticated shopping malls began to sprout up, and Webb's City lost its allure. Other retailers adopted Webb's loss-leader sales techniques. Webb finally sold out in 1972, and the store didn't last much longer than that.

But Webb's legend outlived him. In 2000, the local drama team of Bill Leavengood and Lee Ahlen turned the story of Webb's City into a musical by the same name that includes a piece called the "Breadline Shuffle."

Webb would have loved it.

OLDSMAR FLEA MARKET
180 Race Track Rd. S.
(813) 855-5306
www.oldsmarfleamkt.com
One of the largest outdoor markets around, the Oldsmar Flea Market is open Saturday and Sunday, but hosts a farmers' market on Fridays. ATM's are on site. Live entertainment on Saturday and Sunday afternoons. No pets are allowed unless they are carried or are in a stroller.

TAMPA INDOOR FLEA MARKET
11612 N Nebraska Ave.
Tampa
(813) 391-4162
The Tampa Indoor Flea Market, across the street from International Flea Market, is open Thursday and Sunday, 11 a.m. to 6 p.m., and Friday and Saturday, 11 a.m. to 8 p.m.

WAGON WHEEL FLEA MARKET
7801 Park Blvd.
Pinellas Park
(727) 544-5319
Open 8 a.m. to 4 p.m. every Saturday and Sunday, rain or shine, the Wagon Wheel Flea Market is one of the largest flea markets in the area.

FURNITURE

We aren't lacking in furniture stores in the Tampa Bay area. But the two places listed here are a bit unique. People camped outside the new IKEA store when it opened a few months back, and IKEA is pretty picky about where they put their places. So we feel justified in pointing it out to you. Rooms To Go, on the other hand, has stores everywhere in the Tampa Bay area and around the world. But Tampa is their home, so we get to brag a bit on them, too.

IKEA
1103 N. 22nd St.
Tampa
(813) 623-5454
www.ikea.com/us/en/store/tampa

IKEA has come to Tampa! The two-story Swedish furniture and housewares emporium—one of fewer than 50 in the nation, at this writing—sells everything from soup ladles to sofas. And, while the showroom may be big enough to try the stamina of the most seasoned shopper, the furniture is decidedly on the space-saving side.

IKEA's cafeteria-style restaurant upstairs sells Swedish meatballs served with mashed potatoes, gravy, and lingonberry sauce, as well as other meals, giving us a taste of Sweden in this Latin enclave. Downstairs, just past the checkout counters, is a Swedish market selling everything from a frozen version of the meatballs served upstairs to several varieties of herring, Swedish cookies, and other goodies. Plus there's a bistro that sells hot dogs, cinnamon rolls and—oh, wait. This isn't the Restaurant chapter, is it? IKEA is open Monday through Friday from 11 a.m. to 9 p.m., Saturday from 10 a.m. to 9 p.m., and Sunday from noon to 6 p.m.

ROOMS TO GO
11540 U.S. 92 E.
Seffner
(813) 623-5400
www.roomstogo.com
A 1988 leveraged buyout of his family's northeastern furniture store gave Jeffrey Seaman the opportunity to try something new. In 1991, Seaman opened his first Rooms To Go furniture store in Tampa. Rooms To Go offered shoppers a new way of buying sofas, end tables, lamps, and rugs. Instead of separate sections for each item, Rooms To Go featured room packages that people could see for themselves. The concept, and Seaman's other marketing strategies, worked.

Today, Rooms To Go, one of the nation's largest furniture retailers, has stores in at least 13 states and in Puerto Rico. Licensed stores dot the globe from Turkey to Guatemala, and Rooms To Go Kids sells children's furniture. Check the company's Web site or a telephone directory for a listing of outlets in the Tampa Bay area.

MUSIC

SAM ASHE MUSIC STORE
923 McMullen Booth Rd.
Clearwater
(727) 725-8062

13133 N. Dale Mabry Hwy
Tampa
(813) 908-5556
www.samashmusic.com

Whether you're looking for professional-quality instruments or accessories or a beginner's level band instrument, Sam Ashe Music carries a complete line of gear. The Clearwater store is worth a visit, however, because of its setting. When the old Kapok Tree Inn moved out and Sam Ashe Music moved in, the décor stayed. That means you may find a pink guitar slung over a replica of the Venus de Milo or watch light displays playing on the vaulted ceiling. The entrance to the store—one of the nation's largest music stores—is on the backside of the building. After shopping, walk over to the sign in the parking lot that points to the Players School of Music, then peek into the courtyard for a glimpse of what this property used to be. The courtyard and adjacent ballrooms are still popular spots for weddings and proms.

SPECIALTY FOODS

CHUCK'S NATURAL FOOD MARKETPLACE
114 N. Kings Ave.
Brandon
(813) 657-2555

11301 N. 56th St.
Temple Terrace
(813) 980-2005
www.chucksnaturalmarketplace.com

Chuck's Natural Food Marketplace, in two Hillsborough County locations, is an all-organic and non-genetically altered foods grocery shopping experience. You'll find nuts, seeds, flours, herbs, spices, and other bulk dry foods as well as organic and hormone-free eggs and dairy products. For those needing to avoid lactose altogether, Chuck's also carries alternative products. Plus you'll find organic baby food, pet food, cosmetics and skin care products, and a full freezer of organic convenience foods. Chuck's also has a reputation for stocking a wide range of supplements including vitamins, herbs, homeopathic products, teas, and sports nutrition items. Look for the Purple Plate Health Café inside the stores. Chuck's Natural Food Marketplace is open Monday through Friday from 9 a.m. to 8 p.m., Saturday from 9 a.m. to 6 p.m., and Sunday from noon to 6 p.m.

Florida Winery Strikes Gold

Florida Orange Groves, Inc., and Winery
1500 Pasadena Ave. S.
St. Petersburg 33707
(727) 347-4025, (800) 338-7923
www.floridawine.com

If you think wine is about grapes, grapes, and nothing but grapes, think again. You won't find grapes in these wines made by the Florida Winery—just Florida citrus and other fruits. Tangerine Wine? Mango Mamma? Florida Sunset Pineapple? You bet! And many more. The 40 Karat semi-dry white wine, for instance, is made with Florida carrots. Or try the Hot Sun, made with Florida tomatoes and peppers. These aren't just novelty wines—they've won a whole shelf full of medals, awards, and ribbons.

The Florida Winery is open for tasting and tours Monday through Saturday from 9 a.m. to 5 p.m. and on Sunday from 12:30 to 5 p.m. Tours are at 11 a.m. and at 1, 2, and 3 p.m. They are closed on all major holidays. Call ahead for reservations if you plan to bring a group larger than seven people or so.

HALKI MARKET
520 Athens St.
Tarpon Springs

45 Dodecanese Blvd.
Tarpon Springs
(727) 937-6533
www.halkimarket.com

Greek and Mediterranean food items fill the shelves in these two Tarpon Springs stores. More kinds of olives than you knew existed, 23 kinds of olive oil, spices, cheeses, rose petal preserves, pomegranate juice, pastas and pastries, squid, and more. Plus they carry goat milk soaps made in Tarpon Springs and the Aphrodite line of skin care and cosmetic items.

MAZZARO ITALIAN MARKET
2909 22nd Ave. N.
St. Petersburg
(727) 321-2400
www.mazzarosmarket.com

Mamma mia—brace yourself. When you open the door to Mazzaro Italian Market—the main door looks like it's at the rear of the building, by the way—you open yourself to an Old World shopping experience. You'll find a real butcher shop, a cheese department, a take-out or eat-on-the-patio deli, homemade pasta, gelato, and more. There's a brick oven that puts out hundreds of crusty loaves of bread a day. People line up behind the stools surrounding the coffee bar—where they roast and grind their own coffees—and wait for an empty spot. Fridays and Saturdays, Mazzaro's certified sommelier conducts wine tastings. Mazzaro is not your intimate Italian corner. It's loud, packed with people and heavenly smells, and a bit overwhelming at first. Scout around, but don't wait too long to order—the line grows longer by the minute. Mazzaro is open 9 a.m. to 6 p.m. Monday through Friday and 9 a.m. to 2:30 p.m. on Saturday. Mazzaro is closed on Sunday—and they close the whole store for a couple of weeks' vacation during the summer. You can order online, too.

NATURE'S FOOD PATCH
1225 Cleveland St.
Clearwater
(727) 443-6703
www.naturesfoodpatch.com

A large organic produce department, bulk foods and books, housewares and herbs, vitamins and videos, natural body care products, aromatherapy, teas, and assorted other items fill Nature's Food Patch, one of the Tampa Bay area's largest natural foods stores. The deli sells nitrate- and nitrite-free sliced meats plus take-out lasagna, meatloaf, and other entrées and side dishes. The Bunny Hop Café has a mega-sized salad bar that includes soups and desserts, while the Coffee & Juice Bar serves smoothies, herbal teas, Fair Trade organic coffee, and a variety of juices. Nature's Food Patch is open Monday through Saturday from 9 a.m. to 9 p.m. and Sunday from 11 a.m. to 8 p.m.

SPORTS AND OUTDOORS

There's a Peter Glenn Ski & Sports in Tampa, a few Sports Authority stores scattered about, a Hibbett Sporting Goods, a Dick's Sporting Goods in Citrus Park, a Champs sports, and a couple of Play It Again Sports stores. Then there are a couple of indies that play by their own rules.

BILL JACKSON SHOP FOR ADVENTURE
9501 U.S. 19 N.
Pinellas Park
(727) 576.4169
www.billjacksons.com

One minute you're on one of Pinellas County's busiest highways; the next you've pulled off and are winding your way through pine trees and palmettos toward adventure. What started out as an army surplus store in a ramshackle building shortly after World War II has turned into five acres of a unique outdoor sporting goods store and instruction site. Want to learn to SCUBA dive? Or kayak? Start with the basics in the huge indoor pool. Heading for the Colorado slopes, but it's been a decade or more since you skied? Regain your skills on Tampa Bay's only indoor ski slope. From topo maps to target shooting ranges, Bill Jackson's is a shopping adventure in itself.

OVERHEAD SURF SHOP
John's Pass Village
12991 Village Blvd.
Madeira Beach
(727) 398-7873
www.www.overheadsurfshop.com

Let's put it this way—the staff bio page on the Overhead Surf Shop's Web site includes photos of each staff member catching waves and skimming surf. They can give you tips on doing a flat 540 or a backside 360—or on the best places in the Tampa Bay area to skim, surf, and skate. Their place at John's Pass Village is filled with boards and gear, clothing, footwear, sunglasses, and more. They can also put you in touch with local contests and groups. Call their WAVE Line at (727) 398-7873 for a recorded rundown on the current wave action in the area.

THE RUNNING CENTER
14308-E N. Dale Mabry Hwy
Tampa
(813) 908-1960
www.runcenter.com

The Running Center is where Tampa Bay runners bring their feet to be shod, whether those feet are running sprints or marathons. Owner Bill Davison has spent decades selling running shoes and equipment. Look for helpful articles on his Web site—articles like "Gait Analysis" and "Don't Get Married to Your Shoes," for sport-specific information. You'll find clothing and accessories here, too, and lots of information about local races and events.

SPECTATOR SPORTS

Around the Tampa Bay area, we don't have to turn on the TV to know when the Tampa Bay Buccaneers are playing. Bucs flags fly from flagpoles in front of houses draped with reddish-orange and black bunting. Inflatable helmeted hulks face off against each other on front lawns, and local delis prepare platters for football-watching parties.

And that's nothing compared to the show that goes on at Ray J stadium during a Bucs home game. We may not have the winningest team in the NFL—although don't forget they've won one Super Bowl and come close on a couple of others—but they're our team. We've sent a good number of players to the All-Star games. And we host the Outback Bowl each January.

We spit sparks over the Tampa Bay Lightning, our NHL team that won the Stanley Cup a few years back. And our MLB Rays beat out the competition to become the American League champs and came oh-so-close in the 2008 World Series against the Phillies.

That was a bit ironic. We may have almost as many Phillies fans in Tampa Bay as Rays fans. That's because the Phillies have made Clearwater their spring training home since 1947.

In fact, this area was the birthplace of baseball's spring training program, and St. Petersburg is home to Minor League Headquarters. Later in this chapter we'll be taking a closer look at how the Grapefruit League developed and at who plays where today.

We've also fielded a professional soccer team, the Tampa Bay Rowdies, that played here from 1975 to 1993 in the now-defunct North American Soccer League. But the Rowdies are set to make a comeback in 2010 as part of the United Soccer League First Division. There's even talk of them getting their own stadium.

No, we don't have a NASCAR track. Why bother, when we can turn downtown St. Petersburg into an IndyCar series course each year for Grand Prix and LeMans series racing? And we have our share of short track racing—we'll tell you where to find dirt racing.

Then there's the PGA championship tournament at Innisbrook in northern Pinellas County, the World Championship Ironman Triathlon in Clearwater, and the NOOD Regatta sailing from St. Petersburg. Where's basketball in all this, you ask? We're getting there. No NBA team—yet. But we hosted the 2008 Women's Final Four and the 2009 Southeastern Conference Men's Basketball Tournament, and we're on the NBA circuit as a venue.

Which brings us to alternate leagues and college sports.

Well, we've got the Arena Football League's Tampa Bay Storm, and we've made a couple of stabs at American Basketball Association teams—the ThunderDawgs and the Tornadoes gave it a shot, but hit the rim and bounced out. And we cheer on the University of South Florida Bulls when they play various sports.

Then there are the other kind of sporting events that involve horses, dogs, and the luck of the draw. Thoroughbred horse racing and greyhound racing have been part of Tampa Bay since the 1920s. But in the last few years, they've had some competition from casino gambling. We'll take a closer look at what has happened.

This chapter is organized alphabetically by sport Auto Racing, Baseball, Equestrian Events, Football, Golf, Hockey, Sailing, Soccer, Thoroughbred and Greyhound Racing and Gambling, and Triathlon. Within each sport, we'll look at the major teams and venues.

So—got your team jersey on? Then let's take in a game . . . or two or three.

AUTO RACING

EAST BAY RACEWAY PARK
2VHL Promotions, Inc.
6311 Burts Rd.
Tampa
(813) 677-7223, (877) 457-5611
www.eastbayracewaypark.com
East Bay Raceway Park, "Clay by the Bay," is a one-third of a mile oval clay (dirt) track that hosts racers from around the region in 360 Sprints, Late Model, Limited Late Model, Mini Stocks, and Street Stocks classes. And those are just the regular races. Sometimes there are Antique Race Cars, Open Wheel Modified, 4-Cylinder Bombers, Go Karts, and others. East Bay Raceway Park is an American Speed Association (ASA) member track and is home to the Winternationals (special event ticket prices apply). Tickets are $12 for adults, $7 for youth ages 13 to 17. Children ages 12 and under are free. Racing starts at 6:30 p.m., weather permitting. Food and beverage concessions are on site.

HONDA GRAND PRIX OF ST. PETERSBURG
Acura Sports Car Challenge of St. Petersburg
25 2nd St. N., Ste. 160
St. Petersburg
(727) 898-INDY (4639) ext. 225
www.gpstpete.com
This three-day racing weekend is as much festival as it is race. This past year, the Honda Grand Prix of St. Petersburg was the inaugural race of the IndyCar Series, and the Acura Sports Car Challenge of St. Petersburg was one of only two street races in the American LeMans Series run in 2009.

You have to hand it to the folks in St. Petersburg. They don't just stick this race out in a back pasture somewhere. No, they run it in the city's living room, as it were, sending these road-hugging sleek machines zooming past the Mahaffey Theater and later right through the heart of downtown with high-rise buildings on either side. Not only does the city invite in some fairly loud guests who tear around like there's no tomorrow, but it also rearranges the furniture for them and says, "Have at it." How many other cities would close off one of their airport runways and make it part of the 1.8-mile, 14-turn racetrack? And for three days, no less! Such a pity the drivers of the two Indy Lights races (one on Saturday, one on Sunday), the American Le Mans Series race on Saturday, and the IndyCar Series on Sunday don't get to see that gorgeous waterfront they're streaking past.

Spectators, however, can enjoy that view, the roar of racing engines, and festival activities. Order tickets over the phone or online. General admission tickets this past year started at $25 with reserved seating starting at $60. In addition to the spinning tires, another wheel sometimes turns—this one a giant Ferris wheel to give visitors a bird's-eye view of the race circuit ($5 per ride). There's also live music and, of course, food.

BASEBALL

TAMPA BAY RAYS
Tropicana Field
1 Tropicana Dr.
St. Petersburg
(727) 825-3250
http://tampabay.rays.mlb.com
You'd think we would have gotten a major league baseball team—pardon the pun—right off the bat. Weren't we the ones who invited the Cincinnati Reds to play an exhibition game here back in 1908 and got the whole spring training thing going? Haven't we been the home for Minor League Baseball since 1973? And haven't other teams used us to leverage bigger and better stadiums elsewhere by threatening to move here? We almost got the Giants in 1993, but were left standing at the altar when the baseball powers that be didn't approve the match.

Then there was the whole Thunderdome thing. We tried the "if we build it, they will come" ploy and designed a domed stadium in 1990 called the Florida Suncoast Dome. Somebody did come, but it wasn't a MLB team. Instead, the new NHL team, the Tampa Bay Lightning, came in 1993, and the Suncoast Dome became the

Thunderdome. The Tampa Bay Storm, an AFL team, played here, too. It took the players' strike of 1995 to motivate baseball's decision makers to approve Tampa Bay for an expansion team, beginning in 1998.

Once we knew we were getting a baseball team, the Tampa Bay Devil Rays, we had to refurbish an almost new building. Tropicana bought the naming rights and, even after PepsiCo bought Tropicana, the stadium is now called Tropicana Field or "The Trop." The roof turns orange when the Rays win a home game.

When the team finally started playing, there was more controversy. Some people didn't like the name Devil Rays—even if they were supposed to be named after a type of stingray and not after something more diabolical. And how do you create a costume for a stingray mascot?

Perhaps it's not surprising then, that after being ignored, jilted, and somewhat resented for taking so long to get here, the Rays have taken a while to come into their own. They are now just the Rays—no more devilry, at least to outward appearances—with a twinkling star as the logo and a cute, furry mascot, named Raymond, spreading sunshine everywhere.

In 2008, the Rays earned the American League championship and made the Phillies work for their World Series title. We've traded youthful fantasies of a dream team for the rock-solid reality of a long-term commitment with a major league franchise. We're talking about building a bigger home.

Tickets: The easiest way to buy tickets is online. Or you can call (888) FAN-RAYS (888-326-7297). Tropicana Field's box office is open Monday through Friday from 9 a.m. to 5:30 p.m., Saturday from 9 a.m. to 3 p.m., and Sunday from noon to 4 p.m. On game days, the box office opens at 9 a.m. and remains open until 30 minutes after the game. Tickets can also be purchased at the Rays' Tampa office (400 N. Tampa Street, Ste. 110) open Monday through Friday from 10 a.m. to 6 p.m. Or go to the Concierge Desk at International Plaza where there is a Ticketmaster outlet.

Parking: Buddy up, go green, and park for free at Tropicana Field if you have four or more people in your car. Otherwise, parking is $15 ($10 at the remote lots). Preferred parking ($30 peak and marquee games, $20 regular games) in lot 4B saves some steps and is the most direct exit from the game. Season ticket holders can purchase reserved parking at a discount. Wheelchair-accessible parking spaces are in lots 1, 6A, and 7A. Other public and commercial parking lots surround Tropicana Field. A free shuttle runs during some games. The Rays and Escort Bus Lines (888-571-7778) also provide bus service from various points in Pinellas, Hillsborough, and Manatee Counties.

Owner: Stuart Sternberg

Mascot: Raymond, the "Canus Manta Whatthe-fluffalus" or Seadog.

Spring training: The Rays play home games at Charlotte Sports Park in Port Charlotte, Florida.

Amenities: Tropicana Field is MLB's only field with artificial turf and all-dirt base paths (not just sliding areas around the bases). The Trop wins the "Best Sports Arena" award in our book, featuring creative murals, interactive play areas throughout the stadium, and the Hitters Hall of Fame. Look for the tank of cownose rays just behind the right center field wall—yes, you can touch them. Kids ages 12 and under are invited to run the bases after Sunday home games.

More info: Go to the Rays' Web site, click on the "Tropicana Field" tab, then select "Tropicana Field A–Z Guide," which will tell you everything from how to get players' autographs to what to do if you need wheelchair assistance. (Okay, so it doesn't quite make it all the way to Z. It's still a very comprehensive list of information.)

MINOR LEAGUE BASEBALL
9550 16th St. N.
(P.O. Box A)
St. Petersburg (33731)
(727) 822-6937
http://web.minorleaguebaseball.com

Established in 1901, Minor League Baseball's offices bounced around from New York to North Carolina to Ohio to St. Petersburg, where they have been since 1973. Today, Minor League Baseball oversees 251 clubs in 20 leagues, in four different classifications, whose almost 7,000 players suit up and "Play ball!" before more than 43 million paying fans each year. Minor league clubs play in Canada, the Dominican Republic, Mexico, the United States, and Venezuela. The Professional Baseball Umpire Corp, a wholly owned subsidiary of the National Association of Professional Baseball Leagues, also has its offices at MiLB's headquarters in St. Petersburg.

Spring Training Teams

NEW YORK YANKEES
George M. Steinbrenner "Legends" Field
1 Steinbrenner Dr.
Tampa
(813) 875-7753
www.steinbrennerfield.com
The New York Yankees have been coming to the Tampa Bay area for spring training off and on since 1924, but this facility, built in 1996, provides fans with an 11,000-seat stadium with field dimensions identical to those at Yankee Stadium. Legends Field is also home to the Class-A Florida State League Tampa Yankees and the Hillsborough Community College Hawks baseball team. Located across the street from Raymond James Stadium, the two complexes share parking facilities. There is a pedestrian bridge over Dale Mabry Highway connecting the two complexes. Parking in the general parking lot is $10 ($8 per game with the advanced season book).

PHILADELPHIA PHILLIES
Bright House Field
601 Old Coachman Rd.
Clearwater
(727) 441-9941 (offices)
(727) 467-4457 (tickets)
Tampa Bay area baseball fans were hard pressed to choose between favorite teams during the 2008 World Series. The hometown Tampa Bay Rays were the American League champions. But the Philadelphia Phillies, who have been coming to Clearwater for spring training since 1948, were the National League champions. It's

pretty hard to begrudge them the title—this time. Bright House Field is also home to the Florida State League 2008 Class-A Champs, the Clearwater Threshers. The stadium features a full 360-degrees concourse and a Kid Zone play area.

TORONTO BLUE JAYS
Dunedin Stadium
373 Douglas Ave.
Dunedin
(727) 733-9302 (offices)
(727) 733-0429, (800) 707-8269 (tickets)
Yes, we fly the Maple Leaf and sing "O, Canada" along with the "Star Spangled Banner." There's even LaBatt Blue on tap. It's the least we can do to welcome the Toronto Blue Jays to Dunedin each year, as we have since 1977 when the Blue Jays first flapped their wings. Dunedin Stadium is also home to the Florida State League Class A Dunedin Blue Jays and the Dunedin High School Falcons. *Sports Illustrated* rated Dunedin Stadium as one of the top five minor league stadiums in the country.

> **i** The Florida State League 2008 Class-A Champs, the Clearwater Threshers, are so called because they leave their opponents stunned as the thresher shark does when it slaps prey with its tail. The Thresher mascot's name is Finley.

EQUESTRIAN EVENTS

BOB THOMAS EQUESTRIAN CENTER
Florida State Fairgrounds
4800 U.S. 301 N.
Tampa
(813) 740-3500
www.bobthomasequestriancenter.com
From rodeos to dressage, there's an equestrian event being held almost every week of the year at the Bob Thomas Equestrian Center at the Florida State Fairgrounds. Check the calendar on their Web site for more information.

(Q) Close-up

The Grapefruit League

Baseball has been around in one form or another for as long as kids have hit rocks with sticks.

How baseball grew from one person hitting a rock with a stick into the highly formalized, highly regulated game between two teams we play today in the United States is for anthropologists to figure out. Baseball's growth in the Tampa Bay area is a little easier to see.

After the Civil War, ball clubs existed mainly in the northeastern United States. Ballparks were outdoors, so the game truly was played by the "boys of summer." When the season was over, ball players found odd jobs to tide them over until spring.

Each spring, club owners regrouped their teams and got everyone in shape before the first big game. They also picked up extra money—and new audiences—by doing "barnstorming" tours in warmer southern states. Sometimes the traveling professional teams played local teams—as was probably the case when the Cincinnati Red Stockings, a professional club for almost 40 years, played an exhibition game against the semi-pro St. Petersburg Saints in 1908.

Before long, club owners realized there was a market waiting to be tapped in the south. Why not train in the south, play some unofficial games to get the players warmed up before the real season began, and charge people to come watch them play? Less, of course, than they'd pay for an official game up north.

Local city officials saw this as a way to bring new business to the area. In 1913, Tampa Mayor D. B. McKay pledged to cover up to $100 per player in team expenses if the Chicago Cubs would train in Tampa. The Cubs came in February and practiced at Plant Field, adjacent to Henry B. Plant's Tampa Bay Hotel. No doubt there were some Chicagoans wintering at the hotel who relished getting the inside before-the-season scoop on how their Cubs were likely to fare in the coming months.

Another group of die-hard baseball fans already existed in Tampa's Ybor City. The Cuban League had been around since the 1870s. In fact, the Cincinnati–St. Petersburg game in October 1908

FOOTBALL

TAMPA BAY BUCCANEERS HEADQUARTERS
One Buccaneer Place
Tampa
(813) 870-2700
www.buccaneers.com

No other event may have so signified the Tampa Bay area's coming-of-age as did the awarding of an NFL expansion team franchise in 1974. In a hundred years, we had gone from being an isolated outpost to being a metropolitan community capable of supporting a team of pigskin gladiators in the football arena. On the surface, we looked all grown up.

Then the Tampa Bay Buccaneers kicked off in 1976, and promptly lost their first 26 games. During their first 20 years, the Bucs lost more games than they won.

There were some strong seasons. In 1979, the Bucs were the NFC Central Champs, and they have reached the playoffs several times. Bucs players have been part of All Stars teams, and Lee Roy Selmon, the Buc's first ever draft pick, was inducted into the Hall of Fame in 1995.

A lot has been written about the Bucs. Sports analysts and armchair quarterbacks have hashed over everything from the original "Creamsicle" team colors and uniforms to "Bucco Bruce," the swashbuckling mascot more evocative of Errol took place just before the Reds went on to Havana in November to play a number of teams there, including Cuban teams and an American Negro team, the Brooklyn Royal Giants.

In February 1913, the newly ensconced Chicago Cubs took on the Havana Athletics in a three-game series in Tampa. Nearly 6,000 people showed up. Ybor City businesses closed early so workers could attend the games.

Sweet, thought northern club owners. *Sweet,* thought southern city officials. Before long, other southern cities were actively recruiting teams to come and hold spring training in their communities.

St. Petersburg's mayor, Al Lang, wasted no time. In 1914, Lang persuaded the St. Louis Browns to come to St. Petersburg for spring training. Al Lang also knew people from Pittsburg—the laundry he'd owned up there probably washed a good many Pittsburg sports players' uniforms—and other northern cities. The Phillies came to St. Petersburg from 1915 to 1918. In time, enough teams came to Florida that the Grapefruit League developed. The Cactus League, based in Arizona, began in 1946.

Al Lang Stadium opened in St. Petersburg in 1947 and was rebuilt in 1977. Over the years, both Hillsborough and Pinellas Counties have seen baseball legends come and go.

Babe Ruth hit his longest homer ever—587 feet—at Plant Field in a 1919 game between the Boston Red Sox and the New York Giants. Today, Plant Field is part of the University of Tampa. A commemorative marker sits in front of the John Sykes College of Business on the UT campus.

Today, the Philadelphia Phillies train in Clearwater, as they have every year since 1947. The Toronto Blue Jays have had only one spring training site—Dunedin, just north of Clearwater—since becoming a team in 1977. The New York Yankees trained in St. Petersburg from 1924 to 1942, from 1946 to 1950, and again from 1952 to 1961. In 1996 they moved to Tampa where they have been ever since.

And where do the Tampa Bay Rays play during Grapefruit League season? Why down south a ways, of course, in Port Charlotte.

Flynn than of Blackbeard the Pirate, to bad trades and hard luck. So the uniforms changed from orange and white to black, pewter, and red. A grimacing skull over two crossed swords emblazoned on a ragged flag skewered on a third saber now is plastered on Bucs everything.

Still the Bucs struggled. We struggled with watching them.

What few people have mentioned is the psychological disadvantage that comes with being an expansion team in an area that itself is still growing up—in an area defined for a long time more by transplanted and part-time residents than by year-round, single-minded citizens. Until very recently, we as a region had little sense of our own history. Our lack of civic confidence led us to publicly question whether we were ready to assume big-time responsibilities. We were like a gawky adolescent tall enough to slam-dunk the ball without even jumping, but without the confidence and coordination to make it look effortless. The Bucs reflected that image.

Having an NFL team, having the Bucs helped pull us into full-fledged adulthood.

We hosted our first Super Bowl in 1984 and have hosted three others since then. Every New Years' Day since 1986, football fans have watched Tampa host the Outback Bowl, a college football showdown between the third pick SEC team and the third pick Big Ten Conference team.

Since 1996, the Bucs, too, have demonstrated maturity, being playoff contenders more often than not. They have done it with flair, with theatrics, and with compressed-air cannons booming at every Bucs touchdown from a full-scale replica of an early 1800s pirate ship moored in Raymond James Stadium's Buccaneer Cove. They have done it with players and staff who have been—by and large—committed to more than a paycheck and who have earned the respect of the community.

We are no longer a wide-eyed ingénue in the civic world. And the Bucs, with a win in Super Bowl XXXVII in 2003 (end of the 2002 season), are no longer a team on the verge of growing up.

Tickets: Buy tickets online, or visit or call (813-879-2827 or 800-282-0683) the Buccaneers' ticket office at One Buccaneer Place Monday through Friday from 8:30 a.m. to 5:30 p.m. E-mail the ticket office at buccaneersticketoffice@buccaneers.nfl.com. Tickets can also be purchased on game day only at Raymond James Stadium box office (813-350-6502) located between Gates C and D.

Parking: Print a map from the stadium Web site (www.raymondjames.com/stadium). You can purchase reserved season parking through the ticket office. Otherwise, day of game parking is first-come, first-served and costs $25 per space. RV parking is in lot 14 and costs $50 per space. Parking lots open four hours prior to Buccaneer home games for tailgate partying. Save yourself some grief and read through all the dos and don'ts on the Web site before coming.

Owner: Malcolm Glazer. The Glazer family also owns a soccer team in England.

Mascot: Captain Fear, the Buccaneer, who lives on a diet of Falcons (taste like chicken) and who lives in the captain's quarters of the pirate ship.

Pre-season training: The Bucs train at their brand new facility, One Buccaneer Place, just a hop, skip, and jump from Raymond James Stadium.

Amenities: Raymond James Stadium, nicknamed Ray J, seats 65,856 fans in theater-style seating. Two huge video scoreboards allow fans to see multiple shots of the action on the field. Budweiser's Good Sport program offers a free soft drink to a group's designated driver or a cab ride home for fans faced with a potential drunk-driving situation. Stop at the Information booth for designated driver wrist tags or to call for a Safe Ride home. Also stop at the Information booth for a tag-a-fan or tag-a-kid bracelet to help lost fans or children back to their proper seat.

TAMPA BAY STORM
St. Pete Times Forum
401 Channelside Dr.
Tampa
(813) 276-7300
www.tampabaystorm.com
The Storm play at the St. Pete Times Forum—or did play there. The Arena Football League, an indoor football league, cancelled its 2009 season because of financial problems. However, they've said they'll be back in 2010. The league was founded in 1987. In 2003, the same year the Bucs won Super Bowl XXXVII, the Tampa Bay Storm won Arena Bowl XVII.

UNIVERSITY OF SOUTH FLORIDA BULLS
USF Athletic Department
ATH100 4202 E. Fowler Ave.
Tampa
(813) 974-2125
www.gousfbulls.com
One of college football's newer teams, the Bulls began as a 1-AA independent team in 1997, 40 years after the university broke ground. In 2005, the team joined the Big East Conference, and they were nationally ranked by an AP poll in September 2007—a rarity for a team so young to become so prominent so quickly. The Bulls play their games at Raymond James Stadium.

GOLF

OUTBACK STEAKHOUSE PRO-AM
TPC Tampa Bay
5300 W. Lutz Lake Fern Rd.
Lutz
http://outbackproam.com
April brings the Outback Steakhouse Pro-Am at TPC Tampa Bay, part of the PGA Champions tour, played just north of Tampa in Lutz (pronounced

Loots). TPC Tampa Bay, part of the Heritage Golf Group, gives players of varying skill levels the challenge of playing a par-71, 7,000-yard course (from the championship tees, or 5,036 yards from the forward tees). At the same time, TPC Tampa Bay sits in a more rural part of Hillsborough County, and it's not unusual for the non-tournament, early-morning gallery to consist of armadillos and egrets—maybe even a deer or two. In fact, TPC Tampa Bay, designed by Bobby Weed with player input from Chi Chi Rodriguez, is one of only two courses in the Tampa Bay area the Audubon Society has designated as an Audubon Cooperative Sanctuary.

The Outback Steakhouse Pro-Am pairs pro players like Tom Kite, Nick Price (this past year's pro winner), and Hale Irwin with celebrity players like Michael J. Fox, George Lopez, and Vinny Testaverde. A daily pass is $30, a weekly pass is $70, or go for the Green-Hopper Party Pass ($95 for one day, $185 for the week).

TRANSITIONS CHAMPIONSHIP

**Copperhead Course at Innisbrook Resort &
Golf Club**
36750 U.S. 19 N.
Innisbrook
(727) 942-2000, (800) 456-2000
www.innisbrookgolfresort.com
www.transitionschampionship.com
Two major golf tournaments come each year to the Tampa Bay area, both run by non-profit organizations that make sure local charities benefit from the events. In March, the Professional Golfers' Association Tour comes to the par-71 Copperhead course at Innisbrook (see Accommodations chapter for resort info) for the Transitions Championship. Golfers this past year competed for a $5.4 million purse.

Considered by many golfers to be Florida's finest course, Copperhead is both technically demanding and aesthetically stunning. Originally designed by Larry Packard in 1970, the Copperhead's 7,300+ yards challenge the world's top golfers with narrow fairways lined with trees, rolling hills creating blind spots, and reflective ponds luring errant balls to a watery demise.

Gallery and other tickets to the Transitions Championship can be yours by using the contact information given above. This past year's tickets started at $69 for a daily pass (plus you'll need a parking pass—those started at $20). Various events are held at the resort, including activities for children, along with the tournament itself.

HOCKEY

TAMPA BAY LIGHTNING HOCKEY CLUB
St. Pete Times Forum
401 Channelside Dr.
Tampa
(813) 301-6500
www.lightning.nhl.com
A funny thing happened while we were waiting for baseball. We built a stadium thinking we'd one day get down on bended knee and offer a diamond. Instead, these guys in skates showed up and started playing something called hockey.

Hockey? Since when does Florida have hockey teams?

Since team owners figured out there are enough northern transplants and retirees in the Sunshine State to jump-start a fan base for a new team. And they also figured out that Olympic hockey victories spurred an interest in young Floridians learning the game.

So, since 1992, we've had a hockey team—one that played for a few years in what was supposed to be our baseball stadium, but which became the Thunderdome. It was a makeshift arrangement that worked until something better came along.

That something better was the Ice Palace in Tampa, built as a permanent home for the Lightning beginning with the 1996 to 1997 season. Since then, the *St. Petersburg Times* bought the naming rights and the building is now known as the St. Pete Times Forum—appropriate because the building also hosts concerts, basketball games, and other events.

That doesn't mean things have been as smooth as fresh ice for the Lightning. They've gone through multiple owners, multiple coaches, and multiple players. But the team persisted, and the Lightning won the Stanley cup in June 2004. (Who plays hockey in the summer?)

Then came the NHL lockout that cancelled the 2004 to 2005 hockey season over labor disputes. Since returning to the ice in the fall of 2005, the Lightning have seemed to be unable to recapture the concentrated energy needed to take them past the quarterfinals.

We're a patient people, however. We figure it's only a matter of time before the scattered lightning blips we've seen recently unite and become focused high-voltage winning bolts.

Tickets: Buy tickets online, or visit or call the ticket office (813-301-2500) at the St. Pete Times Forum on non-game days Monday through Friday from 9 a.m. to 6 p.m. or Saturday from 9 a.m. to 2 p.m. On game days, the box office opens at 9 a.m. (including Sunday) and stays open until the end of the game. You can also email the ticket office at boxoffice@tampabaylighting.com.

Parking: Some parking is available in the attached South Regional Parking Garage, which, despite its name, is on the west side of the building. More parking is available in lots in the Channelside area. Fees vary. Purchase reserved parking in advance when you buy your tickets.

Owner: Oren Koules, Len Barrie, Mark Burg, Russell Belinsky, Dr. Richard C. Lehman, Irwin Novack, Craig Sher, Jordan Zimmerman

Mascot: ThunderBug, born on Bugtober 7, 1992 and whose favorite songs are *"The Hockey Song,"* by Stompin' Tom Connors, and *"Lightning Strikes,"* by Lou Christie

Pre-season training: Training camp for the Tampa Bay Lighting generally begins in September at the St. Pete Times Forum.

Amenities: The St. Pete Times Forum seats 19,758 hockey fans (20,500 for basketball). Look for the Energy Team—which might be jugglers or stilt-walkers—providing entertainment before the face off. Stop at the Information booth for designated driver wrist tags or to call for a Safe Ride home—or for a tag-a-fan or tag-a-kid bracelet to help lost fans or children back to their proper seat.

i Watch for the Lightning, through their non-profit Lightning Foundation, to develop a sled hockey team for players with physical impairments that prevent them from strapping on a pair of skates. We have a feeling that won't prevent them from heating up the ice!

SAILING

Neither of these events is actually a "professional" event—but they require more than just casual skill and commitment, so we'll include them here.

NOOD REGATTA
www.sailingworld.com/nood-regattas
St. Petersburg is one of nine stops on the Sperry Top-Sider NOOD (National Offshore One Design) Regatta each year. The St. Petersburg Yacht Club (11 Central Ave., St. Petersburg, 727-822-3873) hosts some 1,500 to 2,000 boats each year for the four-day event that includes three days of racing in 19 design classes. Sailors from around the country—including some America's Cup and Olympics competitors—make the circuit. The NOOD Regatta was begun in 1988 by *Sailing World* magazine.

REGATTA SOL DEL SOL
www.regatadelsolalsol.org
The Regatta Sol del Sol isn't just a "race you to the corner" kind of race. This race begins at the St. Petersburg Yacht Club in St. Petersburg, Florida, U.S.A., and ends at the Club de Yates Isla Mejures, Isla Mejures (off of Cancun), Yucatan Peninsula, Mexico. Yup—400-plus nautical miles across the open waters of the Gulf of Mexico. The race has taken place for more than 40 years, usually involving about 30 yachts, each with a crew of about five people. A support team of trawlers follows with extra supplies and "just-in-case" kinds of help. The race takes about four days, depending on the weather.

Close-up

Tour the Stadiums

Wonder what the players see when they take the ice on game day at the Forum? Or what it's like to sit in the dugout at Tropicana Field? Or to prepare for the gridiron in the Bucs' locker room at Raymond James Stadium? Each stadium offers behind-the-scenes tours of the facilities. Wear your walking shoes!

Note: Be prepared to pay cash for these tours. The tours are arranged through the marketing department rather than through the box office. They don't have access to credit card machines.

Raymond James Stadium
Tampa Sports Authority
4201 N. Dale Mabry Hwy
Tampa
(813) 350-6545
(813) 879-2827, (800) 795-2827 (ticket office)
www.raymondjames.com/stadium

Put on your game face and take the field at Raymond James Stadium through the Bucs' tunnel, tour the locker rooms, and visit the club lounge areas. Sit high above the field in one of the private suites, then explore the pirate ship. It's all part of the tour offered by the Tampa Sports Authority. Tours are offered every Tuesday, Wednesday, and Thursday at 2 p.m. You'll want to get there early, however, as you'll need to check in with the security guard at Lot B (on Himes Avenue), make your way to the Tampa Sports Authority office, and register for the tour. Cost is $5 for adults, $3 for seniors age 65 and up and for children ages 6 to 15. Children age 5 and under are free. Cash only—there is an ATM machine outside the office. No reservations are needed, but you can call (813) 350-6500, ext. 0, to confirm that a tour will be offered that day.

St. Pete Times Forum
401 Channelside Dr.
Tampa
(813) 301-6500
www.lightning.nhl.com

With seven separate levels and three decks, the St. Pete Times Forum becomes an ice rink, hosting the NHL Tampa Bay Lightning, then morphs into a basketball arena, tennis courts for tournament play, or a concert venue. Visitors to the Forum can see the different club areas, get a commentator's perspective from the press box, and sit on a Zamboni. You'll learn, too, about the extensive recycling program at the Forum that goes beyond aluminum cans and plastic bottles. The Forum has won Green awards at the county and state levels. The Forum prefers to give tours to groups of 15 or more people on Tuesday and Thursday, by appointment only. Cost is $5 per person and the tour lasts about 90 minutes. Call (813) 301-6500 to make arrangements.

Tropicana Field
1 Tropicana Dr.
St. Petersburg
(727) 825-3250
http://tampabay.rays.mlb.com

Check the Web site for days the tour is offered. Times are 10 a.m. and 2 p.m. Tours last 90 minutes and take you to the Rays' dugout, to the interactive Right Field and Left Field Streets, to the cownose rays' touch tank, to the Ted Williams Museum and the Hitters Hall of Fame, and other places throughout Tropicana Field. Cost is $8 for adults, $7 for seniors ages 55 and over, and $6 for children ages 12 and under. Cash is preferred. Park in lots 6 or 7 at Gate 1 in front of the Trop. Call (727) 825-3495 or email ballparktours@raysbaseball.com at least 24 hours in advance to reserve your spot. Group rates are available for groups of 20 or more.

SOCCER

TAMPA BAY HELLENIC
Ed Radice Sports Complex
14720 Ed Radice Dr.
Tampa
www.uslsoccer.com/teams/2009/8986511
.html

Tampa Bay Hellenic is a USL Women's soccer team organized in preparation for, according to USL, the return of a Women's Professional Soccer League. For now, Tampa Bay Hellenic is an amateur athletic organization and a player development team. Players have competed at the collegiate and post-collegiate levels in at least four countries. Tampa Bay Hellenic's schedule is posted at the Web site above. Tickets are listed at $80 for a seven-game family season pass (two adults and three youth), $25 for an individual season pass, and $18 for a season pass for a child under age 12.

TAMPA BAY ROWDIES
3837 Northdale Blvd., Ste. 367
Tampa
(800) 813-3294
www.tbrowdies.com

Before there was football in the Tampa Bay area, there was *futbol*—soccer, in American-ese. Yes, the Bucs were awarded a franchise in 1974, but they didn't actually play their first game until 1976. The Rowdies, on the other hand, played their first game in1975.

Not only did the Tampa Bay Rowdies play in 1975, they won the North American Soccer League title in the 1975 Soccer Bowl—not bad at all for a brand-new team.

From there, it gets complicated.

The Rowdies played NASL indoor games at St. Petersburg's Bayfront Center Area in 1975 and from 1979 to 1984, winning the 1980 NASL indoor championship. They played outdoor NASL games at Tampa Stadium from 1975 to 1983. Then the NASL went out of business.

Cornelia Corbett became sole owner of the Rowdies and the team played as an independent for two years before joining the American Indoor

Soccer Association for the 1986 to 1987 season. Then—keeping track of all this?—the Rowdies joined the American Soccer League. Not the 1921 to 1933 or the 1933 to 1983 versions of the ASL, but the 1988 version, an eastern counterpart to the West Coast Soccer Alliance. In 1990, the ASL merged with the Western Soccer League and they formed the American Professional Soccer League.

Between 1975 and 1993, when the team disbanded, the Tampa Bay Rowdies played in four different leagues and played independently for a couple of years.

This time around, the new Tampa Bay Rowdies will be part of the United Soccer Leagues, playing in the USL First Division. The United Soccer League has several divisions designed to develop new players—similar in concept to the minor league system in baseball. Currently, there are 11 first division USL teams with 3 more, including the Rowdies, scheduled to begin playing in 2010.

There's no mascot at this point, no team, not even a coach. But the owners have committed to building the team its own soccer-friendly stadium somewhere in northwest Hillsborough County. Already they're selling season tickets. And they ran clinics at area summer camps in 2009.

Will they succeed? Two thoughts: First, the last time the Rowdies were here, they spawned an incredibly strong youth soccer movement that still fills fields around the Tampa Bay area. Second, soccer is *the* game in much of the rest of the world. Changing demographics in the United States would make it seem reasonable to expect a larger fan base this time around.

Tickets: You can email the Rowdies at tickets@ tbrowdies.com or call (888) 757-6934. We'd love to give you a box office location, but one hasn't been built yet.

Parking: None yet.

Owner: Andrew Nestor, Hinds Howard, David Laxer, Jeffrey MacDonald

Mascot: None yet.

Pre-season training: First they need a coach and a team. After that, our guess is that they'll start at the Ed Radice Sports Complex where the Tampa Bay Hellenic (see page 178) play.

Amenities: Watch for the Rowdies to develop the Tampa Bay Rowdies Academy—a premier youth soccer academy designed to feed players into the USL system.

THOROUGHBRED AND GREYHOUND RACING AND GAMBLING

Pari-mutuel wagering has been legal in Florida since 1934. Through the years, dog racing, horse racing, and jai alai games have attracted many fans. Recently, however, competition from other forms of entertainment and from casino gambling on reservation lands have changed dog and horse track operations. Currently poker—a form of pari-mutuel betting—is allowed at dog tracks and horse tracks. The dogs don't actually have to run at the track, either, as long as a video simulcast of a race is playing.

See the Close-up below for more on the history of gambling in the Tampa Bay area.

DERBY LANE
10490 Gandy Blvd.
St. Petersburg
(727) 812-3339
www.derbylane.com
Greyhound racing times are Monday through Saturday evenings; 6:30 gates open and 7:30 post time. Matinee races are Wednesday and Saturday; 11:30 a.m. gates open and 12:30 p.m. post time. Poker Room is open Sunday through Thursday from 1 p.m. to 1 a.m. and from 2 p.m. to 2 a.m. Friday and Saturday. Dining options include the Derby Club Restaurant (buffet, no children under age 10), two lounges, a coffee shop, and concessions in the mezzanine area.

LUCKY'S CARD ROOM
Tampa Greyhound Track
8300 N. Nebraska Ave.
Tampa
(813) 932-4313 ext. 301
www.tampadogs.com

What is Pari-mutuel Betting?

Pari-mutuel betting is when people bet against each other. It's easy to bet against each other when it's just one or two people and they pay up as promised after the race.

But when there are a lot of people betting—like at a horse or dog race—people pay their money before the race begins. A turf accountant (bookmaker) takes the money, holds it while the race is being run, and pays the winners after the race.

The turf accountant takes a percentage of the money bet as a fee for performing this service.

Of course, it's become more complicated than that. Now the turf accountant also calculates the odds of a particular horse winning, placing (coming in second), or showing (coming in third).

With banked games, on the other hand, everybody bets against "the house" or the bank. Instead of just being a passive holder of other people's money, the house bets, too.

People generally have not been allowed—with the exception of jai-alai—to gamble on games involving humans competing with each other. Athletes could be bribed or coerced to throw a game—to deliberately lose or to lose by a certain number of points. Cheating would be very difficult to control, and people could lose a lot of money on rigged games.

Officially, it's still Tampa Greyhound Track. But the races are simulcast from Derby Lane and from six other locations around the state. Simulcast

⊙ Close-up

Tracks and Casinos

Visitors to the Tampa Bay area used to find greyhound dog racing at two area tracks and thoroughbred horse racing at one track. Visitors used to watch and bet on jai-alai games (similar to lacrosse) at a fronton in Tampa.

Today, only one dog track holds races. But its main business is poker. Tampa Bay Downs, the horse track, also offers poker in addition to horse races and golf. The jai-alai fronton closed in 1998.

HISTORY LESSON

The ancient Greeks awarded laurel crowns to the fastest and the strongest of their athletes. The Romans raced horses harnessed to chariots in the Coliseum. From Little League onward we push our children to throw farther, hit harder, run faster, jump higher—to win. Something in us urges us to pit ourselves, and our animals—or our cars—against each other.

Historically, racing thoroughbred animals has been considered the sport of queens (greyhounds) and kings (horses) and, by extension, of the upper crust of society. But, while many people cheer on the Kentucky Derby competitors, many of the same people don't cheer on the gambling that goes with the horse racing.

In the United States, horse racing began a full century before the American Revolution. In 1665, the first thoroughbred horse racetrack was built on Long Island. By 1890 there were more than 300 tracks in the United States. Sometimes the gambling that went with the racing was legal by default—there were just no laws against it. Sometimes, as with Prohibition laws, law enforcement officials just looked the other way.

Derby Lane, today the oldest continuously operating greyhound racing track in the nation, was built in St. Petersburg in 1925 for greyhound racing. Tampa Bay Downs opened in 1926 for horse racing. But Florida didn't legalize pari-mutuel betting until 1931 when, because of the Depression, the state needed money to pay teachers, state employees, and other bills.

Some people thought legalizing pari-mutuel gambling was better than having a sales tax or state income tax. And there had been some cases of gamblers being cheated by crooked racetrack owners. Bringing the gambling under state control and taxing it seemed to answer both problems.

Supporters of legalizing pari-mutuel gambling in Florida had estimated the state would receive $1 million per year in revenue. By 1940, the state was receiving almost $4.4 million each year, and by 1957 the figure was $25 million. Over the years, gambling expanded to include dog racing, harness racing, and jai-alai. Horse breeders moved into the state, creating a side industry.

Times change, however. Car racing began to displace animal racing. Animal rights activists questioned the care that racing animals receive. Other competition developed over the years. Bingo was legalized. So-called "cruises to nowhere" began taking passengers out into the Gulf just past the 3-mile limit of state legal control for an evening of casino gambling.

And the state government started competing for gambling dollars. In 1988, Florida began selling lottery tickets to increase funding for education. Whether because of the lottery or for other reasons, revenues at the tracks declined that year.

THE SEMINOLE TRIBE OF FLORIDA AND GAMBLING

The Seminole people who stayed in Florida after 1858 lived mostly in the Everglades and other wild areas. They survived by hunting, fishing, and farming. By the early 1900s, as those wild areas began to be developed, the Seminole became a tourist attraction. People would go see the Seminole wrestle alligators. The Seminole also began to lose land they had been living on to developers.

In 1934, however, Congress passed the Wheeler-Howard Bill, known more commonly as the Indian Reorganization Act, as part of the New Deal programs. Tribes could vote not to be included, and many tribes boycotted the election, thinking it would just mean more government control.

In Florida, of the 500 or so Seminole eligible to vote, only 21 actually voted. All 21 voters approved the act, so the government included the Seminole tribe in the provisions. The bill aimed at improving education and health care for native tribes. But it also provided a way by which tribes could become self-governing and preserve tribal lands. The bill also exempted native tribes from paying state and local taxes.

At first, the Seminole paid little attention to the bill. They raised cattle, and in 1947 filed a petition to recover land lost in the 1800s. In 1957, however, the Seminole wrote and ratified a constitution. The federal government officially recognized them as the Seminole Tribe of Florida. Most Seminole lived on two reservations—Big Cypress, just north of Alligator Alley, the east-west stretch of I-75 that runs from Naples to Ft. Lauderdale, and Brighton, on the northwest side of Lake Okeechobee.

Today, the Seminole Tribe of Florida has six non-contiguous reservations in Florida: Big Cypress, Brighton, Fort Pierce, Hollywood, Immokalee, and Tampa. Tampa is the northernmost of the six.

In the 1970s, the Seminole took advantage of their exemption from paying state and local taxes to begin selling tax-free cigarettes on their reservations. The tribe's budget grew from $12,500 in 1957 to $4.5 million by 1976.

By 1979, bingo had become the Tribe's biggest source of revenue. In 1981, federal courts affirmed the right of the tribe to conduct high-stakes bingo games on their reservations. Other tribes around the country, especially in California, followed the Seminole's lead. Because the issues involved federal agreements and decisions, state governments affected had little voice in the matters.

In 1988, Congress passed the National Indian Gaming Regulatory Act to allow states to determine what level of gambling would be allowed on the reservations, but the act also established the National Indian Gaming Commission as part of the federal Department of the Interior.

The Seminole Tribe continued to pursue its land claims against the federal government. In 1992, they received a settlement of around $10 million.

Over the years, the Seminole Tribe has invested in various business ventures—including aircraft manufacturing, citrus production, and turtle farming. In 1996, they acquired additional reservation property in Tampa. In 2002, under a licensing agreement with Hard Rock International, the Tribe began building two Hard Rock Casinos—one in Tampa and one in Hollywood—both on reservation property. The casinos opened in 2004.

In March 2007, the Seminole Tribe made its biggest investment yet. The Tribe paid $965 million for the Hard Rock business—at the time, 124 cafés in 45 countries, four hotels, two casinos, two concert venues, the world's largest collection of rock memorabilia, and other assets.

In November 2007, Governor Charlie Crist signed a compact with the Seminole tribe, which permitted the tribe to operate various high-stakes card games and slot machines in Seminole-owned casinos in Florida in return for money paid to the state each year. The state legislature protested, saying they had not been involved in the decision. The Department of the Interior approved the compact.

Since then, the legislature, the governor, and the Florida Supreme Court have gone back and forth over whether Crist's action was legal and appropriate. Owners of other pari-mutuel facilities say the agreement is unfair because they can't offer the same kinds of gaming the Seminole-owned facilities can.

Meanwhile, the gambling continues at the Hard Rock Casinos in Tampa and Hollywood.

wagering also takes place on harness racing, thoroughbred racing, and jai-alai games from other Florida locations. Lucky's Card Room is open every day from noon to midnight. Dining facilities are open from noon to 10 p.m.

SEMINOLE HARD ROCK HOTEL & CASINO
5223 N. Orient Rd.
Tampa
(813) 627-7625, (866) 502-PLAY (7529)
www.seminolehardrocktampa.com
The casino offers slot machines, high-stakes slot machines, high-stakes poker, blackjack, and other casino games. For resort information, see description in Accommodations chapter.

TAMPA BAY DOWNS
11225 Racetrack Rd.
Tampa
(813) 855-4401, (866)-TBDOWNS (823-6967)
www.tampabaydowns.com
Horse racing gates open at 11 a.m.; post time for the first race is 12:25 p.m. Grandstand admission is free on weekdays and $2 on weekends. Clubhouse admission is $3. Parking is free. Valet parking is available for $5. Simulcast wagering on thoroughbred racing, harness racing, dog racing, jai-alai, and other events is available. Poker at The Silks operates seven days a week from 12:30 p.m. to 12:30 a.m., with doors opening at 11:30 a.m. The Downs Golf Practice Facility (813-854-4946) opens Monday at 10 a.m., Tuesday through Sunday at 8:30 a.m., and closes every day at 9:45 p.m.

TRIATHLON

IRONMAN WORLD CHAMPIONSHIP 70.3
www.ironman.com
One Saturday each November, bikes take over many Pinellas County roads. These cyclists aren't out for a scenic tour—they're competing in the Ironman World Championship 70.3.

The original Ironman Triathlon began in Hawaii in 1978, when a group of athletes debated whether runners, swimmers, or cyclists were the most fit. To settle the question, they competed in a 2.4-mile swim, followed by a 112-mile bike race, and concluded with a 26.2-mile run—140.6 miles, all told, in one event. The race caught on and developed into a worldwide circuit of races, with the championships still held in Hawaii.

In 2005, the World Triathlon Corporation formed a half-triathlon series, and Clearwater became the host city for the Ironman World Championship 70.3. Around 2,000 competitors from all parts of the world swim 1.2-miles off of Clearwater Beach, bicycle a 56-mile route that takes them in a loop around the northern part of the Pinellas peninsula's midsection, then run a 13.1-mile course through Clearwater. They compete for a $100,000 purse.

PARKS AND RECREATION

Yes, we have a wild side. The Tampa Bay area may be part of a major metropolitan region, but deer (no antelope or buffalo, however) still play in our wooded areas, and you can still pitch a tent on either side of Tampa Bay for a real back-to-nature experience.

Or maybe you're just looking for a place to picnic that has some kid-powered rides like swings and merry-go-rounds (remember those?). We have plenty of parks of all sizes with loads of recreational opportunities in the Tampa Bay area.

Florida has a great state park system with clean facilities—and with many opportunities to experience Florida as it was before facilities, clean or otherwise, were invented. Our state parks in the Tampa Bay area lie along the Hillsborough River in the east and along the Gulf of Mexico in the West—Caladesi Island State Park is accessible only by boat. (An urban state park in Ybor City is listed in the Attractions chapter.)

We don't mean to brag, but—oh, why not? In November 2008, American Trails gave Florida its first ever "Best Trails State in America" award for its statewide and state-sponsored greenways and trails system. The Florida Office of Greenways and Trails manages more than 80,000 acres of greenways and over 400 miles of trails in the state (www.dep.state.fl.us/gwt). In this chapter, we'll tell you about Greenway and Blueway trails here and about the Rails-to-Trials program of which some of our trails are parts.

Both Hillsborough and Pinellas counties make parks a priority. You'll find camping, BMX bicycle courses, fishing piers, walking trails, disc golf, and other activities in our county parks. You'll especially want to check into the programs and trails at the Brooker Creek and Weedon Island Environmental and Education Centers in Pinellas County.

You don't have to be a city resident to use our city-owned parks. Boyd Hill Nature Park in St. Petersburg has a nature center and a pioneer village. Moccasin Lake Park in Clearwater hosts campfire-and-marshmallow programs.

There are loads of recreational centers in the area with summer camps for kids, teen activities and centers, fitness programs for all ages, and more. We can't list them all, but we'll give you enough information to get you started.

We've divided this chapter into three main sections: state parks, county parks, and city parks and recreation centers. A fourth section at the end tells about beach parks, regardless of in whose jurisdiction they lie. Throughout the chapter, look for close-ups and sidebars with information about boat launching, fishing licenses, pier fishing, and charter boat fishing trips.

So lace up your sneakers, fill your water bottle, grab the insect repellant and sunscreen, and let's explore the Tampa Bay area's great outdoors!

STATE AND REGIONAL PARKS

Tampa/Hillsborough County

ALAFIA RIVER STATE PARK
14326 South County Rd. 39
Lithia
(813) 672-5320
www.floridastateparks.org/alafiariver

Alafia River State Park's off-road bicycle trails draw riders from around the state. Three major loops constructed and maintained by the Southwest Association Mountain Bike Pedalers (SWAMP; 813-689-5109; www.swampclub.org) make for challenging rides for all levels of experience. Helmets are required for all ages on the bike trails.

There also are plenty of places to fish, camp, canoe or kayak, and ride horseback at Alafia River State Park. Bring your own canoe or kayak and your own horse—no rentals are available. The picnic area has a children's playground with swings and slides. Campsites for RVs and tent campers have electrical service, water, and restroom facilities. Primitive camp areas are also available.

Events at Alafia River State Park include the Alafia Fat Tire Festival (bikes) and a Cross-Country Marathon, both in November.

Because of the number of activities at Alafia River State Park, the admission fees are a bit more complicated than at some of the other state parks. There's a $4 daily fee for a vehicle with two to eight passengers, $3 for a single passenger vehicle. Pedestrians, bicyclists, and extra passengers pay $1. Horses pay, too—or at least their handlers pay $6 per horse, up to two horses per day (plus tax) or $14 per tow vehicle and trailer. Camping fees are $18 per night, plus tax, with an eight-person maximum per site. Daily equestrian fees are not included in the camping rates.

HILLSBOROUGH RIVER STATE PARK
15402 U.S. 301 N.
Thonotosassa
(813) 987-6771
www.floridastateparks.org/hillsboroughriver
CSO: Hillsborough River State Park Preservation Society, Inc., http://lolralph.tripod.com/HRSPPS

Hillsborough River State Park, located in northeastern Hillsborough County and built in the 1930s with New Deal funds, is a good choice for people who want to ease into roughing it. An in-ground, man-made swimming pool (as opposed to ye olde swimming hole complete with alligators, snakes, and other critters), the Outpost concession area to keep shopaholics from going into withdrawal, and a full-facility camping area provide a semblance of civilization in a back-to-nature setting.

Go canoeing, kayaking, or bicycling—bring your own or rent one at the Outpost. Do some fishing, hiking, or bird-watching. Visit Fort Foster, the only standing replica of a Second Seminole War fort in the United States, or the Interpretive Center to learn more about the history of the area. Gather around the communal campfire each Friday evening for a ranger-led program about the park.

And in October, Hillsborough River State Park becomes the Haunted Woods, complete with ghostly terrors—all in good fun, of course.

The daily entrance fee is $4 per vehicle with up to eight people per car. Camping fees are $20 per night, plus tax. The fee to use the swimming pool (not open all year) is $2 per day for everyone ages 6 and up (ages 5 and under are free), and the tour of Fort Foster costs $2 for adults, $1 for children ages 6 to 12 (ages 5 and under are free). Fort Foster tours are conducted Saturday at 2 p.m. and Sunday at 11 a.m., weather permitting.

LITTLE MANATEE RIVER STATE PARK
215 Lightfoot Rd.
Wimauma
(813) 671-5005
www.floridastateparks.org/littlemanatee river
CSO: Friends of Little Manatee River (www.friendsofthelittlemanatee.com)

Twelve miles of equestrian trails and eight equestrian campsites make Little Manatee River State Park in southeastern Hillsborough County popular with horse owners. There are also hiking trails, fishing spots, and canoeing and kayaking along the river. Canoes are available for rent, and some evenings there is a communal campfire circle.

Doing the Stingray Shuffle

Many of our parks include beaches and other saltwater areas, so we'd better teach you our local dance—the stingray shuffle.

Stingrays are flat, bottom-feeding fish that love the shallow areas close to beaches, especially during the warmer months of the year. Swimmers who blithely run out to the waves risk stepping on a ray. Rays who get stepped on do what we might do if someone attacked us—fight back.

A stingray has a venomous barb, sometimes as long as 8 inches. Think of being stung by a frying pan–sized wasp, and you have an idea of what it might feel like. The barb is slimy, too, and the wound can get infected.

Thankfully, rays are very shy and would much rather be left alone. We need to let them know we're in the area. They'll move along, and both they and we will breathe sighs of relief. Hmmm . . . do sea critters sigh with relief through their gills or some other way?

Here's how we let stingrays know we're in the area—we do the stingray shuffle.

As your toes touch the water,
Sh-sh-sh-shuffle
You know you really oughter
Sh-sh-sh-shuffle
Keep your tootsies a-sliding
Sh-sh-sh-shuffle
To tell rays who are hiding
Sh-sh-sh-shuffle
There's a giant coming through
Sh-sh-sh-shuffle
Then they won't sting you!
Sh-sh-sh-shuffle

Okay—so Shakespeare we're not.

But if it helps you remember to slide your feet slowly along the sand as you wade out into the surf, we'll take the jibes. Don't forget to do the stingray shuffle on your way back out of the water.

If a ray stings you, get medical attention immediately. If you can't get to a doctor right away, soak the wound in hot, soapy water. The heat breaks down the protein-based venom and the soap helps prevent infection—sometimes the slime on the barb is worse than the venom.

Full-hookup campsites, including two ADA-accessible campsites, are available for RVs, and there are also primitive camping areas for overnight hikers and others wanting a little more solitude.

The daily admission fee is $4 per vehicle with up to eight people per vehicle. Camping and other fees apply. Firewood can be purchased for $5 a bundle at the ranger station.

LOWER HILLSBOROUGH WILDERNESS PARK
East of I–75 and north of U.S. Hwy 301

The Southwest Florida Water Management District oversees this 16,000-acre preserve in Hills-

About Florida's State Parks

Florida Division of Recreation and Parks
3900 Commonwealth Blvd.
Tallahassee
(850) 245-2157
www.floridastateparks.org

We're not the only ones who think Florida has a great state park system. The National Recreation and Parks Association has recognized the Florida state park system as the "Nation's Best State Park Service" not once, but twice since 1999. You'll find Gold Medal Award–winning parks, programs, and management at the seven Florida state parks in Hillsborough and Pinellas Counties.

Florida's state park system preserves both Florida's natural resources and its cultural resources. Preserving natural resources means such things as restoring the original landscape by eliminating invasive plants or by rebuilding beaches. Preserving cultural resources means restoring historic buildings, conserving furnishings and other artifacts, and placing them in the context of their surroundings.

The first national park, Yellowstone, so designated in 1872, marked the beginning of a national movement to protect some areas from development. In Florida, the Olustee (Civil War) Battlefield near Jacksonville was the first area designated as a state memorial in 1909. A century later, Florida's state park system has grown from one memorial to more than 160 sites, including 100 miles of shoreline and 700,000 acres of land.

Florida boasts the nation's first underwater park (John Pennekamp Coral Reef State Park, 1959), the world's largest and deepest single spring (Edward Ball Wakulla Springs State Park (600,000 gallons per minute, 185 feet deep), the nation's largest variety of wild orchids (Fakahatchee Strand Preserve State Park), and the world's longest fishing pier (Skyway Fishing Pier State Park).

Florida state parks, with a few exceptions, are open 365 days a year from 8 a.m. to sunset. Admission fees vary, as do the facilities and programs offered at each park. Alcohol is not permitted in state parks, except in licensed facilities and during state-sanctioned events.

Check each park's pet policies, and be prepared to offer proof of rabies vaccination. Many parks have equestrian trails—horses must have proof of a negative Coggins test. Florida state law requires all bicyclists under age 16 to wear helmets, but some park rules require helmets for all ages on off-road trails.

Campfires may be prohibited during dry seasons. Many parks have a Citizen Support Organization (CSO) to help with funding and special events. Many CSOs have their own Web site with additional information borough County northeast of Tampa. SWFWMD manages two recreational sites in the park—the Jefferson and Oakridge Equestrian Areas. These two sites have minimal facilities.

Within the Lower Hillsborough Wilderness Park are Hillsborough River State Park, Hillsborough River State Canoe Trail, the Old Fort King Trail, and a number of Hillsborough County parks. The primary purpose of the Lower Hillsborough Wilderness Park is to store water. Thirteen miles—one-fourth the length—of the Hillsborough River flows through the park.

St. Petersburg/South Pinellas County

EGMONT KEY STATE PARK

4905 34th St. S., #5000
St. Petersburg
(727) 893-2627
www.floridastateparks.org/egmontkey
CSO: Egmont Key Alliance
www.egmontkey.org

Egmont Key is the first island reached by ships approaching Tampa Bay from the Gulf of Mexico. Because of its gatekeeper position and its size, Egmont Key has played several roles in the Tampa Bay area's history, including holding Seminole prisoners for relocation to the Arkansas Territory, as a Union navy base during the Civil War, and as a fort during the Spanish-American War era. The Tampa Bay Pilots Association has maintained its operations on Egmont Key since 1926.

There are hiking trails, swimming and fishing spots, and ruins to explore on Egmont Key.

Egmont Key, also a National Wildlife Preserve, is one of the few state parks where pets are not allowed. All visitors must be off the island by sunset. If you take the ferry over and miss the ferry back to Fort DeSoto, the park ranger will arrange for a water taxi, and you will be liable for the cost.

Admission is free, but access is by boat or ferry only. Tampa Bay Ferry (727-398-6577, ext. 3, or 727-867-6569; www.hubbardsmarina.com/um/egmont.html) cuurently provides service, boarded from Bay Pier at Fort DeSoto, a Pinellas County park (see description below). The ferry costs $20 for adults and $10 for children ages 11 and under. Snorkeling and other equipment can be rented from Tampa Bay Ferry. Flip flops are not allowed on the ferry—be sure you have sandals with backs, water shoes, deck shoes, or sneakers. The sand on Egmont Key can be very hot, so you'll want thick soles if you're planning on doing much walking.

SKYWAY FISHING PIER STATE PARK

4905 34th St. S., #5000
St. Petersburg
(727) 865-0668
www.floridastateparks.org/skyway

After the original Skyway Bridge collapsed in 1980 when a freighter struck one of the western columns during a violent storm, the new Sunshine Skyway Bridge was built in 1987. Rather than destroy the old bridge entirely, the double-span approaches were left on either side of the bay to be used as public fishing piers. Today, only one span on each side is being used (Tampa/Manatee side and St. Petersburg side), due to the deterioration of the older span.

With four miles of fishing pier, the Skyway is now the longest fishing pier in the world. Visitors can drive to their fishing spot, park, and fish right off the bridge while watching cruise ships, tankers, freighters, and other boat traffic pass in and out of Tampa Bay.

The telephone number above is for Pier Associates, Inc., a contracted service provider, which operates the concession and bait shops. Restrooms are available on the piers, as well. The piers are lit at night. The piers also attract birds looking for a handout, which is not permitted for the health of the birds and the safety of the humans.

The Skyway Fishing Pier is open 24 hours a day, every day of the year. The fee for a 24-hour period is $3 per car, $2 per adult, or $1.50 for seniors and for children ages 6 to 12. Children age five and under are free. Pets are not allowed on the piers. Skyway Fishing Piers are on both the north and the south sides of the Sunshine Skyway Bridge off of I–275/U.S. 19.

Clearwater/North Pinellas County

ANCLOTE KEY PRESERVE STATE PARK

1 Causeway Blvd.
Dunedin
(727) 469-5942
www.floridastateparks.org/anclotekey
CSO: Friends of Anclote Key State Park &
Lighthouse, Inc. (www.anclotecso.com)

Four islands make up Anclote Key State Park: Anclote Key, North Anclote Bar, South Anclote Bar, and Three Rooker Island. Anclote Key, the largest of the four, has a primitive camping area on the northern end of the island. Facilities there include grills, picnic tables, a pavilion, and a composting toilet. The lighthouse is at the south end of the island, where there is another picnic area. There are no garbage cans on the island, so be prepared to pack out your garbage. There is also no fresh drinking water on the island—be sure to pack plenty.

Access to Anclote Key State Park is by boat only, as the park lies 3 miles off of the coast of Tarpon Springs in line with the mouth of the Anclote River. Most of the park is in Pasco County, but the lighthouse, South Anclote Bar, and Three Rooker Island are in Pinellas County. Anchor offshore, or take the ferry from the Tarpon Springs Sponge Docks (SunLine Cruises at 727-944-4468 or Sponge-O-Rama at 727-943-2164).

Admission and camping are free, but you must register with the ranger to camp on Anclote Key. You also cannot be "dropped off" on Anclote Key to camp—you must have a way off the island at any time. Have the following information ready before you call (727-638-4447): Boat registration number, number of campers, arrival and departure dates, and an emergency contact phone number. If you take your own boat over, you'll need to park your vehicle and trailer somewhere. One spot is Holiday Recreation Complex (2830 Gulf Trace Blvd., Holiday, 727-934-4198), which charges $5 per night.

CALADESI ISLAND STATE PARK

1 Causeway Blvd.
Dunedin
(727) 469-5918
www.floridastateparks.org/caladesiisland

Named America's Number One Beach for 2008 by Dr. Beach himself (www.drbeach.org), Caladesi Island is our tropical, this-side-of-heaven paradise. The western side of the island features miles of white sand beaches and an unobstructed view of the Gulf of Mexico. The sea-grass flats off the eastern side shelter stingrays, dolphins, and other sea life. Kayak through the mangrove tunnels rimming the east side of the island and it's easy to think yourself back a century or more.

As with Anclote Key, Caladesi Island State Park is accessible only by boat or by ferry. Ferry service (727-734-1501) to Caladesi leaves from Honeymoon Island State Park hourly beginning at 10 a.m. The ferry will drop you off for a four-hour stay at the marina, where there is a café (www.romantichoneymoonisland.com), restroom facilities, beach access, and nature trails. (See Honeymoon Island State Park description for entrance fees.) Ferry fees are $10 per adult, $6 for children ages 4 to 12. Children under four years old are free. No pets are allowed on the ferry, but pets are allowed on parts of the island.

Admission to Caladesi Island State Park is $4 for up to eight people per private boat. Kayakers pay $1. Overnight on-board camping at the marina is available online at www.reserveamerica.com.

To sail or paddle over to Caladesi Island, many people launch canoes, kayaks, and small boats from the Dunedin Causeway, a 2.5-mile road leading from Dunedin to Honeymoon Island State Park. Public beaches line both sides, and free parking is allowed on the sand close to the road. Pull off and park on the south side near where the windsurfing rentals set up their wares. Paddle out to the channel, and look both ways for boat traffic. When it's clear, paddle briskly across the channel. You can then paddle to the sandy north end, skim over the sea-grass flats on the northeast side, or follow the marker directions in the next paragraph to the marina and the kayak trail.

Here are the directions from the State Park Web site: "From Marker 14 on the Dunedin Causeway Channel, which runs parallel to the causeway between Hurricane Pass and the Intracoastal Waterway, follow a compass heading of about 212 degrees for approximately 1 mile. Follow the channel markers into the Caladesi Island State Park marina. (Note: Do not turn 212 degrees from Marker 14 on the Intracoastal Waterway. Look for Marker 14 on the Causeway Channel, which has a brown park sign on it.)"

For paddlers without compasses, follow the island's east side about a mile south (along the edge of the mangroves) and look for the channel markers leading into the marina. The marina is nestled quite a ways into the interior of the island and will not be visible from the causeway.

HONEYMOON ISLAND STATE PARK
1 Causeway Blvd.
Dunedin
(727) 469-5942
www.floridastateparks.org/honeymoon
island

Located just across Hurricane Pass from Caladesi Island, Honeymoon Island State Park has a more rugged feel to its beaches. The island's north end, where the waves often get to surfing size, by Florida standards, seems particularly wild and desolate.

Honeymoon Island State Park, so named in 1939 when a developer built 50-some thatch-roofed honeymoon bungalows on the island, has miles of nature trails, swimming and snorkeling areas, and a café/concession area. Kayaks and beach supplies can be rented at the concession stand.

Honeymoon Island State Park's Pet Beach offers several miles of sand for pets to enjoy with their people. Rangers conduct occasional guided tours, and interpretive exhibits help visitors understand the ecosystems on the island.

Admission to Honeymoon Island State Park is $5 for up to eight people per car or $3 for a single-occupant car. Just want to run out and see the sunset? Beginning one hour prior to sunset, the fee drops to $3 per vehicle. There is no overnight camping on the island.

COUNTY PARKS

As if all those state parks weren't enough, come see what our counties and cities have to offer!

HILLSBOROUGH COUNTY PARKS, RECREATION, AND CONSERVATION DEPARTMENT
10119 Windhorst Rd.
Tampa
(813) 635-3500
www.hillsboroughcounty.org/parks

Check the Web site periodically to see what's listed on the "Calendar of Events." You'll find everything from administrative and policy meetings to wine tastings and fun runs.

Hillsborough County Parks, Recreation, and Conservation Department manages 70,000 acres of parklands with 42 recreation centers located throughout the county. Friends of the County Parks, a not-for-profit citizens' organization that meets each third Thursday of the month, provides financial and other kinds of support to the Parks, Recreation, and Conservation Department. Their mascot, Squiggy, attends PRC functions. Keep an eye out for this gigantic and enormously friendly squirrel.

Hillsborough PRC provides the following services to residents of Hillsborough County:

Athletic Services

In addition to lighting and maintaining sports fields and working with independent sports leagues to coordinate the use of facilities, provide some equipment, and certify coaches and other youth volunteers, Hillsborough PRC also provides:
- Youth basketball for children ages 5 to 17
- A Leaguerettes slow-pitch softball program for girls ages 5 to 17
- An adult slow-pitch softball league with more than 200 teams including senior teams, umpires, and referees
- Track and field meets

Blueways and Boat Ramps

Blueways, paddling trails for kayaks and canoes, are featured at the end of this chapter. Boat ramps are listed in the Gone Fishin' Close-up.

Conservation Services

Since 1987, Hillsborough PRC has purchased and managed environmentally sensitive lands, the largest local preservation effort in Florida. Almost 45,000 acres currently are managed by the PRC. Another 44,000 acres have been approved and are waiting to be funded. Anyone—landowner, concerned citizen, or a committee—can nominate lands to be acquired.

Construction and Maintenance Services

This department builds and maintains buildings and structures associated with the parks and recreational facilities.

Greenways and Trails Programs

Greenways are open-space corridors of land that tie different parts of the county together. When combined with trails, greenways provide a system of non-motorized transportation (walking and biking). The map on their Web page shows you where existing corridors and trails are. The Hillsborough Greenway Committee is responsible for planning and supporting the greenway projects.

Hillsborough PRC maintains over 100 miles that make up 24 paved and unpaved trails in unincorporated Hillsborough county for recreational use by walkers, skaters, bikers, and horseback riders. The trails also provide an alternative transportation system. Trails range from a mile or two to 42 miles in length. Some trails connect with other trails in other counties. You can find information about each trail at www.hillsboroughcounty.org/parks/parkservices/trailgrid.cfm.

Parks and Recreational Services

Hillsborough PRC operates 56 recreational parks and facilities ranging from dog parks to fully staffed facilities with programs for all ages and interests. The PRC participates in the Computers for Kids program that encourages donations of used, but working, IBM-compatible computers to recreation facilities for use in after-school and summer programs. The PRC can always use volunteers, too. Check their Web page for ways to help.

Picnic shelters and campground spots can be rented by calling (813) 931-7368 or online at www.hillsboroughcounty.org/parks/rentals.

i Three Hillsborough County Parks offer overnight camping: E. G. Simmons Park in Ruskin, Edward Medard Park in Plant City, and Lithia Springs Park in Lithia.

Special interest classes range from aerobics, art, and animated books to yoga and Zumba. Visit www.hillsboroughcounty.org/parks/recreation/allspecialinterestclasses.cfm for a list of classes, days and times, and facilities.

Programs especially for teens include arts and athletics programs, Girls Clubs, Teen Court, teen camps and councils, and other activities. For more information, call (813) 635-3500 or go to www.hillsboroughcounty.org/parks/recreation/teenprogram.cfm.

Therapeutic services for persons with disabilities are offered at the All People's Life Center at 6105 East Sligh Ave., Tampa. Services include in-school and after-school recreation programs, a summer day camp program called Camp Sparks, Special Olympics programs for mentally challenged residents, and the BlazeSports program for physically challenged residents (see Blaze-Sports and Saddles sidebar, in this chapter). Additional therapeutic equestrian programs are available at the Bakas Equestrian Center (see the BlazeSports and Saddles sidebar in this chapter). Call (813) 744-5978 for information about therapeutic services at All People's Life Center or go to www.hillsboroughcounty.org/parks/recreation/therapeutics.cfm.

PINELLAS COUNTY DEPARTMENT OF ENVIRONMENTAL MANAGEMENT
512 S. Ft. Harrison Ave.
Clearwater
(727) 464-4761
www.pinellascounty.org/environment

In addition to dealing with such things as air quality, beach erosion, and watershed management, Pinellas County's Department of Environmental

BlazeSports and Saddles

Most of us are familiar with the Special Olympics sports program, which, since 1968, has made it possible for people of all ages to participate in competitive sports.

A newer program lets people with physical challenges compete in sports, too. An outgrowth of the 1996 Paralympics Games held in Atlanta, BlazeSports programs provide people with challenges such as spinal cord injury, visual impairment, cerebral palsy, and amputation with an organized, competitive, year-round sports program. BlazeSports athletes compete in everything from soccer to swimming, water skiing to tennis.

Hillsborough County's All People's Life Center has been offering BlazeSports programs since 2002, when they became one of 10 charter BlazeSports groups in the country. Today, there are 63 BlazeSports groups.

In 2008, Hillsborough County athlete Sarah Goldman and Andy Chasanoff, BlazeSports coordinator for Hillsborough County's PRC, were selected to participate in the Paralympics Academy held in Beijing concurrently with the Olympic Games.

The BlazeSports at All People's Life Center is open to anyone with a physical challenge who is at least six years old.

The Bakas Equestrian Center (www.bakasridingcenter.com) in northwestern Hillsborough County works with PRC and with Hillsborough County Schools to provide riding sessions to physically and mentally challenged children and adults. Horseback riding—even seemingly passive riding—helps improve muscle tone and balance, among other benefits.

For more information about the BlazeSports programs, contact Andy Chasanoff, sports coordinator, at (813) 744-5307. For more information about the Bakas Equestrian program, contact Beth Harre-Orr at (813) 264-3890.

Management also oversees four preserve areas—two with extensive education centers and programs. Pets are not allowed in the preserve areas.

PINELLAS COUNTY PARKS & RECREATION DEPARTMENT
631 Chestnut St.
Clearwater
(727) 464-3347
www.pinellascounty.org/park

Pinellas County Parks & Recreation Department manages 12 green parks, four smaller neighborhood parks, three beach parks—including two that have been named to best-beaches lists—six beach access areas, four boat ramp/marina areas, a golf course, the Pinellas Trail, the Florida Botanical Gardens and Heritage Village (see Attractions chapter) and the Pinellas County Extension office. Pinellas County has numerous large lakes and parks surrounding them. Lake Tarpon in the north is so big it has two Pinellas County parks on its shores—A. L. Anderson Park on the west side, and John Chestnut Sr. Park on the east side.

Here we'll tell you about three of our favorite green parks and the Pinellas Trail. Look for spotlights about the beaches and boat ramps elsewhere in this chapter.

i Pinellas County parks are generally open from 7 a.m. until dark. At the entrance of each park, a wooden clock with movable hands shows visitors what time the park closes that day. Well-behaved pets on leashes—with well-trained owners who clean up after their pets—are allowed in most parks.

BROOKER CREEK PRESERVE AND ENVIRON-MENTAL EDUCATION CENTER
3940 Keystone Rd.
Tarpon Springs
(727) 453-6800
www.brookercreekpreserve.org

Brooker Creek Preserve features 8,000 acres of Florida wild lands with miles of hiking trails, ranging from a just-over-half-mile high-and-dry boardwalk to a 4-mile wilderness hike. Check to make sure the trails are open before starting out. Some guided hikes are scheduled. The Environmental Education Center features 22 interactive exhibits, a resource center for research and study, and a gift shop. Workshops and speakers often give presentations. Overnight parking is not allowed—make sure you have finished your hike at least an hour before sundown. The preserve is open from 7 a.m. to an hour before sunset each day.

LAKE SEMINOLE PARK
10015 Park Blvd.
Seminole
(727) 549-6156

Lake Seminole Park sits in the middle of Pinellas County on the east side of a good-sized lake that spills into Boca Ciega Bay—the same bay that the first Spanish explorer, Pánfilo de Narváez, may have pulled into when he first landed here. In addition to boat ramps, fishing, water skiing, and other water sports on the lake itself, the park has several smaller ponds in which people catch bass and bluegill. Because of its proximity to the bayou, the spillway areas and some of the little creeks are popular spots to catch blue crabs.

You'll find a paved walking/skating/biking trail, softball fields and volleyball areas, a play-

ground area, and a hill that kids love to roll down. Lake Seminole Park is a popular spot for weddings and, because it is centrally located, for gatherings of all kinds.

MOBBLY BAYOU PRESERVE
423 Lafayette Blvd.
Oldsmar
(813) 749-1261

The 396-acre preserve is co-managed by Pinellas County Environmental Department and the City of Oldsmar's Leisure Services department. Facilities include restrooms and picnic shelter, hiking trails, canoe and kayak launch, fishing pier, and an observation platform. The telephone number given is for the City of Oldsmar.

PHILIPPE PARK
2525 Philippe Parkway
Safety Harbor
(727) 669-1947

Philippe Park, the oldest of the Pinellas County parks, sits on the upper end of the west side of Old Tampa Bay and is where Odet Philippe (sometimes spelled Odette Phillippe) had his citrus groves. Visitors can climb an Indian mound up a short trail and then walk down the other side on a set of winding stone stairs. The live oaks and other hardwood trees provide lots of shade throughout the park.

On the south end of the park is a sheltered beach area. When the tide is out, visitors can walk several hundred feet out into Tampa Bay. A boat launching area, playground, and horseshoe pits are at the north end of the park near the entrance. Check the park calendar for occasional guided hikes.

SAWGRASS LAKE PARK
7400 25th St. N.
St. Petersburg
(727) 217-7256

Sawgrass Lake Park's 400-plus acres contain one of the largest maple swamps on the Gulf Coast of Florida and comprise one of the top birding sites in Florida. A mile-long boardwalk leads

The Pinellas Trail

The Fred Marquis Pinellas Trail runs down the west side of Pinellas County along an old railroad corridor stretching from Tarpon Springs in the north to downtown St. Petersburg in the south. Including spurs to Honeymoon Island and other spots, the trail provides 50 miles of paved surface. Ten overpasses keep foot and bike traffic separate from motor traffic.

But the Pinellas Trail isn't just about pedaling, skating, jogging, or walking. The trail takes its more than 90,000 users each month through nine cites and towns, along waterways and streams, past roadside art, and under shade trees dripping Spanish moss. Riding the trail can be an endurance test or it can be a serendipitous holiday jaunt to stop and see what's going on at this art district and at this park and then at this barbecue place.

The county maintains the trail, but the citizens' support organization, Pinellas Trails, Inc. (www.pinellastrails.org), has provided the benches, water fountains, rest areas, and other amenities along the way.

Pinellas Trails, Inc., has also written a detailed trail guide that describes every foot of the trail from Tarpon Springs to St. Petersburg. The guide lists restaurants and public restrooms along the way, tells trail users where they can take shelter if a rainstorm pops up, where the many bike repair shops and rental stores are, and how to report an emergency along the trail using the trail marker numbers. The guide can be downloaded from their Web site, or printed copies are available at most bike shops in the area.

Look for Mark Fuller's *Track Two* stylized railroad signs, a public art project, as you pass through each community on the trail.

We're not the only ones who think the Pinellas Trail is one fantastic parkway. In October 2007, the Pinellas Trail was recognized as the Rails-to-Trails Conservancy, Inc.'s Trail of the Month and the Trail is now one of the first few members of the Rail-Trail Hall of Fame (www.railstotrails.org).

Other Trails

The City of Clearwater's Ream Wilson Clearwater Trail runs east from the Long Center to Safety Harbor city limits. Eventually, the trail will run to Clearwater Beach.

The Progress Energy Trail is another Pinellas County north-south trail running closer to the east side of the county from Weedon Island, in the south, to the East Lake area, in the north.

Pinellas Trail Office
12020 Walsingham Rd.
Largo
(727) 549-6099
www.pinellascounty.org/trailqd/default.htm

to an observation tower overlooking Sawgrass Lake. A half-mile dirt trail winds through an oak hammock.

An Environmental Education Center contains exhibits and displays, and staff members offer field trips and guided nature tours for school students and other visitors. The education center and staff are a cooperative venture of Pinellas County Parks & Recreation Department, the Pinellas County School District, and the Southwest Florida Water Management District.

Restrooms and one picnic shelter are located at near the Environmental Education Center.

SHELL KEY PRESERVE
Off the coast of Tierra Verde
(727) 453-6900
www.pinellascounty.org/environment
Shell Key Preserve's 1,800 acres comprise one of the largest remaining undeveloped barrier island areas in Pinellas County. Shell Key Preserve is accessible only by boat and there are no facilities in this area. A permit is required to camp in the designated area, and campers are required to bring, use, and remove a portable toilet. Read the rules and apply for a permit online, or call the number listed above for more information. The preserve is open 24 hours a day.

WEEDON ISLAND PRESERVE
Cultural and Natural History Center
1800 Weedon Dr. N.E.
St. Petersburg
(727) 453-6500
www.weedonislandpreserve.org
Visitors can explore many of Weedon Island Preserve's 3,700 acres on foot or in canoe or kayak. Guided hikes and guided canoe tours are offered, or there is a self-guided version. There are 2 miles of boardwalk and paved trails with observation platforms and tower plus almost 3 miles of unpaved trails. Two well-marked canoe and kayak trails wind in and out of the mangroves surrounding Weedon Island. Canoes and kayaks can be rented on weekends and holidays. Call in advance for weekday rentals. The Cultural and Natural History Center has exhibits about the area's earliest known residents, an art gallery, and a gift shop. There is a vending machine on site. Weedon Island Preserve is open 7 a.m. to sunset every day. The center is open Wednesday through Sunday from 10 a.m. to 4 p.m. and is closed on holidays.

CITY PARKS

Most communities in Hillsborough and Pinellas Counties have a parks and recreation department. This guide looks only at what's available in Clearwater, St. Petersburg, and Tampa, but check other towns, too. Municipalities' phone numbers and Web sites are listed in the Relocation chapter.

Clearwater

CITY OF CLEARWATER PARKS & RECREATION DEPARTMENT
Municipal Services Building, 1st Floor
100 S. Myrtle Ave.
Clearwater
(727) 562-4800
www.clearwater-fl.com/gov/depts/parksrec
In addition to managing parks and recreation facilities at more than 100 sites throughout Clearwater, the Parks & Recreation Department also answers questions about tree trimming, offers athletic and recreational programs—including summer camps—to residents of all ages, houses the city's Office on Aging and Office of Cultural Affairs, and oversees Clearwater festivals and events.

Listed below are a few Clearwater Parks & Recreation Department facilities.

THE LONG CENTER
1501 N. Belcher Rd.
Clearwater
(727) 793-2320
The Long Center has a fully equipped fitness center, gymnasium, football and soccer fields, trails, an Olympic-size swimming pool, and a heated training pool. Clubs and activities at the center range from dance classes to woodcarving, and various sports leagues meet here. The Long Cen-

ter also offers programs for homeschooled students and they have an all-abilities playground. Call for class schedules and fees. The Long Center and the aquatic complex open at 6 a.m. Monday through Friday, and at 8 a.m. on Saturday. They close at 10 p.m. Monday through Thursday and at 7 p.m. on Friday. The aquatic complex closes at noon on Saturday, but the recreation complex is open until 5 p.m. on Saturday. The complexes are closed on Sunday.

ℹ️ Remember when we said Florida is flat? Lose that thought if you bicycle the Ream Wilson East-West trail connecting Safety Harbor with the Long Center and central Clearwater. Just east of McMullen-Booth Road and just north of Drew Street, the trail descends so steeply there's a grade warning sign, just like truck warning signs you see on highways elsewhere.

CLIFF STEPHENS PARK
600 Fairwood Ave.
Clearwater
The City of Clearwater has two disc golf parks that interconnect—Cliff Stephens and Northeast Coachman (1120 Old Coachman Rd.). For descriptions of a dozen or so disc golf courses in the area, most designed by local resident and multi-titled disc golf champion CR Willey, go to Tampa Bay Disc Sports Club's Web site (www.tampabaydiscsportsclub.com). On the left rail, are links to a list of disc sport events, upcoming tournaments, a discussion board, and local stores selling disc golf equipment.

Multiple title-holding disc golf champ Ken Climo also is a member of the Tampa Bay Disc Sports Club. Look for the link on the TBDSC site to Climo's site—he provides helpful information about getting that fickle flier to fall firmly into the basket.

STATION SQUARE PARK
612 Cleveland St.
Clearwater
Talk about urban open space—this little park, sandwiched between two downtown buildings,

is a lovely spot for small events. There's not much in the way of green grass, but a small amphitheater, fountains, and thoughtful landscaping make this a refreshing midday retreat for office workers looking for a spot to eat lunch outdoors.

St. Petersburg
CITY OF ST. PETERSBURG PARKS DEPARTMENT
Parks Administration Office/Athletic Operations Office
1400 19th St. N.
St. Petersburg
(727) 893-7335 (parks)
(727) 893-7298 (athletics)
www.stpete.org/parks
St. Petersburg is probably best known for its string of downtown waterfront parks that provide an *au naturel* backdrop to a multitude of events and festivals. But there are other parks in St. Petersburg—137 of them, at last count, totaling about 2,300 acres. There are playgrounds, dog parks, disc golf courses, boat ramps, and programs and facilities for everyone. In 2008, the city built the nation's first public municipal jai alai court at its Jack Puryear Park (5701 Lee St. N). Go to the National Jai Alai Association's Web site (www.national-jai-alai.com) for more information. St. Petersburg's Recreation Department also handles sports programming in the parks.

BOYD HILL NATURE PRESERVE
1101 Country Club Way S.
St. Petersburg
(727) 893-7326
www.stpete.org/boyd/index.asp
The Country Club Way address should be a clue that Boyd Hill Nature Preserve isn't out in the middle of nowhere. But step into this 245-acre preserve in the middle of residential St. Petersburg, and you'll soon feel as though you're out in the wilderness. Explore five distinct ecosystems, view the bird of prey aviary, or even camp overnight. Tram tours are a great way to get an overview of Boyd Hill Nature Preserve. They run every day at 1 p.m. and also at 10 a.m. on Satur-

day. Boyd Hill Nature Preserve opens at 9 a.m. Tuesday through Friday, at 7 a.m. on Saturday, and at 10 a.m. on Sunday. The preserve closes at 8 p.m. Tuesday through Thursday, and at 6 p.m. Friday through Sunday. The preserve is closed on Monday and Thanksgiving, Christmas, and New Year's Day. Check Boyd Hill's blog at www .boydhill.blogspot.com for a calendar of events and information about camps. Admission to the preserve is $3 for adults, $1.50 for children ages 3 through 16. Children under age 3 are free. Tram tours cost $2. No pets are allowed, and annual passes are available.

Pinellas Pioneer Settlement, located adjacent to the Boyd Hill Nature Preserve, offers living history exhibits and reenactments. Visit them at 3130 31st St. S., St. Petersburg, or on the Web at www.stpete.org/boyd/pioneer.asp, or call (727) 893-7326 for more information.

DELL HOLMES PARK
2741 22nd St. S.
St. Petersburg
www.stpete.org/parks/dellholmes.asp
Located on the north end of Lake Maggiore, Dell Holmes Park offers 20 acres of tree-shaded peace and quiet—and fishing, golfing, and play areas, too. Fish off of the pier, take a lap around the fitness trail, practice your swing on the driving range, or tap a few balls into the cup on the putting green. Let the kids play on the playground. Then grill up some hotdogs or burgers and enjoy the sounds of nature. Dell Holmes Park is open from just before sunrise to just after sunset each day. Call the Parks Department at (727) 893-7335 for more information.

GISELLA KOPSICK PALM ARBORETUM
North Shore Drive and 10th Avenue N.E.
Just north of the Vinoy Resort
What do you do with a two-acre, city-owned miniature golf course that the city can't afford to maintain any longer? That was the question that faced the City of St. Petersburg in 1976. The answer? Turn it into a palm arboretum, of course. Stroll along winding brick paving and view more than 100 species of palms and cycads, includ-

ing the King Sago. (Not to be outdone, there's a Queen Sago and an Emperor Sago, too.) Look for the Teddy Bear Palm, the Old Man Palm, and the Gru-Gru Palm. Signs give their more formal scientific names, where they're from, and other information. There are benches and drinking fountains at the arboretum and the pathway is wheelchair friendly. Free parking is nearby. Guided tours are available on request—call (727) 893-7335 for more information.

Tampa

CITY OF TAMPA PARKS AND RECREATION DEPARTMENT
1420 N. Tampa St.
Tampa
(813) 274-8615
ww.tampagov.net/dept_parks_and_ recreation
Tampa's 178 city parks, totaling more than 3,500 acres scattered throughout the city, have much to offer. Some of them have playgrounds. Some are more for pooches than for people. Some have community centers with after-school and other programs. Some have swimming pools, art studios, or fishing piers. All have lots of Florida sunshine and outdoor air.

The city's Web site lists all parks and facilities, as well as the activities each park offers, at www .tampagov.net/dept_parks_and_recreation/ park_search/parkslis.asp. To rent picnic shelters at any of the parks that have shelters, call (813) 274-8184.

Here's a quick look at four City of Tampa parks or recreation center programs.

AL LOPEZ PARK
4810 N. Himes Ave.
Tampa
Al Lopez Park is open from 5 a.m. to 10 p.m. The Hunt Community Center (813-348-1172) at the park offers after-school and other programs for children ages five to seventeen. Along with 132 acres of land with picnic facilities, trails, a dog park, and a fishing pier, there is also a futuristic Evos play system accessible and attractive to

children of differing abilities. Look for the "Talking Tot Turf."

CAL DICKSON TENNIS CENTER
4011 Watrous Ave.
Tampa
(813) 259-1893
The focus is on tennis here. The Cal Dickson Tennis Center serves up eight courts, private tennis lessons, and group tennis classes—plus picnic areas and restrooms. Bring your racket.

DR. MARTIN LUTHER KING, JR., RECREATION COMPLEX
2200 N. Oregon Ave.
Tampa
(813) 259-1667
In addition to an after-school program here, there's also an art studio (813-259-1607) offering classes to people of all ages who want to explore their creative sides. Dr. Martin Luther King, Jr., Recreational Complex also has a gymnasium, a swimming pool (open seasonally—call 813-259-1606), shuffleboard, and other activities.

WAYNE C. PAPY SEMINOLE HEIGHTS ATHLETIC CENTER
6925 N. Florida Ave.
Tampa
(813) 231-5273
Tampa's Gymnastic and Dance Program has its home here at the Wayne C. Papy Seminole Heights Athletic Center—plus this is where the city's Athletic Office (813-231-5270) is located. Yoga and Bunco activities are offered for adults and seniors.

BEACHES

The beaches section is in alphabetical order rather than by geographic area. Some beaches face the Gulf of Mexico, while others front Tampa Bay.

BARRIER ISLAND BEACHES IN PINELLAS COUNTY
www.pinellascounty.org/park/beaches.htm
There are a number of beach access areas along the Pinellas County barrier islands, many of which have parking, restrooms, and shower towers. Some of them have picnic shelters or benches.

For information about beach access areas, go to the Web site and download the 11-page Beach Access Guide to discover the hundreds of ways to get to your own waiting-to-be-discovered favorite beach. Madeira Beach, for instance, has 17 public access areas with 556 parking spots. Each page includes a detailed map and a chart listing the various amenities to be found at each spot.

BEN T. DAVIS BEACH
7650 W. Courtney Campbell Causeway
Tampa
A Tampa City Park, Ben T. Davis Beach is at the upper end of Tampa Bay on the northeast side near the Rocky Point area. Located at the east end of the Courtney Campbell Causeway and with access on the south side of the road, Ben T. Davis Beach has a concession stand, shelters, grills, beach volleyball, and the three Ss—surf, sand, and sun. Lifeguards are on duty from Memorial Day weekend to Labor Day weekend. Whiskey Joe's Bar and Grill adjoins the property, so be prepared for party crowds at times.

i We share our beaches with a variety of protected animals. Please help us be good neighbors and respect marked—and even unmarked—bird and turtle nesting areas. Remember to properly dispose of all fishing line, cigarette butts, and other trash. Plants, also, are protected and may not be removed or damaged. It is illegal to feed wild animals.

CYPRESS POINT PARK
5620 W. Cypress St.
Tampa
Behind you rise the skyscrapers of downtown Tampa. In front of you are the waters of Tampa Bay. Cypress Point Park offers beaches and a canoe and kayak launch spot plus shelters, restrooms, and a couple of short trails. Plus it faces west—think sunsets on the beach just a hop,

Close-up

Gone Fishin'

This is no fish story—in the Tampa Bay area you can drop a hooked worm over the side of a boat to a panfish, slow-roll a spinnerbait for a big ol' bass, or sling a nose-hooked baitfish to a cruising tarpon out in the Gulf of Mexico.

In fact, Florida is the number one state when it comes to number of anglers, dollars spent on sport fishing, and number of boat registrations. We take our sport fishing seriously and we know that good fishing doesn't just happen. Here's what you need to know to get you started.

LICENSES

Florida Fish and Wildlife Conservation Commission manages fishing and hunting in the State of Florida—and also maintains more than 200 freshwater boat ramps throughout the state, marks paddling trails, and has developed the Great Florida Birding Trail. Fees from licenses help pay for these and other programs.

If you are age 16 or older, you need a license for both freshwater and saltwater fishing. One major exception is if you are on a charter fishing vessel—just be sure the vessel holds a group fishing license.

To see other exemptions, go to www.myfwc.com/license/licpermit_recreationalhf.htm or pick up a copy of the latest fishing regulations at most sporting goods stores, bait shops, and county tax collectors' offices. Licenses sometimes can be purchased at these spots, too, or you can buy an instant license online.

The Tampa Bay area is in the Southwest region for FWC purposes. You can reach FWC in Tallahassee at (850) 488-4676 or online at www.myfwc.com.

REGULATIONS

Fishing regulations specify what you can catch, as well as when, where, and how. Different lakes in the same county might have different regulations. There are separate regulations for individual lakes, for freshwater and saltwater fishing, and for shellfish, frogs, and other water animals. *FWC Fishing Regulations* lists guidelines and also offers fishing tips, color pictures of each species of fish, even a coupon or two from advertisers.

OTHER RESOURCES

Most sporting goods stores and bait shops carry other publications filled with fishing stories, ads for guides, and fishing reports from around the region. Here are a couple of publications and a Web site or two to look for:

All About Fishing (www.aa-fishing.com) is a Web site with fishing information for each state, including tips on fishing for several freshwater species. You'll also find links to tournaments, clubs, and other activities.

Florida Fishing Weekly is a weekly tabloid filled with updates on fishing hot spots and how to maximize your angling time as well as articles by some of the best sports and outdoor journalists in the state. Subscribe to the print edition, visit the Web site—where you can find a list of bait and tackle shops in your area—or even catch them on FloridaFishingWeekly.TV. Go to www.floridafishingweekly.com or call (800) 293-9662 to subscribe.

Florida Sportsman magazine focuses primarily on fishing, but includes information about other outdoor activities, too. Check www.floridasportsman.com for information on subscribing and for their radio and television programming schedules.

Onshore-Offshore magazine is a free, full-color, glossy magazine that covers the Florida fishing scene. Articles—with lots of photos—in a recent issue included "Springtime Spanish Macks: Lure, Bait or Fly—A Guarantee," "River Cats on Cheddar," and "What Length Fly Rod?" Copies distributed to local sporting goods dealers tend to be picked up quickly; read the latest issue online at www.onshoreoffshore.com.

Saltwater Angler magazine (www.saltwaterangleronline.com), published monthly, covers saltwater fishing on the West Coast of Florida from Crystal River to Boca Grande. Readers will find information about tournaments and seminars; features about fish migratory patterns and particular species; how-to, where-to, and when-to articles; as well as motivational photography. *Saltwater Angler* magazine claims a circulation of about 25,000. Editor is Paul Arcos.

The Snook Foundation, a non-profit organization, represents anglers on snook-related fishing issues, including conservation efforts. Plus you'll find fishing information, articles, and photos.

WHAT ARE THE FLORIDA MIDDLE GROUNDS?

The Florida Middle Grounds is a hard-bottomed region in the middle of the Gulf of Mexico known since at least the 1880s for its good fishing.

The southern portion is about 90 miles or so northwest of Tampa Bay. Many charter and private boats head out at night from Tampa Bay area marinas while anglers sleep in bunks aboard ship. The boats arrive at the Florida Middle Grounds shortly before dawn. The fishing starts at daybreak and doesn't let up until well after dark. Then the fishermen catch a few more hours' sleep while the boat crew motors back to port.

CHARTER BOAT FISHING TRIPS

Charter boat trips—sometimes called party boats—head out from several area marinas. www .TampaBayCharter.com has information about different kinds of charter fishing trips and a directory of licensed captains from which to choose, plus articles about what to bring, what to leave at home, and what to expect when you head out to sea.

BOAT RAMPS IN HILLSBOROUGH AND PINELLAS COUNTIES

For a list of public boat ramps in Hillsborough County, go to www.hillsboroughcounty.org/parks/parkservices/boatweb.pdf.

For a list of public boat ramps (both fresh- and saltwater access) at nine Pinellas County parks, go to www.pinellascounty.org/park/ramp_fee.htm. Boaters pay a parking fee of $5 to park their trailers at most Pinellas County parks. Look for a self-serve box in the boat-trailer parking area or purchase an annual pass online for $100.

The City of Clearwater's Marine and Aviation Web page gives detailed information about the Clearwater Municipal Marina and the Seminole Boat Ramp at the marina. Go to www.clearwater-fl.com/gov/depts/marine_aviation/index.asp.

The City of St. Petersburg's Web page on fishing has information about places to fish, regulations, fishing piers, and boat ramps. Go to www.stpete.org/parks/fishing.asp.

The City of Tampa's park finder page lists five parks with public boat ramps. Go to www.tampagov.net/dept_parks_and_recreation.

www.TampaBayAngler.com.boatramps.htm lists public boat ramps on both sides of the bay.

Remember to clean your trailer and boat thoroughly after each use so plants and microscopic critters don't get transferred from one body of water to another.

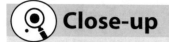

Close-up

Life's a Beach

The Tampa Bay area is home to some of the best beaches in the United States. And we're not just making that up. Dr. Beach says so.

Dr. Who?

No, *Dr. Who* is a British television sci-fi TV show character with a cult following.

Dr. Beach has a bit of a cult following, too. Ever since he gave a somewhat off-the-cuff answer to a reporter about his favorite beaches back in 1989, people have relied on Dr. Beach to tell them which are the best beaches in the country.

Dr. Beach is really Dr. Stephen P. Leatherman, a professor of environmental studies at Florida International University in Miami. He also is the director of FIU's Laboratory for Coastal Research. Dr. Leatherman has studied beach and coastal issues around the world.

Bottom line—Dr. Beach knows what he's talking about.

Dr. Beach's Web site (www.drbeach.org) contains a wealth of information about what makes for a healthy beach and how to treat beaches that are a bit under the weather.

Every Memorial Day weekend, Dr. Beach releases his Top 10 Best Beaches list. In 2008, Caladesi Island State Park was the top beach in America—including beaches in Hawaii. In 2005, Fort DeSoto Park's north beach was the top beach in America.

skip, and a jump from your office. Cypress Point is a Tampa City Park.

DAVIS ISLANDS SEAPLANE BASIN
864 Severn Ave.
Tampa 33606
At the end of the Davis Islands and adjacent to the Yacht Club Basin, the Davis Islands Seaplane Basin has a beach with an off-leash area for dogs. You'll find a boat ramp and a canoe and kayak launch area, too, in this Tampa City park.

E. G. SIMMONS PARK
2401 19th Ave. N.W.
Ruskin
(813) 671-7655
Not only are there miles of sandy beaches at E. G. Simmons Park, there are also two campgrounds with almost 90 sites (water and electricity at each site and a dump station at each campground). The campground area is set among shade trees

and there are showers, picnic tables, and fire rings. Located on the southeast side of Tampa Bay near U.S. 41, E. G. Simmons Park has 469 acres to explore on foot or in a canoe. There is a boat ramp (no ramp or day use fee). The park opens at 6 a.m. every day and closes at 6 p.m. in the fall and winter, at 7 p.m. in the spring, and at 8 p.m. in the summer. Campsite rental is $12 per site ($10 for seniors ages 55 and older). There is no concession stand or store, but civilization is only a couple of miles away. This is a Hillsborough County Park.

FORT DESOTO PARK
3500 Pinellas Bayway S.
Tierra Verde
(727) 582-2267
**www.pinellascounty.org/park/05_ft_desoto
.htm**
Fort DeSoto Park, Pinellas County's largest park, may not have it all—don't seem to recall any snowboarding there—but it has a lot. Comprised of

more than 1,100 acres on five islands, Fort DeSoto Park provides overnight camping, a historic fort and museum, more than 7 miles of waterfront with 3 miles of white sand beach, a boat launch facility, picnic shelters—including some really large ones for big events—swimming areas, a canoe and kayak trail, hiking trails, and concession areas. Fort DeSoto Park is one of few places where you can fish two bodies of water in the same day. One of the park's two fishing piers—each with food and bait concessions—is on Tampa Bay (500 feet long); the other is on the Gulf of Mexico (1,000 feet long). To make campground reservations, go online or call the campground office at (727) 582-2267. Fort DeSoto is a Pinellas County Park.

PICNIC ISLAND PARK
7409 Picnic Island Blvd.
Tampa 33616
In Tampa's early days, a railroad spur that came out here, as this used to be Port Tampa—Henry B. Plant's effort to monopolize boat travel. Today you'll find a pier from which to fish, picnic shelters with grills, a playground, beaches, and an island to explore plus a boat ramp and canoe and kayak launch. Picnic Island is a Tampa City Park.

SAND KEY PARK
1060 Gulf Blvd.
Clearwater
(727) 588-4852
**www.pinellascounty.org/park/15_sand_key
.htm**
Just south of Clearwater Beach and just over Clearwater Pass, Sand Key is 95 acres of dual identity. Part park, part beach, it all adds up to one-stop outdoor enjoyment. Walk over one of the nine boardwalks to the beach, where you can rent a cabana, use the bath house, swim, stroll the beach, and shower off at one of the nine shower towers before heading home—or to the park. Sand Key's park side has picnic shelters, a dog park area, and a playground. Not quite either beach or park, there's also a salt marsh bird nesting area with viewing benches. Sand Key Park also houses an interdepartmental artificial reef program. It's a Pinellas County Park.

Bay Area Blueways

Both Hillsborough County's (www
.hillsboroughcounty.org/blueways) and Pinellas County's (www.pinellas county.org/Plan/blueways/default .htm) blueways Web pages have maps, paddling regulations, equipment checklists, and tips. The Pinellas page includes information about the Florida Circumnavigational Saltwater Paddling Trail, segments of which are in the Tampa Bay area.

Guided trips and Paddling Clubs:

ClubKayak.com. Click on the link to the Tampa Bay Sea Kayakers to learn about club activities.

Florida Paddling Trails Association (www.floridapaddlingtrails.com) Web site lists commercial guides, paddling clubs, and trail associations in Florida.

Canoe Escape, Inc. (813-986-2067 or www.canoeescape.com) offers guided trips down portions of the Hillsborough River and shuttle service for self-guided trips.

Clearwater Marine Aquarium (727-447-0980 or www.cmaquarium.org) offers half-day guided kayak tours of several areas in north Pinellas County.

Sweetwater Kayaks (727-570-4844 or www.sweetwaterkayaks.com) offers guided tours for all ages through Weedon Island Preserve.

ANNUAL EVENTS AND FESTIVALS

Ｗe recognize that many people who come to the Tampa Bay area come here to get away from the rush and the slush and want nothing more than to lounge by a pool or on a sandy beach.

If that's what you want, we'll be more than happy to hand you a towel and a tube of sunscreen, fix you something cool to sip on surfside, and post "Do Not Disturb" signs around your sandy sanctuary. We'll promise not to wake you until it's time for you to go back home, and then we'll do it reluctantly.

But while you're slipping into la-la-land, please excuse us if we tiptoe off and party on without you.

We have much to celebrate here in the Tampa Bay area. Almost every weekend you'll find us paying homage to something from seafood to strawberries, jamming with jazz greats, rejoicing in reading, or recreating the Renaissance. There are festivals and re-enactments for history buffs, ethnic festivals celebrating cultures from Celtic to Cuban, and festivals like Guavaween you have to see to believe. You can marvel as sheep dogs work a herd of sheep, shout "*Opa!*" as you cheer on Hellenic dancers, or watch a Japanese tea ceremony.

No real pirates in our history? We celebrate the power of a collective imagination by paying tribute to a pirate who, in all probability, never really existed. Different organizations create their own krewes, dress up in exotic costumes, parade and party, and generally carry on—and not just for one day. It's a long story—one you'll find spotlighted in this section.

We tend to party hearty day and night. Night parades and fireworks often cap off a full day or even weekend of activities. Some festivals span both sides of Tampa Bay.

Most events have activities for children ranging from face-painting to hands-on craft tables or story-telling centers. A few aren't suitable for children, and we'll tell you ahead of time. Many events are free, while some charge a nominal fee. Most include food vendors serving sweets and savories to munch while you stroll. Savvy shoppers know that festivals are some of the best places to buy truly one-of-a-kind gifts.

So come wander through tent mazes holding sculptures and other artwork by top-notch artists from around the world who come here during the winter months to display their creations in the Florida sunshine. Have your child's face painted to resemble a tiger, or stuff yourself with strawberry shortcake.

There are even a few festivals out on the beaches. Just remember to respect those "Do Not Disturb" signs. Poor things. They just don't know what they're missing.

We've organized this chapter according to the calendar year, January to December, and then in alphabetical order. And we've noted where the event takes place right up front.

Some of these events are "moveable feasts," meaning they may be held, for example, in late February one year and early March the next. We've tried to list them in the earlier month, but we can't promise they will stay there.

Some events have multiple parts, often spanning more than one month. We've listed the main event under its proper month, and noted the peripheral events in the description.

Come join the party!

JANUARY

TAMPA BAY BLACK HERITAGE FESTIVAL
Events throughout the Tampa Bay area
(813) 223-1111 ext. 143, (888) 224-1733
ext. 143
www.tampablackheritage.org
TBBHF, which began in 2000, bills itself as a 10-day event that focuses on contributions of people of African heritage. But if you think that means 10 days of dull history lessons, think again. Artists, authors, and businesses showcase their work in a two-day street festival that includes entertainers, unique villages, crafts, plenty of activities for children, and health screenings for people of all ages. Parades and other events honor Dr. Martin Luther King Jr., and a themed movie is shown at the historic Tampa Theatre. The Soul Roll Invitational Skate Jam brings thousands of roller skaters to Tampa for one humongous skate party, while spoken word events, museum exhibits, an interfaith service, and speakers and seminars feed the mind and the heart. Past speakers and presenters have included the Reverend Jesse Jackson as well as Danny Glover and Felix Justice portraying poet Langston Hughes and Dr. Martin Luther King Jr.

The event begins the Thursday before Dr. Martin Luther King Jr. Day and concludes the following Saturday. Some events, including the street festival, are free. The semi-formal Heritage Gala includes a silent auction, dinner, and show featuring an iconic entertainer. Tickets for this event begin at $60. Tickets for the day-long Women in Business Conference begin at $135.

> **i** Grab a hat, sunglasses, and sunscreen, even for our winter festivals. Some folks wear a light, long-sleeved coverup for extra protection. Remember to apply sunscreen under the chin—reflected rays can burn skin, too. And drink lots of water. We want you to enjoy every moment.

TARPON SPRINGS EPIPHANY CELEBRATION
St. Nicholas Greek Orthodox Cathedral
17 E. Tarpon Ave.
Tarpon Springs
(727) 937-3540
www.epiphanycity.org
Don't miss the January 6 Tarpon Springs Epiphany Celebration, which commemorates the baptism of Jesus Christ in the River Jordan. Greek-language church services begin at 8 a.m. with the liturgy at 9:30 a.m., both held at St. Nicholas Greek Orthodox Cathedral. At noon the Archbishop offers the blessing of the waters, and then everyone processes to Craig Park at Spring Bayou (one block west of Alternate U.S. 19 at W. Tarpon Ave.). Here, thousands of spectators sit on folding chairs and blankets. Several dozen Greek male teens wait on boats for the Archbishop to bless, then throw a white cross into the water. A dove is released, the cross is tossed, and the young men dive in after it, hoping for the special blessing awarded to the one who retrieves the cross.

Then it's *Glendi* time—party time, that is. The big *Glendi* (festival) is at the Spanos-Pappas Community Center's Theofilos Hall, 348 N. Pinellas Ave., where the *opa*s and the Greek food and the traditional dancing go on from early afternoon until 9 p.m.

Locals say the Tarpon Springs Epiphany Celebration is the largest of its kind in the world. If you go, be prepared for crowds—the town more than doubles in size. There are several free city parking lots in the historic downtown district near the church and street parking is permitted unless posted otherwise. Several paid parking lots are located in the sponge docks area—an attraction in itself. A trolley runs between the two areas. (For more information about Tarpon Springs, see the Attractions chapter. For more information about the Greek Orthodox Church, see the Worship chapter.)

⊗ Close-up

Gasparilla

Downtown Tampa
(813) 251-8844
www.gasparillapiratefest.com
www.gasparillaextravaganza.com

Pirates invade Tampa each January, manning the world's only fully rigged 18th century pirate ship, and turn this otherwise conventional city into a pirate fest extraordinaire.

Probably *the* festival in the Tampa Bay area, Gasparilla gets its name from a supposed Spanish pirate, Jose Gaspar, a larger-than-life legend whose story likely is more fiction than fact.

Regardless, we plant tongue firmly in cheek and begin a Mardi Gras–like celebration of all things piratey in late January and tag "Gasparilla" onto other events all the way into March. We even named our football team after Gaspar's buccaneers. So, me hearties, come meet this mythical maverick of the Caribbean.

THE GALLANT GASPARILLA

Here's what we know to be true: Pirates plied the waters off of both sides of Florida—mostly in the Keys and up the east coast—up until the mid-1800s. Further south, down near Boca Grande, lies a good-sized barrier island called Gasparilla. That's it for verifiable facts.

What does the legend say? Depends on which version you hear. Most start with Jose Gaspar being born in Spain in 1756. He served in the Spanish navy until 1783 when he decided to become a pirate, either a) because he was humiliated and ashamed of his country when the English defeated the Spanish navy or b) because he had been falsely accused by a jealous woman of stealing the Spanish crown jewels (this bad-boy version has him, at age 12, kidnapping a girl and holding her for ransom).

The legend says Gaspar, now Gasparilla, and his crew plagued the Gulf side of Florida from their hideout, the island Gasparilla, and in their ship, also called *Gasparilla*, with take-no-prisoners ferocity. Even beautiful young women kept alive as concubines were spared being beheaded only until the next batch was captured. In all the tales told of his dastardly doings, however, Gasparilla retains his gallant, cultured nature.

Gasparilla's exploits and adventures came to an end in 1821 when Gasparilla decided to retire. On the very day he and his crew were to divvy up the swag accumulated over almost 40 years of plundering ships and pillaging towns, a British merchant ship came into view. Gasparilla decided to take one last trophy, and set course accordingly. But, curses! As Gasparilla neared, the British flag came down and the American flag of the pirate-hunting USS *Enterprise* unfurled. Gasparilla refused to surrender. He wrapped the anchor chain around himself and hurled himself into the sea.

Most of his crew died or were later hanged. A few escaped. One version of the story has a few pirates still on the island guarding the undivided treasure. When they saw what was happening, they moved the dozen or so treasure chests inland and buried them before scattering.

Not quite a hundred years later, Tampa's civic leaders decided to liven up a spring festival by invading the city as pirates, albeit as pirates on horseback. They formed Ye Mystic Krewe of Gasparilla and held the first Gasparilla Carnival on May 4, 1904. And the rest, as they say, is history.

FESTIVAL HISTORY

From the first 1904 invasion of Tampa by a motley krewe of locals-turned-pirates-for-a-day, the festival caught the collective imagination. In 1954, the festival became a bit more authentic with the pirates invading, not on horseback from land, but from a 165-foot replica of an 18th century pirate ship.

The 1990s marked another sort of growth, when the exclusive krewes opened their ranks to African-Americans, women, and other groups. While Ye Mystic Krewe Gasparilla remains all-male, with fees and dues estimated to be in the thousands of dollars, other krewes invite participants of all backgrounds to don a costume—including those representing other periods and peoples—and come play pirates. During the rest of the year, krewes are involved in various charitable fundraising and volunteer efforts. Today, upwards of half a million people party in the streets of Tampa during Gasparilla.

GASPARILLA EXTRAVANGZA

This pint-sized version of Gasparilla, usually held the week before the invasion, features activities for the whole family. The area's youngest buccaneers (age five and under) gussy up their wagons and strollers, bikes and trikes, and then parade down Bayshore Boulevard in the Preschooler Stroll. Older children have their own Children's Gasparilla Parade later in the day, complete with marching bands, floats, and visiting area krewes. Bike Safety Rodeos and other children's activities and vendors fill Bayshore Boulevard between Bay-to-Bay and Watrous/ Orleans Avenues. Air pirates invade the skies with parachute teams and vintage aircraft. An evening "Piratechnic" Extravaganza fireworks show recreates an imaginary sea battle that leaves folks cheering.

All events are free. Reserved bleacher seating for the Children's Gasparilla Parade begins at $14.

GASPARILLA PIRATE FEST

A free, all-day Street Festival in downtown Tampa begins mid-morning and continues until long after the sun goes down. Live entertainment appears on multiple stages, Midway games and rides and all sorts of frolicsome fun keep the party going. Want the best view of the invasion? Buy a ticket to the Buffet Brunch at the Tampa Convention Center where you can fill your trencher with definitely non-piratey fare (no hardtack), enjoy live music, and watch the *Jose Gasparilla* sail up and demand that the mayor surrender or else! In the afternoon, the victorious (oops, did we give it away?) captain of Ye Mystic Krewe of Gasparilla swaggers down the 3.5 mile Parade of the Pirates, along with bands, floats, and assorted revelers. Crowds line the parade route, vying for the largesse tossed by the pirates in the form of baubles, beads, and doubloons. After the parade, revelers party hearty at the Street Festival. (Caution to parents: After the parade ends and after the sun goes down, things can get a bit . . . piratey.)

Admission to the Street Festival and Parade are free. Reserved bleacher seating for the Parade of the Pirates begins at $28 per seat (children two and under are free). Tickets to the Buffet Brunch begin at $58 for adults and $48 for children ages 3 to 12 (children 2 and under are free).

Parking is a bit tight. Check the Web site also for a list of paid parking areas and shuttle information (shuttle fee is $5 for adults, children with an adult ride free). Vehicles parked where they shouldn't be get pirated away by local law enforcement and violators pay a hefty ransom to get them back.

Tickets to reserved seating and ticketed events are best purchased online and go on sale October 1. You may bring your own snacks, but glass containers and coolers are not permitted (small, soft-sided coolers are permitted for child care and medical needs). Many vendors accept cash only. Pets are prohibited; strollers are not. There are no strollers or wheelchairs for rent. Restroom facilities are Port-o-lets. The event goes on rain or shine, but may be cancelled in the event of severe weather.

OUTBOUND VOYAGE

After several weeks of yo-ho-hoing, Ye Mystic Krewe of Gasparilla departs. Live entertainment at Channelside Bay Plaza begins at noon. Later, the krewe sails into the sunset. The partying, however, continues.

PINELLAS FOLK FESTIVAL
Heritage Village
11909 125th St. N.
Largo
(727) 582-2123
www.pinellascounty.org/heritage
Want to see a sheep sheared, its fleece spun into yarn, and the yarn crocheted into a shawl? Head to Pinellas County's Heritage Village, a 21-acre collection of historic buildings from around the county, where each January history comes to life, as it has since 1983. Watch long pine needles become intricately woven baskets, visit a sugarcane field, or listen to the clang of metal against metal at the blacksmith's shed. Folk musicians and storytellers perform on three stages, and antique cars are on display. As always, there are plenty of food and crafts for sale.

The festival runs 10 a.m. to 4 p.m. Parking at Heritage Village is limited, but a shuttle runs from outlying parking areas (follow the signs) for those who don't want to or can't walk over the uneven ground. The festival and parking are free, but donations are always appreciated. (Go to the Attractions chapter for a more complete description of Heritage Village.)

FEBRUARY

FLORIDA AFRICAN AMERICAN HERITAGE CELEBRATION
Heritage Village
11909 125th St. N.
Largo
(727) 582-2123
www.pinellascounty.org/heritage
Set in Pinellas County's living history center, Heritage Village, this one-day festival highlights the cultural contributions of local African American communities. An all-day GospelFest competition features performances by church choirs from around the area, while jazz and blues artists jam it up elsewhere in the park and youths pound out complex rhythms in a step competition. Spoken word performers and historical re-enactors who have participated in past festivals have included actor Bob Devin Jones and primal instrument maker Abasi Ote.

Festival hours are 11 a.m. to 5:30 p.m. Parking at Heritage Village is limited, but a shuttle runs from outlying parking areas (follow the signs) for those who don't want to or can't walk over the uneven ground. The festival and parking are free, but donations are always appreciated. (Go to the Attractions chapter for a more complete description of Heritage Village.)

FLORIDA STATE FAIR
4800 U.S. 301 N.
Tampa
(813) 621-7821, 1-800-345-FAIR (3247)
www.floridastatefair.com
All of Florida, it seems, converges on Tampa each February for a 12-day celebration of all things Florida! Walk through the Rabbit and Poultry Barn to see myriad breeds of chickens, for instance, or to watch a costumed demonstrator spin yarn from the fur of a rabbit sitting on her lap. Try your hand at milking a cow, or watch a lamb being born in the Moo-ternity Ward. Dog shows and equestrian events test both animals and their trainers. Move on to the Florida Living Center where Florida woodworkers display fine furniture they have created, and students from across the state display their artwork. Watch soap being made in Cracker Country, and see a Florida panther at the Florida Fish and Wildlife Conservation Commission Exhibit.

The midway has all those twisty-turny, whirly-swirly rides, including some milder rides for little tykes, and games. The La Plaza Hispanic Village hosts a daily lineup of bilingual activities and entertainment, and local performers fill smaller stages throughout the fairgrounds. Top-name entertainers like Mickey Gilley, Ronnie Milsap, and Helen Cornelius draw crowds to the larger stages.

Admission at the gate is $12 for adults and $6 for children ages 6 to 11. Children age 5 and under are free. Pay full price if you must, but you can save as much as a third (pay $8 or $4) by buying tickets before the first day of the fair at various local stores. The fair also offers Senior Days, Student Days, and other discounts. Wristbands for the midway rides start at $25; again, look for discounted days and times. Credit cards are accepted for admission and concert tickets (Gate 1). Gates open at 9 a.m. each day. Midway and closing hours vary. No pets, no re-entry, and no grumps allowed—it's the fair! Call the office for information about camping spaces at the fairgrounds.

i As tempting as midway food is— where else can you fill up on funnel cakes or try chocolate-covered bacon?— folks watching waistlines or wallets head to the Ag(riculture) Hall of Fame Building (to your left as you enter Gate 3, building AA on the map). Volunteers man a small café inside, serving lower-cost salads, soups, and sandwiches featuring Florida foods.

GREEK FESTIVAL
Holy Trinity Greek Orthodox Church
409 Old Coachman Rd.
Clearwater
(727) 799- 4605
www.holytrinityclwtr.org
Didn't get to the Epiphany Celebration in Tarpon Springs last month? You can still get your fill of *spanokopita, mousakka,* and *baklava* at the Annual Clearwater Greek Festival. For three days each February, the Holy Trinity Greek Orthodox Church congregation literally opens their doors to visitors. Grilled *gyro* and *souvlaki* sandwiches with Greek fries are sold under an enormous blue-and-white striped tent in the parking lot, also where Greek music plays non-stop. Periodically, a rhythmic clapping announces traditionally costumed Hellas dancers processing into the tent to perform.

Follow the crowd into Matheos Hall to shop for Greek music, jewelry, spangled scarves, and other finery, to purchase full meals featuring lamb shanks, lemon chicken, and other specialties, or to see cooking demonstrations. (For a description of Greek food, go to the Restaurants chapter.)

Take time to visit the church itself, with its distinctive mosaics and ceiling. One of the priests

explains the Orthodox religion and the symbolism in the artwork.

A children's area with games and other activities is next to the big tent. Parking is free and close at hand. Entrance fee is $2 each.

RENAISSANCE FESTIVAL
11315 N. 46th St.
Tampa
(813) 983-0111
www.renaissancefest.com
There must be a time and space warp on the grounds of Tampa's Museum of Science and Industry. How else can we explain people stepping from the streets of modern Tampa into a 16th-century English village where knights on horseback joust for the favor of their lady loves, jugglers and gypsies wander the streets and entertain passersby, and the queen invites guests to join her for tea? That's what happens each weekend in late February through early April when the Bay Area Renaissance Festival casts its spell over central Florida.

In addition to themed weekends and special events, the festival hosts the Florida State Highland Heavy Game Championships (think tossing telephone poles end over end), the Florida State Longbow Competition, and the Florida State Belly Dance Competition. Lots of rides and activities plus an extensive marketplace and food vendor list—Mongolian barbecue or cheesecake-on-a-stick, anyone?—keep visitors from suffering fat wallet fatigue or the hunger pang blues.

Pets are welcomed to the festival, although pet owners must register their pets. Gate-price admission is $16.95 for adults, $8.95 for children ages 5 to 12, and $13.95 for seniors age 62 and up. Children age 4 and under are free. Various discounts are available for groups and when purchasing tickets in advance. Festival hours are 10 a.m. to 6 p.m., rain or shine.

SANT' YAGO KNIGHT PARADE
Downtown Ybor City
(813) 248-0721
www.knightparade.com
Shiver me timbers and lock the little ones away

for safe keeping—or at least do so once the more than 100 lighted floats have wound their way after dark through Ybor City in the Illuminated Knight Parade. Lots of pirates, lots of food and drink, lots of noise as spectators—some in costumes of their own—do just about everything they can to get pirates to toss them strings of beads, beads, and more beads. Sponsored by the (Gasparilla) Krewe of the Knights of Sant' Yago (St. James), a Tampa Bay area krewe dedicated to preserving Latin heritage and culture, the parade culminates in one wild piratical party that fills the streets of Ybor until the wee hours.

The parade is free, but reserved seating begins at $25. A section toward the end of the parade is designated as a Family Zone.

MARCH

THE FLORIDA STRAWBERRY FESTIVAL
2202 W. Reynolds St.
Plant City
(813) 752-9194
www.flstrawberryfestival.com
Eat strawberries just about any way you like during the 11-day Florida Strawberry Festival held just east of Tampa. Top-name entertainers like Taylor Swift, Jeff Foxworthy, and Kool and the Gang pay homage to these juicy gems, and there's a midway full of twisty-turny rides and games for everyone. Youngsters can go for a whirl in the Big Berry at the Kiddie Korral ride area or see what Granpa Cratchet is up to. See cows puttin' on the ritz at the Dairy Costume Ball or watch pigs and steer be auctioned off. Check out the Hometown Salute to America where Floridians show off their baking and handicraft skills. Two parades and lots of contests fill the days and nights.

And those ruby-red globules of goodness? Load up on strawberry shortcake, preserves, milkshakes, cobbler, pie, chocolate dipped strawberries, and more shortcake. When you're filled to the brim, take a flat or two home with you. There's just no such thing as being strawberried out.

Hours are 10 a.m. to 10 p.m. daily. Admission is $10 for age 13 and up, $5 for children 6 to 12. Children age five and under are free. There is an extra charge for some entertainment. No pets. Strollers, wagons, and wheelchairs can be rented at the festival. Check the festival Web site for a page full of helpful tips.

INTERNATIONAL FOLK FAIR
St. Petersburg International Folk Fair Society (SPIFFS)
330 5th St. N.
St. Petersburg
(727) 235-9095
www.SPIFFS.org
Comprised of 30 member societies representing ethnicities from around the world, SPIFFS is the only independent multiethnic organization of its kind in the United States. SPIFFS offers a speakers' bureau, has several dance groups willing to perform ethnic dances, and maintains a language bank of volunteers who translate and interpret in legal and medical cases or when foreign dignitaries visit.

Each March, SPIFFS members host a three-day International Folk Fair with music, dancing, martial arts, and other activities from countries around the world. You might see a Thai *Grit Sada Pee Nee Han* blessing dance, a Scottish sword dance, or the African Urban Ballet Dundo-dole. Watch craftsmen from various countries make lace or dye eggs or carve wood. Sample ethnic dishes you've watched being prepared. Talk to people from other countries and learn different ways of doing things. In addition to local performers, past guest artists have included Celtic musician Colin Grant-Adams and the Russian folk group Barynya, starring Misha Smirnov of "Superstars of Dance."

The Folk Fair is held at the Vinoy Park (701 Bayshore Dr. N.E.). Admission is $10 for adults, $8 for seniors, $5 for youth ages 10 to 17, and free for children under age 10. Admission on Friday from 3 to 5 p.m. is free for everyone. The Folk Fair runs Friday from 3 to 9 p.m., Saturday from 10 a.m. to 10 p.m., and Sunday from noon to 6 p.m.

St. Patrick's Day in Tampa Bay

Many of the Irish pubs in the area—and a few other places that become Irish for the day—offer shamrock shenanigans of various sorts. Check the Nightlife section for a listing of Irish pubs and a brief note about their St. Patrick's Day events.

Dunedin St. Patrick's Day Street Festival
Downtown Main Street
Dunedin 34698
(727) 736-4994
www.flanagansirishpub.net.
For a family-friendly sort of top o' the mornin', head to Dunedin (just north of Clearwater) where there's a bit of a street festival along the downtown portion of Main Street. This Scottish community raises its glass to its Irish cousins starting around 11 a.m. The celebration is sponsored by Flanagan's Irish Pub (see Nightlife chapter), and alcohol is limited to pub property, but the street fest includes Irish dancing, performances by local pipe bands, and other entertainment. The festival area is also a stop along the Pinellas Trail, a paved biking, walking, and skating trail running north-south along most of Pinellas County's west side (see Parks and Recreation chapter for more about the Pinellas Trail).

Rough Riders' St. Patrick's Day Parade
Ybor City
(813) 248-1898
www.tampa-roughriders.org
In Ybor City, the 1st U.S. Volunteer Cavalry "Rough Riders," an official Gasparilla krewe commemorating President Theodore Roosevelt's forces, hold a St. Patrick's Day night parade. Marching bands, floats, and lots of beads being tossed make this the area's largest St. Patrick's Day—er, night—celebration. The parade starts at 8 p.m. and ends at 10 p.m., in time for wee lads and lasses to head for home before the more spirited folk arrive. Parking is limited in Ybor City. Consider taking the streetcar from the Channelside area or from the Dick Greco Plaza covered stop near the Embassy and Marriott hotels and across from the Tampa Convention Center.

MACDILL AIRFEST
MacDill Air Force Base
Tampa
(813) 828-SHOW (7469)
www.macdill-airfest.com
One weekend a year, MacDill AFB opens its gates to the public and puts on a humdinger of an open house air show on behalf of all branches of the military, including the Coast Guard. Volunteers from the Army, Navy, Air Force, and Marines, as well as some civilians working for SOCOM, make up the United States Special Operations Command (SOCOM) Parachute Team, which performs jumps at the MacDill AirFest that include free-fall, formation, and stacked canopy maneuvers.

Overhead exhibits include Ed Hamill and the Air Force Reserve Biplane show, a narrated aerial display choreographed to period music, the U.S. Air Force Thunderbirds' precision maneuvers, and a host of other flying feats performed in aircraft old and new. When they're not craning their necks skyward, visitors can wander the tarmac and explore airplanes like the gigantic KC-10 Extender up close and climb-into-the-cockpit personal. Military crews are on hand to answer questions. The Thunderbird pilots sign autographs after their performance.

The MacDill AirFest is a free, two-day, 9 a.m. to 5 p.m. event. Two gates open to the public at 8 a.m. and remain open until the lots are full. There is no admission after 2 p.m. Driving while talking on a cell phone is prohibited on MacDill property. No weapons, pets, bicycles (on the tarmac), skateboards, rollerblades, scooters, fireworks, coolers, glass containers, or large tote bags are allowed. You may bring beach chairs, cameras, and cash for the plentiful food and beverage vendors. Smoking is allowed in designated areas only. HARTline buses extend service to MacDill for the event; call (813) 254-4278 or go to www.goHART .org for information.

TAMPA BAY BLUES FESTIVAL
Vinoy Park at 701 Bayshore Dr. N.E.
St. Petersburg
(727) 502-5000
www.tampabaybluesfest.com
Bring a lawn chair or beach blanket to St. Petersburg's Vinoy Park, an open-air grassy park near downtown, for three days of blues by the bay. Past performers include Delbert McClinton, Koko Taylor, Marcia Ball, Taj Mahal, and other world-renowned blues artists. Fans soak up sound and sun, while supporting a local charity, Pinellas Association for Retarded Children (PARC).

Gates open at 12:30 p.m. each day and the festival continues well after dark. Parking is at Al Lang Field (First Street and First Avenue S.). or other nearby parking garages, with a free shuttle running along First Street. One-day tickets are $30; a three-day pass is $75. Backstage passes begin at $150. Food and beverage vendors (including beer and wine) and arts and crafts vendors line the area. Cash only—an ATM machine is on site. No pets, no coolers, no food or drinks, and no professional recording devices are allowed. Small umbrellas are permitted near the back.

APRIL
BEACH GOES POPS
Pass-a-Grille Beach
9th Ave. and Gulf Way
St. Pete Beach
(727) 363-0849
www.beachgoespops.com
It's Friday, and you need to ease into the weekend. Or it's Saturday and you've checked off some of those household to-do items and puttered around the yard. Time to reward yourself for getting through a hard week by stepping out. Pack up the beach chairs and a blanket and mosey on down to Pass-a-Grille beach where you'll find good food, good company, and oh-so-good music by which to savor the sunset. There's an Art in the Park show and a variety of music artists ranging from soft-rock to jazz and dance music—nothing heavy. Tap your toes and sway away.

The highlight is the Beach Goes Pops Orchestra from 7:30 to 10 p.m. each evening. Music director and conductor Robert Romanski, also artistic director for a number of music groups in the Tampa Bay area, gathers 35 or so local professional musicians for this once-a-year outdoor concert. Big band music, patriotic songs, maybe some Sinatra—it's easy listening fare played by top-notch musicians with the sunset as a backdrop. Doesn't get much better than that.

The concert is free. Food vendors open and the music begins at 4 p.m. Local restaurants sell food and beverages (soft drinks, beer, and wine), reserve your seaside table for dinner catered by Mise en Place, or bring your own picnic. You can sit on the beach or there's a paved plaza area next to the Hurricane (see the Restaurants chapter for both) where you can set up. Kids can romp on the beach. Friendly dogs on leashes are welcome. Note: It's Florida, but it's April. The evenings can get chilly. Bring a sweater or jacket just in case.

FESTIVAL OF STATES FAMILYFEST
400 Bayshore Dr. N.E. (Straub Park North)
St. Petersburg
(727) 821-9888
www.festivalofstates.com

There's fun for all ages at the Festival of States FamilyFest, held on one of St. Petersburg's waterfront park, but the emphasis is on youth at this event. With lots of food vendors and two areas of live entertainment—local youth performers and others—as well as free make-it-take-it booths, rock climbing wall, inflatables, and other activities, you'll be taking home happy kids who will sleep well. The day begins at 10 a.m. with a parade full of bands and floats and krewes and clowns that start from Central Avenue and Fifth Street, head east to Bayshore Drive, then turn north to the park.

The parade and FamilyFest end a celebration that began in January with the All County MusicFest celebration of music programs in the schools. Festival sponsors underwrite the registration fees for art and writing students to enter the Scholastic Art & Writing Awards competition—winners here move on to New York to vie for national recognition.

Clown Alley clown school, taught by a graduate of the Ringling Brothers Barnum and Bailey Clown College is another part of the celebration. Cost is $17 for five evenings of hands-on clowning around, and graduates get to join the Clown Alley float in the parade.

There's also a 5K run, some beauty/scholarship contests and a coronation ball, and an illuminated night parade a couple of weeks before the day parade and FamilyFest. No wonder the Festival of States, over 100 years old, is considered the largest civic-sponsored event in the South!

The FamilyFest is free, but some of the rides aren't. You can buy an all-day wristband for $10 or individual tickets for $1 each.

DUNEDIN HIGHLAND GAMES AND SPRING CLAN GATHERING
Highlander Park
1920 Pinehurst Rd.
Dunedin
(727) 733-3197 (Chamber of Commerce)
www.dunedinhighlandgames.com
The two-day Dunedin Highland Games, held the first weekend in April, caps a Scottish Events Week that began with a Military Tattoo the weekend before (the last weekend in March). No, we're not talking military insignia body art. This tattoo is a military drum performance or display of might. The Dunedin Military Tattoo at Dunedin High School's Memorial Stadium (1651 Pinehurst Rd.) has become one mighty performance. Area pipe and drum bands—there are more of them than you might think—gather on the field along with Celtic dancers and representatives from more than 30 clans. Past guest performers have included the University of South Florida's Herd of Thunder Show Band.

The Highland Games draw crowds to watch kilted athletes toss the caber—a log about the size of a telephone pole—end over end, throw a 20-pound sack of hay with a pitchfork backwards over a high bar, or throw a 100-pound rock further than the current record of 15 feet, 2 inches. These games pre-date the ancient Greek Olympics and aren't for lightweights.

There's more piping, drumming and dancing—including free workshops for visitors who want to learn—sheepdog demonstrations, food (try the Scottish ginger cake) and drink, and arts and crafts. Admission is $10 for adults; children ages 12 and under are free with a paying adult. No pets. Parking is in an adjacent field or at nearby Dunedin High School (a shuttle runs between the two spots).

MAY

ASIAFEST
St. Pete Times Forum
401 Channelside Dr.
Tampa
(813) 864-4500
www.asiafest-tampabay.com
AsiaFest celebrates the cultures of as many as 15 separate Asian and Pacific groups living in the Tampa Bay area. Dancers and other performers in colorful traditional clothing fill the St. Pete Times Forum and the plaza outside. Past performances have included a Cambodian blessing dance (*Robam Choun*), an Indian *Kolattam* sacred folk dance, a Japanese *Soran-Bushi* folk dance, and many others. The Philippine Performing Arts

Dance Company's (see Arts chapter) bamboo ensemble (music) and the Woun Korean Performing Group's drum dance allow visitors to experience music outside Western conventions. AsiaFest is held in conjunction with the Tampa Bay Dragon Boat Races, an updated version of a 2,000 year old Chinese sport. Go to the Tampa Bay Dragon Boat Institute's Web site at www.tampabaydragon boats.com to learn about dragon boat racing and about the 2011 International Dragon Boat Championship races to be held in Tampa.

Admission to AsiaFest is free. Ethnic food and beverage vendors are outside on the plaza while arts and crafts vendors are located inside. Pets on leashes are allowed in the outdoor areas. There are a number of paid parking areas in the vicinity.

FUN 'N' SUN FESTIVAL
Events throughout Clearwater
301 Drew St. (Coachman Park)
(727) 562-4700 (City of Clearwater)
www.myclearwater.com
For more than 50 years, the City of Clearwater has hosted the Fun 'n' Sun Festival that usually runs late April through early May. The lineup of events has changed through the years, based on the interests of the organizations sponsoring various events. Fun runs, horseshoe tournaments, scrapbooking seminars, and a brunch with the birds have been featured activities.

There's usually an ethnic component—last year's was a Japanese Lantern Festival celebrating Clearwater's 50-year relationship with sister city Nagano, Japan—and an outdoor come-and-play day. But the three concerts are the biggest draw. Held at the end of the festival, each concert features a different style of music—oldies, smooth jazz, and country—sponsored by a local radio station. Two of the concerts are free (premium seating costs $20), but the jazz concert is by paid ticket only (starting at $10 in advance). There are activities for the kids, and the usual food and beverage vendors. Friday's concert is from 5 to 11:30 p.m., Saturday's is from noon to 11:30 p.m., and Sunday's is from noon to 9:30 p.m. Parking is scattered in various parking lots throughout the downtown area.

RUSKIN TOMATO FESTIVAL
E. G. Simmons Park
2401 19th Ave. N.W.
Ruskin
(813) 645-6028
www.ruskintomatofestival.org
Part country music jam, part farmer's market, part living history exhibit, the two-day Ruskin Tomato and Heritage Festival celebrates the area's best-known product, the Ruskin tomato—topping salads and tacos for generations. Upwards of 7,000 people come out to munch on fried green tomatoes, swamp cabbage, smoked mullet, and barbecue; to see how steam engines and antique tractors revolutionized agriculture; and to enjoy craft demonstrations and down-home bluegrass music. Free sliced tomatoes are offered, and free tomato plants are given to the first thousand or so attendees. Kids can ride a mechanical bull, bounce and bungee 'til they're good and tired, and then make some craft items in the workshop.

Admission is $5 for ages 13 and up. Young 'uns ages 12 and under are free. Cash only—an ATM machine is on site—for admission, activities, and food tickets, which are called—what else?— Tomato Bucks. Children's activities range from $1 to $5 each. Pets are not encouraged, but those bringing a responsible owner—at the other end of a short leash and with pooper-scooper in hand—will not be turned away.

Ruskin sits in southern Hillsborough County directly across Tampa Bay from south St. Petersburg, which means festivalgoers coming from Pinellas County may find it faster to go across the Sunshine Skyway Bridge and up U.S. 41. Parking is free, as is the shuttle service to the main gate. E. G. Simmons Park is a Hillsborough County Park on the water (see Parks and Recreation chapter). The park has restroom facilities, a playground, and beach areas.

TASTE OF PINELLAS
Vinoy Park
701 Bayshore Dr. N.E.
St. Petersburg
(727) 898-7451 (All Children's Hospital)
www.tasteofpinellas.com

Dozens of Pinellas County chefs bring their best dishes to the Taste of Pinellas in St. Petersburg's waterfront Vinoy Park for a three-day smorgasbord of sweet and savory samplings that benefits All Children's Hospital. Eat your way from seafood to soul food to crème brulee and cheesecake, while enjoying the live entertainment and balmy breezes coming across the bay. A large children's area with inflatables and other activities keeps the younger set occupied between tastes of pizza and burgers—or sushi! Saturday night ends with fireworks.

Admission is free; food tickets are $5 for 8 tickets, and most tastes cost between 6 and 12 tickets. Children's area requires a wristband—$15 for the whole day. Restroom facilities are Port-o-lets around the park. The park is grassy but flat, so strollers and wheelchairs work well. Credit cards are accepted and an ATM machine is on site.

Park in any of various downtown garages and ride the free shuttle to the park. No coolers or outside food or beverages are allowed. No pets, please, including birds and snakes. Service animals are, of course, permitted.

JUNE

JOHN LEVIQUE PIRATE DAYS
John's Pass Village
150 John's Pass Boardwalk
Madeira Beach
(727) 391-6025 x303
www.johnspassfestivals.com
Legend has it that when John Levique (sometimes spelled "Levick") retired from piracy, he buried his treasure on one of the barrier islands along the west coast of the Pinellas Peninsula. He became a turtle farmer and, in 1848, took a load of turtles to New Orleans. When he returned, he found that a hurricane had blown through the island, creating a pass into Boca Ciega Bay. Unfortunately, the pass was right where Levique had buried his treasure—and so the pass became known as John's Pass.

Because a turtle farming festival conjures up less exciting images than John Levique Pirate

Days, visitors can expect three days of skullduggery fun. After a water battle and invasion, pirates parade and then "pillage the village." Jugglers, pirate artists, and other performers provide plenty of entertainment. Past activities have included a black powder weapons demonstration, a drum circle, a children's costume contest, and a treasure hunt.

Admission is free. Parking is very limited at the pass and on the beach, so plan to park at Madeira Beach Middle School (on the mainland) and take the free shuttle to the village. (See the description of John's Pass Village in the Attractions and Kidstuff chapter.)

ST. PETE PRIDE
Downtown St. Petersburg
(727) 388-9435
www.stpetepride.com
Held in June to commemorate the June 28, 1969, raid by police on the Stonewall Inn in New York's Greenwich Village and resulting riots, St. Pete Pride observes the event and celebrates the changes that have taken place in the last forty years. The Pride Promenade and Festival features a three-blocks long rainbow flag carried through part of St. Petersburg's streets along with floats, flag, rifle, and other drill teams, costumed characters (many in drag), and music. Tents with food, beverage, and other vendors fill a multiblock festival area. Along with the daytime parade, past events have included a nighttime reception at the Museum of Fine Arts and a nighttime comedy concert at an area resort. St. Pete Pride is the largest Pride event in Florida, and one of the largest in the nation. Admission is free.

JULY

July Fourth Celebrations

Many Tampa Bay area cities and towns sponsor fireworks displays that are free to anyone who looks up and can generally be seen for several miles. Listed below are a few past events—check local listings for updated plans.

BEACH BLAST ON TREASURE ISLAND
Bilmar Beach Resort
10650 Gulf Blvd.
Treasure Island
(727) 360-4121
www.bilmarbeachresort.com
Beach blanket bingo and kite-flying demonstrations have been among the activities at this Fourth of July festival on the beach. Live music, too, and fireworks shot out over the Gulf of Mexico. Look for the fun on the beach behind the hotel. Admission is free.

BRANDON BLAST
Westfield Mall
459 Brandon Town Center
Brandon
(813) 661-MALL (6255)
www.westfield.com/brandon
The Brandon Blast and Rock, Rib, and Ride Festival features live music, inflatable bounce houses, a Punt, Pass, and Kick football competition, a rib cook-off, and more during the day. The Festival benefits the Greater Brandon Community Foundation. Brandon generally hosts a community parade, too. Fireworks start around 9 p.m., but folks arrive early to get a parking spot.

CHANNELSIDE BAY PLAZA
615 Channelside Dr.
Tampa
(813) 223-4250
www.channelsidebayplaza.com
Folks start gathering as early as 2 p.m. for activities. Live music begins at 6 p.m., and fireworks go off at 9 p.m. The Florida Aquarium and the Tampa Bay History Center, both within walking distance, sometimes stay open late and have special ticket prices. The American Victory Museum & Ship, docked behind the Florida Aquarium, sometimes has festivities. These places plus Cotanchobee Park, next to the Tampa Bay History Center, are all great places to watch the show, which is launched from a barge in Garrison Channel. Parking is tight, but there are plenty of parking lots. Come early, and plan to stay awhile.

CLEARWATER CELEBRATES AMERICA
Coachman Park
301 Drew St.
Clearwater 33755
(727) 562-4700
www.clearwater-fl.com
Gather in Coachman Park, then enjoy the Mostly Pops Orchestra with John and Mary K. Wilson, starting round 7:30 p.m. John Wilson is one of our local TV news anchors (see Media chapter). Plus, there's an arts and crafts show, food and drink vendors, children's activities, and more. Gates open at 4 p.m. No pets, coolers, umbrellas, etc. Fireworks begin about 9 p.m.

i What can we say? It's illegal to shoot off fireworks here, but it's legal to sell them. You'll see lots of fireworks vendors setting up tents around the end of June. People sign a paper saying they're going to use them for various legal purposes—none of which include July 4th festivities. We prefer letting the experts put on the show.

ST. PETERSBURG'S FOURTH OF JULY CELEBRATION
Several Downtown Locations
(727) 892-5700
www.stpete.org
Activities are held throughout the day at various venues. Children's activities and live music are at North Straub Park beginning about 4 p.m. and WFLA's listener's party (www.970wfla.com) is at the Vinoy Park, also beginning about 4 p.m. The Pier (www.stpete-pier.com) and BayWalk Plaza (www.newBayWalk.com) each have music, street performers, and other activities throughout the day. Fireworks begin about 9 p.m., and anywhere along the water front is a good place to see them.

AUGUST/SEPTEMBER

We take a bit of a festive break in August. School starts in mid-August for many students and teachers, and the summer sun is at its hottest. Check the local papers for smaller events, or head to a local park and celebrate the natural beauty of the area. Then again, you may want to head to a local mall and celebrate the invention of air conditioning.

OCTOBER

CLEARWATER JAZZ HOLIDAY
Coachman Park
301 Drew St.
Clearwater
(727) 461-5200
www.clearwaterjazz.com

Saxophones simper and brushes caress the cymbals during the four-day Clearwater Jazz Holiday that has featured such top-name artists as Kenny G, Natalie Cole, Zydeco, and the Ramsey Lewis Trio over its 30-year run. Coachman Park, overlooking the Intracoastal Waterway on Clearwater's west edge, is the perfect place to spread out a blanket or plop down a lawn chair. Let the music roll over you in sweet waves of sound as you watch the sun make its way toward the horizon.

Best part? It's free! A ton of volunteers work year-round raising money and then work the festival itself to keep expenses down. Their efforts don't stop with this weekend, however. They also support music students with scholarships and workshops—all to keep the jazz flowing to a new generation.

Check the Web site for exact times of this Thursday through Sunday event. Upscale food and beverage vendors, many from area restaurants, offer full meals or a la carte items while other merchants sell souvenirs. A Tot Spot area features a rock-climbing wall, crafts, and games to keep younger visitors occupied. Leave pets, coolers, umbrellas, skates, glass containers, and all edibles at home. Event coordinators suggest ID tags on small children.

FESTIVAL OF READING
Bayboro Harbor
140 7th Ave. S.
St. Petersburg
(727) 893-8523
www.festivalofreading.com

Logophiles and bibliophiles rejoice—have we got a festival for you! Writers of every genre gather on the University of South Florida's downtown St. Petersburg campus for a day of author talks, panel discussions, and book signings. You might hear Dennis LeHane describe the research he did for one of his made-into-a-movie novels. Or listen to Sandra Tsing Loh, writer/performer and NPR commentator, share how she moves back and forth between the written and the spoken word. The festival's main sponsor is the *St. Petersburg Times*, so look for *Times* columnists and critics to talk about reading, writing, and reviewing. More than 50 writers participated last year.

The outdoors Author's Alley marketplace features booksellers, community groups, and other vendors. Most of the author talks and panel discussions are held indoors. Children's authors and entertainers whet young appetites for reading, plus there is a hands-on craft area and face painting.

The festival is free and runs from 10 a.m. to 5 p.m. Food and beverage vendors are on hand, but don't look for an endless menu. Campus eateries are also open.

GUAVAWEEN
Downtown Ybor City
(813) 248-0721
www.cc-events.org/gw

Think Halloween times Mardi Gras squared, multiplied by guava, and you've got the basis for Guavaween. History says that one of the area's early citizens tried to grow guava commercially here, but was unsuccessful. In a marketing ploy, however, Tampa was dubbed the Big Guava (think New York's Big Apple), and the name stuck. Creative types developed the myth of Mama Guava, a wild-child offspring of pirate Jose Gaspar and a swamp cabbage (don't ask) raised in a convent where she flustered the sisters by singing "Guava Maria" and other similar songs. Eventually she discovered her mission in life—to take the "bore" out of Ybor. Hence, Guavaween.

Before dark, things are somewhat tame so as not to frighten the little guavitas and guavitos. There's a Family Fun Fest from 10 a.m. to

3 p.m. with local entertainment on two stages, a children's parade and costume contest, a pet costume contest, a spooky story time, and more. Cost is $5 per person. Children under age 12 and who are in costume (note that they mean it) are free.

The Night of Costumed Revelry runs from 2 p.m. to 3 a.m. Revelers gather at 8 p.m. for the Mama Guava Stumble Parade. Prizes are awarded for the most original entries and anyone can enter (register on the Web site ahead of time). Three stages with live entertainment (past performers have included Big Daddy Kane, Theory of a Deadman, and Basic Rock Outfit) keep the party going. Advance ticket sale prices begin at $15.

(Ask someone else to tell you the story of Papa Guava. This is a family-friendly travel guide.)

JOHN'S PASS SEAFOOD FESTIVAL
John's Pass Village
150 John's Pass Boardwalk
Madeira Beach
(727) 391-6025 x303
www.johnspassfestivals.com
The John's Pass Seafood Festival honors the tons of fresh seafood caught by the commercial fishermen who make this their home port by hosting such activities as a fishing expo, an oyster-eating contest, and crab races. There is also a juried arts and crafts show that attracts artisans from around the region, a children's Halloween costume contest and trick or treating from shop to shop, and non-stop live entertainment. So come for the sautéed scallops and grilled snapper. But plan to stay for a whole lot more. Admission is free. Park at Madeira Beach Middle School on the other side of the Madeira Beach Causeway and take the free shuttle to John's Pass Village. At the north end of the village, there is a children's activities area.

NOVEMBER

CIGAR HERITAGE FESTIVAL
Ybor City Museum State Park
1818 East 9th Ave.
Tampa
(813) 247-1434

Think it's easy to roll a cigar? Come watch live cigar-rolling demonstrations at the Cigar Heritage Festival in Ybor City and you might think differently. Especially if you happen to attend the festival during one of their Guinness-certified attempts to roll the world's longest cigar. At the 2006 festival, for instance, Wallace and Margarita Reyes rolled a 100-foot cigar!

Cigar-rolling isn't the only thing to see at the Cigar Heritage Festival. Artist demonstrations, a children's area, dominoes, cooking demonstrations of traditional Cuban, Sicilian, and Spanish foods, live entertainment, and food and beverage (including beer) vendors are on hand in the museum garden area. Cigar Dave broadcasts his WFLA-970 show from the festival. Plus the regular Ybor City Saturday Market is in Centennial Park, right across the street from the museum. Visitors won't even have to the miss the big game—they'll have TVs tuned to football games and comfy couches.

Admission is $5, which does not include admission to the museum. Children ages 11 and under are free. The festival runs from 10 a.m. to 5 pm. Some metered parking is available on surrounding streets, or there are two parking garages with a few blocks of the museum—one on 9th Ave. near 13th St. and one at 15th St. and 5th Ave. Or park in the Channelside area and take the trolley. (For more information about the museum, see the Attractions chapter.)

PLANT CITY PIG JAM
Randy Larson Softball Four-Plex
1900 South Park Rd.
Plant City
(813) 754-3707, (800) 760-2315
www.plantcity.org
We're not talking just any 'cue here. The Plant City Pig Jam is sanctioned by the Kansas City Barbeque Society (KCBS) and also hosts the State BBQ Championship. Thousands of dollars in cash prizes—and all-important bragging rights—go to the winning professional chefs, who come from around the country to work their barbecue magic on ribs, pork, brisket, and chicken. Amateur and youth chefs compete for other prizes.

The all-day event runs from 10 a.m. to 5 p.m. and admission is free, although parking is $5 per vehicle. There are loads of activities for children; vendors selling beverages, grills, sauces, and other goodies; and all-day live music. The best part, however, is that after the judging starts—just before noon—most of the barbecue that was on the grill goes up for sale. Mmmmmmm.

RIBFEST
Vinoy Park
701 Bayshore Dr. N.E.
St. Petersburg
(727) 528-3828
www.ribfest.org
Must be something about November that brings out the barbecue sauce. This three-day festival in downtown St. Petersburg also features a rib competition and lots of live entertainment and fun. Previous RibFests have included classic car shows, a job and training fair, and a motorcycle show. A Family Fun Zone for kids runs from 11 a.m. to 5 p.m. and features both live entertainment such as Shana Banana and games and crafts. $12 lets kids play all day on the giant inflatables and other activities. Live music on two stages starts around 6 p.m. on Friday and at 1 p.m. on Saturday and Sunday. Music ends at 10 p.m. on Friday and Saturday and at 8 p.m. on Sunday. Past performers have included Styx, Natalie Stovall, and the Pink Floyd tribute band Wall of Echoes.

Yes, there are ribs, too. Circuit competitors from around the world vie for accolades. We reap the benefit, buying plates of barbecue for a good cause. Admission is $10 in advance (check the Web site) and $15 at the gate. Children age 12 and under are free when accompanied by an adult. No pets, no coolers, no food or beverages, and no audio or video recording. Bring chairs and blankets. Park in any of various downtown garages and ride the free shuttle to the park.

THE SUNCOAST DIXIELAND JAZZ CLASSIC
Suncoast Classic Jazz, Inc.
P.O. Box 1945
Largo
(727) 536-0064
www.jazzclassic.net

Notice the word "Dixieland" in the title of this festival. The Suncoast Dixieland Jazz Classic, the largest of its kind on the east coast, is about the early days of New Orleans jazz, ragtime, and swing. The weekend party starts with a poolside parade—think feather boas, flapper dresses, and parasols—and features lots of dancing. Don't know how to swing dance? No problem! Instructors lead a swing dance session that will have you on your feet in no time. Attend ragtime piano sessions, or bring your washboards and banjos and jam along with trumpets, trombones, and other instruments—this music laughs trouble in the face and sends it packing.

The three-day festival starts just before noon on Friday at the Sheraton Sand Key Resort (1160 Gulf Blvd.) with venues split between the Sheraton and the Marriott Suites on Sand Key (1201 Gulf Blvd.), and the festival runs through Sunday evening. Performers and Dixieland jazz fans come from around the country, and performers have included Sonny LaRosa's World's Youngest Jazz Band (all players are age 12 or under), Wally's Warehouse Waifs, and Mighty Aphrodite Jazz Band.

General admission (early registration) is $90 for the three-day event.

DECEMBER

FIRST NIGHT ST. PETERSBURG
Multiple venues in downtown St. Petersburg
P.O. Box 1915
St. Petersburg
(727) 823-8906
www.firstnightstpete.com
Ring in the New Year with family-oriented festivities along St. Petersburg's waterfront park area. Count down to midnight with fireworks on the hour—a teaser at 8 p.m., a family show at 9 p.m. so sleepy-eyed little ones can celebrate, more fireworks at 10 and 11 p.m. and then the main show at midnight. In between times, you might find a ragtime piano player at a nearby church, see acrobats in a bank lobby, or make a mask at the Dalí museum. They've even had public ice skating.

The fun begins at 5:30 p.m. and ends with the midnight fireworks. Admission is $10 for adults and $5 for children ages 6 to 12. Children age five and under are admitted free. Buy tickets online or at a few designated spots in St. Petersburg. You do not have to be a resident of the city in order to attend. There are several free parking areas and several paid parking areas downtown. The venues are within walking distance of each other, and the Looper trolley runs (25 cents per ride—exact change, please) until midnight. Restrooms are at each of the public parks and at many of the venues.

H. B. PLANT HISTORICAL MUSEUM
401 W. Kennedy Blvd.
Tampa
(813) 254-1891
www.plantmuseum.com
The Henry B. Plant Museum in Tampa is well worth a visit any time of year (see Attractions chapter). At Christmastime, however, the museum takes on an extra special holiday touch. From December 1 through 23, visitors to the museum enjoy a Victorian Christmas Stroll with rooms decorated to reflect an old-fashioned 19th-century Christmas. Carolers perform in the evening accompanied by period instruments, and complimentary spiced cider and cookies are served on the veranda. Admission is $10 for adults and $5 for children 12 and younger.

DAY TRIPS AND WEEKEND GETAWAYS

The Tampa Bay area sits smack-dab in the middle of a very diverse region.

Drive north, and you're in a more rural area—you'll see cows grazing off both sides of the road—with small towns like Brookesville and Inverness, historic state parks, and game management areas that have some great campgrounds. Mermaids, too, and not the cartoon version. You'll also find the state's oddest citizen. There have even been Elvis sightings. Further north is Tallahassee, Florida's capital city and home of Florida State University.

To the east is the Orlando area with more theme parks than you can probably see in a year. Go even further east—we live in probably the only state where you can drive coast to coast in just a few hours—and you've got the Atlantic beach areas of Daytona, home of the Daytona International Speedway, and Cape Canaveral with its Kennedy Space Center.

Just south over the Sunshine Skyway Bridge, if you're in Pinellas County, or off of I–75, if you're in Hillsborough County, is the Bradenton-Sarasota area with the Ringling Museum of Art, some great shopping, and Myakka River State Park. Drive further south, and you come to the Fort Myers/Naples area where Thomas Edison had a winter home.

Motor west by boat to the Middle Grounds for some great fishing, or cruise to Mexico.

We'd love to tell you about the whole enchilada, but we're limiting this chapter to the smaller circle. Half circle, actually—we've already covered the Middle Grounds in the Parks and Recreation chapter's fishing Close-up.

So we'll go as far north as Crystal River, on the Gulf Coast, as far east as Orlando, and as far south as Port Charlotte/Punta Gorda. For those of you who like to keep track of such things, we'll be touching on places in these counties (north to south): Citrus, Sumter, Lake, Orange, Hernando, Pasco, Polk, Osceola, Manatee, Hardee, Sarasota, De Soto, and Charlotte.

Pack your bag, then, and let's go!

NORTH BY NORTHEAST

Let's start by driving north from Pinellas County on historic U.S. 19.

Since 1926, this highway has run from Lake Erie, Pennsylvania, through Pittsburg down to Asheville and then down the south side of the Great Smokey Mountain National Park, through Atlanta and then Albany, Georgia, and slipping west around Tallahassee before hugging the west coast of Florida down to Pinellas County. The tin-can tourists of not quite a hundred years ago chugged their way south along the same route on which we're travelling north.

Some of the sights we're going to see were here back then, too. But not many people paid attention to them. They were to eager to get to where we just left. In any case, our first stop will be about 50 miles north of Tarpon Springs.

Weeki Wachee Springs State Park was just Weeki Wachee Springs up until a few years ago. The name has changed a bit, but mermaids still swim in these magical springs. What? You didn't know we had mermaids in Florida? Read the Close-up to find out more about them.

Meantime, here's what you need to know about Weeki Wachee Springs State Park, one of Florida's newest state parks. Bring swimsuits and towels because Buccaneer Bay has lots of water fun. Swish down water slides, drift down a river in a tube, or let the under-six crowd play in their own Caribbean Cove. After drying off, head on over to the other side of the park and take a riverboat cruise, see the animals, and definitely watch the mermaids play—or rent a canoe or a kayak, snorkel, or dive in the springs (guided dives only).

Located at the junction of U.S. 19 and SR 50, the address is 6131 Commercial Way, Spring Hill. Phone (352) 592-5656 for information or go to either http://weekiwachee.com or www.florida stateparks.org/weekiwachee. Weeki Wachee Springs has seasonal days and hours, so double check the Web site before you go. Because Weeki Wachee has so recently been brought into the Florida State Park system, the information given here may change.

Parking is $3 per vehicle or $10 for oversized vehicles (includes sales tax). Admission on days Buccaneer Bay is closed is $13.95 plus tax for adults, $10.95 for children ages 6 to 10. Children under age 6 are free. Admission on days Buccaneer Bay is open is $24.95 plus tax for adults, $16.95 for children age 6 to 10. Children under age 6 are free. Two-day tickets and season passes are also available. Holders of the Florida State Park Annual Family/Individual Entrance Pass get a 33 percent discount on admission. Check the Web site for other specials. Concession stands sell a variety of foods. Picnic tables are available only when Buccaneer Bay is open.

Homosassa Wildlife State Park is just a half hour or so north of Weeki Wachee Springs State Park along U.S. 19. Homosassa Springs also was a private attraction before being brought into the Florida State Park system, but here the emphasis is on animals and wildlife.

We'll take the pontoon boat ride down Pepper Creek to the wildlife park area, and we might see alligators and otters, limpkins and osprey as we float along. Once at the wildlife park, we'll walk along an elevated boardwalk to see deer, bobcats, bears, a Florida panther, and other animals—including a hippopotamus—in one of the few places in Florida where we can see these animals up close.

Walk underwater without getting wet? We can at the Fish Bowl, where manatees and fish play in the spring environment. This is not an enclosed fish bowl, so the creatures come and go—there's always something different to see. A hands-on children's center and informative and interesting ranger talks mean we'll walk away having learned something we didn't know before.

Homosassa Springs Wildlife State Park is open every day of the year from 9 a.m. to 5:30 p.m., but the last tickets are sold at 4 p.m. Admission is $9 for adults, $5 for children ages 3 through 12. Children ages 2 and under are free. Group rates and season passes are available. Pets are not permitted in the park, and smoking is not allowed anywhere in the park. The Manatee Café and two gift shops are open when the park is open. The Remember When Restaurant (352-628-1717), located above the Visitor Center, is open from 9 a.m. to 8 p.m. Monday through Thursday and from 9 a.m. to 9 p.m. Friday through Sunday. Homosassa Springs Wildlife State Park's official address is 4150 S. Suncoast Blvd., Homosassa. Call the park (352-628-5343) or go to www.floridastateparks.org/homosassasprings for more information.

i An African hippo in a Florida wildlife park? Homosassa Springs used to be a privately owned attraction with exotic animals. When the state purchased the park, they relocated the animals. But area residents didn't want the hippo, a retired movie star, to leave. Governor Lawton Chiles made him an honorary Florida citizen, so he could stay the rest of his life.

Yulee Sugar Mill Ruins Historic State Park is less than a mile southwest of Homosassa Springs. David Levy Yulee had his 5,000-acre sugar plantation here, and Homosassa Springs was part of his property, too. Union troops burned Yulee's home in 1864, but they couldn't find the sugar mill. This is the only surviving sugar mill from pre–Civil War days in the United States.

Interpretive panels help visitors understand what they are seeing. Call ahead (352-795-3817) to request a one-hour guided tour or a talk about the site, about Yulee, or about the agriculture of the day. The site is open every day from 8 a.m. to sundown. Admission is free. Pets on leashes are allowed, and there are picnic tables and rest-rooms in the park.

Crystal River Archeological State Park, 15 miles or so up the road from Homosassa Springs, takes us even further back in time. Only about 6 miles long from its spring-fed source to the Gulf of Mexico, Crystal River was home to pre-Columbian people who built a complex community here. Climb carefully constructed stairs to the top of an almost 30-foot high mound and try to imagine what life was like several thousand years ago. A visitors' center contains exhibits and information about the area, and you can call ahead to request demonstrations, slide programs, tours, and other activities.

Today the area is home to wildlife, and the park is part of the Great Florida Birding Trail (ADA accessible). Take the Heritage Eco-Boat Tour ($10—children under six are free) to see the coastal marsh and marine estuary. Fishing is allowed in designated areas. Pets on leashes are welcome (except in the Visitor Center).

Crystal River Archeological State Park, also a National Historic Landmark, is open every day from 8 a.m. to sundown. The Visitor Center is open from 9 a.m. to 5 p.m. and is closed Tuesday and Wednesday. Admission is $2 per vehicle (up to eight passengers). Pedestrians, bicyclists, and extra passengers pay $1. The address of the park is 3400 N. Museum Point, Crystal River. Call (352) 795-3817 or go to www.floridastateparks.org/crystalriver for more information.

i Going from the pre-Columbian to the post-Einstein era, the 4,700-acre Crystal River 3 Nuclear Power Plant also lies along Crystal River. The facility includes four fossil fuel–generated plants and one nuclear-generated plant.

From Crystal River, we'll drive east on Gulf-to-Lake Highway to Inverness where we'll put on our blue suede shoes.

The Old Courthouse Heritage Museum in Inverness, built in 1912, evokes the solid-as-brick community pride people seemed to have in abundance back then. Over the years, however, the interior of the courthouse was modernized to add air conditioning and other amenities, and much of its original beauty was covered over and lost. When the Citrus County Historical Society wanted to apply for grants to restore the second-floor circuit courtroom, they could find only a few photos of its original appearance.

But a 1961 Elvis Presley movie, "Follow that Dream," was filmed in various Florida communities. The last part of the movie took place in a courtroom—the un-modernized, original second-floor circuit courtroom of the Inverness Courthouse. MGM allowed the Citrus County Board of Commissioners to take still photos of the film, the grant was approved, and the courtroom was restored.

Visitors today can stand where Elvis stood and can also view other exhibits about the real history and heritage of the area. The Old Courthouse Heritage Museum (One Courthouse Square, Inverness) is open Monday through Friday from 10 a.m. to 2 p.m. Admission is free, but donations are gratefully accepted. Call (352) 341-6436 or go to www.cccourthouse.org for more information.

From Inverness, we'll need different wheels. Or good walking shoes. We'll take the **Withla-coochee State Trail** southeast back down to Pasco County. This 46-mile paved trail, the lon-gest paved rail-to-trail in Florida, is for bicyclists and pedestrians. To do all 46 miles, we'd have to backtrack north to Dunellon. On this trip, we're only going to do about 35 miles from Inverness to the Trilby Trailhead. Got plenty of water and a hat? Let's go! We'll pass the Withlacoochee State Forest on the west and Fort Cooper State Park on the east. If it's early morning, we'll have some shade. But much of the trail is in the open. We might see some wild turkeys as we come over a rise. No doubt we'll see some cows—maybe deer or a fox. We'll pass Brooksville, the county seat of Hernando County, and end up not too far from Dade City. If it's January, we'll be just in time for the Kumquat Festival. But if it's October, we'll take in the San Antonio Rattlesnake Festival, for sure!

There is no fee to ride the trail. The trail passes through an occasional city park where there are restrooms and water. An unpaved equestrian trail runs alongside parts of the bike trail. The trail is mostly flat and is well marked.

KUMQUAT FESTIVAL
Dade City
(352) 567-3769
www.kumquatfestival.org

Most of the orange groves have gone from Pinellas and Hillsborough Counties, but citrus is still a way of life in Pasco County. At the Kumquat Festival each January, visitors sample kumquats and calamondins, small sweet-sour citrus fruits that are eaten skin and all. Munch on kumquat pie, cookies, or bread while walking through the farmers' market in downtown Dade City or checking out the car and truck show in a nearby parking lot. An arts and crafts show, a quilt show, wagon rides, and other activities round out this glimpse into rural Florida life. For locals, the festivities began earlier in the week with a recipe contest, a beauty contest, and events for growers. The festival itself is a Saturday-only event. Admission is free. Take I-75 north out of Tampa, exit at SR 52, and go east to Dade City. Parking is wherever you can find it; then walk toward the city center. It's a small town and noone gets lost.

RATTLESNAKE FESTIVAL
San Antonio
(352) 588-4444
http://rattlesnakefestival.com

Yes, there are snakes at the two-day Rattlesnake Festival, run by R.A.G.E., aka Rattlesnake and Gopher Enthusiasts. But they're under the control of trained handlers who will show you how they milk the venom from snakes and tell you why snakes are important. There are also gopher and turtle races. Now, they just might mean gopher as in gopher tortoise. But, with this group, we never know what we might find. In addition to all that, there's live entertainment, an arts and crafts show, the Rattlesnake Run, and the Miss Rattler Pageant. Plus they'll have the grill going with loads of their famous barbecued chicken

cooking. Admission and parking are both free. The snake show and the reptile show cost $5 for adults and $2 for children.

Visitor Centers

You'll find festivals and historical reenactments and loads of other things to do north of the Tampa Bay area by checking the calendars of events on these Web sites:

Citrus County Visitors & Convention Bureau
9225 West Fishbowl Dr.
Homosassa
(352) 628-9305, (800) 587-6667
www.visitcitrus.com

Hernando County Convention & Visitors Bureau
30305 Cortez Blvd.
Brooksville
(352) 754-4405, (800) 601-4580
www.naturallyhernando.org

Pasco County Office of Tourism
7530 Little Road, Ste. 340
New Port Richey
(800) 842-1873
www.visitpasco.net

DUE EAST

Go east, young man, woman, or child, and before long we'll leave this humdrum little planet with its—ho-hum—lakes and rivers and—yawn—historic monuments and—bo-ring—real-life world. Go east on I-4. Turn off just before reaching the real-life city of Orlando and turn in to a world of fairy dust and pirates and talking mice. You know where we mean.

Central Florida has become an Enchanted Empire with dozens of little kingdoms competing for tourist currency. We'll visit the biggies—not that there's much we can add to what's already been said—and we'll stop by some of the lesser-known fiefdoms. Even dinner theater

Orlando-style is an over-the-top adventure—look for a separate listing of some of these. In more-or-less alphabetical order—because there are many kingdoms to some of these realms—let's jump aboard our magic carpets and take a ride into the imaginary.

DisneyWorld. Magic Kingdom. Epcot. Animal Kingdom. Typhoon Lagoon Water Park. Blizzard Beach Park. Hollywood Studios. Wide World of Sports Complex. Disney Resort Hotels. Within each of these themed parks and resorts are worlds within worlds. From Cinderella's Castle (with a Bibbidi Bobbidi Boutique which transforms little girls into princesses) in the Magic Kingdom to the DisneyQuest Interactive Theme Park (a 5-story building in Downtown Disney where guests can design their own roller coaster—and then ride it!), all the possibilites leave us feeling as overwhelmed as Mickey Mouse in "The Sorcerer's Apprentice" sequence from *Fantasia*.

We could close our eyes and pick a park to visit. Or we can pre-plan our trip online. One way to get oriented quickly is to click on the "Plan" tab near the top of the DisneyWorld Web site home page. Be forewarned that these planning guides assume guests will be staying at one of the Disney resort hotels. Click your way through an imaginary vacation, however, and you'll be given lots of information and helpful hints. Then it's easy to go back and plan for real

Visitors don't have to stay in a Disney resort hotel to visit the theme parks. Pitch a tent or bring a camper to Disney's Fort Wilderness Campground. Spaces start at $43 per night plus tax and include a nightly Chip 'n' Dale marshmallow roast sing-along plus a classic Disney movie.

There are many other less expensive hotels in the Orlando area. Or chip in with another family and rent a house in the area (search online for "Vacation Home Rentals Orlando").

Disney World is located off of I–4. Just follow the signs. Call (407) 939-6244 or go to http:// disneyworld.disney.go.com for more information.

The Holy Land Experience re-creates the biblical world of 2,000 years ago—with modern conveniences. Enter through the gates of Jerusalem and find a street market with vendors hawking their wares. See a replica of the Wilderness Tabernacle that Moses and his people built and carried with them through their wanderings, a replica of the Qumran Caves, and a replica of Herod's Great Temple. Throughout the Holy Land Experience, there are theatrical presentations and musical shows. The Scriptorium, with its nonsectarian Center for Biblical Antiquities, houses the Van Kampen Collection of scrolls, manuscripts, and early printed editions of the Bible.

i Have a child who is too small to go on some of the rides? Take advantage of Disney's rider swap policy. While one adult stays with the little one, the other enjoys the ride. As soon as that adult returns, the other gets to ride without having to wait in line all over again.

The Holy Land Experience, owned by Trinity Broadcasting Network, is unabashedly Christian in its orientation and presentations. Visitors of all faiths, however, can learn from the historically accurate replicas that help us see a long-ago time in a far-away place that still is at the center of world affairs. A children's area with climbing wall, misting station, and other activities, plus cafés and shops keep modern families happy.

Admission is $35 for adults ($30 online), $20 for children age 6 through 12 ($15 online), and $30 for seniors age 55 and up ($25 online). Children age five and under are free. Two-day and season passes are also available. Visit for free on your birthday. The Holy Land Experience is open Monday through Saturday from 10 a.m. until 6 p.m. The address is 4655 Vineland Rd., Orlando, and can be reached from I–4 off of Exit 78. Call (407) 872-2272 or (800) 447-7235, or go to www .holylandexperience.com for more information.

International Drive is just a street in Orlando. But with six major theme parks, more than 100 hotels, almost 500 shops, and more than 150 restaurants, that's quite a street! It has a free I-Ride Trolley and its own Web site (www.international driveorlando.com) with loads of information and a Virtual (or printed) Vacation Guide.

Mermaids Discovered in Florida

Once upon a time, there was a Land of Flowers where the sun shone most of the time.

On the west side of this Land of Flowers, *La Florida*, many springs of water bubbled up from the ground. Even though these springs were very near the salty sea, the water from the springs was sweet and fresh. Even though the land above the springs was hot and humid, the water in the springs was clear and cold.

The Seminole called the springs *Weeki Wachee*, meaning either "little spring" or "winding river." Maybe it meant both. Weeki Wachee is a little spring—although it is so deep the bottom, or what divers think is the bottom, more than 400 feet down, wasn't found until 2007.

By humans, that is.

Weeki Wachee is also a river. Only 12 miles long, Weeki Wachee River winds its way from the springs to the Gulf of Mexico. Twelve miles isn't a very long distance for mer-people.

No one knows for sure when the mer-people first swam upstream from the Gulf and came to play and then to live in the springs. Being very shy, the mer-people may have been living in Weeki Wachee Springs even before the Seminole came.

What we do know is that, over time, a garbage dragon made his cave in the magical springs. The mer-people hid in the deep underground caverns because the garbage dragon had taken over their playground.

THE GARBAGE DRAGON

Before there were garbage trucks, landfills, and incinerators, people had to get rid of their own trash the best they could. Some people burned their old papers, fed food scraps to the pigs and chickens, and made compost out of vegetable scrapings. But what do you do with broken tools, old refrigerators, and cars that quit running?

Out of sight, out of mind was what some people thought. Sometimes people took things deep into the woods, where no one but the animals ever went, and left them there. Some people dumped things into rivers and springs. Back then, there weren't as many people as there are now, so people didn't worry about filling up the rivers—there were so many rivers, and they were too big to fill. That's what some people thought, anyway.

Down under Weeki Wachee Springs, however, the mer-people were quite distressed at what was happening. To them, the garbage was very much in sight. But they had no way of making land people stop dumping things into their watery home. They needed a knight in shining armor to rescue them from the garbage dragon.

In another part of *La Florida*, near another area with springs bubbling out of the ground, a boy named Newton Perry was growing up. Even though he was a human boy, he seemed to be part fish. He swam in the Silver Springs every day he could, going deeper and staying down longer each time.

He became the swim coach at his high school when he was 16. On the swim team at the University of Florida, Newt became an All-American swimmer. People started calling him "the Human Fish."

The American Red Cross used pictures of Newt in their 1920s aquatics manual. Writers and photographers for *Life* magazine came to Silver Springs and wrote articles about Newt and his sisters. One film shows Newt swimming underwater for almost four minutes.

Newt didn't know about the garbage dragon underwater in the springs on the other side of *La Florida*. There were other dragons above the water, and Newt was sent to fight them. Because of his swimming skills, the Human Fish became a frogman. He taught other soldiers how to be frogmen, too, and helped train U.S. Navy SEALS. He'd become a newt, a fish, a frogman, and a seal.

Once the dragons above water had been driven away, Newt came back to *La Florida*.

THE MER-KNIGHT TO THE RESCUE

Newt began to explore other springs. The people who owned Silver Springs had a glass-bottomed boat. People came from all over to see the beautiful springs underwater. Newt thought maybe he could find a way to show off the beautiful underwater world at another spring. So he started diving in other springs, trying to think of a way to show people who couldn't dive in the water what an underwater spring was like.

When Newt Perry visited Weeki Wachee Springs and saw the garbage dragon, he knew he had to do something. So he put on his armor—fins to make his feet work better in the water, a wet suit to keep him warm in the cold water, shiny metal air tanks on his back—and his helmet—a mask so he could see clearly underwater.

The knight in shining armor leaped into Weeki Wachee Springs and attacked the garbage dragon. He pulled out mattress springs and refrigerators. He pulled out rusted cars and old tires. He pulled out tools and other junk.

The mer-people peeked out from the underground caverns and watched the mer-knight drive the garbage dragon away. When the garbage dragon was gone, the mer-people came out to play in the springs with the mer-knight.

And Newt Perry got an idea. Would the mer-people help? First, Newt figured out a way to build an underwater theater with windows looking into the springs. Then he asked the mer-people to help him put on a show. The mer-people, still very shy, talked it over. They had a different idea. If Newt could teach land men to be frogmen, why couldn't he teach land people to be mer-people?

So that's what Newt did. He taught local people—mostly teenaged girls—how to swim under the water and to breathe using air hoses instead of air tanks. He taught them how to do ballet underwater, and how to eat and drink underwater.

And the Weeki Wachee Springs mermaids started putting on shows for people. Before long, people came from all over the United States to watch the mermaids play with the fish.

Then, in the 1970s, another dragon came along. This one didn't dump garbage into the springs. Instead, it put on a bigger and better show in a place called Orlando. No one wanted to come see the mermaids any more. People talked about closing the shows at Weeki Wachee Springs. But then a funny thing happened.

The more people talked about closing the mermaid shows, the more people realized that this was a special part of Florida. And not just Florida. Where else in the United States—maybe even the world—could people watch mermaids and mermen in a real, natural springs?

Maybe the mer-people worked some of their mer-magic.

In any case, in 2001, the Southwest Florida Water Management District bought the springs. They also bought a 400-plus acre chunk of land around the springs. In 2008, Weeki Wachee Springs became a Florida State Park.

People from all over still come to see Newt Perry's dream of an underwater mer-people show. And if you look wa-ay in the background, toward the deepest caverns, you just might see some of the real mer-people peeking out, watching the show, too.

SeaWorld Orlando has something some of the other theme parks don't have. Rides, yes—including a 400-foot tower, with a slowly rotating carousel car that gives you a leisurely six-minute view of the Orlando area, a combination roller coaster-flume ride that takes you on a thrilling ride to the lost city of Atlantis, a flying coaster ride that's the only one of its kind in the world. Shows, yes—sea lions and otters help take Pirate Island; dolphins, birds, and actors combine to create Blue Horizons; and, of course, there's Shamu, the killer whale. Lots of exhibits, places to eat (see the Makahiki Luau in the Dinner Theater listings), and more. But the pace at SeaWorld is just a tad more relaxed—maybe it's the soothing underwater views of sea creatures living out their lives unconcerned with what's going on above the water. In any case, SeaWorld Orlando is located at 7007 SeaWorld Drive, Orlando, just off if I–4 at the Central Florida Parkway, and the park opens every day at 9 a.m. Closing times vary depending on the time of year, and some show are only offered at night. The Sky Tower costs an additional $3. Call (407) 351-3600 or (888) 800-5447, or go to the Web site at www.seaworld.com for more information.

Universal Studios, Universal Islands of Adventure, WET'N WILD, and City Walk. More than just a kingdom, Universal claims to be—what else?—a whole "universe of action and thrills." Universal Studios features rides and entertainment built around many of its iconic movies, characters, and TV shows—*Jaws*, *The Simpsons*, *Shrek*, *Terminator 2*, *Barney*, *E.T.*, *Men in Black*, and others. Go behind the scenes and see how make-up can turn the most mild-mannered human into an otherworldy monster. This is more than 3-D and not just rides—*Shrek 4-D* lets you feel as well as see the ogre's world, and zapping aliens is part of the fun on the *Men in Black* ride.

Universal Islands of Adventure takes visitors through another set of characters and movies from *The Cat in the Hat* to *Jurassic Park*, *Spider-man*, and the *Incredible Hulk*. WET'N WILD is a fully loaded water park, and City Walk is 30 acres of themed restaurants, nightclubs, shops, and entertainment venues. City Walk sits on its own island with bridges leading to both Universal Studios and Universal Islands of Adventure. Between the two theme parks, Universal Orlando Resort features Blue Man Group's twist on entertainment. There's also a Hard Rock Hotel and other resorts nearby.

The Universal complex is off of I–4 at exit 75-A. The address is 6000 Universal Blvd., Orlando. Call (407) 363-8000 or go to www.universalorlando.com for hours, ticket prices, and other information.

Visitor Centers

Find festivals and loads of other things to do east of the Tampa Bay area by checking the calendars of events on these Web sites:

Lake County Welcome Center
20763 U.S. 27
Groveland
(352) 429-3673
www.lakecountyfl.gov/visitors

Orlando/Orange County Convention & Visitors Bureau, Inc.
8723 International Drive, Ste. 101
Orlando
(407) 363-5872
www.orlandoinfo.com

Dinner Theater Orlando Style

At most dinner theaters, you eat a meal and then watch a play. At dinner theaters Orlando style, you become part of the play. The settings surround you, the stories engulf you, and the word "spectacular" comes to mind.

The prices can be a bit spectacular, too, but with a little searching you can find ticket brokers offering discounts to fill empty seats or as part of packages. The ticket prices, however, are only the beginning. Once inside, you will find other opportunities to spend the coin of the realm—including cash bars, photos with the stars, gift shops, and fees to have an unsuspecting person in your party knighted or otherwise recognized. Be prepared, and decide ahead of time how much you want to spend. Don't forget to add sales tax to the ticket prices and other fees.

Many of these places—especially those with shows that include animals—warn that people with allergies and other conditions should attend at their own risk and that many of the shows use stroboscopic and pyrotechnic effects.

The reviews on all of these places are very mixed. Serving dinner to a thousand people or more at a time means there may be a choice of entrée, but the rest of the menu may be fixed and the quality may not be that of a restaurant where meals are prepared to order. The focus on these places, however, is on the entertainment and the theatrics. Reservations, sometimes as much as 72 hours in advance, are required for most shows.

ARABIAN NIGHTS
6225 W. Irlo Bronson Memorial Hwy
Kissimmee
(407) 239-9223, (800) 553-6116
www.arabian-nights.com
Scheherezade, teller of the thousand and one tales, is the heroine of this tale—told over a kingly feast and enacted in front of the royal guests. But this is no mere stage production told by jesters and mummers and two-legged troupers. This is equestrian theater with horses, horses, and more horses—20-some acts set in far-off locations and various times and involving different types of horseback riding, tricks, and acrobatics. The show runs every night but check the calendar or call to find out the times for a particular day. Tickets can be purchased over the phone (the online sales tab was under construction last time we checked).

CAPONE'S DINNER & SHOW
4740 W. Irlo Bronson Memorial Hwy
Kissimmee
(407) 397-2378, (800) 220-8428
www.alcapones.com
Ya gotta know da secret passwoid ta get inta dis place, ya know wud we mean? Think Prohibition-

era speak-easy when the hooch and the jazz flowed, flappers flapped, and gangsters muscled their way into the action, and you've got the picture of Capone's Dinner & Show. Most of the time you'll get Mama Capone's Italian buffet-style feast with turkey, ham, and pot roast thrown in for good measure. Capone's only seats 350, so reservations are a must. Showtimes are 7:30 p.m. every night of the year. Tickets are $49.99 for adults and $29.99 for children age 4 to 12. Reservations are by phone only. Note: Some of the reviews suggest that parental discretion may be advised for this show.

MAKAHIKI LUAU
SeaWorld Orlando
7007 SeaWorld Dr.
Orlando
(888) 800-5447
www.seaworld.com
Aloha! Tropical foods and South Sea Islands entertainment—plus, of course, a flowered lei and complimentary island beverage—awaits you at the Makahiki Luau at SeaWorld Orlando's Sea Fire Inn. Fire dancers spin flaming torches and guests are invited to learn the hula. Tickets are $46 for adults and $29 for children ages 3 through 9. Children 2 and under may attend, but a reservation is required. You do not have to pay admission to SeaWorld to attend the luau. Check the calendar for seasonal show days and times.

MEDIEVAL TIMES DINNER & TOURNAMENT
4510 W. Irlo Bronson Memorial Hwy
Kissimmee
(866) 543-9637
www.medievaltimes.com
As 21st-century guests to the castle cross a drawbridge over a magical moat, they find themselves in the 11th-century palace of King Philippe and as guests at a four-course dinner. For their entertainment, knights of the realm battle with swords and joust on horseback, the Falconer's birds of prey soar, and Andalusian stallions display their skills. Medieval Times Dinner & Tournament first began in Spain in 1973, came to Kissimmee in 1983, and now has nine locations in North

America. Medieval Times is open every day, but check the online calendar as days and times vary. Medieval Times offers a midday show some days. Tickets start at $58.95 for adults and $37.95 for children ages 12 and under.

PIRATES DINNER ADVENTURE
6400 Carrier Dr.
Orlando
(407) 248-0590, (800) 866-2469
www.piratesdinneradventure.com

Brigands abound in this maritime dinner production. Guests become crew of one of six "ships" surrounding a 300,000-gallon indoor lagoon, in which is anchored an 18th-century Spanish galleon. Pirates pillage, a princess is in peril, and the audience must help save her. A pre-show appetizer buffet and a post-show Buccaneer Bash (party time) add to the experience. The Pirates Dinner Adventure is open every day, but showtimes vary. Check the online calendar. Tickets start at $58.95 (plus tax) for adults and $38.95 for children ages 3 through 11. Children 2 and under are free. A show-only special ticket is $29.95 for both adults and children.

OUTTA CONTROL MAGIC COMEDY DINNER SHOW
Wonder Works
9067 International Dr.
Orlando
(407) 351-8800
www.wonderworksonline.com

Magic, impersonations, and improv comedy mixed with all the pizza, salad, and popcorn you can eat make this show, part of the Wonder Works experience located in the Pointe Orlando Entertainment Complex. Wonder Works, located in an upside-down building, mixes hands-on science and technology (ever been inside a soap bubble?) with Orlando magic to create what they call a "theme park for the mind." Admission to Wonder Works is $19.95 for adults, $14.95 for children ages 4 to 12 and for young-at-hearts ages 65 and older. Admission to Outta Control Magic Comedy Dinner Show is $24.95 for adults and $16.95 for children and seniors. Combina-

tion tickets and group rates are also available. There are two dinner shows every day—one at 6 p.m. and one at 8 p.m. Reservations are recommended, but walk-ins are welcome.

SLEUTHS MYSTERY DINNER SHOW
8267 International Dr.
Orlando
(407) 363-1985, (800) 393-1985
http://sleuths.com

If you love whodunnits where the audience is given a shot at solving the mystery in settings ranging from a fox hunt where it isn't just a fox being hunted to a class reunion with anything but class, Sleuths Mystery Dinner Show is just dying to have you as their guest. With a choice of three theater sizes ranging from 75 to 250 seats, and with a number of mystery productions running at any given time—including one in Spanish—Sleuths Mystery Dinner Show offers a variety of mystery dinner experiences. Sleuths Mystery Dinner Show is open every day and sometimes offers midday shows. Tickets are $52.95 for adults and $23.95 for children ages 3 through 11.

SOUTH BY SOUTHEAST

We should probably title this section Southeast by South, but that doesn't have quite the same ring. Not that it makes a whole lot of difference, but we don't want to lose any travelers along the way. So look sharp, and pay attention here. We'll be taking you to an eclectic mix of dry bones, to a boat in a moat in the middle of nowhere, to the circus, and to other places in between.

We'll start by heading east on SR 60. Just past the Hillsborough County line, we'll come to the little town of Mulberry. Slow down and look for U.S. 37, aka S.E. First Street. Turn south (right), go one block, and there is a white building that looks like the old train depot it used to be.

The **Mulberry Phosphate Museum** is in what used to be the train depot. Built in 1899, the depot today houses a collection of exhibits about the railroad, about the nearby phosphate industry, and about the dinosaur bones that have been discovered in the ore containing the phosphate. You'll see a complete baleen whale skeleton here, which some scientists estimate to be 10 million years old. You can actually handle a saber-toothed tiger skull. Outside is a dragline bucket used in the mining of phosphate. Also outside is a pile of ore the kids will love sifting through in search of fossils and bones. Yes, it's likely they will find some—that's why they call this area Bone Valley. The Mulberry Phosphate Museum is located at 101 S.E. 1st St, Mulberry. The museum is open Tuesday through Saturday from 10 a.m. to 4:30 p.m., and admission is free. Donations are gratefully accepted.

i If you're into EarthCaching—like geocaching, but you take pictures of places you've been instead of leaving trinkets—the dragline bucket at the Mulberry Phosphate Museum is an official EarthCache site. Go to www.geocaching.com and search for "Digging Phosphate in Bone Valley EarthCache" to learn more about this adventure.

Bok Tower Gardens, a National Historic Landmark, is less than half an hour southeast of Cypress Gardens on U.S. 27. Built in the mid-1920s by Edward William Bok, who had retired in 1919 after 30 years as editor of *the Ladies' Home Journal*, Bok Tower Gardens consists of acres of gardens and bird sanctuary areas, a 205-foot-tall carillon Singing Tower, and the Pine Ridge Nature Preserve and Trail. Bok intended this place as a refuge for humans and birds, and there is a hushed serenity about the place. Carillon concerts at 1 and 3 p.m. each afternoon serenade the gardens with the majestic sound of bells. The 60-bell carillon housed in the Singing Tower is not open to the public, but the Great Brass Door and the wrought iron gates on the north side of the tower are magnificent. Various concerts, art programs, and other events take place at the gardens. The Bok Tower Gardens, built on Iron Mountain, one of Florida's highest points at 298 feet above sea level, is open every day from 8 a.m. to 6 p.m. The Visitor Center and Blue Palmetto Café are open from 9 a.m. to 5 p.m. Admission is $10 for adults,

$3 for children age 5 to 12. Children under age 5 and members are free. Picnic areas are off the main parking lot. Bok Tower Gardens has an unattended "pet pen" where pets can stay, for a fee, while their owners tour the gardens. Ask at the Visitor Center about an Exhibition Basket to help children enjoy their visit to Bok Tower Gardens. The address is 1151 Tower Blvd., Lake Wales. Call (863) 676-1408 or go to www.boktowergardens.org for more information.

Also on the property is the 1930s-era Pinewood Estate, the winter home of C. Austin Buck, vice-president of Bethlehem Steel at the time. This estate was acquired by Bok Tower Gardens in the 1970s. Tours of the estate are offered at noon and 2 p.m. each day. Admission is $6 for adults, $5 for members and for children ages 5 to 12. Children under age 5 are free.

Lake Kissimmee State Park is just a short jog to the east of Bok Tower Gardens on SR 60. From designed and cultivated gardens, we'll transition into the unmanicured Florida wilds— except for the campground area, that is. Lake Kissimmee State Park sits surrounded by three lakes—Lake Kissimmee, Florida's third largest lake, Lake Rosalie, and Tiger Lake—so there are plenty of boating and fishing opportunities. Plus there are 6 miles of horse trails and a 13-mile hiking trail with primitive camp areas. If it's a weekend between October 1 and May 1 and we wander down a short trail not far from the campground, we'll find ourselves back in 1876 chatting with a "cow hunter" at the Cow Camp. He's been out in the boonies a while with no one to talk to but the herd of scrub cattle he's been rounding up. Ask him what he thinks of President Ulysses S. Grant, and we just might get an earful. Then again, he might prefer to show us around his humble abode and talk turkey—as in the wild turkeys that live in the area. Lake Kissimmee State Park is open from 7 a.m. to sundown every day. Admission is $4 per vehicle (two to eight passengers), $3 for a single occupant vehicle, $1 for pedestrians, bicyclists, and additional passengers. Camping fees apply. Call (863) 696-1112 or go to www.floridastateparks.org/lakekissimmee for more information. The park's address is 14248 Camp Mack Rd., Lake Wales. Cow Camp hours are 9:30 a.m. to 4:30 p.m. on holidays year-round and on weekends from October 1 to May 1. Groups of 15 or more can request the Cow Camp living history program at other times during the year.

Solomon's Castle, a good hour's drive southwest from Lake Kissimmee State Park, sits in the middle of nowhere—or about as close to nowhere as you can get and still be somewhere. And what a somewhere! Like the Bok Tower, Solomon's Castle is the product of one man's imagination—one man with a decidedly tongue-in-cheek perspective on life. Howard Solomon eschewed noted architects and sculptors, scrounging materials for his castle from unlikely sources—such as printing press plates for the castle siding—and creating visual puns throughout the grounds and the castle. The castle contains galleries with more than 300 of Solomon's sculptures created from recycled materials. We'll take the guided tour so we don't miss any of Solomon's quirky humor—be sure to bring a full supply of "I can't believe I fell for that one" groans. The Boat in the Moat restaurant serves lunch and dinner(sandwiches, salads, hot meals). We can even stay overnight in the castle tower's Blue Moon Room. Solomon's Castle is a popular spot for weddings and parties. Solomon's Castle is open from 11 a.m. to 4 p.m. every day (except Monday from October 1 through June 30). The Boat in the Moat restaurant stays open until 9 p.m. on Friday and Saturdays (and for groups by special arrangement on other evenings). Solomon's Castle does not accept credit or debit cards.

Solomon's Castle's address is 4585 Solomon Rd., Ona. However, it actually sits halfway between Ona (SR 64) and Myakka City (SR 70) off (Hardee) County Road 665. Go to the Web site (www.solomonscastle.org) for directions or call (863) 494-6077.

The **Punta Gorda/Port Charlotte** area lies an hour or so south of Solomon's Castle on U.S. 17. Punta Gorda, on the south side, and Port Charlotte, on the north side, face each other across Charlotte Harbor. There are lots of beaches and

---

Visitor Centers

You'll find festivals, events, and loads of other information about the areas southeast and south of the Tampa Bay area at these sites. Remember to check these places for coupons and discounts to attractions, restaurants, and lodging.

Charlotte County
Charlotte Harbor Visitor & Convention Bureau
18501 Murdock Circle, Ste. 502
Port Charlotte
(941) 743-1900, (800) 652-6090
www.charlotteharbortravel.com

Osceola County
Kissimmee Convention & Visitors Bureau
1925 E. Irlo Bronson Memorial Hwy
Kissimmee
(407) 742-8200
www.visitkissimmee.com

Polk County
Central Florida Visitors & Convention Bureau
600 N. Broadway, Ste. 300
Bartow
(800) 828-7655
www.visitcentralflorida.org

Sarasota County
Sarasota Convention & Visitors Bureau
701 N. Tamiami Trail
Sarasota
(941) 957-1877, (800) 800-3906

---

parks—we might take a guided wading tour of the estuary at the Charlotte Harbor Environmental Center (www.checflorida.org or 941-575-5435 for the Alligator Creek station). Shop, spa, or stay at Fisherman's Village waterfront mall, resort, and marina (www.fishville.com or 800-639-0020). Check out Rick Treworgy's Muscle Car City (http://

musclecarcity.net or 941-575-5959) and his collection of more than 200 cars from the 1920s to the early 1970s (open 9 a.m. to 5 p.m. Tuesday through Sunday; admission is $10 for adults, and children under age 12 are free). Eat at the Muscle Car City Diner (open 7:30 a.m. to 4 p.m. Tuesday through Saturday).

Starting this past spring, more of us than usual have trekked down to Port Charlotte. That's because our own Tampa Bay Rays head down there for spring training. (Where else would a Florida team go during the winter but to a Florida town just a little further south?) When the Rays aren't at the Charlotte Sports Park (2300 El Jobean Road, Port Charlotte), the Charlotte Stone Crabs (www.stonecrabsbaseball.com), a Cal Ripken–owned Minor League Baseball team, plays there.

For more information about the Punta Gorda/Port Charlotte area, go to the Charlotte County Chamber of Commerce Web site (www .charlottecountychamber.org) or call them at either (941) 639-2222 or (941) 627-2222.

Myakka River State Park, less than an hour north on I-75 from Port Charlotte, is east off the exit onto SR 72. Myakka River State Park is one of the oldest and largest in the Florida State Park System—and they offer airboat tours on the world's two largest airboats or a backcountry tram ride ($12 adults, $6 for children ages 6 through 12 for each ride) and other activities. There's lots of fishing, camping, hiking, bicycling, and birding in this 58-square-mile park—horse trails, too. Guests can stay in one of five cabins made of palm logs in the 1930s by the Civilian Conservation Corps (they've been modernized a bit) or in the campground. Kids who complete an activity sheet (available at the Ranger Station) become Junior Rangers. Myakka River State Park's address is 13208 SR72, Sarasota. The basic entrance fee is $5 per vehicle (two to eight passengers). Call (941) 361-6511 or go to www .floridastateparks.org/myakkariver/default.cfm for a list of activities and other fees. The park is open every day from 8 a.m. to sundown.

When we're ready to leave Myakka River State Park, we'll backtrack on SR 72, cross I-75, and take U.S. 41 north to get to our next destination.

Sarasota, another gorgeous west-coast-of-Florida community, lies about 9 miles north of Myakka River State Park. It offers more beaches, more rivers and waterways, more places to explore, and more things to do.

Let's start with the **John & Mable Ringling Museum of Art** (www.ringling.org), the grounds of which house several museums and exhibits. The Ringling Museum of Art contains original European masterworks—paintings by Rubens, van Dyck, Tintoretto, El Greco, and many other artists—as well as an extensive Asian art collection. The building is a work of art in itself, and the garden contains full-sized casts of such sculptures as Michelangelo's *David*. Then there's the Cà d'Zan ("House of John") 56-room mansion, built in 1925 and patterned after the Doge of Venice's palace. Filled with furnishings and artwork, this is the second museum in the Ringling complex. The third museum, the Circus Museums, celebrates Ringling's most famous legacy—the Ringling Family Circus. The Circus Museums contain parade wagons, costumes, posters, and John and Mable Ringling's private rail car.

Also on the grounds of the Cà d'Zan is the **Historic Asolo Theater**. Built in 1798 in Asolo, Italy, the theater was dismantled in the 1940s and brought to Sarasota. Today, it hosts performing arts including opera, theater, and dance. The John & Mable Ringling Museum of Art complex is open every day except Thanksgiving, Christmas, and New Year's from 10 a.m. to 5:30 p.m. and is located at 5401 Bay Shore Road, Sarasota. Call (941) 359-5700 for more information.

St. Armands Circle, on St. Armands Key, just over the causeway from the Ringling complex, is an upscale shopping and dining area (www .starmandscircleassoc.com or call 941-388-1554). With more than 140 shops and restaurants, most people manage to while away the hours quite nicely. Check their events calendar, too—there's usually something special going on.

Then we'll travel north from Sarasota on U.S. 41, cross over the Manatee River at Bradenton, and take U.S. 301 east toward Ellenton. We have two more stops to make before heading home to the Tampa Bay area.

The **Gamble Plantation Historic State Park** is South Florida's only surviving pre–Civil War era plantation house. Most of us think of Tara from *Gone With the Wind* when we hear the word "plantation." The Gamble house, owned by Major Robert Gamble who had a large sugar plantation, gives a truer picture of what mid-19th-century plantation life was like. Admission to the park, open every day from 8 a.m. to sundown, is free. The Visitor Center is open 9 a.m. to 5 p.m. Thursday through Monday and is closed Thanksgiving, Christmas, and New Year's Days. Guided tours ($5 adults and $3 for children) are available six times a day on days when the Visitor Center is open. There are picnic tables and restrooms on the grounds.

Prime Outlets Mall in Ellenton, just east of the Gamble Plantation on U.S. Hwy 301, has out-let stores from places like Saks Fifth Avenue Off 5th, Polo Ralph Lauren Factory Store, and other name-brand outlet stores—130 of them, to be exact. Prime Outlets Mall, located at 5461 Factory Shops Blvd., Ellenton, is open Monday through Saturday from 10 a.m. to 9 p.m. and Sunday from 10 a.m. to 7 p.m. They are closed Easter, Thanksgiving Day, and Christmas Day. For more information, call (941) 723-1150 or (888) 260-7608, or go online to www.primeoutlets.com/locations/ellenton.aspx.

To get back home, we'lll take I–75 north to Tampa, or we'll turn off I–75 at I–275 and go north over the Sunshine Skyway Bridge to St. Petersburg.

We don't know about you, but we could use a vacation after all this traveling.

RELOCATION

So you've decided to make the Tampa Bay area your home. Wonderful! We're glad to have you come and be a part of our community.

You probably have a gazillion questions. Don't know if we have a gazillion answers, but we can give you lots of phone numbers and Web sites that will connect you with people who will have the answers.

We'll start by listing the various cities within Hillsborough and Pinellas counties and the many chambers of commerce you'll find here. Some of these offices have guides to help you find your way around a specific smaller community or to give you information about business opportunities in the area.

And we'll take a tour—we kid you not—through the telephone directory. Most people are amazed at the wealth of information they find in our telephone directory.

Some things you'll want to know are common to both sides of Tampa Bay.

We'll tell you where to go—and what to take with you—to get a Florida driver license and license plates for your car. Buying a house during hurricane season can be a bit tricky because timing is everything when it comes to buying the property insurance you need in order to close on a mortgage—so we'll talk about property insurance, property taxes, and water issues.

Everyone needs a helping hand at some point. Or maybe you're one of those people—bless you!—whose sleeves are perpetually rolled up, and you're ready to volunteer to make our community even better. You'll find a list of organizations just waiting for your call.

We haven't forgotten about pets. Pet owners will find information about dog parks, licensing, and other issues.

Despite what our mothers told us, we'll be up front about money and politics in the Tampa Bay area. We'll talk in general terms about area industries and businesses. And, unlike some states, Florida is a closed-primary state, so we'll tell you where to register to vote and a bit about the Florida political process.

We'll try to ease your mind about the one thing we hope doesn't happen each year from June 1 to November 30—hurricane season. Not that we take hurricanes lightly. No way, no how. But we've learned how to prepare the best we can. We'll pass along the things we've learned about hurricanes and about other natural nuisances—like mosquitoes, for instance.

Those are the biggies. If your specific question isn't answered here, then please call one of the other resources we've listed.

And if you start to feel a little overwhelmed by all this practical information, go play in the sunshine or on a beach for while. That will help you remember why you're moving here, right?

We've organized this chapter into the following topics: Driver's Licenses and Auto Tags, Economy and Industry, Hurricanes and Other Weather Emergencies, Local Government, Pets and Other Animals, Real Estate, Support Services, Voter Registration and Elections, and Water Issues.

Close-up

Quick List of Local Governments and Chambers of Commerce

TAMPA/HILLSBOROUGH COUNTY

Hillsborough County Government
(813) 272-5900 (7 a.m. to 11 p.m., 365 days a year)
www.hillsboroughcounty.org

Plant City, City of
(813) 659-4200
www.plantcitygov.com

Tampa, City of (Hillsborough County Seat)
(813) 506-6420
www.tampagov.net

Temple Terrace
(813) 989-7100
www.templeterrace.com

PINELLAS COUNTY

Pinellas County Government
(727) 464-3000
www.pinellascounty.org

Clearwater, City of (county seat)
Includes Clearwater Beach
(727) 562-4250
www.clearwater-fl.com

Belleair, Town of
(727) 588-3769
www.townofbelleair-fl.gov

Belleair Beach, City of
(727) 595-4646
www.cityofbelleairbeach.com

Belleair Bluffs, City of
(727) 584-2151
www.belleairbluffs.org

Belleair Shores, Town of
(727) 593-9296
http://belleairshore.com

Dunedin, City of
(727) 298-3000
www.dunedingov.com

Gulfport, City of
(727) 893-1000
www.ci.gulfport.fl.us

Indian Rocks Beach, City of
(727) 595-2517
www.indian-rocks-beach.com

Indian Shores, Town of
(727) 595-4020
www.myindianshores.com

Kenneth, City of (generally called Kenneth City)
(727) 544-6655

Largo, City of
(727) 587-6700
www.largo.com

Madeira Beach, City of
(727) 391-9951
www.madeirabeachfl.gov

North Redington Beach, Town of
(727) 391-4848
www.townofnorthredingtonbeach.com

Oldsmar, City of
(813) 855-4693
www.ci.oldsmar.fl.us

Pinellas Park, City of
(727) 541-0700
www.pinellas-park.com

Redington Beach, Town of
(727) 391-3875
www.townofredingtonbeach.com

Redington Shores, Town of
(727) 397-5538
www.townofredingtonshores.com

Safety Harbor, City of
(727) 724-1555
www.cityofsafetyharbor.com

Seminole, City of
(727) 391-0204
www.myseminole.com

South Pasadena, City of
(727) 347-4171
http://ci.south-pasadena.fl.us

St. Pete Beach, City of
(727) 367-2735
www.stpetebeach.org

St. Petersburg, City of
(727) 893-7171
www.stpete.org

Tarpon Springs, City of
(727) 938-3711
www.ci.tarpon-springs.fl.us

Treasure Island, City of
(727) 547-4575
www.mytreasureisland.org

CHAMBERS OF COMMERCE
Florida Chamber of Commerce
136 South Bronough St.
(P.O. Box 11309)
Tallahassee (32302-3309)
(850) 521-1200
www.flchamber.com

Hillsborough County

Greater Plant City Chamber of Commerce
(813) 754-3707, (800) 760-2315
www.plantcity.org

INDO-US Chamber of Commerce
(813) 637-0156
www.indo-us.org

New Tampa Chamber of Commerce
(813) 293-2464
www.newtampa.org

North Tampa Chamber of Commerce
(813) 961-2420
www.northtampachamber.com

Puerto Rico Chamber of Commerce Tampa
(813) 884-0267
www.puertoricanchamber.net

South Tampa Chamber of Commerce
(813) 637-0156
www.southtampachamber.org

Tampa Bay Beaches Chamber of Commerce
www.tampabaybeaches.com
(727) 360-6957

Tampa Bay Hispanic Chamber of Commerce
(813) 414-9411
www.tampahispanicchamber.com

Tampa Chamber of Commerce
(813) 228-777
www.tampachamber.com

Temple Terrace Chamber of Commerce
(813) 989-7004
www.templeterracechamber.com

West Tampa Chamber of Commerce
(813) 253-2056
www.westtampachamber.com

Ybor City Chamber of Commerce
(813) 241-8838
www.ybor.org (look for Visitor Center link)

Pinellas County

Clearwater Beach Chamber of Commerce
(727) 447-7600, (888) 799-3199
www.beachchamber.com

Clearwater Regional Chamber of Commerce
(727) 461-0011
www.clearwaterflorida.org

Dunedin Chamber of Commerce
(727) 733-3197
www.dunedin-fl.com

Greater Palm Harbor Area Chamber of Commerce
(727) 784-4287
www.palmharborcc.org

Gulfport Chamber of Commerce
(727) 344-3711
www.gulfportchamberofcommerce.com

Largo/Mid-Pinellas Chamber of Commerce
(727) 584-2321
www.largochamber.org

Pinellas Park/Gateway Chamber of Commerce
(727) 544-4777
www.pinellasparkchamber.com

Safety Harbor Chamber of Commerce
(727) 726-2890
www.safetyharborchamber.com

St. Petersburg Area Chamber of Commerce
(727) 821-4069
www.stpete.com

Seminole Chamber of Commerce
(727) 392-3245
www.seminolechamber.net

Tampa Bay Beaches Chamber of Commerce
(727) 360-6957
www.tampabaybeaches.com

Tarpon Springs Chamber of Commerce
(727)-937-6109
www.tarponspringschamber.com

Treasure Island Chamber of Commerce
(727) 360-4121
www.treasureislandchamber.org

Upper Tampa Bay Regional Chamber of Commerce
(813) 855-4233
www.utbchamber.com

DRIVER LICENSES AND AUTO TAGS

FLORIDA DEPARTMENT OF HIGHWAY SAFETY AND MOTOR VEHICLES
(850) 617-2000
www.flhsmv.gov

The Florida Department of Highway Safety and Motor Vehicles oversees the Florida Highway Patrol, the Division of Driver Licenses, and the Division of Motor Vehicles. Sounds simple, yes? Consider, though, that mobile homes—while they are still mobile, at any rate—are considered motor vehicles, and you'll understand why this department also has jurisdiction over some facets of the mobile home industry. Think about all the various types of commercial motor carriers, freight-carrying vehicles, boats, and boat trailers, and all of a sudden what was simple has become quite complex.

We say all this to help you understand that these offices usually are very busy. Go to the Department's Web site and click on "Office Locations" on the left rail for a list of offices in each county. Appointments are not mandatory, but are recommended, and they can be made on line. Plan extra time, call or go online ahead of time to find out what paperwork you need to bring with you, and remember to pick up your sense of humor on the way out the door.

Driver Licenses

As of this writing, it is fairly easy to exchange an out-of-state driver license for a comparable Florida license. Bring a certified birth certificate (not a copy) or your passport to prove you are a U.S. citizen, a marriage certificate or court order verifying any name changes, proof of social security number, and proof of residential address (a utility bill, for example). Non-citizens must bring valid Department of Homeland Security documents, proof of social security number (if you have one), and proof of residential address (a utility bill, for example). Go to the Web site for a list of acceptable documents.

You will be given and must pass a vision test. The fee is $27 and, if you are under age 80, the license may be valid for up to eight years. Motor-cyclists pay an additional $7 and must complete a motorcycle safety course (see the Web site for a list of course sponsors).

Teen drivers in Florida, and their parents, can go to a State of Florida Web site (www.flhsmv.gov/teens) for information about licensing and other laws. Florida grants driving privileges in stages: Learner's License (minimum age is 15), Intermediate License (ages 16 and 17 with graduated privileges for each age), and Full Privilege License (minimum age is 18).

ℹ️ For a copy of the *Florida Driver's Handbook*, the *Florida Commercial Driver's License Handbook*, or the *Florida Motorcycle Handbook*, go to www.flhsmv.gov/handbooks or stop by any of the Driver License Offices and pick up a printed copy. Spanish and Creole versions are available, too.

Auto Tags

Newcomers have 10 days from the time they become employed, enroll children in public school, or establish residence in Florida to register their motor vehicle in Florida. County tax collectors' offices register motor vehicles in the State of Florida (see list of sites).

The form to register your motor vehicle will ask for your Florida driver license number, so get a Florida driver license first.

Second, in order to get Florida license tags, you must have vehicle insurance from a company licensed to do business in Florida. You can find out what kind of insurance you will need by going to the State of Florida's Web page at www.flhsmv.gov/ddl/frfaqgen.html.

Third, complete and print out form HSMV 82040 or HSMV 82042 (available online at www.flhsmv.gov/dmv/forms/btr/milpak/82040.pdf). At the bottom of the form, you'll see a section asking for the Vehicle Identification Number. You must have an authorized person fill out this section—and there will be an authorized person at the county tax collector's office. It may save you a bit of time, however, to have this done before you go.

Next, take your proof of Florida insurance, your original out-of-state title, and the form with you to the county tax collector's office (see list of sites). Every person listed as "owner" on the out-of-state title must sign the application or all applicants must be present.

ℹ️ **You never know when someone will need a bit of seemingly obscure information. So, just in case this applies to you, here is the link to the PDF form you will need if you have modified your golf cart to a low-speed vehicle: www.flhsmv.gov/dmv/forms/bfo/86064.pdf.**

ECONOMY AND INDUSTRY

You name it, we've got it—in terms of industry, that is. From tomato growers to high-tech computer circuit board manufacturers, businesses in the Tampa Bay area are involved in many segments of the economy (see related Sidebar). While we've taken our share of financial blows, that diversity helps us roll with the economic punches somewhat better than some other parts of the country.

ℹ️ **Generally speaking, Florida is a "right-to-work" state, meaning union membership cannot be made a term of employment. Generally speaking, Florida is also an "at-will employment" state, meaning employment can be terminated by either employer or employee without cause. "Generally speaking" means check with an attorney instead of assuming either of these terms applies to your case or anyone else's case.**

As of September 2009, for example, Bureau of Labor Statistics showed the unemployment rate in Florida was 11.2 percent, compared with 3.4 percent in North Dakota and 14.8 percent in Michigan. The Tampa Bay area's unemployment rate was 11.7 percent, compared with 7.2 percent in the Fort Walton Beach and Gainesville areas and 16.2 percent in the Palm Coast area.

We've had our share of home foreclosures, as well. But it's not the first time this has happened. In fact, our real estate market today bears an eerie resemblance to that of the 1920s.

Back then, land prices rose because people were convinced more people would come here to live and the area would grow someday in the future—and most people thought it would be sooner rather than later. Prices were based on future expectations rather than present realities.

And when the future didn't work out quite the way people thought it would—or at least not as quickly as they thought it would—people didn't have enough money to make their payments.

Knowing all of that doesn't make it any easier for people who have had to sell their homes or have lost money. But maybe it will help us not make the same kinds of mistakes again. At least not for another hundred years or so.

In any case, RealtyTrac figures for the first half of 2009 put Florida (3.08 percent) along with Nevada (6.25 percent) and Arizona (3.37 percent) in the top three states with the highest foreclosure rates and Florida (along with California and Arizona) in the top three states with the highest foreclosure totals. Locally, the 2008 foreclosure rate in the Tampa Bay area (Tampa/St. Petersburg/Clearwater) was 4.14 percent, the thirteenth highest in the nation.

Foreclosures and falling property prices affect the amount of property tax collected. Job losses mean less money to buy things, which affects the amount of sales tax collected. Lower tax revenues have meant local and state governments and local school boards have had to do some trimming.

Not all is doom and gloom. After all, we just got an IKEA store (see Shopping chapter)—one of only 48 in the nation. Somebody must think we're doing something right.

ℹ️ **Interested in relocating your whole business here? Contact the Tampa Bay Partnership, an organization of 150 or so businesses in a seven-county region surrounding Tampa Bay. They'll help you find commercial real estate and navigate Florida's business world. Call them at (800) 556-9316 or go to www.tampabay.org for more information.**

Top Tampa Bay Area Businesses

To give you an idea of how diverse our economy is, top Tampa Bay area businesses include a steel manufacturer, a financial services provider, an electronics manufacturer, a public utility, and a home oxygen provider. Some top Tampa Bay area businesses (in alphabetical order) are:

- **Checkers Drive-In Restaurants.** Checkers/Rally's Restaurants 4300 West Cypress St., Ste. 600, Tampa, (813) 283-7000, www.checkers.com—Franchised drive-in restaurants.

- **Gerdau Ameristeel Corp.** 4221 W. Boy Scout Blvd., Tampa, (813) 286-8383, www.gerdauameristeel.com—Steel mills and fabrication shops producing rebar, nails, railroad spikes, wire mesh, and steel sheet piling.

- **Jabil Circuit, Inc.** 10560 Dr. Martin Luther King Jr. St. N., St. Petersburg, (727) 577-9749, www.jabil.com—Electronic components and circuitry.

- **Kforce, Inc.** 1001 East Palm Ave., Tampa, (800) 395-5575, www.kforce.com—Professional and technical staffing provider.

- **Lincare Holdings, Inc.** 19387 U.S. 19 N., Clearwater, (727) 530-7700, www.lincare.com—Home oxygen and respiratory therapy provider.

- **MarineMax, Inc.** 18167 U.S. 19 N., Ste. 300, Clearwater, (727) 531-1700, www.marinemax.com—Recreational boat and yacht sales.

- **OSI Restaurant Partners, LLC.** 2202 N. West Shore Blvd., 5th Floor, Tampa, (813) 282-1225, www.osirestaurantpartners.com—Five restaurant chains including Outback Steakhouse, Bonefish Grill, Carrabbas, Flemings, and Roy's.

- **Raymond James Financial, Inc.** 880 Carillon Pkwy, St. Petersburg, (727) 567-1000, www.raymondjames.com—Financial investment and banking services.

- **Rooms to Go.** 11540 U.S. 92 East, Seffner, (888) 709-5380, www.roomstogo.com—Retail furniture sales.

- **Tech Data Corp.** 5350 Tech Data Dr., Clearwater, (727) 539-7429, www.techdata.com—Computer sales and information technology distributor.

- **TECO Energy, Inc.** 702 Franklin St., Tampa, (813) 228-1111, www.tecoenergy.com—Public utilities holding company and coal mining.

- **WellCare Health Plans, Inc.** 8725 Henderson Rd., Tampa, (813) 290-6200, www.wellcare.com—Medicaid and Medicare managed health care plans.

Another way to look at top businesses, however, is based on how many people they employ. Pinellas County School District is the top employer in Pinellas County (15,000 employees). Hillsborough County School district is the top employer in Hillsborough County (25,000 employees).

i Even before a hurricane actually hits, fire departments and police departments may not be able to respond to calls for help. Once sustained winds reach tropical-storm strength, emergency response vehicles stay in their stations until it's safe to come out again.

HURRICANES AND OTHER WEATHER EMERGENCIES

It's been a while since we've taken a direct hit from a major hurricane. That makes it easy to become a bit blasé about how dangerous they can be and how much damage they can do. Going through all the rigmarole of gathering supplies and closing schools and evacuating can become a bit tedious.

Until, that is, we remember that, before the 1848 hurricane, there was no pass in the barrier islands off Pinellas County where John's Pass is now. Or until we see damage in other places.

Even an indirect pummeling by the outer bands of a hurricane or tropical storm can damage homes and endanger lives. So read the Close-up about hurricanes carefully and plan ahead.

i In different parts of the world, hurricanes are called typhoons or cyclones. Regardless of what they are called, hurricanes help regulate the global temperature.

LOCAL GOVERNMENT INFORMATION

STATE OF FLORIDA
(866) 693-6748
www.myflorida.com
The State of Florida's Web site is fairly easy to navigate and offers entry through portals on the left rail: Visitor, Floridian, Business, Government, and Get Answers. Tabs at the top of the page also offer simple help in finding a State of Florida agency.

Emergency Help Information

Web Sites
Many of these sites have information in Spanish and some have sections for children. Many cities in Pinellas and Hillsborough counties have Web pages with specific information for each community.

- FEMA Citizen Corps: www.citizen corps.gov
- Florida Division of Emergency Management: www.floridadisaster.org
- City of Tampa Emergency Information: www.tampagov.net/inform ation_resources/emergency_info/index.asp
- Hillsborough County Emergency Management: www.hillsborough county.org/emergency
- National Hurricane Center: www.nhc.noaa.gov
- Pinellas County Emergency Management: www.pinellascounty.org/emergency
- Weather Channel: www.weather.com

During an Emergency
- Hurricane Information Desk (City of Tampa): (813) 232-6890
- Citizen Information Center (Pinellas County): (727) 464-4333

Close-up

Playing the Hurricane "What If" Game

Parents sometimes help their children prepare for new situations by playing the "what if" game. Asking a child going into kindergarten, "What if you drop your lunch tray? What would you do?" helps the child plan for those times when things don't go smoothly. Figuring out ahead of time how to ask for help calmly or how to pick up the mess and then get another lunch is better than waiting until the tray spills and the child panics.

Here in the Tampa Bay area, we do something like that every year, all year. Officially hurricane season is June 1 through November 30. But sometimes storms ignore the calendar.

In March 1993, for instance, a storm popped up that packed a hurricane-like wallop just 50 miles or so north of our area. In Pasco County, 8,000 homes were destroyed, many by a tidal surge that swept over even two-story homes. Twenty-six people in Florida were killed, 18,000 homes in Florida were destroyed, and U.S. 19 was under several feet of water as far north as Citrus County.

So how do we plan ahead for something as potentially devastating as a hurricane? We keep the "what if" game in mind all year long. That way we're always ready for the unexpected.

Learn what happens during a hurricane. Many hurricanes that affect this area begin as storms that form in the Atlantic Ocean off the coast of Africa. As the storms blow across the Atlantic Ocean, they sometimes start spinning in a circle and they sometimes grow into a system with many storms in it.

If the winds of an organized storm system stay under 39 mph, the storm system is called a *tropical depression*. A storm system with sustained winds blowing between 39 mph and 73 mph is called a *tropical storm* and is given a name by the National Hurricane Center. According to the Saffir-Simpson Hurricane Scale, if the winds go to 74 mph or higher, the storm system is called a *hurricane*. Hurricanes range in strength from a Category 1 (winds between 74 and 95 mph) to a Category 5 (wind speed is higher than 155 mph).

Hurricanes cause two types of damage: wind damage and water damage.

Wind damage comes not just from the winds of the storm itself, but also from tornadoes that form in the storm. These tornadoes usually are not the monsters we see in the Midwest, but more often are smaller ones that form quickly, touch down briefly, and dissipate quickly. Even so, they can do lots of damage. Waterspouts are tornadoes that form over water rather than over land.

Water damage comes partly from intense rains during a storm. But the greater danger is from the water the wind pushes in from the ocean—the tidal surge that can bring a wall of water several feet high rushing onto land and then sucking everything not fastened down back out to sea.

ACT NOW: The National Hurricane Center's Web site (www.nhc.noaa.gov) has extensive information about how hurricanes form and how they are tracked, as well as up-to-the-minute weather information. The Weather Channel Kids' Web site (www.theweatherchannelkids.com—click on the Weather-Ready tab) helps kids understand hurricanes and other weather.

Learn what is likely to happen where you live and work. Each county in Florida has been mapped to show high spots, low spots, and other information.

The maps tell us in what Evacuation Zone we are located. Evacuation Zone A areas are the most likely to have tidal surge water, even in a tropical storm or Category 1 hurricane. Evacuation Zone E areas probably won't have tidal surge water unless a Category 5 hurricane hits.

If you live or work in a mobile home, it doesn't matter what evacuation zone you are in. You *must* evacuate when Zone A evacuates.

ACT NOW: Find out in what Evacuation Zone you are located. In Hillsborough County, go to www.hillsboroughcounty.org/emergency. Click on "Hurricane Information" (on the left rail) and follow the links to maps or an evacuation zone locator. Or call the Hurricane InfoLine at (813) 272-5900 to find out your evacuation zone and where the closest shelters are.

In Tampa, go to www.tampagov.net/dept_emergency_management/index.asp for maps and information.

In Pinellas County, go to www.pinellascounty.org/emergency. Click on "Know Your Zone," and look at maps or type in your address to learn your zone and where the closest shelters are. You can also call (727) 453-3150 to hear your home's evacuation zone (land line phones in Pinellas County only). Or call Pinellas County Emergency Management at (727) 464-3800.

Learn what your options are. What if you have to evacuate, where will you go? How will you get there? When will you have to leave? What will you take with you? What will you have to do to your house before you go? What about your pets? What about medicines and important papers?

If you stay, what will you need if the power goes out for several days? How will you prepare your home to minimize wind and water damage? What if stores are damaged and can't open for several days? What if you are on oxygen or use other medical equipment needing electricity?

ACT NOW: Pick up a *Surviving the Storm* guide (it may have a different title in different counties or in different years) at the nearest post office or library. These guides have maps, lists of shelters, lists of things to do before a storm hits, lists of things to take with you if you have to evacuate, and other information.

Look for the HEAT (Hurricane Evacuation Assessment Tool), an online planning help on both counties' Web pages.

Pinellas County Emergency Management presents several hurricane-readiness programs to organizations and businesses. Check their schedule for classes held at libraries, or call (727) 464-4600 to request a presentation.

Hillsborough County also presents hurricane-readiness programs to organizations and businesses, and organizes a Hurricane Expo at the beginning of hurricane season each year. Call (813) 301-7174 for more information.

Look for CERT (Community Emergency Response Team) classes offered by some cities and counties to learn how to help yourself and others during disasters.

Make a plan and practice the plan. If you're going to evacuate, drive to where you're planning to go. Then pretend thousands of other people are evacuating, too. Do you need to have an alternate route or leave earlier? If you're staying put, buy some waterproof tubs and start an emergency kit now. Store shelves empty quickly when hurricanes approach.

Plan what to do after the hurricane. More people are injured or killed after the storm has passed because of gas leaks, downed power lines, fallen trees, and other dangers. Be very cautious after the storm. Don't assume the police or fire department will be able to respond right away. Roads may be damaged, or there may be too many people who need help. You may be on your own for hours or even days.

BARRIER ISLANDS GOVERNMENT COUNCIL—BIG-C

c/o Mayor Jim Lawrence
Town of Indian Shores
19305 Gulf Blvd.
Indian Shores 33785
(727) 595-4020 Ext. 0
www.barrierislandscouncil.com

This intergovernmental council represents 11 waterside Pinellas County communities including Belleair Beach, Belleair Shore, Clearwater, Indian Rocks Beach, Indian Shores, Madeira Beach, North Redington Beach, Redington Beach, Redington Shores, St. Pete Beach, and Treasure Island.

HILLSBOROUGH COUNTY GOVERNMENT

601 E. Kennedy Blvd.
Tampa 33602
(813) 272-5900 (7 a.m. to 11 p.m., 365 days a year)

Seven commissioners oversee Hillsborough County government. The commissioners appoint a county administrator who runs the day-to-day operations of Hillsborough County. The Hillsborough Board of County Commissioners meets the first and third Wednesdays of each month on the second floor of the County Center building in Tampa, the county seat (address above). Meetings begin at 9 a.m. and are also aired live on Hillsborough Television (HTV).

Hillsborough County's 1,072 square miles (including 24 square miles of inland water area) is mostly unincorporated. Three incorporated municipalities—Tampa, Plant City, and Temple Terrace—occupy 163 square miles. The population of the three cities totals just over 400,000. The population of the unincorporated area of Hillsborough County is just over 800,000.

HILLSBOROUGH COUNTY CITY-COUNTY PLANNING COMMISSION

601 E. Kennedy Blvd., 18th Floor
Tampa
(813) 272-5940
www.theplanningcommission.org

Representatives from the cities of Plant City, Tampa, and Temple Terrace, plus from unincorporated Hillsborough County, meet to discuss common issues.

PINELLAS COUNTY GOVERNMENT

315 Court St.
Clearwater
(727) 464-3000
www.pinellascounty.org

Seven commissioners oversee Pinellas County government, and they appoint a county administrator to manage the operations. The Pinellas Board of County Commissioners meets on the fifth floor of the County Courthouse (address above) the first Tuesday of each month at 9:30 a.m. and the third Tuesday of each month at 3 p.m. (agenda items) and 6 p.m. (citizen input and scheduled public hearings). Zoning matters are discussed at these meetings. Board meetings are televised live on Pinellas County Connection TV (PCC-TV).

The total population of the incorporated areas is almost 650,000. The population of unincorporated Pinellas County is not quite 300,000. Twenty-four incorporated cities or towns exist in Pinellas County. Pinellas County's Web site gives an information summary for each municipality, including population, area, services provided, type of government, and other bare-facts information. Go to www.pinellascounty.org/munic ipalities.htm. Palm Harbor (www.pinellascounty .org/community/ccc/palm-harbor.htm) and Lealman (www.pinellascounty.org/community/ccc/ lealman.htm) are recognized as two distinctive neighborhoods within the unincorporated area of Pinellas County.

PINELLAS PLANNING COUNCIL

600 Cleveland St., Ste. 850
Clearwater
(727) 464-8250
www.co.pinellas.fl.us/ppc

Representatives from each of the 24 cities and towns in Pinellas County, plus representatives

Citizen Universities and Leadership Programs

Citizen Universities or Academies

Citizen universities or academies help residents understand the inner workings of city or county governments. They usually are free or have a minimal materials charge.

Clearwater Citizen Police Academy
(727) 562-4167
www.clearwaterpolice.org/cpa.asp

Learn about traffic enforcement and SWAT weapons plus other aspects of law enforcement. Cost is free for this nine-week course that meets weekly (days vary) from 6 to 9 p.m. Classes are held several times a year, and registration is required.

Clearwater Senior Academy
(727) 562-4167
www.clearwaterpolice.org/cpa.asp

Three weekday sessions focus on issues of particular interest to seniors including the state attorney's Triad Program (reducing victimization of the elderly), fire safety, and services available to seniors. Cost is free.

Hillsborough County Government Leadership University
Office of Neighborhood Relations
(813) 272-5860
www.hillsboroughcounty.org/onr

Learn how Hillsborough County operates by taking this 10-week free course that takes residents behind the scenes at various county departments and discusses planning for future growth.

Pinellas County Citizen University
(727) 464-4600
www.pinellascounty.org/citizenu/default.htm

Find out what it takes to make a county work by taking this free 10-week course giving behind-the-scenes information on everything from balancing the budget to planning for a hurricane evacuation. Cost is $30, which includes a T-shirt and all materials.

St. Petersburg Citizens Police Academy
(727) 893-7128
www.stpete.org/police

St. Petersburg residents, business owners, and non-residents who work in St. Petersburg can attend the free Citizens Police Academy to learn how the city's police department operates, how the K-9 units are trained and used, and more. Classes meet one evening a week.

Leadership Programs

Part of a national association of leadership organizations, these programs typically offer a 10-month program of periodic meetings (one full day per month) that may include overnight trips to the state capitol, a law enforcement "ride along," and other activities. Participants produce a class project. Tuition ranges from $1,250 to $2,500. Some programs allow installment payments, and some offer scholarships. Leadership Pinellas has a Youth Leadership program for students in grades 10–12.

Leadership Hillsborough
http://leadershiphillsborough.com

Leadership Pinellas
(727) 585-8889
www.leadershippinellas.com

Leadership Tampa Bay
(813) 486-8917
www.leadershiptampabay.com

from the unincorporated parts of Pinellas County and from the Pinellas County Schools system, meet to determine county land use issues.

TAMPA BAY REGIONAL PLANNING COUNCIL
4000 Gateway Centre Blvd., Ste. 100
Pinellas Park
(727) 570-5151
www.tbrpc.org
Representatives from 43 jurisdictions within four counties—Hillsborough, Manatee, Pasco, and Pinellas—plus state-appointed representatives address regional issues through the Tampa Bay Regional Planning Council.

PETS AND OTHER ANIMALS

ANIMAL POISON CONTROL
(800) 548-2423
We mention this number up front because here in the Tampa Bay area we lose a pet every now and then to a non-native toad called by various names—marine toad, giant toad, cane toad, or its scientific name *Bufo marinus*. These toads are found only in a few places in Florida, but the Tampa Bay area is one of those places. They're rare here, too. But they are around.

All toads secrete toxins that can irritate pets and humans—always wash your hands and be careful of rubbing your eyes if you've handled any toad. Most regular toads are much smaller than an adult-sized fist. But the *Bufo marinus* is so big and its secretions are so potent, it can kill a small animal. A full-grown *Bufo marinus* is 6 to 9 inches long, which is bigger than the fist of most adults.

The *Bufo marinus* is attracted to pet food and will sometimes get into a pet's food bowl, if it is left outside. Then the animal either bites into the toad by mistake or attacks the toad because it has invaded the pet's territory. Symptoms include drooling, crying, head-shaking, loss of coordination, and convulsions—symptoms similar to epilepsy. One key indicator of toad poisoning is that the dog's gums turn red. If you suspect your pet has been poisoned by a toad, flush its mouth, especially the gums, with water. Be careful that the animal doesn't swallow the water. Call your veterinarian immediately, or the animal poison control center.

Animal Laws and Licenses

HILLSBOROUGH COUNTY DEPARTMENT OF ANIMAL SERVICES
440 N. Falkenburg Rd.
(P.O. Box 89159)
Tampa (33689-0402)
(813) 744-5660
www.hillsboroughcounty.org/animalservices

PINELLAS COUNTY ANIMAL SERVICES
2450 Ulmerton Rd.
Largo
(727) 582-2600
(727) 582-2608 (Rabies/Bite/Quarantine Line)
(727) 582-2604 (Lost or Found Pets Hotline)
www.pinellascounty.org/animalservices/default.htm
It's against the law to feed the squirrels, ducks, and other animals in many areas. We're not trying to be spoilsports. Feeding wild animals hurts them—and sometimes comes back to hurt us. Feeding wild animals teaches them to rely on humans instead of their own natural hunting or gathering skills. We usually feed wild animals the wrong kind of food, and they develop a kind of malnutrition. Feeding animals sometimes results in the animal biting the hand that's feeding it—literally.

You can read about animal laws—both county ordinances and state laws—in Pinellas County at www.pinellascounty.org/animalservices/law.htm. Hillsborough County's laws can be found at www.hillsboroughcounty.org/animalservices/ordinance. Note that these are the county offices for each area. Individual cities may have other requirements.

Basically, however, most dogs, cats, and some other animal pets must have rabies vaccinations, be licensed, and be on a leash when outdoors.

Dog Parks

Many parks in the Tampa Bay area have dog parks—enclosed areas where dogs and owners can socialize with each other. Listings of dog parks can be found at:

- City of Clearwater: www.clearwater-fl.com/gov/depts/parksrec/news/dp_opening.asp
- City of St. Petersburg: www.stpete.org/parks/dogparks.asp.
- City of Tampa: www.tampagov.net/dept_parks_and_recreation (search for "dog parks")
- Hillsborough County: www.hillsborough county.org/parks (search under "Recreation Facilities")
- Pinellas County Parks' Paw Playgrounds: www.pinellascounty.org/park/paw_playgrounds.htm.

Mosquito Abatement

Mosquitos, gnats, no-see-ums—all those pesky, biting insects can also carry diseases. The counties spray and use other means to control biting insects. We need to do our part, too, by emptying planters, pots, kiddie pools, birdbaths, and other outdoor containers so mosquitoes can't breed in them. It doesn't take much water, and it only takes a few days, to have a swarm of skeeters around.

HILLSBOROUGH COUNTY MOSQUITO & AQUATIC WEED CONTROL DEPARTMENT
(813) 635-5400
www.hillsboroughcounty.org/publicworks/transmaintenance/mosquitocontrol

PINELLAS COUNTY MOSQUITO CONTROL
(727) 464-7503
www.pinellascounty.org/publicworks/div_highway-mosquito.htm

Wildlife Removal

The Tampa Bay area—even in the most developed subdivisions—is home to an abundance of wildlife. Raccoons, possums, and armadillos live in trees and palmetto thickets—and sometimes dig their burrows under houses. Alligators live in retention ponds and drainage ditches as well as ponds and lakes. Most of the time, we manage to live with critters around us. But sometimes they can become an expensive or dangerous nuisance.

For information about removing nuisance wildlife, go to the Florida Fish and Wildlife Conservation Commission's Web site at www.florida conservation.org and look for the "Wildlife Assistance" link. To report a nuisance alligator, call (866) 392-4286.

REAL ESTATE

In this section we're supposed to tell you about the various neighborhoods in the area—whether they're mostly single-family homes, apartments or condos, or public housing. Given that we're dealing with two counties here, that kind of detail could fill a book all by itself.

Instead, we'll give you some "get-started" places to do your own research.

You also need to know that buying a house—more accurately, buying homeowner's insurance—during hurricane season can be a bit tricky. Plus, you'll want to know about property taxes.

Discovering Local Neighborhoods

Enter a zip code into www.NeighborhoodLink .com's search option and you'll find almost instant basic info about the average home value and general demographics in that area. Homeowners associations and other neighborhood groups are also listed. Some of them have active sites within www.NeighborhoodLink.com, and some don't.

www.City-Data.com gives detailed information about particular zip codes. Sixty-six people of Danish ancestry, for instance, live in the 34695 zip code area, according to this page. Scroll about halfway down the page, and you'll find a list of neighborhood links. Click on one of these and you'll get almost block-by-block detailed information.

Municipal and County Information

The City of Clearwater's Department of Development and Neighborhood Services can be

(Q) Close-up

White-Pages Rafting

The *Verizon White Pages* and *Verizon Yellow Pages* are distributed free to every address in the area—regardless of what local telephone service is used. That makes them a good vehicle for important public information.

Ready for a quick white-pages rafting trip through the printed version of the *Verizon White Pages*? You might be surprised at what tidbits you'll find. Want to know what time zone Rock Springs, Wyoming, is in? What the warning signs of an imminent lightning strike are? What to take with you to a hurricane shelter? Read on.

Local Area Codes: Before we start, we'll call your attention to one local quirk—local area codes. Most Pinellas County telephone numbers have a 727 area code (Oldsmar is 813). Most Hillsborough County telephone numbers have an 813 area code. But a call from St. Petersburg to Tarpon Springs (both in Pinellas County) is a long distance call. You have to dial a 1 and 727 and then the number.

A call from Clearwater to Tampa, on the other hand, is an extended area call. Do not dial 1. Dial the area code and then the number. You will be charged a flat rate of 30 cents per residential call. St. Petersburg to Tampa is a long distance call. Clearwater to other areas in Hillsborough County may be a long distance call. (See the note on Calling Instructions below to find detailed information on what to dial and when.)

It can be annoying to get the cheerful recording advising you that the 1 is not required and to hang up and dial again. We're just grateful we're not in Pasco County where they have three different area codes.

Color Coded Pages: Before you open the directory, look at the closed pages. Notice that there is a small white section, then a small blue section and a small green section, followed by a large white section. This color pattern may be repeated a couple more times.

If you live in St. Petersburg, the first large white section will be St. Petersburg exchange numbers and the second large white section will be Clearwater exchange numbers. If you live in Clearwater, the sections are reversed. The third section includes Tarpon Springs numbers.

Tampa area phone directories will have a similar geographical arrangement.

Note that numbers for the Keystone-Oldsmar area, in northwest Pinellas County, are included at the end of the large white second section.

FIRST SMALL WHITE SECTION AND WHAT'S IN IT

Emergency Phone Numbers: Inside front cover—You'll find the obvious 911 and the Poison Control Number (800-222-1222). But you'll also find a list of other emergency hotline numbers for help with everything from missing children to domestic abuse to suicide prevention to alligator removal and the FBI.

Ads: There may be a page or two of ads. Keep going.

Customer Info Guide: This is Verizon's table of contents and quick information on how to reach Verizon. Contact information is given in a number of languages. *Verizon White Pages* counts this as page one. (Note: Page numbers given are approximate, as they may change from year to year.)

Other Local (Telephone) Service Providers: Contact information for various other local service providers listed on pages two through four.

The Basics and Beyond: Everything you ever wanted to know about setting up, maintaining, or disconnecting Verizon phone service is found on pages five through eight.

General Information/Calling Instructions

Florida area code map: Page 9

General Information/In Case of Emergency

General Information/Other

Blank pages for caregiver information and other notes and ads

BLUE SECTION

The blue section is the Government Pages. You'll find phone numbers here for each department within each city, for instance, as well as for county, state, and federal offices. If the city information you want isn't in the first blue section, try the second blue section, as that information is given by geographic location.

You'll find county information for all three area counties—Hillsborough, Pasco, and Pinellas. Schools for all three counties are also listed in the County section of the blue pages.

Trust us—it's easier to look up government phone numbers here than in the white pages.

GREEN SECTION

Green pages are a Zip Code Index. The index is sorted alphabetically by city, then by named streets and then by numbered streets. As with the blue city section, the zip code information may be given by geographic area.

reached at (727) 562-4665 or online at www
.clearwater-fl.com/gov/depts/devel_svc/neigh
borhoodservices.

The City of St. Petersburg's Neighborhood
Partnership page (www.stpete.org/neighbor
hoods/index.asp) lists 71 neighborhoods. Click
on any of the 71 links to read a brief description of
the neighborhood including what kind of homes
are there, its history, and what the boundary
streets are. A 72nd neighborhood, Midtown, is
listed separately on the city's main page.

The City of Tampa's Neighborhood and
Community Relations page (www.tampagov.net/
neighborhoods) lists almost 60 neighborhood
associations and has other information to help
you get to know a particular neighborhood.
Click on "Find a Neighborhood" on the left side.
Or enter a specific address in the "My Tampa
Address" feature on the right (scroll down) to find
out everything from the voting precinct to the
evacuation zone for that address.

Hillsborough County's Office of Neighborhood Relations Web page (www.hillsborough
county.org/onr—click on "Neighborhood Listing"
link on left rail) has a map dividing Hillsborough
County into 24 regions. Click on one of the
regions to get a list of homeowners associations
in that area.

Pinellas County has a Web page (www.pin
ellascounty.org/resident) just for newcomers to
the area. Click on the "Property Report" in the
middle of the page and enter an address to find
everything from where the closest recycling centers are to what crimes have been reported in the
neighborhood.

Neighborhood and Civic Association Coalitions

Tampa/Hillsborough County

Tampa Homeowners, an Association of Neighborhoods (THAN), maintains its online presence
at www.tampathan.org. THAN's forty-two members are homeowner organizations and civic
associations in Tampa. Call (813) 837-8011 for
more information.

St. Petersburg/South Pinellas County

The Council of Neighborhood Associations (St.
Petersburg) has a Web page at www.conastpete
.org, maintains a blog page at www.conastpete
.org/blog, and is on NeighborhoodLinks at www
.neighborhoodlink.com/stpetersburg/cona. Their
mailing address is CONA , P.O. Box 13693 , St.
Petersburg 33733.

Clearwater/North Pinellas County

Clearwater Neighborhood Coalition consists of
40 neighborhood associations in the City of
Clearwater and represents about 15,000 families.
Their Web site (www.clearwatercoalition.com)
was under construction at the time of this writing. Contact the City of Clearwater at (727) 562-
4585 to be put in touch with the current officers.

The Council of North County Neighborhoods, Inc., consists of 14 groups in unincorporated north Pinellas County. Their mailing address
is Council of North County Neighborhoods, Inc.,
C/O Law offices, 800 Tarpon Woods Blvd., Palm
Harbor, FL 34685. Their Web site is www.cncnpc
.org/contactus.html.

Finding a Florida Real Estate Agent

FLORIDA ASSOCIATION OF REALTORS
7025 Augusta National Dr.
Orlando
(407) 438-1400
www.floridarealtors.org

**GREATER TAMPA ASSOCIATION OF REAL-
TORS, INC.**
2918 W. Kennedy Blvd.
Tampa
(813) 879-7010
www.gtar.org

**INDEPENDENT REAL ESTATE PROFESSION-
ALS OF PINELLAS, INC.**
www.pinellasirep.org

**NATIONAL ASSOCIATION OF INDEPENDENT
REAL ESTATE BROKERS**
7102 Mardyke Lane
Indianapolis, IN 46226
(317) 549-1709, ext. 133
http://nationalrealestatebrokers.org

PINELLAS REALTOR ORGANIZATION
4590 Ulmerton Rd.
Clearwater
(727) 344-7767
www.tampabayrealtor.com

PROPERTY INSURANCE

FLORIDA INSURANCE COUNCIL
2888 Remington Green Circle, Ste. A
Tallahassee
(850) 386-6668 ext. 225
www.flains.org

The idea behind insurance, of course, is that everyone chips in a bit to help out the unfortunate person whose house burns down. If we've been chipping in and it happens to be our house that burns down—even if we've only been chipping in a short time—then we're very grateful that the pot of money is there to help us. We have a harder time seeing our premiums as a form of benevolence when we pay them year after year and never need to make a claim.

But what happens if everyone's house burns down all at the same time? There might be enough money in the pot to replace all the houses one time, but what if the same thing happens again next year before the pot of money has had a chance to build up again?

That's essentially the property insurance dilemma that has faced Florida the last several years.

In 2004, four major hurricanes hit Florida. The last time that happened, according to the Florida Insurance Council, was in 1886 in Texas. It's doubtful that any insurance claims were paid in 1886 in Texas, but insurance companies in 2004 paid billions of dollars in Florida hurricane-related claims.

Three more hurricanes hit Florida in 2005. Other damage was caused both years by tropical storms. And Florida wasn't the only state where insurance companies had to pay hurricane-related claims. Many insurance companies won't write property insurance policies in Florida because, they say, they can't afford to keep paying claims over and over again without charging higher rates than Florida will allow.

But Florida has known this might be a problem even before 2004. In 1993, after Hurricane Andrew hit south Florida in 1992, the state formed the Florida Hurricane Catastrophe Fund (Cat Fund; www.sbafla.com) using taxpayer funds as a backup, low-cost "just-in-case" reinsurance fund—kind of like insurance companies insuring themselves against catastrophic claims.

The 2004 to 2005 hurricanes depleted the Cat Fund and added surcharges to Florida policyholders' bills. The surcharges were supposed to replenish the fund. But many people don't want to pay higher insurance rates, so the fund is not being replenished to the degree other people think it ought to be.

There are a whole lot of other pieces to this puzzle—too many to try to describe here. Suffice it to say, it's definitely a puzzle. So what do those of us who live here do?

In 2002, the Florida State Legislature created Citizens Property Insurance Corporation, a not-for-profit, tax-exempt corporation, by merging the Florida Residential Property and Casualty Joint Underwriting Association (which provided homeowners with property coverage statewide) and the Florida Windstorm Underwriting Association (which provided designated coastal area residents with wind-only coverage). Many of us whose insurance companies stopped covering homes got insurance through Citizens.

More recently, however, the Florida State Legislature decided Citizens was carrying too many policies and assuming too much risk. So they created the Depopulation Program to transfer some Citizens' policies back to private—usually smaller—companies.

The state has created a "Shop and Compare Rates" page to help residents navigate this maze (www.shopandcomparerates.com).

In the meantime, people are still buying and selling property. Life goes on.

Here are a couple things you need to know about property insurance in Florida:

Flood insurance is NOT included in most homeowners' policies—it's extra, and you have to ask for it. The National Flood Insurance program's Web site is www.floodsmart.gov. And here's FEMA's page about flood insurance (www.fema.gov/news/newsrelease.fema?id=47721)—note the 30-day waiting period before the insurance goes into effect and possible exceptions to the 30-day wait.

Pinellas County flood zone maps are online at http://gis.pinellascounty.org. Hillsborough County flood zone maps are online at http://gisweb.hillsboroughcounty.org/gis/publicviewer.

The hurricane deductible may be as much as 2 percent of the value of the home. That means a home valued at $100,000 could have a deductible as high as $2,000, rather than the standard $500 deductible for other damage. This is the practice in other hurricane-prone states besides Florida. This is one compromise we've made to keep insurance rates lower.

Beware "the box." Or at least be flexible about the date you close on property during hurricane season. Mortgage companies require property insurance to take effect the date of closing. But if a hurricane is near, insurance companies may not be able to write the policy until after the hurricane is gone. Different insurance companies define the geographic "box" differently, but it's usually tied to the National Hurricane Center issuing a tropical storm or hurricane watch notice. Here's a Florida Insurance Council article about insurers not writing new policies during an active hurricane threat (www.flains.org/content/view/574/26/).

FLORIDA OFFICE OF INSURANCE REGULATION
200 East Gaines St.
Tallahassee
(850) 413-3140
www.floir.com

PROPERTY AND OTHER TAXES

FLORIDA DEPARTMENT OF REVENUE
5050 West Tennessee St.
Tallahassee
(850) 488-5050
http://dor.myflorida.com/dor

HILLSBOROUGH COUNTY PROPERTY APPRAISER
16th Floor County Center
601 E. Kennedy Blvd.
Tampa
(813) 272-6100
www.hcpafl.org

PINELLAS COUNTY PROPERTY APPRAISER
2nd Floor County Courthouse
315 Court St.
Clearwater
(727) 464-3207
www.pcpao.org

The Florida Department of Revenue oversees taxes, including sales tax and property tax, and also collects and distributes child support payments. Florida has no state or local personal income tax.

Of course, few people want to pay taxes, but most people want all the services provided by programs funded with tax dollars.

Because Florida allows citizens to propose laws via amendments to the state constitution (see Voter Registration and Elections later in this chapter), we have passed some initiatives that have limited property taxes for a given number of years. Then we've told the legislators to figure out how to pay for schools and other programs with less money.

How Does Your Florida Garden Grow?

Gardening in Florida can be a challenge even if your thumb glows emerald. Our sandy soil, summer heat, strict watering guidelines, and other obstacles can make a gardener's confidence wilt. Never fear. You have an ally who will test the Ph level of your soil, teach you how to make a rain barrel and to use it to water your newly xeriscaped—planted with Florida-friendly plants—garden, and tell you how to get rid of those cinch bugs feasting on your lawn.

The County Extension Offices in Pinellas and Hillsborough counties are extensions of the University of Florida's Institute of Food and Agricultural Sciences. Local extension offices offer ongoing classes and workshops. Many of the classes are free. Some may charge for materials. They can also put you in touch with gardening clubs.

But the Extension Offices offer more than just gardening classes. They also offer classes in financial management, health and nutrition, food safety, going green, and other topics. The Extension Offices also coordinate the 4-H programs in the area. Another group with loads of help for Florida gardeners is the Florida Native Plant Society.

Hillsborough County Extension Office
5339 South CR 579
Seffner
(813) 744-5519
http://hillsborough.extension.ufl.edu

Pinellas County Extension Office
(located at the Florida Botanical Gardens)
12520 Ulmerton Rd.
Largo
(727) 582-2100
http://pinellas.ifas.ufl.edu

Pinellas Chapter of the Florida Native Plants Society
P.O. Box 1661
Pinellas Park 33780-1661
(727) 544-7341
www.pinellasnativeplants.org

Suncoast Native Plant Society, Inc. (Hillsborough County)
P.O. Box 1158
Seffner 33583-1158
(813) 967-4538
www.suncoastnps.org

We have also disagreed on how land should be valued. Should land stay valued at the price we paid for it and adjusted only for inflation and the cost of improvements? Or should the potential use of the land be considered, too?

Property taxes in Florida are so complicated we won't try to summarize them here. If you plan to purchase property in Florida, check with the property appraiser's office before you buy to find out what your tax assessment would be. Do this even if you have looked to see what the previous property owner was paying in taxes—they may have bought their property during a time when property taxes were capped at a particular rate. Ask if you qualify for the Homestead Exemption.

SUPPORT SERVICES

Both of the Tampa Bay area's 211 programs provide a clearinghouse of programs and information to people who need help and to people who want to volunteer their services. Volunteers who answer these lines have information from thousands of community service organizations at their fingertips. Or you can go online and search the database yourself to find information on everything from children's immunizations to substance abuse treatment centers.

Florida Department of Children and Families Hotline Numbers

- Abuse Hotline: (800) 96-ABUSE (962-2873); TDD: (800) 453-5145
- ACCESS Response Unit: (866) 76-ACCES (762-2237). The Automated Community Connection to Economic Self-Sufficiency allows applicants to apply online at www.myflorida.com/accessflorida for help with food, financial, or medical needs.
- Adoption Information: (800) 96-ADOPT (962-3678); out of Florida (904) 353-0679
- Domestic Violence Hotline: (800) 500-1119
- EBT Customer Service: (888) 356-3281. Electronic Benefits Transfer is the system used to administer Food Stamps, now called the Supplemental Nutritional Assistance Program.
- Emergency Financial Assistance for Housing Program : (877) 891-6445
- Food Stamp Fraud Hotline: (866) 76-ACCES (762-2237). Effective October, 2008, the Food Stamp program changed its name to Supplemental Nutritional Assistance Program with benefits administered through the Electronic Benefits Transfer system—but it's still called Food Stamps on the Hotline list.
- Report public assistance fraud online at www.dcf.state.fl.us/access/reportfraud/mainform.aspx.
- SUNCAP Hotline: (866) 762-2237. SUNCAP is another Food Stamp program for people receiving Social Security benefits.

---

211 TAMPA BAY (HILLSBOROUGH COUNTY)
Dial 211 from any cell or land phone
(813) 234-1234 (outside of Hillsborough County)
http://www.211atyourfingertips.org

211 TAMPA BAY CARES (PINELLAS COUNTY)
Dial 211 from any cell or land phone
(727) 210-4233 (administration)
www.211tampabay.org

Alcoholics Anonymous

Both Hillsborough and Pinellas Counties have Spanish language Alcoholics Anonymous meetings. Some meetings have American Sign Language interpreters. Information about Al-Anon and other support groups are available at the numbers below.

PINELLAS COUNTY INTERGROUP, INC.
Central Office
8340 Ulmerton Rd., #220
Largo
(727) 530-0415
(727) 530-0415 (24-hour helpline)
www.aapinellas.org

TRI-COUNTY CENTRAL OFFICE, INC. (HILLSBOROUGH COUNTY)
8019 N. Himes, Ste. 104
Tampa
(813) 933-9123
(813) 933-9123 (24-hour helpline)
www.aatampa-area.org/meetings.html

Domestic Abuse Help

CASA (COMMUNITY ACTION STOPS ABUSE)
St. Petersburg
(727) 895-4912
www.casa-stpete.org

INTERVENTION ENTERPRISES, INC.
Tampa
(813) 933-8865
www.interventionsinc.com

THE HAVEN OF RCS (RELIGIOUS COMMUNITY SERVICES)
Clearwater
(727) 441-2029
(727) 442-4128 (24-hour helpline)

WESTERN JUDICIAL SERVICE
Tampa
(813) 930-9595
www.westernjudicial.com

Gamblers Anonymous

Gamblers Anonymous meetings in Florida are listed at www.gamblersanonymous.org/mtgdirfl .html. The hotline number for the Tampa Bay area is (866) 442-8622.

Non-Profit Development Assistance

NON-PROFIT LEADERSHIP CENTER OF TAMPA BAY
1111 N. West Shore Blvd., Ste. 215
Tampa
(813) 287-8779
www.nlctb.org
Have a great idea to help fill a need in the community and you want to know how to start a non-profit agency? Or you already have a non-profit organization, but now you need help connecting with funders? The Non-Profit Leadership Center of Tampa Bay, a consortium of non-profit agencies in the Tampa Bay area, offers programs on topics ranging from board member training to event planning.

VOTER REGISTRATION AND ELECTIONS

FLORIDA DIVISION OF ELECTIONS
(850) 245-6200
http://election.dos.state.fl.us/voter-registration/voter-reg.shtml

HILLSBOROUGH COUNTY SUPERVISOR OF ELECTIONS
Earl Lennard, Supervisor
2514 Falkenburg Rd.
Tampa
(813) 744-5900
www.votehillsborough.org

PINELLAS COUNTY SUPERVISOR OF ELECTIONS
Deborah Clark, Supervisor
13001 Starkey Rd.
Largo
(727) 464-6108
www.votepinellas.com

Each of these Web sites has information about where to pick up a Voter Registration form, which you can also get online. You will also find extensive information about the elections process on these sites. Because most of the basics are common to voter registration in other states, we'll only call your attention to a couple of points that might be different.

Florida is a closed primary state. You have to be a registered Republican to vote in the Republican primary, a registered Democrat to vote in the Democratic primary, etc. The only exception is if all candidates for a particular office have the same party affiliation and will be unopposed in the general election. In that case, any registered voter may vote in the primary election.

In the general election, all voters receive the same ballot and can vote for any candidate, regardless of party affiliation.

Florida citizens can propose amendments to the Florida Constitution. The direct initiative process involves several steps including forming a political action committee, filing the initiative with the Division of Elections, and collecting sig-

League of Women Voters

Since 1920, the League of Women Voters has worked to help citizens of both genders to understand and participate in the political process. The league, a non-profit organization, has as its mission statement: "The League of Women Voters, a nonpartisan political organization, encourages informed and active participation in government, works to increase understanding of major public policy issues, and influences public policy through education and advocacy."

- The League of Women Voters of Hillsborough County, P.O. Box 1801, Tampa 33601-1801, (813) 831-9774, www.hclwv.org
- The League of Women Voters of North Pinellas County, P.O. Box 6833, Clearwater 33756, (727) 447-1564, www.lwvnorthpinellas.org
- The League of Women Voters, St. Petersburg, P.O. Box 11775, St. Petersburg 33733, (727) 896-5197, www.lwvspa.org

costs and revenues of the affected governments (usually both state and local).

Citizens can also call a constitutional convention to amend the state convention. The State Legislature, the Florida Constitution Revision Committee, and the Florida Taxation and Budget Reform Commission can also propose amendments to the state constitution.

Proponents of citizen initiatives say the process allows citizens to force the legislature to act on issues it would rather not tackle. Opponents of citizen initiatives say they circumvent the legislative process and allow special interest groups with big advertising budgets to further their agendas.

i In 2002, Florida voters approved a constitutional amendment prohibiting confining pregnant sows in spaces too small for them to turn around. The provisions of the amendment didn't go into effect until November, 2008—by which time the two businesses in the state that would have been affected by the amendment were no longer in business.

WATER ISSUES

SOUTHWEST FLORIDA WATER MANAGEMENT DISTRICT (SWFWMD)
Tampa Service Office
7601 U.S. Hwy 301
Tampa
(813) 985-7481
(800) 836-0797 (Florida only)
www.swfwmd.state.fl.us

Local newscasters refer to this organization as "Swiftmud." The Southwest Florida Water Management District is one of five such districts in Florida charged with managing the state's water supply, protecting water quality and natural resources, and overseeing flood protection plans. SWFWMD's Web site is full of information about water issues and about things that don't seem, at first glance, to be related to water.

The *Recreation Guide*, for instance, has much information about SWFWMD's 360,000 acres of

natures on a petition asking that the initiative be placed on the ballot for voters to decide.

The Florida Supreme Court must approve the language of the initiative. The initiative must be about only one topic and must be constitutional. Once the Florida Supreme Court approves the initiative, the committee has up to four years—the longest time allowed by any state that allows citizen initiatives—to collect signatures on a petition asking that the initiative be placed on the ballot.

Once enough signatures are gathered, the Financial Impact Estimating Conference must determine, if possible, the estimated financial impact the amendment would have on both public conservation lands, many of them Florida Wildlife Management Areas, and the camping, fishing, and hunting on these public lands. SWF-WMD's *Florida Friendly Landscaping* guides and workshops help homeowners and business owners keep water use down while still maintaining an attractive landscape. Their *Education* page has loads of activities for students of all ages.

HILLSBOROUGH COUNTY WATER RESOURCES SERVICES
925 E. Twiggs St.
Tampa
(813) 272-5977
www.hillsboroughcounty.org/water

PINELLAS COUNTY UTILITIES
14 S. Fort Harrison Ave.
Clearwater
(727) 464-4000
www.pinellascounty.org/utilities
Water restrictions have been in place for years now. People can only water lawns and wash cars, for example, on certain days and during certain hours. Check with the city you live in to find out what the watering days are or go to one of the above Web sites for more information.

EDUCATION AND CHILD CARE

Education is what you make of it—in the Tampa Bay area or anywhere else.
We offer plenty of educational opportunities—intellectual water to drink, so to speak—here in the Tampa Bay area.

Our public school systems are among the largest in the nation and our schools place well in various rankings. *Newsweek*, for instance, ranked 14 Tampa Bay area high schools among the top 5 percent of public high schools in the nation in its "Top of the Class 2008" listing.

We'll start by talking about child care. Both Hillsborough and Pinellas counties have agencies responsible for licensing day care centers and child-care workers. They also regulate aftercare and summer programs for school-aged kids. And they have other resources for parents, too.

Then we'll give you the scoop on the public school systems here in the Tampa Bay area. We'll give you a mini-glossary of terms you'll hear so you can begin making some sense of the alphabet soup the education bureaucracy serves up.

But public schools aren't the only options parents have.

The Roman Catholic Diocese of St. Petersburg lists more than 50 schools ranging from early childhood centers to high schools. Other private schools, both religious and secular, operate on both sides of Tampa Bay.

Homeschooling has become more and more common in Florida, and many parents in the Tampa Bay area teach their children at home. Sometimes groups of homeschooling parents form cooperatives that offer enrichment opportunities for the children, and we'll give you information about those.

From there, we'll tour adult and higher education institutions in the Tampa Bay area. We'll look at the University of South Florida's campuses on both sides of the bay, at St. Petersburg College and the University Partnership Center, at Eckerd College and its Program for Experienced Learners, and at other colleges and technical institutes.

Finally, we'll explore some non-typical places to learn such as the public libraries—which offer a whole lot more than just books!— the Extension Office, and more.

An observation before we move on: Part of what makes our country great is that we recognize there's more than one way to do things. Nowhere does this show up quite so clearly, perhaps, as in how different places approach education and child care.

In Florida, for example, each county is one school district. In other states, each city may have its own school district—with or without consolidated purchasing programs in place. In Hillsborough County, some child-care programs come under the Department of Children's Services. In Pinellas County, the same programs come under the Department of Health.

Both are equally valid ways of operating. Just be aware that similar information might be found in two different places depending on which side of Tampa Bay you're on.

Thirsty yet? Good! Let's start learning about learning in the Tampa Bay area.

i Keep your children's immunization records handy if you are moving to Florida. Before you can enroll your child in day care, preschool, school, or summer camp, you must have the records transferred to a Florida Immunization Certificate (DOH 680) by a Florida physician or a Florida health department. If you don't have the records, your child may have to start getting the shots all over again.

CHILD CARE, PRESCHOOLS, AFTER-SCHOOL CARE

State of Florida

FLORIDA DEPARTMENT OF CHILDREN AND FAMILIES
1317 Winewood Blvd.
Building 1, Room 202
Tallahassee
(850) 487-1111
www.dcf.state.fl.us/childcare
In addition to managing programs including Medicaid, Food Stamps, foster care, and adoption, among others, Florida Department of Children and Families oversees licensing of child-care facilities including day care, preschools, after-school programs, and summer camps. The Web link we've given you above will take you straight to the page about child care.

i In the "for what it's worth" category, for Department of Children and Families (DCF) and judicial purposes, Florida is broken into six regions and from there into 20 circuits. Hillsborough and Pinellas Counties are both in the Suncoast Region. But Pinellas County is part of the Sixth Judicial Circuit while Hillsborough County comprises all of the Thirteenth Judicial Circuit.

Hillsborough County

CHILD CARE RESOURCE & REFERRAL
5701 E. Hillsborough Ave., Ste. 2301
Tampa
(813) 744-8941, ext. 428
www1.sdhc.k12.fl.us/~early.child/index.htm

Child Care Resource & Referral is part of Hillsborough County School's Department of Early Childhood School Readiness Programs. You'll find information about special education pre-K programs and about Florida's Voluntary Pre-K (subsidized) program here. But this is the number you call to find infant day care, too.

THE EARLY LEARNING COALITION OF HILLSBOROUGH COUNTY
1002 E. Palm Ave., Ste. 100
Tampa
(813) 202-1000
www.elchc.org
The Early Learning Coalition funds the Child Care Resource & Referral service (see above), which is administered by Hillsborough County Public Schools (listed below). ELCHC is concerned about the quality of education being offered as opposed to operational procedures (safety issues, for example).

HILLSBOROUGH COUNTY CHILD CARE LICENSING PROGRAM
8900 N. Armenia Ave., Ste. 210
Tampa
(813) 272-6487
Operated through Hillsborough County's Department of Children's Services, the Hillsborough County Child Care Licensing Program makes sure facilities comply with a host of regulations and requirements, conducts routine inspections, and provides training for child care workers. Click on "Choosing Child Care" to find a link to obtain inspection reports on a child-care facility (www.myflorida.com/childcare/providers).

HILLSBOROUGH COUNTY DEPARTMENT OF CHILDREN'S SERVICES
3110 Clay Mangum Lane
Tampa
(813) 264-3821
www.hillsboroughcounty.org/childrens services
Here you'll find Hillsborough County's Child Care Licensing Program, as well as emergency shelter care, family counseling and treatment

programs, Head Start, respite shelter care, and other services.

HILLSBOROUGH COUNTY HEAD START/ EARLY HEAD START
3639 W. Waters Ave., Ste. 500
Tampa
(813) 272-5140
www.hillsboroughcounty.org
In Hillsborough County, the Head Start programs are part of the county administration. Hillsborough County Head Start has several centers around the county and also partners with Hillsborough County Public Schools and Nova Southeastern University to provide other services. Click on their "Related Links" page for a whole slew of other resources.

HILLSBOROUGH COUNTY PUBLIC SCHOOLS
Early Childhood School Readiness Programs
5701 E. Hillsborough Ave., Ste. 2301
Tampa
(813) 744-8941
www1.sdhc.k12.fl.us/~early.child/index.htm
The Early Childhood School Readiness Programs include day care, child care centers, and school age programs (all called school readiness), Florida's Voluntary Pre-K program, Head Start programs, and Pre-Kindergarten Exceptional Education programs.

Pinellas County

COORDINATED CHILD CARE OF PINELLAS, INC.
10601 Belcher Rd. S.
Largo
(727) 547-5700
www.childcarepinellas.org
Among the services provided by Coordinated Child Care, a non-profit organization funded by the Juvenile Welfare Board and by the Florida Department of Children and Families, are:
- Child Care Resource and Referral of Pinellas, 727-547-5750 or 866-764-0436

- Operation Military Child Care, a Department of Defense initiative to help deployed parents, same number as above
- Child care scholarships through a number of agencies
- Voluntary Pre-K, a state subsidized pre-kindergarten program, 727-547-5782

i Some schools in both Hillsborough and Pinellas Counties have preschools—either as pre-kindergarten classes in elementary schools or as day cares in high schools. Many churches have preschools on site. Sometimes the preschool is part of the church's outreach programming. Sometimes the preschool just leases facilities from the church during the week.

EARLY LEARNING COALITION
5735 Rio Vista Dr.
Clearwater
(727) 548-1439
www.elcpinellas.net
This coalition oversees the education children in day care and preschools get as opposed to overseeing the operational aspects, which are governed by the Pinellas County License Board. Their "Links" page has a number of links to helpful resources.

PINELLAS COUNTY HEAD START/EARLY HEAD START
2210 Tall Pines Drive, Ste. 200
Largo
(727) 547-5900
www.pinellascountyheadstart.org
Pinellas County Head Start/Early Head Start operates several centers in Pinellas County.

PINELLAS COUNTY LICENSE BOARD FOR CHILDREN'S CENTERS AND FAMILY DAY CARE HOMES
Pinellas County Health Department Center
4175 East Bay Dr, Ste. 350
Clearwater
(727) 507-4857
www.pclb.org

The Pinellas County License Board's Web page
is primarily for administrators of day care operations, after-school care programs, summer
camps, etc., but there are a couple of links for
parents. Look for a link to Child Care Resource
and Referral of Pinellas (a service provided by
Coordinated Child Care of Pinellas, listed above)
and also for a link to obtain an inspection report
on a child-care facility.

i Perry C. Harvey Sr. was a Tampa
longshoreman. He was also a thinker
and a doer. Harvey was president of Tampa's longshoreman's union for 30 years.
Tampa's U.S. Congressman Sam Gibbons
(1963–1997), credited Harvey with coining
the term "head start," which became the
name of the National Head Start Association
championed by Gibbons.

PUBLIC SCHOOL SYSTEMS

FLORIDA DEPARTMENT OF EDUCATION
Office of the Commissioner
Turlington Building, Ste. 1514
325 W. Gaines St.
Tallahassee
(850) 245-0505
www.fldoe.org

From Early Learning/Pre-Kindergarten to the
upper levels of the State University system, the
Florida Department of Education oversees it all,
administers federal grants, and compiles data
and statistics on the state of education in Florida.
Some things you need to know about Florida
public schools:

Districts: Each county in Florida is one separate and unified school district. Other "districts"
include Florida Virtual School (see in the Close-up
about special programs), and some stand-alone
schools like the Florida School for the Deaf &
Blind.

FCAT: The Florida Comprehensive Assessment
Test is given to students at different grade levels.
Students in grades 3 through 10 take the Reading
and Mathematics FCAT. Students in grades 4, 8,
and 10 take the Writing FCAT. Students in grades
5, 8, and 11 take the Science FCAT. Students take
the tests sometime during February and March.
Data from the tests are used to determine student mastery of skills and to hold schools and
districts accountable for student learning. You'll
hear people call this the "F-Cat."

No Child Left Behind (NCLB): No Child Left
Behind is the name given to a federal act that
required a means of measuring how well schools
and school districts—and even states—were
teaching children. NCLB also was supposed to
allow parents more choices in deciding which
school their children would attend. The FCAT
(see above) and School Grades (see below) are
part of Florida's response to NCLB. One of the
choices parents have is the Florida Virtual School
(see below under Alternative Programs). You may
hear people call NCLB the "nicklebee."

School Grades: Schools in Florida earn letter
grades (A through F) based on many criteria,

Homeschooling in Florida

In 1985, Florida law officially allowed parents to teach their children at home. Today more than 56,000 children in Florida are registered with public school districts as being home schooled. Other students are registered with private home school organizations that provide testing and other cooperative resources.

Florida's Department of Education and local school districts caution that home education programs are considered non-accredited schools, meaning most home schooled students will not be issued a standard high school diploma.

Homeschooled students may participate in interscholastic extracurricular activities (sports, band, etc.), and they are eligible for the Florida Bright Futures Scholarship program.

For more information:

Florida Department of Education
Office of Independent Education and Parental Choice (IEPC)
(800) 447-1636
www.floridaschoolchoice.org/information/
home_education/faqs.asp#transfer
This Florida DOE Web page has information about home schooling and charter schools.

Hillsborough County Public Schools
Home Education
(813) 272-4995 / Home Education Information Hot Line
www.sdhc.k12.fl.us/homeeducation

Pinellas County Schools
Partnership Schools and Home Education
 (727) 588-5199 / Home Education Information Hot Line
www.pcsb.org/CI/partnership/homeschool
.html

Other Support Services
Florida Parent-Educators Association
(877) 275-3732
www.fpea.com
FPEA is a statewide organization of parent-educators. Both Hillsborough and Pinellas Counties are in District 5. FPEA's Web site offers a "how-to-get-started" guide and a list of support groups and helps, twenty-six of which are in Hillsborough and Pinellas Counties. They also host an annual convention with workshops, vendors, and other activities.

Fellowship of Christian Homeschoolers
www.homeschoollife.com/sysfiles/member/
index_public.cfm?memberid=125

Pinellas Parent Educators Association
www.homeschool-life.com/fl/ppea

but mostly on how well their students do on the FCAT and other tests, how much improvement is made from year to year (Annual Yearly Progress or AYP), etc. To see the grade a particular school or school district has earned, go to http://school grades.fldoe.org).

Sunshine State Standards: The State Board of Education decides what students should be expected to achieve at different grade levels and for different subjects. To see what the Sunshine State Standards are for each grade and subject, go to www.fldoe.org/bii/curriculum/sss/sss1996.asp.

HILLSBOROUGH COUNTY PUBLIC SCHOOLS
901 E. Kennedy Blvd.
Tampa
(813) 272-4000
www.sdhc.k12.fl.us
Hillsborough County Public Schools, the eighth largest school system in the United States, serves

just over 180,000 students in its K-12 programs. Hillsborough County Public Schools has 139 elementary schools, 43 middle schools, 25 high schools, two K-8 schools, 26 charter schools, and 2 career centers.

Go to www.sdhc.k12.fl.us/choice to learn about your various options and for information about enrolling. If your child has never attended school in Hillsborough County before, you will need to complete a paper application before you can do anything else. You will need your state-issued photo I.D. (driver license or I.D.) and proof of address (utility bill, rental agreement, or lease), your child's birth certificate, child's Social Security number, most recent report card, and Florida Certificate of Immunization (DOH 680). Call 813-272-4000 to find out where to apply based on where you live.

PINELLAS COUNTY SCHOOLS
301 4th St. S.W.
Largo
(727) 588-6000
www.pinellas.k12.fl.us
www.pcsb.org

With almost 105,000 students in grades K–12, Pinellas County Schools is the 25th largest school district in the nation. Pinellas County has 80 elementary schools, 23 middle schools, 17 high schools, 5 exceptional schools, 9 charter schools, and 5 secondary or alternative education centers.

Go to any Pinellas County School to begin the enrollment process. Bring a state-issued photo I.D. (driver license or I.D.) and proof of address (utility bill, rental agreement, or lease). You will be issued a user I.D. and a password. Use the computer at the school or go online at home (www.pcsb.org) to reserve a seat at the close-to-home, magnet, or fundamental school of your choice. Seats are assigned on a space-available basis, so be prepared with a second or third choice. Once you have been assigned a school, take the child's birth certificate, child's Social Security number, proof of residency, most recent report card, Florida Certificate of Immunization (DOH 680), and physical examination certificate to the assigned school.

NON-PUBLIC SCHOOL SYSTEMS

The Florida Department of Education has information about the requirements private schools must meet and a listing of private schools, including military and boarding schools. Go to www.floridaschoolchoice.org/information/private_schools.

There are a number of non-public schools in the Tampa Bay area. Some are religious schools, while others are private, non-religious schools.

THE EPISCOPAL DIOCESE OF SOUTHWEST FLORIDA
7313 Merchant Court
Sarasota
(941) 556-0315
www.episcopalswfl.org/episcopal_schools

The Episcopal Diocese lists nine schools in the Tampa Bay area serving only pre-elementary age children and seven schools serving children in the elementary grades and higher. Three of those schools include high schools. The schools are open to non-Episcopalians.

FLORIDA COUNCIL OF INDEPENDENT SCHOOLS
1211 N. Westshore Blvd, Ste. 612
Tampa
(813) 287-2820
www.fcis.org

The Florida Council of Independent Schools has more than 150 member schools throughout Florida. Sixty of those schools are in Central Florida, which includes Hillsborough and Pinellas Counties.

ROMAN CATHOLIC DIOCESE OF ST. PETERSBURG
Office of Catholic Schools and Centers
P.O. Box 40200
St. Petersburg
(727) 347-5539
www.dioceseofstpete.org

The Office of Catholic Schools and Centers lists 16 early childhood education centers, 28 elementary schools, 6 high schools, and 2 special education schools. Non-Catholic students may enroll.

◉ Close-up

Hillsborough and Pinellas Schools Special Programs

The programs listed here differ from the special services offered in most schools, such as gifted programs and Title I services, which typically involve a few students meeting with a remedial reading or math teacher one or more times a week. They also differ from honors or advanced placement classes. These special programs involve the character of the entire school and may require a different level of commitment from parents and students. Parents may even have to provide transportation to and from the school.

In addition to the geographically close-to-home or zoned schools, there are six types of special schools or programs. Some schools have application deadlines, so start investigating early.

Career Academies (career and technical education) allow high-school students to blend career and technical training with academic subjects. Some students can earn industry certification as part of the program, helping them to step into the work world after graduation or to move on to advanced technical training or college.

Programs in Hillsborough County include the Academy of Computer Game Design, Firefighter/ EMT, Plant Biotechnology, and others. Programs in Pinellas County include the Academy of Architectural Design and Building Technologies, Academy of Finance, Automotive Academy, Jacobson Culinary Arts Academy, and others.

Charter schools are funded by the public school system, but have their own boards of directors, hire their own teachers, and may have other rules, requirements, and curricula—Athenian Academy in Dunedin, for instance, offers language immersion in Greek and Spanish to elementary school students. Parents apply directly to a charter school rather than going through the school district.

Fundamental Schools generally require parents to attend conferences and parent meetings, require students to do daily homework and abide by a stricter dress code, and stress the academic basics.

Magnet Schools are offered at all grade levels (except, in some cases, kindergarten) and have very specialized curricula in addition to academic classes. Some magnet programs have additional entrance requirements.

A sampling of magnet programs around the Tampa Bay area include Animal Science (Hillsborough, elementary), Center for Mathematics and Engineering (Pinellas, elementary), Law & Public Service (Hillsborough, middle), Center for the Arts & Communication Studies (Pinellas, middle), Urban Teaching Academy (Hillsborough, high), and Center for Wellness and Medical Professions (Pinellas, high). International Baccalaureate programs are offered on both sides of Tampa Bay.

Partnership Schools bring the private sector and the public sector together to provide students with experiences outside the classroom. Partnership Schools in Hillsborough County are the Rampello K–8 (Downtown Partnership) and the Roland Park K–8 (Westshore Business Alliance). Partnership Schools in Pinellas County include the Modesta Robbins Partnership School (Chi Chi Rodriguez Academy, part of the First Tee Golf program, for students in grades 4 through 8) and the Early College Program (dual enrollment at St. Petersburg College, allowing students to earn an associate of arts degree concurrently with their high school diploma).

Virtual Schools offer classes online, with teacher interaction and with parents as learning coaches.

ADULT PUBLIC EDUCATION

Both Hillsborough and Pinellas County Schools offer adult education programs ranging from GED classes to Technical Education Centers that offer certification in various industries including Air Conditioning, Automotive, Cosmetology, and others. Adult Literacy, English for Speakers of Other Languages, Motorcycle Rider Safety courses, and Citizenship courses, as well as other programs make the public school systems a valuable technical education resource for adults.

HILLSBOROUGH COUNTY PUBLIC SCHOOLS
Adult and Community Education
(813) 740-7750
www.ace.mysdhc.org

PINELLAS COUNTY SCHOOLS
Adult and Community Schools
(727) 588-6321
www.pinellas.k12.fl.us/workforce/adultand
communityed.html

COLLEGES AND UNIVERSITIES

ECKERD COLLEGE
4200 54th Ave. S.
St. Petersburg
(727) 867-1166, (800) 456-9009
www.eckerd.edu
Eckerd College, located at the southern tip of the Pinellas Peninsula, began in 1958 as Florida Presbyterian College. Eckerd College is still related by covenant to the Presbyterian Church (USA) and is a private, coeducational college of liberal arts and sciences—the only national private liberal arts college in Florida. The Commission on Colleges of the Southern Association of Colleges and Schools has accredited Eckerd College to award the baccalaureate degree.

In addition to drawing students from around the world to its residential student community, Eckerd College's Program for Experienced Learners allows working adults to earn their degrees through creative programming and intensive study. PEL courses are offered on several satellite campuses around the Tampa Bay area. Eckerd College also offers continuing education opportunities through the Osher Lifelong Learning Institute and Elderhostel. Eckerd College has been included on numerous "Best-of" lists. (See the Arts chapter for information on the Writers in Paradise seminar.)

HILLSBOROUGH COMMUNITY COLLEGE
District Administrative Office
39 Columbia Dr.
(P.O. Box 31127)
Tampa
(813) 253-7000, 866-253-7077
www.hccfl.edu
Hillsborough Community College has grown from its 1968 beginnings to include four campuses and two satellite locations. Since 2008, they also have become one of the few community colleges in the nation with its own residence hall, Hawk's Landing. Hillsborough Community College is accredited by the Southern Association of Colleges and Schools.

Hillsborough Community College's locations include Brandon, home to HCC's Honors Institute; Dale Mabry, the largest campus, which specializes in health sciences and technology; the MacDill Education Center at MacDill Air Force Base, which is open to both civilians and military personnel; Plant City, which houses the institute of Florida Studies Program and the environmental centers; SouthShore (Ruskin), which offers a university-partnership program so students can earn bachelor's and master's degrees; and Ybor City, the college's headquarters for law enforcement, fire science, and related disciplines, but which is also known for its arts programs (see listings in Arts chapter).

INTERNATIONAL ACADEMY OF DESIGN AND TECHNOLOGY
5104 Eisenhower Blvd.
Tampa
(888) 315-6111
www.academy.edu
The International Academy of Design and Technology began in 1977 with an emphasis on

design and merchandising. Today, IADT, accredited by the Accrediting Council for Independent Colleges and Schools to confer associate's, bachelor's, and master's degrees, offers courses in fashion and interior design, computer animation, digital photography, and recording arts, as well as other courses.

ST. PETERSBURG COLLEGE
District Office
6021 142nd Ave. N.
Largo
P.O. Box 13489
St. Petersburg 33733-3489
(727) 341-4772

Founded in 1927 as a private, non-profit community college, St. Petersburg College today is a public institution with 10 learning sites around Pinellas County. In 2001, St. Petersburg college became the first community college in the state to offer four-year degrees in addition to its two-year curriculum. St. Petersburg College is accredited by the Commission on Colleges of the Southern Association of Colleges and Schools to award both associate's and bachelor's degrees.

St. Petersburg College's locations include the Allstate Center at the southern end of the Pinellas Peninsula, which houses the Southeastern Public Safety Institute; the Caruth Health Education Center in mid-Pinellas, which offers medical and veterinary courses; the Clearwater Campus, home to a number of design programs as well as the Program for the Deaf and Hard of Hearing; the EpiCenter and EpiCenter Corporate Training Center in Largo, which provides technology management programs; the Palladium, a performing arts facility (see Arts chapter); the Downtown Campus, offering a variety of courses; the Midtown Campus, which hosts the Center for Achievement; the St. Petersburg/Gibbs Campus, the oldest of the current campuses (opened in 1942), which is home to the college's Music Center and Planetarium; the Seminole Campus, which hosts the University Partnership Center and the eCampus operations; and the Tarpon Springs Campus, home of the Leepa-Rattner Museum of Art (see Arts chapter).

STETSON UNIVERSITY COLLEGE OF LAW
1401 61st St. S.
Gulfport
(727) 562-7800
www.law.stetson.edu

Florida's oldest law school, Stetson University College of Law, part of Stetson University in DeLand, has been training lawyers since 1900. In 1954 Stetson University College of Law moved from the middle of the state to Gulfport in Pinellas County. Located in what used to be the Hotel Rolyat, built in 1925, Stetson University College of Law is noted for its trial law, international law, and elder law programs, and it has published the *Stetson Law Review,* an academic journal, since 1970. In 2004 Stetson University College of Law began offering evening classes at the Tampa Law Center (1700 N. Tampa Street, Tampa). The College of Law is accredited by the American Bar Association Section of Legal Education and Admissions to the Bar.

UNIVERSITY OF SOUTH FLORIDA
4202 E. Fowler Ave., ADM241
Tampa
(813) 974-2011
www.usf.edu

Founded in 1956, the University of South Florida began holding classes in 1960 with a group of 2,000 students meeting in five buildings. Today, USF is the ninth largest public university in the nation, serving more than 46,000 students on campuses in five separate locations around the Tampa Bay area. USF's research contracts and grants total more than $360 million each year and it offers more than 200 degree programs at all levels. For a more detailed description of USF Health, see the Health Care, Wellness, and Senior Living chapter.

USF's campuses include the main Tampa campus, which houses USF health, the athletics program (USF is a member of the Big East Athletic Conference), and a number of other programs and colleges; the Downtown Center, which offers business management programs; the Polytechnic campus in Lakeland, the state's only polytechnic campus, which offers science and technology programs; the St. Petersburg campus, which offers graduate and undergraduate programs in arts and sciences, business, and education programs; and the Sarasota-Manatee campus, which offers nursing, engineering, education, and business programs.

The University of South Florida is accredited by the Commission on Colleges of the Southern Association of Colleges and Schools.

UNIVERSITY OF TAMPA
401 W. Kennedy Blvd.
Tampa
(813) 253-3333
www.ut.edu

The University of Tampa, located on the grounds of the Henry B. Plant's Tampa Bay Hotel (see Accommodations chapter), is a private, four-year liberal arts college. In 1933, Tampa Junior College moved into the recently closed hotel and, shortly after, became the University of Tampa. Today the University of Tampa awards both bachelor's and master's degrees in a number of programs. UT's Evening College allows working adults to complete college courses.

In addition to being accredited by the Commission on Colleges of the Southern Association of Colleges and Schools, the University of Tampa's John H. Sykes College of Business holds accreditation from the Association to Advance Collegiate Schools of Business and has one of Florida's largest MBA programs. Additionally, the University of Tampa is an associate member of a European accrediting association, the European Council of International Schools.

OTHER PLACES TO LEARN

County Extension Offices

We mentioned the County Extension Offices back in the Relocation chapter as good places to find gardening classes. And they are—you can learn how to compost, find out how to conserve water by making rain barrels, and learn about wildlife in the area.

But the extension offices offer more than just gardening classes. They also offer classes in financial management, health and nutrition, food safety, going green, and other topics. The extension offices also coordinate the 4-H programs in the area.

The County Extension Offices in Pinellas and Hillsborough counties are extensions of the University of Florida's Institute of Food and Agricultural Sciences. Local extension offices offer ongoing classes and workshops. Many of the classes are free. Some may charge for materials. If they don't have the answer to your questions, they have a whole university system to ask.

HILLSBOROUGH COUNTY EXTENSION OFFICE
5339 South CR 579
Seffner
(813) 744-5519
http://hillsborough.extension.ufl.edu

PINELLAS COUNTY EXTENSION OFFICE
(located at the Florida Botanical Gardens)
12520 Ulmerton Rd.
Largo
(727) 582-2100
http://pinellas.ifas.ufl.edu

Fine Arts Centers

We listed these in the Arts chapter, so we'll not repeat the information here. But we will remind you that they offer hands-on classes in everything from painting to photography and more.

Libraries

Libraries today are about more than just books. Today's libraries offer banks of public computers, which allow people to access electronically archived information and to use basic computer programs to create and send documents. Many libraries have archives of historical documents and photographs that are open to public research. Most libraries lend CDs, audio books, and DVDs.

Contact the appropriate county's Public Library Cooperative for information about:

Bookmobiles bring books to people instead of waiting for people to come to the library.

Children's programs including story times, summer reading programs, and teen programs.

Database subscriptions can be expensive. Most libraries offer patrons home access to some electronic databases. The reference librarian has access to others, if you can't find what you need.

Homework hotlines and other homework help programs are available at many libraries.

Literacy and ESOL programs, are offered, including programs for the deaf and hard of hearing.

Meeting rooms for organizations are generally free or available at a nominal charge.

Talking Book Library offers Braille and recorded books, periodicals, and other literature.

Voter registration information and materials are at all public libraries.

HILLSBOROUGH COUNTY PUBLIC LIBRARY COOPERATIVE

Tampa-Hillsborough County Public Library
900 N. Ashley Drive
Tampa
(813) 273-3652
www.hcplc.org
www.hillsboroughcounty.org/library/

Call the phone number listed above to reach any of the Tampa-Hillsborough County branch libraries or to reach the Hillsborough County Public Library Cooperative—they all share one direct number. The Hillsborough County Public Library Cooperative includes the Tampa-Hillsborough County Public Library, Bruton Memorial Library in Plant City (813-757-9215) and Temple Terrace Public Library (813-506-6770).

i More than one Tampa Bay area library was begun thanks to Philadelphia philanthropist Andrew Carnegie, who funded more than 2,500 public libraries between 1883 and 1929. One of Carnegie's requirements—one we take for granted today—changed library operations dramatically. Carnegie required libraries to allow patrons to browse books for themselves. Prior to that, librarians retrieved books, which patrons requested.

PINELLAS PUBLIC LIBRARY COOPERATIVE
1330 Cleveland St.
Clearwater
(727) 441-8408
www.pplc.us

The Pinellas Public Library Cooperative provides services to a number of libraries in the unincorporated areas of Pinellas County and to these member libraries:

- Clearwater (727-562-4970, www.myclear water.com/cpl)
- Dunedin (727-298-3080, www.dunedingov .com)
- East Lake Community (727-773-2665, www .eastlakelibrary.org)
- Gulf Beaches (727-391-2828, www.gulf beacheslib.org)
- Gulfport (727-893-1074, www.tblc.org/gpl)
- Largo (727-587-6715, www.largo.com)
- Oldsmar (813-749-1178, www.oldsmarlibrary .org)
- Safety Harbor (727-724-1525, www.tblc.org/ shpl)
- Seminole (727-394-6905, www.spcollege.edu/ scl)
- St. Petersburg (727-893-7724, www.splibraries .org)
- St. Pete Beach (727-363-9238, www.tblc.org/ spb)
- Tarpon Springs (727-43-4922, www.tblc.org/ tarpon)

The Seminole Community Library has a joint-use agreement with St. Petersburg College and adjoins the college's Seminole campus.

HEALTH CARE, WELLNESS, AND SENIOR LIVING

We all get sick from time to time. Accidents happen and we get injured.
It's nice to know skilled people and well-equipped facilities in the Tampa Bay area have us covered. We'll be telling you where those facilities are and for what services they're noted.

Good health, however, is about more than recovering from sickness or injury. Good health means staying well, physically and mentally. That takes action on our part. Here we'll tell you about programs that can give you a boost toward living a healthy lifestyle.

When it comes to senior living, let's just say we've had lots of experience in that field. There was a time when the Tampa Bay area—St. Petersburg, in particular—was nicknamed "God's Waiting Room" and was noted for its number of seniors and retirees.

Those were the days of the fabled green benches that dotted the downtown sidewalks. That was back when the town boosters were pitching St. Petersburg, land of sunshine and carefree living, as the perfect place to winter—figuratively as well as literally.

The benches weren't always green. The first benches were orange, set out by a local real estate agent and one of St. Petersburg's early mayors, Noel Mitchell. The benches were a means of advertising Mitchell's real estate business. Other businessmen followed suit. Before long, St. Petersburg was awash in a mish-mash of colored benches.

In 1916, Mayor Al Lang decreed the benches should be one standard size and color—green. We're not talking just a few benches here. By the 1950s, there were as many as 8,000 benches, most of them installed back to back on the curb side of the sidewalk.

The reality was that the benches weren't just for seniors. The benches heard the whispers of lovers, the chattering of gossips, the dickering of businessmen. They seated, in many respects, St. Petersburg's social salons.

Part of St. Petersburg, that is. The benches did not hear much of what African-American society was saying. The reality was that the benches were understood to be for whites only.

Regardless of the realities, the image prevailed of St. Petersburg as a city of retirees whiling away their remaining days sitting in the sunshine on green benches. So much so that in the early 1960s at least one national meat packer thought it futile to advertise its products in St. Petersburg papers—people in St. Petersburg being too old to chew meat.

The benches are now gone, but we still have a larger percentage of seniors than other places in the United States.

As a nation, not quite 13 percent of our population is age 65 or older. In Florida, 17 percent of the population is age 65 or older. Tampa hovers around 12 percent of its population being age 65 or older. St. Petersburg matches Florida's 17 percent or so. Almost 20 percent of Clearwater's population, on the other hand, is age 65 or older.

So we understand the need for specialized services. In fact, our Neighborly Care Network has been providing those kinds of services for almost 50 years.

You've heard of Meals on Wheels? Pinellas County is where the first federally funded Meals on Wheels program began back in 1968, the same year the nation's first Adult Day Care Center opened—yup, right here. One of the more popular services our senior agencies provide is employment—many of our seniors want to work, whether as paid employees or as unpaid volunteers.

While we are proud to provide these kinds of services to our older residents, we are equally proud of our intergenerational community, working together to maximize this life's opportunities.

And, yes, our newspapers and television stations carry ads for meat.

HEALTH CARE AND WELLNESS

Not only do we have hospitals and other medical facilities strategically placed around the Tampa Bay area, we're also home to the University of South Florida's medical program (look for a Close-up later in this chapter) and to two other highly acclaimed research and care centers—H. Lee Moffitt Cancer Center & Research Institute, and the Johnnie B. Byrd, Sr., Alzheimer's Center & Research Institute. The Shriners Hospitals for Children have their Shriners International Headquarters in Tampa and an orthopaedic hospital here, too.

Government Agencies

State Health Departments

FLORIDA AGENCY FOR HEALTH CARE ADMINISTRATION
2727 Mahan Dr.
Tallahassee
(888) 419-3456
www.ahca.myflorida.com
The Florida Agency for Health Care Administration administers the $16 billion Medicaid program that serves more than two million Florida residents, licenses health care facilities in the state, and shares health care data through the Florida Center for Health Information and Policy Analysis.

To find a health care facility, or to compare health care facilities, go to http://FloridaHealth Finder.gov. If you have Medicaid questions, go to www.mymedicaid-florida.com, or contact one of the field offices listed below.

FLORIDA DEPARTMENT OF HEALTH
4052 Bald Cypress Way
Tallahassee
(850) 245-4147
www.floridashealth.com
Florida Department of Health registers all birth,

death, marriage, and divorce certificates; grants licenses to some health care professionals and permits to some facilities including tattoo parlors; monitor's Florida's environmental health issues such as rabies programs, beach water quality, and mosquito control; and has programs dealing with everything from nutrition to AIDS.

i Want to find out how local hospitals compare in terms of mortality and infection rates? Or how a particular nursing home is faring? Then go to www.florida healthfinder.gov.

MEDICAID AREA OFFICE 5 (PASCO AND PINELLAS COUNTIES)
525 Mirror Lake Dr. N., Ste. 510
St. Petersburg
(727) 552-1191, (800) 299-4844

MEDICAID AREA OFFICE 6 (HILLSBOROUGH AND FOUR OTHER COUNTIES)
6800 N. Dale Mabry Hwy, Ste. 220
Tampa
(813) 871-7600, (800) 226-2316

County Health Departments

County Health Departments can help you with back-to-school physicals and immunizations and with registering for a special-needs hurricane shelter (for people meeting certain medical criteria). They provide a host of other services, too, including performing inspections at restaurants and health care, child-care, and other facilities.

HILLSBOROUGH COUNTY HEALTH DEPARTMENT
1105 E. Kennedy Blvd.
Tampa
(813) 307-8015
www.hillscountyhealth.org

Health care: In addition to six health centers around Hillsborough County, the Hillsborough County Health Department also has an Immunization and Refugee Center (813-307-8077), a Nutrition Administration Center (813-307-8074), and a TB Health Center (813-307-8047).

Wellness programs: Click on the "Community Health" link for information on wellness programs including the Family Reunion Program, designed to help families form healthy habits together.

PINELLAS COUNTY HEALTH AND HUMAN SERVICES DEPARTMENT
2189 Cleveland St., Ste. 230
Clearwater
(727) 464-8400

647 1st Ave. N.
St. Petersburg
(727) 582-7781
Pinellas County Health and Human Services Department provides prescription drug assistance, medical care to our community's indigent and uninsured, dental assistance, and other care programs.

PINELLAS COUNTY HEALTH DEPARTMENT
205 Dr. Martin Luther King St. N.
St. Petersburg
(727) 824-6900
www.pinellashealth.com
Health care: Pinellas County Health Department has five centers, three offering dental services in addition to other health services, two satellite clinics, and an office center. The Pinellas County Health Department offers a full range of health services including child car seat safety and tobacco prevention programs.

Wellness programs: The PCHD's Wellness Web site at www.pinellaswellness.com has much healthy-living information. See the Healthy Choices Restaurant sidebar elsewhere in this chapter.

PINELLAS COUNTY HOUSING AUTHORITY
11479 Ulmerton Rd.
Largo
(727) 443-7684
www.pin-cha.org

Finding affordable housing can be a challenge for the disabled and the elderly. Pinellas County Housing Authority offers some solutions. Additionally, they maintain a list of privately owned—often the owner is a religious or other not-for-profit organization—buildings that accept government assistance and set rent prices based on a sliding scale. For the list of subsidized apartments in Pinellas County, go to www.pin-cha.org/documents/subsidizedapartmentslist.pdf.

TAMPA HOUSING AUTHORITY
1529 W. Main St.
Tampa
(813) 253-0551
www.thafl.com
The Tampa Housing Authority's Web page provides a link to www.gosection8.com, which has a map showing available Section 8 housing anywhere in the country. Or go to www.thafl.com/depts/assist_housing/subsidized.asp to find a list of subsidized housing in Hillsborough County.

Hospices
THE HOSPICE FOUNDATION OF THE FLORIDA SUNCOAST
5771 Roosevelt Blvd.
Clearwater
(727) 586-4432
www.thehospice.org
The Hospice of the Florida Suncoast, which provides services to patients and their families in Pinellas County, is the largest community-based, not-for-profit provider of hospice services in the nation. In addition to providing supportive medical services to patients in hospitals, nursing homes, and at home, the hospice also provides counseling, helps accessing community and financial resources, advance care planning, and other services. SteppingStones4Kids.org helps families with seriously ill children or who experience the death of an infant or an older child. The hospice operates a number of community care centers, the AIDS Service Association of Pinellas, one on-site care facility in mid-Pinellas County with another being planned for north Pinellas County, and three thrift stores.

Close-up

USF Health's Corner on the World of Medicine

A remarkable world exists in a corner of the University of Florida's main Tampa campus. Florida Department of Transportation traffic maps suggest that about 50,000 cars pass by this corner every day. The people who come here—to work, to learn, to get well—know that what happens inside the buildings on this corner, quite literally, is changing the world.

A TRIP AROUND THE BLOCK

The University of South Florida's main Tampa campus sits in north Tampa, across the street from MOSI—the Museum of Science and Industry. The campus's main entrance is on East Fowler Avenue, halfway between Bruce B. Downs Boulevard and 50th Street. Our visit begins halfway up Bruce B. Downs Boulevard just past Lake Behnke. The first cluster of buildings we see houses USF Health—formerly, USF Medical Center.

In 1965, only five years after the University of South Florida opened, the Florida State Legislature established the College of Medicine at the University. But building a college—the program, not just the building—takes time. The first class enrolled in 1971. The College of Nursing (1974) and the College of Public Health (1984) followed.

Within each of these colleges are schools, such as the College of Medicine's School of Physical Therapy; programs, such as the Doctorate of Nursing Practice degree offered by the College of Nursing; and unparalleled opportunities, such as the Master's International Peace Corps program offered by the College of Public Health. This first group of buildings represents that first core cluster of colleges, now USF Health.

Sitting south of those buildings and on the east side of the lake is the Shriners Hospital for Children. Since 1985, Shriners Hospital for Children has provided free orthopaedic care for children regardless of their ability to pay and regardless of whether they needed financial assistance. (See sidebar elsewhere in this chapter.)

Northeast of Shriners Hospital for Children is the H. Lee Moffitt Cancer Center & Research Institute, established by the Florida State Legislature in 1986 with cigarette tax money. More than 272,000 people come to the Moffitt Cancer Center for outpatient services each year. The partnership between USF, Moffitt, and other physicians and health care facilities brought the Blood and Marrow Transplant Program (1989), now the largest blood and marrow transplant center in the southeastern United States, and the Lifetime Cancer Screening Center (1993) to the USF campus.

Just north of the Moffitt Cancer Center is the Vincent A. Stabile Research Building, a 2003 expansion of the Moffitt Research Institute. Research at the Moffitt Research Institute includes work to develop a cancer vaccine, melanoma research, and other studies. The Eye Institute is near the Moffitt Research Institute.

Moving further north and east, we come to the Carol and Frank Morsani Center for Advanced Health Care. The focus at the Morsani Center for Advanced Health Care—and at the South Tampa Center for Advanced Health Care near Davis Islands—is on team care and patient convenience and comfort.

North and east of the Morsani Center for Advanced Health is the Johnnie B. Byrd, Sr., Alzheimer's Center and Research Institute on East Fletcher Avenue. Established by the Florida State Legislature in 2002, the Byrd Alzheimer's Center and Research Institute has partnered with a number of universities and other organizations around the nation to conduct research, including clinical drug trials.

Just west of the Byrd Institute and directly north of the Morsani Center is a cluster of buildings housing Health Sciences, Psychiatry, and the School of Physical Therapy, added to the College of Medicine in 1998.

Continuing west, we come to the Luis de La Parte Florida Mental Health Institute, which monitors mental health law and policy, collects data, and conducts research in various fields ranging from autism to aging.

South and west from the Florida Mental Health Institute—we're now near the corner of Bruce B. Downs Boulevard and East Fletcher Avenue—we come to the College of Public Health, established in 1994. Still further south is the Children's Medical Services Building and the USF Health Clinic and Endoscopy Center.

Then we're back where we started. But if we cross Bruce B. Downs Boulevard via the elevated walkway, we're at Tampa James A. Haley Veterans' Hospital, one of USF Health's teaching hospitals. And closer to East Fowler Avenue, somewhat removed from the rest of Health Services area, is the University Diagnostic Institute.

OUTLYING FACILITIES

The Children's Research Institute is at All Children's Hospital in St. Petersburg. Bay Pines VA Health Care System and Tampa General are teaching hospitals for USF Health students.

H. Lee Moffitt Cancer Center & Research Institute
12902 Magnolia Dr.
Tampa
(888) 663-3488
(813) 745-4673, (800) 456-3434
www.moffitt.org

Johnnie B. Byrd, Sr., Alzheimer's Center & Research Institute
4001 E. Fletcher Ave.
Tampa 33613
(813) 866-1611
www.byrdinstitute.org

Louis de la Parte Florida Mental Health Institute
University of South Florida
13301 Bruce B. Downs Blvd.
Tampa
(813) 974-4602
www.home.fmhi.usf.edu

Shriners Hospital for Children
12502 USF Pine Dr.
Tampa 33612-9411
(813) 972-2250
www.shrinershq.org/Hospitals/tampa

The University of South Florida
4202 E. Fowler Ave., ADM241
Tampa
(813) 974-2011
www.health.usf.edu

LIFEPATH HOSPICE
12973 Telecom Parkway, Ste. 100
Temple Terrace
(813) 877-2200, (800) 209-2200
www.lifepath-hospice.org
LifePath Hospice serves patients and their families in Hillsborough County with end-of-life care, providing medical support services, palliative care, counseling, and help in navigating the healthcare and community assistance programs. The National Institute has accredited LifePath Hospice for Jewish Hospice, and they provide a Children's Grief Center. LifePath Hospice operates three community resource centers, one of which includes an on-site care facility, two other on-site care facilities, and two thrift stores.

Hospitals

In the interest of space, we've chosen only a select program or two within each hospital to spotlight. Visit each hospital's Web site to find a full listing of centers, programs, and services provided.

Tampa/Hillsborough County
BRANDON REGIONAL HOSPITAL
119 Oakfield Dr.
Brandon
(813) 681-5551
www.brandonhospital.com
Health care: Brandon Regional Hospital provides a full range of health care services, but is particularly noted for its Joint Commission certified Stroke Center and for its Cardiac Center. The Baby Suites obstetrical unit includes a Neonatal Intensive Care Unit.
Wellness programs: Print out fact sheets on a comprehensive A to Z listing of illnesses and conditions on Brandon Regional Hospital's "Health Info" tab. Call and ask about their Health Library.

KINDRED HOSPITAL
4801 N. Howard Ave.
Tampa
(813) 874-7575
www.kindredhealthcare.com
Healthcare: Kindred Hospital provides long-term care for patients dependent on medical technology such as ventilators or who have medically complex conditions.
Wellness programs: Sometimes the wellness of the family of an acute-care patient is overlooked. Not at Kindred Hospital, which lists support services on their Family Education page.

i Kindred Hospital's Web site offers one of those "art in unexpected places" moments. Click on their Kaleidoscope Gallery to view artwork and poetry by Kindred patients from around the country.

MEMORIAL HOSPITAL OF TAMPA
2901 W. Swann Ave.
Tampa
(813) 873-6400
www.memorialhospitaltampa.com
Health care: In addition to providing general medical services, Memorial Hospital of Tampa has a Sleep Center and offers interventional radiology treatment and inpatient psychiatric services.
Wellness programs: Click on the "Health Resources" tab on the Web site for a Health Illustrated Encyclopedia.

SOUTH BAY HOSPITAL
4016 Sun City Center Blvd.
Sun City Center
(813) 634-3301
www.southbayhospital.com
Health care: In addition to providing general medical services, South Bay Hospital offers an extensive Rehabilitation Center offering everything from Cardiac and Pulmonary Rehabilitation to Wiihabilitation—utilizing Nintendo's Wii as a rehabilitative tool.
Wellness programs: Look for the h2u—Health2You—link for information about a wellness program for people age 50 and up.

SOUTH FLORIDA BAPTIST HOSPITAL
301 N. Alexander St.
Plant City
(813) 757-1200
www.sjbhealth.org

Health care: Part of the BayCare Health System, South Florida Baptist Hospital houses the Pete Beaty Surgical Center, a Heartburn Treatment Center, and a Weight Management for Kids program in addition to general medical services.

Wellness programs: Click on "Classes and Events" to find a listing of classes offered, including a Car Seat Check Up Event and a Teen Talk for Boys.

ST. JOSEPH'S CHILDREN'S HOSPITAL

3001 W. Dr. Martin Luther King Jr. Blvd.
Tampa
(813) 870-4000
www.stjosephschildren.com

ST. JOSEPH'S HOSPITAL BAYCARE HEALTH SYSTEM

3001 W. Dr. Martin Luther King Jr. Blvd.
Tampa
(813) 870-4000
www.stjosephstampa.com

ST. JOSEPH'S WOMEN'S HOSPITAL

3030 W. Dr. Martin Luther King Jr. Blvd.
Tampa
(813) 879-4730
www.stjosephswomen.com

Health care: Part of the BayCare Health System and a ministry of the Franciscan Sisters of Allegany, St. Joseph's Hospital, including the Children's and Women's hospitals, is the largest not-for-profit health care provider in Hillsborough County. In addition to providing general medical services, St. Joseph's Hospital is noted for its Cancer Institute, its Heart Institute, and its Stroke and Neuroscience program. St. Joseph's Children's Hospital has a Children's Heart Center, a pediatric intensive care unit, a pediatric cancer team, and a pediatric emergency/trauma center. St. Joseph's Women's Center has a Women's Healthy Heart Center, a Breast Center, and a High-Risk OB Center.

Wellness programs: St. Joseph's Hospital is noted for its Healing Gardens, which provide emotional and spiritual respite for patients and their families. Click on the "Classes and Events" tab to find a comprehensive listing of wellness classes offered.

TAMPA GENERAL HOSPITAL

1 Tampa General Circle
Tampa
(813) 844-7000
www.tgh.org

Health care: Tampa General Hospital has been affiliated with the University of South Florida's College of Medicine since its beginning almost 40 years ago. Tampa General Hospital has the area's only Level I trauma center, with five medical helicopters serving 23 surrounding counties. Tampa General Hospital also has one of only four burn centers in Florida and is one of the leading organ transplant centers in the country. The Children's Medical Center offers one of just three outpatient pediatric dialysis units in Florida and has a sick-child day care program.

Wellness programs: Check Tampa General Hospital's Web page for healthy-living articles, events, and even replays of real surgeries.

TAMPA JAMES A. HALEY VA MEDICAL CENTER

13000 Bruce B. Downs Blvd.
Tampa
(813) 972-2000
www.tampa.va.gov

Tampa James A. Haley VA Medical Center serves military veterans living in southwest Florida. See the Military chapter for a listing of their clinics and other services.

TOWN & COUNTRY HOSPITAL

6001 Webb Rd.
Tampa
(813) 888-7060
www.townandcountryhospital.com

Health care: In addition to providing general medical services, Town & Country Hospital offers an Alcohol and Drug Recovery Center, a Bone and Joint Replacement Center, and a Digestive Health and Endoscopy Center.

Wellness programs: Click on their "Community Education" tab at the top of the page for a listing of classes and events.

UNIVERSITY COMMUNITY HOSPITAL
3100 E. Fletcher Ave.
Tampa
(8130 971-6000
www.uch.org
Health care: In addition to providing general medical services, the University Community Hospital—Carrollwood offers a Spine Center and a Diabetes Care Institute. University Community Hospital (Fletcher Ave.) offers the Pepin Heart Hospital and Dr. Kiran C. Patel Research Institute (www.pepinheart.org), an Occupational Health Service Center, and an Orthopaedic Care Center.
Wellness programs: Check their "Calendar of Events" for classes including Drive Alive 55 and Heart Health Lunch and Learn Seminar.

UNIVERSITY COMMUNITY HOSPITAL— CARROLLWOOD
7171 N. Dale Mabry Hwy
Tampa
(813) 932-2222
www.uch.org

St. Petersburg/South Pinellas County
ALL CHILDREN'S HOSPITAL
501 6th St. S.
St. Petersburg
(727) 898-7451
www.allkids.org
Health care: Children from around the region may be referred to All Children's Hospital because of the range of pediatric specialties and subspecialties the hospital offers. Affiliated with the University of South Florida's College of Medicine, All Children's Hospital also has a Neonatal Intensive Care Unit.
Wellness programs: Go to All Children's Hospital's Web site and click on the yellow box (left rail) labeled "Community Programs" for a list of wellness programs. You'll find everything from musical cartoons touting the use of sunscreen to a weight management and fitness program for families to take on together.

BAY PINES VA HEALTH CARE SYSTEM
10,000 Bay Pines Blvd.
Bay Pines
(727) 398-6661
(877) 741-3400 (after hours)
www.baypines.va.gov
Bay Pines VA Health Care System serves military veterans living in southwest Florida. See the Military chapter for a listing of their clinics and other services.

BAYFRONT MEDICAL CENTER
701 6th St. S.
St. Petersburg
(727) 823-1234
www.bayfront.org
Health care: In addition to providing general medical services, Bayfront Medical Center hosts Pinellas County's only trauma center, a Level II Adult and Pediatric trauma center served by Bayflite helicopters, and, as part of their Institute of Neurosciences, is one of only five Level IV Regional Epilepsy Centers in Florida. In December 2009, Bayfront's obstetrics unit, Baby Place, moved to nearby All Children's Hospital.
Wellness programs: Bayfront Rejuvenations offers aesthetic medical services.

EDWARD WHITE HOSPITAL (HCA)
2323 9th Ave. N.
St. Petersburg
(727) 323-1111
www.edwardwhitehospital.com
Health care: In addition to providing general medical services, Edward White Hospital has a Center for Wound Care and Hyperbaric Medicine, a Joint Commission–certified Primary Stroke Center, and a Sleep Disorders Clinic.
Wellness programs: Click on their "Upcoming Events" link to learn about scheduled classes on topics such as Armchair Aerobics and the Better Breathers Club.

NORTHSIDE HOSPITAL

6000 49th St. N.

St. Petersburg

(727) 521-4411

www.northsidehospital.com

Health care: In addition to providing general medical services, Northside Hospital is a Tampa Bay Heart Institute (www.tampabayheart.com), has a Spine Care Center, and is a post-graduate osteopathic teaching hospital.

Wellness programs: Click on their "Upcoming Events" link to learn about support group meetings, CPR classes, and other events.

PALMS OF PASADENA HOSPITAL

1501 Pasadena Ave. S.

St. Petersburg

(727) 381-1000

www.palmspasadena.com

Health care: In addition to providing general medical services, Palms of Pasadena Hospital also provides specialized services in treating intestinal conditions, provides aquatic therapy, and recently opened a Voice Center specializing in speech and language therapy.

Wellness programs: Click on their "Health Resources" tab for a Health Illustrated Encyclopedia.

PINELLAS CARE CLINIC

3554 1st Ave. N.

St. Petersburg

(727) 321-4846

www.stanthonys.com

Health care: An outreach program of St. Anthony's BayCare Health System (see next listing), Pinellas Care Clinic serves HIV-positive adults.

ST. ANTHONY'S BAYCARE HEALTH SYSTEM

1200 Seventh Ave. N.

St. Petersburg

(727) 825-1100

www.stanthonys.com

Health care: A ministry of the Franciscan Sisters of Allegany, St. Anthony's provides general health care services in addition to having a Heart Center, a Breast Center and an American Stroke Association recognized program.

Wellness programs: The "Health Information" Web link leads to a list lof healthcare articles.

ST. PETERSBURG GENERAL HOSPITAL (HCA)

6500 38th St. N.

St. Petersburg

(727) 384-1414

www.stpetegeneral.com

Health care: In addition to providing general medical services, St. Petersburg General Hospital offers minimally invasive Robotics Surgery, is a Joint Commission–certified Primary Stroke Center, and has a Women's Center obstetrics unit.

Wellness programs: Click on the "Upcoming Events" link on St. Petersburg General Hospital's home Web page to learn about childbirth and other classes offered.

Clearwater/North Pinellas County

HELEN ELLIS MEMORIAL HOSPITAL

1395 S. Pinellas Ave.

Tarpon Springs

(727) 942-5000

www.hemh.org

Health care: Part of the University Community Health System, Helen Ellis Memorial Hospital offers a Women's Center and a Transitional Care Unit (skilled nursing facility) in addition to general medical services.

Wellness programs: Search Helen Ellis Memorial Hospital's "Calendar of Events" for meetings of the Ostomy Support Group or for events such as Foot/Ankle Screenings.

LARGO MEDICAL CENTER (HCA)

201 14th St. S.W.

Largo

(727) 588-5200

www.largomedical.com

Health care: In addition to providing general medical services, Largo Medical Center is a Tampa Bay Heart Institute (www.tampabayheart.com) and home of the Florida Knee & Orthopedic Pavilion. Largo Medical Center is also home to the largest osteopathic teaching program (D.O.) in the southeastern United States.

Shriners Hospitals for Children

Leave Tampa International Airport headed for Clearwater's beaches across SR 60, and you're struck by the beauty of the journey.

Then come to a spur of land sticking down into the bay called Rocky Point. You have to get across Rocky Point, with its office buildings and restaurants, before you can continue the rest of the way across Tampa Bay.

Notice the white building on the south side of SR 60 on Rocky Point. There's a statue in front of a man carrying a child. He's carrying something else, too. If you caught the red light, you'll have time to notice the other item he's carrying is a crutch.

Shriners International Headquarters (www.shrinershq.org) on Rocky Point in Tampa is the headquarters for a group of Masons.

In 1870, a Mason attended a party given by an Arabian diplomat that featured a musical comedy. The play ended with a spoof of the audience being inducted into a secret society.

He and another Mason felt their Masonic group needed to lighten up a bit. So they started a secret society with a Middle Eastern theme—hence the red fezzes the Shriners wear and the fact that they call their meeting places shrines. This also explains why we'll often see the Shriners riding miniature motorcycles and other vehicles in parades—they still want to have a bit of fun.

The idea spread and by 1900 there were 55,000 Shriners and 82 temples or shrines.

About that time, the Shriners took on a big project. Polio killed many children and crippled others. The Shriners started hospitals to treat children with polio, even if they couldn't pay.

After the polio vaccine was developed in the 1950s, the Shriners broadened their hospital missions to include any type of orthopaedic condition—amputation, scoliosis, juvenile rheumatoid arthritis, and other conditions. When they learned there was only one pediatric burn unit in the United States, and that was on a military base, the Shriners established four pediatric burn hospitals.

Today, the Shriners operate 22 hospitals in the United States, Canada, and Mexico. Recently, however, declining membership and other factors have made it difficult for the Shriners to continue funding the hospitals. One hospital in Texas was damaged by Hurricane Ike and hasn't reopened yet.

In the meantime, children continue to receive therapy and equipment at Shriner Hospitals and to attend special Shriner summer camps. The East-West Shrine Game, a college football all-star bowl game and fundraiser will be coming to Orlando in 2010.

And the Shriners continue to help kids get across a rocky point in their lives so they can continue on life's journey.

Shriners Hospital for Children—Tampa
12502 N. Pine Dr.
Tampa
(813) 972-2250

Shriners International Headquarters
2900 Rocky Point Dr.
Tampa
(813) 281-0300

Wellness programs: Print out fact sheets on a comprehensive A to Z listing of illnesses and conditions on Largo Medical Center's "Health Info" tab. Call and ask about their Health Library.

MEASE COUNTRYSIDE HOSPITAL
3231 McMullen Booth Rd.
Safety Harbor
(727) 725-6111
www.measehospitals.com

Health care: Mease Countryside Hospital is part of the Morton Plant Mease BayCare Health System. In addition to providing general medical services, Mease Countryside Hospital is a Joint Commission–certified Stroke Center and has a Sleep Disorder Center and a Women's and Children's Center that includes a Level III Neonatal Intensive Care Unit.

Wellness programs: Morton Plant Mease offers a wide range of health care classes, including Ladies' Night Out classes on women's health issues and a Hip Hop Dance Class (not all classes may be available at all locations). Click on the "Register for Classes" tab at the top of the main page.

i Mease Dunedin Hospital, opened in 1937, was a labor of love. Since 1926, Dr. Jack Mease had worked in Dunedin, building his own small sanitarium and laboratory. But times were hard. Dr. Mease thought about moving, until Dunedin's residents said they would help him build a hospital. They did—brick by brick, taking partial payment in medical services.

MEASE DUNEDIN HOSPITAL
601 Main Street
Dunedin
(727) 733-1111
www.measehospitals.com

Health care: Mease Dunedin Hospital is part of the Morton Plant Mease BayCare Health System. In addition to providing general medical services, Mease Dunedin Hospital is a Joint Commission–certified Stroke Center.

Wellness programs: Mease Dunedin Hospital offers a wide range of health care classes, including an Arts, Cancer, and Healing class and Boot Camp for New Dads (not all classes may be available at all locations). Click on the "Register for Classes" tab at the top of the main page.

MORTON PLANT HOSPITAL
300 Pinellas St.
Clearwater
(727) 462-7000
www.mortonplant.com

Health care: Morton Plant Hospital is part of the Morton Plant Mease BayCare Health System. Morton Plant Hospital is actually a complex of hospitals including the Morgan Heart Hospital, the Powell Cancer Pavilion, the PTAK Orthopaedic and Neuroscience Pavilion, and others.

Wellness programs: Morton Plant Hospital offers a wide range of health care classes, including Spanish language classes (such as Clasa Para Preparación de Parto) and an Over the River and Through the Woods Grandparenting Class (not all classes may be available at all locations). Click on the "Register for Classes" tab at the top of the main page.

SUN COAST HOSPITAL (HCA)
2025 Indian Rocks Rd.
Largo
(727) 581-9474
www.suncoasthospital.net

Health care: Sun Coast Hospital, now a facility of Largo Medical Center, began in 1957 as an osteopathic hospital and grew into the largest osteopathic post-doctoral teaching program in the southeastern United States. Sun Coast Hospital has a Joint Commission certified Stroke Center and a Behavioral Health Center.

Wellness programs: Print out fact sheets on a comprehensive A to Z listing of illnesses and conditions on Largo Medical Center's "Health Info" tab. Call and ask about their Health Library.

Mental Health and Counseling Services

FLORIDA DEPARTMENT OF CHILDREN AND FAMILIES

Mental Health Services for Hillsborough and Pinellas Counties
9393 N. Florida Ave. Rd.
Tampa
(813) 558-5700
www.dcf.state.fl.us/mentalhealth

LOUIS DE LA PARTE FLORIDA MENTAL HEALTH INSTITUTE

University of South Florida
13301 Bruce B. Downs Blvd.
Tampa
(813) 974-4602
www.home.fmhi.usf.edu

The Florida Mental Health Institute gathers data and conducts research about various behavioral and mental conditions including autism, aging issues, and substance abuse and is the Baker Act Reporting Center for the Florida Agency for Health Care Administration. Departments include Mental Health Law and Policy, Aging and Mental Health Disparities, and Child and Family Studies. The Institute also houses an extensive research library.

MENTAL HEALTH CARE, INC.

5707 North 22nd St.
Tampa
(813) 272-2244
www.mhcinc.org

Mental Health Care, Inc., is an online resource and referral center for information about mental health conditions and mental health care professionals and services.

NATIONAL ALLIANCE ON MENTAL ILLNESS, PINELLAS COUNTY

NAMI Pinellas County, Florida, Inc.
466 94th Ave. N.
St. Petersburg
(727) 791-3434
www.nami.org

The National Alliance on Mental Illness offers training, education, and support group services as well as advocating on behalf of mentally ill people.

NORTHSIDE MENTAL HEALTH CENTER

12512 Bruce B. Downs Blvd.
Tampa
(813) 977-8700
www.northsidemhc.org

Northside Mental Health Center provides both short-term residential treatment and outpatient services to people with persistent and severe mental health disorders.

PERSONAL ENRICHMENT THROUGH MENTAL HEALTH SERVICES, INC. (PEMHS)

11254 58th St. N.
Pinellas Park
(727) 545-6477
www.pemhs.org

PEMHS maintains a suicide hotline, six inpatient programs, and seven community-based programs for children and adults, including a program at Pinellas County Juvenile Detention Center.

SUNCOAST CENTER, INC.

4024 Central Ave.
St. Petersburg
(727) 327-7656
www.sccmh.org

Suncoast Center, Inc., provides more than 40 mental health programs at sites throughout the Tampa Bay area. Programs address the mental health needs of children and families, including the Medical Foster Care program; of adults, including substance abuse programs; and of seniors.

i For 24-hour help, call the Suicide Hotline at (727) 791-3131 or, for other forms of mental health assistance, call (727) 541-4628 (also a 24-hour helpline).

Professional Associations

HILLSBOROUGH COUNTY DENTAL ASSOCIATION
34049 Woodland Circle
Ridge Manor
(813) 541-4056
www.hcdafla.com

HILLSBOROUGH COUNTY MEDICAL ASSOCIATION
606 S. Blvd.
Tampa
(813) 253-0471
www.hcma.net

HILLSBOROUGH COUNTY OSTEOPATHIC MEDICAL SOCIETY
P.O. Box 2025
Largo
(727) 581-9069
www.hcoms.org

PINELLAS COUNTY DENTAL ASSOCIATION
(727) 323-2992
www.smilepinellas.com

PINELLAS COUNTY MEDICAL ASSOCIATION
4900 Creekside Dr., Ste. G
Clearwater
(727) 541-1159
www.pinellascma.org

PINELLAS COUNTY OSTEOPATHIC MEDICAL SOCIETY
P.O. Box 2025
Largo
(727) 581-9069
www.pcomsociety.com

Wellness Centers

BARDMOOR OUTPATIENT CENTER
8787 Bryan Dairy Rd.
Largo
(727) 394-5900
www.suncoastymca.org/bardmoor-youth
.htm?id=p

The Bardmoor Outpatient Center is part of the Morton Plant Mease BayCare Health System. A YMCA Fitness Center and Nature's Table Café are located on the ground floor of the center.

What's a D.O.?

A D.O. is a Doctor of Osteopathy. An M.D., or Medical Doctor, is considered an allopathic doctor.

You'll find both in the Tampa Bay area.

In fact, the Pinellas County Osteopathic Medical Society claims to have largest countywide membership of D.O.s—more than the number of D.O.s in 38 other states.

Many of our hospitals have physicians of both types on staff. Both the Hillsborough and the Pinellas County Medical Association count physicians of both types among their members.

So what exactly is a Doctor of Osteopathy?

Like an M.D., an osteopathic physician learns about diseases, can prescribe medicine and perform surgery, and can be found in every subspecialty. But an osteopathic physician has additional training in the relationship between the musculoskeletal system of the human body and disease.

The first school of osteopathy was founded in 1892 in Missouri. You can learn more about osteopathic medicine at the American Association of Colleges of Osteopathic Medicine's Web site, www.www.aacom.org.

Healthy Choices Restaurants

More than 200 restaurants in the Tampa Bay area participate in Healthy Choices Restaurant, a program developed initially by the Pinellas County Health Department. The program has grown to include Hillsborough and Pasco Counties.

Restaurants submit their menus to the health department nutritionist. In order to qualify as a Healthy Choices Restaurant, the menu must offer two or more of the following options or the restaurant must agree to a "Just Ask" policy. The qualifying options are "Heart Healthy" low- or reduced-fat items, take half home on request, cook-to-order options such as offering grilled instead of fried or no butter added, and offering vegetables, fruit, salad, or rice instead of french fries.

Look for the "Healthy Choice Restaurant" decal at the entrance of the restaurant. It looks like a table setting with a plate in the center that says "Just Ask." Or look for a listing of participating restaurants at www.pinellashealth.com/hcrestaurants/healthychoicesrestaurants.asp.

CHEEK-POWELL WELLNESS CENTER
Cheek-Powell Heart and Vascular Pavilion
455 Pinellas St.
Clearwater
(727) 462-7656

PALM HARBOR WELLNESS CENTER
32672 U.S. 19 N.
Palm Harbor 34684
(727) 772-2222
The Cheek-Powell and Palm Harbor Wellness Centers are part of the Morton Plant Mease Bay-

Care Health System. Each offers fitness programs, including one tailored to the needs of adolescents, nutrition classes and coaching, massage therapies of many types, and personal training. Child care is offered (call in advance). The centers are open from 4 a.m. to 11 p.m. Monday through Friday and 6 a.m. to 8 p.m. Saturday and Sunday. Go to www.mpmhealth.com, click on "MPM Facilities," and look for Wellness Centers.

PINELLAS WELLNESS CORNER
Pinellas County Health Department
205 Martin Luther King St. N.
St. Petersburg
(727) 824-6900
(727) 820-4114 (Office of Chronic Disease Prevention)
www.pinellashealth.com/wellness
This virtual Wellness Corner, includes recipes, exercises to do at your desk, and lots more. Join the 100 Mile Club or check out the Kidz Bite Back page which features a "kid-created, kid-led, and kid-spread campaign" to expose the Big Fat Industries and the Couch Potato Companies. You'll find more information about the Healthy Choices Restaurants program in the sidebar on this page.

SENIOR SERVICES

The services listed in this section presume a wide range of interests, abilities, and needs.

STATE OF FLORIDA'S ELDER HELPLINE
(800) 96-ELDER (963-5337)

FLORIDA DEPARTMENT OF ELDER AFFAIRS
4040 Esplanade Way
Tallahassee
(850) 414-2000
www.elderaffairs.state.fl.us

HILLSBOROUGH COUNTY DEPARTMENT OF AGING SERVICES
County Center, 25th Floor
601 E. Kennedy Blvd.
Tampa
(813) 272-5430
www.hillsboroughcounty.org/aging

Hillsborough County Department of Aging Services provides a wide range of programs and services including respite care for caregivers, community care for the elderly, senior centers, senior adult day care programs, and other services. Check their Calendar of Events for programs like the Seniors' Prom, the Tampa Bay Senior Games, Seniors' Day in the Park, and other events. Hillsborough County's Elder Helpline is (813) 273-3779.

PINELLAS COUNTY HEALTH AND HUMAN SERVICES DEPARTMENT
2189 Cleveland St., Ste. 230
Clearwater
(727) 464-8400

647 1st Ave. N.
St. Petersburg 33701
(727) 582-7781
Pinellas County Health and Human Services Department provides prescription drug assistance, medical care to the indigent and uninsured in our community, dental assistance, and other care programs including elderly assistance programs.

CITY OF CLEARWATER OFFICE ON AGING
100 S. Myrtle Ave.
Clearwater
(727) 562-4830
www.clearwater-fl.com/gov/depts/parksrec/aging/index.asp
Clearwater's Office on Aging is part of the Parks and Recreation Department. Clearwater is tackling its "age wave" head on by providing services such as an Aging Well Center at the Long Center (see Parks and Recreation chapter), scheduled to open in early 2010. Also at the Long Center, the city hosts the Good Life (Senior) Games, part of the Florida Sports Foundation (www.flasports.com/page_seniorgames.shtml). The city's police department offers a Senior Academy (see below).

CLEARWATER SENIOR ACADEMY
(727) 562-4167
www.clearwaterpolice.org/cpa.asp

The Clearwater Police Department offers the Clearwater Senior Academy, three weekday sessions focusing on issues of particular interest to seniors including the state attorney's Triad Program (reducing victimization of the elderly), fire safety, and services available to seniors. Cost is free.

CITY OF ST. PETERSBURG OFFICE ON AGING
(727) 893-7102
www.stpete.org/recreation/seniors.asp
The City of St. Petersburg's Office on Aging is part of the city's Recreation Department. A number of programs, including Neighborly Senior Services offices, a Women's Resource Center, and Suncoast Mental Health Services, as well as organized activities, are offered at the city-sponsored senior centers, located at:
- Azalea Adult Center: 600 72nd St. N., (727) 893-7150
- Bay Vista Adult Center: 7000 4th St. S., (727) 893-7124
- Enoch D. Davis Center: 1111 18th Ave. S., (727) 893-7134
- Roberts Adult Center: 1330 50th Ave. N., (727) 893-7755
- Sunshine Senior Center: 330 5th St. N., (727) 893-7101

CITY OF TAMPA PARKS AND RECREATION DEPARTMENT
Barksdale Senior Citizens Center
1801 N. Lincoln St.
Tampa
(813) 348-1180
www.tampagov.net/dept_parks_and_recreation
The City of Tampa's Barksdale Senior Citizens Center offers programs and activities ranging from low-impact aerobics to social dancing, art classes, and other activities. Each year, the city also hosts the Tampa Bay Senior Games, a program affiliated with the Florida Sports Foundation (www.flasports.com/page_seniorgames.shtml).

Non-Government Agencies

ALZHEIMER'S ASSOCIATION FLORIDA GULF COAST CHAPTER
Chapter Headquarters, Florida Gulf Coast
9365 U.S. 19 N., Ste. B
Pinellas Park
(727) 578-2558

Hillsborough Office
309 N. Parsons Ave.
Brandon
(813) 684-1296
www.alz.org/flgulfcoast
The Alzheimer's Association Florida Gulf Coast Chapter serves as a clearinghouse of information about Alzheimer's and related legal issues, financial matters, and help for caregivers. Their "Living with Alzheimer's" tab at the top of the Home page provides links to pages about African Americans and Latinos and Alzheimer's, as well as pages of information written in Chinese, Korean, Spanish, and Vietnamese.

AREA AGENCY ON AGING OF PASCO-PINELLAS, INC.
9887 4th St. N., Ste. 100
St. Petersburg
(727) 570-9696
www.agingcarefl.org

MEALS ON WHEELS OF TAMPA
550 W. Hillsborough Ave.
Tampa
(813) 238-8410
www.mealsonwheelstampa.com
Meals on Wheels of Tampa, which began in Tampa in 1975, prepares and delivers between 500 and 600 meals each day to Tampa residents.

NEIGHBORLY CARE NETWORK
13945 Evergreen Ave.
Clearwater
(727) 573-9444
www.neighborly.org
Neighborly Care Network provides Meals on Wheels, senior dining centers, transportation to medical appointments and grocery stores, the

Neighborhood Pharmacy, Alzheimer's Care support groups for caregivers, homemaker/companion services, and other programs and services to help seniors remain in their homes for as long as possible. Many of the programs are state or federally subsidized, but many of the services are fee-based.

WEST CENTRAL FLORIDA AREA AGENCY ON AGING, INC.
5905 Breckenridge Pkwy, Ste. F
Tampa
(813) 740-3888
www.agingflorida.com
Both Area Agencies on Aging manage public funds, private grants, and donations for senior services for their designated geographical areas. The West Central Florida Area Agency on Aging, Inc., includes Hillsborough County and several other counties in its service area. Look for the SHINE (Serving Health Insurance Needs of Elders) program for help in navigating the Medicare, Medicaid, and private insurance mazes. The Pasco-Pinellas Web site includes a page just for caregivers (www.agingcarefl.org/caregiver).

Assisted Living Facilities (ALFs) and Nursing Homes

The Area Agency on Aging of Pasco-Pinellas, Inc., has a page on their Web site called "How to Select an ALF or Nursing Home" (www.aging carefl.org/aging/selectalf). This page provides detailed information about the following topics and gives Florida-specific answers:
- What is the difference between an ALF, a skilled nursing facility, and a nursing home?
- What risk factors indicate it may be time to consider an ALF or nursing home?
- What about financial assistance?
- What about residential care facilities for people with Alzheimer's?
- What should I look for in an ALF or nursing home?
- What is a care manager or placement service?
- How can I find inspection reports on ALFs and nursing homes?

- What is an elder law attorney?
- What legal issues do I need to consider?
- What services are available to elderly veterans?
- How do I report a problem with an ALF or nursing home?

AMERICAN ASSOCIATION OF HOMES AND SERVICES FOR THE AGING (AAHSA)
2519 Connecticut Ave. NW
Washington, D.C.
(202) 783-2242
www.aahsa.org

FLORIDA AGENCY FOR HEALTH CARE ADMINISTRATION
2727 Mahan Dr.
Tallahassee
(888) 419-3456
www.ahca.myflorida.com
The Florida Agency for Health Care Administration that administers Florida's $16 billion Medicaid program and that licenses health care facilities, including nursing homes. See the full listing at the beginning of this chapter for Medicaid information. Go to http://FloridaHealthFinder .gov for information about facilities.

ASSISTED LIVING FEDERATION OF AMERICA
1650 King St. Ste. 602
Alexandria, VA
(703) 894-1805
www.alfa.org
ALFA is a professional organization representing companies that operate professionally managed assisted living facilities. Click on the "For Consumers" tab at the top of the page for information about and help finding local ALFs.

FLORIDA ASSOCIATION OF HOMES AND SERVICES FOR THE AGING
1812 Riggins Ln.
Tallahassee
(850) 671-3700
www.fahsa.org
In addition to monitoring legislation affecting aging at the national and state levels, the Association of Homes and Services for the Aging has created the Center for Aging Services Technologies to create products specifically to help people manage the aging experience. AAHSA also has created the Institute for the Future of Aging Services, an independent research organization on aging. Both the national and the state Web sites have help pages on selecting care.

NATIONAL ASSOCIATION OF PROFESSIONAL GERIATRIC CARE MANAGERS
3275 West Ina Rd., Ste. 130
Tucson, AZ
(520) 881-8008
www.caremanager.org
If you are trying to manage care from a distance or if you need help navigating the caregiving maze, you may find a professional care manager helpful. Use this association's locator feature to find a professional care manager in your area.

NATIONAL CENTER FOR ASSISTED LIVING
1201 L Street N.W.
Washington, D.C.
(202) 842-4444
www.ncal.org
NCAL represents long-term care providers. Look for the link "Resources for Consumers" for help in locating a facility.

WORSHIP

Churches, synagogues, mosques, temples—or an all-but deserted beach under the star-spangled dome of heaven, echoing with the endless music of waves breaking on shore.

Whatever your religious affiliation and whatever kind of worship experience you prefer, you'll more than likely find others who share your faith here in the Tampa Bay area.

In the History chapter, we noted that people lived here and had a history even before the histories were written down. In the same way, people here most likely had religious beliefs even before there were organized churches and synagogues, mosques and temples.

Not counting the religion of the Tocobagans or attempts by the Spanish to establish missions in the Tampa Bay area in the 1500s, the first organized church here was a Methodist congregation in Tampa.

In 1846, the Reverend John C. Ley, of the Georgia-Florida Methodist Conference, rode into town after working his way down the Florida peninsula, preaching where anyone would listen, and staying with settlers where he found them.

Ley didn't waste any time once he reached Tampa. His diary indicates he opened a church in an already existing building made of salvaged lumber, organized a congregation, and appointed a class leader soon after arriving. Called Church by the Sea, the building was destroyed in the 1848 hurricane. In 1852, the congregation built the area's first building intended for use as a church.

By then, a Baptist congregation had organized and soon built a church.

Reverend Edmond (sometimes spelled Edmund) Lee, a Presbyterian preacher who owned a general store in Manatee, poled his rowboat up the shoreline from Manatee to Tampa, and preached there beginning in 1854.

In 1860, St. Louis Catholic Church in Tampa was officially constituted, a part of the Roman Catholic Diocese of St. Augustine. The church was named partly in honor of Father Luis Cancer de Barbastro, the priest martyred in Tampa Bay in 1549. In 1888, the parish had three pastors die in succession during a yellow fever epidemic, and Jesuits from New Orleans came to take over the church.

In 1898, ground was broken for a new church to be built on the site of St. Louis Catholic Church. The church was dedicated in 1905 and renamed Sacred Heart Church.

On the other side of Tampa Bay, the Reverend Joseph Brown, a Virginian, arrived in Clearwater Harbor and began preaching in 1868. By 1871, the group there had organized today's First Presbyterian Church of Dunedin.

Episcopalians have had an official presence in the Tampa Bay area since at least the late 1880s. In 1887, English immigrants built St. Bartholomew's Episcopal Church in southwest St. Petersburg. About the same time, another group of Episcopalians was organizing what would become the Church of the Ascension in Clearwater.

People of the Jewish faith have been a part of Florida's earliest years. The first person of Jewish ancestry elected to the United States Congress was Senator David Levy Yulee, elected in 1845 when Florida became a state. (See Parks and Recreation chapter to learn more about where Yulee lived.) His father, Moses Elias Levy was Florida's first Education Commissioner.

Herman Goglowski, also of the Jewish faith, served as mayor of Tampa, not once, but four different times beginning in 1866.

The first Jewish congregation in the Tampa Bay area, however, did not form until 1894. Congregation Schaarai Zedek still meets today, as do congregations of Conservative, Orthodox, Reform, and Traditional practices of Judaism.

The Jewish experience in the Tampa Bay area has not always been positive. Especially in the years right after the Civil War and again in the 1920s, both times of active Ku Klux Klan activity, Jews in Florida were persecuted. Part of the persecution was religious. Part of the persecution was because Jewish businesses sometimes hired African Americans when other white-owned businesses wouldn't. Sometimes the persecution took the form of exclusion from clubs and activities. Sometimes the persecution was more overt.

Sometimes other groups have endured mudslinging and attacks on their faiths and traditions. We didn't say you'd find paradise in the Tampa Bay area. Nevertheless, for the most part, we have learned to live together and to respect each other's differing beliefs.

i One of the earliest funerals conducted at Sacred Heart Catholic Church in Tampa was for a Lutheran woman named Smith, who had died in 1903 while staying at Henry Plant's Tampa Bay Hotel. In gratitude, the woman's sons—the Smith Brothers of cough-drop fame—donated the Italian marble main altar for the new church.

TODAY'S TAPESTRY OF FAITHS

The Tampa Bay area's population has always been somewhat transient, which has been a factor in its becoming home to people of many different faiths. When other areas were being filled up with settlers, sometimes settlers of a particular faith, the Tampa Bay area of Florida was still just a tiny backwater wilderness outpost. The Tampa Bay area's first settlers were mostly military people, coming to Fort Brooke from many parts of the country and moving on before too long. The turnover of military personnel likely meant people of many faiths passed through here.

Later, the people who rode Plant's railroad south were northern developers and wintering millionaires and tourists, also from many parts of the country. These people brought with them the faiths of several religions and of several denominations.

Other peoples of other faiths have come here over the years. In the early 1900s, Tarpon Springs became a destination for Greek sponge divers looking for work and new opportunities. They brought their Greek Orthodox rites and beliefs with them. In the Annual Events and Festivals chapter, we told you about the Feast of the Epiphany celebrated at St. Nicholas Greek Orthodox Church in Tarpon Springs. But the Greek Orthodox Church isn't the only Orthodox Church in the area. You'll find Antiochian Orthodox, Russian Orthodox, Serbian Orthodox, Syrian Orthodox, and Ukranian Orthodox churches—maybe others, too—in the Tampa Bay area.

i The Orthodox Churches use a different calendar than the Western Churches do. Don't be surprised if you find Easter celebrations—called Holy Pascha or the Feast of Feasts—going on at different times in the Tampa Bay area.

The area's first organized Islamic community, the Islamic Society of the Tampa Bay Area, came together in 1974.

From the earliest days of the Tampa Bay area's history, immigrants from the Caribbean Islands have brought other beliefs and perspectives. Asian immigrants have brought their Buddhist, Hindu, and other beliefs to the Tampa Bay area.

All of which means Tampa Bay area tapestry of faith is woven with diverse faiths and beliefs.

Our Lady of Clearwater?

Just before Christmas 1996, a customer visited a Clearwater office building made with exterior glass walls and noticed on one side of the building what appeared to be a gigantic rainbow-colored image. The image resembled a somewhat abstract version of the Virgin Mary as she is often portrayed in paintings.

A local television station filmed the walls of the building and showed it on its noon newscast. Within two hours, people were coming from all parts of the Tampa Bay area to see the image. They didn't stop coming.

Before long, Clearwater police had to start directing traffic. They brought in portable toilets because the office building itself was private property and couldn't handle that many people.

During the two weeks from just before Christmas to just after New Year's, almost 450,000 people came to see the image. Within the first two months, police estimated more than 600,000 people, six times the city's population, had visited the building.

Some people came to pray. Some people left flowers and lined the area near the wall with lit votive candles.

Scientists who examined the glass said it was a natural discoloration, maybe caused by sprinklers around the building. But they couldn't explain why the discoloration was in that shape.

The building, on U.S. 19 in Clearwater, is still there, and people still come, although not in the same numbers as before.

Police no longer direct traffic. An overpass has gone up at the intersection, so drivers heading south on U.S. 19 no longer have red-light time to ponder the image.

The image itself has been damaged—twice.

The first time, less than six months after the image was filmed, someone threw acid on the image. Eventually, the marks from the acid disappeared, leaving the original image unharmed.

The second time was in 2004. A local teenager shot steel balls with a slingshot through the upper panes of glass. The part of the image that formed Mary's face and head was destroyed.

By then a group called Shepherds of Christ, which had begun in Ohio several years earlier, had purchased the building and turned it into a shrine and prayer center. One of the members wrote a song he referred to as the "Our Lady of Clearwater song."

Today, mostly empty white plastic chairs sit facing a large crucifix placed near the window. Other shrine areas with statues are nearby. A woman, dressed in a white skirt, white blouse, and wearing a short white veil, hands visitors literature. A sign by a box requests donations to help make payments on the building.

Inside the building a gift shop sells books, DVDs, and relics. In another room, a picture of the unbroken image is projected on a screen. Beginning at 6:30 each evening, people sit in chairs and pray along with a voice being broadcast, according to another woman in white, from the group's home church in China, Indiana.

The Diocese of St. Petersburg has cautioned people to be skeptical.

The Shepherds of Christ Ministries building is located at 21649 U.S. 19 North in Clearwater, just south of Drew Street. The gift shop can be reached at (727) 725-9312, and the group's Web site is www.sofc.org.

EXPLORING THE RELIGIOUS LANDSCAPE

Regardless of your religious affiliation—or non-affiliation—we hope you'll take the time to discover the incredible breadth of religious expression in the Tampa Bay area. Learning about each other is part of what it means to be in a community.

We're not going to try to tell you about every single religion or denomination. We have a very good Yellow Pages that lists just about every religion we've ever heard of and a few we hadn't until we read through them all.

We'll give you a list of denominational associations in the area and tell you where to find ones that provide extensive social services. We'll also look more in depth at four groups.

The Church of Scientology's Flag Service Organizations building—a religious retreat center for its members, who come from around the world—is in Clearwater. The Roman Catholic Diocese of St. Petersburg, which includes several counties, has its headquarters in St. Petersburg. The Episcopal Diocese of Southwest Florida moved its diocesan offices to Sarasota a few years back, but the cathedral is still in St. Petersburg. You have just read about what some people call a religious phenomenon that occurred in Clearwater in the 1990s, one that still finds pilgrims coming to the site.

There also are a number of religious coalitions, interfaith ministries that fill food pantries and offer other services to the people of our communities. We have a few religious colleges in the area, some religious radio stations, and one of the nation's first Christian television stations, but you'll find those in the Education and Media chapters, respectively.

BAPTIST

SUNCOAST BAPTIST ASSOCIATION
6559 126th Ave. N.
Largo
(727) 530-0431
www.suncoastbaptist.com

Autonomous Religious Organizations

Florida Council of Churches
3838 W. Cypress St.
Tampa
www.floridachurches.org
The Florida Council of Churches lists 23 (Christian) member denominations from throughout Florida and three affiliated organizations. They find common cause in addressing social issues.

Gulf Coast Jewish Family Services
4041 Icot Blvd.
Clearwater
(727) 479-1800, (800) 888-5066
www.gcjfs.org
Gulf Coast Jewish Family Services has Jewish roots, but it is a non-sectarian social services agency serving 31 counties in West Florida. They provide mental health, elder, and family services, including residential treatment centers. They are the home of the Florida Center for Survivors of Torture. Michael A. Bernstein is president and CEO.

Metropolitan Ministries
2002 N. Florida Ave.
Tampa
(813) 209-1011
In 1972, 13 downtown Tampa churches joined forces to consolidate their efforts to reach the hungry and homeless in Tampa. Reverend Morris Hintzman is president.

Religious Community Services
503 S. Martin Luther King Jr. Ave.
Clearwater
(727) 584-3528
www.rcspinellas.org
Religious Community Services operates the largest food bank in Pinellas County, a domestic abuse shelter, a homeless shelter, and a thrift store. Duggan Cooley is president and CEO.

Suncoast Baptist Association lists about 75 Southern Baptist churches. Most are located in Pinellas County, but a few are in Pasco and Hillsborough Counties. The moderator is Donnie Holley. A link on the Web site leads to the Florida Baptist Children's Home.

TAMPA BAY BAPTIST ASSOCIATION
1060 West Busch Blvd.
Tampa
(813) 935-3839
www.tbba.org
Tampa Bay Baptist Association lists more than 170 Southern Baptist churches and missions in Pasco and Hillsborough Counties. The executive director is Tom Biles. Tampa Bay Baptist Association lists a Christian Counseling Center (813-935-3917) on site.

CATHOLIC

ROMAN CATHOLIC DIOCESE OF ST. PETERSBURG
6363 9th Ave. N.
(P.O. Box 40200)
St. Petersburg
(727) 344-1611
www.dioceseofstpete.org

CATHEDRAL OF ST. JUDE THE APOSTLE
5815 5th Ave. N.
St. Petersburg
(727) 347-9702
www.cathedralofstjude.org
The Catholic Diocese of St. Petersburg, encompassing 11 counties and ranging from Crystal River in the north to Fort Myers in the south, was established in June 1968. In 1984, the southern portion of the Diocese became the Diocese of Venice, leaving Pinellas, Hillsborough, Pasco, Hernando, and Citrus Counties in the Diocese of St. Petersburg.

Today, the Diocese of St. Petersburg, part of the Archdiocese of Miami, serves approximately 425,000 Roman Catholics through 74 parishes and seven missions. The Office of Catho-lic Schools and Centers lists 16 early childhood education centers, 28 elementary schools, 6 high schools, and 2 special education schools.

Catholic Charities (www.ccdosp.org) provides a number of social services under two basic headings: Life Ministry (counseling, immigration issues, adoption, etc.) and Shelter Ministry (farm worker housing, HIV/AIDS housing, single-parent family housing, etc.).

The Diocese of St. Petersburg operates WBVM 90.5 SpiritFM radio station, broadcasting to central Florida, and publishes a Diocesan magazine called *Gathered, Nourished, Sent.*

Bishop Robert Lynch was consecrated bishop of the Diocese of St. Petersburg in January 1996 at the Cathedral of St. Jude the Apostle in St. Petersburg. Bishop Lynch even has a blog, *For His Friends* (http://bishopsblog.dosp.org).

EASTERN RELIGIONS

BUDDHIST PEACE FELLOWSHIP
Tampa Bay
www.bpf.org
This Web page has links to Non-sectarian Buddhism, Mahayana Buddhism, Theravada Buddhism (Vipassana), and Vajrayana/Tibetan Buddhism groups meeting in the Tampa Bay area—33 sites in all. Additionally, there are links to Buddhist groups meeting in other parts of Florida.

ISLAMIC SOCIETY OF TAMPA BAY AREA
7326 E. Sligh Ave.
Tampa
(813) 628-0007
www.istaba.org
There are six Islamic mosques in Hillsborough and Pinellas Counties. The Islamic Society of Tampa Bay Area has a preschool/day care program, a weekend religious school for children, an afternoon religious instruction program for children, a food pantry, and a medical clinic—Red Crescent Clinic of Tampa (www.redcrescenttampa.org). Mohammad Sultan is director and imam.

KHAAS BAAT
18313 Cypress Stand Circle
Tampa
(813) 758-1786
www.khaasbaat.com

Khaas Baat is a print and online publication for Indian Americans in Florida. The "Faith" page on their Web site lists 12 Hindu temples or groups in Hillsborough and Pinellas Counties.

EPISCOPALIAN

EPISCOPAL DIOCESE OF SOUTHWEST FLORIDA
7313 Merchant Court
Sarasota
(941) 556-0315
www.episcopalswfl.org

ST. PETER'S EPISCOPAL CATHEDRAL
140 4th St. N.
St. Petersburg
(727) 822-4173
www.spcathedral.net

The Episcopal Diocese of Southwest Florida, part of the Anglican Communion, was formed in 1969 when the Diocese of South Florida was divided into three parts. Today, the Diocese of Southwest Florida reaches from Brooksville in the north to Naples in the south and serves about 36,000 people in 77 parishes. The Diocese operates Dayspring Retreat and Conference Center in Ellenton (www.dayspringfla.org), just south of Tampa.

The Right Reverend Dabney T. Smith was consecrated bishop of the Diocese of Southwest Florida in March 2007.

The Episcopal Church has had a presence on or very near the site of its cathedral building in downtown St. Petersburg since 1889. Over the years, the original small, wooden mission chapel was expanded many times to its present cathedral-like size. The architecture, a style called "Florida Ecclesiastical" or "Florida Gothic," has remained mostly consistent.

The church lists nine schools serving only pre-elementary age children and seven schools serving children in the elementary grades and higher. Three of those schools include high schools.

The Episcopal Church in the Tampa Bay area was a founding partner of and still supports three homes providing transitional housing for homeless families with children, an AIDS ministry, and other area services.

JEWISH

THE JEWISH COMMUNITY CENTER OF PINELLAS
5023 Central Ave.
St. Petersburg
(727) 347-4522
www.pinellasjcc.org

The Jewish Community Center of Pinellas offers summer camp and classes for adults and children. Jay Kaminsky is president.

THE JEWISH FEDERATION OF PINELLAS AND PASCO COUNTIES
13191 Starkey Rd., Ste. 8
Largo
(727) 530-3223
www.jewishpinellas.org

In Pinellas County, the Federation offices are separate from the Community Center. Bonnie Friedman is executive director of the Federation.

TAMPA JEWISH COMMUNITY CENTER AND FEDERATION
13009 Community Campus Dr.
Tampa
(813) 264-9000
www.jewishtampa.com

The Tampa Jewish Community Center offers a number of programs and activities including summer camps, preschool, and fitness programs. Gerry Gould is CEO. The Tampa Jewish Federation lists 12 congregations (Conservative, Orthodox, Reform, and Unaffiliated) in Hillsborough County.

PRESBYTERIAN

PRESBYTERY OF TAMPA BAY
4704 Kelly Rd.
Tampa
(813) 868-4800
www.presbyteryoftampabay.com

The Church of Scientology's Flag Service Organization

In 1975, a group called the United Churches of Florida bought the Fort Harrison Hotel in downtown Clearwater. United Churches of Florida was funded by the Church of Scientology, which refurbished the 11-story building and made it a retreat center.

Opened on New Year's Eve, 1926, the Fort Harrison Hotel was one of the area's premier hotels for many years. The hotel housed soldiers during the first two years of World War II, and it housed the Philadelphia Phillies when they first came to Clearwater for spring training after the war. In May 1965, Keith Richards and Mick Jagger wrote the bulk of "(I Can't Get No) Satisfaction" when the Rolling Stones stayed at what was then the Jack Tar New Fort Harrison Hotel in Clearwater.

Gradually, as happened to cities around the country, areas around Clearwater grew. New attractions in outlying areas pulled people from the downtown sections. With fewer visitors to downtown Clearwater, the hotel deteriorated. Then the Church of Scientology bought the hotel and began acquiring other property, both downtown and elsewhere in the Tampa Bay area.

Today, according to the church's Web site, the Flag Service Organization is a "religious retreat, which serves as the spiritual headquarters for Scientologists from all over the world . . . and is the largest single Church of Scientology in the world."

DIANETICS AND SCIENTOLOGY

The Church of Scientology grew out of the writings of a man named L. Ron Hubbard. Hubbard used the word "dianetics" to describe "what the soul is doing to the body through the mind," according to the local church's Web site. Dianetics Technology seeks to explain the source of and to teach ways to counter seemingly irrational, self-destructive behaviors.

According to Dianetics Technology, as explained in *The Scientology Handbook* (www.scientology handbook.org), people each have eight dynamics or "urge[s] toward survival." The seventh and eighth dynamics are "the urge toward existence as or of spirits" and "the urge toward existence as infinity . . . or God dynamic."

The local Church's Web site says, "[R]esearch into the spiritual aspects of dianetics, led to the discovery of Scientology," which is defined as "the study and handling of the spirit in relationship to itself, to universes and to other life."

The Church of Scientology has adopted an eight-pointed cross as one of its trademarked symbols. The Church says each of the eight points represents one of the eight dynamics.

CONTROVERSY

Over the years, the Church of Scientology has been the source of controversy here and around the world.

According to the church's press office Web site (www.scientologytoday.org), the basis of most of the controversy stems from those "who feel their vested interests are threatened." People and groups with those vested interests, according to the church, have opposed the church's positions on everything from prevailing psychiatric practices beginning in the 1950s to the definition of a tax-exempt church in the 1980s and 1990s.

In 1993, the Internal Revenue Service recognized the Church of Scientology and its related churches as tax-exempt organizations. That means, among other things, that buildings used for religious purposes don't pay property taxes. That can mean a loss of revenue to cities.

In Clearwater, the church was accused of trying to take over the city government (1977) and settled in a wrongful death suit (1995–2004).

In Clearwater, some people have been concerned that having so many Church of Scientology buildings in the downtown area limits the kind of traffic the area gets, thus stifling other kinds of business growth.

In May 2009, Wikipedia, the online encyclopedia that anyone can edit—to add information or to correct erroneous entries—imposed a very rare ban on some computers that were repeatedly editing entries about Scientology. Some people tried to make Scientology appear more favorable. Other people tried to discredit Scientology. After three previous Scientology-related arbitration cases in as many years, Wikipedia decided enough was enough and banned certain people from making changes to articles about Scientology.

SCIENTOLOGY IN THE TAMPA BAY AREA

Two independent schools in the Tampa Bay area, Delphi Academy of Florida and Clearwater Academy International, are licensed to use Applied Scholastics educational materials and services, which are based on the writings of L. Ron Hubbard. The Citizens Commission on Human Rights, an independent organization founded by the Church of Scientology, lobbies against psychotropic drugs. Volunteers who are members of Scientology form Scout troops and participate in area health fairs.

According to the church's Web sites, each Church of Scientology is separately incorporated and has its own board of directors, who also provide ecclesiastical management. Florida incorporation records list Lena Linda as president of the Church of Scientology Flag Service Organization, Inc.

In addition to the Flag Service Organization building, the Church of Scientology owns several other buildings in downtown Clearwater that are used for "auditing" (process of applying dianetics) purposes. They also own other hotels and buildings in the area, which are subject to property taxes.

Aside from these buildings, there are six other churches and missions in the Tampa Bay area:

Belleair Bluffs: Church of Scientology Mission of Belleair, 2907 W. Bay Dr., (727) 501-9996

Clearwater: Church of Scientology Mission of Clearwater, 100 N. Belcher Rd., (727) 443-4111

Plant City: Church of Scientology Life Improvement Center Plant City, 102 Collins St., (813) 752-0148

St. Petersburg: Church of Scientology Life Improvement Center of St Petersburg, 336 1st Ave. N., (727) 895-5404

Tampa: Church of Scientology Tampa, 3617 Henderson Blvd., (813) 872-0722

Ybor City: Church of Scientology Life Improvement Center of Ybor City, 1619 E. 8th Ave., (813) 242-4201

Church of Scientology
Flag Service Organization
International Religious Retreat
210 S. Fort Harrison Ave.
Clearwater
(727) 445-4387
www.scientology-fso.org

The Presbytery of Tampa Bay lists 77 congregations in seven counties serving 24,000 members. Among other ministries, they support Beth-El Farmworkers Ministry, Inc., Thornwell Home for Children, and Eckerd College Center for Spiritual Life. Dr. Gerry Tyer is the Executive Presbyter and Stated Clerk.

SALVATION ARMY (WORSHIP CENTERS)

CLEARWATER CITADEL CORPS

1625 N. Belcher Rd.
Clearwater
(727) 725-9777
www.uss.salvationarmy.org/uss/www_uss_clearwater.nsf

The Clearwater Citadel Corps provides a transitional living center for people in difficult circumstances in addition to offering other programs and services.

SALVATION ARMY OF HILLSBOROUGH COUNTY

Community Worship Center
1100 W. Sligh Ave.
Tampa
(813) 549-5285

Riverview Area Corps
7409 U.S. 301, Ste. 200
Riverview
(813) 672-8139
www.salvationarmyflorida.org/uss/www_uss_tampa.nsf

ST. PETERSBURG AREA COMMAND

3800 9th Ave. N.
St. Petersburg
(727) 323-2222

1400 4th St. S.
St. Petersburg
(727) 822-4954
www.salvationarmyflorida.org/uss/www_uss_stpetersburgac.nsf

The Salvation Army in St. Petersburg has a number of social services programs including a rehabilitation facility and a children's village.

UNITED METHODIST

GULF CENTRAL DISTRICT

(includes Pinellas County)
1498 Rosery Rd. E.
Largo
(727) 585-1207
www.gcdistrictumc.org

The Gulf Central District stretches from Crystal River in the north to Bradenton in the south and numbers about 70 churches. The social services organization for the Gulf Central District is the United Methodist Cooperative Ministries, which provides English classes to non-English speaking people, legal aid, and other services. Reverend John Powers is the district superintendent.

SOUTH CENTRAL DISTRICT

(includes Hillsborough County)
202 W. Reynolds St.
Plant City
(813) 719-7270
www.flumc-scdist.org

The South Central District of the United Methodist Church reaches from Tampa to Lakeland and numbers about 90 churches and missions. Reverend Sharon Austin is the district superintendent.

MEDIA

Want to get to know the Tampa Bay area quickly?

Other than reading this book, of course, one of the best ways is to read a local newspaper. Or turn on the radio and hit the scan button. Listen a minute or two to each station, and you'll see that our musical and talk show tastes run the gamut.

Reading a variety of papers, and listening to and watching a variety of stations, gives us additional eyes with which to see our community. Otherwise, we're a bit like the proverbial six blind men each touching a different part of an elephant and each thinking he had hold of a snake (trunk), a cloak (ear), or a tree (leg)!

In this chapter we'll give you a heads-up on the various magazines, newspapers, radio stations, and television stations originating here. Then there are the weekly newspapers, the alternative newspapers, and the magazines published here—the list goes on. Suffice it to say, we're not hurting for news or the means to tell it.

Our Pulitzer Prize–winning daily papers, the *Tampa Tribune* and the *St. Petersburg Times*, as well as many of our weekly papers, stay on top of what's going on in the world as well as at City Hall, in county commission meetings, and in the state legislature. They give us insight into the sports played here, and they help fill our calendars with festivals and other activities.

Pay attention to the ads, too—even if "50% Off Boat Trailer Hitches" aren't on your need-to-buy list at the moment. Ads tell us more about the local economy—there's water nearby and people can afford boats—in a minute than we sometimes think.

The history of this region would be vastly different without first its newspapers and later its radio and television stations. Without the *St. Petersburg Times'* "Negro News Page," begun in 1939—we've forgotten what a bold statement that was back then—the path to integration in this area may have been harder than it was.

Without an AM news-talk radio show, ordering products online might still be a far-off fantasy—but that's how Home Shopping Network got started (see Shopping chapter).

Maybe most important of all, newspapers introduce us to each other. We cheer for the USF jazz professor who wins a Guggenheim Fellowship. We pray the young babysitters-to-be at an All Children's Hospital child care class remember the graphic lesson about shaken-baby syndrome. We vicariously join a hip-hop class with a forty-something, curious reporter.

This book follows in the tradition of the *Tampa Herald*, the area's first newspaper. First published in January 1854, its pages reveal much about the details of life in long-ago Tampa. This book, too, is a record—a snapshot, if you will—of the Tampa Bay area, which not only tells today's readers what to expect when they come here, but also leaves future readers a record of what life was like in this place, at this time.

Readers interested in how news organizations gather, process, and package information can look for a Close-up about the Poynter Institute, a think-tank training center for journalists and other media professionals.

As the newsboys used to cry: Read all about it!

ℹ️ We have used the words "circulation" to mean an independently confirmed number of newspapers or magazines distributed; "distribution" to mean the number of copies of a publication the publisher says it distributes; and "readership" to mean the number of estimated readers of all the publications distributed. Five people in one household might read the same single newspaper, for instance.

MAGAZINES

In this section we've included only magazines with content about some aspect of life in the Tampa Bay area. Magazines about fishing the Tampa Bay area are listed in the Gone Fishin' Close-up in the Parks and Recreation chapter. Elsewhere in the chapter you'll find a listing of publishers of other magazines and publications. We're proud they choose to make their businesses' home here.

CIGAR CITY MAGAZINE
P.O. Box 18613
Tampa
(813) 373-9988
www.cigarcitymagazine.com

Cigar City Magazine is a labor of love for publisher Lisa M. Figueredo and her staff. It shows in the detail on every page. Published bimonthly, *Cigar City Magazine* articles feature the history and culture of Ybor City. Recent articles have featured Ybor City's Cigar City Mafia, a Roller Derby team, and the artists who designed the labels wrapped around early 20th-century cigars. You'll find some fiction stories here, too, and many of the illustrations are old photographs. *Cigar City Magazine* claims 13,000 subscribers and 25,000 copies sold at 51 area outlets.

FAMILIES ON-THE-GO
P.O. Box 55445
St. Petersburg
(727) 522-2274, (813) 814-5702
www.familiesonthego.org

Families on-the-Go publishes two editions—one for Hillsborough County and one for Pinellas County—every two months and can be found in area supermarkets, doctors' offices, libraries, and other places. It is also sent home with children in some preschools and private schools. *Families on-the-Go* provides information about education, parenting, and wellness. Combined distribution is about 120,000. Barbara Doyle is owner and publisher.

FLORIDA TREND
490 1st Ave. S., 8th Floor
St. Petersburg
(727) 821-5800
www.floridatrend.com

Florida Trend, with a circulation of just over 56,000 and owned by Times Publishing Company, focuses on business news in Florida, but you'll also find articles on removing tattoos and what's coming up at area performing arts centers. *Florida Trend* recognizes restaurants with the Golden Spoon Awards. Check out the "Great Florida Restaurant Guide" on their Web page—it's one of the special sections published throughout the year, along with "Florida Small Business," "Logistics and Supply Chain Management," and "Best Companies to Work for in Florida." *Florida Trend* has won numerous industry awards for both writing and design. Publisher is Bruce Faulmann.

FORUM
The Florida Humanities Council
599 2nd St. S.
St. Petersburg
(727) 873-200
www.flahum.org

Each issue of FORUM features one aspect of Florida. FORUM has studied "Cracker Country," telling us about Florida's first cowmen and Florida folk music radio stations today. FORUM has also looked at where Florida is headed, discussing such things as climate change and changing demographics. FORUM, published quarterly by the Florida Humanities Council, has a circulation of about 50,000.

TAMPA BAY ILLUSTRATED
5110 Eisenhower Blvd., Ste. 165
Tampa
(813) 739-6670
www.tampabayillustrated.com

Tampa Bay Illustrated features Tampa Bay area globetrotters, who share their take on exotic destinations or local eateries with scrumptious fare, and spotlights area events, all lusciously illustrated, of course. Plus you'll find who-was-seen-where photo pages. Tampa Bay Illustrated, published by Palm Beach Media Group, has a circulation of about 20,000, and claims a readership of 100,000. Publisher is Ronald J. Woods.

TAMPA BAY MAGAZINE
2531 Landmark Dr., Ste. 101
Clearwater
(727) 791-4800
www.tampabaymagazine.com

Tampa Bay Magazine has featured the best "People, Places, and Pleasures" in the Tampa Bay area. That means you might read about a local artist—and see some of his work—or about a local restaurant—and vicariously taste the food. Tampa Bay Magazine is published every two months by Tampa Bay Publications, Inc.

TAMPA BAY METRO MAGAZINE
Metro Life Media, Inc.
4856 W. Gandy Blvd.
Tampa
(813) 835-7700
www.tampabaymetro.com

Tampa Bay Metro Magazine, focusing on Tampa's metro areas, might feature Hyde Park kitchens or write about a savvy new business in the area. Published monthly by Metro Life Media, Inc., and distributed in area bookstores and supermarkets, Tampa Bay Metro's publisher is Stephen Parag II.

TAMPA BAY PARENTING MAGAZINE
P.O. Box 82255
Tampa 33682-2255
(813) 949-4400
www.tbparenting.com

Parenting isn't for the faint of heart, that's for sure. In Tampa Bay Parenting Magazine you'll find helpful articles about topics like juvenile diabetes, selecting just the right summer camp, and stirring up healthy recipes with kid appeal. Tampa Bay Parenting Magazine, which is published monthly by Lucy Loo, Inc., claims a circulation of 30,000. The publisher is Angela Ardolino.

DAILY NEWSPAPERS

ST. PETERSBURG TIMES
490 First Ave. S.
St. Petersburg
(727) 893-8111
www.sptimes.com

TAMPA TRIBUNE
200 S. Parker St.
Tampa
(813) 259-7711
www.tampatrib.com

Our two daily newspapers have vastly, different business plans. The Tampa Tribune is part of Media General, a conglomerate of news and other media outlets. The St. Petersburg Times is owned by a nonprofit organization, the Poynter Institute. Each in its own way has blazed new trails in today's media world.

It used to be that newspapers were owned by one person—the archetypical fearless editor, doing nothing but battling the malevolent overlords at city hall and other equally dastardly doers of evil, publishing the truth, the whole truth, and nothing but the truth, so help him or her Johannes Gutenberg. Right?

Not quite.

Many of yesterday's editors were printers of government documents and religious pamphlets who put together a newspaper on the side. Their international news was gathered from letters sent home by ship captains or soldiers.

Then merchants learned advertising meant more business, and newspapers learned merchants' advertisements in their newspapers' pages boosted their profits.

For a time, newspapers made hefty profits. Outside companies began buying newspapers to fund other projects. Sometimes those companies owned competing news organizations. Sometimes those companies were ones the news organizations had been reporting about.

News organizations merged. Others went out of business. Anyone with a computer could start a news service online. But what happens if the only news available becomes whoever can shoot information through the Web the quickest, regardless of how accurate the aim is? Does whoever has the biggest mouth win?

Wikipedia, the online reference source based on the premise that each person is equally committed to the absolute truth and will edit articles accordingly, recently dealt with that issue. They banned certain people from editing certain articles. (See Worship chapter)

All of which makes it an interesting game of marbles for news publishers and broadcasters, editors, reporters, and other media employees. For readers, too.

The *Tampa Tribune* and Media General

In 1926, Virginia newspaper owner John Stewart Bryan found his way to Tampa.

Tampa had had a number of newspapers since January 1854, when the *Tampa Herald* began. The *Herald* became the *Florida Peninsular* less than a year later. Tampa's first daily newspaper, the *Tampa Daily News*, started as a weekly in 1887, but began publishing daily in 1896.

In 1895, Wallace Fisher Stovall formed the Tampa Tribune Publishing Co., and began a weekly paper called the *Tampa Tribune*. Stovall had other papers, too. In 1925, he apparently sold the company—or at least interest in it—to a group of Tampa businessmen.

Things were going well at that time in Florida—you can read about the Plant railroad and hotels, the discovery of phosphate, the growth of tourism, and the real estate boom in the History chapter.

Then in 1926, the boom went bust. The owners of the *Tribune*, also investors in area banks, looked at their investments a bit differently than they had the previous year.

Enter John Stewart Bryan, from Richmond and by then president of the American Newspaper Publisher's Association. In 1927, he and partner Samuel Emory Thomason, previously vice-president and general manager of the *Chicago Tribune*, bought the Tampa Tribune Publishing Co. A *Time* magazine article from 1927 lists the purchase price as $900,000.

Two years later, Thomason went back to Chicago and started the *Chicago Daily Times*.

Bryan held on to the *Tampa Tribune*. Over the years, The Tribune Co. grew to include the *Tampa Tribune*, the *Tampa Times*, WFLA-TV, and WFLA radio.In 1966, the Bryan family's Richmond Newspapers, Inc., acquired control of The Tribune Co. In 1969, Media General was formed.

In 2000, Media General set a new, 21st-century standard for the nation's news organizations by opening the Tampa News Center, which converged the newsrooms of the *Tampa Tribune*, WFLA-TV, and TBO.com. This convergence, or sharing of newsroom resources across various media platforms, has advantages—two heads being better than one—and disadvantages—corporate bosses tend to think only one head—and one salary—is needed.

Of more concern is how many fewer eyes are now observing and reporting on events in ever-larger communities.

Seventy-some years later, you could say the *Tribune* is still a part of the Bryan family, although it's now part of their company, Media General. John Stewart Bryan III is chairman of the board, and the *Tribune*'s interests are well represented among board members.

Media General is a publicly traded company now, which means investors generally expect growth, dividends, and profits—and think less about the intangible benefits news organizations bring to a community.

The *St. Petersburg Times* and the Poynter Institute

The other side of Tampa Bay had newspapers, too. In 1873, Reverend Cooley S. Reynolds, who had started Tampa's first newspaper almost 20 years earlier, started Clearwater's first newspaper, the *Clearwater Times.*

In 1884, the *West Hillsborough Times* (Pinellas was still part of Hillsborough County at that time) began publishing in Dunedin. Six months later, the three men who had started the paper sold it to Arthur C. Turner, who moved the paper to Clearwater.

In 1892, Turner sold the *West Hillsborough Times* to Richard James Morgan, who moved it to St. Petersburg and changed the name to the *St. Petersburg Times.* Morgan sold it to others, who, in 1901, sold the *St. Petersburg Times* to three St. Petersburg businessmen, one of whom was W. L. Straub, for $1,300.

In 1912, publisher Paul Poynter came to St. Petersburg from Indiana and became smitten with the *Times.* Within two days of hitting town, Poynter bought the paper, keeping W. L. Straub as editor. They formed Times Publishing Co. When Straub died in 1939, Poynter's son, Nelson, became editor.

Nelson Poynter became president of Times Publishing Co., as well as editor, when his father

died in 1950. He also became principal stockholder in Times Publishing Co.

The *St. Petersburg Times* grew by expanding into Pasco, Hernando, and Citrus counties.

In 1975, Nelson Poynter formed a non-profit educational institution called the Modern Media Institute. When he died in 1978, he left his stock in Times Publishing Co. to the Institute (see the Poynter Institute sidebar, below).

But Nelson Poynter had only owned the majority interest in Times Publishing Co. A relative and heirs owned the rest and eventually sold it outside the family. The issue wasn't resolved until 1990, when Times Publishing Co. bought the remaining stock back and gave it to what had been renamed the Poynter Institute.

Where the Media Marbles Are Today

Today, Media General owns three metropolitan newspapers on the East Coast, including the *Tampa Tribune*; 21 smaller daily papers in five states; more than 250 other weekly newspapers and other publications; 18 television stations, including WFLA-TV in Tampa; more than 75 online news enterprises; a non-news online enterprise, DealTaker.com; two game companies; and assorted real estate. In short, Media General owns more daily newspapers than any other company in the southeastern United States.

Here's what Media General owns and operates in Tampa:

- Daily paper: *The Tampa Tribune*
- Television station: WFLA-TV
- Online: TBO.com and CentroTampa.com
- Weekly papers: *Centro Tampa, Brandon News and Tribune, Carrollwood News and Tribune, Northeast News and Tribune, Northwest News and Tribune, Plant City Courier and Tribune, South Shore News and Tribune, The Sun, The Suncoast News* (four editions for Pasco North, Pasco West, Pasco East, and North Pinellas), and the *MacDill Thunderbolt.*
- Monthly publications: *The FishHawker* (a community in Hillsborough County) and the *Bloomingdale Gazette* (the official publication of a homeowner's association).

The Poynter Institute

The Poynter Institute
801 3rd St. S.
St. Petersburg
(888) 769-6837
www.poynter.org

Housed in a not-very-big building across the street from the University of South Florida's St. Petersburg campus, the Poynter Institute is part school, part retreat center for journalists from around the world.

Reporters, editors, photographers, and broadcasters come to Poynter for mid-career pick-me-ups. They come to pick up new skills that reporters didn't need in newsrooms 10 or 20 years ago—skills like putting together a podcast. Or shooting video and editing it into a coherent two-minute spot to be uploaded to the Web.

Journalists also come to Poynter to wrestle with hard-to-answer questions like, "When do you refer to a person's race when you're writing an article?" or "Should mug shots of people who have been arrested—but not convicted—be posted online?"

Journalists also come to Poynter to be reminded of why they work nights and weekends for less pay than many of their friends in other professions are making now.

They share stories of how what they have written or posted has made a difference in their communities. They talk about evil exposed and ordinary lives validated by their work.

The surroundings themselves boost journalists' spirits.

Nelson Poynter's old manual typewriter sits on a stand with some paper beside it. Journalists are invited to type a note to themselves and to be encouraged. A life-sized bronze statue of a man reading a newspaper sits in the garden—a reminder of the solid, undergirding power of accurate, proportional information delivered in a timely and compelling manner.

For the rest of us who need to understand how news gets to us—who filters what, why, and how—www.poynter.org can be a valuable tool. Explore their Web site and read articles on many of the same issues being reported in the newspapers and on TV and radio. But they'll be discussed with an eye toward how much coverage should be given to celebrity shenanigans, how journalists in Afghanistan ferret out their information, and what to do when officials stonewall reporters asking tough health care questions. Read the feedback, too, because not everyone agrees about what constitutes bias in reporting or how much a news organization influences events by its choice of what to broadcast first or most.

You don't need a password to browse, and there's a lot to learn.

- The weekly newspapers owned by Media General are published by the *Tampa Tribune*. All weekly papers except the *MacDill Thunderbolt*, which is published on Friday, are published on Wednesday. Each has an online link on TBO.com.

Here's what the Poynter Institute owns through Times Publishing Co. and Times Media Services, Inc.:

- Daily paper: The *St. Petersburg Times*, including various regional editions; *tbt* Tampa Bay Times*, a free tabloid

- Online: Tampabay.com, PolitiFact.com (matches what politicians say with what they do)
- Weekly papers: The papers published by Tampa Bay Newspapers, Inc. These wholly owned, but independently published, affiliate papers are listed separately under Weekly Newspapers.
- Magazine: *Florida Trend*
- Other publications: *Congressional Quarterly* and *Governing Magazine* in Washington, D.C., *Senior Living Guide*

Times Publishing Co. does not own any television or radio stations, but partners with Bay News 9 for political and sports coverage and with Clear Channel Radio Tampa Bay for hurricane coverage.

WEEKLY NEWSPAPERS

There are many, many weekly papers in the area—ethnic papers, religious papers, niche publications focusing on particular topics. Here, we'll list only the most widely circulated or longest running papers in the area. Check coffee shops and other small restaurants for distribution racks carrying an assortment of small papers, and pick up a local paper to read with your morning latte.

BARRIER ISLANDS GAZETTE
118 107th Ave.
Treasure Island
(727) 360-7315
www.barrierislandsgazette.com
The *Barrier Islands Gazette* publishes news about the Pinellas County barrier islands from Clearwater Beach to St. Pete Beach on the first and the 16th of each month. The gazette includes news, editorials, dining, entertainment, and classified sections. Publisher is William Edwards and circulation is about 30,000.

CENTRO TAMPA
202 S. Parker St.
Tampa
(813) 259-8183, (888) 214-4881
www.centrotampa.com

Centro Tampa, published every Friday, claims to be the Tampa Bay area's leading weekly Spanish-language newspaper. Content includes local news, consumer information, sports, entertainment, editorials, and classified ads. A Media General publication, *Centro Tampa* has its own Web site, but also has a tab on TBO.com. Circulation is about 55,000.

ℹ **Other Spanish-language weekly newspapers include *La Prensa Tampa* (www.impre.com/laprensafl/home.php), *Nuevo Siglo* (www.nuevosiglotampa.com), and *Siete Dias* (www.7dias.us), which also publishes a Spanish-language magazine, *La Guia Tampa Bay* (www.issuu.com/laguiadel golfo/docs/guia_jun_tampa_issu).**

CLEARWATER GAZETTE
2401 W. Bay Dr.
Bldg. 100, Ste. 125
Largo
(727) 446-6723
www.clearwatergazette.com
The *Clearwater Gazette* comes out every Thursday, just as it has every Thursday since 1950. Covering events at six City Halls in the greater Clearwater area, as well as social news the larger papers often don't have room for, the *Clearwater Gazette* also includes columns by the County Sheriff and one of the County Commissioners. The *Clearwater Gazette* is a free paper distributed at various local north-county libraries, businesses, condos, and homes. Sandy Pollick is owner and publisher. Circulation is about 17,000.

CREATIVE LOAFING TAMPA
810 N. Howard Ave.
Tampa
(813) 739-4800
tampa.creativeloafing.com
Creative Loafing Tampa, the area's third largest newspaper, is a privately owned, weekly alternative paper that focuses mostly on arts and entertainment, although you'll find some news and witty political commentary, too. Reviews are in-depth and wide-ranging. Caution: Salty lan-

guage and adult topics throughout make this a "parental discretion advised" kind of publication. Publisher is Sharry Smith. Creative Loafing, Inc., has papers in other major U.S. cities.

FLORIDA COURIER
5207 E. Washington Blvd.
Tampa
(813) 620-1300
www.flcourier.com

The *Florida Courier* is a statewide publication covering black communities, including those of West Indian and Caribbean origin, in Florida's metropolitan areas. The *Florida Courier*, owned by Central Florida Communicators Group, Inc., and published each Friday, is available free at stores, churches, and other spots. Circulation is 75,000 statewide. Publisher is Dr. Charles Cherry.

FLORIDA SENTINEL BULLETIN
2207 21st Ave.
Tampa
(813) 248-1921
www.flsentinel.org

The *Florida Sentinel Bulletin* has been putting out a paper every Tuesday and Friday in Tampa since 1945, but its history goes back to 1919. That's when W. W. Andrews started the *Florida Sentinel* newspaper in Jacksonville. The paper folded in 1929, but son Cyril Blythe Andrews resurrected the paper in Tampa in 1945. He also purchased the *Tampa Bulletin* and merged the two into today's *Florida Sentinel Bulletin*. Today, the paper is the only African-American newspaper in the state publishing twice weekly, is printed in-house, and has the fourth generation of the Andrews family at the helm. The paper is distributed to households and newsstands in Hillsborough, Pinellas, and Polk counties. Circulation is about 25,000, and the publisher is S. Kay Andrews Wells.

LA GACETA
3210 7th Ave. E.
Tampa
(813) 248-3921
www.lagacetanewspaper.com

La Gaceta has printed more history on its pages than most other weekly newspapers in the Tampa Bay area. In 1922, Victoriano Manteiga, a *lector* or reader in the Ybor City cigar factories, began publishing a Spanish-language newspaper for the area. But the content wasn't confined to happenings around Ybor City or even just in Tampa. *La Gaceta's* readers had international ties and so international news was part of its pages. In the 1940s English, and then Italian, news and columns were added, making it the nation's only trilingual newspaper for many years. Today, the paper's editor and publisher is Patrick Manteiga, grandson of the founder.

THE NEWS
P.O. Box 271880
Tampa 33688
(813) 909-2800
www.cnewspubs.com

The News is an independent publication covering the northwestern Hillsborough communities of Citrus Park, Lutz, and Odessa. Published every Wednesday, *The News* has a circulation of 10,300. Publisher is Diane Mathes.

PINELLAS NEWS
533 4th St. N.
St. Petersburg
(727) 894-2411
www.pinellas-news.com

The *Pinellas News* prints news from all parts of the Pinellas County community, is available countywide through coin boxes, and mails copies to subscribers throughout the United States. Circulation is 1,200. The *Pinellas News* has been owned by Potter Media, Inc., since 1993, and the publisher is Robert Potter.

TAMPA BAY BUSINESS JOURNAL
4890 West Kennedy Blvd., Ste. 850
Tampa
(813) 873-8225
www.tampabay.bizjournals.com/tampabay

Tampa Bay Business Journal is part of American Business Journals, Inc., which publishes a host of other local business-related products. *Tampa Bay Business Journal*, issued each Friday, provides focused coverage of local businesses and business-related issues in a seven-county area. Their online edition provides continuous coverage, and they offer a daily e-mail subscription service. The paper is available by subscription or can be found at many bookstores and newsstands. *Tampa Bay Business Journal*'s publisher is Bridgette Mill. Distribution is about 8,500 plus a daily e-mail subscriber base of about 15,000.

TAMPA BAY NEWSPAPERS, INC.
9911 Seminole Blvd.
Seminole
(727) 397-5563
www.tbnweekly.com
Seven weekly newspapers—*Beach Beacon, Belleair Bee, Clearwater Citizen, Dunedin Leader, Largo Leader, Pinellas Park Beacon,* and *Seminole Beacon*—are published by Tampa Bay Newspapers, Inc., a wholly owned but independent affiliate of Times Publishing Company. In addition to covering local city council meetings in the mid-Pinellas and beaches areas, Pinellas County commission meetings, and Pinellas County Schools meetings, Tampa Bay Newspapers' publications include feature articles, entertainment reviews, sports articles, editorials, and classified ads. Combined circulation is about 120,000. Publisher is Dan Autrey.

THE WEEKLY CHALLENGER
2500 Dr. Martin Luther King Jr. St. S.
St. Petersburg
(727) 896-2922
www.theweeklychallenger.com
The Weekly Challenger has been publishing news about and for the African-American community in the Tampa Bay area for over 40 years. Publisher and owner is Ethel Johnson, and the circulation is 10,000.

BIWEEKLY AND MONTHLY NEWSPAPERS

C & N PUBLICATIONS, INC.
490 Alt. U.S. 19
Palm Harbor
(727) 789-8980
www.cnpubs.com

C & N Publications publishes a dozen free monthly community newspapers (*East Lake Eagle, Countryside Cougar, Top o' the Bay Journal, Largo Today,* et al.), which are direct-mailed to every home in a particular geographic area within mid- and northern-Pinellas County. These are franchised newspapers filled with "good for you" features and spotlights on area businesses, and also include local police crime reports. Because they are direct-mailed, circulation figures are not available.

JEWISH PRESS OF PINELLAS COUNTY
JEWISH PRESS OF TAMPA
P.O. Box 6970
Clearwater 33758
(727) 535-4400, (813) 871-2332
www.jewishpress.us
Jewish Press of Pinellas County and *Jewish Press of Tampa*, published biweekly most months, cover news of interest to the Jewish community. *Jewish Press of Pinellas County* is mailed to about 6,500 subscriber households, and *Jewish Press of Tampa* is mailed to almost 5,000 subscriber households. Additional copies are dropped at local synagogues, businesses, and other places. Owned by the Jewish Press Group of Tampa Bay, Inc., the publisher is Jim Dawkins

KHAAS BAAT
18313 Cypress Stand Circle
Tampa
(813) 758-1786
www.khaasbaat.com
Since 2004, *Khaas Baat* has been covering news about the Indian-American community throughout Florida. The English-language monthly publication is mailed to subscribers and is distributed at South Asian grocery stores and restaurants. Published by Khaas Batt Communications, the paper's distribution is about 25,000.

THE INTERNET

Online news sources have become a predominant source of information for many people. Putting the news online takes more than just uploading a printed file to a Web site. People read things online differently than they do in print, and the number of items that can be seen peripherally is different.

As an example, readers glance at headlines in the print edition of a newspaper to decide what they want to read. But in that same glance, they also take in the approximate length of the article. The length of the article tells them how important the editor thought the article was and about how much time it might take the reader to read it.

A link to an online article generally doesn't give that kind of information. But there might be more headlines, or links, to more articles on the front page than there would be in a print edition.

Print and online editions published by the same news organization often have different editors, who make independent decisions about how articles are placed for readers to view. Online newsrooms may have their own reporters shooting video and doing audio podcasts, or they may be relying on the print or broadcasting reporters to do it all—which can be a bit like trying to be the plumber, the electrician, and the painter on a remodeling job, all at the same time.

These online news sites each are part of a company that also either prints or broadcasts news:

- BayNews9.com: See listing under Television Stations
- SPTimes.com: See listing under *St. Petersburg Times* newspaper
- TampaBay.com: See listing under *St. Petersburg Times* newspaper
- TBO.com: See listing under *Tampa Tribune* newspaper

RADIO

Children's

1380 AM/WWMI
www.radio.disney.go.com
Radio Disney targets the younger crowd and their parents—ads are for private schools and home improvements—and you'll hear people like Miley Cyrus, Jordin Sparks, and the Jonas Brothers. Homework tips and reminders to "ask mom and dad" are tossed into the mix.

Classical/Jazz

89.7 FM/WUSF
www.wusf.usf.edu/wusf-fm
We've put this University of South Florida station under the heading of classical/jazz. However, you'll also hear National Public Radio essays, *A Prairie Home Companion*, *Car Talk*, and a host of other programs in between the music.

Contemporary

1590 AM/WRXB
www.wrxb.us
Urban contemporary might describe the music on WRXB—but you'll hear interviews and talk, too.

93.3 FM/WFLZ
www.933flz.com
Beyonce, Jamie Foxx, and Kelly Clarkson are some of the artists you'll hear on WFLZ. Weekend programming includes *American Top 40 with Ryan Seacrest* and *Rewind Sunday* that digs way back into the music of the 90s.

94.9 FM/WWRM
www.newmagic949.com
Christina Aguilera, Lifehouse, Madonna, Jason Mraz, and Shania Twain make for a magic mix on WWRM, the New Magic. Music during the day, talk and other programming, and "what's happening in the area" kind of news plays here.

95.7 FM/WBTP
www.957thebeat.com
The Beat goes on and on at WBTP where they play hip-hop and R&B artists like Fast Life Yungstaz, Letoya, and Kid Cudi. Sign up for their VIP club or check out their Sunday Morning Glory Playlist.

100.7 FM/WMTX
www.wmtx.com/main.html
They call this The Mix, and that's what you'll find. A mix of music—upbeat, adult contemporary artists like Theory of a Deadman, Fastball, Miley Cyrus, and others—and news, health, sports, and other tidbits mixed in throughout the day.

Country

99.5 FM/WQYK
www.wqyk.com

Country pure and simple is what you'll hear on WQYK—Jason Aldean, Trace Adkins, Martina McBride, and more. Plus there are contests and concerts and remote broadcasts. *The Polka King*? Guess you'll have to tune in midday to find out.

103.5/WFUS
www.us1035.com

WFUS bills itself as "Tampa Bay's best country," so you won't be surprised to find Valerie Hart, Keith Urban, Toby Keith, and more. Look for a link on their Web site that takes you to Bucs Country—home of the Tampa Bay Buccaneers.

Ethnic

760 AM/WLCC
www.laleytampa.com

La Ley's mix of Latin music includes Patrulla 81, Arroyadora, Sergio Vega, and others. Plus you'll hear laid-back banter between the music and some times for call-in-and-talk-back spots.

1300 AM/WQBN
www.q1300.com

Spanish language radio Super Q, "La Clasica de la Bahia," plays the music of Latin artists from many countries—think Orlando Vallejo and others—and also hosts talk shows on a variety of topics.

1520 AM/WXYB
www.wpso.com

The Web site says this is Greek radio and TV, but you'll hear a mixture of international programming—Greek, Polish, Italian, Arabic, Spanish, Indian, and English. You might hear news, music, or religious programs. From 8 a.m. to 2 p.m. each weekday, WXYB is the home of Hillsborough Community College's Hawk Radio. Listen to Hawk Radio 24/7 on the Internet (www.hawkradio.com).

1550 AM/WAMA
www.lainvasora1550.com

Think Tigres del Norte, Vicente Fernandez, Conjunto Primavera, Alicia Villareal, and other Latin music artists when you think La Invasora.

92.5 FM/WYUU
www.925maxima.com

This CBS affiliate, Spanish-language radio station plays Latin music and more Latin music so listeners can dance their workday away—wonder if there have been any studies done along that line?

96.5 FM/WVVD-LP
Iglesia Cristiana La Nueva Jerusalem—Spanish Catholic programming.

News/Talk

860 AM/WGUL
www.860wgul.townhall.com

WGUL makes no bones about being a Townhall.com station "designed to amplify . . . conservative voices in America's political debates." Along with local news, traffic, and one-minute movie reviews, you'll hear interviews and discussion about various issues.

970 AM/WFLA
www.970wfla.com

There's a mix of local news and commentary by such national radio personalities as Todd Schnitt, Rush Limbaugh, Mark Levin, and others on WFLA. (Note: WFLA radio is not affiliated with WFLA TV.)

1250 AM/WHNZ
www.whnz.com

"Impact Radio" is how WHNZ describes itself. Monday through Friday mornings you can hear the latest from the *Wall Street Journal*. The rest of the day it's a mix of health, finances, and news. The Web site includes sports and other news.

1340 AM/WTAN
www.tantalk1340.com

Want to create your own radio program? Lease an hour from WTAN and go for it! Programming topics here range from health to financial—but you'll also hear some music, and a show on bowling.

1470 AM/WMGG
www.radiogenesis.net/newstalk820

Business news is the focus on this station, which used to be at a different place on the dial, with different call letters, with a different format, and with different owners. That explains why, when you go to the Web site, you'll see 820WWBA. Call in with a tax question, or listen to the discussion surrounding foreign investments.

Oldies/Classics

101.5 FM/WPOI
www.1015thepoint.com

Remember the 1980s? It wasn't all that long ago, so maybe "oldies" is a bit premature. The Point plays Aerosmith, Bon Jovi, and U2, and keeps listeners current as to what's happening around the Tampa Bay area. Early risers can listen between 6 and 7 a.m. for the Nearly Impossible Question to get their brains working.

104.7 FM/WRBQ
www.tampabaysq105.com

Tampa Bay's Q105 has been playing oldies since forever. Of course the definition changes a bit each decade. Now you'll hear Three Dog Night and Fleetwood Mac along with the Beatles' "Twist and Shout." Local radio personality Mason Dixon has got to have one of the Tampa Bay area's longest running morning shows, *Mason in the Morning*.

107.3 FM/WXGL
www.1073theeagle.com

Tampa Bay listeners fly with The Eagle's line-up, which includes Paul McCartney, Doobie Brothers, Lynyrd Skynyrd, The Cars, and more—classic hits from not so long ago. Sign up online to be a Frequent Flyer.

Religious

570 AM/WTBN
www.bayword.com

Programs from nationally known radio preachers and personalities like Chuck Swindoll, John MacArthur, Dr. David Jeremiah, and Joni Eareckson Tada are broadcast over WTBN. You'll hear movie reviews and commentary, as well.

680 AM/WGES
www.genesis680.com

Spanish-language religious programming includes *Buenos Dias Familia*, *Iglesia el Rey Jesus with Pastor Kerwin Castillo*, plus afternoon music and evening broadcasts of Tampa Bay Rays' games.

88.9 FM/WYFE
www.bbnradio.org

Part of the Bible Broadcasting Network, WTIS broadcasts sermons, radio drama like Pacific Garden Mission's *Unshackled*, and other religious programming.

90.5 FM/WBVM
www.spiritfm905.com

Spirit FM plays contemporary Christian music throughout the day interspersed with prayer, the Mass, and other family-friendly programming. Sunday evening from 6 p.m. to midnight the programs are in Spanish and include Latin contemporary religious music and prayer.

91.7 FM/WFTI
www.familyradio.com

Part of the Family Radio network, WFTI airs *Family Bible Reading Fellowship*, *Radio Reading Circle*, parenting shows, and other religious programming.

Rock

97.9 FM/WXTB
www.98rock.com

97.9 is close enough to 98.0 that that's what you'll hear WXTB call themselves—98Rock. Sign up on their Web site if you want to be a Rock-a-holic. Otherwise tune in for your daily dose of heavy rock—98 minutes non-stop beginning at 9 a.m.

Sports/Sports Talk

620 AM/WDAE
www.620wdae.com

WDAE calls itself "The Sports Animal," and you'll hear the play-by-plays as the Tampa Bay Rays slug it out with the Mets or the Rockies or whoever the foe *du jour* is. Bucs, Lightning, Gators, and Storm games, too, are covered as well as golf, racing, and other members of the sports menagerie.

1010 AM/WQYK
www.1010sportsonline.com

For the times when you can't play sports or watch sports, there's talk sports on 1010 AM radio—11 hours each day of talkin' Rays baseball, Bucs football, Lightning hockey, and other sports. Plus you'll hear play-by-plays and sports updates.

1040 AM/WHBO
www.espn1040.com

You'll hear ESPN more than you will the call letters of this station. Mostly you'll hear sports talk and sports talk and more sports talk. Plus they'll broadcast the games and related commentary.

Variety

88.5 FM/WMNF
www.wmnf.org

Right—how do you categorize a station that plays Latin music, bluegrass, the *Polka Party Express*, alternative, metal, and jazz, plus has other programs ranging from one on Buddhism to one on poetry? Variety works. WMNF is a non-profit, truly community radio station.

i *Radio Years: Central Florida's Great Radio Stations of the Past* is **the Web site for radio history buffs. You'll find complete histories—photos and audio clips, too—of all the radio stations in Polk County, plus histories for many stations in the Tampa Bay area, at www.radioyears .com.**

TELEVISION STATIONS

With cable and satellite extending our viewing range, we could list all the stations in the world as ones available here in the Tampa Bay area. Not. We'll list only ones that broadcast from here, including a couple of government channels and one cable channel. Most of these stations also have cable slots, so you'll want to check your cable schedule for the correct channel number. Since the change to digital broadcasting, many of these stations stream more than one channel.

BAY NEWS 9
Hillsborough Bureau
4400 Martin Luther King Jr. Blvd.
Tampa

Pinellas Bureau
700 Carillon Pkwy, Ste. 9
St. Petersburg
(727) 329-2300
www.baynews9.com

Bay News 9 is a Bright House Network Cable channel providing 24-hour news, weather, and other coverage of the Tampa Bay area in both English and Spanish. Feature spots include cooking, home improvements, gardening, local travel, and entertainment. Bright House Sports Network (www.bhsn.com) covers local sports in the Tampa Bay and Orlando areas.

WCLF-TV CHANNEL 22
Christian Television Network
6922 142nd Ave. N.
Largo
(727) 535-5622
www.ctnonline.com

WCLF-TV signed on in the fall of 1979 as an independent, Christian television station, making it one of the oldest religious television stations in the nation. Today, it is the flagship station in a network of 13 stations in the Southeast and Midwest, plus it has an online site. CTN-produced programming includes *The Good Life, Homekeepers, Gospel Voice,* and *Christian Fitness,* among others. Other programs broadcast on WCLF-TV include *The 700 Club* and *Gaither Homecoming* shows.

WEDU-TV CHANNEL 3
Florida West Coast Public Broadcasting, Inc.
1300 N. Blvd.
Tampa
(813) 254-9338, (800) 354-9338
www.wedu.org
WEDU-TV is a PBS member station broadcasting to 16 counties in west central Florida. You'll find *NewsHour with Jim Lehrer, Sesame Street, Antiques Roadshow, Great Performances*, and more. Locally produced programs include *A Gulf Coast Journal, Florida This Week, Suncoast Business Forum*, and *Up Close*. WEDU-TV also airs The Florida Knowledge Network, produced by the Florida Department of Education. WEDU-DT1 (digital 3.2) broadcasts programs in Spanish.

WFLA-TV CHANNEL 8
Florida Communications Group
200–202 S. Parker St.
Tampa
(813) 259-7716, (813) 228-8888
www.wfla.com
WFLA-TV, which signed on the air in 1955, has been an NBC-network affiliate station for more than 50 years. Owned by Media General, WFLA-TV calls itself News Channel 8 and shares quarters with the *Tampa Tribune, Centro,* and TBO.com, also owned by Media General. Its news team has won numerous Emmys and other awards, and the station is considered number one in the Tampa Bay area marketplace. NBC programming includes *The Today Show, Oprah Winfrey Show*, and *Entertainment Tonight*.

WFTS-TV CHANNEL 28
WFTS ABC Action News
4045 N. Himes Ave.
Tampa
(813) 354-2828, (877) 833-2828
www.abcactionnews.com
Part of the Scripps TV Station Group, WFTS-TV is an ABC-network affiliate station. WFTS began in 1981 as an independent station and changed ownership several times before becoming an ABC affiliate in 1994. The station formed a news department at that time and has since won several awards. ABC programming includes *Good Morning America, Jeopardy!,* and *Wheel of Fortune*.

WFTT-TV CHANNEL 50
2610 W. Hillsborough Ave.
Tampa
(813) 684-5550
www.foro.univision.com/univision/board?
board.id=705098947
Channel 50 began broadcasting in 1988 as WBHS, Home Shopping Network's station. Univisión Communications, Inc., bought the station in 2002, and began a Spanish-language news network called Telefutura. Today, WFTT-TV is owned by Univisión, operated by Entravision (owners of WVEA-TV, with whom WFTT-TV shares facilities), and is part of the Telefutura network. Programs include *Veredicto Final* and *Betty la Fea* plus movies and local paid programming.

WMOR-TV CHANNEL 32
WMOR-TV
7201 E. Hillsborough Ave.
Tampa
(813) 626-3232
www.wmortv32.com
Owned by the Hearst Corporation, WMOR-TV is an independent station airing syndicated programming, movies, and other shows. Its D-2 channel is known as This TV and airs mostly movies.

WTOG-TV CHANNEL 44
WTOG-TV CW 44
365 105th Terrace N.E.
St. Petersburg
(727) 576-4444
www.cw44.com
Owned by CBS Corporation and serving as the Tampa Bay area station for CW Television Network, WTOG-TV airs syndicated programs, mov-

ies, and reality shows such as *America's Next Top Model*.

WTSP-TV CHANNEL 10
WTSP-TV/10 Connects
11450 Gandy Blvd.
St. Petersburg
(727) 577-1010
www.wtsp.com

WTSP-TV first went on the air as WLCY-TV, an ABC affiliate, in 1965. Today, WTSP is owned by Gannett Company and is a CBS affiliate. Over the years, WTSP-TV's news department has introduced the area's first news helicopter, the first portable microwave transmitter, the first use of a computer in weather forecasting, and the first use of Doppler radar. CBS programming includes *The Early Show, NCIS*, and the *Late Show with David Letterman*.

WTTA CHANNEL 38
My TV Tampa Bay
7622 Bald Cypress Place
Tampa
(813) 886-9882
www.wtta38.com

The frequency occupied by WTTA-TV was originally the home of the Tampa Bay area's first television station, WSUN-TV, which began broadcasting in 1953. WSUN-TV closed in 1970, and it wasn't until the late 1980s that WTTA-TV began broadcasting on the same frequency. Today, WTTA-TV is owned by the Sinclair Broadcasting Group. Programming includes *Deal or No Deal, Masters of Illusion, American Choppers*, and other syndicated programming.

WTVT-TV CHANNEL 13
3213 W. Kennedy Blvd.
Tampa
(813) 876-1313
www.myfoxtampabay.com

WTVT-TV first began broadcasting as a CBS affiliate station on April Fool's Day of 1955. Today, WTVT-TV is owned and operated by Fox Television Stations, Inc. The Fox 13 News team includes many award-winning journalists. Programming

on WTVT-TV includes *Regis and Kelly, So You Think You Can Dance*, and *House*.

i Fox 13's news anchor, John Wilson, and his wife, singer Mary K. Wilson, perform at Tampa Bay area events. Son Mark Wilson also anchors a Fox 13 newscast. Son Paul Wilson owns an advertising business and sings. Son Patrick Wilson played Raoul, Le Vicomte de Chagny, in the film *Phantom of the Opera*, and has earned Tony nominations for his stage work.

WUSF-TV CHANNEL 16
WUSF Public Broadcasting
4202 E. Fowler Ave.
TVB100
Tampa
(813) 974-8700, (800) 741-9090
www.wusf.usf.edu

Broadcasting from the University of South Florida since 1966, WUSF-TV receives programming from PBS, American Public Television, and other public networks. You'll find *History Detective, Barney, Nature,* and *Great Performances* among their listings. Locally produced programs include the Emmy award–winning *Expedition Florida, The University Beat*, and *Power Yoga for Mind and Body*.

WVEA-TV CHANNEL 62
2610 W. Hillsborough Ave.
Tampa
(813) 872-6262, (813) 998-3662
www.wveatv.com

Owned by Entravision Communications Corporation since 2001, WVEA-TV is a Spanish-language station and an affiliate of Univisión. WVEA-TV, the Tampa Bay area's first Spanish-language television station, began broadcasting in the early 1980s on channel 50. Programming includes local news, movies, and programs such as *Mañana es Para Siempre* and *Don Francisco Presents*. WVEA-LP carries the Home Shopping Network on channel 46.

WXPX CHANNEL 66
(212) 757-3100
www.iontelevision.com

Channel 66 began in 1994 and was founded by Home Shopping Network founder Bud Paxson (see Shopping chapter) after he left HSN. Paxson Communications has become ION Media Networks, which still owns the WXPX-TV. Today, the station is licensed just to the south of us in Bradenton, but you'll see it listed in Tampa Bay area TV guides. Programming is primarily syndicated reruns of top shows like *Boston Legal*, *M*A*S*H*, and *NCIS*.

Government Channels

WPDS-TV CHANNEL 14
Pinellas County Schools
301 4th St. S.W.
Largo
(727) 588-6357
www.wpds.tv
WPDS-TV has been broadcasting news and information about Pinellas County Schools since 1989. Today, coverage of school board and other meetings, programs highlighting students and schools around the county, interviews with school officials, and science and history documentaries WPDS-TV have won a number of national, and even international, awards for their productions. WPDS-TV can be found on Bright House Networks Channel 614, Knology Channel 14, and Verizon Channel 46.

HTV-22
Hillsborough Television
(813) 272-5362
www.htv22.org
HTV-22 airs on Bright House 622 and Verizon FiOS 22 and can also be viewed online. Programming includes Hillsborough County government meetings, Port Authority meetings, and Southwest Florida Water Management District meetings, plus *Informes Latino* and *Jobline*.

PCC-TV
Pinellas County Connection TV
(727) 464-4724
www.pinellascounty.org/tv

You can watch PCC-TV online or on three area cable channels: Bright House 622, Knology 18, or Verizon 44. County commission meetings, school board meetings, and other proceedings are part of the programming. But you can also learn about native plants and preparing for hurricanes, or see stories about Pinellas County residents.

PUBLISHERS

These publishers don't necessarily publish material about the Tampa Bay area, but their businesses are headquartered here.

BIZED
AACSB International
777 S. Harbour Island Blvd., Ste. 750
Tampa
(813) 769-6500
www.aacsb.edu
Published by the Association to Advance Collegiate Schools of Business, *BizEd* is a magazine for and about the world of business education. Published bimonthly, *BizEd* has a circulation of about 15,000, most of whom are college educators.

FAIRCOUNT MEDIA GROUP
United States HQ
701 N. West Shore Blvd.
Tampa
(813) 639-1900
www.faircount.com
Faircount Media Group publishes annual magazines and reports for a number of industries including defense (*National Museum of the Marine Corps*), government (*Alaska 50—Celebrating Alaska's 50th Anniversary of Statehood*), scientific and medical (*MRI Whole Body Scanner*), and sports (*Payne Stewart's Guide to Golf*).

GOING PLACES
AAA Auto Club South
1515 N. Westshore Blvd.
Tampa
(813) 289-5931
www.aaasouth.com/current_issue/home.asp

AAA Auto Club South's travel magazine, *Going Places*, takes members to places around the world as well as on motor trips throughout Florida, Georgia, Tennessee, and Puerto Rico.

LIGHTNING PUBLICATIONS, LLC
5009 W. Rio Vista Ave.
Tampa
(813) 881-0887
www.lightningpublications.com
This publisher's magazines—*Black and White Photography*, *Furniture and Cabinetmaking*, *Woodcarving*, *Woodturning*, and *Woodworking Plans and Projects*—are published in the United Kingdom, but the company's headquarters are in Tampa. They also publish home improvement books and DVDs.

WOMEN'S RUNNING MAGAZINE
1499 Beach Dr. S.E., Ste. B
St. Petersburg
(727) 502-9202
www.womensrunning.com
Founded by St. Petersburg businesswoman Dawna Stone, *Women's Running Magazine,* formerly *Her Sports + Fitness*, offers women-specific coverage of the running world.

THE MILITARY

I t's not surprising to find a strong military presence in an area that once was the headquarters for the Southern Division of the United States Army. Fort Brooke, established in 1823 soon after Florida became a state, brought federal troops to the then isolated area of Tampa Bay. Federal troops meant federal dollars to be spent at local establishments. Tampa grew, at least in part, because of Fort Brooke.

Today we are home to MacDill Air Force Base, in turn home to several joint commands involving every branch of the military, and to two United States Coast Guard facilities.

Where there are military bases, there are also military veterans and military retirees eligible for various benefits and services on or near military bases. Military personnel also mean military families. So we'll list the veterans' hospitals in Hillsborough and Pinellas, about Bay Pines National Cemetery, and veterans' organizations. We'll also give you information about 4-H groups just for military kids and other resources for military families.

THE ANTEBELLUM ARMY

Florida became a state in 1821 after the United States was the surprising victor in a long tug-of-war involving Spain, England, and, to a lesser extent, France, over the Florida peninsula (see History chapter).

The United States fought the Creek and Seminole people in the Creek War (1813–1814) and in the First Seminole War (1817–1818). General Andrew Jackson commanded the United States Army during those wars, which were fought primarily in southern Alabama and Georgia.

The History chapter recounts in detail how Brevet Colonel George Mercer Brooke, who had been brevetted during the War of 1812 for meritorious action in defending Fort Erie in 1814, brought four companies of soldiers to the largely uninhabited Tampa Bay area.

i Before the United States military established a system of giving medals to recognize bravery in battle, soldiers were rewarded with brevets—field promotions that were more honorary than anything else. The soldier wasn't entitled to any more pay, but he could use the title in correspondence. Brevet promotions occurred through the Civil War.

Brooke established what was then called Cantonment Brooke—more of a depot than a fortified fort—in January 1824 at a spot where the Hillsborough River (sometimes spelled "Hillsboro") emptied into the Hillsborough Bay, a finger of the larger Tampa Bay..

On December 28, 1835, two Fort Brooke companies under the command of Major Francis Langhorne Dade were ambushed north of Tampa near Bushnell, and 108 soldiers were killed.

By then, Brevet Colonel George Mercer Brooke was a Brigadier General overseeing the building of roads between Fort Howard and Fort Winnebago in Wisconsin. Colonel Zachary Taylor, one of the officers under Brooke's command, later served at Fort Brooke and, later still, became President,

Cantonment Brooke became Fort Brooke in 1835, and, for a short time, was the headquarters of the Southern Division of the United States Army during the Second Seminole War.

By 1858, Fort Brooke had been all but abandoned by the federal government. They still held title to this prime chunk of real estate in Tampa. Tampa's mayor, Captain James McKay, tried to get the federal government to turn the property over to the City of Tampa. They refused. So McKay tried to buy the property from the federal government. They refused that, too.

Instead, the United States Department of the Interior offered to rent the property to McKay. McKay posted a $1,000 bond and took possession of the property on January 1, 1861. Ten days later, Florida seceded from the United States, and the Confederate Army moved into the fort.

i Brevet Colonel George Mercer Brooke brought his wife to Tampa. Their son, John Mercer Brooke, born in Tampa in 1826, graduated from one of the earliest classes of the forerunner of the U. S. Naval Academy in 1847. In the mid-1850s, John Mercer Brooke invented the first deep-sea sounding device to map the ocean floor, making possible the Trans-Atlantic telegraph cable, laid in 1858.

CIVIL WAR INCIVILITIES

With the Confederate Army at Fort Brooke holding the harbor and the Confederate Navy on Egmont Key holding the lighthouse, U.S. Navy troops arrived. Union troops soon took over Egmont Key, but not before Confederate troops had removed the lens from the lighthouse.

The only actual Civil War battle in the Tampa Bay area occurred in 1863 near Ballast Point. Confederate troops ambushed Federal troops returning from burning a couple of McKay's ships. A few men were killed and captured on either side.

Fort Brooke came to an inglorious end when three Federal gunboats landed in Tampa one spring day in 1864, and not a Confederate soldier was there to stop them. They were all rounding up cattle in the interior or were foraging further south. The Federal troops pulled down Fort Brooke's stockades, destroyed the cannon and machine shops, and ransacked the town. A month later, the Federal troops decided Tampa wasn't worth bothering with, and they left.

Federal troops occupied Fort Brooke from 1866 until 1869 as part of the Reconstruction terms. The fort was decommissioned in 1883, and its land sold for development.

THE RETURN OF THE ARMY

Fifteen years later, the Army was back, ostensibly to protect property in Cuba owned by the American sugar companies. When the U.S.S. *Maine* blew up in Havana harbor in February 1898, a court of inquiry determined it was a mine that caused the explosion. The United States declared war on April 25.

Henry Plant pitched Tampa—and his Tampa Bay Hotel—to the United States Army as the perfect base of operations. Why go to all the bother of building a fort? So Army officers, including Colonel Teddy Roosevelt, came and stayed in the hotel. Enlisted men camped out on the grounds.

But would the Spanish navy sail north? A small fort, Fort Dade, was built on Egmont Key, but the Spanish threat never materialized. Fort Dade became the quarantine site for soldiers returning from Cuba. At one time 300 people lived at Fort Dade, which had a school, a movie theater, and a hospital.

Fort Dade was deactivated in 1923. But during World War II, Egmont Key was used as a lookout for U-Boats and as a practice bombing range.

COAST GUARD

The second branch of the military in the Tampa Bay area may well have been the United States Revenue Cutter Service, the forerunner of today's U.S. Coast Guard.

In the early 1800s, Revenue Cutter vessels combated piracy and smuggling off Florida's Gulf Coast. During the Second Seminole War, eight small cutter vessels slipped through the inland marshy areas in search of Seminole people hiding to avoid being removed from the area.

The Revenue Cutter Service became the United States Coast Guard in 1915.

In the mid-1920s, Prohibition brought a new challenge: stopping rumrunners coming from Cuba. With the development of aviation, the Coast Guard adopted aircraft to help locate smugglers far out at sea. In 1934, the Coast Guard established an air station in St. Petersburg.

In 1939, President Roosevelt transferred the Lighthouse Service to the Coast Guard. The local Coast Guard stations assumed responsibility for the lighthouses on Egmont Key and Anclote Key.

WORLD WAR II AND AFTER

The years leading up to and including World War II saw increases in the number and types of military personnel in the Tampa Bay area.

The U.S. Maritime Service (Merchant Marines), charged with moving supplies to the front, trained in St. Petersburg from 1939 to 1950.

The U.S. Navy oversaw shipbuilding at the Port of Tampa.

The U.S. Marines came to Dunedin, just north of Clearwater—not because there was a base there, but because that's where the scion of the Roebling family had created an "Alligator."

Donald Roebling—whose great-grandfather John Roebling had designed the Brooklyn Bridge and whose grandparents Washington and Emily Warren Roebling had built it—had a mechanical mind, a workshop in his Dunedin estate, and a mission. It bothered Roebling that many of the more than 2,500 people killed in 1928 when a hurricane destroyed the dikes surrounding Lake Okeechobee, causing massive flooding, died because rescuers couldn't get to them.

Roebling set to work. In 1935, he came up with an amphibious tractor that, instead of wheels and tires, had cleated, paddle-tread tracks. Roebling paid a local manufacturing company to build the prototypes. A 1937 *Life* magazine article about Roebling's "Alligator" caught the attention of United States Marine Corps, but there was no real military need for such a vehicle at the time.

By 1939, however, war seemed imminent, and the Marines asked Roebling to make some modifications. They also sent an Amphibian Tractor Detachment to learn how to maneuver the 'gators and to do field repairs. By the time the Landing Vehicle, Tracked—LVT or amtrac—started rolling off the assembly line in 1941, the Marines were ready to take them overseas.

The U.S. Army bought the Don CeSar Hotel in 1942 at its assessed value of $450,000 and turned it into a hospital for wounded soldiers. Other hotels in the area were pressed into service as ready-built housing and training sites for soldiers. The Vinoy was used, in part, to train bakers and cooks. The Belleview Biltmore housed soldiers stationed at area airfields.

One of those airfields was in west Tampa. Drew Field Municipal Airport had opened in 1928. During World War II, Drew Field was leased to the U.S. government for use as a signal-air-warning training school and for combat air training.

The government gave Drew Field back to the City of Tampa in 1945. Because the U.S. Army Air Force had greatly enlarged Drew Field during World War II, commercial airline operations were moved to Drew Field in 1946. Eventually, Drew Field grew into today's Tampa International Airport (see Getting Here, Getting Around chapter).

On the other side of Tampa Bay, the 304th Fighter Squadron trained at the Pinellas Army Airfield. After the war ended, the U.S. government turned the facility over to Pinellas County. The county developed the airfields into today's St. Petersburg-Clearwater International Airport.

In addition to Drew Field, the Army used two other airfields. Hillsborough Army Air Field now sits under Busch Gardens. Southeast Air Base, built in 1939 at the tip of the Interbay Peninsula, became MacDill Field in 1941.The Southeast's largest training center for bombers, MacDill Field became a major staging area for Army Air Corps crews and planes serving in Europe.

The United States Air Force became a separate branch of the military in 1947. After World War II, MacDill Field grew to become MacDill Air Force Base.

In 1976, the Coast Guard needed more room for their air operations, so the air station moved to facilities at the St. Petersburg-Clearwater International Airport. The USCG Air Station Clearwater became the service's largest air station in 1987.

Tampa and St. Petersburg Coast Guard offices merged into one command, Sector St. Petersburg, in 2005.

MILITARY FACILITIES TODAY

MACDILL AIR FORCE BASE
Tampa
(813) 828-1110
www.macdill.af.mil
MacDill AFB is home to the 6th Air Base Wing, which includes among its missions everything from air refueling to civil engineering, and to the Air Force Reserve's 927th Air Refueling Wing. The United States Central Command and the United States Special Operations Command also have their headquarters at MacDill along with more than 50 other mission partners, including the National Oceanic and Atmospheric Administration and the U.S. Department of Agriculture's Anti-Medfly operation. Base locator phone numbers for the various branches are:

- Air Force, (813) 828-2444
- Army, (813) 827-6910
- Marine Corps, (813) 827-5875
- Navy, (813) 827-5875

UNITED STATES COAST GUARD
Air Station Clearwater
15100 Rescue Way
Clearwater
(727) 535-1437
www.uscg.mil/d7/airstaclearwater

Sector St. Petersburg
600 8th Ave. S.E.
St. Petersburg
(727) 824-7506, (727) 824-7534

155 Columbia Dr.
Tampa
(813) 228-2191
http://homeport.uscg.mil/stpetersburg

VETERANS' FACILITIES

Administrative Offices

ST. PETERSBURG VA REGIONAL OFFICE
9500 Bay Pines Blvd
(P.O. Box 1437)
St Petersburg (33731-1437)
(800) 827-1000
www.vba.va.gov/ro/south/spete/index.htm

Cemeteries

BAY PINES NATIONAL CEMETERY
10,000 Bay Pines Blvd.
P.O. Box 477
St. Petersburg
(Bay Pines 33744-0477)
(727) 398-9426
www.cem.va.gov/cems/nchp/baypines.asp
Dedicated in 1933, Bay Pines National Cemetery holds the remains of more than 27,000 veterans and, in some cases, their spouses. Space is available for cremated remains.

Health Care, Hospitals, and Outpatient Clinics

BAY PINES VA HEALTH CARE SYSTEM
10,000 Bay Pines Blvd.
Bay Pines
(727) 398-6661
(877) 741-3400 (after hours)
www.baypines.va.gov

DUNEDIN VA OUTPATIENT CLINIC
1721 Main St.
Dunedin 34698
(727) 734-5276
Open Monday through Friday 8 a.m. to 4:30 p.m.

JAMES A. HALEY VETERANS' HOSPITAL
13000 Bruce B. Downs Blvd.
Tampa
(813) 972-2000
www.tampa.va.gov

ST. PETERSBURG VA OUTPATIENT CLINIC
10,000 Bay Pines Blvd.
Bay Pines
(727) 398-6661
Open Monday through Friday 7:30 a.m. to 4 p.m.

Veterans' Centers

ST. PETERSBURG VET CENTER
2880 1st Ave. N.
St. Petersburg
(727) 893-3791
www2.va.gov/directory/guide/facility.asp?ID=557

Semper Paratus (Always Ready)

The United States Coast Guard is—wrongly—sometimes seen as less than fully military. In the very early years of our country, the Revenue Cutter Service took the place of the decommissioned United States Navy.

For a while, the Coast Guard was part of the Department of Transportation, except in time of war.

Today, however, the United States Coast Guard is considered one of the five branches of the United States military and is part of the Department of Homeland Security.

In addition to providing search-and-rescue services, today's United States Coast Guard defends our waterways against pirates, drug smugglers, human traffickers, and other criminals. The Coast Guard maintains waterway buoys and channel markers to keep water traffic flowing smoothly, and they help mop up after hurricanes and other natural disasters.

Coast Guard crewmembers sometimes die in the line of duty.

On January 28, 1980, the Coast Guard cutter *Blackthorn*, commissioned in 1944, had just left the Port of Tampa where she had spent three months being overhauled. Her missions over the years had included breaking ice on the Great Lakes, tending buoys on the California coast and in the Gulf of Mexico, and helping in numerous rescue missions. *Blackthorn* was returning to active duty, with 50 crewmembers aboard.

The tanker *Capricorn* was coming in as *Blackthorn* and a Russian passenger ship *Kazakhstan* were going out. When the passenger ship passed *Blackthorn*, *Kazakhstan*'s bright lights obscured the views of both the *Capricorn* and the *Blackthorn* crews. There was confusion about which way each boat should turn, and the tanker and the cutter collided. Then *Capricorn*'s anchor caught hold of *Blackthorn*'s hull and ripped it open. *Blackthorn* capsized almost immediately and 23 of her crew died.

The *Blackthorn* memorial in St. Petersburg is at the north end rest area of the Sunshine Skyway Bridge, which is about 2 miles north of where the collision took place. *Blackthorn*'s home, Coast Guard Sector Field Office Galveston, keeps a buoy permanently lit honoring *Blackthorn* and her lost crew.

TAMPA VET CENTER
8900 N. Armenia Ave., #312
Tampa
(813) 228-2621
www2.va.gov/directory/guide/facility
.asp?ID=559

Veterans' Organizations

THE AMERICAN LEGION
District 15 (includes Hillsborough County)
District Commander
Kathryn Ferrin
(813) 643-2430
www.floridalegion.org/postlocator/district15.php

District 16 (includes Pinellas County)
District Commander
Ray Maya
(727) 430-6292
www.floridalegion.org/postlocator/
district16.php

DISABLED AMERICAN VETERANS
VA Regional Office
9500 Bay Pines Blvd., Room 232
Bay Pines
(727) 319-7444
www.dav.org/veterans

JEWISH WAR VETERANS
Albert Aronovitz Post #373
Post Commander
Leon E. Blumberg
5100 Burchette Rd. #1507
Tampa
(813) 767-2605
www.jwv-tampa.org

VETERANS OF FOREIGN WARS
(352) 622-5126
http://myfloridavfw.org

Veterans' Publications
VETERANS POST
1441 Dr. Martin Luther King Jr. St. S.
St. Petersburg
(727) 822-8387
www.veteranspostnews.com
Veterans Post newspaper publishes monthly news of interest to veterans. It is distributed in area veterans' hospitals, organization meeting places, and by subscription. Look inside the print edition for a comprehensive listing of veterans' organizations and auxiliary groups meeting in the Tampa Bay region. Click on the "Links" line on the main page of the Web site for an even more comprehensive listing of organizations and events of interest to veterans.

Other Support Services
AMERICAN RED CROSS (ARC)
(877) 741-1444 (24-Hour Military Helpline)

HILLSBOROUGH COUNTY EXTENSION OFFICE
5339 S. CR 579
Seffner
(813) 744-5519
http://hillsborough4hschoolenrichment.ifas
.ufl.edu/4hmilitary.html
In addition to hosting 4-H clubs on base at Mac-Dill Air Force Base—and in all U.S. military bases in England—the Hillsborough County Extension Office has other programs to help military families. Operation Military Kids helps children and teens of Army Reserve and National Guard troops understand and cope with a parent's being deployed and with adapting to military culture. Operation Child Care helps with short-term child care for children whose Army Reserve or National Guard parents are part of Operation Iraqi Freedom or Operation Enduring Freedom.

NORTH PINELLAS BRANCH ARC
2481 Sunset Point Rd.
Clearwater
(727) 446-2358

SOUTH PINELLAS BRANCH ARC
818 4th St. N.
St. Petersburg
(727) 898-3111

TAMPA HEADQUARTERS ARC
3310 W. Main St.
Tampa
(813) 348-4820
www.redcrosstbc.org
Congress has charged the American Red Cross with keeping families and service members connected during times of crisis. The Tampa Bay Chapter of the American Red Cross conveys emergency messages to active-duty troops, provides emergency financial and travel assistance, provides counseling and connections to other social services for troops and their families, and helps veterans claim financial benefits.

INDEX

ABOUT THE AUTHOR

Anne W. Anderson has explored the Tampa/St. Petersburg area for over 30 years and has written about Florida's West Coast for the St. Petersburg Times and Tampa Bay Newspapers, Inc. In addition to being a freelance journalist, she writes children's stories, liturgical dramas, ad copy, poetry, and grocery lists. Anne teaches seminars and short courses about writing, children and media, and liturgical drama. She and her husband live in Safety Harbor, Florida, surrounded by kids and grandkids, except for one son who returned to the mountains and lives in Colorado.